INTASC Standard	Description of Teacher Performance	Text Chapter/ Page Number
Principle 7	Plans instruction based on knowledge of subject matter, students, the community, and curriculum goals.	Ch. 1: pp. 10–19 Ch. 2: pp. 42–46 Ch. 3: pp. 71–74; Ch. 4: pp. 104–121; 124–126; 132; 135–137 Ch. 5: pp. 145–146; 148–150; 158–165; 173 Ch. 6: pp. 200–202 Ch. 8: pp. 285–288 Ch. 11: pp. 382–386
Principle 8	Understands and uses formal and informal assessment strategies.	Ch. 4: pp. 109–111; 121–124 Ch. 5: pp. 148–150; 165 Ch. 6: p. 201 Ch. 10: pp. 345–346 Ch. 11: pp. 368–369
Principle 9	Reflects on teaching.	Ch. 1: p. 1 Ch. 5: pp. 144–146; 148–151; 153; 156–158; 162–165 Ch. 8: pp. 289–293 Ch. 11: pp. 378–380 Ch. 13: pp. 447–448 Ch. 14: pp. 465–468; 479–482 Ch. 15: pp. 488–490; 497–498
Principle 10	Fosters relationships with colleagues, parents, and agencies in the larger community.	Ch. 1: pp. 5–10; 28–29 Ch. 2: pp. 58; 61; 63–65 Ch. 3: pp. 70–74; 76–79 Ch. 5: pp. 146; 156–158 Ch. 6: p. 210 Ch. 7: pp. 219–224; Ch. 10: pp. 342–45 Ch. 11: pp. 376–380 Ch. 13: pp. 425–431; 442–446; 449–451 Ch. 14: pp. 465–466 Ch. 15: pp. 493–496

Those Who Can, Teach

Tenth Edition

Kevin Ryan

Boston University

James M. Cooper

University of Virginia

Houghton Mifflin Company   *Boston*   *New York*

Sponsoring Editor: Sue Pulvermacher-Alt
Senior Development Editor: Lisa Mafrici
Project Editor: Jane Lee
Editorial Assistant: Talia Kingsbury
Senior Production/Design Coordinator: Jodi O'Rourke
Senior Designer: Henry Rachlin
Senior Manufacturing Coordinator: Jane Spelman
Marketing Manager: Nicola Poser

Cover Image: © José Cintrón

Printed in the U.S.A.

Library of Congress Control Number: 2002109666

ISBN: 0-618-30704-4

456789-DOW-06 05 04

Brief Contents

iii

Contents

6 What Should Teachers Know About Technology and Its Impact on Schools?   177

7 What Are the Ethical and Legal Issues Facing Teachers?   215

PART FOUR   The Teaching Profession   394

Preface

This book, *Those Who Can, Teach*, is a book of questions. In fact, it was written in the first place to answer the question, "What are the things people beginning their formal study of education should know?" We have organized the chapters of our book around a series of questions that are likely to be of special concern to prospective teachers, and that we believe are key to the central issues and concerns of teaching and learning. We hope that these questions provide direction and focus to readers' study well beyond the time they spend with this book. In addition, for those who are simply considering careers in teaching, we believe that the search for answers to these questions will help them clarify their career goals.

Purpose and Audience

Those Who Can, Teach is intended as a basic text for courses variously titled "Introduction to Education" or "Foundations of Education." We originally wrote this book because we couldn't find the kind of textbook our own students and the students of many of our colleagues needed and wanted—a book that involves prospective teachers in the real issues of schooling and education and that gives them a clear view of the skills and knowledge they will need to be successful professionals.

Content of the Tenth Edition

Those Who Can, Teach, Tenth Edition, presents a frank, contemporary examination of the field and foundations of education and, especially, the teaching profession. Although the text is firmly based in educational research and scholarship, it seeks to convey the important knowledge and issues in the field of education in a way that effectively bridges educational research and classroom practice. For this purpose, we rely heavily throughout the book on a narrative style, using the words of practicing teachers wherever we can in an effort to place the book's content in very human terms.

We have organized the book around four themes, each theme representing one of the four parts. Part One, "Schools and Students," opens with an examination of what defines a school and a review of its competing purposes. This is followed by two chapters, which focus on the diversity of the American students and the new and old social issues surrounding them. We then discuss what it is that schools are trying to teach elementary and secondary students, and we deal with some of the tensions around this critical topic. Part Two, " Teachers," explores three important dimensions of a teacher's work: first, what it takes to be an effective teacher; second, what the growing emphasis on educational technology is all about and what the teacher should be able to do; and third, what the ethical and legal issues are surrounding the work of the teacher. Part Three, "Foundations and the Future," deals with "something old and something new." The practice of education rests on a body of thought and experience. Therefore, we attempt to lay out the primary lines of thought, or educational philosophies, that speak to teaching and learning. On the other hand, American schools, in particular, are part of a unique national experiment to educate all the people to the fullest extent possible. The chapter entitled "What Is the History of American Education?" paints a "warts-and-all" picture of our attempts to fulfill that high ideal. This part ends with a close look at one of the most talked about and pressing issues facing educators: reform of our schools. We give this special attention because new teachers will undoubtedly be entering schools that are struggling to change. Part Four, "The Teaching Profession," examines teaching from a number of vantage points: what the current job situation is in various parts of the country and in the different levels and subject specialties; what a new teacher can expect from students, fellow teachers, administrators, and others; and what it mean to be a member of a profession. This part ends with a final chapter on the all-important question, "Why teach?" Having studied education, thought about and probably fantasized about teaching, this chapter enables readers systematically to reflect on whether teaching is the work for them.

▓ *Features of the Revision*

Teaching, learning, and the condition of our schools have been in the headlines almost continually in the three years since our last edition. Education is big news from Main Street to Pennsylvania Avenue. As the link between education and the well-being of both the individual and the nation becomes more obvious, both real change and proposals for change are more in evidence. In this edition, therefore, we have tried to sort out the most significant developments without losing sight of the enduring issues facing students and teachers.

Among the most significant changes in this edition are:

- **New "Open to Debate."**   We, the authors, are long-time friends and colleagues. Writing and revising *Those Who Can, Teach,* has been a work of professional interest and of friendship. But even in the best of professional relationships and friendships, folks differ. And, as you will soon see, that is surely the case with us! Although we have overwhelming agreement on the contents of this text, there are some sticky wickets where we just cannot agree. Rather than fudge and paper over these differences, we thought it would be useful for readers to see where we differ and what we individually believe. Thus, "Open to Debate." For those readers who go on to become teachers, reading these debates should surely prepare you for life in the faculty lounge.

- **New "Voices from the Classroom."**   One of the frequent complaints made by new teachers is that "no one ever told us what it is really like out here in the trenches." Although these complaints are sometimes unfair (people tried to tell them, but they weren't listening!), we have, nevertheless, from the very first edition of this book tried to reflect, through case studies and reports of teachers, the real world of schooling. In this tenth edition we are expanding that effort with this new feature, "Voices from the Classroom." We solicited contributions from a number of our former students and their teacher-friends, and we are enormously pleased with what they wrote. Each chapter has a reflection or comment on one of the chapter's key topics. Most contributors are new teachers; a few are veterans. All tell it like it is.

- **New "Pause and Reflect" Questions.**   We all live in a world of information overload, if not overkill. College students, in particular, have to plow through masses of written material. Educators in recent years have been pointing out that, unless we stop and reflect on what we read, our chances of holding the information and having it become *meaningful* are greatly reduced. On the other hand, if we stop and consider an idea and evaluate it in the light of our own experience, then we *own* the information. We have put our own stamp on it and, therefore, we hold it more strongly and clearly in our memories. With this in mind, in each chapter we have placed three or four "Pause and Reflect" stops, each containing two or three question for your consideration. We urge you to use this new feature.

Continuing Features

As you are probably well aware, education is a dynamic field of study and practice. Americans, young and old, make a huge investment in their schools. We are continually examining them; we are continually criticizing them; and we are continually changing or modifying them. As in previous editions of *Those Who Can, Teach,* we are responding to the changes in schools with changes in this book:

- Our earlier focus on student diversity and multiculturalism has been updated and expanded to reflect the changing demographics of our schools. The growing concern in society and among educators over ethics and character is also mirrored here.

- Our courts, too, have been busy handing down decisions, which are having profound effects on our schools. We keep students updated on the directions of the decisions.

- Our society's ever-changing answer to the question, "What is most worth knowing?" is, of course, mirrored in the school's curriculum, and we have thoroughly updated the new curricular emphasis and school reform movements.

- A huge new topic on the educational scene is standards-based education, and we have treated its many implications for teachers in a number of chapters. To help make the connection between standards and content crystal clear, we've included a correlation chart in the front of the book. The ten core principles of INTASC are correlated to the chapters and pages in the tenth edition.

- Educational policies, of which standards-based education is but one example, have had a great impact on everyone involved in our nation's schools and make great differences in the everyday lives of beginning teachers. Therefore, we have continued and updated a feature from the ninth edition called "Policy Matters!". This feature is designed to help students be informed of current policy developments, highlighting key topics such as alternative licensure, teacher induction programs, and censorship issues.

- Reflecting technology's omnipresence in education today, we have expanded our coverage of educational technology with resources, such as software programs and URLs, and references to standards that are found in the dedicated technology chapter and throughout the text.

- We continue to believe that it is important for teachers to have a knowledge and appreciation for some of the outstanding teachers, both from the past and the present. For example, in this edition we have added a biographical sketch of the controversial Chicago educator, Marva Collins.

- Home schooling is a challenging new issue for educators, and we have a first-hand report from a mother who has chosen to educate her children at home.

Although much is new in the tenth edition, many features have been retained. Chief among them is the book's informal writing style. We have tried to communicate the seriousness surrounding professional topics and, at the same time, weave in some humor and create a sense of conversing directly with the reader. The text describes extensively the experiences of classroom teachers, often in their own words. Frequently, these experiences happened directly to us when we were teaching in public schools. We believe (and hope) that this writing style and heavy use of narrative give the text a greater sense of reality.

Both of us have been classroom teachers and are long-time teacher educators. As such, we have, from our very first edition to this tenth edition, continually tried to keep one question uppermost in our minds as we have labored on this book: What does the new teacher need to know and be able to do in order to succeed in today's school? Answering that question is the challenge and the mission of *Those Who Can, Teach*.

■ *Accompanying Teaching and Learning Resources*

The tenth edition of *Those Who Can, Teach* is accompanied by an extensive package of instructor and student resources.

- *Kaleidoscope: Readings in Education,* **Tenth Edition,** is a companion book of readings that can be used either in conjunction with the text or as a separate volume. This collection of more than seventy selections, approximately 35 percent of which are new in this edition, contains works by some of the most distinguished scholars in education, along with the writings of practicing teachers. Many of the authors and reports of research cited in *Those Who Can, Teach* are included in this book of readings. We have specially marked several key classic readings in education. Also, an easy-to-use chart in *Kaleidoscope* cross-references topics discussed in *Those Who Can, Teach* with the readings in *Kaleidoscope*.

- *Instructor's Resource Manual with Test Bank,* prepared by Leslie Swetnam of Metropolitan State College of Denver, includes a transition guide, sample syllabi, student objectives, chapter overviews, supplementary lecture and discussion topics, class activities, student study guides, practice quizzes, selected references and media resources, School Observation activities, and a section of 5–6 case studies with discussion questions. The test bank contains multiple-choice, short answer, and essay questions. The IRM includes a cross reference to *Kaleidoscope,* the companion reader.

- **HMClassPrep CD with HM Testing Version 6.0** provides instructors with a variety of teaching resources in an electronic format, allowing for easy customization to meet specific instructional needs. Files encoded on the disk include: A brand new PowerPoint package for classroom presentations and Word files from the *Instructor's Resource Manual* which can be easily edited, including lecture outlines, class exercises, debate issues, chapter quizzes, answers to discussion and review questions, comments on the cases, and video guide information.

- **Blackboard and WebCT Cartridges** text and study guide content made platform-ready for online courses.

- **You Can Teach! Multimedia for Reflection CD-ROM,** a free student CD, provides "Videos Resources with Reflection Questions" (topics of videos include: history of education, the digital divide, gender bias in the classroom,

A Guide to the Features in the Tenth Edition

Many pedagogical features have been included to enhance the student's learning and the text's usefulness.

What Social Problems and Tension Points Affect Today's Students?

3

Chapter Preview Rarely a day goes by on which educational issues fail to make headlines in newspapers across the country. Violence in schools, rampant teenage drug use, inequality of educational opportunity, sex education programs, and youth suicides are only a few of the issues that we read about daily. Underlying these issues are problems that complicate young people's efforts to get an education, such as crippling poverty and child abuse and neglect. This chapter explores some of the most sensitive and controversial issues in American education. Naturally, in such a short space we can treat each topic only briefly. However, we urge you to pursue additional reading on each issue.

This chapter emphasizes that:

● Many school-age children are affected by critical problems that directly influence their lives and often spill over into the classroom. Among these problems are severe poverty, homelessness, teenage parenting, child abuse, alcohol and drug abuse, and adolescent suicide.

● Violence and vandalism are not confined to urban school[s], problems in all of our schools and in our society.

● School dropout rates, although improving, reflect dispariti[es] groups and foreshadow future societal problems.

● Access to equal educational opportunity for poor and disa[dvantaged] is an elusive goal in American education.

● Charter schools and school voucher plans are controversi[al] choice.

● Gender issues affect the curriculum, classroom interactio[n] ment levels.

● Sex education remains as controversial as ever, althoug[h] acquired immune deficiency syndrome (AIDS) has streng[then]ment for proponents of sex education.

CHAPTER PREVIEW

The **Chapter Preview** provides an outline of the major topics and subtopics that will be discussed. This outline gives you a mental framework to arrange the information you will learn in the chapter.

MARGINAL NOTES

These **marginal notes** help clarify concepts being discussed, and will help you find key concepts while you study and review the chapter.

As pregnant teenagers struggle with the decision of whether to drop out of school, educators are finding ways to encourage pregnant teenagers and young mothers to stay in school and graduate.
(David Young-Wolff/PhotoEdit)

many cases unreported

America is losing sight of its children. In decisions made every day we are placing them at the bottom of the agenda, with grave consequences for the future of the nation.
—ERNEST BOYER

effects of abuse

the teacher's responsibility

working with local health officials to ensure that pregnant teenagers receive prenatal care and parenting advice. They are also encouraging these young women to stay in school and graduate. In many cases, the schools are permitting young mothers to bring their babies with them to school. To prevent teenage pregnancies, some schools have established clinics where birth control devices can be obtained, and sex education programs (discussed later in the chapter) have become common and controversial.

If you are planning on teaching in secondary schools, you should give some thought to what you would do if one of your students informs you that she is pregnant or that he has gotten his girlfriend pregnant. Know both your legal and ethical responsibilities in these cases. If you plan to teach in an elementary school, be prepared to work with very young parents, perhaps even your own age.

Abused and Neglected Children

The education of the young brings us into contact with humanity's best impulses. Occasionally, however, we see the wreckage of its darkest and most vicious urges. For many years, the phenomenon of child abuse was known only to a small percentage of social workers and law enforcement people. More recently, we have become aware of the magnitude of this problem and the variety of forms abuse can take, including physical or mental injury, sexual abuse, negligent treatment, and maltreatment. Because of the hidden nature of child abuse and neglect, reliable figures on it are somewhat difficult to obtain. Professionals in the field acknowledge that most cases are unreported. Nevertheless, almost 3 million incidents of child abuse or neglect are reported to child-service agencies each year. More than 800,000 of these reported cases are substantiated. Almost three-fifths of the victims of maltreatment suffered from neglect, about one-fifth experienced physical abuse, and about one-tenth were victims of sexual abuse.[19] Parental substance abuse was reported as a major contributing factor in child abuse cases.

The toll that abuse and neglect take on children's physical, emotional, and psychological development is difficult to assess. Children subjected to violent treatment also sustain injuries that cause serious learning problems in school. These children may be withdrawn or have trouble concentrating. They suffer enormous stress, and their self-esteem is low. They sometimes have excessive needs for control because they have experienced such helplessness. Ironically, they may be more likely to abuse their own children in the future.

The classroom teacher will not directly encounter the problem of abuse very often. However, in all fifty states, educators are legally responsible for reporting suspected cases of child abuse. Teachers must be aware of potential signs of abuse and know school policy and procedures for reporting suspected abuse. (See the chapter entitled "What Are the Ethical and Legal Issues Facing Teachers?" for a discussion of teachers' legal obligations regarding suspected child abuse.) Potential signs of abuse include the following:

TECHNOLOGY ICONS

In order to integrate the extensive supporting technology with the text, these **technology icons** indicate topics that are covered in greater depth on either the companion web site or the new "You Can Teach! Multimedia for Reflection" CD-ROM.

■ *"latch-key" children*

■ *child care issues*

home to an empty house or apartment after school is standard for an estimated 4 million "latch-key" children in our country.

For parents of younger children not yet in school, working outside the home raises the issue of adequate childcare. If both parents or the only parent is working full time, who is taking care of the children? Grandparents and extended family used to pitch in and help, but today it is less common for a family to settle in one location near relatives for extended periods. Parents who have to work, especially single parents, can easily be caught in a bind, and they often must settle for whatever child care they can find or afford.

In addition to limiting the amount of time children spend in close contact with their parents, the trend toward two-career and single-parent families also has a direct impact on the schools. In the past, young people were actively involved outside of school in family and community, but today the school is being urged to play a larger role in expanding and guiding the limited experiences of children. Schools are being asked to deal with the new problems being brought to them by the facts of modern family life and our changed economy. Many schools have responded to child care needs by offering both before- and after-school programs. For example, many schools provide both breakfast and lunch programs. Schools may offer enrichment and recreational programs or on-site day care after school to address student and parental needs. Some schools even stagger their bus schedules to accommodate students who stay for after-school programs. As mentioned in the "Who Are Today's Students in a Diverse Society?" chapter, many schools offer nontraditional programs that coordinate agencies dealing with health, and social and recreational services. These interagency programs enable the schools to deliver needed social and health services to students and their families to promote success in school.

In the past, teachers could count on more support from families; now teachers often find it difficult to even get in contact with many parents. In this situation, the more dramatic social problems such as poverty and homelessness take on even greater urgency for the schools.

■ *schools play a larger role*

 Reflect on the relationship between families with the video resources on your CD-ROM.

PAUSE AND REFLECT

The **Pause and Reflect** questions provide an opportunity for you to stop reading and think about the main points of the section you have just read and how they relate to your own experiences.

PAUSE AND REFLECT

❶ Does your own family background reflect traditional or emerging family patterns? How do you think your upbringing will affect your ability to teach students from different family situations?

❷ How can you prepare to work effectively with a variety of parents and caregivers?

■ *Poverty*

■ *the widening income gap*

The rich are getting richer and the poor are getting poorer. This well-known phrase describes the extremes of different socioeconomic levels in our society today. The poorest 40 percent of American citizens receive 14 percent of the national income, whereas the wealthiest 20 percent receive more than 47 percent.[9] In 2001, the number of impoverished Americans was 31.6 million, or 11.7 percent of the population.[10]

Numerically, the majority of poor Americans are white; however, the rate of poverty is higher among minorities. Almost 8 percent of whites, 23 percent of African Americans, 21 percent of Hispanic Americans, 26 percent of Native Americans, and less than 11 percent of Asian Americans live below the poverty line ($18,267 for a family of four in 2001).[11]

Visit this chapter of the web site to link to up-to-date statistics on this topic.

VOICES FROM THE CLASSROOM

Christa Compton has taught high school English in Columbia, S.C., for nine years. She was South Carolina's Teacher of the Year in 2001.

Families and School

My students show up with hearts burdened by terrible losses. Angela's father was murdered when she was very young, and she still grieves for a man she only vaguely remembers. Marcus was put up for adoption at birth by his teenage mother, and his adoptive mother died of cancer two years ago. Peter is angry because his mother recently moved out of the house, and he blames her for breaking up their family. Many other families have been torn apart by divorce, and fathers are increasingly absent in their children's lives.

All of this means I have to work hard to earn students' trust, an especially difficult task with those who have been disappointed by other people they have trusted. If students don't find a sense of belonging at home, it becomes even more important to find it at school, so I try to create a supportive community within the class. I un-

cover the story of each kid's life and design activities that build relationships among the students. Throughout the year, we write sympathy cards when one of us is grieving, applaud the students who make the honor roll, welcome back the students who return from an absence, and do whatever we can to express concern for each class member.

It helps to observe their behavior and moods from day to day. Sometimes just a quiet comment can reassure them that someone cares. At other times, students reveal their anxieties in a written assignment, so I write notes on their papers to let them know that I am there to support them.

They desperately want someone to pay attention—to praise their successes, to notice when they are sad, to share the daily torments and victories that are the hallmarks of adolescent life. When they feel dismissed, I can provide encouragement. When their lives are chaotic and unpredictable, I can offer safety and consistency. I might be the one person they can count on, and I refuse to let them down.

Visit the web site for more Voices from the Classroom.

VOICES FROM THE CLASSROOM

These authentic voices offer interviews with real teachers, administrators, and other school personnel, who give tips and advice regarding one of the chapter's key topics.

will also require more sensitivity in daily interactions, such as when asking students to bring a note from "your mother." It would perhaps be better to say "your parent" or "the person who takes care of you."

■ **Family Relationships**   Family composition affects the amount of time

John Berloan, Hillsborough Community College

Dorothy G. Brown, Fayetteville State University

June Edwards, SUNY College at Oneonta

Gail Figa, Florence-Darlington Technical College

Richard Gallian, University of North Texas

Barbara Graham, Ball State University

Francis Guldbrandsen, University of Minnesota, Duluth

Linda A. Hoover, Shippensburg University

Carol Lorek, Northern Arizona University

Ron Petrich, Augsburg College

Lynn Stallings, Kennesaw State University

Steven A. Schmitz, Central Washington University

A special acknowledgment is due to Marilyn Ryan for the substantial intellectual and psychological contributions she made to the several editions of this book.

Writing and revising a book is a multifaceted process. Many people provide advice—some solicited and some not. We believe, however, that our best source of advice on this book and its companion, *Kaleidoscope*, has been the team we've worked with at Houghton Mifflin. Lisa Mafrici, senior development editor, has been the one who has gracefully orchestrated the coming together of the many pieces of this book and *Kaleidoscope*. Sue Pulvermacher-Alt, senior sponsoring editor, has the responsibility of overseeing the "big picture" surrounding this project and *Kaleidoscope*. We are enormously appreciative of her dynamic and thoughtful leadership. Jane Lee, project editor, has deftly handled the copyediting process and all of the final stages of production. The developmental editor for this edition has been Sheralee Connors, who has been a terrific source of good ideas, cartoons, quotes, and practical suggestions. A good revision editor has to have a fine sense of what to keep and what to drop. We are convinced that Sheralee is a gifted poker player because she truly "knows when to hold 'em and knows when to fold 'em," and all of this with the greatest of tact.

Finally, we acknowledge the thousands of students for whom this book is written. Your new learning as you become teachers is central to our work as authors. We value your feedback on how we are doing and invite you to respond by sending us your comments through the Houghton Mifflin web site.

Kevin Ryan
James M. Cooper

Part One

Schools and Students

The makeup of children in America's schools is changing dramatically. Our culture is becoming increasingly diverse, especially in its ethnic and racial composition. About 37 percent of the children enrolled in our schools are minorities, and the percentage increases each year. Children are also innocent victims of many of society's ills—poverty, drug abuse, disorganized and disintegrating families, to name a few—that greatly affect schools' ability to teach youngsters effectively.

As a new teacher, you must understand these social factors because they may affect your own and your students' ability to respond to their intellectual, physical, emotional, and ethical needs. All of these variables make the task of teaching challenging.

What Is a School and What Is It For?

Chapter Preview People take education courses for several reasons. Three in particular are common. First, as citizens, people need to know how a major institution like the school system works so that they can make informed choices within their communities and at the voting booth. Second, as parents or potential parents, they need to know a great deal to be intelligent partners with the schools in their children's education. Third, those who are considering a career in teaching need to understand the profession they may enter. This text, by and large, is written with this third group in mind.

In past editions of this text, we started the text by asking you, prospective teachers, why you want to teach. We asked you to consider your own motivations and examine unfamiliar aspects of teaching. We believe that "Why do I want to teach?" is one of the most fundamental questions any prospective teacher can ask him- or herself. Before progressing further into this chapter, take a moment to think about why you want to teach, and write down what you think is motivating you *today* to become a teacher. As you will see throughout this book, we believe that effective teachers, indeed effective people in many areas of life, succeed in part because they are mindful of what they are doing. They reflect on their attitudes and performance, always looking for ways to improve. This practice of **reflection** is a habit you can use even now, as part of your career choice process. We think that recording what you think today, revisiting your thoughts throughout the term, and then noting what you think at the end of your class will help solidify any choice you make about teaching. We hope that by the end of the semester (and the end of reading this text), you will develop a greater understanding of what it means to teach, what teachers do, how schools operate within their communities and society, and a number of other issues you will need to consider to make a wise decision about whether teaching is right for you. We will return to this highly personal and central question, "Why teach?" at several points throughout the text, especially in the chapter devoted to that question.

_____

_____

_____

_____

Have you written down some reasons that you think you may want to teach? Have you imagined yourself in front of a classroom teaching? Have you daydreamed about being some student's favorite teacher? Keep your ideas in mind as we start our exploration of teaching. We encourage you to take time to revisit the previous page several times throughout the term and add to your thoughts or change them as you gather new information. To begin our exploration, let's consider some seemingly simple questions, "What is a school, and what is it for?"

In this chapter, you will see that there is no single answer to our question, "What is a school?" This and many other questions asked in this book are too large and elaborate to be adequately answered here. We pose them and talk about them anyway to aid you in forming your ideas about the issues that lie behind them. It seems unlikely that you can make a good career choice if you lack a fundamental understanding of the institution you are considering entering, and if you hope to survive and be happy within an institution, you will need to know how it is put together and how it works. For example, you need to know what the institution says it is doing and what, in fact, it actually does. You need to know a particular school's expectations of you as a teacher so that you can decide how to respond or if you wish to respond at all. Finally, if you hope to improve the schools—that is, make them better because of your involvement with them—you need to have a realistic view of what is now going on in the schools and develop your vision of what the schools can and should become. This chapter emphasizes that:

- Education is a large, all-encompassing endeavor, whereas schooling is simply one aspect of an education.

- The purpose of school determines much of what happens in school. You can determine the aims of school by reading formal statements of purpose and by relying on your own experiences in and observations of schools.

- You can understand schools by comparing them with models or abstract representations of reality.

- Schools are cultures and therefore play a critical part in passing on a society's values to the young.

- Research is giving us more accurate answers to the age-old question "What is a good school?"

What, then, is a school? This may not sound like a profound question; in fact, it probably seems rather tame, but as senator and linguist S. I. Hayakawa once wrote, "If fish were scientists, the last thing they would study would be water." We think it is important to examine schools themselves, something so much a part of our lives that they become almost invisible to us. What follows is the first of many questions where we ask you to pause and seriously reflect on what you know about a particular issue.

PAUSE AND REFLECT

How would you answer the question, "What is a school?"

_____

_____

_____

Your reaction to this question reflects who you are and what your experience with school has been. Perhaps you responded in one of the following ways:

- A school is an agency that weans children from the protective warmth of the family and trains them for what society has decided is useful work.

- A school is a place where they fix your mind so you think like everyone else.

- A school is where children fall in love with learning.

- A school is a tax-supported baby-sitting agency.

- A school is a place where young savages have a chance to become civilized by engaging the world's most precious wisdom.

- A school is a place where we explore who we are and how we can become full, creative human beings.

- A school is a fun place.

- A school is a tax-supported institution where the dead wisdom and worn-out skills of the past are force-fed to the young.

- A school is where education takes place.

Each of these descriptions says a great deal about the school experience of the person who formulated it. Our conviction is that your definition of *school* is a cognitive map that greatly affects how you put together information and impressions of schools.

Education and Schooling

In simpler, premodern societies, when a boy could learn to be a man by following his father around and imitating the men of the village and a girl could learn to be a woman by doing the same with her mother and the other women, schools were not necessary. Formal schooling became a social necessity when the home and the community were no longer effective or competent at training the young through informal contacts. Most modern societies have realized that education is too important to be left to chance. Whereas important things are sometimes learned on street corners, and grandparents often are excellent teachers, the formal educative process is simply more reliable. There are nagging doubts, however, that herding youngsters into school buildings for six or seven hours a day, five days a week, is the most effective way to educate our children.

    In fact, it has been quipped that today, children interrupt their education to go to school. The distinction between schooling and education implied by this remark is important. Like school, education has myriad definitions. We have sprinkled a

Learn more about ancient schooling in the video resources on your CD-ROM.

few such definitions here and there throughout the book for you to sample. Before we go further, though, we should look at the two concepts in more detail.

Education

■ *definition of education*

For the moment, let us say that **education** is a process of human growth by which one gains greater understanding and control over oneself and one's world. It involves our minds, our bodies, and our relations with the people and the world around us. Education is also characterized by continuous development and change. The end product of the process of education is learning.

All of us have two educations: one which we receive from others; another, and the most valuable, which we give ourselves.

—John Randolph

Education is much more open-ended and all-inclusive than schooling. Education knows few bounds. It includes both the formal learning that takes place in schools and the entire universe of informal learnings, from hooking a worm on a line to

■ *takes place everywhere*

burping a baby. The agents of education can range from a revered grandparent to the guests on a late-night television talk show, from a child with a disability to a distinguished scientist. Whereas schooling has a certain predictability, education quite often takes us by surprise. We go to the movies to relax and come home with a vivid sense of poverty's corrupting influence. We get into a casual conversation with a stranger and discover how little we know about other religions. Education is a lifelong process; it starts long before we begin school and should be an ongoing part of our entire lives.

Schooling

■ *definition of schooling*

In contrast to education, **schooling** is a specific, formalized process, usually limited to the young, and whose general pattern traditionally has varied little from one setting to the next. Despite minor variations in teaching practices among schools, for example, schooling remains a rather uniform practice throughout the United States. Throughout the country, children arrive at school at approximately the same time, take assigned seats, are taught by an adult, use the same or similar textbooks, do homework, take exams, and so on. The topics they learn—from phonics to the three branches of American government—have usually been mandated in advance.

Schools are created for the express purpose of providing a certain type of educational experience, which we call the *curriculum*. Teachers receive preparation and are employed to fulfill the purposes of schooling as defined by the curriculum. The curriculum, which will be discussed more fully in the chapter entitled "What Is Taught?", represents what a community believes young people need to know to develop into good and productive adults, or it at least includes what the school policymakers in a particular community believe young people need to know. In effect, a school's curriculum represents a **social bet**. It is what the older generation thinks the young will need to live well in the twenty-first century. If the curriculum turns out to be a losing bet, the individual and social consequences are severe.

■ *curriculum as a social bet*

Keeping the differences between education and schooling clearly in mind is often particularly difficult for the people who should be most sensitive to them—that is, teachers who *do* education *in* schools. People enter teaching because they wish to educate others. They may be committed to a particular educational philosophy. Usually, however, the everyday experiences of working in a school cause their allegiances to shift from abstract educational ideals to the network of personalities and ideas surrounding the particular schools where they teach. They become invested in schooling, in the way things are—that is, the routines of homework, quizzes, and detention—and to varying degrees, they tend to lose focus on education. For this reason alone, it is important for the teacher to keep alive the questions, "What is a school for?" and "What is my contribution to this child's and this class's education?" We will have more to say on this topic when we get to examining your ideas in the chapter entitled "What Are the Philosophical Foundations of American Education?".

I have never let my schooling interfere with my education.
—MARK TWAIN

PAUSE AND REFLECT

❶ Which have been the most important learnings in your life—those from your nonschool education or from your schooling?

❷ What do you think has been the most important thing you have learned in school, and what has been the most important thing you have learned outside of school?

Four Basic Purposes of School

By distinguishing between education and schooling, we may have somewhat clarified the question, "What is a school?", but we also need to understand the *purposes* of schools if we are to understand fully what role they play in society.

One thing you may think you know best is school. After all, many of you have spent the better part of your lives in schools. Isn't it obvious what schools are and what they do? Perhaps. Yet most of us tend to think of schools in limited ways. Our own experiences within a relatively few schools influence what we think about all schools and what we understand of schools in general. For that reason, it is important to look at schools from different vantage points to gain more perspective on schools as a whole by looking at them from a more distant view.

As benign as the question, "What should schools do?" may seem, it is the kind of question that can stir fierce arguments amongst different groups. It can rattle the foundation of a community if residents have conflicting views about what their community's schools should do. The issue masks serious

The function of schools that comes first to most people's minds is the intellectual function.
(© Elizabeth Crews)

questions about what different people think of contemporary American culture and society and what they want from them. What you should understand, however, is that questions about school, such as what it is and what it should do, are by no means new questions. People have argued, discussed, and written about what schools should do for hundreds of years.

To help illustrate that point, we have included several quotes about schools. Some were written centuries ago; others have been written in the past decade. As you read each quote, think about how each speaker characterizes the functions of schools and education and also think about your own schooling.

■ **Intellectual Purposes**   Jacques Barzun is a cultural historian who writes frankly about the current state of schools in America. As you read his quote, try to decide what Barzun sees as the primary purpose of schools.

> What do we really want from our schools? . . . Given the public's muddled feelings about brainwork (which is what "excellence" refers to) and the parental indifference up to now about what their children are being taught, the school has a double fight on its hands: against ignorance inside the walls and against cultural prejudice outside, the prejudice lying so deep that those who harbor it do not even know they do. . . . The difficulties of schooling . . . do not change. . . . Difficulties remain. It will always be difficult to teach well, to learn accurately, to read, write and count readily and competently; to acquire a sense of history and develop a taste for literature and the arts. . . . For this purpose no school . . . is ever just right; it is only by the constant effort of its teachers that it can even be called satisfactory.[1]

—JACQUES BARZUN

Reflect on the intellectual purposes of schooling with the image in this section of your CD-ROM.

■ *primacy of intellect*

If you said that Barzun is emphasizing the academic or *intellectual* purposes of schools, you would be right. One longstanding purpose of schools has been to foster the intellectual development of the young. Barzun is one among many who contend that promoting academic learning is the single most important purpose of schools.

Most people who highlight the intellectual purpose of schools believe that the development of reason, through intellectual pursuits, leads to individual en-

rationality makes us human

lightenment. Rationality, or the ability to know, to think, to reason, is seen as an attribute distinct to humans, and, more importantly, the capacity that *makes us human*. Many of those who rank intellectual purposes as the highest priority see school as the one institution most common to all people. They believe, therefore, that promoting intellectual development in schools is essential so that all children have the opportunity to become rational human beings.

The intellectual purpose of school is included in every school's mission. The way it is manifested, however, can look different from school to school. Some schools exist for the sole purpose of helping students develop their intellects. You may have heard about or even attended a secondary school that requires students to study "the Great Books" or that requires five or six core academic subjects for all students. Other schools include the study of academic disciplines along with numerous co-curricular activities.

"Great Books" and core academics

▓ **Political and Civic Purposes** Now, let's consider another quote. It highlights a different purpose of school. You will be able to tell by the writing style that it was written some time ago; however, the idea the writer expresses is one that has been a constant in American public schools since their beginning.

> [E]ven under the best forms [of government], those entrusted with power have, in time . . . perverted it into tyranny; and it is believed that the most effectual means of preventing this would be to illuminate . . . the minds of the people at large, and more especially to give them knowledge of those facts, which history exhibiteth . . . [that] they may be enabled to know ambition under all its shapes. . . . [2]

—THOMAS JEFFERSON

You will read more about Jefferson's contributions to the American public schools in the chapter entitled "What Is the History of American Education?". For now it is simply important to see that Jefferson hoped that American schooling would help establish and sustain the United States of America, an infant nation. One of the overriding concerns of the early political leaders was, in fact, how people would learn to be American citizens and *not* English subjects.

schooling to sustain democracy

With this quote, the *political and civic* purposes of schooling are underscored. Jefferson thought schools could help people learn how to govern themselves wisely and justly.

The need for schools to prepare students for their political and civic lives persists to this day. In your own schools, you may have seen political and civic purposes emphasized through voter registration drives, citizenship education programs, even community service and outreach programs, but schools also promote these purposes by *how* they teach the students to read, to write, and to discuss ideas rationally.

In the course of history, education has served every purpose and doctrine contrived by man. If it is to serve the cause of human freedom, it must be explicitly designed for that purpose.
—GEORGE S. COUNTS

As we will discuss later in the chapter, some believe that schools should prepare students for an especially active role, as citizens who actively work to improve their society. The only sure way for any country to have a well-informed citizenry is through the systematic education that schooling can bring. That need may be more or less prominent during certain times, but the political purposes of schools has always been one of the primary reasons public schools exist.

■ **Economic Purposes**   Let's consider one more perspective and see how you would link it to your own school experiences. Jean Anyon, an educational researcher, has investigated the connection between economics and schooling for a number of years. She wrote the article in which this excerpt appeared in 1992.

> When inner city students and their access to the range of services provide a realistic expectation that education will lead to better jobs, life, and future, as is expected in most middle-class and affluent homes, then the students will have a reason to make an educational effort. Realistic expectations that education will make a substantial, positive difference in the lives of their students may also motivate teachers and other school staff to a higher level of performance. At that point teachers, principals and a quality curriculum can more easily make a difference in the lives of the inner city poor.[3]
>
> —JEAN ANYON

What is the question that Anyon raises about the connection between a student's schooling and his or her occupation? What are the criticisms she seems to be leveling against schools in American society? As this quote suggests, many Americans feel that schools primarily serve an *economic* purpose—that is, they believe that schools help students obtain the skills and knowledge required to attend college or to get a job.

Americans generally expect that more schooling leads to greater personal wealth, and they are right. Think about how you approach your own college education. If you and the student body of your campus were interviewed right now about why you are attending college, many of you would say that you attend college because you expect to earn a more comfortable living with a college degree than without one, and you are probably right. On the whole, high school graduates do obtain higher-paying jobs than those who didn't complete high school, and college graduates earn more than high school graduates.

Americans also expect that schools will prepare students for their future, regardless of whether that includes a college education. High schools support that expectation by including courses of study that are *college preparatory* or *vocational*. Many Americans accept without question that schools guide students into curricular tracks that seem matched to their abilities and inclinations so that the mathematically inclined students will enroll in such courses as calculus and advanced placement (AP) physics and the labor-oriented students will enroll in machine shop or computer repair courses. The tacit assumption underlying the economic purposes of schools is that well-schooled people and people *appropriately schooled* are vital to a strong national economy, regardless of whether they become business leaders or laborers. We will see later in the chapter that Anyon, among others, has questioned the practices that rest on this assumption, pointing out that curricular tracking and instructional practices are not always related so much to students' individual abilities as to their expected role in the work world.

The economic purposes of schooling have profound effects both on the individual student and society as a whole. You may have heard news accounts of the need for a "well-educated work force" or the "new demands of working in high-tech industries." Pundits pronounce to one another what the new global economy will demand, and those predictions often trickle down to schools. For instance, many school systems have placed renewed emphasis on teaching world languages so that bilingual Americans are able to do business in other countries.

■ *the job sorting role of schools*

Reflect on the economic purposes of schooling with the image in this section of your CD-ROM.

On the other hand, school isn't all work. The social functions of school are important, too.
(© Bob Daemmrich)

■ **Social Purposes**　We have identified intellectual, political, and economic purposes of schools, but one more purpose has yet to be identified. This can be called the *umbrella purpose* for schools because it is so all encompassing. Consider this last quote and think about what it means.

> If . . . education has a collective function above all, if its object is to adapt the child to the social milieu in which he is destined to live, it is impossible that society should be uninterested in such a procedure. . . . It is, then, up to the State to remind the teacher constantly of the ideas, the sentiments that must be impressed upon the child to adjust him to the milieu in which he must live.[4]

—ÉMILE DURKHEIM

Reflect on the social purposes of schooling with the image in this section of your CD-ROM.

This quote draws attention to the *social purpose* of schools. How would you paraphrase this quotation? At some point in your life, you may have heard that schools also teach "social skills." What exactly does that mean to you? You may have heard the old adage, "It's good to be smart, but if you can't get along with people or don't know how to work with others, then it doesn't make much difference how much you know. . . ."

Émile Durkheim was a French sociologist in the early twentieth century. One of his primary interests was the school's responsibility in promoting a healthy social order. For him, schools existed to help mold or guide students into what their society needed and expected of them. A teacher's job was to help students understand their role in the broader social order.

■ *adapting the child to society*

Durkheim's idea that schools must work to help students adapt to social expectations holds currency with many, even today. Think of how many times elementary school teachers impress on pupils how important it is to share with each other. Who decided that we needed to learn to share? Think of how frequently middle and high school teachers remind students to give their best effort on their homework or a project. What does "best effort" mean? Why not encourage students to "kick back and go with the flow"? Those are two simple illustrations of how schooling helps children learn and adapt to social conventions. Because the social nature of schooling is so important, we will return to it later in the chapter.

PAUSE AND REFLECT

❶ Thinking back on your high school experiences, how were these four purposes (intellectual, political, economic, and social) evident in your schooling? Was one more dominant than the others? Which one? Why was this one purpose more dominant in your particular community?

❷ Which of these four purposes of education do you believe ought to be given the greatest weight in the organization of schools?

Models of School

The broad purposes of schools may be complex enough to be difficult to distinguish at first look. Is there another way, another set of lenses, with which to bring into focus these large, amorphous ideas about schools? Models can make these abstract ideas more concrete for us.

■ *descriptive models*

A *model* is a representation of reality. All of us create mental models to help sort out the sounds and sights we encounter daily and to organize them into sensible patterns. Scientists use theoretical models to predict events and to explain why certain things have occurred. Models can also be useful as we attempt to answer the question, "What is a school?" The following paragraphs briefly describe a few such models. As you read, think about how well each model describes the schools you know and which of the four basic purposes of school each model most strongly emphasizes.

■ *The School as Trainer of the Good Worker*

According to this model, the school's essential task is to turn children into good, productive workers, adults who will contribute to the current economic system. Students are gradually fashioned, like raw material, into the finished product: docile workers. Their teachers are their first real supervisors, who ready them to obey happily and unquestioningly the orders of the "higher-ups." Not every student who experiences this model of schooling receives the same training, however. In Jean Anyon's research she found that students were educated for the kinds of work that matched their families' socioeconomic status. In working-class neighborhoods, elementary school children's experience included "being told to follow directions, copying teachers' notes, answering textbook questions, or coloring and assembling paper cutouts."[5] This model of schooling, Anyon argued, would train students to become productive, docile workers, able to follow directions from supervisors. In contrast, those children in elite schools in the most affluent neighborhoods were encouraged to think logically, make systematic decisions about their work, or discuss their own analyses of social studies problems. That kind of education, according to Anyon, prepares those students well for having similar jobs as their parents, who are often decision makers and leaders, such as corporate executives.

■ The School as Social Escalator

In this model, the school is seen as the vehicle by which one rises in society. School is the royal road to economic well-being and social prominence. Although, as Jean Anyon suggests, this model may not be equally applicable to all students, many parents and students still see success in school as the ticket to the upper rungs of the community. The model of school as a preparer for college, described next, often supports this view of schools. Although athletic or artistic success in school escalates some students to prominence, academic achievement provides the boost for most. Failure or poor performance in school acts as a "de-escalator" for many students.

■ The School as Preparer for College

Here the school prepares the student for more schooling. As a result, the here and now is not nearly as important as the future. Using this model, the curriculum of the secondary school is justified to the degree to which it prepares students to do college-level work. Likewise, the elementary school curriculum is justified to the degree to which it prepares students for success in secondary school. Increasingly, preschool is justified to the degree it readies children for elementary school. Students' current needs and interests are given slight attention because the focus is on the demands of the curriculum at the *next level up*. This model often strongly emphasizes student performance on standardized tests, and districts that follow this model often publicize the average test scores or the percentage of students who continue on to postsecondary education. Those indicators demonstrate to the community just how well the school is performing. When the school earns a reputation for its students' high test scores, the community, in turn, becomes desirable for prospective homebuyers. Jay Mathews (1999) writes about the public high school in Mamaroneck, NY. Because so many of its students completed AP courses, performed exceptionally well on the exams, and were admitted to the most prestigious colleges in the country, parents and the school board resisted *any* change in the curriculum. The parents' perspective was that the school shouldn't tinker with success.[6]

> *School is not preparation for life, but school is life.*
> —JOHN DEWEY

■ The School as Shopping Mall

In this model, the school, particularly the high school, is a large structure made up of different customer-oriented enterprises, all competing for the "business of student-customers." We will discuss this model in detail later in the chapter, when we talk about students' everyday experiences in schools.

■ The School as Developer of Human Potential

The school attempts to ensure that each individual develops her or his intellectual, social, and physical capacities to the fullest possible measure. The teachers are specialists in identifying students' strengths and needs and in matching the instructional program to these strengths and needs. The cornerstone of the school is the uniqueness of each child, and the school is designed to be flexible and have a positive impact on the child. By focusing on the individual child, the school runs the risk of preparing self-oriented, highly individualistic students.

■ The School as Family

The school-as-family model focuses on establishing a caring community in which the child's emotional and familial needs are addressed, especially if families are not able to respond to those needs. In response to changing family conditions many schools offer such programs as extended day or after-school care. More than just a great baby-sitter, the teacher in this model nurtures the students' development not only in the intellectual arena but also in the emotional and moral arenas.

■ The School as Social Panacea

Here the school becomes the society's problem solver. This model is similar to the family model, but has a more targeted purpose. If poverty exists or parents are neglecting their responsibilities, the school takes on the problem and acts as a panacea, offering a remedy that can benefit the whole society. Whereas schools once were limited to passing on the moral and intellectual heritage to students, schools in this model "do what is needed." Driver's education, multicultural education, sex education, drug education, and AIDS education are all examples of the school attempting to solve new social problems.

■ The School as Acculturator

Reflect on the model of school as an acculturator with the image in this section of your CD-ROM.

The school in this model brings together people of divergent backgrounds who must accommodate themselves to one culture. Reflecting Thomas Jefferson's view, the school's role in the United States is to teach "the American way of life." In acculturating students, schools pass on the customs, values, and social patterns of the dominant group to immigrants and others who have been excluded from full participation in this society. According to this view, the school is a melting pot whose function is to minimize the influence of minority ethnic, racial, and religious influences.

The acculturation function of schools, however, extends way beyond acquainting newcomers to American ways. Let's explore a little more deeply what the terms *society* and *culture* mean and how these two entities affect the roles of schools.

PAUSE AND REFLECT

❶ Which of these models corresponds most closely to your elementary and secondary school experiences? If you had to select one as the model for a school in which you would like to teach, which would it be?

Schools as Cultures

■ meaning of culture

A *society* is a grouping of individuals bound together by various connections. Some of the connections might be shared geographic space or similar racial features, but what really connects people is their shared culture. A *culture* is composed of beliefs about what is right and wrong, good and bad. It also includes the dominant ideas, stories and myths, artistic works, social habits, and organizations of a group. Another key aspect of culture is language and the ways people use it in relationship to one another. Every group of people who live together in relative harmony can be said to share a culture. Someone once defined culture as simply "just the way we are 'round here." Without a common culture, every time we walked into a room or passed someone on the street, we would grope for a way to respond. Our culture tells us what to do.

All sorts of cultures exist. A family possesses a culture. The U.S. Marine Corps possesses a culture. After a few weeks and months, a college dorm assumes a distinctive culture. A school also possesses a culture. Think about it: each school you have attended has had its own culture—a set of beliefs, values, traditions, and ways of thinking and behaving—that distinguishes it from other social institutions and other schools.

Cultures, including **school cultures,** can be good or bad, leading to good human ends or poor ones. A strong, positive school culture engages the hearts and minds of children, stretching them intellectually, physically, morally, and socially. A school with a weak, negative culture may have the same type of physical plant, student-teacher ratio, and curriculum as a neighboring good school, but it may fail to engage students. Everyone, students and teachers, goes through the motions, but with few of the positive effects that the strong-culture school provides.

■ Socialization

Because a human being comes into the world vulnerable and "not quite ready for prime time," adults play a crucial role in the child's survival. Besides food, shelter, and loving care, adults pass their culture on to their young. A major part of any culture is the skills and attitudes necessary to function in that particular society. In our contemporary American society, we expect that most people will try hard to get along with one another, work cooperatively, and look after their families. Schools, as one of the most common institutions in the United States, have a significant role in teaching young people how to be social in the American context.

This task of passing on a society's culture to the young is called **socialization**, defined as the general process of social learning whereby the child learns the many things he or she must know to become an acceptable member of a particular social environment. Besides the family and the school, the major socializing agencies in the life of a young person are peer groups, religious institutions, youth organizations, political and economic institutions, the mass media, and, in some cases, work environments. Each of these agencies has its own values, norms, and mores that it attempts to teach so that the individual child will know how to act and behave in a manner acceptable to other agency members. Some agencies, such as the school, are formally created and organized, and some, such as the peer group, are informally created and organized. Every school attempts to socialize children by getting them to value those things the school teaches both explicitly and implicitly. The more successful students tend to accept these values, whereas many of the less successful ones reject the ways of thinking and behaving that the school tries to teach.

What are these values, and how are they communicated to students? One researcher suggests that schools value several specific ways of thinking and behaving.[7] One is compliant behavior as opposed to personal initiative. Students soon learn to give the teacher what she or he wants or expects. Reward systems

POLICY MATTERS !

School Dress Codes

What's the Policy?

No issue in education is of greater concern than student behavior or discipline. In the wake of the Columbine High School shootings in 1999, in which the killers dressed in "Goth" or "trench-coat Mafia" outfits, came a rash of suspensions across the nation over inappropriate dress.

One of the leading school policy options in this arena is the adoption of school uniforms. Currently, 20 percent of the nation's school districts use uniforms, although most of these districts have a voluntary school uniform policy.

In addition, many schools enforce a dress code. For example, some schools may forbid students to wear clothing that advertises alcohol and tobacco products. In 2001, many schools adopted restrictions on girls' clothing, as extremely low-slung jeans became fashionable.

How Does It Affect Teachers?

The way students conduct themselves in school is of intense interest to everyone, including parents, administrators, and teachers. Many schools such as those in Long Beach, Calif., which has had a very successful uniform policy for years, attribute dramatic declines in school violence and misbehavior to uniforms. If students are not distracted by their own or others' clothing or misbehavior, they and their teachers are able to spend more time on the teaching and learning tasks that are central to education.

In schools without uniforms, teachers may find themselves responsible for interpreting and enforcing the specifics of a general dress code. If they do not handle violations effectively, teachers could create even more distraction than the student who wears the inappropriate clothing.

What Are the Pros?

Proponents say that school uniforms offer a concrete and visible means of restoring order and discipline to the schools. Instead of kids fighting one another over designer jackets or the latest hot sneaker or creating an economic pecking order based on who can afford the "in" clothing, there is

---

used by schools teach students to "read" both the teacher and the system to determine just what is expected to get the grade, the teacher's attention, or the sticker with the smiling face. Similarly, competitiveness is learned through the examples of athletics, grading systems that compare students to one another, and ability grouping to separate students into classes according to their achievement. The many ways in which students learn what a school values include how the school allocates time to subjects of study, the rules established for the school, and even the architecture of the school.

■ *reading school cultures*   As a future teacher, you should work to be able to *read cultures*. What rules of behavior, rituals and ceremonies, and accepted patterns of teacher-student interaction are communicated to students at a particular school? Does the "climate" of the classroom and the school suggest warmth, support, and nurturing

The dead might as well try to speak to the living as the old to the young.

—WILLA CATHER

of individuals, or do you observe a mood of disinterest, regimentation, and antipathy among staff and students? Most importantly, what is the school's deeper message about what stance its students should take toward the current culture?

greater economic equality because everyone wears the same clothes.

Also, requiring dress codes or uniforms for public school students appeals to an intuitive belief that increased structure will improve students' behavior, attitudes, and learning. In this country, school uniforms are associated with private and Catholic schools, which are perceived to be more orderly and safe and offer a better learning environment than public schools. Similarly, a clear dress code can offer a sense of structure to students that will allow them to concentrate on matters other than their clothing.

What Are the Cons?

Those opposing school uniforms see this policy as un-American, attempting to stifle children's individuality and sense of distinctiveness and perhaps even depriving them of their rights. Opponents of uniforms also point out that research results are mixed. One recent study of 5,000 tenth graders, for example, found that "sophomores in schools requiring uniforms were no less likely than their more casually dressed peers to fight, smoke, drink alcohol, take drugs, or otherwise get in trouble in schools."*

Dress codes create problems too, especially those that are vague or unevenly enforced. Students and teachers may expend energy dealing with clothing issues that could be more productively used.

What Do You Think?

1. **Have you had any firsthand experience teaching or observing students who are required to wear school uniforms? If so, what did you observe?**
2. **Do you favor a schoolwide uniform policy? Why or why not?**
3. **How would you, as a teacher, go about approaching a student who was violating the school's dress code?**

*David Brunsma and Kerry Rockquemore, *Journal of Educational Research*, American Educational Research Association: Washington, DC, September/October, 1998.

SOURCES

Jessica Portner, "Schools Ratchet Up the Rules on Student Clothing, Threat," *Education Week,* May 12, 1999.

Debra Viadero, "Uniform Findings," *Teacher Magazine on the Web* (January 1999). Available at: **http://www.edweek.org/tm/**.

 Visit the material at the web site to learn more about this policy issue.

Schools as Transmitters or Re-creators of Culture

Underlying the various models of school discussed earlier are different purposes and therefore different curricular emphases. Two models are especially prominent on the American educational scene: (1) the school as the social institution where the young receive from the older generation the very best of their culture and (2) the school as the social institution where the young learn skills and become agents of social change.

■ *Transmitting Culture*

In the model of the school as acculturator, schools exist to advance society by ensuring that the young know and appreciate the dominant ideas and values of their society's culture. The goal of cultural transmission in the American public

schools reflect culture

schools is to teach the American way of looking at the world and the American way of doing things. Without even being conscious of it, our teachers instruct our young in our version of reality and our way of handling the real world, and so, too, do the schools of other countries. Schools in northern India, for instance, differ markedly from those in Ghana, and both have sharp differences from their counterparts in the United States. However, the schools of each country are attempting to perform a similar function: to transmit the unique culture of the country to its newest members, the young.

This desire to ensure that the young share the common culture may explain why in many U.S. school systems, we teach American history in the third, seventh, and eleventh grades. It can also explain why, for instance, we give little attention to the history of China, even though China is the most populous nation on earth and has one of the world's oldest and richest cultural heritages.

Usually people who view schools as transmitting culture talk about society as an organism, a living thing that can thrive or deteriorate based on how well different elements of society function together. When a society is healthy, its various components (the government, schools, communities, families, and individuals) each do what they ought to be doing and they each work in concert with each other. Conflict, from this point of view, is negative, and society should work toward finding consensus among various groups and toward eliminating any conflict. From this perspective then, it is vitally important that the older generation, including parents and teachers, help the young find value and meaning in their own culture so they too will internalize its values and contribute to its smooth functioning.

need to understand other cultures

■ **Acculturation and Diversity**   Several dangers lurk in this tendency of schools to concentrate on transmitting the dominant culture. If schools offer the young an understanding of only the prevailing culture, the result may be an attitude of smug cultural superiority, which often leads nations and individuals to foolish actions. In cultural terms, what we do not know we often do not respect, and without mutual respect, people easily become enemies.

In recent decades, instantaneous electronic communications, missile-delivered nuclear weapons, and interdependent national economic structures have increasingly made the world a global village, and our students must learn how to function in this new world.

arrival of new cultures

Moreover, in recent decades the United States has experienced an enormous immigration from Southeast Asia, the Middle East, Central America, and elsewhere. These new Americans tend to be young. They and their children are hungry for education. Although they are eager to learn American ways and American culture, teachers and students need to be respectful of the cultures these students bring with them.

Visit the material at the web site to link to more information about acculturation and diversity.

Sometimes, schools, as part of acculturating children, tend to pull them away from their individual ethnic backgrounds. For example, one out of five of our students go home at night to families where English is a second language. As they become acculturated, using English becomes more important for these children, and their first languages become something private and rarely used in public. Other school models, more commonly, try to acculturate the child while supporting his or her ethnic heritage. Elementary schools in Calexico, Calif., serve large populations of newly arrived Mexican children. Teachers design the classrooms so that English and Spanish languages and cultures are honored. According to Mike Rose, who visited and wrote about one Calexico school, children learn to operate effectively in both languages.[8]

acculturating immigrant students

Students participate in a frog dissection activity.
(© Bob Daemmrich/The Image Works)

The presence of new Americans can be a valuable resource in the effort to increase multicultural understanding and appreciation. Therefore, although American schools need to transmit American culture, we must realize that what we call "American culture" has always embraced many cultures. Nevertheless, the primary responsibility of the schools to assist foreign-born students in the acquisition of a high level of English proficiency stands. We will return to this thorny issue when we discuss multiculturalism in the chapter entitled "Who Are Today's Students in a Diverse Society?".

■ *Reconstructing Society*

Some of the issues just mentioned, including threats from international terrorists and nuclear weapons; a highly interdependent world economy; large numbers of immigrants; and the hunger, suffering, and social injustices rampant in our modern world, have led some educators to the view that schools must become the tool of social reconstruction. Instead of seeing schools as places where the collective wisdom of the past dribbles down to those who have the capacity and interest to make use of it, these educators assume a much more active, even assertive, role for the school. From this perspective, schools and teachers should work toward activating student interest and commitment to improving society. Unlike those who wish to transmit culture, educators who wish to reconstruct society accept the existence of conflicts between different groups and look at them as important ways to understand these groups' view of social problems.

■ *school as social leavener*

These **social reconstructionists** see the school forming the young into agents of change and also participating in the decision about how society needs to change. They have little reverence for the accumulated wisdom of the past and more concern for the world's problems and the necessity to create a new order. They see the successful student not so much as a cultivated person but as

Reflect on social reconstructionism with the image in this section of your CD-ROM.

an autonomous citizen ready to join with others to tackle the world's ills and help in the reconstruction of society.

Even among social reconstructionists, however, a wide range of emphases and views are evident. Social reconstructionists fall into two broad categories: *democratic reconstructionists* and *economic reconstructionists.*

■ Democratic Reconstructionists

Democratic reconstructionists see the solution to certain trends and current issues, such as racism, poverty, and the destruction of the ecosystem, in an aroused and skilled citizenry.[9] The school's mission, then, is to prepare students for vigorous participation in their government. The focus of schooling is on developing knowledge of democratic processes, critical thinking skills, and group process skills so the student can fruitfully work with others for social improvement. In more active programs, students actually select, study, and work on a community environmental problem, such as the polluting of landfills with unrecycled garbage.

■ Economic Reconstructionists

Economic reconstructionists tend to take a harsher view of the dominant culture and see schools as the pliant servants of those in power. Instead of humanistic institutions attempting to free individuals from their own lives' limitations, schools are institutions operating for the economic powers-that-be. The influence of corporate values is seen in many phases of school life, from the way textbooks are used to our widespread use of testing.[10] Moreover, economic reconstructionists often argue that schools *claim* to serve the needs of all while, in fact, serving the needs of the elites, or those with the most power. Economic reconstructionists usually see schools as disguising that fact, either by their own naivete or by their willing support of the system that already exists. Because of their deep suspicions of, and sometimes outright disgust with, capitalism, economic reconstructionists are often called *neo-Marxists.*

■ *Paulo Freire*

One noted economic reconstructionist is the Brazilian educator Paulo Freire. Freire's first book, *The Pedagogy of the Oppressed,* describes his work with poverty-stricken, illiterate peasants in his native Brazil.[11] As Freire tried to teach these adults to read, he saw they were trapped in an economic and social web over which they had little control. He saw, too, that the normal mechanisms of education, such as grading and control by the teacher, imposed on the peasants passivity and subservience to authority. For Freire, the typical methods and routines of schooling are a form of oppression in that they keep people from becoming fully human. To counter this, Freire taught literacy by helping the peasants to (1) name their problem (a polluted water supply); (2) analyze the problem (sewage contamination of the springs); and (3) collectively take action (design and build a new sewage system) to solve the problem. In this manner, education becomes a tool both to develop the human potential of people, such as the ability to read, and to free them from oppressive conditions such as poverty and disease.

Although both democratic and economic reconstructionists focus on social problems and try to foster in students the attitudes and skills necessary to solve them, the economic reconstructionists question more deeply the fundamental economic and social arrangements in a society. They see education as a necessary means for restructuring the power structures in a society. For them, money, power, and control of education are tightly bound together. Critics of the social-reconstructionists' approach to education see it as naive and wrong-headed. Critics emphasize that our current economic and social relations are too fragile and serious to be toyed with by innocent and immature children.

■ *critics of social reconstructionism*

■ *the new globalization*

As we gingerly enter the new millennium, a relatively new concept of the world as a highly interrelated and interdependent community is emerging. Increasingly, our students need to be educated in terms of this global interconnectivity, clearly drawing on the best ideas of the past, and also need to be ready to address the fresh demands of a new world. For our educators, that is a big job!

PAUSE AND REFLECT

❶ Which of these two broad purposes, transmitting the culture or reconstructing the culture, has the most appeal to you? Why?

What Do Studies Reveal About the Nature of Schools?

Researchers often look at the everyday events of human life and see patterns of which the rest of us may be only vaguely aware. In the next several pages, we present a few of these studies, focusing first on elementary schools, then middle schools and junior highs, and finally high schools, and examine the patterns the researchers noticed.

■ *Life in Elementary Schools*

■ *Jackson's study*

One of the best perspectives on how time is usually spent in the elementary classroom is provided by Philip W. Jackson's classic study *Life in Classrooms*.[12] Anthropologists have taught us that the humdrum aspects of human existence have cultural significance and that we must look at the most routine events in an elementary classroom if we are to understand what happens there. Are certain trivial acts repeated many times? How often do they occur? What is their cumulative effect on the child? What do they teach the child? Jackson's observations of elementary school classrooms show how revealing the answers to these questions can be.

Have you ever figured out how many hours a child spends in school? In most states, the school year is 180 days. The day typically begins at 8:30 AM and ends at 3 PM, a total of six and one-half hours. Thus, if a child doesn't miss a day of school, he or she spends more than 1,000 hours in school each year. Including kindergarten, the average child will spend more than 10,000 hours in elementary school. How are those hours typically spent?

You may think first of the curriculum, which is so many hours of reading, language arts, mathematics, science, play, social studies, music, art, and so on, but what do students really *do* when they are studying these subjects? They talk to each other or the teacher. They read silently and aloud. They yawn. They look out the window. They raise their hands. They line up. They stand up. They sit down. In short, they do a number of different things, many of them commonplace and trivial. To understand why some of these things happen, we first need to look at what the teacher does.

■ *controlling discussions . . .*

■ The Teacher's Role   Jackson has observed that the elementary school teacher engages in as many as a thousand interpersonal interchanges each day. The teaching-learning process consists, for the most part, of talking, and the teacher controls and directs discussion. The teacher acts as a *gatekeeper*, deciding

Waiting and delayed grati-fication are common occur-rences in elementary school classrooms.
(© Elizabeth Crews)

who shall and who shall not speak. (One may debate whether this *should* be the teacher's role, but clearly most teachers function this way.)

. . . supplies, privileges

The teacher also acts as a *dispenser of supplies*. Because both space and resources are limited and the number of students wishing to use them at any one time is likely to be greater than the supply, the teacher must dole them out. A related function is the *granting of special privileges* to deserving students: passing out the milk, sharpening pencils, taking the roll, or operating the videocassette player. Although little teacher time is involved in awarding these special jobs, they are important because they help to structure the classroom socially as a system of rewards and punishments.

. . . time

Timekeeping is another teacher responsibility. It is the teacher who decides when a certain activity ends and another begins, when it is time to stop science and begin spelling, and when to go outside for recess. In some schools, the teacher is assisted in timekeeping by bells and buzzers that signal when a period is over. As Jackson observes, things happen because it is time for them to occur and not because students want them to happen.

result of crowded conditions

All these teacher functions can be seen as responses to the crowded conditions in the classroom. If the teacher were dealing with one student at a time in a tutorial situation, gatekeeping, dispensing supplies, granting special privileges, and timekeeping would not be necessary, but since a tutorial setting is not possible, much time and energy are spent keeping order. The resulting atmosphere has unavoidable effects on the students. What are some of the consequences for students in crowded classroom conditions?

What Students Experience   One inevitable outcome for students that results from the teacher's "traffic management" functions is *delay*. Because students' actions are limited by space, material resources, and the amount of teacher attention they can command, there are definite limits on their freedom in class. In addition, because the class ordinarily moves toward a goal as a group rather than as individuals, its slowest members often determine the pace of progress.

waiting

Waiting is therefore a familiar activity for elementary school children—that is, waiting in line to get a drink of water, waiting with arm propped at the elbow to be called on to answer a question, waiting to use the scissors, waiting until others have finished their work to go on to the next activity, waiting until four other students have finished reading aloud for a chance to do so, and so on.

denial of desire

Denial of desire is another common experience for the elementary student. A question goes unanswered, a raised hand is ignored, talking out of turn is not permitted, relief of bodily functions is allowed only at specified times. Some denial is necessary and probably beneficial, but one thing is certain: delayed gratification and denied desire are learned in school, and a certain amount of student frustration is bound to develop.

interruptions

Students also experience frequent *interruptions* of many sorts, such as interruptions of seatwork by the teacher to give additional instructions or to clarify one student's question, interruptions when messages from the principal's office are read aloud to the class, interruptions for fire drills, interruptions when the teacher is working with one student and another student misbehaves, and so on. Students are expected either to ignore these intrusions or to quickly resume their activities.

The emphasis on an inflexible schedule contributes to the sense of interruption by often making students begin activities before their interest has been aroused and stop at the height of their interest when the schedule dictates that they must begin another task.

social distraction

A related phenomenon is *social distraction*. Students are often asked to behave as if they were in solitude when in fact they are surrounded by thirty or so other people. During assigned seatwork, for example, communication among students is often discouraged, if not forbidden. To be surrounded by friends, sometimes seated across from one another at a table, and not be allowed to talk is a difficult and tempting situation. As Jackson remarks, "These young people, if they are to become successful students, must learn how to be alone in a crowd."[13]

patience is a necessity

Delay, denial, interruption, and *social distraction,* then, are characteristic of life in elementary classrooms. Given these classroom conditions, it seems likely that the student who either possesses or quickly develops patience would find school more tolerable than the student who lacks it. The ability to control desires, delay rewards, and stifle impulses seems to be characteristic of successful students, whereas less successful students exhibit less patience and more impulsiveness.

Life in Middle and Junior High Schools

little descriptive information

many grade configurations

We know much less about the routines and roles of students and teachers in the middle grades than we do about those in elementary grades. One reason is that researchers have been late focusing on the middle years. Another related and obvious issue, however, is the variety of grade-clustering patterns evident in our schools. A national survey of middle-grade practices and trends found that schools around the country enrolled seventh-grade students in about thirty

Perhaps the greatest of all pedagogical fallacies is the notion that a person learns only the particular thing he is studying at the time.

—B. BRADFORD BROWN

different grade spans. For example, some schools were structured to educate all students in grades K–12; others served primarily elementary and middle grades such as K–8; and yet others served middle to high school students such as grades 7–12. Some schools were structured just for students in the middle grades, but even within this group there was great variety. Middle schools mainly contained students in grades 6–8, but also in 5–8, 5–7, and 6–7. Other schools were strictly 7–8 schools, and another grade configuration of junior high schools structured students in grades 7–9, 6–9, or 5–9.[14]

What difference does it make where students in the middle grades are educated? Researchers at Johns Hopkins University found direct relationships between grade configuration and such important educational characteristics as school goals, report card entries, course offerings, instructional practices, relationships between students and staff, and other trends in middle-grade practices.[15] One factor related to the organization of middle grades was size. In the various schools examined, enrollment in grade 7 ranged from five students to more than 2,250. Consider for a moment the very different educational experiences these students will have in their middle school years in regard to familiarity with peers, class size, teacher contact, and so forth.

■ *varying school sizes*

School goals were also examined across different grade configurations. Regardless of the grade span of their schools, most principals identified mastery of subject matter and basic skills as the most important goals at their institutions. However, secondary goals of educational importance varied by the school organization. As might be expected, principals of K–12 schools assigned more importance to higher-level skills such as reasoning, problem solving, and creative thinking. Principals of K–8 schools put less emphasis on personal growth and developmental issues such as self-esteem and self-knowledge than principals of middle schools.[16]

■ *varying school goals*

The goals that schools set for students influence middle school education in other ways as well, including the curriculum offered and the instructional methods used. The same study found that schools serving younger students, such as K–8, typically offered fewer elective courses such as home economics or keyboarding for students in the middle grades. Seventh- and eighth-grade teachers used drill practices more often and made less use of higher-order thinking activities such as writing essays, using computers, and discussing controversial issues. These schools, however, also reported greater use of such methods as peer- or cross-grade tutoring.[17]

■ *staffing patterns*

Another distinction among schools of different grade configurations was seen in staffing patterns. Classroom structure for students in the middle grades varied from completely self-contained classrooms, in which one teacher taught one group of students all major subject areas, to completely departmentalized schools in which each teacher specialized in a single subject area and taught several different classes of students. As you might expect, schools serving younger students (K+) had a larger percentage of self-contained classrooms, whereas middle schools showed a greater percentage of departmentalized staffing.[18]

■ *licensure patterns*

Teachers also differed by type of licensure held. Teachers with secondary licensure were more likely to be subject matter oriented, and middle-grade students who were taught by subject matter experts showed higher levels of achievement. On the other hand, teachers who were licensed in elementary education were likely to be more student centered and tended to focus on both the academic and personal development of individual students. The research indicated that relationships between students and teachers in self-contained classrooms tended to be more positive.[19]

So we see a variety of educational experiences occurring along a number of dimensions in the middle grades. Is one means of educating students in the middle grades best? Probably not. The many aspects of diversity we have just examined, from grade configuration to school goals to teacher orientation, appear to present a series of trade-offs in educating students in the middle grades. What is consistently being identified as important for educating students in the middle grades, however, is that the developmental needs of early adolescents must be acknowledged and considered in developing and organizing programs.

■ *Life in High Schools*

No aspect of our public educational system has recently received more study than our high schools. This is probably because we are worried about our teenagers and dissatisfied with the educational experiences we are providing them. Although conducted with reform in mind, the studies, some of them hardly new, provide important insights into how students and teachers live and carry on in our high schools. For instance, in 1983 the Carnegie Foundation for the Advancement of Teaching released a study, *High School: A Study of Secondary School in America,* intended to guide discussion about needed reforms in American secondary education. In this investigation of fifteen supposedly unique schools, the researchers found striking commonalities among them.[20] Typically, a school day is divided into six or seven fifty-minute periods (although in recent years, high schools around the nation have been experimenting with a wide variety of class-time structures). Hall passes, dress codes, and rules against smoking are often part of life in a high school. From most principals' points of view, absenteeism, class cutting, and parents' disinterest are moderately serious problems; fights, thefts, and vandalism are more serious problems.[21] High school is a place where young people experiment with growing up, find the support that may not be available at home, and attempt to accomplish a variety of goals ranging from marking time to finding social acceptance to preparing for intellectual challenges. Although some high schools have departed from this picture, this description still fits the great majority of our schools.

■ **Inside Classrooms**   What happens in classrooms during those typical six- or seven-period days? In a review of instructional practices in American classrooms, Larry Cuban concluded that the high school of today is *remarkably similar to the high school of the 1890s.*[22] Cuban gathered descriptions of more than 1,200 classrooms. He examined how classroom space was arranged; the ratio of teacher talk to student talk; the manner of grouping the teacher used for instruction (whole-class, small-group, or individual); the presence of learning or interest centers used by students as part of a normal school day; and how much physical movement students were allowed within the classroom. Cuban found that, just as in the 1890s, today's high school classes are characterized by whole-class instruction, teachers talking most of the time while students listen, little student mobility, and a narrow range of activities completed by the entire class at one time.

Ernest Boyer, the lead researcher in the Carnegie study, and fellow observers found similar characteristics. They noted, for example, a standardized use of classroom space: rooms equipped with rows of desks for thirty or more students, a teacher's desk at the front of the rows, and the traditional black or

Visit the material at the web site to link to more information about middle and junior high schools.

■ *high school similarities*

Visit the material at the web site to link to more information about research on high schools.

■ *same as the 1890s*

green chalkboard. The use of time is also routine, consumed by procedural tasks like taking attendance and keeping records, although relentlessly interrupted by announcements on the intercom, pep assemblies, photo sessions, and many other distractions.[23] Boyer also describes teachers' powerlessness over the factors that influence the quality of instruction they can deliver: the number of students in a class, the lengths of school days and periods, the formats of report cards, the courses that will be taught, and even the textbooks that will be used. Pressures of time and heavy student loads invite traditional, teacher-centered instruction such as lecturing, question-and-answer sessions, and routine homework assignments. Too often, students play passive roles in classrooms dominated by regimentation and conformity.[24]

pressure on teachers

■ Multiple Purposes   Tracing the history of the high school, Ernest Boyer concluded, "[H]igh schools have accumulated purposes like barnacles on a weathered ship."[25] Americans seem to want high schools to accomplish everything. The resulting confusion of goals is evident in the variety of goal statements adopted by the states for their schools, in the written goals found in teachers' manuals or school district curriculum guides, and in teacher and student responses when asked about school goals.

multiple goals

In an attempt to accomplish these multiple purposes, high schools have developed a comprehensive curriculum with many elective courses. How do students decide what to take and what not to take among dozens or, in some cases, hundreds of courses? Students report that their choices are guided more by parents and peers than by guidance counselors or teachers.[26] Boyer and his colleagues conclude that students' academic programs may be shaped most decisively by the "tracks" in which they are enrolled. *Academic* tracks stress the traditional subjects of English, mathematics, science, and foreign languages as preparation for college. A *general* track usually allows a greater number of elective courses and less rigorous versions of the traditional subjects. *Vocational* tracks may include a combination of academic and job-related courses; students in these tracks are preparing for a job after graduation. Because of the variations in courses required for these different tracks and the differing standards for student achievement among them, a high school education can take on myriad meanings.

influence of tracking

Reflect on the shopping mall high school with the image in this section of your CD-ROM.

■ The Shopping Mall High School   Another group of researchers suggest that the high schools' characteristics resemble those of a shopping mall, with an emphasis on variety and choice for the consumer,[27] a model mentioned earlier in this chapter. Given a diverse student body with many different interests, high schools have offered a diverse curriculum in an attempt to provide something for everybody. Students are expected to make their own course selections; the schools maintain neutrality in regard to students' or parents' choices among the many alternatives offered. The customer has the final word.

Staying with the shopping mall metaphor, the study found that some customers (students) are serious about buying, others are just browsing and looking for ideas on what to buy, and still others are at the mall to meet their friends and "cruise." Faced with customers with such different levels of commitment, teachers reach accommodations, or treaties, that promote mutual goals or keep the peace. For example, some teachers make their deals crystal clear when they advise students, "Don't get into my class if you don't want to work." If students don't want to play by these rules, they don't have to take the course.

classroom "treaties"

Kids may do poorly in school not simply because they aren't motivated to study or because they lack ability, but because they are intent on maintaining their standing in a crowd that regards academic achievement as uncool.

—B. Bradford Brown

Most classroom treaties are not this formal or public, however; rather, they are *tacit* arrangements made to accommodate students and teachers in a manner satisfactory to all. If teachers preach or push too hard, some students resist. To avoid resistance, individual teachers strive to find the appropriate balance in their classrooms between requiring academic rigor and allowing students to opt out of learning entirely. As one teacher commented, "I think I get along fairly well with most of the kids, but to be perfectly truthful, I think I get along because I don't put a lot of pressure on them."[28]

■ *specialty shops*

Within the shopping mall high school can be found "specialty shops," the niches for students and families wanting more learning and school engagement. These can include top-track programs, special education programs, vocational and technical education programs, and extracurricular programs like marching band or football. Because the students in these programs have been designated as special, they tend to receive special attention. In contrast, the average or unspecial students are generally ignored by the specialty shops; they do not receive the additional commitment of time, personal relationships, and intensity of learning generally given to specialty-shop students.

■ *differences in opportunities*

School personnel were not precise about who the middle students were, using terms such as *average, general, normal,* and *regular,* so the researchers concluded, "Few characteristics of the shopping mall high school are more significant than the existence of unspecial students in the middle who are ignored and poorly served."[29] These students have no important allies or advocates. Their treaties are characterized by avoidance of learning, not engagement. Schools may try to nurture these students' self-esteem, but do not make academic demands on them. As a result, parents of these students occasionally demand a specialty program for their children or transfer them to private schools where purposes are more focused and attention is more personal. Without these opportunities to experience the purpose, push, and personalization of a specialty shop, the unspecial students become the losers in the educational marketplace.

As one reviewer of this study notes,[30] the researchers' evidence supports generalizations made by previous high school observers. For example, although students may have equal access to a high school education, enormous differences may exist in the opportunities available to them within their schools. Effective schooling is marked by a consensus of purpose, high expectations for students, and a supportive climate, and the treaties notion of this study emphasizes the power that teachers and students have to negotiate the quality of education. What can schools and teachers do to help *all* students be winners? The suggestions are many, but reading the shopping mall high school study may provide a starting point for thinking about the problem.

■ *exceptions to the norm*

These pictures of life in high school classrooms contrast with glimpses of teachers who challenge their students to think, to express themselves creatively, and to struggle with difficult questions. Students in such classes are pushed to perform as individuals; their teachers share a vision for them that includes high expectations of success. Which picture is more characteristic of high school life? Did the reform movements of the 1980s and 1990s create conditions in schools that will encourage teachers to teach well in the 2000s? At the time they finished their study, Boyer and his team believed the time was ripe for a true renewal of high school education. As the new century began, however, this renewal had yet to take place in most high schools, and new calls for reform were emerging.

PAUSE AND REFLECT

❶ The high school years are often said to be "the best years of your life." Do you agree with this assertion and why? If not, what could and should be done to change the high school experience?

A New Call for High School Reform

In 1996 the Carnegie Foundation for the Advancement of Teaching and the National Association of Secondary School Principals released a joint report entitled *Breaking Ranks: Changing an American Institution*. This national study offered many suggestions for improving the quality of American high schools. Among the factors cited for particular attention were personalization, coherence, time, and technology.[31]

Personalization   Finding American high schools too large, impersonal, and rigid, the report recommends that high schools break into units of no more than 600 students so that teachers and students can get to know one another better. Each teacher should be responsible for no more than ninety students each term. Every student should have a *personal adult advocate* who knows him or her well and follows the student's progress throughout high school. No student should be able to remain anonymous, and each student should feel special to some adult in the school. Each student should have a *personal progress plan*. Just as every student with a disability must have an individualized education program (IEP), described in the chapter entitled "Who Are Today's Students in a Diverse Society?", a student's progress plan would set learning goals that are continually reevaluated.

personal adult advocate

Coherence   High schools should identify the essentials that all students must learn to graduate. Instead of organizing the school by disciplinary departments, the report calls for a reorganization that more closely links the various subject matter areas so that learning makes more sense to students in terms of the real world and the application of what they know. Tests must also be aligned with what is taught so that both are consistent with each other.

connect subjects to real world

Time   Flexible, innovative scheduling should replace the fixed fifty-minute periods that dictate the amount of instructional time devoted to each course. The Carnegie unit (the standard type of course credit) should be abandoned or revised so that it no longer equates seat time with learning. Instead, high schools should identify a set of *essential learnings* in literature and language, math, social studies, science, and the arts, the areas where students must demonstrate achievement to graduate. Furthermore, schools should operate twelve months a year.

identify essential learnings

Technology   High schools should develop long-term plans for using computers and other technologies in all aspects of learning and teaching. Each high school should have a technology resource person to consult with and assist the staff.

develop technology use

One thing we can be certain of is that the American high school will continue to be a center of controversy and concern. Worrisome achievement scores and outbursts of violence, such as those in the late 1990s, will keep public attention focused on this segment of our educational system. Reform is in the air, and we'll discuss it in some depth in the chapter entitled "How Should Education Be Reformed?".

VOICES FROM THE CLASSROOM

Denis Gray is a law and justice teacher at Brighton High School in Boston, Massachusetts.

What Is a Good School?

I teach in an urban high school, and it's a good school. For me, there are three criteria for what makes for a good school:

1. The vast majority of its teachers want to have maximum impact on students through instruction.

2. Students have internalized the value of education and want to learn.

3. Most importantly, the educational and ancillary needs of all students are met.

To say the least, making this a reality in the lives of students does not go unchallenged. Students continually test us to determine whether we are "for real." Someone has said, "Students do not care what you know until they know that you care." Difficult students, in particular, test us. They test our patience, our self-control, our professionalism, our integrity, our faith, and our hope. Then, there are the self-doubt questions, "Am I a good teacher?", "Could my actions be interpreted as racist?", "What could/should I be doing that I'm not?"

There are many models and methodologies for instructing and learning. Most of them assume that students *want* to learn. Yet the reality is that for many students, there is a profound disconnect between education and success. They see that multimillion-dollar athletic contracts are signed by high school students. Colleges that should know better are not interested in ensuring that their athletes graduate. Many of our parents shower their children with the latest designer clothes and sneakers. Many of my students have part-time jobs to ensure that they always have pocket money. In their minds is the question, "If I get what I want now, why do I need an education?" Then there are issues of alienation and mistrust. Many students view the education we are trying to give them as the attempt by the "establishment" to "mess with their heads."

Of the three criteria, I believe No. 3 to be the most important. Today's urban school, as a matter of social conscience, must address the psychosocial needs of its students as never before. Today's teacher, as a matter of personal conscience, is required to assume many roles in students' lives, including being parent, protector, counselor, and confidant. It is a tough and complex job, but it's a job I love.

 Visit the web site for more Voices from the Classroom.

What Is a Good School?

school as human "product"

First, not all schools are good schools. Second, good schools do not just happen. They are made. A school is the product of people's intellectual and physical energies, and, at any particular moment, the way a school happens to be reflects efforts that have gone into creating and maintaining it. Like towns and civilizations, schools also rise and fall. They are human creations—dynamic and continually on the move.

No school, at least in the authors' experience, is "right" or "good" for all students, but although we believe this is true, we also believe that some schools are strikingly better than others—that is, some schools provide a significantly better education for a much larger percentage of their students than do others. These schools, referred to in the educational literature as **effective schools,** are the focus of this section.

One major problem associated with this question of effectiveness is what criteria to apply. Effective or good in what dimension? In engaged and happy students? In a teaching staff with high morale? In the percentage of students who get promoted or graduate? Go on to college? What kinds of colleges? How many succeed in business or professional life? In athletics? Socially? Ethically? *Effective,* as currently defined in most of the educational research literature, refers to students' achievement test scores in basic skills such as reading and mathematics. Although such tests measure skills that are hardly the only objectives of education, achievement in these academic areas is an important and widely acclaimed outcome of schooling. Also, achievement in reading and mathematics is easier to measure than good citizenship, artistic development, or interest in ideas.

Characteristics of an Effective School

definition of effective schools

Beginning more than twenty years ago, a number of educational researchers began looking for the qualities of effective schools.[32] Among the most significant characteristics they found to be correlated with high achievement in the basic skills were high expectations for student performance, communication among teachers, a task orientation among the staff, the ability to keep students on task, the expenditure of little time on behavior management, the principal's instructional leadership, the participation of parents, and the school environment.

The Teacher's Expectations Through their attitude and regular encouragement, teachers in effective schools communicate to students their belief that the students will achieve the goals of instruction. In effect, the teachers get across to students a "can-do" attitude about learning.

high, "can-do" expectations

Communication Among Teachers Teachers in effective schools do not operate in a vacuum, each in his or her isolated classroom. Instead, they talk among themselves about their work. They converse about one another's students. They know the curricular materials and activities that go on in one another's classrooms, and they are helpful to one another. In short, effective schools have teachers who are good colleagues.

high degree of colleagueship

Task Orientation The faculties of effective schools are highly task oriented. They begin instruction early in the class period and end instruction late in the period. The staff approach their teaching responsibilities with a serious air and waste little time in class. Whether the classes are formal or informal, underneath the surface of events lies a seriousness of purpose that is communicated to students.

serious attitude

Academic Engaged Time *Academic engaged time* (or *academic learning time*) refers to the amount of time students are actually engaged in relevant content-related activities. Research has demonstrated a tight link between the amount of time devoted to academic learning tasks and students' achievement.[33] This characteristic involves the ability of a teacher to get students engaged in academic tasks, such as reading or solving math problems, and to keep their attention on these instructional activities.

keep students working

Behavior Management We have all been in classrooms with teachers who spent huge chunks of time trying to quiet students to get them "on task" or who, in the course of correcting one student, disturbed all the rest, causing a ripple of

maintain classroom order

Good communication among teacher, student, and parents is key to good teaching.
(© Bob Daemmrich/The Image Works)

distraction throughout the room. Teachers in effective schools have learned techniques to minimize the time devoted to managing students. They are efficient both in handling discipline problems and in implementing the learning activities. In addition, these teachers do not routinely resort to corporal punishment, because they use other techniques to deal with student behavior.

principal as instructional leader

The Principal   Principals play an important role in effective schools. Instead of being faceless bureaucrats aimlessly shuffling papers, the principals of effective schools are instructional leaders. They have strong views on the purposes of education and are vitally concerned about the quality of teaching and learning in their schools. Still, the principal is perceived as democratic in approach and cooperative in relationships with faculty. The effective principal gains teachers' confidence and clearly communicates to them a vision of what the school should accomplish and how each teacher can contribute toward this end.

parent involvement

Parents   An effective school reaches out and draws in parents instead of ignoring them or keeping them at arm's length. Parents are treated as key members of the learning team, as partners with the professional staff in helping their children achieve academic success. In addition to aiding in students' intellectual achievement, the involvement of parents can help improve their children's self-concepts, work habits, and attitudes toward school.

The School Environment   A school that is unsafe, hostile, and generally unruly is rarely a place of learning—at least not academic learning. On the other

■ *environment conducive to learning*

■ *another view*

hand, an environment that is calm, safe, pleasant, and orderly is conducive to learning.

Different studies often come up with different characteristics. A ten-year study of 140 schools in the Chicago area, which looked for more holistic measures of effectiveness (rather than just academic achievement), came up with a quite different list. Among the characteristics the study found to be associated with successful schools were coherence; good communication within the school community; vital subgroups of teachers (work groups with meaningful responsibilities); a wide range of student incentives (prizes and other forms of recognition); a clear disciplinary policy; and an extracurricular program stressing service to others.[34]

Attempts to answer the question "What is a good school?" are still incomplete. Although the characteristics cited are those identified by several extensive research projects, studies continue. Perhaps the reason the research does not demonstrate these as characteristics of effective schools is that not enough schools exists where these qualities prevail.

> *Achievement consists of never giving up. . . . If there is no dark and dogged will, there will be no shining accomplishment; if there is no dull and determined effort, there will be no brilliant achievement.*
>
> —HSUN TSU, CHINESE PHILOSOPHER

Nevertheless, it appears that whether one is measuring school effectiveness by test scores on math and reading tests or by the more holistic measures, certain features stand out in the schools that most successfully socialize students to behave in ways that the school values. The principal, faculty, and staff in such schools:

- Agree on what they are doing and why something is being done

- Clearly communicate their expectations to students

- Consistently enforce rules

- Provide an environment conducive to the accomplishment of learning tasks and the regular monitoring of students' academic progress

■ *other qualities of effective schools*

We have a strong suspicion that a number of qualities besides those mentioned here dramatically contribute to the making of a good school. Among these characteristics are a pervasive sense of curiosity, a passion for excellence, a strong belief in students' capacity to grow, and an environment of kindness and support.

The Unfinished Work of the Schools

As we mentioned at the start of this chapter, our question "What is a school?" has no single satisfactory answer. Schools are human inventions. People bring schools into being for a variety of social purposes. The overall purposes of schools are to advance the common good and help people live happy and successful lives. However, if schools are to serve a society, they must at least keep pace with that society. Many people who are concerned about our schools feel that the schools are moving very slowly while the rest of society experiences dynamic change. In effect, the schools are out of step with the society, usually being either too far ahead, which is the rarity, or lagging behind (the more common situation) the needs of the people they exist to serve.

■ *need for balance*

As happens often in times of tension, views polarize in the manner suggested in this statement by John Gardner, who was imagining the reactions of future scholars looking back at our age:

The twenty-third century scholars made another exceptionally interesting observation. They pointed out that twentieth-century institutions were caught in a savage crossfire between uncritical lovers and unloving critics. On the one side, those who loved their institutions tended to smother them in an embrace of death, loving their rigidities more than their promise, shielding them from life-giving criticism. On the other side, there arose a breed of critics without love, skilled in demolition but untutored in the arts by which human institutions are nurtured and strengthened and made to flourish. Between the two, the institutions perished.[35]

Nevertheless, the purposes for which schools are brought into being are still vital. People still desire good schools for their children, and, as you will see later in this book, many excellent ideas are being generated and movements are under way for the renewal of our schools.

A Final Word

today's challenges

Some readers may be uncomfortable with the idea that it is their job to renew the schools. Many may feel that becoming a good classroom teacher is sufficient. Teachers, however, are more than technicians in charge of their classrooms. As professional people, they and their colleagues must have a strong and clear voice in deciding how they render their services. It follows that the teacher is not simply responsible for his or her own performance but bears responsibility for the total educational enterprise. To live up to this responsibility requires a deep understanding of the schools and much hard work, but it is the very critical nature of the problems confronting the schools that makes teaching such an exciting occupation today. In the immediate future, education is where the action will be. You have a chance to complete this unfinished work of the schools.

KEY TERMS

democratic reconstructionists (18)

economic reconstructionists (18)

education (4)

effective schools (27)

reflection (1)

school cultures (13)

schooling (4)

social bet (5)

social reconstructionists (17)

socialization (13)

FOR REFLECTION

1 Can you think of some pieces of information you picked up on the street that you later "unlearned" in school? Can you think of some things you learned in school that your experience later taught you were untrue? Which has happened more often? What is your reaction?

2 To what extent did the schools you attended serve the purposes suggested by the various models we described? Can you suggest any models we have overlooked?

❸ Look at the cartoon in the "Education and Schooling" section of this chapter. Is it appropriate to any of the models of schools that we have discussed? Does it seem to you an apt comment on your own education?

❹ Has reading the accounts and research on the various levels of schools caused you to reconsider the grade level at which you would like to teach?

❺ How do you feel about the school as transmitter of the culture rather than of "the truth" or "just the facts"? What are some problems with the school being a transmitter of culture? What happens if the national government takes a very strong hand in this? What examples from history can you think of in which a government used schools to promote a particularly dangerous culture?

❻ How would you describe the cultures of the schools you have attended?

❼ This chapter cites several factors that are associated with good schools. Which five factors are, in your opinion, the most important, and why do you think so?

FOR FURTHER INFORMATION

PRINT RESOURCES

Ernest Boyer, *Basic School: A Community for Learning* (Princeton, NJ: The Carnegie Foundation for the Advancement of Teaching, 1995).

This was the final book of one of education's great practitioners and spokespersons. Practical wisdom is woven into a clear description of the kind of schools we can and should have.

Ivor Pritchard, *Good Education: The Virtues of Learning* (Washington, DC: Judd Publishing, 1998).

Pritchard's book explores the purpose of education and schooling, giving particular attention to the commonly neglected mission of the schools in character and moral education.

Diane Ravitch and Joseph P. Viteritti, *New Schools for a New Century,* ed. D. Ravitch and J. P. Viteritti (New Haven, CT: Yale University Press, 1997).

This collection of essays reflects our nation's struggles with school reform. What emerges is the view that to break away from our current factory model schooling, radical changes, such as charter schools or choice and new contractual arrangements, are needed.

Theodore R. Sizer, *Horace's Hope: What Works for the American High School* (Boston: Houghton Mifflin, 1996).

The third book in Sizer's Horace trilogy, this book embodies the principles espoused by the Coalition of Essential Schools, a reform-oriented association of secondary schools.

WEB RESOURCES

Eisenhower National Clearinghouse, *ENC Online.* Available at: **http://www.enc.org**.

ENC is a rich resource of research-based ideas about school improvement and curricular materials for classroom teachers from kindergarten through twelfth grade, particularly in mathematics and science.

Lee Shiney and Lajean Shiney, *Teacher's Edition Online: Tools for Teachers.* Available at: **http://www.teachnet.com/**.

This web site contains many resources for teachers, including links to information on such topics as classroom management, advice to student teachers, attention deficit disorder, drugs and violence in schools, and gangs.

Who Are Today's Students in a Diverse Society?

Chapter Preview In some ways, children never change. The pictures of children in our classic literature are as true today as when they were first written. Look at the conniving, mischievous Tom Sawyer, the overly curious Alice in Wonderland, or the tenacious Mafatu in *Call It Courage*. These characters are endearing to us in part because we have all known children like them. Real children of today are also very much like the children of yesterday or the children of tomorrow. Certain stages of cognitive, social, emotional, and physical development have been identified, and a similar progression through these stages occurs for everyone. We all have basic psychological and physical needs that cut across racial, cultural, age, and gender boundaries. Understanding these stages of development and areas of common needs gives the classroom teacher insight into student behavior and so helps the teacher develop appropriate classroom experiences. You learn a great deal about these subjects in your courses in child development and educational psychology.

However, it is also important to be sensitive to the great differences among students and to factors in our society that are directly affecting their lives. In this chapter, we hope to make you more fully aware of the diversity in our society and classrooms, the range of abilities among your students, and the schools' attempts to address all this diversity. We also hope to make you more deeply sensitive to the sorts of issues, potential problems, and benefits related to this diversity. This chapter emphasizes that:

- Studies of the demographic makeup of the country indicate shifts in ethnic composition.

- All children have basic needs. Being aware of and understanding these commonalities helps us understand the diverse needs of students.

- Students have many strengths and abilities that extend beyond the traditional emphasis in our schools on linguistic and analytic abilities. Approaches that recognize multiple views of intelligence and differing learning styles emphasize the great diversity in student learning and ability.

- Schools address the individual needs of students through multicultural, bilingual, special education, differentiated instruction, and gifted and talented programs.

- Cooperation between the school and various support agencies, such as community health, childcare, and social services, is increasing.

- To cope in today's classroom, teachers must be aware of many dimensions of student diversity.

Sources of Student Diversity

You will see diversity in your students along a number of dimensions, including who the students are, what they need, and their various kinds of abilities.

■ Racial, Ethnic, and Cultural Backgrounds

■ *racial and ethnic diversity*

Students in your classroom are likely to come from a variety of racial and ethnic backgrounds, representing many different cultures and ways of looking at the world. The term *race* refers to people with common ancestry and physical characteristics, whereas the term *ethnicity* applies to people who share a common culture, usually including language, customs, and religion. With the development of a richer, more varied society, differences in values and family expectations are more and more evident. For example, some families may place a premium on school and higher education, whereas other families may emphasize early entry into the workplace. But even though you will encounter a range of familial expectations for school achievement, all children deserve the best educational experience they can get while in school. Recognition of racial and ethnic differences can provide the understanding and insight needed for more effective instruction.

Diversity in the classroom means that your students will come from a wide range of cultural backgrounds, may speak a first language other than English, and may have a variety of learning abilities and learning styles.
(© Mary Kate Denny/PhotoEdit)

Languages Other Than English

ELL (English Language Learners)

■ *non-English-speaking students*

Some of your students may speak a primary language other than English. More than 3.4 million **limited English proficient (LEP)** students are enrolled in public or nonpublic elementary and secondary schools (about 7.6 percent of the total enrollment) and the number has increased every year for the last decade. Almost 70 percent of all LEP students are concentrated in the states of California (42 percent), Texas (15 percent), New York (6.5 percent), and Florida (7 percent).[1] Across the country, LEP students speak more than 100 different languages. Spanish is the non-English background of the great majority of LEP students (78 percent), followed by Vietnamese (2.7 percent), Hmong (1.8 percent), Cantonese (1.6 percent), French (Haitian) Creole (1.1 percent), and Korean (1.1 percent). All other language groups represent less than 1 percent of the LEP student population.[2]

Visit this chapter of the web site to link to up-to-date statistics on this topic.

Although you might think that these non-English-speaking youngsters are from recent immigrant families, a surprisingly large number of them were born and raised in the United States but have not learned English at home or in their community. About one in seven American children between five and seventeen years old speaks a home language other than English, and the percentage of such young people is growing two and one half times faster than the general school population.[3] Many of them also lack basic skills in the language spoken at home, which makes it more difficult to teach them English at school.

In addition, more than 2 million immigrant youths enrolled in U.S. schools in the past decade, and many of them are non-English speakers. As these children and youth enter schools, most will need to make sense of a new language, a new culture, and possibly a new way of behaving. An important function of teachers and schools is to offer a source of stability for students who are experiencing rapid change in their lives. We will discuss bilingual education programs, provided by schools to help both immigrant and American children, later in the chapter.

Socioeconomic Status

Socioeconomic status (SES) is the term used by the U.S. Bureau of the Census to classify economic conditions of people using a family's occupational status, income, and educational attainment as measures of status. Individuals high in income, occupational prestige, and amount of education are considered to be high in socioeconomic status and are usually seen by others to be upper-class people who are influential in their communities. In contrast, people low in socioeconomic status are seen as being lower-class people who have little prestige or power. Your students will come from families with varied socioeconomic backgrounds. The benefits of being a child from a high-SES family show up in school performance; as such, a child typically does much better academically than a student from a low-SES family. Teachers and schools are challenged to help overcome the debilitating effects of low SES on students from these families. This topic is discussed in more detail in the chapter entitled "What Social Problems and Tension Points Affect Today's Students?".

■ *SES related to school performance*

Gender

Boys and girls are different even when they come from the same socioeconomic, racial, or ethnic group. They are raised differently, and often society has different expectations of them. Treating boys and girls equitably as individuals

■ *avoiding gender stereotypes a challenge*

and not as gender stereotypes is a constant challenge for both male and female teachers. We will discuss this topic in more detail when we look at gender issues in the chapter entitled "What Social Problems and Tension Points Affect Today's Students?".

■ *Sexual Orientation*

■ *schools often hostile toward gay/lesbian students*

You are likely to have gay and lesbian students in your classroom, especially if you teach at the middle or high school level, and you are apt to encounter gay and lesbian parents of students at any level. Schools typically have not been welcoming environments for young homosexuals. Gay and lesbian students have often experienced taunting, harassment, and even violence because of their sexual orientation. As a teacher, you will be challenged to establish and maintain a safe and supportive classroom environment for these and all of your students. Again, see the chapter on "What Social Problems and Tension Points Affect Today's Students?" for a more detailed discussion of this topic.

■ *Diverse Needs*

■ *students with differing needs*

Psychologists and educators have identified a number of basic needs that all individuals experience, including needs for belonging, safety, and self-esteem. However, students in your classroom will develop at different rates and probably will display *diverse needs*. Students will also bring their own individual histories, backgrounds, and conditions that have influenced how and whether certain needs have been satisfied. For example, a child from a stable, secure home may have different needs than a child who has not had this kind of security. Recognizing diverse needs will help you better understand some student behaviors and perhaps increase your insight into how to respond.

■ *Diverse Abilities*

■ *academic diversity*

Another dimension of diversity will be seen in the academic *abilities, achievements,* and *learning styles* of your students. Some students will enter the school environment and immediately do well. Other students will appear not to respond to your teaching. One of your biggest challenges as a teacher will be to provide a variety of experiences and learning encounters to accommodate your students' diverse learning styles and abilities.

As we delve further into the topic of today's students in a diverse society, you will discover that you need to be aware of these sources of diversity to address the educational needs of your students. Let's examine each of these sources in more detail and consider how they will influence your ability to teach effectively.

Racial, Ethnic, and Cultural Diversity

Although American society has always been composed of various races, ethnicities, and cultures, today we are experiencing great cultural diversity.

■ *demographic changes*

The demographic composition of public school classrooms as we enter the twenty-first century reflects that diversity. Although about 29 percent of the total population are members of minority groups, 37 percent of school-age children are minorities, a figure that will continue to increase in the coming years.[4]

Visit this chapter of the web site to link to up-to-date statistics on this topic.

TABLE 2.1   Projections of the U.S. Population Age 0–17, 2000–2020 (millions)

Youth	2000	2010	2020	Change
Total youth*	71.7	73.6	77.8	+8.5%
White, non-Hispanic	45.9	43.0	41.8	−8.9%
Hispanic (of any race)	10.9	13.6	16.4	+50%
Black, non-Hispanic	10.8	11.7	12.9	+19%
Other races†	4.1	5.4	6.6	+61%

Increase in total nonwhite youth = +10.1 million, or +39%

Decrease in total white youth = −4.1 million, or −8.9%

*May not add exactly because of rounding.
†Includes American Indians; Alaskan Natives; and Pacific Islanders.
Source: *Youth Indicators 1996* (Washington, DC: U.S. Department of Education, National Center for Education Statistics, September 1996), p. 16.

As shown in Table 2.1, birth rates among minority groups are higher than those of white Americans, and immigration patterns are contributing to the increasing size of the minority population.

These national averages disguise the fact that minority groups are unequally distributed across the country. The fastest-growing states also have high percentages of minority youth. For example, the four states of California, Texas, New York, and Florida will have more than one-third of the nation's young people by 2010, and the youth population of each of these states will be more than 52 percent minority. By that same year, about twelve states will have more than 50 percent minority youth populations.[5] In the forty-seven urban school districts that constitute the "great city schools," including those in New York City, Los Angeles, and Chicago, an overwhelming majority of students are from minority groups.

increasing minority school population

As might be expected with increasing cultural diversity, teachers will encounter more students whose native language is not English and whose ethnic and cultural backgrounds reflect a Hispanic or Asian heritage. We noted earlier in this chapter, for example, that the four fastest-growing states already are home to most of the students who have a first language other than English.

"melting pot"

At one time, the United States was considered a "melting pot" of many different kinds of people. Immigrants were expected to give up the language and customs of their homelands and adopt the language and customs of their new country. During the nineteenth and early twentieth centuries, schools contributed to the concept of the melting pot by socializing and acculturating immigrant children to American ways while discouraging them from maintaining the ways of their homelands. Many states even passed laws forbidding instruction in any language but English. The basic idea was to produce a society with one dominant culture. This process of incorporating an immigrant group into the mainstream culture is often referred to as *enculturation* or **assimilation.** Many European immigrant groups were easily assimilated into the dominant American culture, but people of color were often prevented from doing so.

Acting White

Two researchers, Signithia Fordham and John Ogbu, studied a predominantly African American high school, Capitol High, in Washington, D.C., to see how students' sense of collective identity enters into the process of schooling and affects academic achievement. They conclude that many African-American students underachieve academically because they are afraid of being accused of "acting white."

Fordham and Ogbu argue that historically subordinate minorities like African Americans have developed a sense of collective identity, or sense of peoplehood, in opposition to the social identity of white Americans. Because African Americans have been excluded from true assimilation in economic, political, social, and psychological arenas, they develop an oppositional cultural frame of reference that includes protecting their identities and maintaining boundaries between themselves and white Americans. For African Americans to behave in a manner that falls within the white cultural frame of reference is to "act white" and is negatively sanctioned by the peer group.

The "teenage peer group" at Capitol High School (99 percent African-American student body) exerted strong pressure to reassure one another of black loyalty and identity by discouraging students from engaging in certain behaviors that were interpreted as "white." Being an academic high achiever was one such unacceptable behavior. Fordham and Ogbu found that many students succumbed to peer pressure and purposely underachieved academically. Many of these students were afraid of being labeled *brainiacs,* a term meaning that a person was smart but also a jerk. Worse yet for male students was to be known as a *pervert brainiac.* To be known as a brainiac was to question a male student's manhood, but to be known as a pervert brainiac left little doubt and was the kiss of death among peers.

Students who wanted to achieve academically and still be considered an accepted member of the peer group tried various strategies to avoid antagonizing their peers, including engaging in athletic activities, acquiring the protection of "tough guys" in return for assisting the latter in their schoolwork and homework, and clowning around. These students were careful not to brag about their academic achievements or to bring attention to themselves, but even in these instances, the researchers conclude, the students would do much better if they did not have to divert their time and attention into strategies to conceal their academic pursuits.

What are the implications of these findings? Clearly, schools must find ways to reinforce black identity that are compatible with academic achievement. Similarly, the African-American community must convince black children that academic pursuit is not synonymous with acculturation into white society. If the community can demonstrate that academic achievement is valued and appreciated, the children will get a different message.

Source: Signithia Fordham and John U. Ogbu, "Black Students' School Success: Coping with the Burden of 'Acting White,'" *The Urban Review* 18, no. 3 (1986), pp. 176–206.

■ *cultural pluralism*

The concept of the melting pot has generally been replaced by the notion of **cultural pluralism**, which calls for an understanding and appreciation of the cultural differences and languages among the nation's citizens. The goal is to create a sense of society's wholeness based on the unique strengths of each of its parts. Cultural pluralism rejects both assimilation and separatism, a philosophy that suggests each cultural group should maintain its own identity without trying to fit into an overall American culture. Instead, it seeks a healthy interaction among the diverse groups in our society—that is, each subculture maintains its own individuality while contributing to our society as a whole. As some commentators put it, cultural pluralism argues for replacing the melting-pot metaphor with that of a "mosaic" or "tapestry" in which the individual parts are still distinct but combine to make a unique whole.

■ Not There Yet

cultural pluralism not a reality

Many people have promulgated cultural pluralism as a desirable goal, but it does not currently exist in the United States. Although racial, ethnic, and cultural diversity do exist, equality among the various groups does not. In general, racial and ethnic minorities do not share equal political, economic, and educational opportunities with those of the dominant culture, even though our society espouses such equality.

Unfortunately, schools have too often been run for the benefit of those in the dominant cultural group, excluding minority groups from receiving the full range of benefits. Schools that embrace cultural pluralism seek to promote diversity and to avoid the dominance of a single culture. Their curricula are infused with the histories and contributions of diverse groups. These schools attempt to use the cultural patterns of the students to provide instruction and promote learning. The goal is for students to be comfortable operating both within their own cultures and in others as well. Students from all racial, ethnic, and cultural groups are urged to participate in the school's various social, athletic, and governmental activities. These schools seek to eradicate the academic achievement disparities among the various racial, ethnic, and cultural groups. In short, the goal for schools that aim for cultural pluralism is that no particular cultural group either dominates or is excluded from those activities and accomplishments that schools value.

Many people, however, resist the notion of cultural pluralism as a desirable goal. These people argue that cultural pluralism will undermine our country's common traditions, historically derived from western European cultures. We discuss these issues later in the chapter when we talk about multicultural education.

culturally responsive teaching

Teaching Implications   One method for teachers who want to acknowledge and accommodate cultural diversity in the classroom is through **culturally responsive teaching.** Many educators have documented how cultural identity, communication styles, and social expectations of students from minority cultural groups often conflict with the values, beliefs, and cultural assumptions of teachers.[6]

> *Understand and be confident that each of us can make a difference by caring and acting in small as well as big ways.*
> —Marian Wright Edelman

The school's middle-class culture often places students from other cultures at a disadvantage in understanding the school's cultural codes and communication styles. Teachers who recognize this can implement an *equity pedagogy*, a style of teaching that uses instructional materials and practices that incorporate important aspects of their students' family and community culture. For example, a teacher whose class contains mostly immigrant children from Central America can place maps of both Latin America and the United States around the room, provide magazines and games in both Spanish and English, and play salsa music as background for certain activities. This teacher might also recognize that for many students from a Latin culture, establishing direct eye contact with an adult authority figure is a sign of disrespect, so she does not establish that expectation of her students. Knowing and understanding your students' cultural backgrounds can help you make your classroom more inviting and can increase their academic achievement.

PAUSE AND REFLECT

1 What are the pros and cons of living in a culturally pluralistic society?

2 In your opinion, is this preferable to a "melting-pot" or assimilationist approach to diversity? Why or why not?

Diverse Needs

In addition to the diversity of racial, ethnic, and cultural backgrounds we have discussed so far, another element of diversity occurs within each individual. We all have basic physical and psychological needs that may vary in their prominence and expression because of individual circumstances. One way to understand the diverse needs of students is to see how one prominent psychiatrist and educator, William Glasser, has conceptualized the basic needs of all individuals.

Glasser's Choice Theory

choice theory

Glasser begins with the premise that each of us is born with fundamental needs for survival, love and belonging, power, freedom, and fun.[7] Throughout our lives, our motivations, actions, and behaviors are attempts to satisfy these needs. Glasser's idea, called **choice theory**, is that if we understand and identify these needs within ourselves, we can make conscious choices about how best to meet them. The recognition of our ability to make choices results in personal empowerment: we have control over how we choose to react to external events and information.

Glasser believes that teachers should empower their students through the use of choice theory. He states that effective teachers combine the needs of students with classroom assignments or activities. By understanding and incorporating basic human needs into the classroom structure, the teacher is teaching in a way that also meets those needs. The more students are convinced that their schoolwork satisfies their needs, the harder they will try and the better work they will produce. For example, when asked what is the best part of school, many students respond, "My friends." According to Glasser, this expresses the students' built-in need for friendship, love, and belonging. Rather than structure classroom settings to suppress this need, such as by emphasizing independent seatwork or teacher lectures, teachers should find ways to let students associate with others in class as a planned part of learning. Glasser refers to this kind of cooperative grouping as the use of *learning teams*.

learning teams, power needs

Teaching students in cooperative learning teams also meets students' needs for power. Using the term *power* synonymously with *self-esteem* or *sense of importance*, Glasser explains that to fulfill this need students must have the sense that someone they respect listens to them. Unfulfilled needs for power often result in a number of undesirable attention-getting behaviors.

Glasser believes these inappropriate behaviors are often misguided efforts to achieve power and are the source of 95 percent of discipline problems in school. In accordance with choice theory, he suggests that teachers structure opportunities for students to fulfill needs for power appropriately during the school day. In addition to learning teams, in which students interact and listen to one another in the learning process, Glasser suggests that teachers provide opportunities for student input and a forum for students to be heard. Glasser also rec-

Schools help students meet social, as well as academic, needs.
(© Bob Daemmrich)

ommends self-evaluation of homework, classwork, and tests. He believes that students need to be encouraged to set their own standards for quality work and to evaluate whether they are meeting those standards. This helps satisfy the need for power and instills an internal standard for achievement in education and work.

Glasser proposes that students' needs for freedom and fun, although important, are not at the core of problems in schools. Students generally understand the need for some structure in dealing with large groups of people, and they realize that rules and regulations must govern behavior in school, even though they limit individual freedom. Although fun is an essential need, students who have a sense of belonging in school and a forum for personal power are already likely to be experiencing fun.

Glasser's theory of personal empowerment provides one interesting way of viewing and identifying a wide variety of student needs. Other approaches such as Abraham Maslow's hierarchy of needs theory may also be useful. The most important point is that teachers must be aware of their students' varying needs and respond accordingly in the classroom.

■ Adolescent Subcultures

how crowds are labeled

Teenagers often satisfy their needs for belonging, power, and fun by forming crowds, or groups that share common characteristics. Most schools have crowds of elites, average students, and outcasts, with various terms used to describe them, including *jocks, preppies, brains, druggies, burnouts, nerds/geeks/dweebs,* and *goths.* Each crowd has attitudes, behaviors, or dress characteristics that distinguish it from all other crowds. As members of these adolescent subcultures, teenagers can express their own attitudes, explore personal relationships, and test themselves against others.

Reflect on adolescent subcultures with the image in this section of your CD-ROM.

Elite groups, such as the jocks and preppies, are the "leading crowd," who enthusiastically participate in, and receive the endorsement of, the school. The outcasts, such as the burnouts or the goths, tend to have an adversarial rather than cooperative relationship with the high school because they believe school doesn't serve their needs well. The outcasts are contemptuous of the elites' interest in student government and athletics, while the elites reject the outcasts' resistance to authority and achievement. Clothing and adornment are probably the most powerful symbolic indicators of category membership, although each crowd also tends to stake out particular territories of the school as its own.

■ *symbols of membership*

Membership in teenage subcultures begins to form in the middle and junior high schools as cliques develop around particular interests such as athletics, academics, student government, drugs, and tastes in music and cars. Often, teens don't even select a group as much as they are placed into one because of their image among their peers. These groups strengthen as the teenagers begin to move away from their families, and peer membership becomes a type of new family where youngsters find comfort and support. By senior year, however, the hold of the subcultures on students has weakened. The students develop more self-confidence, and they seek greater freedom. At this point, the friendship group becomes a drag on their autonomy. Until that happens, however, the teen subcultures exert a strong influence on the values of their members.

Most high schools have done a reasonably good job of making academically and socially oriented students an integral part of school life. They have been less successful with subcultures like the various outcast groups. In fact, because groups like the burnouts or goths reject the schools' values, the schools may be reinforcing their alienation. Finding ways to bring members of alienated subcultures into participation in their schools, bring the loners or outsiders into greater contact with their peers, and channel peer influence as a positive force is a major challenge for high school and middle school educators.

Diverse Abilities

■ *traditional focus on small range of abilities*

In some ways, many of our schools today are not structured to address students' diverse abilities. Most of our schools tend to emphasize a curriculum that specifically targets the predominantly linguistic and analytic abilities needed to do well on commonly used standardized tests. This constricted focus on a limited range of abilities results in an education system that teaches and reinforces only certain types of achievement. Children who are strong in linguistic and analytic tasks are likely to be successful in school and feel a great sense of achievement. Other children, however, who may be very competent or even gifted in nontraditional school tasks may experience frustration or failure in school. Children do not enter school as failures; rather, they acquire this debilitating label from a system that is strongly oriented toward a limited range of student abilities.

As a teacher, it is important to be aware of and help nurture a broad spectrum of abilities and strengths in your students. In the following section, we look at the theory that students may have many abilities and talents not tapped by traditional schooling. We also explore learning styles to see how different students learn and perhaps broaden your views on approaches to teaching. Then we briefly examine characteristics of students along a range of disabilities and talents.

Visit the material at the web site to link to more information about multiple intelligences theory.

■ *Multiple Intelligences*

Howard Gardner, a leading psychologist, proposes that we should move toward educating **multiple intelligences,** of which linguistic and analytic abilities are only two facets. In Gardner's books, *Frames of Mind* and *Multiple Intelligences: The Theory in Practice*,[8] he explains that we all have strengths, weaknesses, and unique combinations of cognitive abilities. Gardner proposes that people have at least eight distinct intellectual capacities that they use to approach problems and create products:

■ *eight different abilities*

1. *Verbal/linguistic intelligence* draws on the individual's language skills, oral and written, to express what's on the person's mind and to understand other people.

2. *Logical-mathematical intelligence* is a person's ability to understand principles of some kind of causal system, like a scientist does, or to manipulate numbers, quantities, and operations, like a mathematician does.

3. *Spatial intelligence* refers to the ability to represent the spatial world internally in the mind, like a chess player or sculptor does.

4. *Bodily-kinesthetic intelligence* is the capacity to use your whole body or parts of your body to solve a problem, make something, or put on some kind of production, like that of an athlete or a performing artist.

5. *Musical intelligence* is the capacity to "think" in music and to be able to hear patterns and recognize, remember, and manipulate them.

6. *Interpersonal intelligence* is the ability to understand other people, an ability that we all need but is particularly important for teachers, salespeople, and politicians.

7. *Intrapersonal intelligence* refers to having an understanding of yourself and knowing your preferences, capabilities, and deficiencies.

8. *Naturalist intelligence* refers to the ability to discriminate among living things (plants and animals) and to have sensitivity toward features of the natural world, such as rock formations and clouds.[9]

Traditionally, schools have tended to reinforce a learning profile emphasizing verbal/linguistic and logical-mathematical abilities and deemphasizing or excluding other possible intelligences.

Reflect on multiple intelligences theory with the graphic on your CD-ROM.

■ **Teaching Implications** In Gardner's theory, abilities in diverse areas would be valued as indicators of intelligence and be considered worthy of further nurturance and development in school. To address these varied intelligences, Gardner emphasizes learning in context, particularly through apprenticeships. Student development in an area like music should be fostered through hands-on practice and experiences. Even traditional subjects should be taught in a variety of ways to address the varied intelligences of both students and teachers. For example, the history of an era might be taught through a number of media and methods, ranging from art and architecture to biographies and dramatic reenactments of events. Assessments should also be tailored to different abilities and should take place in the learning context as much as possible.

■ *fostering diverse abilities*

The theory of multiple intelligences emphasizes the highly individualized ways in which people learn and recognizes that each of us has unique intellectual potential. Acknowledging and fostering individual abilities in a variety of areas is one way teachers can help students. This is an emerging idea in education. The Multiple Intelligences Menus, shown in Table 2.2, offer some ideas for expanding instructional repertoires and infusing variety into lessons. Currently a number of schools across the country are applying the theory in the classroom on a day-to-day basis. The multiple intelligences theory provides a framework for enhancing instruction and a language to describe the efforts. These efforts should contribute to our knowledge and skills in this area.

■ *Differing Learning Styles*

Visit the material at the web site to link to more information about learning styles.

Another approach to individual abilities and differences is the theory of learning styles. A **learning styles** approach to teaching and learning is based on the idea that all students have strengths and abilities, but each student may have a preferred way of using these abilities. Whereas Gardner's theory of multiple intelligences centers on the *content* and *products* of learning and has its roots in an effort to rethink the theory of measurable intelligence, learning styles theory addresses differences in the *process* of learning and the different ways people think and feel as they solve problems, create products, and interact. Some researchers have identified four basic learning styles[10]:

■ *varieties of learning styles*

1. The *mastery style* learner absorbs information concretely; processes information sequentially, in a step-by-step manner; and judges the value of learning in terms of its clarity and practicality. For example, a middle-school student with a mastery learning style might enjoy learning geometry because it helps him or her figure out problems with a building or craft hobby.

2. The *understanding style* learner focuses more on ideas and abstractions; learns through a process of questioning, reasoning, and testing; and evaluates learning by standards of logic and the use of evidence. A geometry student with this style might benefit from testing several triangles to deduce the principle that the angles all add up to 180 degrees.

3. The *self-expressive style* learner looks for images implied in learning; uses feelings and emotions to construct new ideas and products; and judges the learning process according to its originality, aesthetics, and capacity to surprise or delight. A geometry class that included making three-dimensional mobile sculptures by combining classic geometric forms might appeal to a student with the self-expressive learning style.

4. The *interpersonal style* learner, like the mastery learner, focuses on concrete, palpable information; prefers to learn socially; and judges learning in terms of its potential use in helping others. Students with interpersonal styles might enjoy learning geometry in groups, especially if they were able to use what they learned in a project, such as building part of a house for a low-income family.

People also differ in terms of their preferred sensory input for learning—that is, some people learn better visually, some through auditory input, and others tactilely. It's important to understand that various styles are neither good nor bad, just different. It's also important to know that individuals are not locked into any one style but can vary styles to fit different situations and tasks. To find out more about learning styles, consult one of the web sites listed in For Further Information at the end of the chapter.

■ **Teaching Implications**   A learning styles approach to teaching is currently receiving a great deal of attention in education. Although few schools adhere strictly to any one "model," the approach is being applied in varying forms and

TABLE 2.2 Multiple Intelligences Menu

Linguistic Menu

Using storytelling to explain _____

Conduct a debate on _____

Write a poem, myth, legend, short play, or news article about _____

Create a talk show radio program about _____

Conduct an interview of _____ on _____

Logical-Mathematical Menu

Translate a _____ into a mathematical formula

Design and conduct an experiment on _____

Make up syllogisms to demonstrate _____

Make up analogies to explain _____

Describe the patterns of symmetry in _____

Others of your choice _____

Bodily-Kinesthetic Menu

Create a movement or sequence of movements to explain _____

Make task or puzzle cards for _____

Build or construct a _____

Plan and attend a field trip that will _____

Bring hands-on materials to demonstrate _____

Visual Menu

Chart, map, cluster, or graph _____

Create a slide show, videotape, or photo album of _____

Create a piece of art that demonstrates _____

Invent a board or card game to demonstrate _____

Illustrate, draw, paint, sketch, or sculpt _____

Musical Menu

Give a presentation with appropriate musical accompaniment on _____

Sing a rap or song that explains _____

Indicate the rhythmical patterns in _____

Explain how the music of a song is similar to _____

Make an instrument and use it to demonstrate _____

Interpersonal Menu

Conduct a meeting to address _____

Intentionally use _____ social skills to learn about _____

Participate in a service project to _____

Teach someone about _____

Practice giving and receiving feedback on _____

Use technology to _____

Intrapersonal Menu

Describe qualities you possess that will help you to successfully complete _____

Set and pursue a goal to _____

Describe one of your personal values about _____

Write a journal entry on _____

Assess your own work in _____

Naturalist Menu

Create observation notebooks of _____

Describe changes in local or global environment _____

Care for pets, wildlife, gardens, or parks _____

Use binoculars, telescopes, microscopes, or magnifiers to _____

Draw or photograph natural objects _____

Source: Reprinted with permission from Linda Campbell, "How Teachers Interpret MI Theory," *Educational Leadership, 44* (September 1997), p. 18.

■ *disagreements over implementation*

intensities in many schools. Key advocates and researchers of a learning styles approach to education agree that individual strengths and abilities should be emphasized, but they disagree on how to put the theory into practice. Some educators call for a formal assessment of each student's learning style and then a prescription for appropriate teaching methods for that individual. Others believe that students should be assessed and matched with teachers having similar learning styles. Still others warn that current tests are not yet technically adequate and that using these tests may actually harm students because they may

Reflect on teaching students with different learning styles with the image in this section of your CD-ROM.

keys for teachers

result in improper labeling of individuals and their so-called learning styles. Rather than label students as having a particular learning style, many educators argue that curriculum and instruction should offer varied lessons that appeal to a range of strengths, abilities, and learning preferences over time. Teachers need to accommodate different learning styles by systematically varying teaching and assessment methods to reach all students. Differentiated instruction, as described in the "What Is Taught?" chapter, is a powerful way to address academic diversity. Web sites on how to differentiate instruction are listed in the For Further Information section at the end of that chapter. Flexibility and variety are the keys; don't assume that all students learn the way you do, and don't undervalue students just because their learning styles differ from yours. Technology can help in varying instruction and assessment methods. As teachers become more familiar with new technology, they are making use of CD-ROMs, video/audio World Wide Web sites, and other multimedia tools that offer students varied ways to access materials and learning experiences.

PAUSE AND REFLECT

1 Of Howard Gardner's list of intelligences, which are your strongest? How do you know?

2 What are the general characteristics of your learning style? If you don't know, visit one of the web sites on learning styles and take an inventory to discover your preferred ways of learning.

3 How will you account for various learning styles in your students?

Students with Disabilities

types of disabilities

Within the range of diversity your students will display, some will have disabilities. The types of disabilities you may encounter are many. For example, you may have students with mental retardation, emotional disturbance, learning disabilities, attention deficit disorders, speech or language impairments, multiple handicaps, autism, traumatic brain injuries, orthopedic impairments, visual impairments or blindness, and hardness of hearing and deafness. Figure 2.1 shows the percentage and number of students in each of these categories. During the 1999–2000 school year, 5.68 million students, ages six to twenty-one, received federal aid for their disabilities; these students represented 13 percent of the total public school population. About 588,000 additional children, ages three to five, also received federal aid for their disabilities.[11] In the fiscal year 2000, the federal government distributed approximately $4.9 billion to the states for students with disabilities.[12]

Visit this chapter of the web site to link to-up-to-date statistics on this topic.

Teaching Implications   Students with disabilities will likely be in your classroom for varying amounts of the school day, depending on the types and amount of support services they are receiving. How will you deal with the different needs of these children? Most important, remember not to stereotype them. Certainly different disabilities will have different implications for student learning. For example, a student with mental retardation may require repetition and practice to master simple concepts, whereas a student who uses a wheelchair may learn even the most difficult material quickly. Even within the parameters

Figure 2.1
Specific Disabilities Among Children Age 6–21: Total and Percentage for Each Category

Source: *Twenty-third Annual Report to Congress on the Implementation of the Individuals with Disabilities Education Act* (Washington, DC: U.S. Department of Education, 2001), p. II–23.

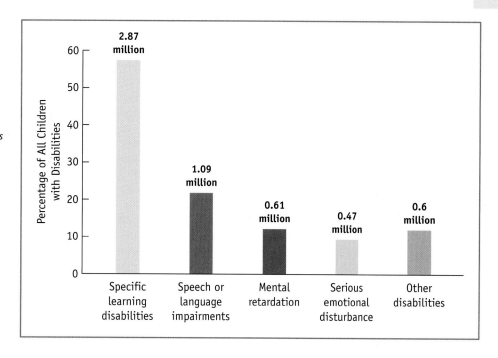

of each type of disability, however, you will probably encounter a wide range of differences. Consider two students identified as having learning disabilities. One may display a low-average intelligence quotient (IQ) and have extreme difficulty in mathematics; the other may have an extremely high IQ and have difficulty in reading. Both of these students have a learning disability, but you would not provide the same instruction for each of them or have the same expectations.

The point is, you should approach instruction for these children as you would for other students in the classroom: expect diversity, anticipate a range of abilities, and look for the particular strengths and learning profiles of each student. A helpful resource for recognizing student abilities and suggesting instructional strategies will be the special education teacher(s) in your school. The more you and a special education teacher can coordinate instruction and services for your students with disabilities, the better the students' educational experiences are likely to be.

▓ *expect diversity*

▓ *Gifted and Talented Students*

One of the most challenging types of students is the gifted or talented child. The term *talented* most often refers to an ability or skill (for example, musical or artistic talent) that may not be matched by the child's more general abilities, whereas the term *gifted* usually includes intellectual ability. The gifted child is extremely bright, quickly grasping ideas and concepts you are teaching and making interpretations or extrapolations that you may not even have considered. Gifted children may also have a creativity that shows itself in original thinking or artistic creations.

Students who are gifted and/or talented are sometimes overlooked when educators talk about students with special needs. However, as one educator says, "Highly gifted children are as far from the norm in the direction of giftedness as the severely retarded are in the other direction."[13] Therefore, they do have special needs.

Breaking Out: One School System's Success with Autistic Children

Robert Goodfellow, age six, has Asperger's Syndrome, a mild form of autism that combines uncanny knowledge and awkward social skills. Students with Asperger's may be masters in mathematics, science, or computers, for example, but require daily drilling on such basics as how to make eye contact, or maintaining appropriate distance from other children.

Before he joined a special program in the Seattle school system, Robert would sit alone in his yard, peeling bark off of sticks he would find. He seemed fascinated by the process of removing the bark, often singing songs over and over again as he worked on the sticks. He also refused to bathe, clip his nails, or comb his hair.

Robert, however, has benefited greatly from a new program in the Seattle school district. With his teachers' encouragement, Robert has channeled his obsessiveness in more socially accepted ways. He has become an expert on the Seattle Mariners baseball team and has learned how to juggle extremely well. His new knowledge about the batting averages and other minutia of the Mariners, plus his juggling, have enabled Robert to relate better socially with his peers. They now admire his new knowledge and skills.

Students with Asperger's syndrome tend to excel in subjects that interest them, but other aspects of school may be difficult for them. For example, the hustle and bustle of recess or lunch can be extremely stressful. The Seattle program aims to help children like Robert function in their world without alienating others by their eccentric behavior. Robert and other Asperger's students attend mainstream classes as much as possible, sometimes with a school aide, and only go to small special education classes when they need to work on a particular skill. The special education teachers function as case managers for the children, monitoring their schedules, serving as their advocates, and teaching them lessons on behavior, social skills, and life skills. Students in grades 1–4 are given visual cue cards to remind them of appropriate classroom behavior, such as raising their hands before speaking and sitting still.

There is no cure for autism disorders, but "high-functioning" people with autism can make useful, even outstanding, contributions to society. The Seattle school district began its program in 1997 with a single elementary-school pilot class for such high-functioning autistic children. Two years later the program was expanded districtwide, and twelve classes are now offered in elementary, middle, and high schools. There are plans to add even more classes in upcoming school years.

Because autism is one of the fastest growing categories of disability in special education, it presents new challenges to school districts. The Seattle program has attracted considerable attention, and educators from around the country and even Japan and Korea have visited to learn more about how to help high-functioning autistic children succeed in school.

Source: Lisa Fine, "Cracking the Shell," *Education Week*, November 21, 2001, pp. 22–29.

Although special educational care and services for students with disabilities have long been recognized and accepted, American education has been slow to accept the notion that gifted children require special adaptations in both curricula and teaching methods. Because the idea of giftedness implies an elitism to many Americans, it seems undemocratic to provide special services to children who already enjoy an intellectual advantage.

high dropout rate

As a result of neglected needs, gifted and talented students drop out of school at rates far exceeding the rates of dropout for their nongifted peers. Many of those who stay in school feel unchallenged and become bored and apathetic. The result is that many of our brightest and most talented minds are being turned off or underdeveloped. Only recently have school districts begun to make serious efforts to identify gifted children and develop special programs for them. We discuss these programs more fully later in this chapter.

■ **Teaching Implications**   If your school or school district has special programs for gifted and talented students, you may be expected to work with resource teachers to help prepare individualized education plans for these students. If you want to teach gifted students instead, your state may be one of the twenty or so that require you to obtain a gifted endorsement to your teaching license. It is more likely, however, that you will discover certain students in your class to be gifted or talented and, lacking any special program, you will be responsible for teaching these students as part of your regular class. What do you need to know?

■ *guidelines for teaching gifted and talented students*

1. Recognize that gifted pupils generally learn the standard curricular skills and content quickly and easily. They need teaching that does not tie them to a limited range,that is not preoccupied with filling them with facts and information, but allows them to use the regular class as a forum for research, inquiry, and projects that are meaningful to them.

If 2 + 3 is always going to be 5, why do they keep teaching it to us?
—*A GIFTED FIRST-GRADE STUDENT*

2. Realize that these students are persistently curious. They need teachers who encourage them to maintain confidence in their own ideas, even when those ideas differ from the norm.

3. Teach these pupils to be efficient and effective at independent study so that they can develop the skills required for self-directed learning and for analyzing and solving problems independently. Allow students of varying abilities to work together in areas of high interest, such as social action research projects.

4. Help students apply complex cognitive processes such as creative thinking, critiques, and pro and con analyses.

5. Expand your ideas concerning what instructional materials are available. Consider businesses, religious groups, national parks, and resource people as sources of potential instructional materials in addition to the textbooks and reference books available in the school. Be sure to investigate any technological resources that are available, including World Wide Web sites and other electronic links to information and knowledgeable people outside the school.

   Use differentiated instructional strategies such as flexible grouping, "tiered" assignments (in which all students explore the same topic but the level of questions or products produced varies depending on students' abilities), learning centers, student contracts, and mentorships. (See the chapter entitled "What Is Taught?" for more on differentiated instruction.)

6. Implement *curriculum compacting,* in which teachers test students on what they already know on upcoming units. Students who demonstrate mastery in advance are allowed to accelerate through the material or pursue enrichment activities while the unit is being taught to the rest of the class.

7. Match students with *mentors* to help develop talent and engage students in relevant and applied problem solving. Mentoring programs encourage independent growth, increased self-confidence, and a willingness to reach out into new, untried areas.

PAUSE AND REFLECT

① Do you have any concerns about your ability to work with students who have disabilities? What do you think will be the most rewarding aspects of working with these students?

② What do you think will be the most challenging aspect of teaching gifted or talented students? How can you prepare for that challenge? What will be most rewarding?

The School's Response to Diversity

■ *help for teachers*

You may be getting concerned about whether you can handle the range of diversities you may face in your classroom. Be assured, however, that you are not in this alone. Various assistance systems have been devised to help the teacher respond to the range of student needs. Besides having other teachers and administrators to help you, most schools have specialists, such as nurses, school psychologists, and counselors, who often can give you valuable advice or direct help to your students. A growing number of parent councils involve parents in giving advice and helping to deal with problems. Teacher aides may be community members who speak the language of substantial minorities in the schools. In-

© Lynn Johnston Productions, Inc./Distributed by United Feature Syndicate, Inc.

terns or students from the local college may help as well, providing another adult in the classroom.

In addition to support personnel, schools have tried to provide special programs to address some dimensions of student diversity. Multicultural and bilingual education, special education, and programs for gifted and talented students have all evolved out of concern that certain types and degrees of student diversity require different educational strategies to ensure an equal opportunity for intellectual stimulation and growth.

■ *Multicultural Education*

■ *definition and goals*

Multicultural education represents one approach to meeting the educational needs of an increasingly diverse student population. Multicultural education values cultural pluralism and seeks to enrich the cultural perspectives of all students. Spurred by the civil rights movement of the 1960s, multicultural education is a response to economic inequality, racism, and sexism in American culture. Originally used in conjunction with improving the lot of "people of color," the term has been broadened to include gender, disability, and other forms of diversity. Its goals include reducing prejudice and fostering tolerance, improving the academic achievement of minority students, building commitment to the American ideals of pluralism and democracy, and incorporating minority groups' perspectives into the curricula of our schools. Like the concept of cultural pluralism on which it is based, multicultural education rejects the notion of the melting pot, whereby minority groups are expected to abandon their group identities and become assimilated into a homogeneous American culture. Equally, multicultural education rejects separatist philosophies that would have each cultural group go its own way without trying to fit into an overall American culture.

Visit the material at the web site to link to more information about multicultural education.

At least five different approaches to multicultural education have been identified, which helps explain why the term often has very different meanings for different people:

■ *different approaches*

1. *Teaching the exceptional and culturally different,* which helps students achieve academically and socially within currently existing schools by building bridges between the students' backgrounds and the schools to make the curriculum more "user friendly."

2. *Human relations,* which attempts to build positive relations among members of different racial/cultural groups and between males and females.

3. *Single-group studies,* which focus on programs that examine particular groups, such as African American studies or women's studies.

4. *Multicultural,* which promotes cultural pluralism by reconstructing the whole educational process around the perspectives of diverse racial, ethnic, cultural, and social classes.

5. *Multicultural and social reconstructionist,* which teaches students to examine inequality and oppression in society and to take action to remediate these inequalities.[14]

Reflect on multicultural education with the image in this section of your CD-ROM.

Multicultural education is not just for members of minority racial or ethnic groups but for all students, including those with western European heritage. A major goal of multicultural education is to help students from diverse cultures learn to cross cultural borders and to participate in a diverse, democratic society. True multicultural education does not consist of only black history or women's history months. Instead of simply adding on information about particular groups, leaving the rest of the curriculum untouched, real multicultural education presents multiple perspectives and viewpoints to help students understand how events and facts can be interpreted differently by various groups. In addition to valuing cultural diversity, multicultural education is based on the concept of *social justice,* which seeks to do away with social and economic inequalities for those who have been denied these benefits of a democratic society. African Americans, Native Americans, Asian Americans, Hispanic Americans, women, individuals with disabilities, people with limited English proficiency, people with low incomes, members of particular religious groups, and individuals with different sexual orientations are among those groups that have at one time or another been denied social justice. Educators who support multicultural education see establishing social justice for all groups of people who have experienced discrimination as a moral and ethical responsibility.

■ *social justice*

■ **An Ongoing Debate**   Many school districts are attempting to permeate their curricula with a multicultural emphasis, believing that attention to multicultural education is our society's best way to combat the prejudice and divisiveness among the different subcultures of our nation. By developing mutual respect for and appreciation of different lifestyles, languages, religious beliefs, and family structures, students may help shape a better future society for all its members.

Some educators, however, are concerned about what they believe are potential dangers of multicultural education in the schools, including all of the following:

■ *concerns and controversy*

- It may destroy any sense of common traditions, values, purposes, and obligations.

- It may divert the schools' attention from their basic purpose of educating for civic, economic, and personal effectiveness.

- It attacks the problem of minority students' underachievement by advocating an emphasis on self-esteem rather than hard work.

- It substitutes "relevance" of subjects studied for instruction in solid academics.

- It may undermine a sense of morality because no universal moral positions are considered acceptable to all elements of our society.

These critics do not argue against the need to preserve and value the achievements of the diverse ethnic and racial groups of our country, but they reject the position that everything is of equal value, that the schools have a responsibility to teach every possible belief and value, and that behavior is moral if it is believed to be so by any group.[15] These critics assert that there are limits to pluralism and that those limits must be articulated by schools and school leaders. Other critics of multiculturalism completely reject the concept of cultural pluralism, preferring an assimilationist perspective whereby schools are charged with forging one dominant American culture in which English is the only acceptable language.

Thus, the major thrusts of multicultural education are not without controversy. Multicultural education has often been cast as a reform movement, designed to address inequity and discrimination resulting from the race, religion, socioeconomic status, gender, age, exceptionality, or language of students.[16] As with any attempt to solve social problems, excesses and overexuberance can occur. Nevertheless, schools do need to accommodate larger minority populations in a way that removes barriers while preserving the basic purposes of schooling.

■ *Bilingual Education*

Students whose native language is not English constitute one of the most conspicuous failure groups in the American educational system. Because of their difficulty in speaking, writing, and understanding English, many of these LEP students fall further and further behind in school, and overwhelming numbers drop out before finishing high school.

Find the full text of the Bilingual Education Act in the text resources on your CD-ROM.

■ *Lau v. Nichols*

The Government Response   To cope with this problem, Congress passed the Bilingual Education Act in 1968 and subsequently amended it a number of times to provide federal funds to develop bilingual programs. Much of the expansion of bilingual programs in the 1970s can be attributed to a series of court cases, the most notable of which was the 1974 U.S. Supreme Court case of *Lau v. Nichols*. The case involved a class action suit on behalf of Chinese-speaking students in San Francisco, but it had implications for all of the nation's non-English-speaking children. The Court found that "where inability to speak and understand the English language excludes national origin–minority group children from effective participation in the educational program offered by a school district, the district must take affirmative steps to rectify the language deficiency in order to open its instructional program to these students."[17] Basing its ruling on the Civil Rights Act of 1964, the Court held that the San Francisco school system unlawfully discriminated on the basis of national origin when it failed to cope with the children's language problems.

Although the *Lau* case did not mandate bilingual education as the means to solve the problem, subsequent state cases did order bilingual programs. With the advice of an expert panel, the U.S. Office of Civil Rights suggested guidelines for school districts to follow, the so-called Lau Remedies. The guidelines "specified that language minority students should be taught academics in their primary home language until they could effectively benefit from English language instruction."[18]

Our common language is . . . English. And our common task is to ensure that our non-English-speaking children learn this common language.
—WILLIAM BENNETT
(FORMER U.S. SECRETARY OF EDUCATION)

■ *different models*

Bilingual Education Models   Students with a native language other than English have two goals in school: learning English and mastering content. Several types or models of **bilingual education** programs have been designed to help them reach these goals. In the *immersion model,* students learn everything in English. Teachers using immersion programs generally strive to deliver lessons in simple and understandable language that allows students to internalize English while learning academic subjects. The extreme case of immersion is called *submersion,* wherein students must "sink or swim" until they learn English. Sometimes students are pulled out for *English as a Second Language (ESL)* programs, which provide them with instruction in English geared toward language acquisition.

The *transitional model* provides intensive English-language instruction, but students get some portion of their academic instruction in their native language.

POLICY MATTERS !

The Battle over Bilingual Education

What's the Policy?

In 1998, voters in California passed an "English only" law, Proposition 227, an initiative that called for ending bilingual education in the state. In 2000, Arizona passed a similar law, Proposition 203. The California law, which took effect in the fall of 1998, requires schools to teach limited English proficient students almost entirely in English except when at least twenty students in a given grade level are granted waivers to the law. If an insufficient number of students receive waivers in a given school, the school district must allow students to transfer to another school that offers bilingual education. Many parents report, however, that the schools have not informed them of their right to choose a bilingual education program. Educators and legislators in other states will be closely following the progress of California's and Arizona's students as they consider implementing similar plans.

How Does It Affect Teachers?

Many teachers are withholding judgment on the effects of Proposition 227 until they have a sense of what it will mean in the long run for Latino student achievement. School districts vary greatly in their strictness or leniency in granting waivers to allow bilingual education programs. School districts that supported bilingual education before Proposition 227 have found ways to keep at least some bilingual classrooms, whereas in school districts without such support, bilingual education has been either eliminated or severely restricted. In the Oceanside school district in San Diego County, for example, of the 159 waiver requests received, only five were approved, which effectively meant that no bilingual programs needed to be offered. Even within a district, waiver rates vary tremendously from school to school. Some schools have even seen an increase in the number of students enrolled in bilingual classes since Proposition 227 was passed. Presently, only 12.5 percent of the state's 1.5 million LEP students remain in bilingual programs.

What Are the Pros?

In the three years following passage of Proposition 227, scores on state standardized tests for English learners have risen, especially at the elementary and middle school levels. For example, many

---

The goal is to prepare students for regular classes in English without letting them fall behind in subject areas. In theory, students transition out of these programs within a few years.

    Maintenance or *developmental* bilingual education aims to preserve and build on students' native-language skills as they continue to acquire English as a second language.

■ *California and Arizona abandon bilingual education*

■ **Controversies** Choosing the best method for educating students who need to learn English has become a divisive political battle. The transitional and-maintenance models of bilingual education are in growing jeopardy, as first California, then Arizona, and now other states threaten these bilingual programs (Figure 2.2). In 1998, California voters passed Proposition 227, which called for LEP students to be taught in a special English-immersion program in which nearly all instruction is in English, in most cases for no more than a year, before moving into mainstream English classrooms. Proposition 227 basically ended transitional and maintenance models of bilingual education in California, except when sufficient numbers of parents specifically request that their children con-

teachers at Ditmar Elementary School in the Oceanside school district report surprise at how well their LEP students have progressed academically in English immersion. Some report rapid gains in students' oral English skills and in their requests to read books in English in the school library.

What Are the Cons?

Some teachers report that their students tune out as the day goes on because they can't keep up in English, whereas others say that they have slowed the academic pace of their classes because it takes much longer to convey information. Still other teachers state that fewer students in their classes are ready to read compared with last year because the students' English vocabulary is much more limited than their Spanish vocabulary. Teachers in the upper elementary grades say that they often pull students out of subjects such as science to do extra work in English so they can read their textbooks.

Lynn Gonzalez, a second-grade bilingual teacher at Ditmar, says, "This has been the hardest year of my life." She feels "enormous pressure" to make the school district look successful by producing English-proficient students by the end of the year, even though her training taught her that

such proficiency takes at least three years. "I'm implementing something that goes totally against my beliefs," she says.

What Do You Think?

1. **Do you support the intent of Proposition 227 to do away with bilingual education models other than structured English immersion? Why or why not?**

2. **If you were teaching LEP students who had had only one year of English instruction, what concerns would you have?**

3. **What might be some motivations for parents to request waivers to Proposition 227?**

 Visit the material at the web site to learn more about this policy issue.

SOURCES

Lynn Schnaiberg, "Calif.'s Year on the Bilingual Battleground," *Education Week,* June 2, 1999, pp. 1, 9–10.

Mary Ann Zehr, "English-Language Learners Post Improved Calif. Test Scores," *Education Week,* September 5, 2001, p. 29.

Duke Helfand, "The Bilingual Schooling Battle Flares Anew," *Los Angeles Times,* February 20, 2002. Available at: **http://www.latimes.com/news/local/la000012930feb20.story?coll=la%2Dcalifornia%2Dmanual**.

Visit the material at the web site to link to more information about bilingual education controversies.

tinue in them. Many parents, administrators, and teachers are concerned that all children, not just LEP students, will be affected as mainstream teachers grapple with students who may be unprepared to deal with grade-level work in English after one year in immersion. The legality of Proposition 227 was challenged in the courts, but in 2001 a federal appeals court upheld the law. By 2001, English-language learners in California elementary and middle schools had improved their overall scores on state standardized tests for the third year in a row, but the scores for high school students had stalled. Supporters of Proposition 227 argue that the test scores improved as a result of the law being implemented. Bilingual education supporters, on the other hand, point out that average scores have risen for all students and that the rate of increase in scores for LEP students still lag behind those of English-speaking students.

Although some educators believe students who use English as a second language should be educated in their native language as well, critics insist such an approach doesn't work. The critics believe the best path to academic achievement for language-minority students in most cases is to learn English and learn it quickly. Too many bilingual programs, they say, place LEP students into

Reflect on bilingual education with the image in this section of your CD-ROM.

Figure 2.2
State Bilingual Education Requirements

Source: Reprinted with permission from *Education Week* as found at **http://www. edweek.org/context/ topics/gallery/biling1.htm**.

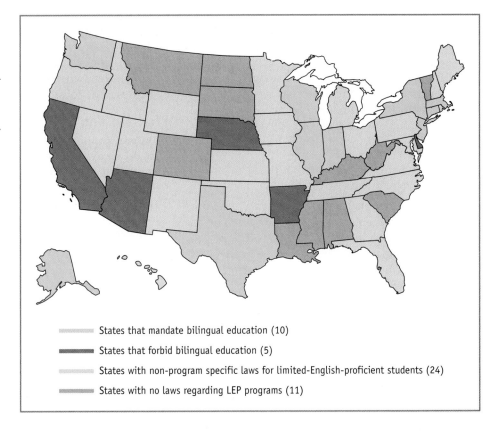

States that mandate bilingual education (10)

States that forbid bilingual education (5)

States with non-program specific laws for limited-English-proficient students (24)

States with no laws regarding LEP programs (11)

bilingual critics support immersion model

many still support bilingual education

need for bilingual teachers

slower learning tracks where they rarely learn sufficient English and from which they may never emerge. These critics basically support an immersion model of bilingual education but oppose the transitional and maintenance models. However, supporters of transitional and maintenance models argue that students can best keep up academically with their English-speaking peers if they are taught at least partly in their native languages while learning English.

In the early 1970s language-minority speakers and their advocates fought for bilingual education as their right, but today many of them are expressing doubts about the effectiveness of bilingual programs. Civil rights and cultural issues are giving way to concerns that non-native English speakers are just not sufficiently mastering the English language. Advocates say, it is not fair to blame bilingual education for the slow progress some students are making. They cite research indicating that instruction in the native language concurrent with English instruction actually enhances the acquisition of English.[19] The problem is not bilingual education, they say, it's that becoming proficient in any second language takes longer than just one or two years. They also point out that there is a shortage of well-qualified, fully bilingual teachers, so in many cases the problem with bilingual classes is not the curriculum but the quality of instruction. Some school systems have used teacher aides who speak the child's language to help connect the child and the school. The use of bilingual peer tutors may also help provide a greater sense of stability.

Despite this controversy, many school districts are in desperate need of bilingual teachers, particularly those who speak Spanish and Asian languages. If you speak a second language or still have time to include learning a language in your college program, you could help meet a serious educational need and, at the same time, greatly enhance your employment opportunities. Speaking a foreign language, especially Spanish, is also an asset for the regular classroom teacher who may have Spanish-speaking students in class.

PAUSE AND REFLECT

1 How can you help prepare yourself for the diversity you are likely to encounter in the classroom?

2 What experiences with diversity will you bring to the classroom? How do you think these experiences help you as a teacher?

■ *Special Education*

Find the full text of the *Education for All Handicapped Children Act (PL 94-142)* in the text resources on your CD-ROM.

■ *Public Law 94–142*

Students with disabilities are another group in our schools who have received special attention to ensure equal educational opportunities. The term **special education** is often used as a designation for services designed for these students.

In 1975, the *Education for All Handicapped Children Act (PL 94–142)* established the right of all students with disabilities to a "free appropriate public education" (FAPE). The law specified that each such student must be provided with an **individualized education program (IEP)** outlining both long-range and short-range goals for the child. Since that time, a number of other federal laws have reinforced and extended the commitment to special education.

■ *early intervention*

Find the *Education of the Handicapped Amendments* in the text resources on your CD-ROM.

■ **Preschool Legislation** *The Education of the Handicapped Act Amendments (PL 99–457),* passed in 1986, provided for early intervention for children from birth to age two who are developmentally delayed. For states that choose to participate, programs must include a multidisciplinary assessment of the child's needs, a written **individualized family services plan (IFSP),** and case management. Services may draw from a variety of areas, such as special education, speech and language pathology, occupational or physical therapy, or family training and counseling, depending on the developmental needs of the child.

PL 99–457 also stated that FAPE must be extended to children with disabilities ages three to five years. Although state and local education agencies administer these programs, they may contract with other programs, agencies, or providers to provide a range of services, such as programs that are home based for part of the day. Families are recognized as playing a particularly important role in preschool education, and instruction for parents is to be included in the IFSP whenever that is appropriate and the parents desire it. When students reach school age, they are covered by the provisions of the Individuals with Disabilities Education Act (IDEA) discussed in the next section.

■ **IDEA and ADA** In 1990, Congress passed two significant federal laws: the *Individuals with Disabilities Education Act (IDEA),* subsequently amended in 1997, and the *Americans with Disabilities Act (ADA).* IDEA amended the Education for All Handicapped Children Act of 1975. ADA ensures the right of individuals with disabilities to nondiscriminatory treatment in aspects of their lives other than education.

Six principles provide the framework of IDEA, around which education services are designed and provided to students with disabilities:

basic provisions of IDEA

- FAPE

- Appropriate evaluation

- An IEP

- **Least restrictive environment (LRE)**

- Parent and student participation in decision making

- Procedural safeguards

IEP's function

Because of the wide variety of disabilities and infinite degrees of severity in which these conditions may be found in individual students, IDEA mandates that an "appropriate education" be defined on an individual basis, using the written IEP first mandated in 1975. The IEP states the child's current levels of educational performance, short-term objectives and annual goals, services to be provided, and criteria and schedules for evaluation of progress. Thus, the IEP helps ensure that the educational goals designed for the child are appropriate to individual learning needs and that these plans are actually delivered and monitored. Provisions must be reviewed and revised annually—more often if necessary. Teachers, parents or guardians, special educators, other professionals, and the child (whenever appropriate) are all involved in the development and approval of the IEP. IDEA also requires that all older students with a disability (usually ages fourteen to sixteen) have an individualized plan for making the transition from school to work or additional education beyond high school through age twenty-one.

least restrictive environment

Like the original act of 1975, IDEA further stipulates that services for students with disabilities be provided in an LRE, meaning students with disabilities should be educated with children who are nondisabled to the greatest extent appropriate. Determination of what constitutes an appropriate environment has been subject to great debate. The social and academic benefits of the regular classroom must be weighed against the unique educational needs and individual circumstances for each child. The term **mainstreaming** has long referred to the practice of placing special education students in general education classes for at least part of the school day while also providing additional services, programs, or classes as needed. More recently, the term **inclusion** has been used to mean the commitment to educate each child, to the maximum extent appropriate, in the regular school and classroom. Compared with mainstreaming, inclusion, particularly *full inclusion,* as it is sometimes called, generally indicates an even greater commitment to keeping students with disabilities in regular classrooms. Thus, it usually involves bringing the support services to the child rather than moving the child to services located in separate rooms or buildings.

mainstreaming

inclusion

pros and cons of inclusion

Controversy over Inclusion   Full inclusion has become a civil-rights issue, compared by some to racial desegregation. Advocates of full inclusion argue that segregated education for students with disabilities is inherently unequal and therefore a violation of the rights of the children who are segregated. They also argue that traditional special education programs have resulted in a costly special education bureaucracy that has not shown the expected benefits in terms of academic, social, or vocational skills. Among the benefits of full inclusion for

Visit the material at the web site to link to more information about inclusion.

children with disabilities, they say, are higher expectations and better socialization, as well as greater acceptance of human differences by nondisabled children.

Critics, on the other hand, say that both teachers and students are being hurt in the following ways in the rush to embrace inclusion:

- Parents of nondisabled children often worry that the curriculum standards will be lowered by the inclusion of students with learning disabilities and that those students with attention-deficit hyperactivity disorder can be a disruption to their classmates and teachers.

- Some special educators voice concern that full inclusion may result in diminished or inadequate specialized services for students who have special needs. They point out that the regular classroom may not be the best setting for every child. Violent or emotionally disordered children, for example, may pose a threat to themselves and their classmates. These educators are wary of eliminating the range of service delivery options currently available in favor of a pure inclusion model. Furthermore, they argue, there is little evidence that inclusion programs strengthen students' academic achievement. (However, the same criticism could be made of many special education programs.)

- Overworked classroom teachers have complained that they are given inadequate resources and training to deal with students with disabilities. Ideally, when students with disabilities are included in regular classrooms, their teachers receive special training and help from a special education teacher who serves as either a co-teacher or a consultant. Cases are cited, however, in which teachers have been given sole responsibility for a class of thirty students, with as many as ten having disabilities. True collaboration between general education and special education teachers is essential for inclusion to work effectively.

special education costs

In too many instances, critics say, when children with disabilities are moved from resource rooms and self-contained classrooms into regular classrooms, the necessary supports do not follow. One reason is that some school districts use the cover of inclusion as a way to cut costs for special education services. Since 1967, when local and state expenses for special education services constituted 4 percent of all school expenditures, these expenses have increased more than fourfold.[20] With voter reluctance to increase school taxes and many school districts facing budget cuts as a result, some school boards and administrators see the inclusion movement as a way to save money by reducing funding for special education. When PL 94-142 was passed in 1975, the federal government set out to pay up to 40 percent of the costs for educating special education students who would be covered by this law. However, it has never come close to that goal. Federal expenditure for special education costs covered by IDEA account for just 15 percent of the total costs, or $6.3 billion in 2001. There is increasing pressure on Congress to live up to its promise to fund 40 percent of IDEA expenditures.[21]

inclusion becoming widespread

Despite criticisms, one thing is certain: inclusion of children with disabilities is becoming increasingly common in American schools. More and more students with disabilities are taking part in regular classroom life with their nondisabled peers. Inclusion seems to thrive in schools that have a shared vision of the school's purposes; strong lines of communication among teachers, administrators, and parents; and cultures of innovation and reform. In many schools with successful inclusion programs, the presence of students with disabilities has

© Lynn Johnston Productions, Inc./Distributed by United Feature Syndicate, Inc.

sparked other reform initiatives such as cooperative learning, peer teaching, team teaching, authentic assessment, and interdisciplinary instruction.

■ **Assistive Technology**   Just as many students use contact lenses or glasses to help them compensate for poor eyesight, students with disabilities may rely on a variety of technology-based innovations to help them learn better. The term **assistive technology** refers to the array of devices and services that help people with disabilities perform better in their daily lives. Devices such as motorized chairs, remote control units to turn on appliances, voice recognition systems, ramps to enter and exit buildings, and computers can all assist people with severe disabilities. Computers are especially important in allowing many students with a range of disabilities to participate in normal classroom activities that would otherwise be impossible, and we discuss their use more in the chapter entitled "What Should Teachers Know About Technology and Its Impact on Schools?".

assistive technology incorporated into IDEA

Congress incorporated definitions of assistive technology in IDEA, declaring that such technology must be provided whenever necessary as an element of free and appropriate public education. Thus, assistive technology must be considered a potential component of the IEP for each student with disabilities.[22] As a new teacher, you should be prepared to encounter situations in which a child uses technology as a medium for interaction and engagement within your classroom.

■ **Teaching Implications**   How can you as a regular education teacher be effective in teaching children with disabilities in your classroom? Here are a few suggestions:

guidelines for teaching students with disabilities

1. Be open to the idea of including students with disabilities in your classroom.

2. Learn about each child's limitations and potential and about available curriculum methodologies and technologies to help the child learn.

3. Insist that any needed services be provided.

4. Pair students with disabilities with children who can help them.

5. Use a variety of teaching strategies, including hands-on activities, peer tutoring, and cooperative learning strategies.

6. Avail yourself of opportunities for co-teaching with a special education teacher.[23]

PAUSE AND REFLECT

❶ Have you had any contact with individuals with disabilities (for example, a relative or neighbor)? What did you learn from this relationship that might be helpful in your teaching?

❷ What is your position on the issue of "full inclusion"? What reservations, if any, do you have?

▓ *Programs for Gifted and Talented Students*

Programs for gifted and talented students exist in every state and in many school districts, but the exact number of students served cannot be determined because not all states and localities collect this information. We do know, however, that by the year 2000, twenty-seven states reported serving almost 2.5 million K–12 gifted students and spending at least $436 million on gifted and talented programs.[24]

▓ *meanings of* gifted *and* talented

▓ **Identifying Gifted and Talented Students**   How do educators decide whether a student is gifted? A survey of definitions of the terms *gifted* and *talented* used by the education departments in each state reveals wide variations. The areas in which states identify gifted and talented students can range from intellectual to psychomotor to artistic, with many variations. In many schools, the definition of giftedness is shifting away from an emphasis on general intellectual ability toward the recognition that giftedness occurs in a variety of areas, such as mathematics, language, spatial ability, and kinesthetics. Through its evolution, the study of giftedness has moved increasingly toward more *inclusive* definitions and away from more *exclusive* ones. Intelligence is now thought to be composed of many factors, not just one or two as was previously thought. Howard Gardner's work on multiple intelligences cited earlier in the chapter demonstrates this more inclusive thinking.

▓ *reliance on scores and grades*

In their assessments of students' intellectual abilities, school districts have, in the past, tended to rely heavily on general intelligence and achievement tests, as well as on teacher recommendations and grades earned in school. There is a danger of letting the tools used to identify the children become synonymous with the *definition* of gifted and talented. To avoid this danger, teachers and administrators must study and interpret the data the tools provide rather than take the data at face value and use them for hard-and-fast cut-off points. Whether to recommend a child for a special program is a decision that should be made by the responsible teacher and other professional educators on the basis of their objective and subjective appraisals of the student, the nature of the gifted program or activity, and the atmosphere in which the student lives and goes to

▓ *avoid cut-off points*

school. Parents should be a significant part of these discussions. The point is that the complexity of the variables involved requires that individual decisions be made by professionals using their best judgments rather than according to arbitrary, predetermined cut-off points on tests.

▓ *minorities underrepresented*

The problem of identification is especially acute for bilingual children and children adjusting to a new culture, as well as for children in other minority groups. A major concern in the identification of gifted and talented students centers on the underrepresentation of economically disadvantaged students, learning-disabled students, and certain minority students. In a national survey

VOICES FROM THE CLASSROOM

Amy Shuler graduated from the University of Virginia in 1999 with a B.A. in Spanish and an M.T. in Special/Elementary Education. She has been teaching special education for four years. Amy Peterman graduated from Virginia Tech in 1995 with a B.A. in History and Political Science. She received her teaching certification from Mercer University in 1998. She is currently working toward her Masters in Elementary Education at Mercer. She has been teaching elementary school for four years.

They teach at Woodland Elementary Charter School in Fulton County, Georgia. The school offers a Special Needs Preschool and a Special Needs Kindergarten and children with moderate to profound intellectual disabilities, behavior disorders, and learning disabilities are represented in all grades.

Collaborative Teaching

Our collaborative teaching (co-teaching) experience began for a one-hour block during science and social studies. We saw that students who were previously isolated because of their behaviors or academic weaknesses experienced pride in their accomplishments and began to strive to meet new goals. This year, we decided to co-teach for segments of language arts, mathematics, and science/social studies.

Co-teaching requires two teachers to work together daily; therefore both teachers not only need to get along, but also need to be flexible, organized, and willing to share responsibilities. Co-teaching is a reflective process; we are always changing to meet our students' academic and social needs.

Common planning is critical to the success of co-teaching. Currently, we plan together on a weekly basis. During our planning time, we design lessons for all subjects and discuss any modifications that we should create before the lesson. For example, we might create vocabulary picture cards or word banks or highlight key parts of the textbook for some students.

We also share teaching responsibilities throughout the day. The general education teacher usually teaches the whole group, whereas the special education teacher circulates throughout the classroom to make sure that students remain on task and receive any accommodations. During the day, each of us also works with a small reading and math group. We feel that co-teaching and planning together allows us to present more creative and exciting lessons and plan more cooperative group projects.

The presence of two teachers working together also helps us address students' social skills. A teacher is always available to immediately prompt discussions or teach appropriate behaviors. The sense of community developed through co-teaching has surpassed all of our expectations. In the beginning of our co-teaching experience, we had to encourage partnerships and friendships. After six months of working together, students are finding ways to include each other in all activities, in spite of their differences. On a recent writing assignment, a fourth grade general education student wrote about her classmate with autism:

> *"If I could trade places with someone for one week, I would trade with Sally (name changed). . . . I am her friend. I like her for who she really is!"*

 Visit the web site for more Voices from the Classroom.

---

of eighth-graders enrolled in gifted and talented programs, only 9 percent of the students were in the bottom quartile of family income, while 47 percent of program participants were from the top quartile in family income.[25] Asian American students are well represented in gifted and talented programs, but African American and Hispanic students are underrepresented in terms of their proportion in the total school population. Thus, educators and parents are concerned that the measures being used to identify gifted and talented youngsters may work to the disadvantage of African Americans, Hispanics, and children from low-income families.

Visit the material at the web site to link to more information about talented and gifted children.

■ **Teaching Gifted and Talented Students**   The two main strategies for serving gifted children are **acceleration** and **enrichment.** With an accelerated curriculum, gifted children can learn at a pace commensurate with their abilities, allowing them to progress to advanced materials faster than their age norms or grade levels. Enrichment activities, on the other hand, provide gifted students with opportunities to go beyond the regular curriculum in greater depth and breadth, to engage in independent or collaborative inquiry that develops their problem-solving abilities, research skills, and creativity.

various approaches

Current educational programs for gifted and talented students are quite varied. Some programs establish special schools that are designed only for gifted or talented students and have special admission requirements. In such schools, stimulating courses can be devised and taught without concern for students who might be unable to keep pace, and teachers and students can be recruited on the basis of their talents.

Other programs adapt and enrich the regular school curriculum for gifted and talented children by grouping these students together for all or part of their instruction. This option normally is more flexible and practical than special schools. Classes can be established on a continuing or short-term basis, in any subject area, with the intention of either enriching or accelerating the student.

inclusion of gifted students

Although special programs and special schools for gifted and talented students do exist, these students are most likely to receive all, or nearly all, of their education in regular classrooms. In many school districts, in fact, separate programs for gifted students are being curtailed or phased out. The two primary reasons for this trend are the spread of a philosophy that favors mixed-ability grouping and the cessation of tracking and a lack of funds for separate gifted programs. The move to meet gifted students' needs within the regular classroom is parallel to the inclusion movement in special education. Some advocates for gifted education programs are disturbed by this trend, concerned that gifted students will be shortchanged in the regular classroom. They fear that teachers will concentrate their efforts on struggling students or that gifted students will be drafted to serve as tutors for these students rather than working to their own potential. Supporters of the current trend, however, believe that most gifted students' needs can be met in the regular classroom if teachers can differentiate curriculum and instruction for them and increase the level of challenge.

Still others argue that it is important to keep a continuum of programs and services available for gifted students. Along with the regular classroom, these educators argue, the options should include pullout programs, special classes, and separate centers and schools. A range of giftedness exists, and whereas some students will do just fine in a regular classroom, others can benefit from different programs.

Nontraditional Programs

All of the school programs discussed so far in this section address student diversity in a somewhat "traditional" way; that is, they have evolved from the notion that the role of the school is to address issues that arise for children in a standard school setting during the course of the school day. However, a number of social conditions may complicate the issue of diversity. Social problems such as poverty, homelessness, or inadequate health care are such pervasive influences in some students' lives that we will discuss them in more detail in the chapter entitled "What Social Problems and Tension Points Affect Today's Students?". The more we examine "today's children," the more we realize that societal conditions and problems affecting our students cut across traditional lines of services delivery.

social services provided through schools

■ **Interagency Cooperation**   In acknowledgment of the complexity and pervasiveness of these conditions and problems in the lives of children, programs are emerging that emphasize interagency cooperation in meeting the needs of individuals. For example, the coordinated school health initiative responds to the risk factors that threaten children and youth by providing coordinated school health services related to student health and success in school. The initiative assesses the health problems in particular school communities, builds consensus on what services should be provided, and puts together a comprehensive approach to improving children's health using agencies that address health, mental health, dental health, social services, recreation, and youth development. The guiding principle of the coordinated school health movement is that schools and communities can do much more with their current resources if they work together in partnership rather than as separate, isolated agencies. At least 900 school-based health centers are operating in the United States.[26]

changing the school environment

■ **The Comer Model**   James Comer, a public health physician and psychiatrist at Yale University, developed an initiative in New Haven, Conn., that emphasized structuring the environment to facilitate learning and development rather than placing blame and trying to change children. The Comer Model attempts to change the climate of demoralized schools and to create a sense of community and direction by bringing together the principal, teachers, aides, and parents to form a school planning and management team. Services of the school social worker, the psychologist, special education teachers, and counselors are coordinated to provide a consultation team to support individual students and teachers as well as the school planning and management team. Comer notes, "Kids don't learn in pieces. That's why it is essential to address the entire social system of the school because of the way the many variables interact and because attitudes, morale, and hope all affect school performance."[27] (See the box on the following page for more on Comer and his model.)

Diversity: A Complex Phenomenon

The school programs described in this section have been designed to address student diversity and create a more equal educational opportunity for children in our school systems. An inherent danger in these approaches to addressing diversity, however, is the tendency to label children and form stereotypic images of who they are. Remember that student performance in school is affected by many factors, including social and cultural trends.

differences, not deficits

We encourage you, as a teacher, to remember that we are talking about *differences* in students, not necessarily deficits. The educational groupings we have been discussing are an administrative convenience, not a naturally occurring segmentation of children. Within each of these groups, each child will vary along a number of dimensions and have very different learning profiles of strengths and weaknesses.

LEADERS IN EDUCATION
JAMES COMER

James Comer is a public health physician and psychiatrist who, through his work with low-income New Haven, Conn., schools, has shown that it is possible for low-income African American children to achieve at high academic and social levels.

After receiving his M.D. from Howard University in 1960, Comer entered the public health service. He became interested in the study of how policies and institutions interact with families and children and began to see the school as the place to improve the life chances for children from difficult home situations. He decided that a career in psychiatry would enable him to address the social problems that plagued the people with whom he worked, and in 1964, he began his psychiatric training at Yale University.

At Yale, Comer worked with the inner-city New Haven schools to find out why they were not helping African-American children and how they could be made to do so. He wanted to give these children the same opportunities in life that education had given him. The more he worked with children, the more he came to believe that schools were the only places where children trapped in poverty and failure could receive the support their families could not give them.

With the help of a Ford Foundation grant, Comer became the director of the School Development Program with the New Haven public schools. A team of educational and mental health professionals consisting of Comer, school administrators and teachers, a social worker, a psychologist, a special education teacher, and other support staff worked to involve parents in developing a social skills curriculum that integrated academic disciplines. The curriculum included four major areas: politics and government, business and economics, health and nutrition, and spiritual and leisure time, all areas in which the students would need proficiency to succeed in school and to lead productive lives. Through the curriculum, the students became more aware of their community and of how their involvement in it could make a difference.

By adopting child development and behavioral science research, the team concentrated on problem solving rather than blame fixing and made decisions based on consensus. This consensus process gave each team member a sense of participation and ownership of decisions. The project was a great success: students' standardized test scores rose dramatically, project schools had higher attendance rates than other New Haven schools, and students graduated to become school leaders in their later schooling.

The Comer Model emphasizes the social context of teaching and learning. No academic learning is possible, Comer asserts, unless there is a positive environment at the school where teachers, students, parents, and administrators like one another and work together for the good of all children. Built around three elements—a school governance team, a mental health team, and parental participation—Comer's model seeks to create schools that offer children stable support and positive role models. With the school and parents working successfully together, no conflict arises between home and school. The students learn desirable values, disruptions at school are reduced, and both teachers and students have more time and energy to focus on academic and social skills learning.

Among the many sites that have successfully implemented Comer's approach, now known as the School Development Program, are Washington, D.C.; Dade County, Fla.; Dallas; Chicago; Detroit; San Diego; and New Orleans. Many school districts have chosen this program's structure and processes as a way to implement site-based management.

 Visit the web site for more information about James Comer.

The Teacher's Response to Diversity

So far in this chapter, we have presented a great deal of information about the diversity of the children you will be teaching. Ultimately, how these children are educated will come down to you and your daily interactions with them in your classroom. How will you deal with diversity?

■ *Teacher-Student Disparity*

■ *the typical teacher*

Consider what we know about the typical teacher today. Women and whites predominate in the teacher force; 73 percent of all public school teachers are women, and 87 percent of those teaching in public schools are white.[28] Profiles of preservice and beginning teachers show similar gender, racial, and ethnic patterns. Most of these teachers, moreover, come from relatively stable family backgrounds. The majority of teachers and future teachers in our classrooms, then, come from very different backgrounds than many of the students they teach. Despite efforts to increase the number of minority teachers (see the chapter entitled "What Are Your Job Options in Education?"), this gap between teachers and students is likely to continue for some time.

As we mentioned in the first chapter, "What Is a School and What Is It For?", the more alike students and teachers are in social and cultural characteristics, the more they share tacit expectations about behavior and academic performance. However, as social and cultural characteristics become increasingly disparate, teachers need to rely on solid pedagogical training to overcome these differences. As an incoming teacher, you will need to know about the commonalities and differences among students, and you need to have learned specific methods and techniques for addressing the plurality of culture and learning styles you will encounter. Too often white educators have been reluctant to recognize that their own backgrounds and the culture of the school have an effect on learning. Rather than thinking of minority students as having a culture that is valid albeit different from theirs, they sometimes think of these students as deficient. Teachers are challenged to recognize the diversity of cultures represented by their students and to address these cultures in their teaching.

■ *preparing for student diversity*

■ *Implications for Teachers*

Given this profile of the cultural discrepancy between students and teachers, how can prospective teachers best prepare? Here are some steps you can take now:

■ *steps to take*

- Seek out experiences to broaden your understanding of societal and cultural commonalities and differences (for example, travel to foreign countries).

- Spend time in communities whose residents differ from you in terms of ethnicity, culture, or language.

- Volunteer in schools that differ from those you attended.

    Once you have your own classroom, what can you do to address diversity there? Here are some guidelines:

- Learn about and appreciate the values and backgrounds of your students.

- Teach to your students' strengths rather than making them feel incapable or deficient.

- Provide a variety of educational experiences, and find ways for all students to achieve recognition from you and peers for being good at something.

- Involve your students' parents or caregivers and other professional staff at the school to coordinate expertise and support so that students get a consistent message.

- Recognize that the schools' traditional emphasis on middle-class values such as individual learning and competition may clash with the values represented by their students' cultures. Teachers can provide opportunities for students to learn ways to succeed in today's dominant culture, but they must also respect the value systems in students' home lives and help them, in positive ways, to bridge the gap between the two worlds.

A Final Word

At one time, the only business of schools was to educate students, but now, because of the increasing complexity and diversity of our students' lives, other needs are being addressed and incorporated into the way schools are approaching "education." A major goal of this chapter has been to make you aware of the complexity of issues that directly affect many children's lives and their ability to get an adequate education. In our complex society, it is no longer feasible for the teacher to try to attend to all students' needs alone. You will need to use all the resources available to you, including parents and other professionals. Some teachers may initially feel threatened by this involvement or have a sense that the classroom is their "turf." As we have seen throughout this chapter, however, our students need the coordinated expertise and support of all school professionals and the crucial link with parents to be given a fair shot at acquiring the good education that is their due.

KEY TERMS

acceleration (63)
assimilation (37)
assistive technology (60)
bilingual education (53)
choice theory (40)
cultural pluralism (38)
culturally responsive teaching (39)

enrichment (63)
inclusion (58)
individualized education program (IEP) (57)
individualized family services plan (IFSP) (57)
learning styles (44)
least restrictive environment (LRE) (58)

limited English proficient (LEP) (35)
mainstreaming (58)
multicultural education (51)
multiple intelligences (42)
socioeconomic status (SES) (35)
special education (57)

FOR REFLECTION

❶ How do you compare to the profile of the typical teacher described at the end of this chapter?

❷ Would you like to be a teacher of gifted or talented children? Why or why not?

❸ What other elements of diversity will you find in your students that have not been discussed in this chapter? How will you be sensitive to these differences?

FOR FURTHER INFORMATION

PRINT RESOURCES

Lisa Delpit, *Other People's Children: Cultural Conflict in the Classroom* (New York: The New Press, 1995).

Asking why schools have such a hard time making school a happy place for poor children and children of color, the author concludes that most classrooms are dominated by a white perspective and too few teachers acknowledge that children of color have perspectives of their own.

Howard Gardner, *Multiple Intelligences: The Theory in Practice* (New York: Basic Books, 1993).

A mixture of previously published articles and lectures and chapters written specifically for this book, all explain the theory of multiple intelligences and how it can be applied in today's schools.

Geneva Gay, *Culturally Responsive Teaching: Theory, Research and Practice* (New York: Teachers College Press, 2000).

The author makes a convincing case for using culturally responsive teaching to improve the school performance of underachieving students of color.

Sonia Nieto, *The Light in Their Eyes: Creating Multicultural Learning Communities* (New York: Teachers College Press, 1999).

This book draws on research in learning styles, multiple intelligences, and cognitive theories to portray the ways in which students learn. It also discusses the social context of learning and the influence of culture on learning.

Marleen C. Pugach and Cynthia L. Warger, eds. *Curriculum Trends, Special Education, and Reform: Refocusing the Conversation* (New York: Teachers College Press, 1996).

Arguing that the reform agenda must address the needs of all children, including those with disabilities, this volume gives practical suggestions for doing so in different curriculum areas.

Guadalupe Valdes, *Learning and Not Learning English* (New York: Teachers College Press, 2001).

This book addresses the difficulties surrounding the teaching and learning of English for second language learners by focusing on the lives and experiences of four Mexican children in an American middle school. Raises important questions about current ESL teaching policies.

WEB RESOURCES

University of Virginia, *Office of Special Education: A Web Resource for Special Education.* Available at: **http://curry.edschool.virginia.edu/go/specialed**.

This web site at the Curry School of Education at the University of Virginia contains much information about special education, including the history of the field and types of disabilities. It also offers discussion groups, electronic addresses of special educators, and much more.

Multicultural Pavilion. Available at: **http://curry.edschool.virginia.edu/go/multicultural**.

This web site at the Curry School of Education, University of Virginia, has many resources for incorporating multicultural aspects into a curriculum.

National Clearinghouse for Bilingual Education. Available at: **http://www.ncbe.gwu.edu/**.

Funded by the U.S. Department of Education, this site contains hundreds of articles, links, databases, and online assistance in the area of bilingual education.

Association for Supervision and Curriculum Development (ASCD). Available at: **http://www.ascd.org**.

ASCD has many resources on multiple intelligences and learning styles. Click on PD (Professional Development) Online Courses, *Multiple Intelligences;* create your own password; and take an online course, complete with audio clips from Howard Gardner and Robin Fogarty.

VARK Questionnaire. Available at: **http://www.vark-learn.com/questionnaire.htm**

This questionnaire assesses whether learners prefer visual, aural, reading-writing, or kinesthetic learning.

Learning Style Inventory. Available at: **http://rrcc-online.com/%7Epsych/LSInventory.html**

This is another test of visual, auditory, or tactile preferences.

Learning Disabilities Resource Community, *Multiple Intelligences Inventory.* Available at: **http://www.ldrc.ca/projects/miinventory/miinventory.php**.

This site tests which intelligence you favor.

Teaching Style Inventory. Available at: **http://www.fcrc.indstate.edu/tstyles3.html**

This test is designed for college instructors but is applicable for K–12 education as well.

Paragon Learning Style Inventory. Available at: **http://www.oswego.edu/~shindler/plsi/taketest.htm**

This inventory is somewhat similar to the Myers-Briggs personality tests used in business that give you a four-letter description of your style.

What Social Problems and Tension Points Affect Today's Students?

Chapter Preview Rarely a day goes by on which educational issues fail to make headlines in newspapers across the country. Violence in schools, rampant teenage drug use, inequality of educational opportunity, sex education programs, and youth suicides are only a few of the issues that we read about daily. Underlying these issues are problems that complicate young people's efforts to get an education, such as crippling poverty and child abuse and neglect. This chapter explores some of the most sensitive and controversial issues in American education. Naturally, in such a short space we can treat each topic only briefly. However, we urge you to pursue additional reading on each issue.

This chapter emphasizes that:

- Many school-age children are affected by critical problems that directly influence their lives and often spill over into the classroom. Among these problems are severe poverty, homelessness, teenage parenting, child abuse, alcohol and drug abuse, and adolescent suicide.

- Violence and vandalism are not confined to urban schools; they are major problems in all of our schools and in our society.

- School dropout rates, although improving, reflect disparities among various groups and foreshadow future societal problems.

- Access to equal educational opportunity for poor and disadvantaged youth is an elusive goal in American education.

- Charter schools and school voucher plans are controversial forms of school choice.

- Gender issues affect the curriculum, classroom interactions, and achievement levels.

- Sex education remains as controversial as ever, although concern about acquired immune deficiency syndrome (AIDS) has strengthened the argument for proponents of sex education.

The children who stream into a teacher's classroom each September bring their own personal histories. Although they may wish to start afresh with the beginning of the new school year, much of who they are is wrapped up in their past and their current out-of-school lives. It is likely that some of these students bear deep scars from their past experiences and that some are currently caught up in desperate widespread social problems. We are not suggesting that you should be Mr. or Ms. Fix-It, taking in troubled children and, with a few quick adjustments to their psyches, sending them out into the world cured. Rather, we wish to make you more fully aware of and more deeply sensitive to the sorts of problems your students will bring to your classroom. We also want you to recognize the healing power of education, which gives structure, purpose, and hope to youngsters whose daily lives often lack these stabilizing and motivating influences.

Social Problems Affecting Students

In the previous chapter, entitled "Who Are Today's Students in a Diverse Society?", we talked about changes in our society that are resulting in increased diversity among today's students. These conditions affect many students' lives, but they do not necessarily prevent them from getting an education. However, some changes or trends in society do pose a more direct threat to the performance of students in school. Many teachers may have difficulty recognizing and adapting to differences that contribute to the problems some children bring to the classroom. As we discussed in "Who Are Today's Students in a Diverse Society?", most teachers come from relatively stable backgrounds. Although this situation can be a source of strength, it also means that children often inhabit different worlds than their teachers. Often there are gaps between teachers' and students' social class and their personal exposure to major social problems.

■ *social class differences*

In our discussion, we deal with several difficult conditions and problems, including poverty, homelessness, child abuse, alcohol and drug use, teenage parenting, adolescent suicide, violence, and school dropout rate. As you will see in the following discussion, these pervasive societal problems do not occur in isolation but actually tend to cluster or overlap. In real life, it is difficult to separate out discrete sources of social problems. The compounding of risk factors contributes to the incredible scope of these problems and places a number of students at risk for not completing or succeeding in school. For such **at-risk students**, as they are often called, the chances are great that they will have difficulty getting an adequate education.

■ *problems tend to cluster*

What are some of these risk factors? Six key measures include the following:

- The child is not living with two parents.
- The household head is a high school dropout.
- Family income is below the poverty line.
- The child is living with a parent or parents who do not have steady, full-time employment.
- The family is receiving welfare benefits.
- The child does not have health insurance.

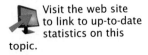
Visit the web site to link to up-to-date statistics on this topic.

We know that these family variables do not necessarily compromise children. Many children from families with these risks overcome the odds to succeed in school and in life. Research indicates, however, that when several of these risk

Figure 3.1
Number of Risk Factors Experienced by Children, 1998

Source: *Kids Count 1999* (Baltimore: The Annie E. Casey Foundation, 1999), p. 10. Reprinted by permission of the Annie E. Casey Foundation.

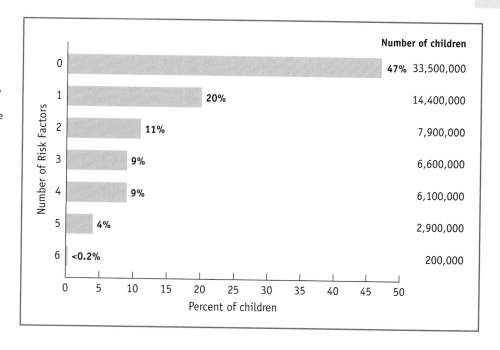

factors are present, fewer children make it. As one prominent author states, "The research . . . shows that the more risk factors are present, the greater the damaging impact of each. But the impact is not just additive—risk factors multiply each other's destructive effects."[1] Nationally, 9.2 million children are growing up with four or more of these risk factors (Figure 3.1). Nearly 30 percent of African-American children and almost 25 percent of Hispanic children are in the high-risk category, compared with only 6 percent of white children (Figure 3.2).[2] Compounding the problem is the fact that multiple-risk families are often concentrated in economically and socially isolated communities that have limited job opportunities, poor schools, low-quality public services, and higher levels of crime and drug use.

▨ *risks multiply with each added factor*

Let's examine some of these risk factors in more detail, starting with the changing patterns of the American family.

▨ *New American Family Patterns*

In recent decades, our society has experienced dramatic changes in how families are structured. The once common image of the "breadwinner" father, a housewife mother, and two children of public school age now accurately describes only 6 percent of households in the United States.[3] So what is the typical family of our students like today? Actually, there is no longer one "typical" family pattern. Rather, a number of economic and societal trends have resulted in families that come in many forms that, in turn, have a pervasive influence on children in school.

▨ *no "typical" family*

▨ *single-parent households*

Family Composition   An increasing number of children are being raised by single parents. Twenty-two percent of all children live only with their mothers, 4 percent live only with their fathers, and 4 percent live with neither parent.[4] A breakdown of the figures by racial group reveals that 23 percent of white children, 72 percent of African-American children, and 35 percent of Hispanic children live in arrangements other than two-parent families.[5]

Figure 3.2
Percentage of Children in High-Risk Category by Race/Ethnicity and Location, 1998*

Source: *Kids Count 1999* (Baltimore: The Annie E. Casey Foundation, 1999), p. 11. Reprinted by permission of the Annie E. Casey Foundation.

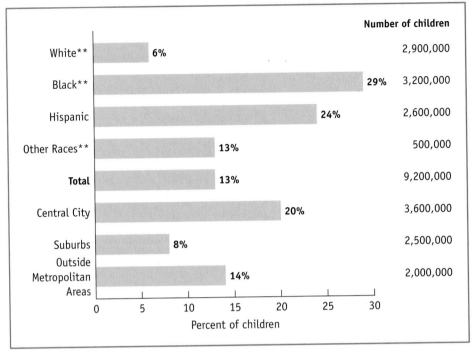

*There were 9.7 million children whose location could not be determined; 1.2 million of the children were high-risk children.

**Non-Hispanic.

Visit the web site to link to up-to-date statistics on this topic.

The rate of divorce has influenced the composition of our families, particularly among couples who have children. More than half of today's new marriages will end in divorce. In addition to divorce, other factors such as births to single parents, separation, and death of a parent contribute to the number of children living in single-parent households or possibly with grandparents or aunts and uncles.

Being a child in a family in which the parents' marriage is conflict ridden and unhappy may be less preferable in some ways than living in a single-parent family, but single-parent families have one major disadvantage: lower incomes. In 2000, the median income for single-mother households was just over $28,116; for married-couple households, the median income was just over $59,346.[6] Single-mother families have been called *the new poor*. It is not just the absence of one parent but the loss of a two-parent income that puts a special burden on these families. More difficult to pin down is the effect of only one parent bearing the daily chores of monitoring, supporting, and guiding the school-age children.

Another result of high divorce rates is the increasing number of children living in blended families with stepparents, stepsiblings, and/or half-siblings. In some cases, divorced parents share physical custody of the children, with the result that the children must split their time between parental households.

As we discussed in the chapter entitled "Who Are Today's Students in a Diverse Society?", you may also have students whose parents are of the same gender.

Changes in American family patterns will likely influence your interactions with students and their parents in a number of ways. For example, in divorce situations it may be difficult to keep both parents informed of their child's progress, or a single parent may have a very heavy workload and may be unable to attend parent-teacher conferences at the usual times. Varied family patterns

teaching implications

VOICES FROM THE CLASSROOM

Christa Compton has taught high school English in Columbia, S.C., for nine years. She was South Carolina's Teacher of the Year in 2001.

Families and School

My students show up with hearts burdened by terrible losses. Angela's father was murdered when she was very young, and she still grieves for a man she only vaguely remembers. Marcus was put up for adoption at birth by his teenage mother, and his adoptive mother died of cancer two years ago. Peter is angry because his mother recently moved out of the house, and he blames her for breaking up their family. Many other families have been torn apart by divorce, and fathers are increasingly absent in their children's lives.

All of this means I have to work hard to earn students' trust, an especially difficult task with those who have been disappointed by other people they have trusted. If students don't find a sense of belonging at home, it becomes even more important to find it at school, so I try to create a supportive community within the class. I un-

cover the story of each kid's life and design activities that build relationships among the students. Throughout the year, we write sympathy cards when one of us is grieving, applaud the students who make the honor roll, welcome back the students who return from an absence, and do whatever we can to express concern for each class member.

It helps to observe their behavior and moods from day to day. Sometimes just a quiet comment can reassure them that someone cares. At other times, students reveal their anxieties in a written assignment, so I write notes on their papers to let them know that I am there to support them.

They desperately want someone to pay attention—to praise their successes, to notice when they are sad, to share the daily torments and victories that are the hallmarks of adolescent life. When they feel dismissed, I can provide encouragement. When their lives are chaotic and unpredictable, I can offer safety and consistency. I might be the one person they can count on, and I refuse to let them down.

 Visit the web site for more Voices from the Classroom.

---

will also require more sensitivity in daily interactions, such as when asking students to bring a note from "your mother." It would perhaps be better to say "your parent" or "the person who takes care of you."

■ **Family Relationships**   Family composition affects the amount of time children and their parents have to spend with each other and can also affect the quality of that time. For a single parent, the combination of a job with the necessities of maintaining a family, such as cooking, cleaning, and grocery shopping, does not allow for a great deal of leisure time to spend supervising and enjoying the children. Many single parents do a fine job of raising their children, but the hardships are considerable.

■ *working parents*

Even two-parent families can face challenges, Many mothers now go to work or return to work when their children are very young. In 32 percent of two-parent families, both the mother and father worked all year, full time.[7] Two-career families must balance the needs of childrearing and family life with the demands of two work environments. Neither Mom nor Dad is as available as she or he used to be to attend daily to children's social, intellectual, and moral development.

America's future will be determined by the home and the school. The child becomes largely what it is taught, hence we must watch what we teach it, how we live before it.

—JANE ADDAMS

About three-quarters of today's students live in families in which either both parents work or the only parent works full time.[8] Now, when many children return home from school, they watch television rather than talk with their parents. Coming

■ *"latch-key" children*

home to an empty house or apartment after school is standard for an estimated 4 million "latch-key" children in our country.

■ *child care issues*

For parents of younger children not yet in school, working outside the home raises the issue of adequate childcare. If both parents or the only parent is working full time, who is taking care of the children? Grandparents and extended family used to pitch in and help, but today it is less common for a family to settle in one location near relatives for extended periods. Parents who have to work, especially single parents, can easily be caught in a bind, and they often must settle for whatever child care they can find or afford.

■ *schools play a larger role*

In addition to limiting the amount of time children spend in close contact with their parents, the trend toward two-career and single-parent families also has a direct impact on the schools. In the past, young people were actively involved outside of school in family and community, but today the school is being urged to play a larger role in expanding and guiding the limited experiences of children. Schools are being asked to deal with the new problems being brought to them by the facts of modern family life and our changed economy. Many schools have responded to child care needs by offering both before- and after-school programs. For example, many schools provide both breakfast and lunch programs. Schools may offer enrichment and recreational programs or on-site day care after school to address student and parental needs. Some schools even stagger their bus schedules to accommodate students who stay for after-school programs. As mentioned in the "Who Are Today's Students in a Diverse Society?" chapter, many schools offer nontraditional programs that coordinate agencies dealing with health, and social and recreational services. These interagency programs enable the schools to deliver needed social and health services to students and their families to promote success in school.

Reflect on the relationship between families with the video resources on your CD-ROM.

In the past, teachers could count on more support from families; now teachers often find it difficult to even get in contact with many parents. In this situation, the more dramatic social problems such as poverty and homelessness take on even greater urgency for the schools.

PAUSE AND REFLECT

❶ Does your own family background reflect traditional or emerging family patterns? How do you think your upbringing will affect your ability to teach students from different family situations?

❷ How can you prepare to work effectively with a variety of parents and caregivers?

■ *Poverty*

■ *the widening income gap*

The rich are getting richer and the poor are getting poorer. This well-known phrase describes the extremes of different socioeconomic levels in our society today. The poorest 40 percent of American citizens receive 14 percent of the national income, whereas the wealthiest 20 percent receive more than 47 percent.[9] In 2001, the number of impoverished Americans was 31.6 million, or 11.7 percent of the population.[10]

Visit this chapter of the web site to link to up-to-date statistics on this topic.

Numerically, the majority of poor Americans are white; however, the rate of poverty is higher among minorities. Almost 8 percent of whites, 23 percent of African Americans, 21 percent of Hispanic Americans, 26 percent of Native Americans, and less than 11 percent of Asian Americans live below the poverty line ($18,267 for a family of four in 2001).[11]

Figure 3.3
Percentage of Children Under 18 Living in Poverty, by Race/Ethnicity and Year

Source: U.S. Bureau of the Census, *Historical Poverty Tables—People* (Table 3: Poverty Status of People by Age, Race, and Hispanic Origin from 1959 to 2001). Available at: **http://www.census.gov/ hhes/poverty/histpov/ hstpov3.html**

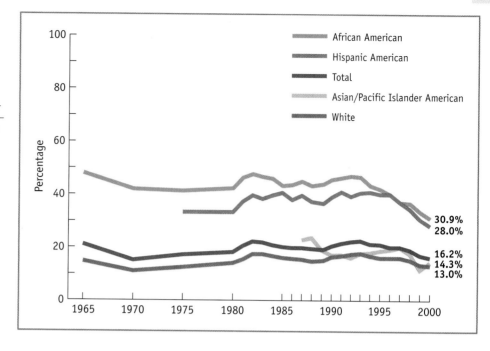

■ *one in six children are poor*

Although poverty rates declined through the 1990s because of a booming economy, the problem of poverty is still pervasive, and the prospects for breaking its grip on children are particularly bleak. Slightly more than 16 percent (11.7 million) of American children live in poverty, the highest rate among all age groups and the highest in any industrialized country. Children make up about one-fourth of the population, but they constitute 36 percent of the poor. More than 55 percent of the children in families headed by females are poor[12] (Figure 3.3).

In the past, poverty was assumed to be the result of unemployment, and for many, this is still true. Nearly 19 million American children, or 26 percent, are growing up in households in which no parent has a full-time, year-round job.[13]

■ *the working poor*

However, many people do hold regular jobs but still find themselves in poverty. After World War II, many high school graduates could get manufacturing jobs that required minimal education yet paid quite well. A high school graduate could support a family of four, buy a house, own two cars, and live comfortably. The American job market has now changed. Many manufacturing jobs can now be done more efficiently and effectively by machines, and many of those that are still done by people have been moved to countries with low-wage workers. The U.S. job market for unskilled workers today is found mostly in fast-food establishments and service jobs that typically pay minimum wage and offer no benefits. Full-time employment at the current minimum wage is not enough to support a family above the poverty line.

Many people in our society have thought that we could eliminate poverty through education and that, through schooling, it would be relatively easy to free people from the chains of impoverishment. The efforts have been well intentioned but often too little, too late and in retrospect, sometimes naive. With poverty so prevalent, schools have a challenging problem, partly because they

■ *two views of schooling*

are not designed to serve poor children. The schools in this country were created and continue to be supported by the middle class to perpetuate the middle-class way of life. There is nothing particularly startling about this. Middle-class

Reflect on how schools serve students in poverty with the image in this section of your CD-ROM.

people want their children to be like themselves or possibly somewhat better. Therefore, they have built and continue to pay for a school system that reflects their values and supports the way of life with which they feel comfortable.

On the other hand, some critics see our schools as part of an enslavement system. They claim that the schools not only do not help develop the individual talents and strengths of poor children but also make these children believe they are losers. After eight to eleven years of schooling, many of these young people see themselves as unable to fit into the middle class and as people who, at best, will do society's menial work. Although some of these critics see this system as a conscious plan of our society, we do not. Such a cynical view suggests that the teachers who are toiling in the urban and rural slums are either people of evil intentions or simply dupes. In our view, many of the most heroic teachers alive are those struggling to aid people oppressed by poverty.

Our past and present inadequacies in educating the children of the poor tempt some to turn away and devote their energies to more solvable problems. We cannot do this. Ours is an evolving society. As a people, we are not finished with our own development. Eradicating the ravages of poverty and its withering effect on children should be at the top of our agenda as citizens of this nation and as educators. Although there are many important and solvable problems to work on, we cannot afford—in justice—to ignore this one.

Homelessness

For families close to poverty, the threat of homelessness is very real. Families in poverty often pay more than one-half of their annual incomes in rent. With such a large percentage of income consumed by rent payments, one incident or emergency in the family can disrupt the tenuous equilibrium and jeopardize the family's ability to maintain a home. Imagine, for example, the domino effect that could occur from mechanical difficulties with the one family car. Even minor repairs costing $50 to $100 may be beyond the family's budget. Without a car, the family breadwinner may be unable to get to work and the children unable to get to day care. It does not take long in such a situation to lose a job or a long-awaited slot in a day care center. If the main earner cannot work, paying rent can soon become impossible. It is easy to see why housing, which consumes so much of annual income, is a particularly vulnerable area for families in poverty.

obstacles for homeless schoolchildren

There are about 1 million homeless children and youth in the United States, and more than 750,000 are of school age.[14] Imagine the obstacles for a homeless child trying to get an education. Uprooted from their homes, many live in shelters or other locations in distant parts of town. Attending school may require extensive transportation, which parents are not likely to be able to afford. Enrolling children in a school near a shelter may be a difficult and intimidating process for parents struggling with daily survival. Many parents, believing they will be homeless only for a short time, may not even try to transfer their child's enrollment. As days turn into weeks and months, the child may miss a great deal of school. If the child is fortunate enough to attend school, other difficulties may arise, such as the stigma of wearing dirty and ragged clothes, being unwelcome by other children or school officials, or being unable to stay awake in class.

Some homeless children are on their own, having run away from home or been ejected from their families. Many of these chronically homeless youth have been physically or sexually abused, and many suffer from drug or alcohol abuse, poor nutrition, inadequate sleep, exposure to the elements, and lack of health care. School can be a stabilizing force in the lives of these children, but it can also exacerbate their problems. In 1987, Congress passed the Stewart B. Mc-Kinney Homeless Assistance Act, with subsequent amendments, to provide protection for the educational needs of homeless children and youth. The legislation provides grants to states to provide for the educational needs of homeless children and requires states to ensure that these children are educated with the rest of the youth in their area and not isolated and stigmatized.[15]

homeless children require teacher's support

You may have homeless children in your classroom; if so, they are likely to require support and understanding from you. Some may be malnourished or physically dirty because they lack access to shower or tub facilities. They may show emotional needs. Other children may make fun of them. Your support and caring could provide them with hope and be crucial in improving their chances for success. Hundreds of local and federal programs serve runaway and homeless youth, and these agencies will help you work with these youngsters. More than anything else, homeless children need homes.

PAUSE AND REFLECT

1. Why do you think it is so difficult for the schools to overcome the effects of poverty on the academic achievement for poor children?

2. What are the challenges in teaching poor children?

3. Are you interested in teaching children from poverty situations? Why or why not?

Teenage Parenting

Visit the web site to link to up-to-date statistics on this topic.

The bad news is that each year almost 900,000 American teenagers get pregnant and give birth to some 500,000 children, by far the highest teenage birthrate among the world's developed countries. The good news is that between 1990 and 1999, the birthrate among girls ages fifteen to nineteen declined from 60 to less than 50 births per 1,000.[16] Still, the annual cost in public funds for teenage pregnancies in America is estimated to be more than $7 billion.[17]

relationship of teen pregnancy and poverty

The consequences of early parenthood for teen fathers are generally not as severe as those for teen mothers. Most teenage mothers are not married and so are particularly vulnerable to poverty. When we combine the difficulties of single parenthood with the likelihood that teenagers will have poor work skills and limited employment experience and, if they find work, will receive low wages, we gain some understanding of the finding that more than half the children from households headed by a female live in poverty. In fact, an 8- to 12-year-old child born to an unmarried, teenage, high school dropout is ten times as likely to be living in poverty as a child born to a mother having none of these three characteristics. Contributing to this condition of poverty is the fact that many young fathers do not provide financial assistance and support to these children. Because about three-quarters of teenage births occur out of wedlock, male parents often feel little responsibility for their children. Only 10 percent of mothers ages 15 to 17 receive child support payments.[18]

steps taken by schools

Teenage parents face not only the enormous task of juggling childrearing and employment but often a premature baby, who is more likely to have health problems and possible learning difficulties. Moreover, poverty often correlates with worse nutrition, less health care, more homelessness, and less education than for more advantaged families. To lessen this problem, many schools are

As pregnant teenagers struggle with the decision of whether to drop out of school, educators are finding ways to encourage pregnant teenagers and young mothers to stay in school and graduate.
(David Young-Wolff/PhotoEdit)

working with local health officials to ensure that pregnant teenagers receive prenatal care and parenting advice. They are also encouraging these young women to stay in school and graduate. In many cases, the schools are permitting young mothers to bring their babies with them to school. To prevent teenage pregnancies, some schools have established clinics where birth control devices can be obtained, and sex education programs (discussed later in the chapter) have become common and controversial.

If you are planning on teaching in secondary schools, you should give some thought to what you would do if one of your students informs you that she is pregnant or that he has gotten his girlfriend pregnant. Know both your legal and ethical responsibilities in these cases. If you plan to teach in an elementary school, be prepared to work with very young parents, perhaps even your own age.

Abused and Neglected Children

The education of the young brings us into contact with humanity's best impulses. Occasionally, however, we see the wreckage of its darkest and most vicious urges. For many years, the phenomenon of child abuse was known only to a small percentage of social workers and law enforcement people. More recently, we have become aware of the magnitude of this problem and the variety of forms abuse can take, including physical or mental injury, sexual abuse, negligent treatment, and maltreatment.

■ *many cases unreported*

Because of the hidden nature of child abuse and neglect, reliable figures on it are somewhat difficult to obtain. Professionals in the field acknowledge that most cases are unreported. Nevertheless, almost 3 million incidents of child abuse or neglect are reported to child-service agencies each year. More than 800,000 of these reported cases are substantiated. Almost three-fifths of the victims of maltreatment suffered from neglect, about one-fifth experienced physical abuse, and about one-tenth were victims of sexual abuse.[19] Parental substance abuse was reported as a major contributing factor in child abuse cases.

> *America is losing sight of its children. In decisions made every day we are placing them at the bottom of the agenda, with grave consequences for the future of the nation.*
>
> ——ERNEST BOYER

■ *effects of abuse*

The toll that abuse and neglect take on children's physical, emotional, and psychological development is difficult to assess. Children subjected to violent treatment also sustain injuries that cause serious learning problems in school. These children may be withdrawn or have trouble concentrating. They suffer enormous stress, and their self-esteem is low. They sometimes have excessive needs for control because they have experienced such helplessness. Ironically, they may be more likely to abuse their own children in the future.

■ *the teacher's responsibility*

The classroom teacher will not directly encounter the problem of abuse very often. However, in all fifty states, educators are legally responsible for reporting suspected cases of child abuse. Teachers must be aware of potential signs of abuse and know school policy and procedures for reporting suspected abuse. (See the chapter entitled "What Are the Ethical and Legal Issues Facing Teachers?" for a discussion of teachers' legal obligations regarding suspected child abuse.) Potential signs of abuse include the following:

- Repeated injuries such as bruises, welts, and burns
- Neglected appearance
- Sudden changes in academic performance
- Disruptive or passive, withdrawn behavior
- "Supercritical" parents who remain isolated from the school and community[20]

Teachers need to realize that even after an abusive situation has been reported and perhaps disclosed, these children's problems in school will not suddenly end. Children who have been abused have a continuing need for emotional safety and stability. They need capable adult role models who can provide varied but predictable activities and measurable classroom achievement. They need trustworthy praise, concrete rewards, and constructive ways to control their classroom environment.

▨ *Alcohol and Drug Abuse*

Many of the trends we have talked about so far in this chapter can severely stress the functioning of families, provoking self-destructive responses. Substance abuse is a particularly destructive response. It may involve the use of alcohol or various other drugs. It may be the act of parents or children. Unfortunately, when one family member gets entangled in substance abuse, the entire family is usually a victim.

▨ alcohol, a major problem

Alcohol is the most commonly abused substance, and the first use of alcohol may occur at a young age, sometimes in elementary school. Historically, the greatest number of alcoholic teenagers have been male students, especially those with low grades, but the gap between males and females seems to be closing. The problem of alcohol abuse among high school students is widespread. A 2001 survey revealed that four out of every five students have consumed alcohol by the end of high school, and nearly two-thirds of twelfth-graders have reported being drunk.[21]

Reflect on student alcohol use with the image in this section of your CD-ROM.

In the same year, the percentages of eighth-, tenth-, and twelfth-graders who reported using an illicit drug during the past year were 20, 37, and 41 percent, respectively (Figure 3.4).[22] Despite slight recent declines, student drug and alcohol abuse remain massive problems. Substance abuse by parents has also increased, with devastating results for children. As indicated in the previous section of this chapter, many child abuse and neglect cases involve parental substance abuse.

▨ physical and emotional damage

What should you do if you suspect one of your students is using drugs or binge drinking? The most important thing is to talk with the school counselor about the situation. He or she has been trained to deal with these problems and can offer you advice on both the legal aspects of the situation and ways to assist the student.

▨ *Adolescent Suicide*

Suicide is third only to motor vehicle accidents and homicide as a leading cause of adolescent death in the United States. Each year about 3,900 people in the 15 through 24 year old age group take their own lives.

▨ suicide patterns

Studies of young people who have attempted suicide and those who have succeeded reveal several patterns. For every teenager who commits suicide, 100

Figure 3.4
Student Drug and Alcohol Use: Percentage of High School Seniors Reporting Use in the Previous 30 Days, by Year and Substance

Source: University of Michigan, Institute for Social Research, *Monitoring the Future*, various years. Available at: **http://monitoringthefuture. org/pubs/monographs/ overview2001.pdf**

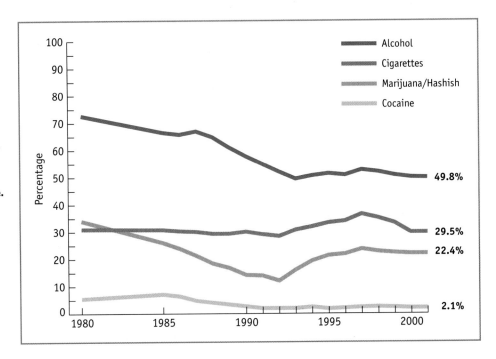

more will try. Every year, one in 13 high school students attempts suicide, and half of all high school students report they have "seriously considered" suicide by the time they graduate. Among those who attempt suicide, the vast majority is female. Girls attempt suicide about three times more often than boys, but boys complete suicide about four times more often than girls.[23] The suicide rate for blacks ages fifteen to nineteen has increased dramatically since 1980 but is still lower than the rate for whites.

risk factors

What puts young people at risk for attempting suicide? Factors include family violence or disruption, mental illness, unemployment, a history of substance abuse, being bullied, and stress in school or social life. Some experts argue that the leading reason why young people are more at risk for suicide now than they were a generation or two ago is the decline of the traditional family unit. To add to the tragedy, young people sometimes engage in copycat suicides. In this "cluster" syndrome, a wave of adolescent suicides plagues an area. In response, hundreds of school districts now offer programs in suicide prevention.

Even though suicide is the third greatest cause of deaths among youth, only one in ten schools has a plan to prevent them. Educators often have the opportunity to recognize children and youths who are suicide risks and to help them get the advice and support they need. Although suicidal behaviors are complex and the warning signs can be ambiguous or misleading, it is important to realize that most young people who commit suicide give warning first to signal their need for help. The American Academy of Child Psychiatry recommends that parents, teachers, and counselors watch for these signs:

warning signs

- Changes in eating and sleeping habits

- Withdrawal from friends, family, and regular activities

- Violent or rebellious behavior

- Running away

- Drug or alcohol abuse

Whom You Will Teach

Percentage of ninth- to twelfth-graders who admitted carrying a weapon at school in the past 30 days: 7

Percentage of ninth- to twelfth-graders who reported being in a physical fight in the previous year: 36

Percentage of teens ages sixteen to nineteen who were high school dropouts: 9

Percentage of three to five year olds who were read to every day in the last week by a family member: 54

Percentage of children under age eighteen who are living in poverty: 16

Percentage of high school seniors who report having used an illegal drug in the previous 30 days: 25

Percentage of students age twelve to seventeen who reported gangs at their schools: 17

Percentage of high school graduates who will not attend college: 27

Percentage of students in grades nine through twelve who had drunk alcohol during the previous thirty days: 50

Percentage of high school students age sixteen to nineteen who have jobs: 30; percentage who work twenty or more hours per week: 11

Percentage of children under eighteen living in single-parent households: 27

Percentage of thirteen year olds who watch television three to four hours per day: 42; five hours or more: 31

Percentage of sixteen to nineteen year olds who participate in volunteer activities for schools and other organizations: 13

Percentage of tenth-graders absent from school seven days or more each year: 26

Percentage of students with disabilities who are served by federal programs: 13

Percentage of eighth-graders who agree or strongly agree with the following statements:

- Teachers are interested in students: 75

- Teachers praise my effort when I work hard: 63

- I often feel "put down" by my teachers: 22

- I don't feel safe at this school: 12

- Students get along well with teachers: 67

Sources: *The Condition of Education 1998 and 2001, Indicators of School Crime and Safety 2001*, and *Digest of Education Statistics 1998 and 2001* (Washington, DC: National Center for Education Statistics); *Youth Indicators 1996* (Washington, DC: U.S. Department of Education); *2001 Kids Count Data Book* (Baltimore: The Annie E. Casey Foundation, 1999); *America's Children; Key National Indicators of Well-Being 2001* (Washington, DC: Federal Interagency Forum on Child and Family Statistics, 2001).

- Unusual neglect of personal appearance

- Radical change in personality

- Persistent boredom, difficulty concentrating, or a decline in the quality of schoolwork

- Frequent complaints about physical symptoms that are often related to emotions, such as stomachaches, headaches, or fatigue

- Loss of interest in previously pleasurable activities

- Inability to tolerate praise or rewards[24]

If you observe such potential indicators of suicidal tendencies, do not try to handle the burden alone. Seek a support network of the guidance counselor, the school social worker, and/or the school psychologist. Recognizing symptoms and getting professional help for students who behave in this way may prevent their suicides and help them develop coping behaviors to deal with their problems.

■ *School Violence and Vandalism*

Massacre at Columbine High School in Littleton, Colo.—15 Die

Gunman shoots eighth-grader in L.A.

Sixth-graders plot to kill their teacher

Student, 14, shoots security guard in D.C.

Fifteen year old shoots and kills classmate

As these headlines indicate, America has become a dangerous place for its children. In urban areas, crime and violence from surrounding neighborhoods have spilled over into the schools, affecting children, staff, and teachers alike. In the suburbs, we have seen some horrible examples of students killing other students. How extensive is the problem of school violence and crime?

Despite the headlines just given, serious violent crime constitutes a small percentage of the total amount of school crime, and homicide is extremely rare. Although the number of multiple homicide events at school has increased and receives national media coverage when it does occur, the chance of suffering a school-associated violent death is less than one in a million. The rate of violent deaths at schools has actually dropped since 1992. Between the 1994–95 and 2000–01 school years, 253 people died in 220 school-related violent incidents, 67 percent of which occurred on school property. Nearly 70 percent of the victims and 37 percent of the perpetrators were students. Nevertheless, schools still remain relatively safe environments for students. Of all the homicides and suicides that occur among school-age children, less than 1 percent are associated with a school,[25] but even that is too much.

■ *school crime statistics*

Factors that contribute to violence, including gangs and bullying, the costs of violence and vandalism, and recent prevention efforts in schools, are discussed below.

■ **Gangs**   Severe violence is often associated with gangs. Once confined to inner-city areas, street gangs are now present in smaller urban areas and suburbs, although in smaller percentages. Urban students are more likely to report street gangs at their schools (25 percent) than are suburban students (16 percent) or rural students (11 percent).[26] The proportion of young people who actually join gangs is quite small, however. The U.S. Justice Department estimates the number of gang members at about 250,000 out of the nearly 47 million Americans ages twelve to twenty-five, the years most closely associated with gang activity.[27]

Children and teenagers join gangs for a variety of reasons: the excitement of gang activity, peer pressure, physical protection, attention, financial gain, a sense of belonging, and sometimes because they feel ignored by the people they should be close to—usually one or both parents. In many cases, youths are not actively discouraged from gang involvement by their parents. Often parents are unaware that their children are engaged in gang activity. Gangs often display clothing, jewelry, or graffiti that distinguish and identify their members. The character of gang activity has become more violent because increasingly, gangs

Reprinted with special permission of King Features Syndicate.

are involved in drug dealing and other criminal activities. The easy accessibility and spread of guns and the greater tendency to use extreme violence to settle disputes or to avenge even the smallest acts of "disrespect" have also contributed to increased violence. Although gang members are often stereotyped as lower class, some are children of middle-class, suburban families who commit acts of vandalism, robbery, and drug dealing out of boredom or feelings of alienation from family and friends.

combating gang influence

How can educators minimize the negative influences of gangs? Useful actions include the following:

- Establish and enforce clear codes of school conduct that stress the unacceptability of gang behavior and the prohibition of weapons.

- Establish programs that stress positive youth involvement as alternatives to gang membership.

- Assimilate gang-oriented students into the mainstream—academically, socially, and through extracurricular activities.

- Create school programs that focus on nonviolent conflict resolution and gang prevention.

- Take quick, decisive actions when instances of gang activity occur on school grounds.

Reflect on the effects of bullying with the image in this section of your CD-ROM.

Bullying   Everyone who has attended school most likely has memories of themselves or friends of theirs being frightened by a bully. Once dismissed as "kids-will-be-kids" behavior, chronic teasing and bullying are now being viewed by educators as dangerous social acts. Recent studies have shown that up to 30 percent of children endure harassment in school and that as many as 7 percent of eighth-graders stay home at least once a month because of bullies.[28] Bullying takes a terrible toll on children. Their schoolwork suffers, and their physical and mental health also suffers. Physical and psychological bullying is often reported to be a contributing cause in adolescent suicide attempts. Bullying is also bad for bullies because they never learn the consequences of their actions.

programs to eliminate bullying

A nationwide program, Bully-Proofing Your School, teaches children to recognize bullying and to develop ways to protect themselves, such as humor and avoidance. Teachers and other school workers also receive training. Civility training is also becoming a popular way to reduce bullying by teaching children how to be kind and compassionate to all people. When the problem persists, some schools have developed **zero-tolerance policies** for aggressive behavior and automatically suspend any student who harasses another. By developing a heightened awareness of bullying and its negative consequences, teachers can

Visit this chapter of the web site to link to more information about stopping bullying.

take actions to make the school environment more hospitable and inviting for all students.

■ **Costs of Vandalism and Violence**   Costs resulting from vandalism or violence include the costs of building repairs, skyrocketing premiums for liability insurance, human costs in terms of injuries to students and teachers, and in extreme cases, even deaths.

Many teachers are injured while attempting either to break up student fights or to halt robberies. Student-teacher disagreements also provoke attacks. Still other teachers are injured not by students but by intruders who may be dealing drugs or who see the elementary schools as buildings with little security and populated by women and children.

■ **Steps to Reduce School Violence**   Concern over school crime and violence has prompted many public schools to take various measures to reduce and prevent violence and ensure safety in schools. Such measures include adopting zero-tolerance policies regarding weapons—that is, carrying a weapon to school will automatically result in expulsion; creating alternative schools for students with a history of violence; requiring students to wear uniforms; employing various security measures such as requiring visitor sign-in and using metal detectors; having police or other law enforcement officials stationed at the school; and offering students and staff various types of violence prevention programs.

Several aspects of school organization can contribute to student aggression, including high numbers of students occupying a small space, imposition of routines and conformity that may anger some students, and poor building designs that may contribute to the commission of violent acts.[29] Most deadly incidents occur during "transition times"—that is, the start of school, during lunch periods, or the end of the school day. Reducing crowding, increasing supervision, and instituting policies for handling disputes during these intervals can reduce the likelihood of conflicts and their resulting injuries. On the other hand, students who enjoy positive interactions with faculty and staff, are academically successful, or participate productively in school activities are less likely to commit acts of violence. One study found that in more than half the cases of school

Bullying is common in schools, producing consequences detrimental to both the bullies and victims. Schools are responding with a variety of programs to reduce the incidents of bullying.
(© Jonathan Nourok/
PhotoEdit)

One cause of dropping out is unrealistic expectations about the world of work. Many students with high hopes for the imagined luxury of a regular income fail to realize that wages in the service sector of employment have deteriorated. Other teenagers may envision starting at the bottom of the work hierarchy and, through hard work, eventually climbing the ladder of success. However, many of them lack job search skills and end up in jobs with limited potential for advancement. Despite this reality, the strong motivation to work often proves too powerful an incentive and results in a student leaving school. The immediate rewards of the workplace lure some students away from the more remote incentives for attaining an education and staying in school.

Tension Points in American Education

This section explores opposing positions on some of the most controversial topics in American education today. Our goal is to equip you, as a teacher, with an understanding of and sensitivity to the exposed nerve endings of American education. Keep in mind the significance of these tension points; they are the result of an attempt to educate children in a pluralistic society. Tension points are inevitable when diverse groups and individuals with different objectives for the schools try to achieve those objectives. Because teachers have a deep responsibility to the schools, it is important that they provide leadership in seeking enlightened solutions to the problems arising from these complex and touchy issues.

One warning is that our coverage of these tension points will acquaint you with some of the key aspects surrounding these issues, but it is not very deep. You should not be satisfied to stop here. It is your responsibility to dig below the surface to find out what these issues really involve. Obviously, all of the tension points in American education cannot be explored in this chapter, but a number of them are addressed in other chapters. For example, equitable school funding, certainly a "hot button" topic, is addressed in the chapter entitled "How Are Schools Governed, Influenced, and Financed?". In this section, we focus on three topics that have generated considerable controversy and debate: access and equality of educational opportunity, school choice, and gender issues.

Before we proceed, take a few moments to assess your own position by answering the following questions about these three controversial topics in American education:

assessing your own position

• What constitutes equality of educational opportunity? Should it be determined by students having equal access to similar resources or by achieving comparable academic results?

• Do you believe in providing preferential treatment to members of groups to compensate for unequal educational opportunities resulting from their race, social class, or financial situation?

• Do you believe parents should be free to choose the public school their child attends, regardless of whether they live in that school's district? Are you in favor of providing parents with government-funded vouchers that they can use to pay their child's tuition at a private or religious school?

• Do schools treat boys and girls equally? What evidence can you provide to support your position?

- Should schools teach sex education? If so, what should be the focus of such programs?

Opinions on these issues are extremely diverse because they touch on our religious, political, or philosophical convictions. Whatever your views, you may find it stimulating and thought provoking to compare your responses with those of your classmates.

■ *Access and Equality of Educational Opportunity*

The United States is a multiracial, multiethnic, and multiclass society. Many people consider it to be one of the most successful mixed societies the world has ever seen. However, it is far from perfect, and many children born into poor or minority-group families face severe disadvantages in their attempts to live decent lives and to climb the ladder of success. Schooling is intended to help individuals in this process. Whether the schools have been helping or hindering the progress of these children has been a source of raging debate for decades.

One fact seems clear: large numbers of poor and minority-group students are leaving school without the academic and occupational skills necessary to function effectively in American society. Who, if anyone, is to blame for this situation? The schools? Teachers and administrators? Is the responsibility that of society as a whole, and are the schools merely being made a scapegoat? Talk to five different people, and you will probably hear five different opinions about where blame should be fixed.

■ *changing definitions of access and equal educational opportunity*

The debate revolves around the ideas of *access* and **equality of educational opportunity**. These are hardly new concepts in American education, but their components have changed dramatically in recent decades. In the nineteenth century, the goal of educational access was to build schools where children lived and to enroll as many of them as possible. By the beginning of the twentieth century, that goal was augmented by a focus on giving students curricular choices, including vocational training, to help prepare them for their different economic and social roles. In the 1930s, 1940s, and 1950s, access to equal educational opportunities focused on removing legal, racial, and economic barriers to schooling. The federal government's role in removing these barriers to school access increased dramatically, especially after the landmark 1954 U.S. Supreme Court decision in *Brown* v. *Board of Education*. This decision held that segregated schools are inherently unequal because the effects of such schools are likely to differ (see the chapter entitled "What Is the History of American Education?"). Thus, a new component was introduced into the concept of educational opportunity: that equality of educational opportunity is defined in terms of the effects, rather than the provision, of schooling. In the *Brown* decision, the Court found that even if the facilities and teacher salaries provided were identical, "equality of educational opportunity" would not exist in segregated schools.

■ *Brown* v. *Board of Education*

Find the full text of the *Brown* v. *Board of Education* decision in the text resources on your CD-ROM.

Before *Brown*, the community and educational institutions were expected only to provide equal resources such as teachers, facilities, and materials. Responsibility for the best use of those resources lay with the child and the child's family. In the decades since *Brown*, many people have come to consider it the responsibility of the educational institution, not the child, to create achievement.

From the 1960s through the 1970s, access and educational opportunity were redefined as they became increasingly tied to results. The removal of racial, linguistic, mental, and physical discrimination as the basis for expanded access was augmented by a focus on measuring learning outcomes among different groups as a test of whether improved access led to real educational opportunity. Others do not accept this assertion, arguing that the school should do its best to provide equal educational resources for all its students but cannot be held accountable for differences in student learning. As one noted educational historian has stated:

> Each redefinition incorporated the view that schools had fallen short of meeting existing goals or that the goals themselves needed modification. This duality was itself revealing. On the one hand, inequalities by region, social class, race, gender, and disability meant that access—in any of its meanings—was always incomplete. On the other hand, even when goals were substantially met . . . new expectations were added to what the schools should accomplish. By the end of [the twentieth] century, those expectations had shifted to an emphasis on academic achievement and a de-emphasis on issues of equity.[32]

▪ *opinions vary regarding poor achievement*

Although it is agreed that many poor and minority children in our schools are not learning at a rate comparable to white and middle-class children, opinions vary considerably as to the locus and cause of the problem. At one extreme are those who think the problem resides in the so-called deficiencies of minority children. Their impoverished home life, their particular cultural milieu, or even their mental capacities are cited as the sources of unequal results in school. At the other extreme are those who claim the problem is in the schools, which neither stimulate nor instruct the minority child with the intensity that is needed. Teachers expect minority children to do poorly, they claim, and this becomes a self-fulfilling prophecy. As described in the "Who Are Today's Students in a Diverse Society?" chapter, this position assumes that it is the school's obligation to diagnose the learner's needs, concerns, and cognitive and affective styles and to adjust its program accordingly. As with most controversies, the answer probably lies somewhere in between: many minority students do come to school with certain deficiencies, but the schools need to learn how to overcome them.

In addition, numerous court cases have challenged the school finance systems in various states, charging that when educational spending in rich school districts exceeds that of poor districts by two or three times, students in the poor districts are not getting access to equal educational opportunities. In a number of cases, courts have ordered legislatures to redesign the school finance system. (See the chapter entitled "How Are Schools Governed, Influenced, and Financed?" for more on the topic of equitable school finance.)

Equality is the result of human organization.
—HANNAH ARENDT

As we begin a new century, the goals of access and educational opportunity have become exceedingly complex as they encompass multiple meanings. Even as America has achieved success in creating greater access to schooling, those very successes have bred discontent and changed expectations as to what access and educational opportunity mean. The current emphasis on elevating academic outcomes for all students has essentially displaced the historic commitment to removing barriers to universal attendance and high school graduation as measures of access. The controversy over access and equity is best seen in the contentious debates about affirmative action. Although affirmative action centers primarily on admission to college, it is also being tested in admissions to select private schools and magnet schools. The issue centers on whether awarding minority students special status in admissions decisions is either appropriate or legal. The larger issue is whether any group defined as *in need*

▪ *controversy over preferential treatment*

LEADERS IN EDUCATION
MARIA MONTESSORI (1870–1952)

Maria Montessori became a proponent of preschool education, an urban educational reformer, and a believer in equal opportunities for women sixty years before any of these issues were matters of widespread concern.

As a child, Montessori excelled in mathematics and thought of becoming an engineer. Later she became interested in medicine and overcame tremendous criticism to become the first woman to enroll in the University of Rome's medical school. After graduating, she lectured on anthropology at the university and became associated with the psychiatric clinic. She developed an interest in children with mental retardation and, suspecting they were far more capable of learning than was commonly believed, founded and headed the Orthophrenic School, where she achieved remarkable results with these children.

Not until she was thirty-six years old, though, did Montessori find her life work. Believing that her methods could be even more effective with normal children, she opened her first school, the Casa dei Bambini (Children's House), to the preschool-age street urchins of Rome. Montessori's school was run on the principle of allowing children freedom within a carefully designed environment and under the sensitive guidance of a trained director. The materials and toys available in the school were prescribed, but the children could handle or ignore them as they wished. The teachers were instructed simply to wait until the child became interested in a particular game or project. A child who was concentrating deeply on a ritual with a toy was not aided or corrected by a teacher unless she or he asked for help.

Montessori discovered that certain simple and precise educational materials evoked sustained interest and attention in young children. Children under five years of age would concentrate on a single task, oblivious to distraction, from fifteen minutes to an hour, and afterward seemed refreshed rather than tired. Montessori's close observations of children led her to conclude that from birth to age six, all children have "absorbent minds" that equip them to learn more quickly and easily than at any later period in their lives. Montessori recognized that small children learn through their senses, and she developed methods of stimulating the child's senses in ways that would improve learning. For instance, children were taught the alphabet with sandpaper letters that they could manipulate with their fingers. Montessori was the first to use flashcards as a sensory stimulus, and she even introduced the hula hoop, which became a fad in the United States in the 1950s. When severely criticized for ignoring discipline, she replied that in the conventional schools she had visited, children were "not disciplined, but annihilated."

Montessori's teaching methods have aroused considerable interest in the United States as a result of recent psychological research that verifies many of her theories. Psychologists and educators have come to agree with her that the period of early childhood is critical in determining a person's intellectual potential. Teachers of underprivileged or poor children in particular claim great success with Montessori techniques. The day care center movement and the early childhood movement in general have been significantly influenced by Maria Montessori's views. In many ways, hers was one of the first compensatory education programs.

 Visit the web site for more information about Maria Montessori.

should receive preferential treatment designed to compensate for unequal educational opportunities resulting from their race, social class, or financial situation. These changed expectations have made the concepts of access and equal educational opportunity a major tension point in American education.

PAUSE AND REFLECT

1 Do you agree that equality of educational opportunity should be defined by its effects rather than by its provisions? Why or why not?

School Choice

Visit the web site to link to more information about school choice.

The United States is recognized around the world as a consumer's paradise. Whether it is soft drinks in the supermarket, jeans in a clothing store, or sports cars at the auto dealer, the principle of choice rules—except in K–12 schooling.

Technically, all parents have a choice as to where they wish to have their children educated. If they do not like the public, state-supported school to which their children are assigned, they can send them to a private or religious school (if there is one in their locale), or they can move to another community where the schools are more to their liking. Another increasingly popular option, as we discuss in the "How Should Education Be Reformed?" chapter, is for parents to teach their own children at home. The only problem with this theory is that not everyone can put it into practice. For the large percentage of parents without the time and ability to conduct home schooling or the resources to pay tuition at private or religious schools, there really is no choice at all. Many people are touting **school choice** as an important aspect of access and educational opportunity. They argue that poor parents should have a choice in the schools their children attend, as wealthier parents do. Being able to choose the school your children attend, they argue, is an important way to ensure access to educational opportunity. If the neighborhood public school isn't doing an adequate job, shouldn't parents have alternative choices of schools?

constraints on parental choice

The advocates of school choice see our current system as monopolistic and want to revolutionize the way we organize education. They want to transfer the decision of where a child must go to school from the school system to the child's parents. They want *market forces* to regulate the schools instead of the educational monopoly that they claim currently operates.

Parents as Educational Consumers Advocates for choice say that the current public schools have no real incentive to better serve students, since salaries and benefits are unaffected by either good or poor student results. The teacher who works sixteen hours a day and gives heart and soul to the school is on the same salary scale as the teacher who is the first one out of the parking lot at 2:30 P.M. On the other hand, if the parent can act as a consumer, choice advocates argue, schools will have an incentive to improve. Free-market principles suggest that "More choice equals more competition equals better products at lower prices." Here, the phrase *better products* means better-educated students.

arguments for school choice

Supporters of school choice say further that the group getting the worst public education today, our urban minorities, stands to benefit the most. As an example, they point to one of the longest-running choice experiments in the country, District 4 in New York City. Central Park East secondary school and the area's elementary schools are part of a network of schools from which

O P E N

T O

D E B A T E

Are the American Public Schools a Government Monopoly?

▶ **KEVIN:** It's clear to me that most American parents . . . who have a choice about where to work, where to shop for goods, and where to get most of the services they use, are, when it comes to educating their own children, forced into a government-run monopoly.

▶ **JIM:** Wait a minute. A monopoly? My dictionary says that a monopoly means having exclusive control over particular goods or services. What about religious schools? What about private schools? That doesn't sound like a government monopoly to me.

▶ **KEVIN:** It does to the millions of parents and students that are trapped in decaying, low-performing urban schools. It does to the millions of poor and minority parents who have no choice but to send their kids to these government-run "public" schools.

▶ **JIM:** Let me guess here. You are proposing some sort of a capitalist educational system, turning the public schools over to corporations to run like little Wal-Marts or Taco Bells. Look, by all means and with all haste, those failing schools need to be reformed and revitalized, but this doesn't mean dismantling our public school system.

▶ **KEVIN:** Personally, I prefer the term "free market" educational system to "capitalist," but that is a small point. Essentially, the idea is, instead of giving the tax dollars collected from citizens to some government bureaucrat, some superintendent of schools, give the dollars back to parents to buy the educational services they believe are best for their kids. The current system is like the government collecting a hefty car tax from citizens and then telling them they can only choose a single brand of government-issued car.

▶ **JIM:** We're not talking here about buying cars or soap flakes. We are talking about educating kids, preparing them to be successful human beings and good citizens. Our free, universal system of public schooling is one of the great success stories in our history. It has been copied around the world. Sure, it can and should be improved, but not by turning it over to corporations whose main goal is to make money. That is a recipe for disaster. Have you forgotten Enron!

▶ **KEVIN:** Listen, a lot of our public schools are Enrons, but they aren't being allowed to fail. We keep pumping money into them, keeping them afloat while generation after generation of kids drowns. What the public schools need is a healthy dose of competition, the same kind of competition that has given us such a vital economy and raised Americans' standard of living to be the envy of the world. Nobody today is copying our noncompetitive schools.

> **JIM:** Actually, that's not true. The Japanese, who excel in taking exams, are very dissatisfied with their educational system that promotes conformity and discourages creativity. They are looking at the American system for ideas. Besides, schooling isn't about competition. Administrators and teacher aren't in it for the money. We, the public, own the schools, like we own the military and law enforcement. What we need is greater public concern and involvement in our schools, not to sacrifice our kids on the altar of corporate competition.

 Visit the web site for more information about this debate topic.

benefits for minorities

parents can select. Not only has parents' satisfaction increased, but more important, the students' achievement has improved substantially. Poor families that would have had little or no choice now have some options.

The choice concept is definitely gaining support across the country. There are at least three kinds of school choice. The least controversial form allows parents to choose from among the various public schools that a school district or state operates. Many school districts have created a variety of schools with different goals and purposes, and allow parents to select the one they want their child to attend. The next, more controversial form of school choice is the charter school concept, and the most controversial form is school voucher plans. The major political parties have staked out positions on the choice issue, with Democrats favoring choice within the current public school system and Republicans tending to support voucher plans. Charter schools draw support from both Republicans and Democrats.

Public School Choice   Many public school systems are offering parents and students options, in addition to the traditional neighborhood school, as to which schools students attend. Some schools have a particular specialty such as mathematics or science. Others are "alternative" schools designed for youth who don't seem to fit well within traditional schools. There are several varieties of public school choice, most of which are fairly noncontroversial. Districtwide or intradistrict choice allows parents to select among the schools within their home district. These school choice options are offered in numerous school districts around the country, including Boston, Seattle, Minneapolis/St. Paul, and District 4 in New York City. Statewide, or interdistrict choice allows students to attend public schools outside their home school district. By 2001, fourteen states, led by Minnesota, had accepted statewide choice plans, and more than twenty states had considered them.[33]

variety of public school choice options

Magnet Schools   These schools represent another form of public school choice. During the 1970s, a number of urban school districts began implementing magnet school programs as a way to reduce "white flight" from the inner cities and as an alternative to forced busing for desegregation purposes. **Magnet schools** are alternative schools designed to provide high-quality instruction in specified areas and in the basic skills. Magnet schools differ from regular schools in three principal ways: (1) magnet schools have a unified curriculum based on a special theme or method of instruction, (2) enrollment is open to students beyond the geographic attendance zone, and (3) students and parents choose the school. In many cases, magnet schools have been established as a method of voluntary desegregation by offering quality education to students who meet admission criteria, regardless of the neighborhoods in which they reside. They are designed to attract (like a magnet) students of all racial and ethnic groups from all areas of the school district; thus, they offer quality education in integrated classrooms.

■ *magnet schools popular*

Magnet schools have been established with considerable success in many areas of the country. Once limited to a few large cities, today magnet schools number about 4,000 elementary and secondary schools, serving more than 2 million students.[34] Offering parents a choice of what school their children will attend is a key factor in the popularity of magnet schools. Another factor is that the federal government spent $110 million in fiscal year 2002 to get magnet schools up and running in more than 100 school districts.

■ *diversity among magnets*

Magnet school programs are diverse. Some emphasize academics: science, social studies, foreign languages, college preparation, and so on. Others stress fine arts or performing arts. Some magnet schools address students with special needs, such as gifted and talented students. Still others take a career or vocation such as engineering or the health professions as their focus. Elementary magnet schools are often identified with a particular teaching style such as emphasis on basic skills, Montessori methods, or open classrooms. Besides diversity, most magnet school programs offer quality.

■ *effectiveness of magnets*

Although originally designed to achieve voluntary desegregation, magnet programs have also been found to help stem enrollment declines, raise achievement levels, and allay community doubts over the general quality of education. These programs have been linked with reduced school violence and vandalism and improved pupil attendance, as well as more positive student attitudes toward school.[35] However, one study found no evidence that magnet schools in themselves contribute significantly to districtwide desegregation.[36] In fact, one researcher argues that considerable segregation occurs inside many magnet schools' classrooms.[37]

Despite these doubts, magnet schools are likely to continue to flourish in the future. Virtually all magnet schools now have long waiting lists, despite the facts that in many schools, students have to travel long distances to school, the class day is longer, and the work is harder than in nonmagnet schools. Their successes have been numerous, and they offer parents and students school choice within the public school system. The secret of their success seems to be an environment with high interest, motivation, and learning for students, along with support and satisfaction for parents.[38] By providing quality education to students of all types, magnet schools offer a promising step in the direction of equal educational opportunity.

📀 Reflect on charter schools with the image in this section of your CD-ROM.

■ **Charter Schools** Recent years have seen a rapid growth in **charter schools,** public schools that usually belong to a particular school district but have been given a charter that provides them with a large degree of independence. Teachers, administrators, parents, and community representatives who wish to open a charter school in a district negotiate an agreement with the school district or other agency authorized to grant charters. As long as they meet the specifications of their charters, these schools are free to control their own budgets, hire their own consultants, design their own curriculum, and infuse the school with their own educational flavor. These schools are, in effect, independent public

■ *school autonomy*

schools. Typically, students are chosen randomly from those who apply to attend the particular charter school.

Because they are independent, charter schools usually have a strong element of **site-based decision making** (also known as *site-based management* or *school-based management*), in which participatory decision making is the mode of operation. In theory, the charter school's site-based decision making provides everyone, including teachers, parents, and students, with more say about what goes on in their school and with a great degree of ownership of and commitment to the decisions that are made.

Charter schools are judged on how well they meet the student achievement goals established by their charter, or contract, and how well they manage their fiscal and operational responsibilities. Although charters generally allow schools to be run with substantial autonomy, charter schools must operate lawfully and responsibly with the highest regard for equity and excellence, or their charters will be taken away. Some charter schools have been closed down, primarily because of financial mismanagement or failure to fulfill the conditions of their charter.

The first charter schools were authorized in Minnesota in 1991. Although strongly resisted at first, at least thirty-eight states have since enacted charter school legislation. By the fall of 2002, more than 2,700 charter schools, mostly elementary, had been established in thirty-six of these states, serving about 576,000 students.[39] The federal government has committed $190 million a year to encourage the growth of charter schools. States vary greatly in the ease with which charter schools may be created and in the number of restrictions and amount of autonomy these schools are granted. Charter schools are most popular in the states of Arizona, California, Texas, and Michigan, where the legislation allowing charter schools is quite permissive.

Many supporters see charter schools as a way to encourage innovation, provide parents with school choice, and still be supportive of the public school system. Opponents wonder why the charter schools should be exempt from regulations while the rest of the public schools must abide by them. They also see charter schools as a form of "voucher light"—that is, a foot in the door toward the creation of **school vouchers.** Evaluations of charter schools' effectiveness are inconclusive at this time. One study, commissioned by the U.S. Department of Education, concluded that through competition, charter schools are exerting pressure on regular schools within the same district to improve.[40] Often, however, evaluations have been carried out by individuals with vested interests in either proving the effectiveness of charter schools or showing that they are ineffective and lack accountability. More time will be needed to see whether charter schools will revolutionize public education or remain just a boutique innovation.

■ **Vouchers**   More controversial than charter schools are school voucher plans. In their typical form, vouchers give the parent-consumer the widest array of choices. In effect, this type of plan gives parents a piece of paper, a voucher worth a certain dollar amount, that they can use to help pay the costs for their child to attend the public or private school of their choice. The school collects a voucher from each student who chooses that school and then turns in its vouchers to the state government for real dollars with which to run the school.

In a pure choice system, all schools would be public schools, the way all department stores are public stores. Advocates of the voucher system believe it would release an enormous amount of competition-driven creativity in our schools. Teachers and administrators would join together to provide high-quality, unique educational programs that would attract students and parents.

Margin notes:
■ *site-based decision making*

■ *support by federal government*

■ *voucher = money*

■ *arguments for vouchers*

Educational institutions would be like most other American enterprises, competing to put out the best possible product—namely, students. Those that succeeded would prosper, attracting many students and therefore voucher dollars. Those schools and teachers that failed to attract or hold "customers" would "go out of business," perhaps to start again with a better idea.

Although the voucher idea is based on well-known free-market principles, it is still relatively novel. No really thorough test has been conducted to see if it can deliver on its interesting promises, but both the Milwaukee and Cleveland school districts are currently implementing voucher plans. These plans, however, are limited to low-income, mostly minority families.

The plans also vary in the amount of money attached to each voucher (about $5,000 in Milwaukee and $2,250 in Cleveland) and in eligibility regulations. In 1999 the state of Florida passed the first statewide school voucher program for children attending "failing schools."

salvation or disaster?

Some education critics see the voucher concept as the savior of education in America. Others see it as a plot to undermine both the public schools and the democratic spirit of the country. Many politicians who support charter schools oppose voucher plans. They see charter schools as providing choice opportunities to parents and encouraging school reform efforts while staying within the public education system, but view voucher plans as draining money from the public schools to spend on private and religious schools. Vouchers reduce funding indirectly by decreasing public school enrollment, which is one of the factors on which governments base their allocations of money to public schools. (Learn more about government allocations in the chapter entitled "How Are Schools Governed, Influenced, and Financed?".)

Opponents of voucher plans have voiced several other objections and concerns:

Reflect on voucher plans with the image in this section of your CD-ROM.

- They argue that voucher plans bring false hopes of school choice because the private schools, not the parents, do the choosing through admissions decisions, and a private school is under no obligation to accept students with vouchers.

- In some proposals, the vouchers are worth only $1,000 to $2,500 per student, limiting the choices of schools for which these amounts would pay the actual costs of tuition.

public funding for religious schools?

- In Cleveland and Milwaukee, religious schools have been the major beneficiaries of the vouchers, which raises concerns about whether spending public dollars for students to attend religious schools violates the principle of church and state separation. In summer 2002, the U.S. Supreme Court ruled in a 5–4 decision that Cleveland's voucher plan, which empowers parents to redeem tuition vouchers at religious as well as nonreligious private schools, does not violate the constitutional prohibition of "establishment" of religion because government aid goes directly to parents who use it at their discretion. This decision is interpreted as giving a green light to states to implement school voucher plans to assist students attending "failing schools," and we will likely see more school voucher plans being implemented.

teacher unions oppose vouchers

- Many voucher opponents, including the two largest teacher unions, suggest that if voucher plans become widespread, the public schools will lose much-needed revenue and be forced to educate children with great needs, whom the private schools would not accept, while lacking the resources to do a good job.

- Finally, voucher opponents contend that applying market forces to educational institutions doesn't make sense because schools should be driven by the need to serve the public good, not the need to earn profits.

Those who support voucher plans offer counterarguments to many of these objections. For example, although funding private and religious schools with public money is very controversial in the United States, it is less so in many other countries. The United States is one of the few developed nations with such strict limits on parental choice of schools. Most other Western democracies fund private or religious schools with public money, although if these schools accept public money, they usually have to meet certain conditions required by the government.

religious schools already get some public money

Voucher supporters also point out that although many people believe U.S. tax dollars fund only public schools, private and religious schools already benefit from public money. The major breakthrough for private and religious schools was the passage of the Elementary and Secondary Education Act of 1965, which funneled millions of dollars into private schools through federal programs. In addition, private schools in many states have been receiving assistance ranging from pupil transportation, textbooks, health services, and general auxiliary services to salary supplements for teachers. In general, state assistance in areas other than transportation, milk, school lunch programs, and textbooks has been attacked in the courts.

private schools relieve burden on public schools

Another argument in support of voucher plans is that the private schools, which provide education for 5 million students a year, are lightening the burden of the public schools. If, for example, the Catholic school system collapsed, more than 2.6 million new students would enroll in the public schools, creating a massive shortage of space, teachers, and money. Advocates of private school aid argue that by partially subsidizing private schools to keep them in operation, the public schools can avoid a deluge of students whom they would be unable to assimilate readily. Private elementary and secondary schools spent $28.4 billion during the 1999–2000 school year.[41] If a substantial number of these schools were to shut down, the public schools would incur a substantial portion of these costs.

A major review of scholarly research on private school vouchers and charter schools conducted in 2001 concludes that there are no clear answers yet about whether they are an effective alternative to the traditional public school. As the lead author of the report states, "The summary of the evidence is that neither the hopes of the supporters nor the fears of the opponents have yet been realized."[42]

The issue of school choice is likely to remain a contentious one for some time to come.

PAUSE AND REFLECT

1 Which form of school choice appeals most to you? Why?

2 Do you support the use of school vouchers for students to attend private or parochial schools? Why or why not?

Gender and Sexuality Issues

Another multifaceted tension point in American education centers on issues of gender and sexuality, particularly equality between the genders, sexual harassment, sexual orientation, and sex education. Our ideas about the roles of men and women and how each should be treated, how schools should behave toward gay and lesbian students, and what role schools should play in educating youth about sex are all closely tied to moral, ethical, and legal issues. As a result, considerable disagreement surrounds these complicated issues. This section explores some of these controversial positions.

Visit the web site to link to more information about gender equality in schools.

■ Equality Between the Genders   Earlier in this chapter, we made the point that racial and ethnic groups have been denied equal educational opportunities throughout our country's history. Another social group, women, has also suffered discrimination and denial of equal educational opportunities. Many women assert, and rightfully so, that societal values and mores have discriminated against them as a class and have significantly limited the development of their human potential. Indeed, strong evidence supports the contention that historically women in our society have been denied educational and employment opportunities routinely extended to men. Whether that condition continues to exist is a matter of controversy.

■ historical discrimination against females

■ differences in socialization

■ Early Differences in Socialization   Women and men experience very different kinds of socialization in our society. From very young ages through adulthood, society holds different expectations for males and females. These expectations, in turn, generate different patterns of behavior toward boys and girls. Whether it is pink or blue clothes, G.I. Joe or Barbie dolls, video games or drawing kits, or football helmets or ballet slippers, boys and girls get different messages from society about what is expected of them. Society tolerates aggressive behavior more in boys than in girls. Boys are encouraged to be independent, whereas girls often are expected to conform to accepted norms.

■ AAUW report

This situation is not confined to the home. The American Association of University Women (AAUW) issued a controversial report in 1992, *How Schools Shortchange Girls,* describing various ways in which girls are adversely treated in schools.[43] In 1998, the AAUW updated those findings in its report, *Gender Gaps: Where Schools Still Fail Our Children.* This latter report contends that, although much progress has been made to reduce academic gender gaps, some still remain. Girls have closed the gap in terms of the number of courses taken in mathematics and science, but gender differences remain in the kinds of courses taken, with boys more often taking advanced courses. Girls are also much less likely to enroll in computer science classes in high school than are boys. On the other hand, girls take more advanced-placement (AP) courses in English, biology, and foreign languages. The report concludes that the goal of school excellence that propels the standards movement is the same goal behind gender equity, yet few states that have adopted standards acknowledge equity issues in their language. Addressing the learning styles of all students, the report argues, is the best way to insure high educational attainment for boys and girls.[44]

Boys often dominate classroom discussions unless teachers take steps to ensure participation on the part of girls.
(© Myrleen Ferguson/PhotoEdit)

Several researchers have charged that gender bias abounds in the schools and is even taught informally in the curriculum. Textbooks, other reading materials, and educational software, despite recent attempts at improvement by publishers and authors, often still portray females as more helpless than males. Although sexism has decreased in many texts, these researchers argue that examples of gender stereotyping, tokenism, and omission often still occur in references to girls and women.

■ **Classroom Interactions**   Numerous observational studies have concluded that teachers treat boys differently than girls, often to the girls' detriment, although teachers are generally unaware of their behaviors that favor boys.[45] For example, at all levels of schooling, male students have more interactions with teachers than do female students. Males are more likely to dominate classroom discussions, whereas females sit quietly. Boys are more likely to call out, and when they do, teachers are apt to accept the call-out and continue with the class. When girls call out, a much less frequent occurrence, the teacher's typical response is to correct the inappropriate behavior. As a result, boys receive more attention simply by demanding it. As Myra and David Sadker, two lead-ing researchers in gender equity research, report, "As victims of benign neglect, girls are penalized for doing what they should and lose ground as they go through school. In contrast, boys get reinforced for breaking the rules; they are rewarded for grabbing more than their fair share of the teacher's time and attention."[46] Although boys receive more criticism from teachers than do girls, they also receive more praise. Boys also receive more precise feedback from teachers than do girls.

In contrast to these findings, a clinical psychologist researcher at Harvard University argues that schools don't accommodate boys' learning styles and classroom needs. Boys perform best, he reports, when they have frequent recess breaks and are able to roam around the classroom. Boys are also more likely to enjoy argument and lively classroom debate, which is often discouraged.[47]

■ **Implications of Classroom Findings**   What are the implications of the findings on gender interactions in classrooms? Older research reports that in subtle and not-so-subtle ways, female students get the message that boys are more important than girls because teachers pay more attention to boys. One explanation is that boys demand more attention than girls, but cultural influences are also at work. The long-term effects of gender bias taught or reinforced in schools are potentially many: fewer women are in professions and occupations that emphasize mathematics and science, such as engineering and medicine; fewer women are in executive leadership positions in business, government, and education; and lower earning power is available to women because of their smaller representation in positions of leadership.

However, some observers challenge the assertion that schools discriminate against girls. They cite the fact that the large gaps between the education levels of women and men that were evident in the early 1970s have essentially disappeared for the younger generation. Although females still lag behind males in science and higher-level mathematics achievement, high school females on average outperform males in reading and writing, take more credits in academic subjects, are more likely to be inducted into the National Honor Society, are more likely to attend college after high school, and are as likely to graduate with a postsecondary degree. Furthermore, two-thirds of all students receiving special education services are boys. If schools were really so biased against females, they argue, why are women doing so well academically?

Certainly women have made tremendous progress in educational attainment. What remains to be seen, however, is how these attainments will be rewarded in

■ *males dominate interactions*

See for yourself how teachers treat boys and girls differently with the video resources on your CD-ROM.

■ *effects of gender bias*

■ *not everyone agrees*

the marketplace. The average earnings of female high school graduates age twenty-five to thirty-four are more than one-third lower than those of male graduates of the same age. Similarly, female college graduates earn, on average, salaries that are only 80 percent of what their male counterparts receive.[48] Women have made important advances recently in gaining equal educational opportunities with men, but our society still seems to favor males when it comes to prestigious jobs and salaries.

Find the full text of Title IX in the text resources of your CD-ROM.

■ **Title IX**   In 1972, Congress passed **Title IX** of the Educational Amendment Act, which states, "No person in the United States shall, on the basis of sex, be excluded from participation in, be denied the benefits of, or be subjected to discrimination under any education program or activity receiving Federal financial assistance." Although the fine print required interpretation, the large print was clear: gender discrimination in educational programs receiving federal financing is against the law.

effects of Title IX

The law has been interpreted to ban gender discrimination in physical education, athletics, vocational education, financial aid, pension benefits, employment and compensation of staff, facilities, and counseling. Athletic programs have received the most public attention. Included under Title IX have been regulations requiring that equal opportunity be provided in all facets of physical education and athletics, such as facilities, game and practice schedules, coaching, travel and per diem allowances, equipment, and supplies. Separate teams have been permissible in contact sports such as boxing, football, and ice hockey. Whenever a school has had a team in a given noncontact sport for one gender only and athletic opportunities for the other gender have been limited, members of the excluded gender must be allowed to try out for the team.

■ **Your Role as a Teacher**   Title IX regulations and the overall attention given to gender bias have greatly helped correct inequities resulting from gender discrimination. It is still clear, however, that the elimination of gender bias and gender-role stereotyping in schools will be a complex procedure requiring the cooperation of teachers, administrators, school boards, counselors, educational publishers, teacher educators, and parents. Your role as a teacher will be especially important. As you interact with your pupils and as you select and use instructional materials, your sensitivity to this issue will help determine the attitudes of our future generations. Here are some steps you can take to address gender inequities:

steps you can take

- Be aware of your own behavior toward boys and girls in your classes.

- Organize classes so students don't segregate themselves by gender.

- Examine instructional materials to ensure that they are not gender biased and that they include features on girls and women.

- Place less emphasis on competition and speed and more emphasis on cooperative activities to ensure that everyone understands and completes the assignment.

- Increase the focus on practical, real-life applications of mathematics and science.

- Structure learning activities so girls will have equal opportunities to participate.

- Help promote a school culture in which gender and ethnic bias are not tolerated.

Much remains to be done. Remember, as with all the other issues we have addressed in this chapter, if you are not part of the solution, you are part of the problem.

Visit this chapter of the web site to link to more information about sexual harassment in schools.

■ **Sexual Harassment**   In 2001, the AAUW commissioned a national survey, as a follow-up to a similar survey conducted in 1993, to investigate a national problem of sexual harassment, or unwelcome verbal or physical conduct of a sexual nature imposed by one individual on another, in our schools.[49] Four out of every five students in grades eight through eleven report experiencing sexual harassment, with girls experiencing it only slightly more often than boys. The psychological effects of harassment seem to be most profound among girls. Teenage girls responded with stories of pervasive and overt sexual harassment. Girls described sexual jokes and taunts; attempts to snap their bras, lift their skirts, and grope their bodies; and other unwanted physical attention. Boys and girls get the message that girls are not worthy of respect and that it is OK for boys to exert power over girls. Spreading sexual rumors and calling a person gay or lesbian were often reported verbal forms of harassment. Most of the harassment occurred in plain view of others—in hallways, lunchrooms, classrooms, assemblies, and playgrounds, and on school buses. We will also see in the next section that harassment related to sexual orientation is commonplace in our schools.

effects of harassment

In 1999 the U.S. Supreme Court ruled that school districts may be sued if they fail to respond to student sexual harassment of other students. The Court emphasized that districts could be found liable only if they were "deliberately indifferent" to information about "severe, pervasive, and objectively offensive" harassment among students. In a separate case involving sexual harassment of a student by a teacher, the Court ruled similarly that a school district could be sued for damages only if district officials were aware of the teacher's harassing behavior and were deliberately indifferent to it.[50] School officials are worried that these rulings may trigger an avalanche of lawsuits against school districts, which could end up costing districts millions of dollars. Schools can work to avoid the problem by drafting a sexual harassment policy; requiring training programs for administrators, teachers, and students; acting quickly when confronted with sexual harassment; enlisting the support of parents; and instituting disciplinary actions against repeat harassers.

prohibited by law

Sexual harassment is prohibited by law, and many schools now have sexual harassment policies that they distribute to students and staff. However, neither boys nor girls are likely to report actual incidents to adults for fear of being labeled a "snitch" or suffering repercussions. The challenge for educators is how to change the culture of harassment in schools and to encourage the use of existing resources to address the problem. All our students, boys and girls, have the right to attend schools whose environments are free from such harassment. As a teacher, you cannot ignore such instances when you see them occur. Choose to make such times "teachable moments" by helping students learn to appreciate the dignity of others and ensuring that the classroom is a welcoming environment for all students.

■ **Sexual Orientation**   Another controversial issue centers on sexual orientation. Regardless of your own beliefs on the subject of homosexuality, if you are going to teach in the public schools, you may very well teach gay and lesbian students.

schools hostile to homosexuals

There is considerable evidence that school is often a hostile environment for young homosexuals. Teenagers tend to ridicule differences in general and homosexuality in particular. Gay and lesbian students are often verbally, and even physically, abused by classmates. Teachers and administrators who condone such name calling as "queer" or "faggot" while prohibiting profanity or racial slurs are also sources of hostility toward homosexual youth. In fact, there have been recent cases where gay students won lawsuits against school officials for failing to maintain a safe school environment and to discipline students who regularly tormented them.

gays, a high-risk population

The hostility that gay and lesbian youth encounter in school is mirrored in the larger society, which bombards them with messages that they are outcasts. This hostility leaves many of them isolated, frightened, and uncertain about their own worth. As a result, gay students are a high-risk population. Many run away from home or are thrown out by parents, abuse drugs and alcohol, suffer from depression, or attempt suicide. One youth risk behavior survey conducted in Massachusetts found that more than one-third of self-identified gay, lesbian, or bisexual teenagers reported having attempted suicide in the previous twelve months.[51] The National Education Association, the American Federation of Teachers, and the Association for Supervision and Curriculum Development have all passed resolutions calling on their members and school districts to acknowledge the special needs of homosexual students, provide supportive services such as counseling and support groups, and implement anti-harassment measures. In 1993, Massachusetts became the first state to ban anti-gay discrimination in public schools, and establish a statewide "safe schools" program. By 2001, four other states had followed suit. In 1997 the U.S. Department of Education issued guidelines spelling out that "gay or lesbian students" are covered by federal prohibitions against sexual harassment.[52]

However, the issue of homosexuality is extremely controversial, and actions urged by these organizations are certain to provoke opposition by some community members who believe such steps would signal that the schools are condoning homosexuality. Some people believe that while touting tolerance, gay and lesbian organizations are actually seeking to promote homosexuality among students. In spite of such controversy, all students, regardless of sexual orientation, have the right to a safe and supportive learning environment. As educators, we also have the responsibility to promote the emotional well-being of all of our students.

■ **Sex Education**

Sex education is more than just knowledge of the mechanics of the sex act and the development and birth of a baby. The physical aspect should not be emphasized at the expense of its psychological and social aspects.

Sex education should communicate that sexuality is normal, is healthy, and has many variations.

Sex education reduces one of life's most profound and mysterious activities to something akin to plumbing, and ends up promoting irresponsible sexual activity.

Sex, love, birth, and family life are all one package and should be discussed in the reassuring warmth of the parents' presence.

Runaway teenage pregnancy rates and the wildfire spread of AIDS make it imperative that the schools teach sex education, especially since parents don't teach it.

■ *controversial topic*

Sex education is a headline grabber in newspapers throughout the country. The preceding statements represent five different attitudes about sex education and give evidence of the controversy surrounding it. Although most people agree that children should be given information about sex, the controversy centers on two issues: (1) is the school the appropriate institution to offer such instruction, and (2) if so, should it limit instruction to strictly factual information, or should the psychological, social, health, and moral aspects of sex also be included in the curriculum?

Some people argue that because sex is such an intimate topic and is closely related to religious and moral beliefs, sex education is the responsibility of the home and the church. Advocates of sex education in the schools respond that they would agree with that position if parents did in fact provide adequate sex information for their children. They argue that, unfortunately, this simply is not the case. The majority of parents fail to assume the responsibility to teach their children about sex. According to advocates of sex education, the public school is the only institution that has access to most children over an extended period, and the responsibility must fall to the school because of the demonstrated failure of the home, church, library, and medical profession to provide effective sex education. Courts have supported state boards of education and local school boards' right to offer sex education in the curriculum.

Goals of Sex Education Preventing teenage pregnancies is a major goal of any sex education program. As we discussed earlier in the chapter, besides endangering babies, early pregnancies are placing the future lives of great numbers of teenage girls in serious jeopardy, interrupting and usually terminating their education. In spite of special counseling and accommodations made for teenage mothers to stay in school, the majority drop out, thus drastically reducing their job and career opportunities.

■ *dropout problem*

Another goal of sex education is to reduce the incidence of sexually transmitted diseases (STDs). It has been estimated that about 3 million American adolescents are newly infected with an STD each year, with chlamydia and gonorrhea being the most commonly acquired diseases.[53] With the alarming spread of AIDS, preventive measures have become a matter of life and death. Almost 50 percent of high school students report that they have engaged in sexual intercourse (49 percent of males and 48 percent of females), but only 57 percent of the teenagers who were sexually active in the previous three months reported using condoms, which, aside from abstinence, are the only relatively safe forms of protection against AIDS.[54] It is estimated that one-fourth of all new human immunodeficiency virus (HIV) cases occur in people ages thirteen to twenty-one, half are among people under age twenty-five, and the majority of these infections are sexually transmitted.[55]

■ *risk of AIDS*

Reflect on different types of sex education with the image in this section of your CD-ROM.

Successful HIV education programs must focus on students' behavior, for that is what puts them at risk. Teenagers report that they know what they should and should not do to avoid transmission of HIV, but their physical urges are stronger than their common sense. This speaks to the need for advice on how to handle sexual feelings and how to evaluate relationships. Students need to be helped to gain the self-control and strength of character to avoid risky and irresponsible behavior.

Types of Sex Education   Arguments over the kind of sex education the schools should offer are just as heated as the controversy about whether to offer it. Some support comprehensive sex education programs that convey sexual activities as a natural and healthy part of life, be it heterosexual or homosexual expression. Others believe this approach negates certain moral or religious beliefs; they would recommend an abstinence-based curriculum that teaches students to abstain from homosexuality and sex outside of marriage. Advocates of the abstinence approach argue that when sex education programs teach both abstinence and the use of contraceptives, students receive a mixed message. These people believe that only message they should receive is abstinence.

Some believe that the large number of STDs, especially AIDS, has strengthened the position of those who argue for comprehensive sex education programs. Providing children with the sex education that will help them understand the risks they face and how to prevent or minimize those risks makes a great deal of sense. Still, some object that this type of sex education, by exciting interest in sexual experimentation, will lead to more promiscuity and increase the risk that it is supposed to reduce.

In fact, in programs that provide information about both contraception and abstinence, evaluators have found no increase in sexual activity. In 2001, the U.S. Surgeon General issued a report on sex education programs, based on a two-year review of scientific papers and conferences. He concluded that comprehensive sex education programs, which combine teaching about the importance of abstinence and providing information about condoms and other methods of contraception, have proven to be most effective. The report noted that the evidence on abstinence-only programs is insufficient to draw evidence-based conclusions on their effectiveness. He also questions the effectiveness of these programs for teenagers who have already become sexually active. In his words, ". . . given that one-half of adolescents in the United States are already sexually active and at risk of unintended pregnancy and STD/HIV infection, it also seems clear that adolescents need accurate information about contraceptive methods so that they can reduce those risks."[56] However, the federal government has weighed in on the side of abstinence-only programs. Since 1996, Congress has committed more than a half billion dollars to abstinence-only education programs and zero dollars to comprehensive sexuality education. President George W. Bush, in keeping a campaign promise, has proposed nearly doubling federal spending on abstinence programs to $138 million for 2003.[57]

In the meantime, it is possible that you will have students in your class or school who are known to have HIV. It is important for you and your colleagues to know school district policy regarding these children and the ways in which the disease can be transmitted. Safeguarding other children while also attending to the rights and needs of the child with the virus requires knowledge, care, and understanding.

■ what kind of program?

Visit this chapter of the web site for an author debate on sex education.

■ research reports

■ be aware of district policy

A Final Word

Given the range of social problems that we have discussed in this and the preceding chapter, it is not surprising to find the schools bearing an ever-growing burden to guide young people's decision making. How well equipped are the schools to handle this task? Too often public education has merely reflected the inequities of our society in its treatment of women, racial minorities, individuals with disabilities or disadvantages, individuals who are culturally different, and so on. Many of the tension points in American education touch on questions of values: Can equity and excellence coexist? If not, which is more important? Can the rights of the majority and minority receive equal protection? The problems implied by these questions are not easily solved, and these tension points will likely be with us for a long time to come.

KEY TERMS

at-risk students (70)

charter schools (94)

equality of educational
   opportunity (88)

magnet schools (93)

school choice (91)

school vouchers (95)

site-based decision making (95)

Title IX (100)

zero-tolerance policies (83)

FOR REFLECTION

❶ What aspects of our culture contribute to the high incidence of child abuse in the United States?

❷ Should schools assume responsibility for educating children about alcohol, drugs, sex, and suicide? Why or why not? If so, what aspects of the current curriculum should be dropped to make room for these topics?

❸ Can you recall any gender-biased behavior that you have observed in schools? Do you think gender bias and gender-role stereotyping are problems in our schools?

FOR FURTHER INFORMATION

PRINT RESOURCES

AAUW Report: Hostile Hallways: Bullying, Teasing, and Sexual Harassment in School (Washington, DC: American Association of University Women, 2001).

This report examines the findings of a student survey on bullying, teasing, and sexual harassment in schools.

James P. Comer, Norris M. Haynes, Edward T. Joyner, and Michael Ben-Avie, eds., *Rallying the Whole Village: The Comer Process for Reforming Education* (New York: Teachers College Press, 1996).

In this text, James Comer and his colleagues describe the process they have employed to coordinate various resources to create effective school communities in areas of low socioeconomic status.

Children's Defense Fund, *The State of America's Children: A Report from the Children's Defense Fund, Yearbook 2001* (Boston: Beacon Press, 2001).

This report makes a compelling case for increasing health and educational programs for children in the United States. Citing numerous shocking statistics, the report makes it clear that the United States, compared with other industrialized nations, is short-changing its children.

Thomas L. Good and Jennifer S. Braden, *The Great School Debate: Choice, Vouchers, and Charters* (Mahwah, NJ: Lawrence Erlbaum Associates, 2000).

This is a well-written coverage of choice topics by two nationally known educational researchers.

Joan N. Burstyn, Geoff Bender, Ronnie Casella, Howard W. Gordon, Domingo P. Guerra, Kristen V. Luschen, Rebecca Stevens, and Kimberly M. Williams, *Preventing Violence in Schools: A Challenge to American Democracy* (Mahwah, NJ: Lawrence Erlbaum Associates, 2001).

This text provides an in-depth ethnographic analysis of violence prevention programs and an assessment of their effectiveness.

WEB RESOURCES

Education Week on the Web. Available at: **http://www.edweek.org**.

Published forty-one times a year, *Education Week* is the nation's newspaper devoted to educational issues, preschool through secondary school. Many of the issues discussed in this chapter are reported on in this periodical, and its web site contains an archive section that permits searches for particular topics and issues, particularly the "Hot Topics" section. The site also includes the archives of *Teacher Magazine*.

Virginia Youth Violence Project. Available at: **http://youthviolence.edschool.virginia.edu**.

The Virginia Youth Violence Project identifies effective methods and policies for youth violence prevention, especially in school settings.

Center for the Study and Prevention of Violence. Available at: **http://www.colorado.edu/cspv**.

This site contains many good ideas, references, programs, and links related to violence prevention.

Program on Educational Policy and Governance. Available at: **http://www.ksg.harvard.edu/pepg/**.

Located at the John F. Kennedy School of Governance at Harvard University, this program issues numerous reports on school choice.

Thomas B. Fordham Foundation. Available at: **http://www.edexcellence.net/**.

This conservative foundation issues many papers and positions supporting vouchers and charter schools.

American Association of University Women. Available at: **http://www.aauw.org**.

The AAUW is an organization of 150,000 college graduates dedicated to equity and education for women and girls. It conducts many studies on gender issues.

Safe and Drug Free Schools Program. Available at: **http://www.ed.gov/offices/OESE/SDFS/**.

A program of the U.S. Department of Education, the site contains descriptions of model programs, research findings, grant opportunities, and links to related sites.

What Is Taught?

Chapter Preview What knowledge is most worth knowing? What should be taught in the schools? The answers to these questions take the form of curricula, and they are often a source of tension among teachers, school boards, education professors, textbook publishers, policymakers, and parents. Currently, these groups are seeking to raise academic standards through common curricular emphases while also accommodating various cultural and ethnic groups' demands for representation in the curriculum.

This chapter emphasizes that:

● The school curriculum, which has evolved over time as a result of shifting purposes, consists of all the organized and intended experiences of the student for which the school accepts responsibility.

● The present curriculum in most subject areas has been greatly influenced by the standards-based reform movement that identifies what students should know and be able to do in each subject area.

● Textbooks have such a strong impact on what is taught in the classrooms that some people argue that texts represent a national curriculum.

● Major innovative instructional approaches used across the curriculum include interdisciplinary teaching, cooperative learning, critical thinking and problem solving, writing across the curriculum, differentiated instruction, and block scheduling.

● The relevance of the schools' curricula to individual and societal problems is a continually debated issue.

Baseball, debating, reading, and biology are all learned in school, along with love and tolerance, independence and frustration, mathematics and dramatics, values and ceramics, woodshop and poise, history and boredom, and computer science and leadership! Some are learned intentionally and others incidentally.

What Is Curriculum?

■ *definition of curriculum*

We define the **curriculum** as all the organized and intended experiences of the student for which the school accepts responsibility. In other words, the curriculum is not just the intellectual content of the subjects taught but also the methods used to teach them, the interactions that occur among people, and the school-sponsored activities that contribute to the "life experience." Educational theorists have identified several different kinds of curriculum, including the formal, extra, and hidden. Let's briefly examine these different kinds of curriculum.

■ *formal curriculum*

The planned content and objectives of language arts, mathematics, science, and all the other subject areas available to students constitute the *formal* or explicit curriculum. The states and the local school boards are responsible for determining the subjects that will be taught in this formal curriculum. Later in this chapter, we will examine the formal curriculum of the schools, including trends and controversies in each of the content areas.

■ *"extra" curriculum*

At one time, such activities as athletics, band, cheerleading, and debate club were considered to be part of the "*extra*" curriculum, whereas the formal courses of study (history, science, mathematics, and English) were considered curricular. However, this distinction is not particularly useful any more because very important learning also occurs outside the classroom.

■ *hidden curriculum*

However, what students learn in the environment of the school extends beyond the planned curriculum of courses or subjects they will take, or the extracurricular activities in which they participate. Classroom observers have noted that the schools also teach a *hidden* or informal curriculum through which the classroom and school, as learning environments, socialize children to the values that are acceptable to the institution and society at large. The messages of the hidden curriculum are usually conveyed indirectly and deal with attitudes, values, beliefs, and behavior. The messages of the hidden curriculum can support or undermine the formal curriculum. When the hidden and the formal curriculum conflict, many observers believe the hidden curriculum carries more weight.

Reflect on the hidden curriculum with the image in this section of your CD-ROM.

What are these attitudes and values, and how are they communicated to students? A major purpose of the hidden curriculum in schools has been to teach students the routines and values for getting along in school and in the larger society. Thus, it tends to have a conservative bias, focusing on preserving the status quo. In the eyes of some critics, the hidden curriculum of the schools works against diversity, equity, and social justice.[1]

One researcher suggests that schools value several specific ways of thinking and behaving.[2] One is compliant behavior as opposed to personal initiative. Students soon learn to give the teacher what she or he wants or expects. Reward systems used by schools teach students to "read" both the teacher and the system to determine just what is expected to get the grade, the teacher's attention, or the sticker with the smiling face. Similarly, competitiveness is learned through the examples of athletics, grading systems that compare students to one another, and ability grouping to separate students into classes according to their achievement. The many ways in which students learn what a school values include how the school allocates time to subjects of study, the rules established for the school, and even the architecture of the school.

As future teachers, you should be able to identify what rules of behavior, rituals and ceremonies, and accepted patterns of teacher and student interaction are communicated to students at schools you visit. Does the "climate" of the classroom and the school suggest warmth, support for diversity, and nurturing of individuals, or do observers describe a mood of disinterest, regimentation, and antipathy among staff and students? Most important, what is the school's deeper message about what stance its students should take toward the current society?

PAUSE AND REFLECT

1 How can you determine the hidden curriculum of a school? What clues would you look for?

Standards-Based Reform Movement

In this chapter, we examine the formal curriculum, those subjects that are taught in schools and some of the forces and instructional approaches that influence how they are taught. The typical school curriculum is organized according to subject-matter divisions, and most of the efforts that go into curriculum development are still concentrated around traditional subject matter.

All that is taught is a commitment to what is thought valuable.

—R. S. PETERS

In the chapter entitled "What Is a School and What Is It For?", we discussed how the curriculum is a *social bet* on what knowledge, skills, and attitudes the older generation thinks the young need to know to prosper, personally and economically, in the twenty-first century. However, there is by no means a consensus among the parties involved in placing this social bet. In fact, curriculum decision making can resemble a battlefield in which conservatives and liberals, religious groups and agnostics, whites and people of color, and many other groups grapple to ensure that their beliefs and perspectives are represented in the school's curriculum. These *curriculum battles* at both the state and local level can be heated because those engaged believe so much is at stake, which, in essence, is the future of the United States.

■ *curriculum battles*

The strongest influence on a **subject-matter curriculum** over the last decade has been the *standards-based reform movement*, designed to promote academic excellence and equity. **Content standards** are statements of the subject-specific knowledge and skills that schools are expected to teach and students are expected to learn. Standards-setters often use the shorthand phrase, "what students should know and be able to do," to communicate the purposes of content standards.

■ *content standards*

In contrast to many other countries, the United States has traditionally had a decentralized system of state and local curricula. The national government has had little influence on what is taught in our nation's schools. During the 1980s and 1990s, however, spurred by concern about the nation's economic competitiveness with other countries, a strong movement emerged toward national curriculum standards, national testing and assessment, and the establishment of national goals. A 1994 law, the Goals 2000: Educate America Act, codified eight national goals (listed in Table 11.1) to guide future educational initiatives and funded different academic groups to develop national standards in the various subject-matter fields. The National Council of Teachers of Mathematics led the way in 1989 by publishing its mathematics standards, and by a decade later,

■ *Goals 2000*

Find the full text of the Goals 2000: Educate America Act in the text resources of your CD-ROM.

TABLE 4.1   Examples of Content Standards from Several States

Language Arts

Grade Level	
K–3	Distinguish different forms of texts such as lists, newsletters, and signs and the functions they serve. (Texas)
2–5	Uses consonant blends, diagraphs, and dipthongs to orally decode words. (Georgia)
8	Produce work in at least one literary genre that follows the conventions of the genre. (Pennsylvania)
9–11	Apply knowledge of Greek, Latin, and Anglo-Saxon roots and affixes to determine meaning of unfamiliar vocabulary. (Kansas)
9–12	Identify strategies used by the media to present information for a variety of purposes (e.g., to inform, entertain, or persuade). (California)

Mathematics

Grade Level	
2	Use place value concepts to represent whole numbers using physical models, numerals, and words, with ones, tens, and hundreds. (Ohio)
7	The student will solve consumer application problems involving tips, discounts, sales tax, and simple interest, using whole numbers, fractions, decimals, and percents. (Virginia)
K–12	All students will regularly and routinely use calculators, computers, manipulatives, and other mathematical tools to enhance mathematical thinking, understanding, and power. (New Jersey)
Advanced Placement Calculus	The student will use integration to solve problems. This will include areas bounded by polar curves, length of a path (including parametric curves), work (Hooke's law), and improper integrals. (Virginia)

Science

Grade Level	
K–5	All students will measure and describe the things around us; explain what the world around us is made of; identify and describe forms of energy; and explain how electricity and magnetism interact with matter. (Michigan)
6–8	Students will know how cells function as "building blocks" of organisims and describe the requirements for cells to live by stating how cells work together to keep the organisim alive. (Illinois)
9–12	All students will analyze claims for their scientific merit and explain how scientists decide what constitutes scientific knowledge; how science is related to other ways of knowing; how science and technology affect our society; and how people of diverse cultures have contributed to and influenced developments in science. (Michigan)
9–12	The student will identify the independent variables, dependent variables, and controls in an experimental setup. (Oklahoma)

Social Studies

Grade Level	
1–3	Construct and interpret maps and other geographic tools, including the use of map elements to organize information about people, place, and environments. (Arizona)
6–8	Describe the social, economic, and political characteristics of Western European society that led to the exploration of the Americas. (Maryland)
9–12	Explain how the design of the U.S. Constitution is intended to balance and check the powers of the branches of government. (Connecticut)

Visit this chapter of the web site to link to more examples of state content standards.

Source: Education World. Available at **http://www.education-world.com/standards/**.

Reflect on your opinions about curriculum standards with the image in this section of your CD-ROM.

Find the full text of the No Child Left Behind Act in the text resources of your CD-ROM.

■ *controversy over standards movement*

most subject-specific teacher organizations had followed suit. By 1996, however, these centralization efforts had lost steam, giving way to a growing consensus that the setting of standards and curriculum should remain the prerogative of the individual states. Interestingly, many states were using the national standards developed by different academic groups in formulating their own state standards. By the beginning of the twenty-first century, virtually every state had developed its own standards for student learning, and many states backed up their new standards with rigorous accountability measures for both students and educators. (For examples of state standards in different subject matter and grade levels, see Table. 4.1.) The Leave No Child Behind Act, signed by President Bush in January 2002, requires states to begin administering annual, statewide assessments in reading and mathematics for grades 3–8 by the 2005–06 school year. For more on this law, see the chapter entitled "How Are Schools Governed, Influenced, and Financed?".

The standards movement was immediately surrounded by controversy. Some critics objected to the attention and money lavished on the development and assessment of standards instead of other pressing educational needs, such as habitable school buildings. Other critics were concerned with the testing that usually accompanied the state standards. Many state legislatures linked student passage of standards-based tests with "high-stakes" outcomes, including graduation from high school or school accreditation. Some legislatures made educators accountable for students' learning the standards and passing the assessment tests. Teachers' jobs and students' future education were suddenly at risk if students failed the tests, and educators and students alike felt much more pressure to succeed. In spite of these criticisms, numerous polls show the public overwhelmingly supports the idea of high standards. The chapter entitled "How Should Education Be Reformed?" discusses the current status of national education standards and assessment in more detail.

PAUSE AND REFLECT

❶ Study the standards for a discipline area in which you are interested. (You can find standards web sites listed at the end of this chapter.) Do you believe they are appropriate for the level of students you would like to teach? Why or why not?

❷ Do you support the use of "high stakes" tests to determine graduation from high school? Why or why not?

What Is the Present Curriculum?

In looking at the courses of study prescribed by the fifty states, we will see that the similarities far outweigh the differences. Parts of this chapter discuss some reasons for this phenomenon, such as the influence of standards-based reform movements in the various states and the uniformity of available textbooks, but for now, let's examine what is presently taught in elementary and secondary schools across the country. At both levels the curriculum is organized into subject-matter areas, which ordinarily are language arts and English, mathematics, science, social studies, foreign languages, fine arts, physical education and recreation, vocational education, and electives. Most of the national organizations representing teachers of these various subject areas have developed content

POLICY MATTERS !

Teaching by Script or Improvisation?

What's the Policy?

Schools and school districts around the country have adopted or considered standardized programs for teaching reading, such as DISTAR, Success for All, and Reading Mastery, that have excellent records in promoting reading success among children but relegate the teacher to a functionary role devoid of creativity.

How Does It Affect Teachers?

Instead of giving teachers suggestions and guidelines on how to use the materials provided, prescriptive reading programs are actually scripted, with specific instructions for how teachers should proceed, including what to do and say. If a student's response is A, then you are to go to question 2; if his response is B, then you should go to question 3. Teachers have almost no flexibility to deviate from the program's procedures and questions.

What Are the Pros?

Several of the most well-known reading programs are very effective and can boast proven track records of helping children, especially those from impoverished backgrounds, to learn to read. One elementary school principal in Houston, for example, brought his low-income students from near the bottom in reading and math to ranking twelfth among his district's 182 elementary schools. He attributes the success to implementing the DISTAR program, a highly scripted direct-instruction program.

What Are the Cons?

A Rice University researcher criticizes these programs as dishonoring the professional craft of teaching. "Educators do not find in this program, or any other package, the depth and breadth and variety of reading styles that they need to get all their kids to read and to find reading purposeful and fun."

Teachers who use these programs are not expected to diagnose students' difficulties, matching their interests and styles with materials selected by the teacher. In contrast, critics suggest, the teacher's role in these programs is to do what the program dictates, with little difference between the master teacher and a bright teaching aide.

What Do You Think?

1. What position do you take regarding the use of these prescriptive programs? What additional information would you like to have about these programs?

2. What would you do if your school or school district adopted one of these programs, even if you were personally opposed to them?

3. What position do you think the parents of your elementary-aged children would take regarding this issue?

Visit the web site to learn more about this policy issue.

SOURCE: William Raspberry, "Classroom Riffs," *The Washington Post,* June 25, 1999, p. A29.

standards of what elementary and secondary students should know and be able to do in each content area. The web sites for these organizations and their respective content standards can be found in the For Further Information section at the end of the chapter.

Visit this chapter of the web site to link to more information about language arts curricula.

Language Arts and English

The *language arts* program seeks to develop in children the skills of reading, writing, speaking, and listening, as well as a knowledge of culture as represented in literature. The importance of language arts cannot be overemphasized because no subject can be successfully studied without adequate language skills. In elementary schools, most language arts programs focus on helping students develop written and oral communication skills, comprehension and problem-solving strategies, creativity, and appreciation for language and literature. At the secondary level, English courses focus on integration of the language arts using literature as the prime motivator. Among the most commonly read works are *Romeo and Juliet, Julius Caesar, The Scarlet Letter, Macbeth, Huckleberry Finn,* and *The Great Gatsby.*

> *I have often reflected upon the new vistas that reading opened to me. . . . As I see it today, the ability to read awoke inside me some long dormant craving to be mentally alive.*
>
> —MALCOLM X

■ **Issues and Trends** Teachers today are selecting literature that is relevant to student interests yet representative of an accepted literary tradition; balancing classic literature selections with works by and about minority groups; instructing students in critical thinking; encouraging writing across the curriculum (discussed later in this chapter); integrating the various language arts by, for example, linking reading and writing together or speaking, listening, and reading; composing and creating in new media forms such as video or World Wide Web presentations; and maintaining a balance between composition and literature in the curriculum. Many English educators are chafing under the pressure to prepare students for state standards-based proficiency examinations that emphasize grammar, spelling, and basic skills, often to the exclusion of explaining classic and modern literature.

■ trend toward new media

Major disagreements exist in the field of reading education. The basic debate is whether reading instruction should emphasize the integration of

"They're words, Eddie. Assembly required."

© Martha Campbell

language arts skills and knowledge in a literature-based approach, commonly known as the **whole language approach**, or focus on phonics instruction, an approach to reading that teaches the reader to "decode" words by sounding out letters and combinations of letters. During the 1970s and 1980s, whole language approaches to reading displaced the phonics approach in many schools. However, discontent with declining reading scores in states that emphasized a whole language approach, notably California, spurred a renewed interest in **phonics**. In fact, the issue has become politically charged, with conservatives supporting phonics and liberals supporting whole language approaches. Although both the whole language and phonics camps have their strong believers, recent research concludes that it is important to teach explicit, systematic phonics within a context of meaningful literature.[3] *Phonemic* awareness, the understanding that sounds make up language, seems to be crucial in the development of good readers. Thus, a balanced use of both approaches, rather than one over the other, seems to be the key to reading instruction.

■ *phonics versus whole language*

■ Reflect on the debate about ways to teach reading with the image in this section of your CD-ROM.

▨ *Mathematics*

Before the 1950s, schools emphasized student mastery of basic computational skills. In the 1960s, a new type of mathematics curriculum, known as the *new math,* emerged. It saw mathematics as a language that both communicates ideas about numbers and describes the quantitative aspects of ideas and objects. As a result, the new math stressed *structure* rather than drill and computational skills. The new math tended to be abstract, and for the average student, its conceptual theories were of little practical use.

■ *"new math"*

Today the traditional approach featuring drill and practice, computation, and memorization tends to be used in courses for non-college-bound students. College-bound students, after studying algebra and geometry, often take optional fourth-year courses that place strong emphasis on structure, learning by discovery, definitions, properties, sets, rigor, statistics, calculus, trigonometry, and other abstract concepts.

■ Visit this chapter of the web site to link to more information about mathematics curricula.

▨ **Issues and Trends** Mathematics at the elementary level emphasizes the use of hands-on manipulatives to aid students in learning about patterns in mathematics and our base-ten system. Mathematical reasoning and problem-solving, rather than the teacher's authority and the textbook, are being urged. Experts in mathematics education are urging teachers to emphasize multiple approaches to solving real problems. These emphases are consistent with the popular constructivist approach to learning, which is based on psychological theories suggesting that people must construct knowledge and meaning for themselves, rather than receiving knowledge passively from teachers or textbooks. (Constructivist approaches to learning are discussed further in the chapters entitled "What Are the Philosophical Foundations of American Education?" and "How Should Education Be Reformed?".) Calculators and computers are becoming more common, even at the elementary level, and especially in later years, as mathematics education focuses less on computational skills and more on developing concepts, relationships, structures, and problem-solving skills. Moreover, the use of computers and computer programming in mathematics classes adds a great deal of practical utility for many students. Not only do computers create interest in the curriculum, but students receive valuable experience that may prove useful as they seek jobs. As described in the chapter entitled "What Should Teachers Know About Technology and Its Impact on

■ *emphasis on problem solving*

■ *use of computers*

Elementary school teachers must build basic understanding in key subjects such as mathematics if students are to succeed in later grades.
(© Bill Aron/PhotoEdit)

Schools?", graphing calculators are seen as important tools to help students understand complex mathematical relationships.

Computers, however, can be misused. A 1998 national study examining the use of computers in schools concluded that computers can be an important learning tool when used in simulations and real-life applications of math concepts, but using computers for repetitive math drills actually hurt students' math scores.[4]

■ *integration of skills*

In addition to using technology and emphasizing problem solving, mathematics programs have been moving away from the traditional compartmentalization of arithmetic, algebra, geometry, calculus, and so on. As newer topics, such as probability, statistics, and computer science, are emphasized, course designers have begun to integrate a variety of mathematics skills and topics in one course or across several courses. The blending of mathematics with other subject areas, including consumer economics and personal finance, will continue as part of the trend toward broadening students' applications of their mathematical understandings and skills.

■ *Science*

Visit this chapter of the web site to link to more information about science curricula.

Science in the elementary grades takes advantage of children's natural curiosity about the world around them—plants, seasons, color, light, sound, and animals. In the upper elementary and middle school grades, the curriculum includes weather and climate, the solar system, electricity, and health-related topics. The secondary school science curriculum is still centered around year-long courses: general science, biology, chemistry, and physics.

■ **Issues and Trends**   Two major questions drive science education reform: where will the next generation of scientists come from, and how can all students be prepared to make informed judgments about such critical and science-based issues as environmental pollution, energy sources, and biotechnology?

Performing well-designed experiments fosters a deeper understanding of key scientific concepts and methods.
(© Bob Daemmrich/ Stock Boston)

■ *Project 2061*

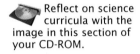 Reflect on science curricula with the image in this section of your CD-ROM.

For reformers, there has been both good news and bad news concerning science education in the United States. The bad news is that American youth don't know much science. The good news is that the country is reaching consensus on how to remedy the problem. The science curriculum has been undergoing dramatic redirection as a result of Project 2061 (named for the year in which Halley's comet is expected to return), an initiative of the American Association for the Advancement of Science. Inquiry-based learning and a hands-on approach are strong elements in science reform efforts. Addressing both elementary and secondary science, the association's recommendations include the following:

• Reducing the boundaries between academic disciplines

• Emphasizing ideas and thinking skills rather than specialized vocabulary and memorization

• Helping students develop a cogent view of the world by including such key concepts and principles as the structure and evolution of the universe; basic concepts related to matter, energy, force, and motion; the human life cycle; medical techniques; social change and conflict; and the mathematics of symbols.[5]

In the science classroom, wondering should be as highly valued as knowing.
—2061 SCIENCE CURRICULUM

The work of Project 2061 appears to have had a strong effect on both the national standards for science education and many state curriculum frameworks, but as yet, it has been slow to change how science is taught in the schools.

■ *Social Studies*

Social studies—the study of people and their ideas, actions, and relationships—is not a discipline in the same sense as mathematics or physics, although it draws

Visit this chapter of the web site to link to more information about social studies curricula.

■ *history dominates*

■ *concern for non-European cultures*

■ *the "new civics"*

Visit this chapter of the web site to link to more information about foreign language curricula.

on the various social science disciplines (history, geography, political science, economics, psychology, sociology, and anthropology), as well as on religion, literature, and the arts, for its content and methods of inquiry. (A *discipline* has been defined as an area of inquiry containing a distinctive body of concepts and principles, with techniques for exploring the area and for correcting and expanding the body of knowledge.[6])

History has traditionally been the leading discipline of social studies at both the elementary and secondary levels, and although other disciplines have made some inroads, it still remains dominant. Recently, efforts have been made to restore geography to the social studies curriculum following assessments that pointed out students' inability to locate countries on maps. Government is also a staple of the social studies curriculum. Altogether, however, the social studies curriculum at both the elementary and secondary levels is a hodgepodge of approaches.

■ **Issues and Trends**   Currently, a major debate rages over whether the social studies curriculum overemphasizes European history and culture at the expense of Asian, African, and Latin American history and culture. Another concern is the representation of women's roles in the history curriculum. Although many textbook publishers are making efforts to include greater representation of women and people of color in their books, critics argue that the efforts seem feeble and contrived. At all levels, textbooks dominate the social studies curriculum.

Civic learning or **civic education** is another issue gaining the attention of social studies educators. Advocates of this new focus call for courses that will acquaint a racially and culturally diverse student population with the heritage common to the American democratic tradition. These new courses would extend the basic study of American law and government to include trends in history, issues in contemporary society, and questions of character and values. Through critical study of case histories and current news reports, students would learn to apply principles of democracy to everyday concerns they will face as citizens. Practical experiences in civic, cultural, and volunteer activities are also strongly recommended. The "new civics" courses may help unify educators calling for issues-centered, traditional, historical, critical thought, and character education approaches to the teaching of social studies.

Standards have been developed by the various national organizations representing history, geography, economics, civics, and social studies. Unfortunately, these subject standards were developed independently of one another and don't relate to one another. However, the National Council for the Social Studies (NCSS) has articulated a framework to foster academic and civic competence by integrating national standards across various social sciences. Ten themes are highlighted in the framework: culture; people, places, and environments; individuals, groups and institutions; production, distribution, and consumption; global connections; time, continuity, and change; individual development and identity; power, authority, and governance; science, technology, and society; and civic ideals and practices.[7]

■ *Foreign Languages*

Compared with citizens in other nations, Americans are woefully unprepared to speak foreign languages. About 50 percent of students in U.S. public high schools are enrolled in a foreign language course, with Spanish and French being the most popular languages taken.[8] On the bright side, more and more elementary schools are offering foreign language programs in recognition of the ease with which young children learn foreign languages.

■ *cultural understanding*

■ **Issues and Trends** Foreign language departments in the public schools are trying to make the study of foreign languages more attractive by expanding their course offerings and integrating language study with concerns for international and multicultural education. Leaders in the field emphasize the cultural foundations of language, asserting that language study increases linguistic competence and cultural sensitivity. The Internet assists students and teachers in gaining greater access to current materials from other countries, thus facilitating teaching and learning. Alternative secondary schools, such as international schools, schools-within-schools, and magnet schools, have also begun to integrate international studies and foreign language study. Attention to techniques used in elementary bilingual education—immersion, partial immersion, or the Foreign Language in the Elementary Schools Program—has focused instruction on developing fluency in speaking, writing, and comprehension. Proficiency-oriented instruction that focuses on what the learner can do with language rather than what the learner knows about language marks modern-day language teaching.

■ *elementary school emphasis*

Early introduction of foreign languages continues to gain support, and concern about U.S. competitiveness in a global economy has led many business leaders and politicians to urge greater emphasis on foreign language instruction. More and more states are responding to these pressures.

■ *The Arts*

Art is humanity's most essential, most universal language. It is not a frill, but a necessary part of communication.

—ERNEST L. BOYER

The arts include visual arts, music, dance, and theater. Art and music in the elementary school are ordinarily taught by regular classroom teachers, although some schools hire specialist teachers in one or both areas. Dance and theater are largely ignored in the elementary school, although children of this age are less inhibited and seem to enjoy these activities more than do secondary students. The small amount of instruction provided in the arts for elementary students contrasts with high school offerings such as drama clubs, orchestras, bands, and dance groups. In most instances, instruction in music or dance during a child's elementary school years takes the form of private instruction outside the public school.

Visit this chapter of the web site to link to more information about curricula in the arts.

■ *aesthetics emphasis*

■ **Issues and Trends** Programs in the arts have tended to emphasize the creation of an art object or the development of a performance, but newer programs center on aesthetic education and art as a way of knowing and perceiving the world. For most students, this trend will be useful.

Reflect on the role of arts in the curriculum with the image in this section of your CD-ROM.

Curriculum specialists have suggested integrating the arts with other subject matter to show the usefulness of the arts and to appeal to a broader range of intelligences. (See the chapter entitled "Who Are Today's Students in a Diverse Society?" for more on the topic of Howard Gardner's theory of multiple intelligences.) There is little doubt that the arts play a crucial role in the development of cultured, educated individuals and that they respond to a deep instinct in humanity. In spite of this recognition, however, the arts remain an endangered species whenever budget cuts occur and when high-stakes assessments

Arts advocates support integrating the arts with the rest of the curriculum. These girls, for example, are studying Macbeth.
(© Bob Daemmrich/ Stock Boston)

of standards in language arts, math, science, and social studies dictate what teachers should emphasize in their classrooms.

Physical Education, Health, and Recreation

■ *emphasis on fitness*

Physical education—education by and through human movement—contributes to physical fitness, skill and knowledge development, and social and psychological development. Currently, physical education curricula are responding to four needs: (1) to develop aerobic capacity to maintain acceptable cardiorespiratory efficiency, (2) to achieve appropriate levels of body fat, (3) to acquire strength to perform expected tasks of living, and (4) to achieve flexibility and abdominal strength to avoid lower back injuries. To address these needs, sports skills are alternated with fitness development through such activities as swimming, jogging, bicycling, and cross-country skiing. Students are given information on exercise and nutrition so they can understand how to balance caloric intake and maintain an appropriate body fat level. Physical education teachers are typically licensed for both elementary and secondary school teaching, but teachers usually seek out the age levels in which they are most interested.

Visit this chapter of the web site to link to more information about the curriculum in this area.

■ *health education*

The health curriculum addresses such topics as injury prevention and safety, prevention and control of disease (including acquired immune deficiency syndrome [AIDS]), substance abuse, nutrition, family life (sexuality), consumer health, and mental and emotional health. More than most academic subjects, health education strives to change students' attitudes and behaviors to get them to take fewer risks and take preventive measures. Many health educators express frustration that health is not identified as a critical component of the K–12 curriculum and questions about health do not appear on high-stakes tests. Because health is not tested, it isn't stressed in schools as much as health educators would like.

Elective Courses

Most high schools today offer their students a number of options regarding the courses they take. Whereas the average high school student graduates with about twenty units (one year-long course represents one unit), large high schools may offer as many as one hundred courses. The average student, then, will probably choose among optional courses according to individual interests and academic or career ambitions.

non-college-bound students

Issues and Trends   Although college preparation has been the major goal of many high schools, recently increased effort has been made to provide comprehensive programs for students not planning to attend college. This trend is especially evident in rural areas, where small, local high schools are being replaced by comprehensive regional high schools. Some of the courses involved, such as technology education, distributive education, home economics, business education, and agriculture, are specifically vocational. Others such as driver education and consumer education have been added to the curriculum because of an obvious societal need or in response to student interest.

more graduation requirements

A trend disturbing those who teach elective courses is the increase in requirements for graduation from high schools, which leaves less time for elective courses. Some argue that a common general education provides the best foundation for future work or academic study; others hope to maintain a large percentage of the curriculum as electives. Issues raised by teachers of elective courses focus attention on the purpose of comprehensive schooling and on what is "basic."

Vocational Courses

Visit this chapter of the web site to link to more information about vocational curricula.

Vocational education has come under fire from those who note its inadequacy in preparing students for careers in high-technology fields or in the country's now dominant service economy. In 1991 the U.S. Department of Labor issued the Secretary's Commission on Achieving Necessary Skills (SCANS) report, which called for all high school students to develop a set of higher competencies and a foundation of skills to be better prepared for the world of work.[9] The report recognizes that both education and businesses will have to change if America is to have a well-prepared work force. The report urges teachers to help students see the relationships between what they study and its applications in real-world contexts and to emphasize real-life problem solving. The federal government also supports a School-to-Work program designed to help students develop skills and understandings that will prepare them to adapt to the changing needs of the workplace. Although aimed particularly for students not planning on going to college, many college-bound students also take advantage of these programs to get a "real-world" grounding for future careers. These programs can take many different shapes, from career academies that feature specialized career-oriented curricula in such areas as health professions, business, or law, to paid internships and co-op experiences. Schools work with local businesses to design courses and experiences that will prepare high school students for particular

School-to-Work partnerships

> *A liberal education is the only practical form of vocational education.*
>
> —CARDINAL JOHN HENRY NEWMAN

kinds of jobs that meet local business needs. Hundreds of thousands of businesses nationwide now participate in School-to-Work partnerships.

more apprenticeship programs?

Reflect on the changing vocational curriculum with the image in this section of your CD-ROM.

"tech-prep" programs

Issues and Trends   Some educators and labor officials urge that the line between academic and vocational education should be blurred and that all youngsters should be provided with more applied learning experiences. Some states such as Oregon are moving to require all graduating high school students to have work experience and a career plan. Further, they argue that the "general education" track in high school, which falls between a college-preparatory track and a strictly career/technical track, should be eliminated. Although just 42 percent of all high school students are enrolled in a general education track, nearly two out of three high school dropouts come from that track. In addition, apprenticeship programs such as those in Germany are being praised. In such a program, students receive on-the-job training with a company for four days a week and participate in classroom instruction on the fifth day. Such programs are designed to help youth move from school to work.

Another promising trend is the development of "tech-prep" programs that link high school and postsecondary study. Tech-prep programs typically involve the last two years of high school and the first two years of college (usually at a community college) and provide an attractive alternative for students who do not plan to attend a four-year college.

PAUSE AND REFLECT

1 What is your view of the issues and trends in your favorite subject field? Are there any other developments that you would like to see?

Assessing Student Academic Performance

Both supporters and critics of contemporary curricula often focus on the results: what do students actually learn from their studies of language arts, math, science, and so forth? The methods of assessing results are themselves highly controversial and will be discussed further in the "How Should Education Be Reformed?" chapter, but in this section, we will look at both national and international studies that attempt to judge the academic performance of American students.

National Assessment of Educational Progress

"nation's report card"

Visit this chapter of the web site to link to the web site for the NAEP.

Since their introduction over thirty years ago, National Assessment of Educational Progress (NAEP) assessments have been conducted periodically in reading, mathematics, science, writing, history, geography, and other fields. Administered to a representative national sample, the NAEP assessments are the primary source on educational achievement in the United States, and they have become known as "the nation's report card." Although almost all the states assess their students' progress on content standards, they don't all have the same standards or use the same tests, so comparisons across states are mainly limited to the NAEP data. Assessment occurs at three grade levels: fourth, eighth, and

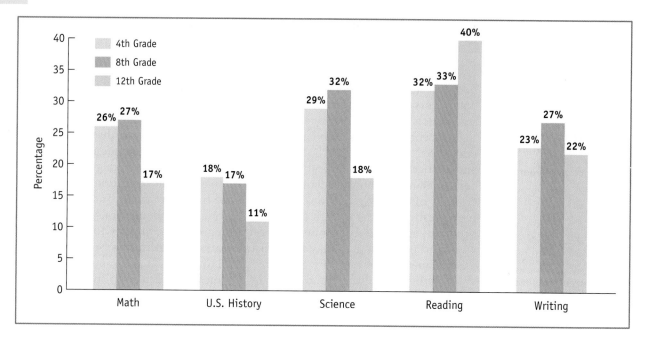

Figure 4.1
Percentage of Students Scoring at the Proficient or Advanced Level on NAEP Assessments in Various Subject Fields

Source: The Nation's Report Card. Available at: **http://nces.gov/ nationsreportcard/site/ home.asp**.

▪ *how are students doing?*

▪ *ignorance of history and geography*

twelfth. Achievement levels are defined as *basic* (denoting partial mastery of knowledge and skills fundamental for proficient work), *proficient* (representing solid academic performance over challenging subject matter for the grade level), and *advanced* (signifying superior performance).

So how are American students doing? See Figure 4.1 for figures on mathematics, science, reading, writing, and U.S. history. In the 2000 science assessments, fourth grade students performed about the same as they had in 1996, whereas eighth-graders did slightly better and twelfth-graders did slightly worse. Twenty-nine percent of the fourth-graders scored at or above the proficient level, whereas the percentage for eight-graders and twelfth-graders were 32 and 18 percent, respectively. Unlike in science, students made significant improvements in the 2000 mathematics assessments. In fact, over the past decade, student achievement on the NAEP mathematics tests has improved significantly for all ages and racial and ethnic groups, as much as one year's worth of mathematics knowledge since 1990 for fourth, eighth, and twelfth grades. Reading scores, on the other hand, remained relatively unchanged from 1992 to 2000, although a modest upward slope has occurred since 1994.[10] The 2000 reading assessment of fourth-graders indicated that 63 percent of the students were at or above the basic level, whereas 32 percent were at or above the proficient level.[11] African-American, Hispanic, and Native-American students continue to score significantly lower than white and Asian-American students, although the gap between African-American and white students has been narrowing. Males continue to outperform females on mathematics and science tests, but the reverse is true on the reading and writing tests.[12] Further NAEP assessments reveal that American students are woefully ignorant of history, geography, and civics. In the 2001 history assessment, a significant percentage of students—33 percent of fourth-graders, 36 percent of eighth-graders, and 57 percent of twelfth-graders—failed to achieve the expectations for the basic level. The percentages of students who reached the proficient or advanced levels at the fourth, eighth, and twelfth grades were only 18, 17, and 11, respectively.[13] In the 2001 geography tests, the percentages of students who reached the proficient or advanced levels at the fourth, eighth, and twelfth grades were 21, 30, and 25, respectively. In every subject field, therefore, a large majority of American students are failing to achieve the proficient level in the NAEP assessments.

■ **International Comparisons**   Compared with the academic performances of students from other developed countries, American students have tended to do poorly, especially middle and high school students. In 1995, the Third International Mathematics and Science Study (TIMSS) tested the mathematics and science knowledge of half a million students at three grade levels—fourth, eighth, and twelfth—in forty-one countries. TIMSS was the largest, most comprehensive, and most rigorous international comparison of education ever done. The general finding of TIMSS is that U.S. students start out performing at high levels in fourth grade, but by the time they graduate, they are performing at unacceptably low levels in both math and science. The two main messages of TIMSS are that (1) U.S. students don't start out behind, they fall behind; and (2) by the time U.S. students finish high school, they are not achieving at the international standards demanded by a global labor market.[14] Of the twenty-one nations that participated in the twelfth-grade tests, the United States outperformed only two, Cyprus and South Africa, in general math and science knowledge. Even our most advanced students, those taking advanced mathematics and physics, scored at the bottom when compared to their counterparts in other countries, and none of the Asian countries, which led the eighth-grade performances, even participated in the twelfth-grade assessments.[15]

poor U.S. performance

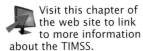 Visit this chapter of the web site to link to more information about the TIMSS.

The TIMSS is not without its critics. A number of nations in the study did not heed the quality control guidelines in selecting the students who would participate. For example, some countries only tested students in programs concentrating on mathematics and science. As a result, TIMSS may tell us more about the differing educational systems than about the students.[16] In spite of the criticisms, it is difficult to find much in the U.S. TIMSS data to cheer about.

possible explanations

A number of explanations are possible for the differences in mathematics and science achievement test scores between U.S. students and those from high-scoring countries, including cultural differences that result in greater value being placed on education in some countries than in the United States, lower expectations for American students, and more American students holding jobs. Moreover, the TIMSS study revealed that the content of U.S. mathematics and science classes is not as challenging or focused as that of other countries. Many middle school students in the United States are still doing elementary arithmetic and introductory science while their international counterparts are studying algebra, geometry, physics, and chemistry. By the senior year of high school, many of our students have stopped taking math and science altogether. Many students never study algebra (about 15 percent), geometry (about 30 percent), advanced algebra (about 40 percent), other advanced mathematics (around 80 percent), chemistry (about 45 percent), or physics (almost 75 percent).[17] TIMSS researchers have characterized the U.S. mathematics and science curricula as being "a mile wide and an inch deep"—that is, they cover many topics but devote little time to any one topic. The United States is number one in the world in one category—the size of the textbooks—which tend to be encyclopedic rather than focused! U.S. teachers, supported by the textbooks they use, teach more topics but in less detail than teachers from high-scoring countries. Furthermore, when contrasted with Japanese teachers, they focus much more on procedures and skills and much less on concepts, deductive reasoning, and

breadth instead of depth

nonacademic activities

understanding. Surprisingly, however, U.S. teachers assign more homework and spend more class time discussing it than do teachers from Japan and Germany.[18]

Another factor is the total amount of time spent on academic pursuits. At the high school level, American students spend much of their school day in such nonacademic activities as counseling, gym, homeroom, driver training, pep rallies, and education about personal safety, AIDS, consumer affairs, and family life. An average of only 41 percent of secondary school time needs to be devoted to core academic work to earn a high school diploma,[19] and that's probably the way most American parents want it. Both parents and students downplay a "nerdish" emphasis on strong academics in favor of preparing "well-rounded" individuals, making it difficult for schools to strengthen their academic requirements beyond a certain point. As long as a majority of Americans feel this way, it seems unlikely that we will see a radical restructuring of schools to emphasize strong academics.

lessons learned from TIMSS

We believe there are several lessons to be learned from TIMSS. First, we need to continue setting clear, high standards for what we expect students to know and be able to do in mathematics and science. Second, we need to align everything else we do with those standards: initial preparation of teachers, selection of texts and other curriculum materials, design of assessments, and the continuing professional development of teachers. The difficulty, of course, is that unlike most of the other countries participating in the TIMSS, the United States is highly decentralized in its educational decision making, thus making it extremely difficult to align the various educational components with the standards.

PAUSE AND REFLECT

1. In your opinion, what best explains the relatively poor performance of U.S. students in international comparisons of student achievement in mathematics and science?

2. Do you think the U.S. should have a national curriculum, as do so many other industrialized nations? Why or why not?

Additional Influences on Curriculum

Although we can examine what is taught in the schools in terms of the subjects offered, the curriculum as students experience it is affected by a number of other factors. The individual teacher, of course, is a major variable in what students actually learn. The classroom and school context also affect the delivery of the curriculum, as does the academic track to which the student is assigned. We will focus on two other major influences on the curriculum that is actually delivered to students: textbooks and emerging instructional approaches.

■ *Textbooks*

textbooks as a national curriculum

Education in the United States is constitutionally the domain of the various individual states—that is, the states are empowered to establish curricula and to organize and finance school systems. Unlike in many other countries, there is no national curriculum established by the federal government and implemented throughout the country. Some educational observers assert, however, that we do have a national curriculum of sorts, called *textbooks*. Several recent studies have

Critics claim that textbooks are dry, devoid of concepts, and "dumbed down" to meet readability standards. In spite of the criticism, textbooks are prevalent in America's classrooms.

(© Jeff Dunn/Stock Boston)

concluded that most of what teachers and students do in classrooms is textbook related. For example, the objectives and goals for student learning are defined by the textbook (even the text you are now reading), learning activities and materials are provided to teachers as part of the textbook package, and tests geared to the textbook's objectives are usually prepared for the teacher's use.

More than twenty states, mainly in the Sunbelt, have a textbook adoption process in which citizens have the opportunity to examine textbooks being considered for statewide adoption and to express their objections to particular books. Because textbook adoption is a multimillion-dollar business, publishing companies must be careful not to include material that influential groups and factions may find offensive.

With the implementation of content standards in the various states, school boards and faculty responsible for adopting textbooks now examine how well textbooks address their state's standards. However, textbook publishers do not often customize their books for each state. Instead, they adapt the books to the standards of states that have a lot of children, and buy a lot of books. Publishers rely on the similarity of standards between states to assure that books geared to the larger states will meet at least some standards in nearly every state. This means that states such as Texas, California, and Florida greatly influence the content of textbooks produced by commercial publishers.

call for better textbooks

A wave of educational reform is directing attention to the quality of the textbooks that determine the curriculum. Some critics claim that texts are "dumbed down" to meet readability requirements; the writing style, designed to meet arbitrary criteria for lengths of words and sentences, can be awkward and stiff. Others believe that textbooks try to include too much material and so lack depth of coverage, a criticism certainly supported by findings from the TIMSS. Critics also complain about typical textbook emphases on skill development instead of the stimulation of students' interest and intellect; these emphases, they say, create texts that are dry, barren of ideas, devoid of concepts, and lacking in the vigorous style that stirs students to comprehend and retain what they read.

Visit this chapter of the web site to link to more information about textbooks.

■ multimedia texts

Critics have noted the shortcomings of many adoption systems that allow too little time and money to support the selection of excellent texts by qualified personnel. Whereas some education personnel call for schools to spend more money on textbooks, many others claim that teachers and curriculum developers rely too much on textbooks and not enough on primary sources.

A recent modification of the traditional textbook involves the use of electronic laser discs. The state of Texas offers school districts the option to use an elementary science program on laser discs instead of textbooks, and about one-half of the districts choose to do so. The multimedia system, called *Windows on Science,* contains eleven discs, plus printed lesson plans and suggested activities for students. The producer of the program, Optical Data Corporation, regularly updates the information on the discs and distributes the new discs to adopters of the program. The discs are also available in either English or Spanish. Besides keeping information current, the technology provides access to rich materials and interesting projects such as using the videodiscs to engage in simulated scientific experiments that otherwise would be impractical. The videodiscs also provide alternative assessments by permitting students to answer questions and follow directions on the disc. Whether laser disc systems or other electronic media will make major inroads into textbook adoptions in other subjects remains to be seen. While lacking the technological pizzazz, conventional textbooks are less expensive and more portable, and do not break down. One thing appears certain: textbooks, in paper or electronic form, are one of the major determinants of our nation's elementary and secondary school curricula, and that situation does not appear likely to change in the near future.

■ *Innovative Instructional Approaches*

Curriculum and instruction are intimately related, and the instructional approaches that teachers use clearly shape how students experience the curriculum. Although these approaches have remained amazingly constant since the 1890s, especially at the secondary level, some alterations to traditional teacher-centered instruction have taken hold.[20] Educators are constantly searching for new ways to deliver the curriculum more effectively. All of the trends discussed here can be used in a variety of subject areas with students of many age and ability levels. We will look at six nontraditional instructional influences on the curriculum: interdisciplinary curriculum, cooperative learning, critical thinking and problem solving, writing across the curriculum, differentiated instruction, and block scheduling.

■ Interdisciplinary Curriculum   Students, particularly secondary students, are often critical of the traditional curriculum, which seems irrelevant to their lives outside of school. They often fail to see how English, history, mathematics, and science relate to them. The curriculum they experience is fragmented and isolated. As one student explained, "Math isn't science, science isn't English, English isn't history. A subject is something you take once and need never take again. It's like getting a vaccination; I've had my shot of algebra. I'm done with that."[21]

Many teachers agree. Noting that the real world is not organized by disciplines but contains situations and problems that cut across disciplinary boundaries, these teachers are returning to an old idea of organizing and teaching the

Reflect on the interdisciplinary curriculum with the image in this section of your CD-ROM.

Figure 4.2
Sample Interdisciplinary Approach

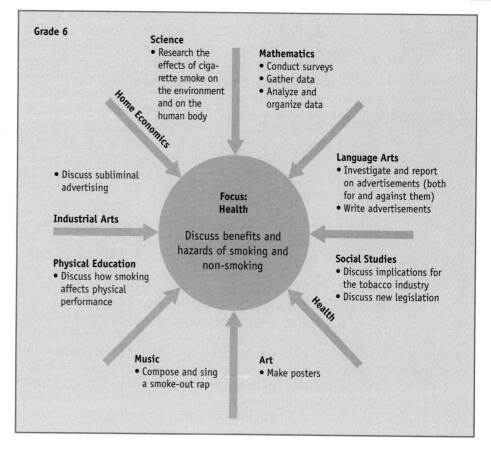

Grade 6

Science
• Research the effects of cigarette smoke on the environment and on the human body

Mathematics
• Conduct surveys
• Gather data
• Analyze and organize data

Home Economics
• Discuss subliminal advertising

Industrial Arts

Language Arts
• Investigate and report on advertisements (both for and against them)
• Write advertisements

Focus: Health

Discuss benefits and hazards of smoking and non-smoking

Physical Education
• Discuss how smoking affects physical performance

Social Studies
• Discuss implications for the tobacco industry
• Discuss new legislation

Health

Music
• Compose and sing a smoke-out rap

Art
• Make posters

---

curriculum in an integrated and interdisciplinary fashion. Although numerous definitions of **interdisciplinary** or **integrated curriculum** exist, the terms are often used synonymously to mean a curriculum that cuts across subject-matter lines to focus on comprehensive life problems or broad-based areas of study that bring together the various segments of the curriculum in meaningful association.

There are many approaches to developing integrated, interdisciplinary curricula. One of the simplest is for two or more teachers from different disciplinary backgrounds to plan and teach their respective subjects together, seeking different disciplinary perspectives on a particular unit of study. For example, an English and social studies teacher might team together to integrate the study of the nineteenth century through the history and literature of that period.

Another approach is *thematic* in nature. A cross-departmental team chooses themes as overlays to the different subjects. "Inventions," for example, is a theme that could combine science and mathematics in the study of machines and their mechanics, reading and writing about inventors in language arts, and designing and building models in industrial arts. Another example, "health," would permit a number of different subjects to be used to better understand specific health topics (Figure 4.2). Still another thematic approach is to identify concepts that apply in different subjects, such as examining how symmetry, patterns, evidence, and proof apply in mathematics, art, science, social studies, and language arts.

teaming teachers from different disciplines

thematic teaching

Visit this chapter of the web site to link to more information about interdisciplinary themes.

arguments for interdisciplinary teaching

Proponents of interdisciplinary curricula argue that the merits far outweigh the extra expenditure of time and effort required. Students benefit by experiencing coherence in the curriculum and connections to real-world situations. Critical thinking and problem-solving skills are developed within specific contexts rather than in isolation. Teachers benefit by having students who enjoy learning and by working collaboratively with other teachers. Although interdisciplinary teaching is enjoying a resurgence of popularity, particularly in middle schools, the disciplinary approach to curriculum in the secondary schools is well entrenched and is being reinforced by the development of national standards within each discipline rather than across disciplines. The tension between disciplinary and interdisciplinary approaches to curriculum development will continue for some time.

Cooperative Learning

Cooperative learning in classrooms is another trend influencing what is taught in the schools. Those who have analyzed the "hidden" curriculum, or the implicit teachings that schools communicate to their students, have observed that American schools tend to reward competitive or individual accomplishment more than cooperative effort.[22] Arguing for cooperative learning techniques, some educators maintain that such techniques can change the ways students learn, their attitudes toward what they are taught, and their perceptions of themselves and others.

definitions of cooperative learning

What is cooperative learning? There are many different forms, but all involve students working in small groups or teams to help one another learn academic material. Cooperative learning strategies are organized, highly structured methods that usually involve formal presentation of information, student practice and coaching in learning teams, individual assessment of mastery, and public recognition of team success. Table 4.2 summarizes several such strategies. By their structure and individual assignments, cooperative learning strategies avoid the problem of letting the hard-working students in the group do the work while the other students get a free ride. Cooperative learning strategies have proven successful across grade levels and in different subjects. The effectiveness of cooperative learning, particularly for achievement outcomes, depends on the particular approach used, but overall positive effects have been found on such diverse outcomes as self-esteem, intergroup relations, acceptance of academically handicapped students, attitudes toward school, and ability to work cooperatively.[23]

Visit this chapter of the web site to link to more information about cooperative learning.

three key characteristics

The success of cooperative learning strategies comes from three important characteristics: group goals, individual accountability, and equal opportunity for success. *Group goals* usually take the form of rewards based on team success in academic tasks. To achieve team success, each member of the group must coordinate the completion of his or her assigned task with the other group members; each team member is indispensable. *Individual accountability* involves assessing each student's mastery of the content, with the results usually given back to the group and the individual. Teammates practice together and support and coach one another, but individuals are assessed in the usual ways. The team's success is often judged by how much each team member improves over earlier assessment. In that way, even the least-achieving student can contribute to the team's success by improving over the first assessment. *Equal opportunities for success* are ensured by team scoring systems based on individual improvement over prior performance. This feature reinforces the perception that student effort, not just innate ability, counts.

TABLE 4.2 Selected Cooperative Learning Strategies

Name	Brief Description	Function
1. Student team learning a. Student Teams Achievement Divisions (STAD)	Four-member mixed learning teams. Teacher presents lesson, students work within teams to make certain all team members have mastered the objectives. Students take individual quizzes. Points awarded based on improvement over previous quizzes.	Appropriate for teaching well-defined objectives with single right answers in most subjects.
b. Teams-Games-Tournament (TGT)	Uses same teacher presentations and teamwork as in STAD, but replaces quizzes with weekly tournaments.	Same as STAD
2. Jigsaw	Each student on team becomes "expert" on one topic by working with members from other teams assigned same topic. Upon returning to home team, each expert teaches the group, and students are all assessed on all aspects of the topic.	Acquisition and presentation of new material, review, informed debate. Promotes interdependence, status equalization. Used in social studies and other subjects where learning from text is important.
3. Jigsaw 2	Same as Jigsaw, except instead of each student being assigned a particular section of text, all students read a common narrative. Each student receives a topic on which to become expert.	Same as Jigsaw
4. Group investigation	Students work in small groups using cooperative inquiry, group discussion, and projects. Students form two- to six-member groups. Groups choose subtopics from a unit, break subtopics into individual tasks, and prepare group reports.	Develop skills of planning, investigating, and reporting.
5. Think-pair-share	Students think to themselves on a topic provided by teacher; then pair with another student to discuss it; then share their thoughts with class.	Generating and revising hypotheses, inductive reasoning, deductive reasoning. Fosters participation and involvement.

helps at-risk students

 Cooperative learning has been found to be a particularly effective instructional tool in teaching at-risk students who benefit from immediate feedback for their learning attempts. It works well because it offers students more involvement in and control over their learning activities. As many schools attempt to do away with tracking and to encourage heterogeneous grouping, cooperative learning provides a means to make all students feel they are essential to the classroom learning process. It enables students to recognize that they all, when given a chance, have something to contribute to everyone's learning. Cooperative learning has quickly become a major instructional method in the United States, particularly in elementary and middle schools.[24]

■ **Critical Thinking and Problem Solving**   A growing interest in helping students become better thinkers and problem solvers is evidenced by the multitude of publications, workshops, curriculum study institutes, journal articles, and course requirements addressing the topics of thinking and problem solving. Although many people favor teaching it, definitions of **critical thinking** vary widely. At the heart of these definitions, however, is the intent to help students evaluate the worth of ideas, opinions, or evidence before making a decision or judgment.

■ *different approaches*

Some educators favor approaches that help students detect bias or identify a wide range of propaganda strategies. The teaching of philosophy is also proposed as a way to provide criteria by which students can judge others' thinking. Still other approaches identify component skills (for example, making inferences, testing hypotheses, identifying assumptions) within the realm of critical thinking and advocate direct instruction in each skill. Socratic questioning (a style of questioning that elicits a clear expression of truth that was implicitly known by the person being questioned) is also suggested as a way to teach the art of thinking.

■ *problem solving*

Problem solving is an element of critical thinking that has received increasing attention and use. **Problem solving** generally refers to the process of either presenting students with a problem or helping them identify a problem and then observing and helping them become aware of the conditions, procedures, or steps needed to solve it. The problem may range from putting puzzles together, to solving simple science or mathematics problems, to solving more complex mental, logical, or social dilemmas. It may be presented as an individual activity, such as when independently predicting outcomes in a reading passage, or may be used with a group, such as when simulating wilderness "survival" activities that require group cooperation. In the many diverse ways of teaching problem solving, the emphasis is on the *process* of reaching a solution. Proponents of problem-solving instruction point out that if students become more aware of their mental processes, they will be able to exercise greater control over their own learning and thinking in future situations. In group problem-solving activities, students may also benefit from interacting with one another and being exposed to the variety of approaches used by peers in solving the same problem.

> *Many highly intelligent people are poor thinkers. Many people of average intelligence are skilled thinkers. The power of a car is separate from the way the car is driven.*
>
> —EDWARD DE BONO

Visit this chapter of the web site to link to more information about critical thinking and problem solving.

What is the role of critical thought in the curriculum? At one time, educators debated whether students can best learn effective thinking through separate courses or as an integrated part of every course. Greater agreement now exists that although students do benefit from stand-alone courses in critical thinking, they must also learn to think within the context of each discipline. The integration of critical thinking into subject areas appears to be the direction of the future, especially since the curricula of the schools are already so crowded.

■ *integration with subject areas*

■ **Writing Across the Curriculum**   The **writing across the curriculum** movement has been a center of curricular interest for a growing number of Eng-

VOICES FROM THE CLASSROOM

Judy Boch graduated from the University of Arizona and obtained a Master's degree in Educational Leadership at Northern Arizona University. She has Administrative licensure and an English as a Second Language (ESL) endorsement. Judy has taught mainly primary grades. She spent four years working as a Collaborative Peer Teacher under a National Science Foundation grant assisting K–6 teachers in their classrooms with math and science. She is currently out of the classroom as a Master Teacher working under the Teacher Advancement Program sponsored by the Milken Family Foundation. In this capacity, Judy observes, evaluates, team teaches, and provides professional development to teachers in the Cartwright Elementary School District in Phoenix.

Triumphs and Setbacks

Up until the time he came to me as a second grader, Raul's content education had been conducted in Spanish. Only in the latter part of first grade did he begin to learn in English. My second grade classroom was labeled *English as a Second Language (ESL)*, but I spoke no Spanish. The only Spanish that Raul heard in the classroom was from a one-hour Spanish aide and from the other children.

I wondered how I was going to reach this obviously bright and talented boy. This was soon made clear during one of our first math lessons. Having been trained in Cognitively Guided Instruction, I gave the children a story problem and asked them to solve it with their own invented strategies. Although Raul couldn't, at first, read the problem, another child translated for him. Raul came alive! He drew pictures and used numbers to model his strategy to the problem. I knew I was taking a risk that day when I asked Raul to share his strategy with the other students. I wondered if I had made a mistake when he grasped for words to explain. But explain he did! He drew his picture on the board, labeled it with numbers, and wrote a number sentence to match the problem. In short phrases, he shared his thinking sequentially.

Raul blossomed after that day. His English began to improve as he continually volunteered to share his thinking in mathematics. In his math journal, Raul wrote:

"Math is my favrit becuz I get to be the techer. It makes me feel prowd."

Unfortunately, Raul's excitement has not continued. This year, as a Lead Teacher on my campus, I visit Raul's classroom once a week. He is learning math through more conventional methods using the traditional algorithms. It is painful to see him using traditional methods that he really doesn't understand and that take him so much longer than his invented strategies. His teacher says he is becoming unfocused and having discipline problems. Although his English has improved considerably, math is no long his great equalizer or passion. My only hope is that Raul rediscovers his love and enthusiasm for mathematics. For if he does not, we have failed him.

 Visit the web site for more Voices from the Classroom.

■ *writing as aid to subject-matter learning*

lish educators since the 1960s. Also called *writing to learn* or *writing to learn in the content areas*, the idea emphasizes writing as a tool for students' learning, not only in English classes but in all subject areas.

How can teachers use the act of writing as the medium through which subject-matter learning takes place? Students in social studies classes may be asked to take a written stand on school issues, moral questions, or political problems. Music students may write their own ballads. Students in science classes may work together to predict the future in story form or to write futuristic headlines and news features. Children in math classes can create their own word problems and keep records of what they have learned, their questions, and their observations. Art classes can write scripts for slide shows and cartoon strips or create illustrated guides and storybooks. Teachers at many grade levels and in many subject areas can ask students to keep informal journals or "learning logs." In these journals students record their responses to what they have read and studied and can then interact with text material and with the teacher's responses to their queries and remarks. These are just a few examples of the many ways teachers use writing as a thinking tool for students to use and apply their knowledge in the content areas.

■ **Differentiated Instruction**   The term **differentiated instruction** is relatively new on the educational scene; however, its practice has been around for a long time. In its simplest form, differentiated instruction tries to respond to student variance rather than adopting a standardized approach to teaching that assumes all learners in a class are essentially alike. The academic diversity of students in today's classrooms is growing, and one instructional approach won't work for all students. (See the chapter entitled "Who Are Today's Students in a Diverse Society?" for more discussion on various kinds of diversity.) As schools are trying to ensure that all students learn what is expected of them, teachers recognize that they need to diversify their instruction to meet individual student needs. Teachers are trying to tailor their instruction to provide appropriate challenges for gifted students, students who lag behind, and those in between.

■ *adapt instruction to meet student needs*

Differentiated instruction is a teaching philosophy based on the premise that teachers should adapt instruction to student differences in reading readiness, learning preferences, and interests. According to Carol Tomlinson, a national expert on differentiated instruction, teachers can differentiate three aspects of the curriculum: content, process, and products.[25] *Content* refers to the concepts, principles, and skills that teachers want students to learn. All students should be given access to the same core content, Tomlinson believes. However, teachers can provide different means (for example, texts, lectures, and demonstrations) to give students access to skills and knowledge. *Process* refers to the activities that help students make sense of and own the knowledge being taught. Teachers can vary the activities to provide some students with access to more complexity and others with more support, depending on their readiness levels, student interest, or learning preferences. *Product* refers to culminating projects that students develop to demonstrate and extend what they have learned. These products can vary also, depending on students' interests or learning preferences. For example, some students might prefer to work as a member of a group while producing a play about the topic being studied, whereas others might prefer to work alone to write a term paper. Differentiating content, process, and product for students requires teachers to know their students, their subject, and their materials. (See Table 4.3 for some strategies for differentiating instruction.) There is no formula for differentiation—no one way to address student differences. Rather, it is a commitment to start with students and to make a match between learner and the material to be learned. Its goal is to maximize the capacities of each student.

> *Any subject can be taught effectively in some intellectually honest form to any child at any stage of development.*
>
> —JEROME BRUNER

Visit this chapter of the web site to link to more information about differentiated instruction.

■ **Block Scheduling**   A 1994 report by the National Education Commission on Time and Learning, an independent panel temporarily convened by Congress, stated that time is "the missing element in the school-reform debate." The report urged that the traditional six-hour school day and 180-day year "be relegated to museums as an exhibit of our education past." Advising schools to be less rigid in how they use time, the report also recommended the use of block

TABLE 4.3　Strategies for Differentiating Instruction

Many teachers accept the desirability of differentiating instruction, but don't know how to go about doing it. Here are some of the many strategies that teachers can use to avoid lockstep instruction.

Stations. Involves setting up different spots in the classroom where students work on different tasks at the same time. This strategy encourages flexible grouping because not all students have to go to all stations all the time.

Compacting. Involves assessing students before beginning a unit of study so they won't have to waste time learning something they already know.

Complex Instruction. Uses challenging materials, open-ended tasks, and small instructional groups. Teachers circulate among the groups as they work, asking questions and probing student thinking.

Choice Boards. Teacher writes work assignments on cards that are placed in hanging pockets. Teacher asks a student to select a card from a particular row of pockets, which gives the student some choice within circumscribed options. Each row represents work at different levels of complexity.

Problem-based Learning. Places students in an active role of solving problems.

Entry Points. Using some of the multiple intelligences identified by Howard Gardner (see the chapter entitled "Who Are Today's Students in a Diverse Society?" for more on this topic), students explore a given topic through as many as five avenues: narrational (presenting a story), logical-quantitative (using numbers or deduction), foundational (examining philosophy and vocabulary), aesthetic (focusing on sensory features), and experiential (hands-on).

Orbital Studies. Involves independent investigations, generally lasting several weeks, around some aspect of the curriculum. Students select their own topics, and work with the guidance of the teacher.

4MAT. Teachers plan some lessons for each of four learning preferences (mastery, understanding, personal involvement, and synthesis) over the course of several days on a given topic. Each learner can approach the topic through preferred modes of learning. (See the chapter entitled "Who Are Today's Students in a Diverse Society?" for more information about learning preferences.)

Source: Carol Ann Tomlinson, *The Differentiated Classroom: Responding to the Needs of All Learners* (Alexandria, VA: Association for Supervision and Curriculum Development, 1999.)

scheduling and an extended school year.[26] As the accompanying box describes, in another innovative twist on the traditional school year, some schools are trying out **looping**, a practice that lets teachers stay with the same students for more than a single year.

▧ *what is block scheduling?*

Block scheduling is a "less is more" approach in which students take fewer classes each school day but spend more time in each class. In theory, block scheduling carves out more time for instruction by reducing the amount of time students spend going from class to class and the time teachers spend taking roll and settling down classes. It was relatively rare a decade ago, but now at least 14 percent of high schools nationwide use some form of block scheduling, including more than 40 percent of the high schools in North Carolina and Virginia.[27] Although block scheduling is not an instructional approach in itself, it does allow and encourage teachers to use cooperative learning, interdisciplinary teaching, critical thinking and problem solving, writing across the curriculum, and other innovative instructional strategies.

▧ *models of block scheduling*

Several models of block scheduling exist. The trimester approach may have classes lasting an hour and twenty minutes; instead of students taking the traditional six classes per semester, they take four each trimester. Courses that used

Looping or Multiyear Teaching

Suppose someone offered you an educational innovation with the following benefits: better teacher/student relationships, improved teacher job satisfaction, extra teaching time, a richer curriculum, increased student attendance, increased student development in social skills and a sense of community, and easy implementation at very little cost. Sound good? Proponents of an old but increasingly common practice called *looping* claim these as among its benefits.

Looping, or multiyear teaching, is a simple concept in which the teacher is promoted with his or her students to the next grade level and stays with the group for several years, typically two but sometimes as many as five. Although not much quantitative research exists on the benefits of looping, qualitative research supports the benefits just mentioned. By keeping the same group of students together with the same teacher, everyone gets to know one another well and feel comfortable in the group. Teachers get to know their students' strengths, weaknesses, and interests. Forging bonds of trust and understanding between teachers and students is at the heart of looping. Teachers who loop have fewer transitions to make at the beginning of the school year and can introduce curriculum topics right away at the start of the second year. They don't have to spend precious instructional time at the beginning of the new year to establish classroom routines and expectations. Instead, teachers can spend the gained time exploring curriculum topics in greater detail.

Administrators argue that looping isn't for everyone, so implementation should be on a voluntary basis. Some administrators urge teaming teachers to implement looping. In that way, students can benefit from different teacher strengths, and if a student has a problem with one particular teacher, another teacher can compensate.

Sources: "Looping—Discovering the Benefits of Multiyear Teaching," *Education Update* 40, no. 2 (March 1998), a publication of the Association for Supervision and Curriculum Development, pp. 1, 3–4; *Looping: Supporting Student Learning Through Long-Term Relationships,* Themes in Education (Brown University: LAB–Northeast and Islands Regional Educational Laboratory, 1997).

to last a semester now last a trimester, and courses that used to last a year now run for two trimesters. In the 4 × 4 plan, students take four 90-minute classes a day and complete them in a semester rather than a full year. In the A/B plan, students take eight 90-minute classes each semester, but classes meet every other day, four on day A and four on day B. Even more models exist.

The research on block scheduling so far is relatively scarce, and what does exist is often contradictory. Anecdotal evidence indicates that students like the new schedule if teachers are good and keep students' interest through various learning activities, but if teachers rely primarily on lectures, which are longer under block scheduling, students complain. The key seems to be to work with teachers to change their teaching models to make better use of the additional time they have each day the class meets. Teachers seem to like the block schedules because they have fewer students each term (for example, 90 instead of 150), and, as a result, they get to know those students better. In addition, block scheduling allows teachers more in-school preparation time. Teachers of certain disciplines such as music and foreign languages tend to dislike models of block scheduling that don't allow students to work each day on those subjects, arguing that developing skill in their subjects requires daily practice. On the other hand, science teachers tend to like block schedules that allow for longer laboratory periods. Some parents and students are concerned about student absences, which in some forms of block scheduling mean they miss more material and find it difficult to make it up.

PAUSE AND REFLECT

1 Have you had personal experience with any of the instructional approaches described above? If so, were they positive or negative? What made them so?

Current Curriculum Controversies

Given a highly pluralistic society and many different educational philosophies represented in America today, it is little wonder that the questions of how and what schools should teach generate much controversy and debate. In this section we will touch briefly on two of the most highly charged curriculum issues.

Reflect on a multi-cultural curriculum with the image in this section of your CD-ROM.

Core Versus Multicultural Curriculum American schools have traditionally played a central role in instilling the ideas and attitudes that maintain our pluralistic society as "one nation." They have helped weave the many ethnic and religious strands together to make a seamless national garment. At least that's the theory. Questions are now being raised about whether schools today provide a shared understanding of our culture, history, and traditions. Does the current curriculum of our schools reflect our national diversity to the exclusion of our national unity? Or is the reverse true?

multicultural curriculum

Proponents of a **multicultural curriculum** argue that minority students, whose representation in the public schools is about 37 percent and increasing every year, experience a Eurocentric, or Europe-centered, curriculum that gives short shrift to the literary and historical contributions of other parts of the world and to minorities within the United States. As a result, the proponents of multiculturalism argue, youngsters of color see the schools' curricula as being irrelevant to them, not reflective of their cultures or backgrounds. Some multicultural advocates take the position that the current school curriculum needs to be broadened to better reflect the contributions of people of color. Cultural pluralism, a fact of our society, needs to be a fact of our school curriculum, they assert.

ethnocentric curriculum

A more extreme position is taken by those who demand that the whole curriculum be oriented to a particular ethnicity. For example, some advocates of an Afrocentric curriculum claim that black schoolchildren can learn effectively only in an environment that recognizes and amplifies their African heritage. The theory is that if students learn of the accomplishments of those who share their ethnic identities, their self-esteem will improve, which will promote learning. When schools emphasize the achievements of African cultures, especially ancient Egyptian culture, and of individuals of African descent, students will have a greater sense of pride and be more motivated to learn. Afrocentric curricula are currently being used in a number of large-city school districts.

core curriculum

In contrast, proponents of a **core curriculum**, a course of study every student would be required to take, argue that ever since the 1970s, schools have focused on celebrating national diversity and pluralism but have failed to help students develop a shared national identity and common cultural framework. As described in the "What Are the Philosophical Foundations of American Education?" chapter, some advocates of a core curriculum, such as Mortimer Adler

The man who doesn't read good books has no advantage over the man who can't read them.

—MARK TWAIN

(*The Paideia Proposal*, 1983), promoted the great literary works that have endured over the years as the basic elements of a core curriculum.

cultural literacy

E. D. Hirsch, Jr., also endorses the great literary works, but goes beyond them in his push for **cultural literacy** (now called **core knowledge**).[28] Hirsch, sees a culturally literate person as someone who is aware of the central ideas, stories, scientific knowledge, events, and personalities of a culture. Cultural literacy is important, says Hirsch, because authors and speakers make allusions and references in their writing and speaking, assuming that the audience understands these references. If a person doesn't understand the reference, he or she will miss the point and not understand the message. If an author writes, for example, of the "luck of Midas," and the reader doesn't know who Midas was, then the point is lost.

Hirsch does not restrict his idea of a core curriculum to the great works of "dead white males," a criticism made of many traditional core curricula; rather, he sees American culture as incorporating the contributions of many ethnicities and subcultures. Hirsch believes that privileged youth gain much of their cultural literacy at home, but since many poor, minority, and immigrant children do not receive cultural literacy at home, it is especially important that they receive it in school. If they do not, Hirsch argues, poor children will not learn those aspects of our common heritage that are necessary to succeed in American society. Hirsch and his colleagues, through the Core Knowledge Foundation, have developed grade-by-grade guidelines for a core knowledge sequence for grades K–8, as well as a series of books entitled *What Every 1st [2nd, etc.] Grader Needs to Know*. Currently, several hundred schools across the country have adopted the core knowledge sequence.

The debate between those who advocate a common curriculum to ensure that all students learn what society has determined is important and those who favor state, local, and individual choice in what is learned will likely continue indefinitely.

Tracking The curriculum that a student receives is influenced by many factors, including aspirations for further schooling, academic ability, motivation, and vocational interests. Based on these and other factors, students are often placed into academic program *tracks* that determine what courses they take, the process being called **tracking**. The track in which a student is placed can open or close future academic and vocational options. The three most common tracks

three common tracks

are academic (stressing the traditional subjects of English, science, mathematics, and foreign languages), general (allowing more electives and less rigorous versions of the traditional subjects), and vocational (preparing students for the

Visit this chapter of the web site to link to more information about tracking.

world of work with a combination of academic and job-related courses). Each track has variations in courses required and different standards for student achievement. Within the academic track, further options exist, including advanced-placement (AP) and honors courses.

During the 1970s and 1980s, tracking came under attack. Several prominent educational researchers produced studies showing that students placed in the lower tracks received an inferior curriculum and less stimulating instruction than students in the academic tracks. Furthermore, these researchers found that poor and minority students were disproportionately placed in the lower tracks, where they had less qualified teachers, less rigorous curricula, and poorer instruction than students in the upper tracks. These researchers also reported that students in the upper tracks did no better than if they had been in mixed-ability classrooms.[29] Tracking became a dirty word, and detracking efforts ensued.

■ *tracking harmful to poor and minorities*

Other educational studies found conflicting evidence that, while detracking does help the educational performance of low-achieving students, high-achieving students are hurt academically.[30] Parents of these high-achieving students exert considerable pressure to ensure that their children have access to honors and AP classes, resisting efforts to detrack the schools. Furthermore, teachers who teach the high-track students often resist efforts to detrack, enjoying the intellectual challenge and prestige that come from teaching these students. The general sense is that tracking benefits high-ability students but hurts low-ability students, whereas the reverse is true of detracking.

■ *strong support for tracking*

Is the Existing Curriculum Relevant to Today's Society?

In this first decade of the twenty-first century, the world community is confronted with staggering problems. There are 6 billion people on our globe and forecasters project 10 billion by 2050. They need food, shelter, and an education that will lead them to fulfilled lives. The twentieth century saw great advances in manufacturing, agriculture, technology, and the growth of information. However, these advances have not been without costs. Acid rain, for example, polluted our vegetation, wildlife, and the very bodies of millions of people. Together, we and the rest of the world need to stop the systemic despoiling of our planet. Diseases such as AIDS have weakened whole continents. New weaponry, such as nuclear missiles and suitcase bombs, daily threaten the world's peace and progress. A despair brought on by hunger and poverty has bred a desperate terrorism in many corners of the world. It is no overstatement to say that we are in a race for global survival.

In the chapter entitled "What Is a School and What Is It For?", we described the curriculum as a social bet. Perhaps the most basic function of all education is to increase the survival chances of the human community. People, however, raise questions in one way or another about the relevance of the education provided to today's students, but before anyone can determine whether a particular curriculum is relevant to today's needs, some difficult issues must be addressed. In that same chapter, we discussed the purposes of schools and different models of schooling, particularly the school as a transmitter of culture and the school as an agent of social reconstruction. In the chapter entitled "What Are the Philosophical Foundations of American Education?", we discuss four schools of

■ *relevance depends on philosophy*

The Saber-Tooth Curriculum

In his classic satire on curriculum irrelevance, Harold Benjamin (using the pseudonym J. Abner Peddiwell) describes how the first school curriculum was developed in the Stone Age. The earliest theorist, according to Benjamin's book, was a man named New Fist, who hit on the idea of deliberate, systematic education.

Watching children at play, New Fist wondered how he could get them to do the things that would gain them more and better food, shelter, clothing, and security. He analyzed the activities that adults engaged in to maintain life and came up with three subjects for his curriculum: (1) fish-grabbing-with-the-bare-hands, (2) woolly-horse-clubbing, and (3) saber-tooth-tiger-scaring-with-fire. Although the children trained in these subjects enjoyed obvious material benefits as a result, some conservative members of the tribe resisted the introduction of these new subjects on religious grounds. But, in due time, many people began to train their children in New Fist's curriculum and the tribe grew increasingly prosperous and secure.

Then conditions changed. An ice age began, and a glacier crept down over the land. The glacier brought with it dirt and gravel that muddied the creeks, and the waters became so dirty that no one could see the fish well enough to grab them. The melting waters from the approaching ice sheet also made the country wetter, and the little woolly horses migrated to drier land. They were replaced by antelopes, who were so shy and speedy that no one could get close enough to club them. Finally, the new dampness in the air caused the saber-tooth tigers to catch pneumonia and die. And the ferocious glacial bears who came down with the advancing ice sheet were not afraid of fire.

The thinkers of the tribe, descendants of New Fist, found a way out of the dilemma. One figured out how to catch fish with a net made from vines. Another invented traps for the antelopes, and a third discovered how to dig pits to catch the bears.

Some thoughtful people began to wonder why these new activities couldn't be taught in the schools. But the elders who controlled the schools claimed that the new skills did not qualify as *education*—they were merely a matter of *training*. Besides, the curriculum was too full of the standard cultural subjects, fish-grabbing, horse-clubbing, and tiger-scaring, to admit new ones. When some radicals argued that the traditional subjects were foolish, the elders said that they taught fish-grabbing not to catch fish but to develop agility, horse-clubbing to develop strength, and tiger-scaring to develop courage. "The essence of true education is timelessness," they announced. "It is something that endures through changing conditions like a solid rock standing squarely and firmly in the middle of a raging torrent. You must know that there are some eternal verities and the saber-tooth curriculum is one of them!" (pp. 43–44).

The Saber-Tooth Curriculum was written in 1939, but its continuing applicability seems to be one of the "eternal verities."

Source: J. Abner Peddiwell (Harold Benjamin), *The Saber-Tooth Curriculum.* Copyright © 1959. Reprinted with permission of the McGraw-Hill Companies. (NOTE: One chapter of this book is reproduced in *Kaleidoscope: Readings in Education*, the companion volume to this text.)

A closed mind is a dying mind.
—EDNA FERBER

■ *two basic oppositions*

educational philosophy: perennialism, progressivism, essentialism, and romanticism. In judging curriculum relevance, all of these matters come into play, because the relevance of a curriculum depends very much on one's basic beliefs about schooling.

At the present time, there are conflicting trends in the academic curriculum, each representing a different philosophy. For example, if one considers the school's primary objective to be the intellectual (or mental) training of students, any curriculum that does not emphasize the mastery of certain subject matter and the training of the mind will be judged as irrelevant. Conversely, if one believes the school should emphasize the development of the "whole child"—the child's emotional and social, as well as intellectual, growth—a curriculum devoted exclusively to English, history, the sciences, mathematics, and foreign languages will be considered inappropriate for many students and thus irrelevant.

What one considers to be a relevant curriculum, then, depends on the philosophical position one takes. At the present time, there are conflicting trends in the academic curriculum, each representing a different philosophy.

In a society as large and pluralistic as the United States, many philosophies and notions of school purpose have committed supporters. How can the schools incorporate in their curricula such diverse ideas of what a school should do? If a certain philosophy is dominant within a given community, the curriculum of the community's schools is likely to reflect that set of beliefs, and those who don't agree will remain dissatisfied. On the other hand, some communities are responding to these diverse philosophical conceptions of the curriculum by providing choice among alternative schools, each with a different curricular emphasis.

PAUSE AND REFLECT

❶ Where do you stand on the tracking issue? Has your own educational background included tracking? How does your background affect where you stand on this issue?

❷ How would you adapt your curriculum to meet the needs of a very diverse group of students?

A Final Word

The rather innocuous word, *curriculum*, and the simple question, "What Is Taught?" contain within them nothing less than the keys to our future. Inevitably, schools will have a curriculum and students will learn it, but the actual *stuff* of the curriculum and how they are encouraged to learn it is the key issue. What knowledge from our past should be represented? What from our vast storehouse of scientific and cultural knowledge will they need? What from our moral heritage will they need to guide themselves and the nation to make the right choices? What form of classroom and school life will encourage the habits of heart and mind that students will need to take up and meet the challenges they face in the world?

Our collective response will lead to a prosperous and noble future or a future of disappointment and decline. What we select for students to learn in our schools will have a profound effect on their individual futures and on the future of our nation. Indeed, given the power and influence of the United States, the impact of our choices will be global, but what does this have to do with you as a future teacher? Plenty! What should be taught? What do students need to know? These questions are, and will continue to be, debated globally at the highest levels of governments, and here in the United States at national, state, and local school board levels. These questions, however, are the special responsibility of teachers, of those who have dedicated their lives to the education of the youth. No small responsibility!

which curriculum for survival?

KEY TERMS

block scheduling (133)

civic learning (civic education) (117)

content standards (109)

cooperative learning (128)

core curriculum (135)

critical thinking (130)

cultural literacy (core knowledge) (136)

curriculum (108)

differentiated instruction (132)

interdisciplinary (integrated) curriculum (127)

looping (133)

multicultural curriculum (135)

phonics (114)

problem solving (130)

subject-matter curriculum (109)

tracking (136)

whole language approach (114)

writing across the curriculum (130)

FOR REFLECTION

❶ In your opinion, should the curriculum emphasize cultural learning common to all Americans, or should it stress the pluralistic nature of our diverse cultural backgrounds? Is it possible to do both?

❷ In your opinion, is the prevalent use of textbooks in the schools a positive or negative influence on teaching and learning? Can you see both the benefits and the dangers? If so, what are they?

❸ What would you do to improve the curriculum of the public schools?

❹ Are there aspects of our current curriculum that you would equate with the *Saber-Tooth Curriculum*? If so, what are they?

FOR FURTHER INFORMATION

PRINT RESOURCES

Elliot W. Eisner, *The Educational Imagination,* 3rd ed. (Upper Saddle River, NJ: Prentice Hall, 2001).

The author presents a stimulating, controversial book regarding forces influencing today's curriculum.

E. D. Hirsch, Jr., *Cultural Literacy: What Every American Needs to Know* (Boston: Houghton Mifflin, 1987).

This provocative treatise asserts that literacy requires the early and continued transmission of specific information—the common knowledge that enables students to make sense of what they read. (See the Core Knowledge Foundation web site at: **http://www.coreknowledge.org**.)

David W. Johnson and Roger T. Johnson, *Learning Together and Alone: Cooperative, Competitive, and Individualistic Learning,* 5th ed. (Boston: Allyn & Bacon/Longman, 1999).

This excellent, comprehensive book was written by two of the leading researchers on cooperative learning.

Richard Rothstein, *The Way We Were? The Myths and Realities of America's Student Achievement* (New York: Twentieth Century Fund Press/Priority Press Publications, 1998).

This analysis of student academic achievement concludes that American students are steadily getting better rather than worse.

Carol Ann Tomlinson, "Differentiating Instruction for Academic Diversity," ed. James M. Cooper, *Classroom Teaching Skills,* 7th ed. (Boston: Houghton Mifflin, 2003).

This chapter guides the reader through the philosophy and strategies for differentiating instruction.

Jon W. Wiles and Joseph C. Bondi. *Curriculum Development: A Guide to Practice,* 6th ed. (Columbus, Ohio: Merrill/Prentice Hall, 2002).

A comprehensive text offering thorough coverage of K–12 curriculum philosophy, curriculum planning, instruction, and curriculum design. It offers separate chapters on developing curriculum in the elementary, middle, and secondary schools.

WEB RESOURCES

American Council on the Teaching of Foreign Languages. Available at: **http://www.actfl.org**.
An executive summary of the national standards for foreign languages can be found at this web site.

Mid-continent Regional Educational Laboratory. Available at: **http://mcrel.org**.
One of ten regional educational laboratories supported by the federal government, this lab has a great set of materials in different subject areas, as well as research reports on effective practice. The web site also offers links to other useful sites.

Special Education and Gifted Education. Available at: **http://www.cec.sped.org**.
This site contains standards for special educators, not for the children they teach.

The following journals and web sites contain many interesting and helpful items for teachers in the respective subject-matter fields. To find both national and state-by-state content standards in the various subject-matter fields, go to *Education World* at **http://www.education-world.com/standards/**.

Art: *Art Education; Arts and Activities, School Arts;* ArtsEdge at the Kennedy Center web site, available at: **http://artsedge.kennedy-center.org/**.

Elementary and early childhood: ERIC Clearinghouse on elementary and early childhood education web site, available at: **http://ericeece.org/**.

English: *English Journal;* ERIC Clearinghouse on reading, English, and communication web site, available at: **http://www.indiana.edu/~eric_rec**; National Council of Teachers of English web site, available at: **http://www.ncte.org**. Includes national standards in English and language arts.

Foreign languages: *Modern Language Journal;* ERIC Clearinghouse on languages and linguistics web site, available at: **http://www.cal.org/ericcll/**; University of Wisconsin Letters and Sciences web site (contains lots of language links), available at: **http://polyglot.lss.wisc.edu/lss/lang/langlink.html**.

Mathematics: *The Mathematics Teacher; School Science and Mathematics;* math forum web site, particularly "Ask Dr. Math," available at: **http://forum.swarthmore.edu/dr.math**; National Council of Teachers of Mathematics, available at: **http://www.nctm.org**. Includes national standards in mathematics.

Music: *Music Educators' Journal;* Music Education Resource Links (MERL) web site, available at: **http://www.cs.uop.edu/~cpiper/musiced.html**.

Physical education: *Journal of Health, Physical Education and Recreation;* American Alliance for Health, Physical Education, Recreation and Dance web site, available at: **http://www.aahperd.org/**. Includes national standards in physical education.

Reading and language arts: *Language Arts, The Reading Teacher;* children's literature web guide, available at: **http://www.ucalgary.ca/~dkbrown/**.

Science: *The Science Teacher, School Science and Mathematics;* Eisenhower National Clearinghouse, available at: **http://www.enc.org**; *Blueprints for Reform: Science, Mathematics, and Technology Education,* available at: **http://project2061.aaas.org**. Includes national science standards.

Social studies: *The Social Studies, Social Education;* history/social studies web site for K–12 teachers, available at: **http://execpc.com/~dboals/boals.html**. National Council for the Social Studies, available at: **http://ncss.org**. Includes national standards in social studies.

Vocational education: *Industrial Education, Journal of Home Economics; Business Education Forum, Business Education Review;* ERIC Clearinghouse on Adult, Career, and Vocational Education web site, available at: **http://ericacve.org/**.

Part Two

Teachers

What exactly do good teachers do, and how do they do it? In recent decades, educators have been developing a deeper understanding of what makes a teacher effective. There are many new teaching methods, new technologies, and new approaches to curriculum. In this section, we aim to give you insights into the issues, challenges, and opportunities for teachers.

What Makes a Teacher Effective?

5

Chapter Preview Effective teaching is much more than an intuitive process. A teacher must continually make decisions and act on those decisions. To do this effectively, the teacher must have *knowledge,* both theoretical knowledge about learning and human behavior and specific knowledge about the subject matter to be taught. A teacher also must demonstrate a repertoire of teaching *skills* that are believed to facilitate student learning and must display *attitudes* that foster learning and genuine human relationships.

This chapter emphasizes that:

- Teachers are required to make many decisions as they plan for instruction, implement teaching strategies, and evaluate outcomes of their planning and strategies.

- Four major types of teacher attitudes affect teaching behavior: (1) attitude toward self, (2) attitude toward children, (3) attitude toward peers and parents, and (4) attitude toward the subject matter.

- A teacher should have an intimate knowledge of the subject matter being taught, both the instructional content and the discipline from which it derives.

- To be able to recognize and interpret classroom events appropriately, a teacher should be familiar with theoretical knowledge and research about learning and human behavior.

- Effective teachers demonstrate a repertoire of teaching skills that enable them to meet the different needs of their students. Research has identified a number of these skills in, to name a few areas, classroom management, effective questioning, and planning techniques.

We once knew a teacher who was described as having not twenty years of experience but one year's experience twenty times. The message was that this teacher had stopped growing and developing as a professional after the first year. As someone just starting in your teaching career, this may seem like a remote possibility. After all, there's so much that you know you don't know, and you're eager to learn as much as you can. It is relatively easy, however, to fall into comfortable patterns of teaching, especially after you have gained a few years of experience.

How can you avoid this complacency and stagnation? One way is to maintain your curiosity and develop habits of inquiry and reflection. More and more teacher educators are coming to believe that although it is important to prepare beginning teachers for initial practice, it is even more important to help them develop the attitudes and skills to become lifelong students of teaching. Ideally, rather than relying on authority, impulse, or unexamined previous practice, teachers will continually examine and evaluate their attitudes, practices, effectiveness, and accomplishments. This process of examination and evaluation is often called **reflective teaching.** Reflective teachers ask themselves such questions as, "What am I doing and why?", "How can I better meet my students' needs?", "What are some alternative learning activities to achieve these objectives?", "How could I have encouraged more involvement or learning on the part of the students?" Even when lessons go well, reflective teachers analyze the lesson to determine what went well and why, and how else things might have been done.

■ *developing the habit of reflection*

Developing the habits of inquiry and reflection should begin in the teacher education program. Experiences with schools, teachers, and students will give you many opportunities to reflect on what has occurred. You can use journal writing, observation instruments, simulations, or videotaping to help you examine teaching, learning, and the contexts in which they occur. Comparing your perspectives with those of classmates, professors, and school personnel will broaden your interpretations and give you new insights. As you reflect on your experiences, you will come to distrust simplistic answers and explanations. Nuances and subtleties will start to become clear, and situations that once seemed simple will reveal their complexities. You are likely to encounter and think about moral and ethical issues.

Teachers make moral and ethical decisions every day. When teachers decide how they treat students and others, they make ethical decisions. When they elect to create a classroom climate that fosters trust, safety, and cooperation, they make ethical decisions. When certain examples from history or literature are selected for study, teachers make ethical decisions. In other words, you cannot teach without making ethical decisions. The chapter entitled "What Are the Ethical and Legal Issues Facing Teachers?" discusses this topic in greater detail, but we hope you will study and reflect upon the cases we present throughout this book that reflect moral or ethical issues. By practicing reflective teaching, you will grow and develop as an effective, professional teacher.

Framework for Professional Practice

Visit this chapter of the web site to link to more information about the INTASC standards.

In recent years, there have been several attempts to identify what effective teachers should know and be able to do. The Interstate New Teachers Assessment and Support Consortium (INTASC), which is discussed in more detail in the chapter entitled "What Does It Mean to Be a Professional?", has identified

Planning is an essential skill for any teacher.
(© Frank Siteman/PhotoEdit)

the knowledge, dispositions, and performances that a beginning teacher should possess. These INTASC standards are based on the standards that the National Board for Professional Teaching Standards (also discussed in the "What Does It Mean to Be a Professional?" chapter) has developed for experienced, accomplished teachers. (The web site for the INTASC standards is listed at the end of the chapter.) Many states are working in concert with INTASC to implement the standards as part of the states' teacher licensing requirements.

> *The mediocre teacher tells. The good teacher explains. The superior teacher demonstrates. The great teacher inspires.*
> —WILLIAM ARTHUR WARD

Danielson's Framework for Teaching

domains of teaching responsibilities

Charlotte Danielson has also attempted to define what an accomplished teacher does.[1] Danielson's Framework for Teaching lays out the various areas of competence in which professional teachers need to develop expertise. Danielson organizes the complex activity of teaching into twenty-two components, which are then clustered into four domains of teaching responsibility: (1) planning and preparation, (2) the classroom environment, (3) instruction, and (4) professional responsibilities. A brief review of each of these domains will provide you with a road map of the skills and competencies new teachers need to develop.

Domain 1: Planning and Preparation   How does a teacher design instruction and organize the content of what students are expected to learn? To be effective in this domain, teachers need to demonstrate that they know their content, pedagogy for teaching that content, their students, how to select instructional goals, what resources they have available to them, how to design coherent instruction, and how to assess student learning.

■ **Domain 2: The Classroom Environment** Domain 2 consists of the interactions occurring in a classroom that are non-instructional. Effective teachers create an environment of respect and rapport among the students and with the teacher, establish a culture for learning, manage classroom procedures and student behavior, and efficiently organize the physical space.

■ **Domain 3: Instruction** This domain constitutes the core of teaching—the engagement of students in learning content. To be effective here, a teacher needs to communicate clearly and accurately, use appropriate questioning and discussion techniques, engage students in learning, provide feedback to students, and demonstrate flexibility and responsiveness.

■ **Domain 4: Professional Responsibilities** This domain addresses the wide range of teacher responsibilities outside the classroom. They include reflecting on teaching, maintaining accurate records, communicating with families, contributing to the school and district, growing and developing professionally, and showing professionalism. Teachers who demonstrate these competencies are seen as true professionals and are highly valued by their colleagues and administrators.

This framework for professional practice provides several benefits. First, the framework offers the teaching profession a shared vocabulary as a way of talking about excellent teaching. Second, it assists novice teachers by providing a roadmap to excellence in professional practice. Third, the framework provides a structure for discussions among teachers and sharpens the focus for professional development. Lastly, it communicates to the larger community the array of competencies needed to be an effective teacher.

PAUSE AND REFLECT

❶ In which of these four domains do you feel most confident about your skills? Which domains do you need to work on?

This chapter will discuss some basic characteristics of effective teachers that are part of Danielson's framework. We particularly emphasize the role of the teacher as a reflective decision maker. We begin with a case study of a new teacher who faces problems that many classroom veterans will find familiar. We will then take a critical look at the many teaching decisions that she had to make.

■ *the case of Carol Landis*

CASE STUDY
Carol Landis/ A Case of Classroom Decision Making

As an example of how ordinary teaching situations can lead to useful reflections about effective teaching, consider the case of Carol Landis. Carol is beginning her first year of teaching. She prepared to be a high school social studies teacher, graduated, and accepted a job in her own community, a small city in the Northwest. Most of her students come from solidly blue-collar, working-class backgrounds.

Carol has been assigned three periods of world geography and two periods of American history. We will join her as she prepares the first lesson of a new unit in world geography.

Carol plans to require her ninth-graders to work in groups to prepare panel discussions about a country of their choice. She wants the groups to research the relationships among the geography, political history, and culture of a country and share what they find in panel discussions with the rest of the class. Carol sets these goals for her students: that they work together in groups and that they make effective oral presentations of their research.

■ *Carol's questions*

When planning how to present the assignment to her classes, Carol has many questions. Do these students know how to use the library? If not, will she need to provide directions for using reference materials? Maybe the librarian has already done this, and they will just need a review. Do these students know what *culture* means or understand general concepts that will help them look for relationships among culture, history, and geography? What background do they need before they start researching a specific country? And do these students know how to work in groups? Have they ever participated in a panel discussion? In planning how to help her students complete this assignment, Carol bases her decisions on what she thinks she knows about them as learners.

Although Carol has already planned this assignment to meet her state's curriculum standards in social studies, she is concerned about whether the books in her room and the library will provide the information her students need. What other resources are available? She knows that other teachers have back issues of *National Geographic,* for example. Maybe she could help students use the World Wide Web to access hypertext links that would tie together geography, political history, and culture for their respective countries.

In addition to the panel discussions, Carol has considered having each student submit a written report. For this first research assignment, however, she decides that an oral presentation by the group is appropriate. Later, she will work with the classes on report writing. In the beginning, she wants her students to enjoy her classes, to feel a part of a group, and to get to know one another, and Carol prefers listening to her students to grading written reports anyway, so this assignment fits her style of teaching.

■ *incident with Tom*

Despite her planning, when Carol reflects on her second-period class after the first day of library research, she wonders what went wrong. One group argued the whole period and never did select a country. Maybe she should have assigned groups and not let students choose their own partners. She tried to ignore the group, believing they should work out their own differences and come to a group decision. But what if they never work together? She noticed that another group was completely dominated by one of the top students. He decided what country they would research, he assigned the topics, and he told the others where to look for information. When Carol urged the other members to share equally in the group decisions, they asserted, "Tom always gets A's. We don't mind if he tells us what to do." Carol didn't know how to respond to their concern for grades without insulting Tom, so she said nothing.

Later in the period, Tom asked her what religion predominated in Indonesia. Carol wasn't sure but was afraid to admit her lack of information, so she told him, "Just look it up." Tom responded, "So you don't know either?" Carol testily told Tom that she was not his personal encyclopedia. Now she wonders if she overreacted. Maybe she should have admitted she didn't know. Was Tom challenging her authority, or was he just reacting to the sharp tone in her order to look it up? Did she turn Tom and his group against her?

Carol also wonders whether the other groups worked productively. She spent so much time watching the arguing group and Tom's group that she didn't have time to notice whether the chatter from the other groups was work or play. Maybe it didn't hurt to let the other groups have some fun today, anyway. She can direct her attention to them tomorrow.

There is so much to watch and monitor when students work in groups, Carol realizes. Many questions arise, such as, "Where do I find this?", "Mr. Shaw won't lend me his magazines; what do I do now?", "This library stinks. Why do we have to do this assignment anyway?", and even, "Miss Landis, what did you do this weekend?" Carol wonders if she will ever learn to field all her students' questions and comments and distinguish the words on the surface from the real messages. She also worries about what to do about Ron, who started reading a novel about life in Siberian concentration camps. Carol thinks it is the only book she has ever seen him read. But it won't help his group do their project on Kenya.

Maybe this assignment wasn't such a good idea in the first place, Carol thinks, or maybe she just wasn't up to working with her classes in groups. The stares from the librarian and the study hall teacher indicated that they didn't think she could handle her classes, and Carol hasn't even thought about how she will grade her students' panel discussions. Just thinking about it all exhausts her. How will she ever get through another day with that second-period class?

◼ *Carol's frustrations*

The Teacher as a Reflective Decision Maker

◼ *Carol as decision maker*

Reflect on your own decision-making skills with the image in this section of your CD-ROM.

We present Carol's case to illustrate that the teacher's role can be described as one of a reflective *decision maker*. Indeed, some educational researchers have identified skill in decision making as the most important teaching skill. Some decisions are made as teachers quietly deliberate curricular and instructional goals; many more must be made almost instantaneously as teachers and students interact. Let's look at some of the particular decisions that Carol made or will make, dividing them into three basic stages: planning, implementing, and evaluating.

◼ *Planning Decisions*

Carol wants her students to understand the relationships among geography, history, and culture. But what exactly does she want them to know about these relationships? She must decide the particular kinds of understanding she wants her students to achieve, and this decision affects her choice of teaching techniques.

From a variety of possible techniques, she has chosen independent group work. She has also decided that a panel discussion will provide evidence of her students' learning. These decisions reflect Carol's personal preferences, her goals for her students' learning, and her skills in methods of evaluating their learning. Her decisions are also based on a series of judgments about her students' ability to do research, work in groups, and present panel discussions, as well as on judgments about how long they will need to work together and what resources they will need. Carol may have made some plans for what to do in case her judgments turned out to be wrong, and she needed to adapt her lesson.

Differences Between Expert and Novice Teachers

A number of educational researchers have tried to identify expert and experienced teachers and compare them with novice teachers. These studies have identified various ways in which novice and expert teachers differ.

We can think of an expert teacher as similar to an expert chess player. Expert chess players quickly spot trouble areas in any chessboard pattern; likewise, expert teachers quickly recognize trouble spots in a classroom setting. Experts in chess or teaching draw on their hours of experience to build a repertoire of recognizable patterns. In one experiment, expert and novice teachers were asked to look at a photograph of a classroom and identify the class activity. Experts were better able to "read" the classroom, making inferences about what was happening in the picture. When observed in action, expert teachers also show greater ability to gather information in a short time for multiple purposes. For example, an expert teacher may be able to accomplish many tasks in an opening review session: gather attendance information, identify who did or did not do the homework, and locate students needing help with the next lesson.

In comparison, novice teachers described the surface characteristics of the classroom pictures they saw. And when presented with descriptions of student problems, the novices relied again on the literal features of the problems to suggest solutions. Their analyses did not correspond with the higher-order classifications used by expert teachers.

Experts differed from novices in their approaches to planning as well. In a simulated task of planning, experts focused on learning what students already knew about the subject matter to be learned, while novices planned to ask students where they were in their textbooks and then present a review of important concepts. In other words, experts planned to gather information from the students, whereas novices planned to give information to them.

The research suggests that experts in any field demonstrate skill in planning and in classifying problems and formulating solutions. This is no less true for teachers: the expert teacher shows problem-solving skills like those of other experts, whether in chess, bridge, or physics. The studies also indicate that the process of moving from novice to expert teacher takes considerable time because extensive experience is necessary to develop enough episodic knowledge to interpret information about classrooms.

Sources: David C. Berliner, "Expertise: The Wonder of Exemplary Performances." In *Creating Powerful Thinking in Teachers and Students*, ed. J. N. Mangiere and C. C. Block (Fort Worth, TX: Harcourt Brace College Publishers, 1994), pp. 161–186; Greta Morine-Dershimer, "Instructional Planning." In *Classroom Teaching Skills*, 7th ed., ed. J. M. Cooper (Boston: Houghton Mifflin, 2003), pp. 31–32.

▇ *Implementing Decisions*

Carol, like most teachers, must make many of her decisions almost instantly, as she adapts her teaching to changing classroom conditions. As Carol teaches this lesson or series of lessons, she has to decide when and how to intervene with some of her groups, whether to allow Ron to continue reading a novel, and what responses to make to students' questions.

▇ *Evaluating Decisions*

After the first day's library work, Carol reflects on her interactions with the students, facing decisions about what adjustments to make in her strategies for the next day. As the groups continue to work, she will also face decisions about how to evaluate the impact of her planning and instruction on her students' learning.

In each of these planning, implementing, and evaluating stages of instructional decision making, Carol chooses among alternative concepts her students could learn, approaches to help them learn the concepts, ways to manage the classroom to encourage their learning, and ways to measure their learning. Could her decisions improve with more adequate knowledge, skills, and attitudes?

Aspects of Reflective Decision Making

In the rest of this chapter, we will explore the areas of competence that help teachers make more effective decisions. We, along with many other educators, believe that to be effective decision makers, elementary and secondary school teachers need to have attitudes, knowledge, and skills essential to the teaching profession. Teachers must ask themselves not only, "What am I going to teach?", but also "What should my students be learning?", "How can I help them learn it?", and "Why is it important?" To answer these questions, teachers must be familiar with children and their developmental stages. They must know something about events occurring outside the classroom and about what society requires from the young. They must have enough command of the subject they teach to be able to distinguish what is peripheral from what is central. They must have a philosophy of education that guides them in their role as teacher. They must know something about how human beings learn and about how to create environments that promote learning.

areas of teaching competence

What are the specialized skills and attributes of the effective instructional decision maker? The five areas of competence that we consider essential for a teacher are the following:

1. Attitudes that foster learning and genuine human relationships

2. Knowledge of the subject matter to be taught

3. Theoretical knowledge about learning and human behavior

4. Personal practical knowledge

5. Skills of teaching that promote student learning

Teachers draw on their competence in these five areas to inform the many decisions they make as they plan instruction and as they spontaneously interact with the students in their classes. Figure 5.1 indicates the relationship of these areas of competence to the process of instructional decision making. In the remainder of this chapter, we will examine these areas of competence, now and then referring to the instructional decisions that Carol made and the attitudes, knowledge, and skills influencing her decisions.

What Attitudes Does the Effective Teacher Possess?

Many people believe that the teacher's personality is the most critical factor in successful teaching. If teachers have warmth, empathy, sensitivity, enthusiasm, and humor, they are much more likely to be successful than if they lack these characteristics. In fact, many people argue that without these attributes, an individual is unlikely to be a good teacher.

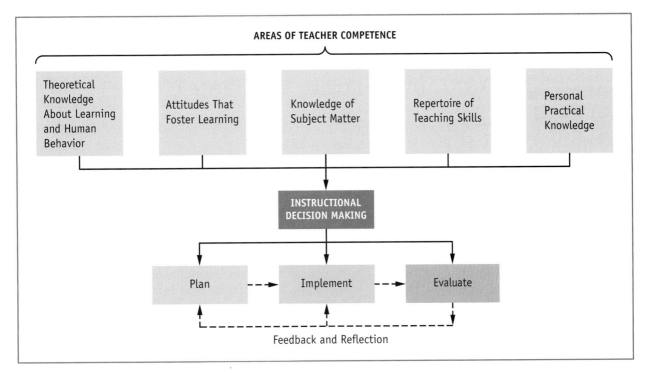

Figure 5.1
Relationship of Teacher-Competence Areas to Process of Instructional Decision Making
Source: James M. Cooper (ed.), "The Teacher as a Reflective Decision Maker," in *Classroom Teaching Skills*, 7th ed. Copyright © 2003 by Houghton Mifflin Company. Reprinted with permission.

For years, educational researchers sought to isolate the characteristics essential to good teachers. In one comprehensive study, the researcher concluded that effective teachers are fair, democratic, responsive, understanding, kindly, stimulating, original, alert, attractive, responsible, steady, poised, and confident. Ineffective teachers were described as partial, autocratic, aloof, restricted, harsh, dull, stereotyped, apathetic, unimpressive, evasive, erratic, excitable, and uncertain.[2]

Unfortunately, this information is not very useful. After all, what human interaction wouldn't be improved if the participants possessed only positive traits? Two researchers, summarizing fifty years of research on teachers' personalities and characteristics, conclude, "Despite the critical importance of the problem and a half-century of prodigious research effort, very little is known for certain about the nature and measurement of teacher personality, about the relation between teacher personality and teaching effectiveness."[3]

■ *definition of attitudes*

A person's *attitudes,* or predispositions to act in a positive or negative way toward people, ideas, and events, are a fundamental dimension of his or her personality. Although the relationship between general personality traits and teacher effectiveness has proven elusive, almost all educators are convinced of the importance of teacher attitudes in the teaching process. Attitudes have a direct but often unrecognized effect on our behavior in that they determine the ways we view ourselves and interact with others.

■ *four categories of teacher attitudes*

We believe four major categories of attitudes affect teaching behavior: (1) the teacher's attitude toward self, (2) the teacher's attitudes toward children and the relationship between self and children, (3) the teacher's attitudes toward peers and pupils' parents, and (4) the teacher's attitude toward the subject matter.

ANNE MANSFIELD SULLIVAN (1866–1936)

The proof is in the pupil. In this case, Helen Keller, a blind and deaf pupil, was a terror. Wily and mean, Helen was also animal-like. Nevertheless, her teacher, Anne Sullivan, enabled her to become an international celebrity.

Sullivan pioneered the teaching of individuals without sight and without hearing. Today we speak of a *deaf culture,* but this term was not used in the era of Anne Sullivan. "Teacher," as Helen always called her, is credited with making it possible to reach students who were thought to have mental retardation.

The daughter of Irish immigrants, Sullivan was born in Feeding Hills, Mass., on April 14, 1866 and entered the almshouse at eight when her mother died and her father abandoned her and her brother. Half-blind herself, she went to the Perkins School for the Blind in Boston at age fourteen without a toothbrush, hat, or coat; her only possessions were a shirt and stockings tied in a bundle.

At age twenty-one, Sullivan took a job offered by the Keller family in Tuscumbia, Ala., to teach the Kellers' daughter, Helen. Helen Keller was an angry and frustrated child, but she was not stupid. Sullivan saw this and began her assault on Helen's locked mind. Within a month, she made contact with Helen in the now famous pump story, immortalized in the drama *The Miracle Worker.* Sullivan fingerspelled words into Helen's hand, each word suiting an action. Finally, Helen, feeling water over her hand, realized the connection between word and object. She had broken the code and realized that everything had a name.

Sullivan's methods were practical. She taught Helen to play through games and exercises, stimulating her to ask the names of the motions. She kept a menagerie of animals for Helen to help her understand movement. She progressed to abstractions like peace and God as soon as her pupil was ready.

Sullivan wanted to make Helen as normal as possible, giving her every experience she could. She worked at teaching her to sit, stand, and walk properly. As soon as Helen could distinguish between right and wrong, "Teacher" sent her to bed for misdeeds. Laziness, carelessness, untidiness, and procrastination were dealt with by ingenuity, humor, and light sarcasm.

Helen used the manual alphabet for three years before she began to speak. When Helen was nine, Sullivan was rewarded with the words "I am not dumb now." It was one of the most dramatic achievements in the history of teaching.

Sullivan's great discovery was that a child should not be taught each word separately by a separate definition but instead should be given endless repetition of language he or she does not understand all day long. Sullivan continually spelled words into Helen's hand to mimic the way a hearing child in the cradle absorbs words. This method had never before been put into practice in the education of a deaf child, especially a deaf-blind one.

When Helen attended a school for deaf pupils in New York, Annie Sullivan went along. At Cambridge School and Radcliffe College, Sullivan attended classes, interpreting instruction and looking up words for Helen. She made herself eye and ear to Helen and supplied knowledge to a starving mind as she fired her pupil's drive to study hard. After college, Sullivan accompanied Helen on worldwide lecture tours as Helen became a famous author and personality.

Extraordinarily close, teacher and pupil spent much of their lives together. The name "Teacher" has been enriched by Annie Sullivan's dedicated life, persistent high standards, and creative instruction.

 Visit the web site for more information about Anne Mansfield Sullivan.

Source: Marilyn Ryan.

The Teacher's Attitude Toward Self: Self-Understanding

If teachers are to help students have meaningful experiences, develop their aptitudes and abilities, face their inner difficulties, and accept themselves as people, they need to know and understand those students. Before teachers can do that, however, they must work at knowing and understanding themselves. Empirical evidence from psychology indicates that people who deny or are unable to cope with their own emotions are unlikely to be capable of respecting and dealing with others' feelings.

recognize own needs as well as students'

For example, unless teachers recognize their own needs and anxieties, they will be unlikely to understand and empathize with their students' needs or expressions of anxiety. They may not recognize that students' inabilities to learn, inattentiveness, impudence, or irritability may be the result of anxiety. Teachers also need to recognize that their own anxieties may make them irritable, causing the students in turn to feel anxious and to show similar symptoms.

Ways to Achieve Self-Understanding   How can one achieve understanding of self and, after achieving it, accept it? A number of potential resources can help promote self-understanding. For example, books by sensitive and compassionate people who have made progress in their own struggles to know themselves can be a valuable aid in self-examination. For prospective teachers, such books might include Sylvia Ashton-Warner's *Teacher,* an account of her teaching experience in a Maori infant school in New Zealand; Tracy Kidder's *Among Schoolchildren;* Herbert Kohl's *36 Children;* and Lisa Delpit's *Other People's Children.*

books about teachers

Another method is **participant observation,** the process of observing a class and recording what you hear, see, and feel as you observe. You then compare your record with the records of other observers. This experience may show you that what you notice in any given situation is determined largely by habits of thought that you take for granted. It may also show that your "objective" perceptions are often projections of your own subjective state, and so it may tell you more about yourself than about the people you have observed.

I touch the future. I teach.

—Christa McAuliffe

observing in classrooms

self-examination

We urge you to regard self-examination as a serious commitment and to undertake it, *as a prospective teacher,* in an effort to make a good decision about whether to teach and to become the best teacher you are capable of becoming.

Carol's self-concept

Remember Carol's attitude toward Tom when he asked for information she didn't have, and recall her seeming "live and let live" attitude toward the argumentative group and the student reading a novel. What may these attitudes about student behaviors indicate about Carol's self-concept? Is she afraid to admit limitations in her knowledge? Does she hesitate to discipline off-task behavior because she thinks her students will no longer like her? How strong is her need for approval? Maybe Carol overreacts to Tom's request for information because she is insecure with the role of teacher and feels threatened by his authority among his peers. Although Carol's case does not give enough information to answer these questions, we can say with confidence that her self-concept will influence her behavior toward her students. As Carol develops a realistic understanding of herself and her needs and anxieties, she will change her attitudes toward her students and improve her relationship with them.

What Would You Do?

1. You are a woman, a beginning teacher in a ninth-grade English course. As the first semester proceeds, you realize that one of your students, Fred, has a crush on you. He is always volunteering to help you pass out papers, and he lingers after class each day to talk to you. He finds out your home address and comes to visit you one Saturday morning. His actions are becoming obvious to the other students, who are starting to kid him about his infatuation. *What would you do?*

2. You are generally recognized as one of the most popular teachers in your school. The students look on you as a friend who can be trusted, and you have told them that if they ever have problems, school-related or personal, they should feel free to come to you. One day Maryanne, a junior in one of your classes, seeks you out. Close to hysteria, she tells you she is ten weeks pregnant. You are the first person she has told. She begs you for advice but insists you do not tell her parents. *What would you do?*

3. You are a fourth-grade teacher. Until recently, you have been quite comfortable in your class of twenty-three children. About three weeks ago, you had to speak to Debbie. Although she is your brightest student, she was continually talking when you were trying to address the class. Since then she has been as cool as ice to you, and you recently discovered a nasty drawing in your desk drawer that was supposed to be you. *What would you do?*

4. You are a white teacher in a somewhat racially tense school. There are seven African-American students in one of your classes. Because you fear alienating the African Americans and being accused of prejudice, you make special efforts to treat them fairly. One day, three of your white students come to see you and accuse you of coddling the African Americans and discriminating against whites. *What would you do?*

5. You teach in a school that uses a letter grading system. You have assigned your students a term paper. You know that one student has spent hours and hours on his report, but its quality is quite poor. The student has already expressed his hope that you will take effort into account when grading the reports. *What would you do?*

■ *The Teacher's Attitude Toward Children*

Children are sensitive observers of adult behavior, and they often see, and become preoccupied with, aspects of the teacher's attitude toward them of which the teacher may be unaware. Consider how a teacher's effectiveness might be reduced by these feelings or attitudes toward students:

■ *negative attitudes*

- A strong dislike for particular pupils and obvious fondness for others

- Biases toward or against particular ethnic groups

- A bias toward certain kinds of student behavior such as docility or inquisitiveness

- An uneasiness in working with children who have disabilities

Few teachers are entirely free of negative attitudes at the outset, and self-awareness can be the crucial factor distinguishing a teacher who is able to control and change these attitudes. Thus, it is important that prospective teachers confront their own attitudes early on, perhaps through case studies, group discussions, role playing, or behavioral records of teaching experiences. When we become aware of our attitudes, we can often control our behavior better, but even then change is neither easy nor automatic. It is difficult to admit to feelings and attitudes that might be considered inappropriate or unprofessional. For example, most teachers would like to believe that they like all their students equally, but this is almost never the case. You will have some students you find charming and others who rub you the wrong way. The important thing is that teachers treat students fairly, which usually means treating them differently. Each child has different needs, and the best way to address these needs equitably is to address them uniquely, including taking into account such factors as race, ethnicity, and gender. As one educator puts it, "If teachers pretend not to see students' racial and ethnic differences, they really do not see the students at all and are limited in their ability to meet their educational needs."[4] The discussion on differentiating instruction in the chapter entitled "What Is Taught?" addresses this issue of treating students differently.

■ *treat students fairly*

■ Teacher Expectations   In general, a teacher's expectation that *all* students can succeed seems to make a difference in students' achievement. As a teacher, you need to believe that all your students are capable of high academic achievement and base your beliefs and behavior on the needs, abilities, and aspirations of each individual student.

■ *cultivating positive attitudes*

Teachers do form expectations about a student's performance, and these expectations seem to relate to the student's achievement. The source of a teacher's expectations may vary: a student's social class, race, or gender; information from previous teachers; test scores; or family background information. Research indicates that some teachers expect certain behaviors from students on the basis of stereotypes that they have about particular racial, ethnic, or socioeconomic groups.[5] For example, Asian-American students may be encouraged to study mathematics or science because teachers believe they are "good" in those subjects, or teachers may expect more from middle-class students than from lower-class students. Often teachers do not recognize these attitudes and beliefs but communicate them nevertheless in both overt and subtle ways, including the use of praise or criticism to guide a student's performance.[6]

Reflect on a teacher expectations with the image in this section of your CD-ROM.

If a teacher expects a student or group of students to behave in a certain way, the teacher's attitude may serve as a **self-fulfilling prophecy**—that is, the

■ *self-fulfilling prophecies*

PEANUTS reprinted by permission of United Feature Syndicate, Inc.

A master can tell you what he expects of you. A teacher, though, awakens your own expectations.

—PATRICIA NEAL (ACTRESS)

students may behave in the predicted manner in response to the teacher's attitude and not as a result of the other factors on which the teacher's expectations are based. Thomas Good and Jere Brophy have suggested a process by which teachers' expectations may encourage certain levels of achievement.[7]

First, the teacher forms expectations of specific behavior and achievement for individual students. Then the teacher's behavior toward these students differs according to the expectations. The students perceive the teacher's expectations from how they are treated; this perception affects their self-concept, motivation to achieve, and aspiration to excel. Over time, students of whom much is expected will perform well, and students of whom little is expected will perform poorly. Thus, the result seems to justify the original expectation and fulfill the teacher's unspoken prophecy. The process is not automatic; teachers' expectations are not always fulfilled, but research indicates that teachers can influence which children do or do not achieve in the classroom.

PAUSE AND REFLECT

1 Can you think of any examples of where a teacher's expectations led to a self-fulfilling prophecy? Describe the circumstances.

2 What attitudes do you possess that you think will have either positive and potentially negative effects on student learning?

3 Do you have negative feelings or expectations about any group or type of people? Can you identify the basis of those feelings? Do you want to change them? If so, how might you try?

■ The Teacher's Attitude Toward Peers and Parents

Much of what we have already said about teachers' attitudes toward themselves and children also applies to their attitudes toward peers and parents. Some attitudes enhance a teacher's effectiveness, and others detract from it.

■ *problems with authority*

Authority/Collaboration One source of conflict may be the teacher's attitude toward those who represent authority (ordinarily administrators but, for prospective teachers, the university supervisor or cooperating teacher). Teachers may find it hard to be themselves while dealing with people who outrank them in position or prestige. Sometimes teachers find they yield too readily to demands from those in authority, and as a result they feel guilty about complying rather than standing on their own convictions. When this occurs, the result is often a continuing undercurrent of resentment toward the person in authority.

Visit this chapter of the web site to link to more information about working with students' families.

If teachers can assume a role of collaboration with those in authority, seeing themselves as part of a valuable partnership in the enterprise of education, they may be able to overcome any predispositions to hostility or any anxiety unwarranted by reality. Resentment of those in authority only prevents communication and understanding.

■ *need for recognition*

Competition/Cooperation Some teachers develop a strong drive to compete with other teachers for recognition from both authority figures and students. They try to have the best lesson plans, to be the "most popular teacher," or to maintain the friendliest relationship with the administration. Such teach-

How Do Teachers Treat Low Achievers?

Researchers have not definitely established why some teachers treat students they perceive as high and low achievers differently, but observations of many classroom teachers reveal that they often behave differently toward these two groups of students. Good and Brophy have summarized these differences:

1. Teachers wait less time for lows to answer a question.

2. Teachers give lows answers or call on someone else for the answer instead of giving clues or providing additional opportunities to respond.

3. Teachers reward lows for inappropriate behaviors or incorrect answers.

4. Lows are more often criticized for failure.

5. Lows are praised less frequently for success than highs.

6. Lows may not receive feedback for public responses.

7. Generally, teachers interact less often with lows, paying less attention to them.

8. Teachers call on lows less often for answers to questions.

9. Teachers seat lows farther from the teacher.

10. Less is demanded from lows.

11. Lows receive more private than public interactions; their activities are more closely monitored and structured.

12. When teachers grade tests and assignments, they give highs but not lows the benefit of the doubt in borderline cases.

13. Lows experience fewer friendly interactions, including fewer smiles and other nonverbal signs of support.

14. Lows receive shorter and less informative feedback to their questions.

15. Teachers make less eye contact and respond less attentively to lows.

16. Teachers make less use of effective but time-consuming instructional methods with lows when time is limited.

17. There is less acceptance and use of lows' ideas.

18. Lows are exposed to an impoverished curriculum.

As a teacher, you should make it a point to reflect on your own behavior toward low and high achievers, making sure that you are treating all your students fairly.

Source: "How Do Teachers Treat High or Low Achievers?" From Thomas L. Good and Jere E. Brophy, *Looking in Classrooms*, 8th ed. Published by Allyn & Bacon, Boston, MA. Copyright © 2000 by Pearson Education. Adapted by permission of the publisher.

ers are striving to be recognized and rewarded. As a result of this attitude, they sometimes cut themselves off from much-needed help and severely limit their ability to be of help to others. Carol Landis has taken an important first step by enlisting the help of other teachers to get the necessary resources for her students. For the benefit of staff and students, teachers need to cooperate and share ideas.

▪ *lack of tolerance*   ▪ **Superiority and Prejudice/Acceptance**   One attitude that never fails to cause trouble for teachers is a feeling of superiority to other teachers or parents of students. They may feel intellectually superior to colleagues, socially superior to students' parents, or both. Some teachers simply have little tolerance for

*Teacher enthusiasm is
usually contagious.*
(© Elizabeth Crews)

people who differ from them in values, cultural background, or economic status, and, as a result, they treat others with disdain and contempt rather than patience and respect. Again, effective teachers—those who work well with colleagues and parents to empower children to achieve—show attitudes of acceptance. In their dealings with other teachers and parents, teachers should be real or genuine, value other people as worthy in their own right, and show empathy.

■ *The Teacher's Attitude Toward the Subject Matter*

■ *must feel enthusiasm*

This section is short because our message is simple: it is most important that whatever subject matter you teach, you feel *enthusiasm* for it. Just as students usually can discern the teacher's attitude toward them, they are also very sensitive to the teacher's attitude toward the subject matter. One of the most striking characteristics of the excellent teacher is enthusiasm for what she or he is teaching. The bored teacher conveys boredom to the students—and who can blame them for failing to get excited if the teacher, who knows more about the subject than they do, doesn't find it engaging?

Some teachers find it difficult to feel enthusiasm for a curriculum they haven't constructed themselves, don't identify with, or don't want to teach. The surest way to guarantee that teachers are enthusiastic about what they are teaching is to allow them to teach what they are enthusiastic about. We do not mean this as a mere play on words. We would rather see an enthusiastic teacher teaching a minor historical topic than an uninspired teacher teaching Shakespeare. As one student put it, "There is nothing worse than sitting in a lesson knowing full well that the teacher is dying to get rid of you and rush back to the staff room to have a cup of coffee." Unfortunately, as more and more states adopt learning standards for students, the latitude that teachers once had to choose content is being greatly curtailed. States expect teachers to teach to the standards, and the high-stakes assessment tests given to students exert considerable pressure on teachers to be certain they "cover the content" contained on the assessments. If you have to teach something you would rather not, try to develop a positive attitude toward the subject. Enthusiasm: if the teacher has it, life in the classroom can be exciting; if it is missing, there is little hope that students will learn much of significance.

PAUSE AND REFLECT

1 Do you have any concerns about your attitudes toward students' parents, school administrators, or other teachers? If you do, what can you do now to improve your attitudes?

2 Can you think of any ways that you, as a teacher, might be able to work up more enthusiasm for a topic that does not, at first, seem very interesting?

3 If you begin to lose your enthusiasm about a certain subject after you have taught it for a few years, what are some ways you might be able to rekindle your interest?

What Subject-Matter Knowledge Does the Effective Teacher Need?

Very simply, prospective teachers need to understand the content of the subjects they teach, as well as the methods of teaching the specific content. Three important components contribute to a teacher's content knowledge. First, teachers need to understand the subjects they teach well enough to analyze and convey their elements, logic, possible uses, and social biases—that is, teachers need to understand the **structure of the** subjects they teach. They primarily learn this content in subject-matter courses they take in college. In the case of Carol Landis, she had learned about social studies topics including history and geography in her college courses.

curriculum content

Second, the teacher must also understand the content of the school curriculum that pupils are expected to know. Unfortunately, most college courses in the specific disciplines don't prepare prospective teachers to actually teach the knowledge that students are expected to learn. Much of what prospective teachers learn from their study of the academic disciplines is not taught to children and so is not directly applicable to teaching. This is particularly true for elementary school teachers, who are called on to teach content that is rarely taught in universities. For example, a mathematics major preparing to teach elementary school may never have occasion to use differential equations or calculus in the content she or he teaches to elementary-age children. Thus, although studying and understanding specific disciplines is crucial, it is not sufficient for effective teaching. A teacher must also study the actual curriculum taught in his or her school. Carol Landis, for example, worked to make her group project contribute to her students' ability to meet their district's standards in social studies. A third type of knowledge shown by effective teachers is **pedagogical content knowledge,** the knowledge that bridges content knowledge and pedagogy. Pedagogical content knowledge represents the "blending of content and pedagogy into an understanding of how particular topics, problems, or issues are organized,

(margin notes)
structure of the discipline
curriculum content
pedagogical content knowledge

POLICY MATTERS!

Raising Standards for Teachers

What's the Policy?

Along with the push to raise academic standards for students in elementary and secondary schools, most states are raising the standards expected of would-be teachers.

How Does It Affect Teachers?

States are now requiring higher grade point averages for students entering teacher education programs. Also, as a prospective teacher, you will most likely have to pass some form of standardized test to become licensed to teach in your state. Candidates for teaching licenses usually must achieve passing scores on examinations that test general literacy and mathematical knowledge, subject-matter knowledge, and professional teaching knowledge. A number of states are also requiring students in teacher education programs to provide evidence that they have met the INTASC standards for beginning teachers. This evidence is often in the form of a teaching portfolio prepared by the prospective teacher.

What Are the Pros?

Teachers are increasingly seen as the most important element in the drive to raise academic standards and increase public confidence in K–12 schools. The perception is that you can raise standards for children and youth, but if you don't have good teachers, you won't make progress.

What Are the Cons?

Higher standards could contribute to a teacher shortage. States are increasing the standards for becoming a teacher just as the demand for teachers is increasing, and many are predicting a shortage of teachers over the next decade. Nationwide, 2.2 million new teachers will be needed in the next decade to meet rising student enrollments and replace retiring teachers. Passing state tests is not always automatic. For example, in 1998, Massachusetts introduced its first-ever licensure exam, and nearly 60 percent of the test takers flunked. The bar for becoming a teacher has been raised, with the predictable result that fewer people will get over it.

The increasing standards may also discourage people from pursuing teaching as a career for fear that they will spend four or five years of teacher education, only to be denied the opportunity to teach because they failed an exam. There is also concern that the exams don't really measure teaching effectiveness, merely general knowledge. Also, some people who would be fine teachers just don't test well. In addition, many educators criticize what they see as a double standard; that is, raising standards for students in teacher education programs but requiring less of students licensed through alternative routes. Finally, many people are concerned that these tests will diminish the pool of minority candidates, who historically have not tested as well as white candidates.

What Do You Think?

1. Is your decision on whether to become a teacher influenced at all by the requirement to pass a test to become licensed? Why or why not?
2. Professions such as law and medicine require tests for licensure. Do you support the idea of testing teachers for licensure? What concerns, if any, do you have about teacher competency tests?
3. What alternative methods can you suggest for states to use to determine teacher competence?

 Visit the web site to learn more about this policy issue.

represented, and adapted to the diverse interests and abilities of learners, and presented for instruction."[8] The skilled teacher draws on the most powerful analogies, illustrations, examples, explanations, and demonstrations to represent and transform the subject so that students can understand it. For example, a physics teacher who possesses pedagogical content knowledge might use the analogy of water flowing through a pipe to explain how electricity flows through a circuit, but he or she would also know the limitations of such an analogy. Education methods courses in the specific subject areas are where you are most likely to learn pedagogical content knowledge. Carol Landis has learned several methods for teaching social studies content and is now in the process of discovering whether the one she has chosen will be effective with her students.

all three types of knowledge essential

These three types of knowledge—of discipline content (including the structure of the discipline), of curriculum content, and of pedagogical content—are, we believe, essential for effective teachers. Did Carol Landis have such knowledge? We suspect not, at least not to the degree that she could communicate information and concepts to her class with the authority and expertise required for effective teaching. In the next section, we will examine more closely another area of the effective teacher's knowledge: theoretical knowledge about learning and human behavior.

What Theoretical Knowledge Does the Effective Teacher Need?

Theoretical knowledge about learning and human behavior equips the teacher to draw on concepts from psychology, anthropology, sociology, and related disciplines to interpret the complex reality of the classroom. The teacher who lacks a theoretical background will have to interpret classroom events according to commonly held beliefs or common sense, much of which is, unfortunately, based on outmoded notions of human behavior.

> *Education must bring the practice as nearly as possible to the theory.*
> —HORACE MANN

Theories-in-Use

Carol Landis operated on the basis of certain ideas, or what some call *theories-in-use,* which differ from pure theories.[9] A *theory* is an unproved explanation of why something happens the way it does. In its simplest form, a theory is a hypothesis designed to bring generalizable facts, concepts, or scientific laws into systematic connection. On the other hand, a *theory-in-use* is something people have in their heads and apply in their dealings with people and the world. Theories-in-use are often unexamined.

typical theories-in-use

We all have these theories-in-use, and they guide us as we make our way through our daily lives. You eat certain foods because you have an idea that they have a healthy effect on the body, or you decide to take a summer job in a public playground, believing that you will get to know children better and that future prospective employers might be pleased or impressed when they hear you have had that kind of experience.

Carol's theories-in-use

As you may have observed, Carol Landis has several theories-in-use. For example, Carol has the theory-in-use that groups should operate democratically and not be dominated by one student. She also has a theory-in-use that some children will perform better in school than others; as a result, she expects certain behavior from certain kinds of students. She also has a classroom management theory-in-use that she should give students some leeway before she resorts to firm discipline. Some of Carol's theories-in-use are clearly questionable. A few may have contributed to her problems that day in the library, and some may cause her more problems further down the line. Notice, however, that Carol was not worried about her theories-in-use. She was worried about what she did and what she will do. She didn't question some of her conceptions. Theories-in-use were the last things she had in mind, but they in fact caused some of her problems.

PAUSE AND REFLECT

1 Has reading about Carol Landis and her theories-in-use helped you identify any of your own theories-in-use or those of teachers you have known? If so, what are some of those theories-in-use?

■ *Why Study Educational Theory?*

The fact that Carol did not reflect on the truth or falsity of her theories-in-use or try to recall some theories she had learned during her teacher education is not uncommon. Indeed, many teachers question the basic usefulness of theory. Many a beginning teacher has been told by a senior colleague, "Forget all that theory they've been giving you in college. Here's what works in the real world." Further, preservice teachers often complain that courses are too theoretical. They want to get out to schools, where the action is. This desire (perhaps it is your own desire) for things that work and ways to cope with real situations is vital, and we do not want to diminish it. As a teacher, you will need practical techniques and solutions to real problems, but to need practical tools does not mean that educational theory is less important.

■ why theoretical knowledge is necessary

The case of Carol Landis illustrates how lack of theoretical knowledge of classroom management can lead to inappropriate behavior on the teacher's part. Both theory and empirical research support the notion of being consistent in your expectations of student behavior, whereas Carol thought it was all right to let students behave as they wished until they crossed her tolerance threshold, at which point she came down hard on them. Carol probably would not have encountered such trouble if more of her theories-in-use had been challenged.

■ good theories are practical

Like Carol, you may have your own theories-in-use, and these need to be challenged and tested. The best way to do this is to pit them against other theories and ideas. We believe, moreover, that theoretical information *is* practical. The problem is not that theory is wrong or unworkable but that many teacher education programs offer students few opportunities to apply theory to practical situations. As the great American philosopher John Dewey said, "Nothing is so practical as a good theory."* Finally, by giving attention to theoretical knowledge now, we are looking ahead to the future. In other words, even if it doesn't interest you much at this point, we want you to know that at a later stage of your development, you will encounter theories that will enlighten and enrich your work with the young.

---

* For the moment we will downplay the fact that John Dewey was primarily an educational theorist.

Teaching: Art or Science?

One of the pioneering investigators of research on teaching, N. L. Gage, professor emeritus at Stanford University, sees teaching as a blend of both art and science. Teaching can be considered an art because teachers must improvise and spontaneously handle a tremendous number of factors that interact in often unpredictable and nonsystematic ways in classroom settings. Teaching cannot be reduced to formulas or recipes for action, in Gage's opinion.

On the other hand, Gage contends that teaching is also a science. Although science can't offer absolute guidance for teachers as they plan and implement instructional strategies, research can provide a scientific basis for the art of teaching. For example, the research on academic engaged time has demonstrated the importance of keeping pupils on task with intellectually challenging, but not too difficult, subject matter.

These two components of teaching, art and science, interact. Empirically derived knowledge of the relationships among teacher behavior, pupil behavior, material to be learned, and desired student learning can guide teachers as they make artistic decisions about their teaching—that is, teachers use their knowledge of the research on these relationships to accomplish the artistry of moving a unique classroom of unique students toward the intended learning.

Is teaching an art or a science? The answer is "yes."

Source: N. L. Gage, *Hard Gains in the Soft Sciences: The Case of Pedagogy* (Bloomington, IN: Phi Delta Kappa, 1985), pp. 4–11.

How Can Theoretical Knowledge Be Used?

A teacher's theoretical knowledge can be used in two ways: to interpret new or ambiguous situations and to solve problems. (Personal practical knowledge, on the other hand, is more limited in applicability and is used primarily to respond to familiar situations. We will discuss personal practical knowledge shortly.)[10]

zone of proximal development

An Example of Using Theoretical Knowledge   Let's consider an example of how theoretical knowledge can help a teacher interpret classroom events and solve the problems arising from them. In educational psychology, there is a concept known as the **zone of proximal development,** a range of tasks that a child cannot yet do alone but can accomplish when assisted by a more skilled partner. In other words, the child is on the verge of being able to solve a problem but just needs some structure, clues, help with remembering certain steps or procedures, or encouragement to try. (This assistance, called **scaffolding,** allows students to complete tasks they can't complete independently.) This zone is where instruction can succeed and real learning is possible. The concept of the zone of proximal development derives from the theoretical work of the Russian psychologist Lev Vygotsky, in which he theorized that a child's culture shapes cognitive development by determining what and how the child will learn about the world.

forming hypotheses and investigating

Now suppose that a student, John, is experiencing difficulty doing some percentage problems in math. You, the teacher, understand that the zone of proximal development is influenced by reasoning ability, background knowledge, and motivation. Therefore, you assess John's ability to understand the problems by watching him try to solve one of them. You ask him to explain to you what he is thinking as he attempts the solutions. Is he missing some important understanding, or is he making some procedural error? Are the problems too difficult, or should he be able to solve them with some assistance? If the latter, what kind of assistance does he need? Who should give him the assistance, you or another student?

You decide that John is not lacking any fundamental knowledge but is very close to understanding the correct procedures. You ask Mary, a student who understands percentage problems pretty well, to come over and think aloud as she works on one of the problems. By thinking aloud and having John follow along, Mary provides John with insight into how she goes about solving the problem. You encourage John to ask Mary questions as she goes over her solution. You now ask John to work a similar problem, also thinking aloud as he tries to solve it. This time, he gets the problem correct. You ask him to do a couple more problems and to raise his hand when he finishes so you can check to see if his understanding carried over to the new problems.

using theoretical knowledge

How did the theoretical knowledge about the zone of proximal development assist you in helping John? First, you had to determine whether John was close to understanding or missing some fundamental knowledge. Was he in the zone of proximal development where additional coaching or assistance would help him, or would you have to reteach some important knowledge that he didn't have? Second, what sort of scaffolding would benefit John? By having both Mary and John think aloud as they solved the problem, mistakes or errors could be easily determined and, if solved correctly, provide a model for John. An understanding of the zone of proximal development and its related scaffolding strategies represents the kind of theoretical knowledge that can help you interpret and solve classroom problems.

taking advantage of opportunities

This example helps show that a teacher needs much more than a common-sense understanding of human behavior. The capable and effective teacher uses theoretical knowledge drawn from various education-related disciplines to formulate and test hypotheses about human behavior in the classroom. In our opinion, the translation of theory into practice cannot be left to chance; you must constantly take advantage of opportunities that allow you to apply theoretical concepts to classroom situations and to receive guidance and feedback from your instructors about the application of these concepts. The field of cognitive psychology, in particular, has recently provided fertile research findings and theoretical concepts for teachers.

Personal Practical Knowledge

practical knowledge differs from person to person

Personal practical knowledge is the set of understandings teachers have of the practical circumstances in which they work. Personal practical knowledge includes the beliefs, insights, and habits that allow teachers to do their jobs in schools. This type of knowledge tends to be time bound and situation specific, personally compelling, and oriented toward action. Teachers use their personal practical knowledge to solve dilemmas, resolve tensions, and simplify the complexities of their work. For example, the personal practical knowledge that Carol Landis must develop ranges from learning whether another teacher will loan his collection of *National Geographic* magazines to other classes to clarifying her beliefs about whether assigning students to groups is better than letting them choose their own groups. Because teachers' personal practical knowledge is so intertwined with them as individuals, researchers have not been able to summarize this knowledge into a codified body of teaching knowledge. Case studies of teachers have, however, provided us with rich images of how teachers use their knowledge to make sense of complex, ill-structured classrooms.

takes time to develop

Teachers' personal practical knowledge definitely influences the decisions they make. Some researchers argue that a well-informed belief system is the most credible basis for rational teacher decisions. They assert that teachers should become aware of the assumptions that comprise their belief systems. Then, as they develop attitudes and habits of practice, these should be reflected on to ensure conformity to accepted educational principles. Carol Landis, for example, is already reflecting on the educational soundness of her belief that students work well in groups with their friends. As you plan instruction, interact in classrooms, and evaluate instructional outcomes, continually testing your attitudes and habits of practice against sound educational principles can help protect you against poor education decision-making.[11]

What Teaching Skills Are Required of an Effective Teacher?

Knowing Versus Doing

Simply knowing something does not guarantee the ability to act on that knowledge. There is a profound difference between *knowing* and *doing*. Teachers may know, for example, that they should provide prompt feedback to their students on written assignments, but they are not always able to act on that knowledge. Teachers may also know how important it is to hold high expectations for all children, regardless of race, ethnicity, or social class, but then not act on that knowledge. No teacher education program can afford to focus only on theoretical knowledge at the expense of the practice, or "doing," dimension of teaching, just as no individual teacher can rely solely on knowledge of subject matter. All prospective teachers need to develop a repertoire of *teaching skills* to use as they see fit in varying classroom situations.

Among the skills that many educators believe are essential to effective teaching are the following:

some essential skills

- The ability to ask different kinds of questions, each requiring different types of thought processes from the student

- The ability to plan instruction and learning activities

- The ability to diagnose student needs and learning difficulties

- The ability to vary the learning situation to keep the students involved

- The ability to recognize when students are paying attention and to use this information to vary behavior and, possibly, the direction of the lesson

- The ability to use technological equipment, such as computers, to enhance student learning

- The ability to assess student learning

- The ability to differentiate instruction based on the students' experiences, interests, and academic abilities

The list of skills just given is far from complete. It does make it clear, however, that teachers need a large repertoire of skills to work effectively with students with varying backgrounds and different educational experiences. Varied approaches are necessary to meet the many needs of students. As Figure 5.1 illustrated, effective use of teaching skills, along with appropriate attitudes, knowledge of subject matter, and theoretical knowledge, leads to better instructional decision making.

■ *Classroom Management Skills*

No other dimension of teaching causes more concern for beginning teachers than managing the classroom and maintaining discipline. "Will I be able to manage and control my class(es) so I can teach effectively?" is a question most beginning teachers ask themselves. Because there is such a great concern about this aspect of teaching, we have chosen to spend some time on this skill area first, before turning, somewhat more briefly, to two others: questioning and planning skills.

Classroom management is "a process—a set of activities—by which the teacher establishes and maintains those classroom conditions that facilitate effective and efficient instruction."[12] Developing teacher-student rapport, establishing productive group norms, and rewarding promptness are examples of managerial behavior. Managerial behavior also includes housekeeping duties like record keeping, and managing time, facilities, and resources in the classroom.

As with most complex teaching skills, classroom management requires a thorough understanding of theoretical knowledge and research findings, as well as practical experience. The knowledge or theory comes primarily from educational, social, and humanistic psychology. As with many other areas of investigation, there is no consensus regarding the one most effective approach to classroom management. Instead there are different philosophies, theories, and research findings, each tending to address particular dimensions or approaches to classroom management. Table 5.1 gives a brief overview of some of these approaches.

The last twenty-five years or so have produced significant new knowledge about effective classroom management practices. The following sections describe some of those findings.

■ **Academic Engaged Time**   Research that focuses on student behaviors, such as academic engaged time, reveals some interesting insights on effective teaching skills.* **Academic engaged time,** also known as *academic learning time*, is the time a student spends being successfully engaged with academically relevant activities or materials. Several research studies indicate that academic engaged time in reading or mathematics is strongly related to achievement in those subjects.[13] Simply put, the more time elementary students spend working on reading or mathematics activities that provide them with successful experiences, the more likely they are to achieve in those areas. Although this finding may not seem very startling, observations indicate that tremendous differences exist in the amount of time individual students spend engaged in academic activities, both across classrooms and within the same classroom.

*On-task behavior, time on task, and academic engaged time are related concepts. *On-task behavior* is student activity that is appropriate to the teacher's goals. *Time on task* refers to the amount of time students spend engaged in on-task behavior. Academic engaged time adds the dimensions of a high success rate and academically relevant activities or materials to the concept of time on task.

Side notes:

Visit the web site to link to more advice on classroom management.

■ *definition of classroom management*

■ *no one approach*

■ *research findings*

TABLE 5.1   Different Approaches to Classroom Management

Name	Major Developers	Characteristics
Behavior modification	B. F. Skinner	Originates from behavioral psychology. Modify student behavior by consistently and systematically rewarding (reinforcing) appropriate student behavior and removing rewards for, or punishing, inappropriate student behavior.
Socioemotional climate	Carl Rogers William Glasser Haim Ginott	Originates in counseling and clinical psychology. Emphasis on building positive interpersonal relationships between students and teachers.
Group process	Richard Schmuck and Patricia Schmuck Lois Johnson and Mary Bany	Originates in social psychology and and group dynamics research. Emphasis on teacher establishing and maintaining effective, productive classroom group. Unity and cooperation, as well as group problem solving, are key elements.
Authority	Lee Canter and Marlene Canter	Views classroom management as a process of controlling student behavior, primarily by using discipline. Emphasizes establishing and enforcing rules, using soft reprimands and orders to desist. *Assertive discipline* is a popular manifestation of this approach.

Source: Wilford A. Weber, "Classroom Management," in *Classroom Teaching Skills*, 7th ed., by James M. Cooper (ed.). Copyright © 2003 by Houghton Mifflin Company. Reprinted with permission.

The research on academic engaged time clearly indicates that a primary goal of elementary teachers (and probably secondary teachers, although the research has been limited mostly to elementary schools) should be to keep students on task. We know that classes that are poorly managed usually have little academic learning time. A major task of teachers is to learn how to manage their classes so that students are productively engaged.

Numerous studies indicate that the most efficient teachers are able to engage their students about thirty minutes a day longer than the "average" teacher. If the most efficient teachers are compared with the least efficient, daily differences of an hour in academic engaged time appear. If this is spread out over 180 days, students of efficient teachers get 90 hours more of academic engaged time than students of average teachers and 180 hours more than students of inefficient teachers! Differences of this magnitude may help explain why students in some classes learn more than students in others.

■ *differences among teachers*

■ **Kounin's Research**   Jacob Kounin's research on classroom management in the elementary school grades explains which skills can help teachers improve their classroom management and keep pupils on task.[14] Kounin discovered that effective managers kept students involved in academic tasks, minimized the frequency with which students became disruptive, and resolved minor disruptions before they escalated into major ones. Of the concepts Kounin identified to describe teacher classroom management behavior, three seem particularly useful.

What Are Some Characteristic Behaviors of Effective Teachers?

In a broad study, educational researcher David Berliner attempted to provide an answer, based on contemporary research on teaching, to the question "What is an effective teacher?" His answer focuses on teacher behaviors that give students the opportunity to spend sufficient time engaged in and succeeding at tasks that help them achieve intended learning. Several of the following behaviors seem to distinguish effective teachers:

- They monitor students' independent work, checking on their progress and providing appropriate feedback, to maintain a high level of student engagement with the task at hand.

- They structure lessons to let students know what is expected of them and what procedures to follow.

- They pace instruction rapidly to deliver a maximum amount of the curriculum to students.

- They ask questions requiring students to analyze, synthesize, or evaluate, demand answers at the same level as the question, and wait at least three seconds for students' answers.

- They communicate high expectations for student success.

- They provide a safe and orderly classroom. Deviant behavior is managed sensibly, and academic achievement is rewarded.

- They foster a convivial atmosphere in their classrooms.

- They capitalize on the instructional and motivational uses of tests and grades.

- They provide feedback to students through praise, the use of student ideas, and corrective forms that allow students to respond appropriately.

This list is not comprehensive; these nine categories of teaching behaviors are only examples of behaviors that distinguish effective teaching, but the relationship of this collection of attitudes, knowledge, and skills to a research base indicates their importance in the repertoire of the professional teacher.

Source: David C. Berliner, "Effective Classroom Teaching: The Necessary but Not Sufficient Condition for Developing Exemplary Schools." In *Research on Exemplary Schools*, ed. Gilbert R. Austin and Herbert Garber (Orlando, FL: Academic Press, 1985), pp. 127–154.

■ *"withitness"*

The first concept he termed *withitness*. Teachers who are "with it" are those who communicate to pupils and so, by their behavior, appear that they know what is going on. Teachers who are "with it" pick up the first sign of misbehavior, deal with the proper pupil, ignore a minor misbehavior to stop a major infraction, and so forth.

■ *smoothness*

The second and third concepts concern the problems of lesson flow and time management. *Smoothness* involves the absence of behaviors initiated by teachers that interfere with the flow of academic events. Examples of teacher behavior that do not reflect smoothness occur when a teacher bursts in on children's activities with an order, statement, or question; when a teacher starts or is engaged in some activity and then leaves it "hanging," only to resume it after an interval; and when a teacher terminates one activity, starts another, and then initiates a return to the terminated activity.

momentum

The third concept, *momentum,* concerns the absence of teacher behaviors that slow down the pace of the lesson. Kounin conceptualized two types of slow-down behaviors: *overdwelling* (when a teacher dwells too much on pupil behavior, on a subpoint rather than the main point, on physical props rather than substance, or on instructions or details to the point of boredom) and *fragmentation* (when a teacher deals with individual pupils one at a time rather than with the group or unnecessarily breaks a task into smaller parts when the task could have been accomplished in a single step).

Kounin found strong correlations between teachers' use of withitness, smoothness, and momentum and their pupils' work involvement and restraint from misbehavior. He discovered that teachers who are effective classroom managers emphasize the prevention of disruptions rather than having to deal with them after they occur. Good managers do this by keeping the students engaged in lessons and assignments through effective application of the skills related to withitness, smoothness, and momentum.

Other Research Findings Many researchers have replicated and extended Kounin's work on classroom management. Here are a few other important recommendations arising from the research:

important recommendations

1. *Establish clearly defined rules and routines.* Clear rules and routines decrease the complexity of the classroom, minimize confusion, and prevent loss of instructional time. Moreover, having students help make the rules increases their commitment to abide by them.

2. *Ensure students' compliance with rules and demands.* To encourage students to comply willingly with the rules and routines, teachers must gain students' cooperation by establishing positive relationships, sharing responsibilities, and using rewards. In addition, teachers must be willing to administer consequences for repeated misconduct in a way that is not threatening or punitive.

Reflect on your classroom management skills with the image in this section of your CD-ROM.

3. *Involve families.* When families understand what the teacher is trying to achieve, they can provide valuable support and assistance, including helping develop and carry out successful behavior management plans.

developing students' responsibility

One school of thought rejects the notion of effective classroom management as a system of rewards and punishments, because these are seen as instruments for controlling people. In this approach, instead of teachers seeing themselves as being in charge and taking steps to maintain that control, they should give up some of the control and help students work together to decide how to be respectful and fair; that is, teachers should help students develop an internal sense of how to work together in a community.[15] The approach may involve times of chaos and uncertainty, but advocates believe that students will learn ethics and democracy in action. One of your responsibilities as a teacher will be to develop a philosophy and a way of operating in the classroom that make sense to you and that accomplish what you value. Your attitude toward the use of rewards and punishments will be part of that development.

Overall, we are learning more about what constitutes effective classroom management behavior. Understanding the related theories and research and practicing the skills that this body of knowledge has identified as effective will help you establish and maintain the conditions that promote student learning. Effective classroom management is a skill that can be taught and learned. (See the insert on Kevin and Jim's Suggestions for Classroom Management Problems.)

Kevin and Jim's Suggestions for Classroom Management Problems

1. *When students misbehave, check your instruction.* Many behavior problems result from problems with instruction. Students are bored or confused, and their response is to get off task and into trouble.

2. *Take the time to ensure that students fully understand your classroom's rules and procedures.* As the old adage has it, "You have to keep school before you can teach school." At the beginning of the year, and again if and when things begin to break down, teachers need to fix in the minds of their students how the class is to be ordered.

3. *Regularly monitor the entire class.* Successful classroom managers frequently scan the class, noticing what each student is doing. Although the teacher need not react to every sign of off-task behavior or deviation from the established procedure, it is important for students to know that what they are doing is being noted.

4. *Move in on repeated or flagrant breaches of conduct quickly and directly.* Do not let things drift. Students will think you are afraid to confront them, and they may end up confronting you!

5. *Correct in private.* As much as possible, deal with student misconduct in private. Don't disturb the rest of the students and get them off task simply to get one or two students back to work. Also, public reprimanding may backfire and get you involved in a game of escalating remarks with a student.

6. *Don't make empty threats.* Do not say you are going to "do" something to a student or the class unless you have thought it over carefully and are really ready to do it. For instance, do not threaten to call the parents of every child in the room and tell them what rotten children they have unless you have a good deal of time—and alternative plans for next year.

7. *Don't put a hand on a student in anger or even annoyance.* Do not even think of striking a student, no matter how much you are tempted. When a situation is emotionally charged, even your well-intended gesture can be misinterpreted. On the other hand, if students are fighting, you may need to restrain them physically for their own good.

8. *Think through behavior problems.* When your class or an individual student is not behaving up to your expectations, treat the event as a problem-solving activity. Do not flail around or get panicky or discouraged. Coolly identify exactly what the problem is, consider possible causes, and test some possible solutions.

9. *Get help.* If management problems persist and you cannot solve them on your own, get help from a colleague or an administrator. Do not let things fester. Do not be shy about asking for help, particularly about discipline problems, which are so common for many beginning teachers.

10. *Be sure there is a back-up system.* If you need to remove a student from your room, you need to know there is a system in place that will back you up.

11. *Be sure your rules accord with schoolwide expectations.* For example, if the school has decided that chewing gum is tolerable and you crack down on it, you can expect to have more trouble than the issue is probably worth.

PAUSE AND REFLECT

1 Do the research findings on academic engaged time surprise you, or do they seem obvious? If you think the findings reflect common sense, why do you suppose teachers vary so much in their ability to keep students engaged?

2 Are you concerned about your ability to establish and maintain a productive classroom environment? If so, what particularly concerns you?

3 We have included a number of suggestions for managing a classroom. Which seem most useful to you, and why? Which do you believe you would find most difficult to use, and why?

▣ *Questioning Skills*

▣ *ineffective questioning*

The questioning process is a central feature of most classrooms. Studies indicate that teachers may ask hundreds of questions in a day's lessons, but they often fail to ask questions that require students to process and analyze information, and their questions require only a rote response of memorized facts. They also tend to rush students' responses, not giving them adequate time to provide varied and thoughtful answers. Some teachers do not direct as many questions to certain groups of students, such as minority students, girls, or "slower" learners, and thus deprive them of the opportunity to interact actively in classroom learning.[16] Mastery of questioning skills contributes to students' learning and thus is important for effective teaching.

Visit the web site to link to more advice on effective questioning.

Through effective questioning techniques, teachers can encourage and promote student participation in discussions.

(© Michael Newman/PhotoEdit)

■ **Wait-Time** Good questioning behavior requires that the teacher provide students with sufficient time to think about and respond to questions. What do you think is the average amount of time a teacher waits for a student to respond to a question she or he has asked? Mary Budd Rowe, a science educator, determined in a series of studies that the teachers she observed waited less than one second before calling on a student to respond. Furthermore, after calling on a student, they waited only about a second for the student to answer before calling on someone else, rephrasing the question, giving a clue, or answering it themselves! How can students think carefully or deeply when they have only one second to respond to a teacher's question?

■ *results of wait-time training*

Rowe followed up these observations with studies designed to train teachers to increase their **wait-time** after questions from one second to three to five seconds. She reported amazing results, including the following: (1) an increase in the average length of student responses, (2) an increase in unsolicited but appropriate student responses, (3) an increase in student-initiated questions, (4) a decrease in failures to respond, (5) an increase in student-to-student interaction, and (6) an increase in speculative responses. In short, she found that longer wait-times led to more active participation on the part of more students and an increase in the quality of their participation. Subsequent research by others replicated her findings. If questions require students to think about material or generate original responses, they need a longer time to think about their answers than if they are being asked only to recall information from memory.[17]

■ **Effective Questioning Techniques** In addition to wait-time, those who have studied the relationship between questioning strategies and student achievement have identified a number of other techniques as signs of effective teaching. This research suggests that teachers do the following:

■ *useful techniques*

1. Phrase questions clearly. Avoid vague questions.

2. Ask questions that are purposeful in achieving the lesson's intent.

3. Ask brief questions, because long ones are often unclear.

4. Ask questions that are thought provoking and demand original and evaluative thinking.

Reflect on your questioning skills with the image in this section of your CD-ROM.

5. Encourage students to respond in some way to each question asked.

6. Distribute questions to a range of students, and balance responses from volunteering and nonvolunteering students.

7. Avoid asking "yes-no" and "leading" questions.

8. To stimulate thinking, probe students' responses or demand support for their answers.

9. Provide students with feedback about their responses, both to motivate them and to let them know how they are doing.[18]

Good teaching is one-fourth preparation and three-fourths theatre.

—GAIL GODWIN

With knowledge and practice, teachers can learn questioning strategies that engage all students in the verbal interaction that supports learning.

▇ *Planning Skills*

▇ *types of planning*

Another skill related to a teacher's effectiveness is skill in planning. The plans teachers make for lessons influence the opportunity students have to learn, because plans determine the content students will experience in a lesson and the focus of the teaching processes. Effective teachers base their plans on a rich store of perceptions of classroom events and of their students' progress toward educational objectives and content standards. This store of perceptions (ways of looking at students and classroom activities) also helps the teacher make adjustments during instruction when plans must be adapted to the immediate situation.

Teachers do four basic types of planning—yearly, unit, weekly, and daily—and all are important for effective instruction.[19] Research shows that experienced teachers don't plan the way curriculum experts recommend—that is, by beginning with instructional objectives and then selecting instructional activities to meet those objectives. Instead, many elementary school teachers begin by considering the context in which teaching will occur (for example, the materials and time available); then they think about activities that students will find interesting and that will involve them; finally, they ponder the purposes these activities will serve. Secondary school teachers, on the other hand, focus almost entirely on the content and preparation of an interesting presentation.[20] This doesn't mean experienced teachers don't have goals, especially in these days of content standards; rather, it suggests that the interest and involvement of their students are paramount. Since research shows that student achievement is related to academic engaged time, planning should include consideration of how to involve students.

Visit the web site to link to lesson plans and advice on planning.

We have looked at three skill areas—classroom management, questioning, and planning—that researchers have identified as competencies demonstrated by effective teachers. (Another important skill relates to the use of technology, to which we devote a whole chapter.) Principals and other school evaluators assess beginning teachers' competence in these and other skills areas as part of their observations of beginning teachers. Standards for new teachers, such as those created by INTASC, discussed earlier in this chapter, also emphasize these skills. Therefore, developing classroom management, questioning, and planning skills should be an important concern for those preparing to teach. Several web sites related to these and other skill areas are listed at the end of the chapter.

A Final Word

We think this chapter is an important one because it provides an overview of what a truly effective teacher needs to know and be able to do. It may have been a frustrating chapter if you concluded that there is no way you can achieve the ideal we describe. We share that frustration, since we ourselves have not attained this ideal in our own teaching, and we're not certain that we ever will. Nevertheless, we continue to aspire to be the type of teacher we have detailed in this chapter. If you too can fix your sights on this conceptualization of an effective teacher and continually work toward this ideal, you are certain to observe positive and rewarding results in your own classroom.

Although we can detail the various proficiencies teachers need, noted educational author Jonathan Kozol cuts to the chase in his description of what he would look for in a teacher:

> [O]bviously we want people who can teach [their subjects]. . . . But if I had to narrow it down to one characteristic, I would always hire teachers whom I wouldn't mind getting stuck with on a long plane flight to California. I would look for people who are capable of making the world seem joyful, people who are a delight to be with, people who are contagiously amusing human beings. To me, that's more important than almost anything else. I would put the emphasis on the capability to create contagious enthusiasm for life. There are a lot of teachers like that, but not enough.[21]

KEY TERMS

academic engaged time (166)

classroom management (166)

participant observation (153)

pedagogical content knowledge (159)

personal practical knowledge (164)

reflective teaching (144)

scaffolding (163)

self-fulfilling prophecy (155)

wait-time (172)

zone of proximal development (163)

FOR REFLECTION

❶ Do you agree that having an enthusiastic teacher teach an unimportant subject is preferable to an uninspired teacher teaching a crucial subject? What implications do you see in this remark? On what assumptions about teachers, students, and subject matter is it based?

❷ What is the difference between common sense and theoretical knowledge?

❸ We have maintained that decision-making skills are important for teachers. What do you think you can do to improve your ability to make good decisions as you plan and deliver instruction?

❹ Can you think of any ways that you, as a new teacher, could speed up the process of gaining personal practical knowledge?

❺ Which of the skills listed in the "Knowing Versus Doing" section of this chapter seem most important to you? What skills would you add to the list? What skills would you subtract from it?

FOR FURTHER INFORMATION

PRINT RESOURCES

James M. Cooper, *Classroom Teaching Skills,* 7th ed. (Boston: Houghton Mifflin, 2003).
This self-instructional book is designed to help teachers acquire basic teaching skills such as writing objectives, evaluation skills, classroom management skills, questioning skills, and interpersonal communication skills.

Charlotte Danielson, *Enhancing Professional Practice: A Framework for Teaching* (Alexandria, VA: Association for Supervision and Curriculum Development, 1996).

This useful book, organized around a framework of professional practice, is based on the PRAXIS III criteria, including planning and preparation, classroom environment, instruction, and professional responsibilities.

Thomas L. Good and Jere E. Brophy, *Looking in Classrooms,* 9th ed. (Boston: Allyn & Bacon, 2003).

This excellent book provides teachers with concrete skills that will enable them to observe and interpret the classroom behavior of both teacher and students.

Bruce R. Joyce, Marsha Weil, and Emily Calhoun, *Models of Teaching,* 6th ed. (Boston: Allyn and Bacon, 2000).

This text describes numerous teaching models based on different assumptions about teaching and learning.

Carol Simon Weinstein and Andrew J. Mignano, Jr., *Elementary Classroom Management: Lessons from Research and Practice,* 3rd ed. (New York: McGraw-Hill, 2003).

This practical book, based on sound research findings, addresses the major issues in establishing and maintaining effective learning environments. Ms. Weinstein has a secondary version entitled *Secondary Classroom Management* (2003), also published by McGraw-Hill.

WEB RESOURCES

AskEric's Lesson Plans. Available at: **http://ericir.syr. edu/VirtualLessons/**.

Access more than 1100 lesson plans submitted by teachers from all over the United States.

Beginning Teachers. Available at: **http://www.nea.org/ bt/1-students/1-1-nres.html**.

The National Education Association offers teachers a wide variety of resources, including the article on "Hints on Effective Questioning Techniques."

Education World. Available at: **http://www.db. education-world.com/perl/browse?cat_id=1846**.

Education World presents a range of information concerning classroom management, including a "database" of nearly 100 teacher resources concerned with classroom management.

Effective Questioning Techniques. Available at: **http://www.oir.uiuc.edu/did/booklets/question/ question.html**.

This online booklet offers ideas to help teachers ask good questions and create environments in which students are encouraged to ask questions.

Preparing a Teaching Portfolio: A Guidebook. Produced by the Center for Teaching Effectiveness at the University of Texas-Austin. Available at: **http://www.utexas. edu/academic/cte/teachfolio.html**

This online resource provides detailed instructions on how to prepare a teaching portfolio.

Electronic Teaching Portfolio Samples. Available at: **http://curry.edschool.virginia.edu/curry/class/edlf/ 589-07/sample.html**.

This site contains sample electronic teaching portfolios from preservice teachers, in-service teachers, and university faculty members.

Expage. Available at: **http://www.expage.com/ ClassroomManagement**.

Expage presents a list of links to web sites dealing with various aspects of classroom management; titles include "Classroom Management Concepts," "Classroom Management Ideas," and "Strategies for Classroom Management," for example.

Funbrain. Available at: **http://www.funbrain.com**.

This site provides games and thousands of assessment quizzes to enable teachers to integrate them into their daily lesson plans.

How Better Questioning Leads to Improved Learning: QUILT. Available at: **http://www.ael.org/rel/quilt/ questng.htm**.

Questioning and Understanding to Improve Learning and Thinking (QUILT) helps make the classroom learning environment more active and student centered.

Interstate New Teacher Assessment and Support Consortium (INTASC). Available at: **http://www.ccsso.org/ intasc.html** and **http://www.ncpublicschools. org/pbl/pblintasc.htm**.

A consortium of state education agencies, higher education institutions, and national educational organizations dedicated to the reform of the education, licensing, and on-going professional development of teachers. Their core standards for beginning teachers can be located at **http://www.ccsso.org/intasc.html** or more directly at the North Carolina department of public instruction at **http://www.ncpublicschools. org/pbl/pblintasc.htm**.

The New York Times. Available at: **http://www. nytimes.com/learning/teachers/index.html**.

This newspaper web site has daily lesson plans for grades 6–8 and 9–12, as well as daily news "snapshot" activities that can be developed into lesson plans for grades 3–5. This site can be a valuable resource for exemplary lessons and activities, especially by allowing users to access related academic standards for many individual states.

Preparing a Teaching Portfolio: A Guidebook. Available at: **http://www.utexas.edu/academic/cte/teachfolio.html**.

This site is produced by the Center for Teaching.

Teachers.Net. Available at: **http://www.teachers.net/**.

This excellent site has an online reference desk, an active chat board, and a lesson plan exchange.

Yahoo!'s Directory of K–12 Lesson Plans. Available at: **http://dir.yahoo.com/Education/Standards_and_Testing**.

This site contains a large variety of resources for testing, assessment, measurement, and benchmarking.

Lastly, the Virginia Department of Education has developed a series of video programs that identify research-based instructional strategies and discuss the use of these strategies in Virginia's classrooms. A list of them is available at no cost on the Mid-continent Research for Education and Learning (McREL) web site at **http://www.mcrel.org/products/learning/index.asp**.

The video series has been developed at each of three levels—elementary, middle, and secondary—and discusses research-based strategies such as homework and practice, similarities and differences, summarizing and note taking, nonlinguistic instruction, reinforcing effort, activating prior knowledge, and teaching skills and processes.

What Should Teachers Know About Technology and Its Impact on Schools?

6

Chapter Preview The use of technology in the classroom has gained attention as an issue in education. As our society continues to embrace new forms of communication, networking, and computer technologies, our schools are scrambling to keep up. In this chapter, we will explore what teachers should know about technology and its use in the educational setting, what roles technology may take in education, and how those roles may change what students and teachers do in the classroom.

This chapter emphasizes that:

- Technology is not new to the field of education.

- Schools are being pressured from many sides to incorporate contemporary technologies into instruction.

- Students can use computers not just for drill but in ways that promote creativity, collaboration, and higher-order thinking.

- Technologies can help teachers change their role from dispensers of information to facilitators of students' learning.

- Teachers can also benefit from the productivity of computers in areas ranging from record keeping to staff development.

- The placement of technology within the educational setting affects how it can be used.

- Issues involving equity, teacher education, infrastructure, and budgeting will need careful consideration as technological tools become more and more integrated into classroom instruction.

■ *a technology-enhanced
teaching scenario*

Patricia Gonzalez issues a challenge to her eighth-grade class: "Where should the next landfill be built in our state?" The students are interested in this topic, which they have heard their parents discuss. To find a solution, Patricia's class works with local city officials, who coach them on the mechanics of a geographic information system (GIS). A GIS, in simple terms, is a collection of electronic tools that translate data to a digital map. The power of a GIS comes from its ability to display several layers of maps on the computer screen at a single time. For example, students can look at a map showing population density and then at another that depicts distance from urban areas. They can also view these two maps together as they struggle to choose the site of their landfill. The GIS tools allow students to zoom in and out on an area as they begin to narrow down their choices for the site. Then they can search the GIS database to make sure they will not disturb any known historic or archaeological sites.[1]

After two weeks of investigation, Patricia's class divides into teams to present their choices. Three sites are offered, and a different group presents the case for each location. The culminating activity requires students to role-play a city council meeting, assuming such roles as city councilor, mayor, geologist, and angry citizen.

Two years later, the same students are still using the geographic information system, but now they are in the field collecting water samples near the landfill that was built. Students meticulously record data, which are transferred to a GIS database. They still work with municipal officials, this time to monitor the safety of the landfill.

This project has many educational benefits:

- The partnership between city government and middle school classrooms lets students learn about the workings of government while contributing to a worthwhile cause in their community.

- Patricia's students learn marketable skills to take with them into the job force.

- The nature of Patricia's lesson is a problem-solving activity. Students work collaboratively to consider things like water leakage.

- The nature of GIS means that it integrates learning from several different subject areas. Students use their math skills, for example, to calculate the slope of different areas and see how the results might affect the landfill.

- The GIS technology allows Patricia to innovate. Posing a dilemma such as the landfill problem would be possible without technology, but the GIS tools allow her students to do what scientists do with the same question: use sophisticated equipment, consider multiple perspectives, and grapple with real, scientific data.[2]

■ *teacher as facilitator*

Patricia Gonzalez's role in the classroom is far from the traditional view of the teacher as sole dispenser of information. Instead, Patricia functions as a facilitator. She allows her classroom to become an active laboratory where students take charge of their learning and hypothesize about solutions. As she circulates around the room, she challenges her students to consider what evidence they will need to convince an area's citizens that their backyards are the best place for the landfill. Patricia is one reference point that students can consult, along with others, including technology, municipal officials, and other students.

GIS software allows users to create customized maps such as the one shown here. (ArcData Online screen capture provided courtesy of ESRI. Copyright © 2000 ESRI, EDT, FEMA. All rights reserved.)

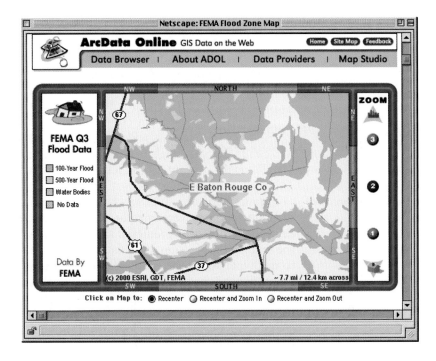

For example, she knows the technology skills required by GIS software, but she relies on the expertise of the municipal officials who use it daily to teach her students while she facilitates.

Has Patricia been replaced by the computer? The answer is no. Teachers, in fact, have an expanded role in this technologically enriched environment, though this role differs from the traditional one. Later in the chapter, we will explore in more detail how teachers can use computer technologies in instruction and what changes this approach can bring to the roles of both students and teachers. First, though, to put contemporary changes in perspective, let's look at the way technology has affected American schools in the past.

A Brief Look at Education's Technological Past

■ *a high-tech wonder of the early 1800s*

Visit the web site to link to more information on the history of educational technology.

Today people usually equate educational technology with computers. But technology in a more general sense is by no means new to education. In the early 1800s, a technological innovation was introduced to classrooms that would prove to have a profound impact on teaching. Although advocates called this new tool "invaluable" and it was installed in classrooms throughout the country, many teachers ignored it at first. Schools had to encourage use of this new technology by preparing training manuals with step-by-step instructions to help teachers integrate the device into their lessons. What was this technological wonder? The chalkboard!

In the old one-room schoolhouses, where students of different ages worked on various individual lessons, the function of a chalkboard was not immediately apparent. During the nineteenth century, however, classroom structure began to evolve from a one-room orientation to the graded classrooms we know today.

When teachers began to teach the same lesson to an entire group of students, the chalkboard came into its own.[3]

■ *TV reaches the classroom*

The twentieth century brought a variety of technological devices that helped teachers use pictures in the classroom, including the filmstrip projector, the overhead projector, the motion picture, and educational television.[4] Such changes were viewed as so significant that in 1913 technological proponent Thomas Edison stated, "Books will soon be obsolete in the schools. Scholars will soon be instructed through the eye. It is possible to teach every branch of human knowledge with the motion picture. Our school system will be completely changed in ten years."[5]

I think there is a world market for maybe five computers.

—THOMAS WATSON, CHAIRMAN OF IBM, 1943

■ *microcomputers become affordable*

Similarly, in the 1980s, when microcomputers became affordable, many software products were introduced to drill students on basic skills, and some educational visionaries predicted the end of classroom instruction and the end of the teaching profession as we know it. Of course, the technology never lived up to the hype. Today the most effective and promising technologies are not those that claim to take over the instruction but those that help with it.

As these episodes show, many grandiose claims have been made about the use of technology to revolutionize the instructional process. But the eventual acceptance of any new technology, from the chalkboard to the microcomputer, has been determined more by the needs and demands of the classroom than by the claims of technology advocates.

Once a technology enters the classroom, the uses to which it is put are affected by what we might call the technology's level of maturity. In education, as in other fields, new technologies tend to go through three stages of application:

■ *typical stages of technology*

1. In the first stage, the technology is applied to things we already do. For instance, when microcomputers were first introduced into education, computer programs were created to simulate flash cards for math drill.

2. As a technology moves into the second stage, it is used to improve on the tasks we do. As an example, a more sophisticated math software application can provide remedial instruction when a student makes the same mistake more than once. It can also expand to cover more math topics and increase motivation by using gamelike activities.

3. In the third stage of maturity, the technology is used to do things that were not possible before. An excellent example is the geographic information system software that Patricia used in our opening case study. Among other things, the GIS software helps students pull together their knowledge and skills from different disciplines in a collaborative manner to solve a problem in their local community. This kind of application uses technology in a way that is innovative rather than just allowing us to do old things in new ways.

Following this pattern, the role of any technology in the classroom will tend naturally to change as the technology matures. In addition, teachers follow a similar progression as they become more comfortable with various technologies. Teachers who are just beginning to use technology may start with applications, like drill and practice software, which are similar to something they already do. As they begin to learn about technology's possibilities, they will move on to applications that allow them to innovate. As we examine different technologies, ask yourself at which stage they can be applied and at which stage you would feel comfortable using them.

1 How have recent developments in technology affected you and your family?

2 When you were in high school, what types of technology were your teachers using? At what stage was the technology applied?

3 Do you think the excitement about computers in education will fizzle as it did for educational television, or will computers go the way of the chalkboard, being seamlessly integrated in a meaningful way?

How Are Schools Being Pressured to Change?

do schools prepare students for modern life?

sources of pressure

Computer and networking technologies are an integral part of our society. It is hard to imagine a world without ATM machines, email, and pay-at-the-pump gas stations, a world with no microprocessors to run your microwave, TV, DVD, automobile, and cellular phone. Now imagine a classroom with no TV, no DVD (not even a VCR), no phone, and no computer. This classroom scenario is easily imagined, for we have all experienced it. Most people agree that schools should prepare students for life in our society. If pervasive use of technology is a fact of life, should the classroom be an exception?

No wonder, then, that schools are feeling pressure to increase their use of technological tools. The pressure is coming from many sources:

1. Parents are placing pressure on schools to use technologies in the classroom. They see a discrepancy between what is taught to their children and the real-world activities they perform every day at work. An example is the debate over the importance of cursive writing as opposed to keyboarding skills: is instruction in handwriting important if most adults will soon be using a keyboard? Parents are concerned not only that their children have access to technology in the classroom, but also that the students learn technology skills to allow them to compete in a job market increasingly powered by technology.

2. Students are placing pressure on schools by knowing more about current technologies than many of the teachers.

3. Teachers are placing pressure on schools because they need both access to technology in their classrooms and training to use the technology effectively. New teachers, in particular, who have used technological tools in college and at home, want to use them in their classrooms.

4. Businesses are placing pressure on schools and governmental agencies to adequately prepare future employees. By 2006, nearly half of all workers will be employed in industries that produce or intensively use information technology products and services.[6] Computer-based information processing power is doubling every twelve months,[7] and the pace of change in technology is significantly faster than even the pace in business, let alone that in education. The pressure on schools to keep up, therefore, is intense.

5. Another pressure stems from the perception that America is falling behind the world in educational attainment. Business and governmental agencies march to the drum of global competition: "If America is to compete with the world, America's schools must be the best!" Regardless of their truth, rallying calls like this add to the pressure on schools to use technology.

Visit the web site to link to more information on technology and content standards.

6. Governmental agencies have moved to support federal, state, and local initiatives to ensure access to technology for K–12 students. Many state departments of education have written "technology skills" into teacher licensure requirements, and national organizations are moving toward specific subject-area technology standards for K–12 students.*

7. Within each of these groups are voices calling for schools to help close the digital divide—that is, the gap between those who are able to benefit from technology and those who are not. These gaps may divide along such lines as race, gender, ability, or geographic location. Citizens are concerned that technology is further deepening cleavages between the haves and have nots of American society.

■ *change equals opportunity?*

Although we have been speaking of "pressures" for change, they can also be seen as opportunities. Many educators welcome the chance to try new curriculum materials and methods in their classrooms or to help bridge the digital divide. There are also new opportunities for teachers with skills in technology, now an important competitive edge in the job market. Most important, perhaps, there are tremendous opportunities for students, as the next section describes.

PAUSE AND REFLECT

1 What other pressures can you add to this list?

2 As a teacher, from where do you expect to feel the most pressure to incorporate technology?

3 Are schools facing pressure to avoid adopting technology?

How Are Technologies Affecting Student Learning?

As our example of GIS software shows, many new technologies have been introduced into the educational setting in the last decade. To facilitate our discussion

During my eighty-seven years I have witnessed a whole succession of technological revolutions. But none of them has done away with the need for character in the individual or the ability to think.

—BERNARD MANNES BARUCH

of these new technological tools, we will group them into content-specific categories, even though some examples will cross disciplines and join subjects, such as social studies and math. Many disciplines use some common technological tools, but how a teacher uses telecommunication in science, for example, will differ from how another uses it in English.

Some computer applications can be classified as **cognitive tools** when they are used to engage and enhance thinking.[8] These tools are applications that manage information in ways

*For one example, see ISTE's National Educational Technology Standards (NETS) (**http://cnets.iste.org/**).

■ *enhance and engage thinking*

that allow users to think more clearly, creatively, and critically. They derive their power from their flexibility and their ability to unleash creativity and foster significant cognitive processes. For example, they allow users to organize information in new ways, evaluate it, and construct personally meaningful representations of it. Cognitive tools are not necessarily meant to make learning easier. Instead, they often require students to think harder, more critically, or more creatively than without the tool.[9] Much of the working world uses cognitive tools for everyday tasks, and we believe that all teachers and students should have similar opportunities. There are many computer technologies that we might consider cognitive tools. Our discussion will include word processors, databases, spreadsheets, telecommunications tools, tutorials, simulations, multimedia software, drill-and-practice programs, and presentation and publishing tools. Table 6.1 summarizes these tools and their educational benefits.

■ *combining instructional techniques and technologies*

Today most educational software applications use a combination of instructional techniques (for example, tutorial, simulation, and interactive multimedia) to achieve the desired outcomes. It would be relatively rare to find an application that neatly fits into only one of these categories. Moreover, teaching approaches that use educational software normally draw from two or more of these categories.

PAUSE AND REFLECT

❶ As you read the following sections, consider how teachers are using particular tools. At which of the stages discussed earlier are teachers making use of these technologies? Are teachers applying the tools to things they already do? Does the technology enhance the teacher's ability? Are teachers innovating with the tools?

■ *English/Language Arts Education*

Teachers of many disciplines will find the tools for developing literacy useful. In this section, we will examine word processors, different software applications to develop reading skills, multimedia presentation and communication tools, including digital video, and ways to combine technologies across disciplines.

■ *ease of editing and rewriting*

■ **Writing with Word Processors**   Although technology has vastly broadened the avenues of expression available to students, writing ability is still highly valued in our culture, and today many students write using word processing software. The **word processor** provides many benefits over paper and pencil. Editing is less tedious when you don't have to laboriously erase several lines of text or even start over. Using a word processor, students can experiment with different sequences for their paragraphs with little effort. In fact, students who learn to write using word processors are more likely to revise their work and make more substantial revisions than students who learn to write without the tool.[10] Built-in spelling and grammar checks in most word processing software help struggling students to focus on their ideas, and the keyboard itself avoids the handwriting obstacle many students face. These aids are controversial, however; they are not foolproof, and some educators believe they are often a crutch. Nonetheless, the more students edit their writing, the more they learn about the

TABLE 6.1   Types of Technology Tools

Technology Tool	Educational Benefits	Example
Word processor	• Easy cut-and-paste procedures and the ability to save and return to a document later encourage editing. • On-screen spell checkers, dictionaries, and thesauruses aid accuracy.	*Alpha Smart,** a portable and user friendly word processor, is especially popular with teachers who work with younger writers.
Multimedia presentation software	• Combining text, audio, video, and virtual environments helps to communicate complex ideas. • Caters to a variety of learning styles.	*PowerPoint* allows students to easily combine a variety of media or even publish a presentation on the Web.
Drill and practice	• Similar to an interactive worksheet that provides feedback for the user and teacher. • Progress through the program depends on mastery of previous level. • Effective at reinforcing a concept.	*Reader Rabbit* is a popular program to reinforce letter recognition, rhyming words, and word families.
Database	• Organizes and stores complex sets of information. • Users can sort through information and filter unwanted data.	The *Valley of the Shadow* web site offers students access to a variety of searchable databases from two communities during the Civil War.
Digital video	• Caters to a variety of learning styles. • Capable of presenting rich and complex information. • Easy editing software empowers students to take a video project from idea to completion.	A digital camera and *iMovie's* easy editing tools allow students to plan, film, synthesize, and present the drama of the Monarch butterfly's metamorphosis.
Graphing calculator	• Quickly generates graphical representations of mathematical functions • Helps users connect graphical, numerical, and algebraic representations of mathematical functions • Allows users to input data from real-time experiments	Students can gather motion data with collection devices connected to the *TI-73* graphing calculator to analyze graphs and look for patterns.
Simulation	• Interactive in nature, simulations allow students to reenact an event. • Students assume roles in the event, making decisions to which the software responds appropriately.	*Decisions, Decisions: Local Government* lets students play the role of a mayor facing a dilemma about the city's economic future.
Spreadsheet	• Allows users to form multiple calculations and to see all answers simultaneously. • A powerful tool to manipulate large sets of data. • Includes easy tools to graph.	Students can study a graph of population demographics in a community and use a spreadsheet program, like *Excel,*† to predict future changes in that society.
Tutorial	• Provides the initial instruction for a topic in a self-controlled, self-paced environment.	Fundamental Math allows teachers to individualize their student's instruction in math.

TABLE 6.1   Types of Technology Tools *(cont'd)*

Technology Tool	Educational Benefits	Example
Tutorial	• Monitors progress and evaluates the student once instruction is complete. • Students' location within the tutorial can be saved.	
Telecollaboration over the Web	• Allows for fast, inexpensive worldwide communication and collaboration. • Organizations support these projects, allowing students to participate in legitimate research.	The GLOBE program supports a project that uses data on acid rain and waste disposal collected and submitted by students around the world.

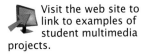 Visit the web site to link to all the web sites mentioned as examples in this chapter.

writing process. In this respect, the word processor engages students and enhances thinking, making it a cognitive tool.

expanded definition of literacy

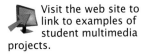 Visit the web site to link to examples of student multimedia projects.

■ **Communicating in Multimedia**   The spread of technology has required an expanded definition of literacy. Students are now becoming literate not just in the written word, but also in video, audio, and multimedia* productions. In the chapter entitled "Who Are Today's Students in a Diverse Society?" we discussed Howard Gardner's theory of multiple intelligences and the concept of learning styles, emphasizing that different individuals learn best in different ways. Students who struggle with written expression may enjoy the chance to publish a web page or create a multimedia presentation instead of submitting a traditional five-page essay. Presentation tools, such as *PowerPoint*, can combine text, graphics, audio, and video to communicate complex ideas. Students can use multimedia authoring programs like *HyperStudio* or *Kid Pix* to create their own interactive presentations or illustrate and present stories.†

These multimedia programs allow users to insert short videoclips into a presentation, but digital video software expands on the video options. Rich movies combining audio, video, and text can now be created with increasingly affordable digital video cameras and easily edited with user-friendly software.‡ For example, students can film a Native-American elder telling an important story from his or her tribal culture as the culminating project for a unit on storytelling. The students learn technical and visual literacy skills while strengthening their ability to analyze and synthesize information.

These programs allow students to use their strengths in expressing themselves while they become familiar with valuable tools for the future. It is relatively

*Multimedia productions combine various media such as text, graphics, video, music, and voice narration.

†*PowerPoint* is a product of Microsoft (**http://www.microsoft.com/**; telephone: 425-882-8080). For *HyperStudio*, contact Knowledge Adventure (**http://www.hyperstudio.com/**; telephone: 800-321-7511). For *KidPix*, contact The Learning Company (**http://www.kidpix.com/**; telephone 800-825-4420).

‡For one example, see Apple's iMovie software (**http://www.apple.com/imovie/**; telephone: 800-MY-APPLE).

SALLY FORTH   **BY STEVE ALANIZ & FRANCESCO MARCIULIANO**

Reprinted with special permission of King Features Syndicate.

easy to publish student work through the **World Wide Web**, commonly called the *Web,* and knowing their work may end up in the public domain motivates students to care more about their creations.[11] Like word processors, multimedia tools are used across the disciplines—from a presentation on the Depression that includes music from the era and clips from President Franklin D. Roosevelt's Fireside Chats to a hurricanes project with graphs, images, video clips, and links to the National Weather Service web site.

■ **Learning to Read**   Multimedia technologies also give students an advantage in learning to read. The *Living Books* series* consists of children's literature titles available on CD-ROM in which the story is represented in many forms or media. For example, the student reads the text on the screen, the computer reads it to the student, and the student sees interactive video and still images illustrating the concept. Some titles are also available in several languages. Multimedia technologies can improve the match between the instruction and students' learning styles, offering a great opportunity to encourage literacy.[12]

■ finding a better match between instruction and learning style

Drill-and-practice programs are the earliest form of educational software or educational game. First used as an interactive worksheet, the software provided feedback to the user, usually by labeling an answer right or wrong, and then presented the next task. Now, many programs monitor the students' progress so they do not move on until they have mastered the current concept. Drill-and-practice programs generally increase the fluency of a skill rather than actually teaching it.[13] For example, products such as the *Reader Rabbit* series† are popular for reinforcing young children's reading skills, such as letter

---

Living Books' titles are available through Broderbund (**http://www.broderbund.com**).
†Reader Rabbit is a product of the Learning Company (**http://www.readerrabbit.com/**; telephone: 800-825-4420).

"Edutainment" Software

A software application that is both entertaining and educational is referred to as "edutainment." Ordinary drill-and-practice software is repetitive by nature, and children can easily lose interest in such mundane tasks. Therefore, software developers added gamelike characteristics to their applications in the hope of motivating users to complete the task. These features also helped to sell the products to students and parents looking for educational activities for the home. The balance between entertainment and education is a delicate one. As you try out educational software, ask yourself whose mind is doing the thinking: the child's or the programmer's?

Today most edutainment software is designed and marketed for the parents of school-age children, not specifically for classroom use. Nevertheless, some software applications with gamelike features, such as *Math Blaster* and *Oregon Trail,** manage to bridge the gap, proving useful in both the home and the classroom. Since parents often ask teachers to recommend software applications for the home, it is a good idea to know what applications available for home use would complement the school's curriculum.

Math Blaster* is manufactured by Knowledge Adventure (http://www.education.com/blaster/BlasterMaster.html**). *Oregon Trail* is a product of Broderbund (**http://www.broderbund.com/**.)

---

recognition, rhyming words, and word families. Teachers also use drill-and-practice programs such as *Reader Rabbit* to diagnose students' ability in reading, as well as other subjects, and assign them to the appropriate group.

Combining Technology and Crossing Disciplines   Technology can facilitate interdisciplinary connections in a powerful way. An example combining several types of technologies and crossing content areas is the *I Lost My Tooth* project.[14] First-grade students around the world use email to share stories and myths about losing their teeth. Using these rich and diverse stories, teachers develop interdisciplinary activities that can make use of a variety of educational tools, both technological and traditional. For example, students study maps, either on computer or on paper, to locate the countries where other children live and ask their "e-pals" about the weather and local heroes of their regions. Students can use drawing software, or old-fashioned crayons, to illustrate their tooth fairy stories. They use their math skills, and perhaps graphing software, to chart the number of teeth lost. In this project, technology is functioning at the second stage we described: facilitating and enhancing what teachers can do.

Reflect on how technology affects student learning with the image in this section of your CD-ROM.

enhancing what teachers do

Science Education

As the case study at the beginning of this chapter showed, technology can allow students to do legitimate scientific investigations on a scale that would be impossible without technology. Technology enabled Ms. Gonzalez to use a constructivist approach to education where her students engaged in building their own knowledge on the basis of their experiences. (See the box on constructivism in this section. See also "The Influence of Psychological Theories" in the chapter

Cognitive Tools and Constructivist Teaching

In the constructivist approach to teaching (discussed in the chapters entitled "What Are the Philosophical Foundations of American Education?" and "How Should Education Be Reformed?"), learning is recognized as an active process. Students engage in constructing their own knowledge on the basis of their previous experiences instead of passively absorbing knowledge as presented by the teacher. This approach to instruction celebrates the differences among students instead of continually trying to build similarities.

Constructivist teachers can find cognitive tools especially helpful. Since cognitive tools do not try to instruct, they do not assume a particular learning style or methodology. A spreadsheet is a good example of this. The student must bring the goals—and the content to achieve them—to the tool, and then the tool will facilitate the student's discovery of knowledge and construction of meaning.

It is important to note that it is *how* the tool is used that makes it constructivist, not necessarily the tool itself. Although cognitive tools are an excellent match for constructivist methods, many software applications can be used in a similar manner. As with many other aspects of teaching, it is the learner's and teacher's ingenuity, creativity, and experience that set the limits of a tool's educational use, not the tool itself.

entitled "What Are the Philosophical Foundations of American Education?" and "What Ought to Be the Elements of Educational Reform?" in the chapter entitled "How Should Education Be Reformed?".) Putting these technologies in students' hands can allow learning to become an active process in which students do the experiments themselves, draw conclusions, and engage in problem solving rather than merely reading about an investigation and memorizing the results.

Although the equipment to conduct many of these experiments is costly, there are ways around these financial obstacles. For example, most city governments own geographic information systems software, and many are interested in partnering with a local school to share their expertise. Many organizations support collaboration between scientists and schools; for a reasonable membership fee, schools receive the technical support they need and an opportunity to work with experts. This section discusses some of these opportunities, ranging from conducting sophisticated local research that contributes to an organized database to collaborating with NASA scientists via teleconferencing technology.

▪ **Scientific Hardware**   Imagine conducting class beside a stream behind your classroom and having the technology to collect a water sample; instantly and accurately find the pH, temperature, and amount of dissolved oxygen in it; and graph the data on the spot. Revolutionary technology in the form of affordable handheld computers, such as the Palm* and accompanying probes, thermometers, and sensors, allow this to happen. No longer are teachers forced to demonstrate stale experiments in the sterile environment of a lab. With the help of relatively low-cost equipment, or an online connection, students can access rich data, do calculations, and test their hypotheses themselves. Science students today do things like measure ozone and sulfur dioxide levels from the air near their schools, use the Web to request images from a professional observatory in Australia to learn about how supernovae form, or monitor the regularity of Old Faithful's eruptions through a live web camera.

▪ *doing "real" science*

*Palms are produced by Palm, Inc (**http://www.palm.com/**; telephone: 800-881-7256).

some concerns

Not everyone is a fan of such projects, however. Some caution, for example, that the many bells and whistles technology offers can reduce science to a "spectator sport" where students sit back and watch machines do the calculations. Furthermore, the complicated calculations that technology allows are often beyond the comprehension of the students involved. They understand the results but not the process required to get there.[15] Educators must address these problems as technology continues to progress.

Communication with Other Scientists The class doing the stream experiment could take their results a step further and **telecollaborate** with students and scientists around the world to examine the effect of acid rain or waste disposal on the earth's water quality. The Global Learning and Observations to Benefit the Environment (GLOBE) program* coordinates such a project. GLOBE allows students to collaborate with expert mentor scientists who will answer questions, engage in the analysis of data, and help students place their measurements in the broader context of global environmental issues. Students and teachers work with other classrooms to collect data at the same time and send it into a computer that aggregates it and returns analyses of all the classrooms' data. The program is a dynamic, legitimate scientific investigation without preprogrammed answers. Students must interpret the results and develop an understanding based on their own experiments.

Telecollaboration projects are becoming more popular across the disciplines as a variety of communications technologies make it easier to connect with schools, universities, experts, and organizations around the world. Many teachers use text-based email. Some opt for videoconferencing, in which students and teachers exchange live audio and video. Projects such as Global Schoolhouse and NASA Quest† provide the technical support and organizational framework to connect students, teachers, and experts using telecommunications.

Enhancing Problem Solving Teachers often wonder what their students are thinking, and technology is providing some ways to discover and understand the cognitive processes students use as they solve problems. At Cedar Way High School, students use the True Roots program‡ to play the role of forensic scientists trying to determine if a girl is correct in asserting that she was switched at birth in the hospital. Using genetic data, students must try to deduce whether the girl is related to the parents who have raised her. The program tracks students' decisions so that the teacher can later analyze the problem-solving strategy students used. Teachers instruct students not to guess or proceed randomly but to have a systematic plan. To reinforce the idea that problem solving should be a logical exercise, classes often use the program two times over three days. Teachers take the middle day to show students the graphs of their problem-solving strategy. Students try again and are graded on their improvement.[16]

understanding students' cognitive processes

Here, technology is functioning at the third stage of progress: offering teachers unique insight into their students' cognitive processes, which would not be possible without this sophisticated technology.

*To learn more, visit the GLOBE web site (**http://www.globe.gov**).

†To learn more, visit the Global Schoolhouse web site (**http://www.globalschoolhouse.org/**) and the NASA Quest web site (**http://quest.arc.nasa.gov/**).

‡True Roots is produced by IMMEX (Interactive Multimedia Exercises) at UCLA (**http://www. immex.ucla.edu**; telephone: 310-649-6568).

GalapagosQuest: **Darwin Meets the Web**

*G*alapagosQuest is an educational web project focusing on grades four through eight organized by Classroom Connect. In 1999 a team of scientists and explorers retraced Charles Darwin's 1835 journey to the Galapagos exploring the animal, plant, and geological components of this chain of islands. Armed with sea kayaks, camping equipment, laptop computers, digital cameras, and a satellite uplink, the team investigated the impact of the earth's changes on the Galapagos Islands. For example, they studied the earth's only marine reptiles and the effects of El Niño on penguin colonies. The scientists posted pictures of animals and habitats as well as logs from their journals on the *GalapagosQuest* web site as they tried to unlock the secrets of this unusual environment. This interactive project allowed students around the world to vote on the course the team followed. Teachers and stu-dents theorized about the evolution of both animal species and the natural habitat, and conversed with the scientists through email. Curriculum materials and lesson plans are available for classrooms that subscribe to the project. The technology provides a means to bring together the context of the Galapagos Islands, the expertise of the scientists, and students around the world for an extraordinary learning journey. Check it out for yourself at **http://quest.classroom.com/archive/ galapagosquest1999/default.asp**.

In the fall of 2002, the team followed Christopher Columbus's sea route through the Bahamas to Cuba. Students helped the team explore the question of where Columbus first set foot in the New World. For more information on this and other quests, visit **http:// quest.classroom.com/quests/**.

▨ *Social Studies Education*

Among other tools, social studies teachers across a broad range of subjects are making use of technological tools that include databases, online archives, electronic simulations, virtual fieldtrips, and spreadsheets.

▨ *organizing knowledge using databases*

▨ **Databases**   **Databases** are powerful tools for organizing information that are used by teachers and students in many content areas. A database software program stores information in the form of records (analogous to a 3″ by 5″ index card) and fields* of data within each record (analogous to the individual lines of data on the index card). The database user is able to sort quickly through the "cards," shuffling them in different orders. For example, if the database contains information from a census, you can view it by last name, age, race, and so on. The computer will also allow the user to filter out those records not relevant to the task—for instance, hiding all records except those of African American women. Database software allows the user to search for information that would otherwise prove too tedious to gather. For instance, a database could be used to compare several decades of infant mortality rates. Done by hand, this task might take several hours; by computerized database, it would take a few minutes.

In addition, the computer's ability to filter information into discrete categories, then sort that information by various criteria, allows the user to manipulate data in ways that are purposeful and useful beyond the data itself.[17] A middle-

---

*A *field* is a container for one piece of information. For example, a first-name field would store the first name for each record.

school class studying socioeconomic statistics could use a world atlas database to examine the relationships between literacy and life expectancy, population and land mass, or average income and crime rates.[18] In these ways, the database can become a cognitive tool allowing students to enhance their thinking rather than a mere collection of information.

■ **Online Archives** Social scientists are digitizing* immense archives and publishing them on the World Wide Web. Without the computer to help organize and manage such large amounts of information, a teacher might be limited to using several photocopied diary entries to expose students to primary sources.† Giving students access to a rich archive that is organized by databases allows them to broaden their understanding of history and do the work of historians. For example, the *Valley of the Shadow* web site‡ contains detailed databases of census results, church records, newspaper articles, military records, and letters about two communities, one southern and one northern, during the Civil War. Users can investigate the answers to questions they pose, such as what was the average number of slaves people held or how did occupations differ in the North and South. Students can incorporate the details they discover into their larger picture of the Civil War, building a richer understanding of the event than facts alone could provide. The role of the teacher changes from dispenser of knowledge to guide through the archives, helping students learn to ask the right questions and examine the sources critically. Students and teachers construct their understanding of history together.

doing the work of historians

teacher as guide through the archives

■ **Simulations** A **simulation,** a representation of an activity or environment, is a time-honored and effective teaching technique. Long before software developers began to use the technique, teachers had their classes simulating a newspaper business or a famous court case. A simulation can be a fun way to explore an environment or a concept that would be too expensive, or possibly dangerous, to handle in reality. For this reason, simulations have proven to be a fertile field for educational software developers. A large variety of computerized simulations are available for classroom use in practically every field.

Decisions, Decisions: Local Government§ is a simulation game in which users assume the role of the mayor of a community facing a dilemma. The town's main employer, a mining company, wants to greatly expand production. The mayor must choose between improved employment opportunities with increased development and keeping the quality of life while risking economic stagnation. The mayor must listen to advisers and weigh the options. The program can be used by the class as a whole, with only one computer, or it can accommodate multiple small groups at individual computers. After students input their decisions, the software reacts and presents them with the results. For example, if the mayor raises taxes, she or he must accept some public dissatisfaction. To come up with every possible scenario and consequence manually would be an

students assume the role of mayor

---

*The digitizing process stores documents in an electronic format that allows them to be viewed on the Web and archived in a more permanent form.

†A primary source is a firsthand account. For example, a soldier who fought at the battle of Gettysburg and described it in his diary provides a firsthand account or primary source.

‡To learn more, visit the University of Virginia's Valley of the Shadow web site (**http://jefferson. village.virginia.edu/vshadow2/**).

§The *Decisions, Decisions* series of software titles is available from Tom Snyder Productions (**http://www.tomsnyder.com/**; telephone: 800-342-0236).

The teacher helps a student use a Photoshop program as others watch. (© David Young-Wolff/PhotoEdit)

overwhelming task for any teacher, but the computerized simulation manages that information easily. The software frees the teacher to be more involved with the students and to mediate instruction.

■ *exploring environments beyond the classroom*

■ **Virtual Fieldtrips**   **Virtual fieldtrips** provide a wealth of opportunities to extend learning. Not limited to social studies, virtual fieldtrips can be used to provide information about a site that students are unable to visit.[19] It is unlikely you will manage a class outing to the Amazon rainforest, for example, but National Geographic's Jason Project* provides a "fieldtrip" through the computer. Hundreds of sites are produced by teachers, agencies, governments, and students themselves. Student-produced virtual fieldtrips are often used in connection with local history. Students conduct interviews and use digital cameras to take pictures of important sites and people in their community. Digital cameras use a disk instead of film to capture an image. By using photo-editing software such as *Photoshop,*† the image can be manipulated or enhanced on the computer screen. Students can put their images of local sites into a multimedia presentation program such as *HyperStudio* or *PowerPoint* and add descriptions. These can then be published on the World Wide Web and viewed by others. Students can see themselves as historians who are contributing to the preservation of their community's story.

Visit this chapter of the web site to link to examples of virtual fieldtrips.

■ *students contribute to local history projects*

■ **Using Spreadsheets to Connect Disciplines**   Though social studies and math are not two subjects that people naturally connect, technology helps

*To learn more, visit The Jason Project web site (**http://www.jasonproject.org/**).
†*PhotoShop* is available from Adobe (**http://www.adobe.com/**; telephone: 800-833-6687).

facilitate such interdisciplinary relationships by providing easy access to rich data. For example, students who visit the National Center for Health Statistics web site* can find data on the number of live births in the United States, create a **spreadsheet** to mathematically manipulate and display the information, then analyze the trends based on their knowledge of U.S. history.[20] A spreadsheet is a software program that allows users to perform multiple calculations. With a simple calculator, students can find only one answer at a time, and for more complex scenarios, this is too limiting. But a spreadsheet will allow the user to see all the numbers and formulas at once. Any change is immediately reflected in the entire sheet. Using the above example, students are able to calculate whether the number of live births increased or decreased over time. As a tool for forecasting and predicting, a spreadsheet might help students understand the consequences of population changes. For example, during a hypothetical epidemic, students can predict the future population changes and hypothesize the societal effects. Technology facilitates these interdisciplinary connections: the World Wide Web offers easy access to numerous sets of rich, real-world data, while the spreadsheet provides a powerful tool to manipulate the data. Social studies problems are analyzed using mathematical and social studies skills, and students are challenged to synthesize data, make predictions, and construct knowledge.

forecasting and predicting changes in society

Mathematics Education

From slide rules to calculators, math teachers have relied on technology for years. This section deals with some of the newer uses of technology in math education, including tutorial software, other software, and graphing calculators.

Tutorial Software **Tutorials** are educational software applications designed to provide the initial instruction on a given topic. They are used in most disciplines. Unlike drill and practice, tutorials present the skill or concept, then check for understanding throughout the process, and evaluate the learner's grasp of the topic once the program is completed. More narrative in nature than drill and practice, tutorial software often has the feel of a book placed on computer.

Somewhat controversial, tutorial software is intended to replace the teacher as the primary agent of instruction for a particular topic. To achieve this, the software is self-contained and self-paced. Small chunks of information are delivered to the learner in a careful sequence of instruction designed to adjust to students' needs, allowing them to achieve success. One tutorial program is *Fundamental Math*.[†] Users move through concepts such as fractions and decimals at their own pace; topics are explained, reinforced, and tested. As with most tutorials, the software may be turned off and the user's location in the program saved for a later time. Generally more flexible than drill-and-practice applications, this type of software is a powerful tool for individualizing instruction and monitoring student progress.

self-contained, self-paced software

*To learn more, visit the National Center for Health Statistics web site (**http://www.cdc.gov/nchs**).

[†]*Fundamental Math* is available from Boxer Learning, Inc. (**http://www.boxermath.com**; telephone: 888-627-5327).

■ **Other Math Software**   Certain mathematics-specific software enhances what teachers can do. For example, *The Geometer's Sketchpad** allows students to explore the relationships among points, lines, planes, and angles in an environment conducive to experimentation. Users are offered a palette of tools for drawing and deriving geometric concepts. This cognitive tool enables the user to explore, question, learn, theorize, fail, succeed, and grow.[21]

■ **Graphing Calculators**   Schools are trying to heed the National Council of Teachers of Mathematics' statement that "Electronic technologies—calculators and computers—are essential tools for teaching, learning, and doing mathematics. They furnish visual images of mathematical ideas, they facilitate organizing and analyzing data, and they compute efficiently and accurately."[22] Electronic technologies help teachers and students with some of the same tasks that were conducted without these aids. Many students find it difficult to make connections among the graphical, numerical, and algebraic representations of mathematical functions, for example, but the speed and ease with which graphs can be generated and manipulated using graphing calculators help students to understand those relationships. Technology also enhances what teachers and students are able to do. Students can use data collection devices[†] connected to their calculators, for example, to conduct their own investigations of mathematical phenomena. Learning becomes more active, and students consult with both technology and the teacher.[23] Technology has not replaced the teacher. As students are gathering the data themselves and manipulating the graphical representations, the teacher watches and analyzes how individual students are solving problems and making sense of mathematical concepts. Technology is enhancing what the teacher is able to do.

■ *Foreign Language Education*

The World Wide Web and **telecommunications** applications open up vast opportunities in foreign language education. Compare assigning a sterile textbook article about French food to connecting your students with e-pals in French-speaking Africa so they can ask about the cuisine themselves. Furthermore, the World Wide Web offers a wide array of current foreign language publications that would be far too difficult and expensive to obtain otherwise. Students will find extensive online newspaper collections in languages as different as Arabic and Portuguese, as well as live radio from Guatemala.

A **news group** is a feature of the Web that can be compared with a large wall full of messages in chronological order. When you subscribe to a news group, you join an online discussion that occurs as people post messages and reply to one another. Teachers nationwide log on to these resources to share ideas, find keypals for their students, and converse with other professionals in their field. For example, ESPAN-L[‡] is a news group for teachers of Spanish, and discussion ranges from cultural notes to grammatical points. Students can also log on to news groups and join a discussion in a foreign language. To participate in this real, interactive chat, students are required to put their communication abil-

Visit this chapter of the web site to link to the National Council of Teachers of Mathematics.

■ *making connections among multiple representations*

---

*Key Curriculum Press produces *Geometer's Sketchpad* (**http://www.keypress.com/sketchpad/**).

[†]One example is Texas Instrument's Calculator Based Ranger (**http://education.ti.com/ product/tech/cbr/features/features.html**; telephone: 800-842-2737).

[‡]To learn more, visit the ESPAN-L web site (**http://www.uv.es/~lemir/Espan_L.html**).

ities to the test. These engaging ways of learning foreign languages are changing the way we teach and encouraging us to be creative and flexible.

Distance Education

School districts vary greatly in location, size, budget, composition of populations, and graduation requirements. Such differences often create educational inequities, particularly when a school district simply cannot afford to provide the quality and variety of courses offered by larger or more affluent districts. **Distance education** is a fast-growing alternative for schools trying to overcome such constraints.

connecting professionals and students

Distance education involves using technology to link students and instructors in separate locations. As we have seen, two-way audio and video allow live interaction between individuals who are hundreds or thousands of miles apart, while the Web allows the rapid exchange of data over distances. Thus, distance education can allow schools to increase educational opportunities by offering courses otherwise prohibited by cost or other constraints.

A congressional report found that distance education can help reverse some of the effects of the nation's long-term population shift from rural to metropolitan areas. This population loss has caused many districts to close or consolidate schools, forcing many rural students to travel long distances.[24] Ironically, the decline of rural populations has often been accompanied by state educational reforms that pressure schools to broaden programs and offer more courses. Many schools find themselves in the awkward situation of having to offer elective subjects for which neither funds nor teachers are available.

Reflect on distance education with the image in this section of your CD-ROM.

An explosion in the availability of online courses has alleviated some of this pressure. The Virtual High School (VHS)* first offered courses in 1997–98 and in 2001, it offered 156 courses to more than 1700 students. Students from around the country use their courses' web sites as their starting point. From there they obtain readings and assignments. Students then log on to a daily discussion group in which the teacher conducts a *netseminar*. This flexible arrangement accommodates a variety of school schedules as well as time zone differences. The convenience and additional time for reflection that come from logging on at any point make the netseminar particularly appealing. Students do telecollaborative projects for the course by exchanging information over the Web. All the makings of a traditional class are present without the face-to-face interaction. Furthermore, schools in more isolated areas or with limited resources can vastly expand the courses they offer to include such diverse classes as Eastern philosophy and the history of aviation. Students below the college level can explore nontraditional academic avenues and connect with peers who have similar intellectual interests. While the VHS intends to enhance the traditional high school experience, other programs are available that offer complete high school curricula for those who are overseas or homebound, or who are nontraditional students.

an alternative to the traditional high school experience

Technology for Students with Special Needs

Technology tools can be of especially great assistance to students with special needs. For those with disabilities, the tools can help level the playing field by

*To learn more, visit the Virtual High School web site (**http://www.govhs.org/website.nsf**).

This computerized voice synthesizer is reopening the world to this mute accident victim. (© Spencer Grant/ Index Stock)

Visit the web site to link to more information about assistive technology.

■ *assistive technology*

■ *vastly improving the quality of life and education for special-needs students*

presenting information in a manner best suited to a student's learning style and particular needs. Although using a software program does not replicate the experience of learning from a teacher, the computer is not constrained by the human variables of limited patience and classroom distractions. Using the right software, an alternative, individualized curriculum can be created for students with special needs, paralleling the standard school curriculum.

In addition to its direct instructional uses, technology plays a second, very important role for special-needs students. The term **assistive technology** describes the array of devices and services that help people with disabilities perform better in their daily lives. (See the chapter entitled "Who Are Today's Students in a Diverse Society?" for a further discussion of assistive technology and special education.) Students with disabilities may rely on a variety of innovations to help them achieve successful inclusion in regular classrooms.[25]

Computers are especially helpful in allowing students to participate in normal classroom activities that would otherwise be impossible. User-friendly keyboard enhancements simplify typing, and assistive technology can be used to control most basic computer applications. ERICA (Eyegaze Response Interface Computer Aid) is one revolutionary technology that opens up opportunities for special-needs students. Using ERICA's system that tracks and records the user's eye movements and pupil dilation across a computer display, the mouse can be controlled with eye movement alone, allowing even extremely immobile students to communicate with teachers and classmates.*

The variety of tools to help special-needs students fully participate in school is constantly expanding. The options include a word-predictor feature† that facilitates keyboarding. After the student types a letter or two, the computer pre-

---

*To learn more, contact ERICA (**http://www.ericainc.com/**; telephone: 434-296-3846).

†One such product is *Co-Writer* by Don Johnston Inc. (**http://www.donjohnston.com/**; telephone: 800-999-4660).

sents a list of likely words, and the student simply selects the correct word rather than typing it out completely. Other aids, such as voice recognition software, which translate a student's spoken words into text on the computer screen, or programs that will read text aloud,* can make writing a satisfying experience for students who struggle in this area.[26] Blind students and their teachers can use braille software, which provides easy-to-use, sophisticated print-to-braille and braille-to-print translations.†

▨ *part of IEPs*

As discussed in the chapter entitled "Who Are Today's Students in a Diverse Society?", assistive technology must be considered a potential component of the individualized education program (IEP) required under law for each child with a disability. Regular classrooms now often include students with disabilities and other students with special needs, and you should be prepared to work with children who use assistive technology in your classroom.

PAUSE AND REFLECT

❶ To what technologies should students have access?

❷ Pick the technology that most interests you in this section, and think about how you might use that technology in your classroom. Would it allow you to improve on something you already did? Would you be innovating with the technology?

❸ Do you have any educational concerns about the use of these technologies in schools?

How Are Technologies Affecting Teaching?

▨ *movement toward standards*

 Visit the web site to link to the International society for Technology in Education (ISTE).

As a teacher, you can expect your students to have to meet some standards relating to technology. Some states give technology only a brief mention in their standards, whereas others have separate standards exclusively for technology. North Carolina requires its students to pass both a multiple choice and performance test.[27] In line with the current nationwide move toward standards-based learning (see "What Ought to Be the Elements of Educational Reform" in the chapter entitled "How Should Education Be Reformed?"), the International Society for Technology in Education (ISTE) has produced national technology standards. For example, before completing eighth grade, students should "design, develop, publish, and present products (e.g., web pages, video tapes) using technology resources that demonstrate and communicate curriculum concepts to audiences inside and outside the classroom."[28] ISTE encourages teachers to teach these skills within the context of their academic curriculum. To this end, ISTE has worked with content specialists to provide resources for incorporating the ISTE technology standards into subject standards for the rest of the curriculum.

DragonDictate is a popular voice-input program available from Software Maintenance, Inc. (**http://www.ddwin.com/dictate.htm**; telephone: 888-343-3773). *IntelliTalk II* is a talking word processor from IntelliTools (**http://www.intellitools.com/**; telephone: 800-899-6687).

†Kurzweil Educational Systems offers software for visually impaired students (**http://www. kurzweiledu.com/products.html**; telephone: 800-894-5374).

This trend is encouraging; however, for technology to be truly integrated as an important part of classroom instruction, several additional shifts must take place in current practices and attitudes. The impact of technology on learning depends more on how teachers use the technology than on the characteristics of the technology itself.

■ A Different Role for the Teacher

Learn more about changes in the teacher's role in the video resources on your CD-ROM.

Integrating technology into your teaching can change the way you deliver content to your classes. Many schools and teachers have been slow to discover the real potential of new technologies, but some new trends are emerging. Technology can be more effective in a teaching environment where computers help to facilitate instruction and foster a constructivist approach to learning, as discussed in "The Influence of Psychological Theories" in the chapter entitled "What Are the Philosophical Foundations of American Education?". As we have mentioned throughout this chapter, a constructivist approach to infusing technology is related to several other classroom characteristics, including the following:

teacher as leader and co-learner

- *Teacher as a Facilitator.* Think back to the scenario at the beginning of this chapter. Patricia Gonzalez, a technology-assisted teacher, was *facilitating* instruction as needed to bring a deeper understanding and relevance to students. Because of the technology the students employed, she was no longer the sole source of information for her class. By using technology to present basic factual and historical information, the teacher is freed to become much more involved in higher-level evaluation of performance. Teachers can monitor students' projects, guiding their efforts and providing feedback. Instead of being a teller and a tester, the teacher can be a leader and a co-learner. In such environments, teachers must view themselves as "coaches" or "facilitators" who guide students as they use technology to discover facts and concepts.

the subject matter drives the technology

- *Embedding Technology in the Curriculum.* With the encouragement of groups like ISTE, described above, teaching technology skills in isolation is giving way to a new model of embedding technology skills within the context of the content.[29] For example, a teacher will teach the mechanics of a program, such as *HyperStudio,* when asking students to create a virtual fieldtrip, as described earlier in the chapter. The subject matter is driving the technology rather than vice versa. In the words of one team of researchers, "we learn best 'with' technology rather than 'from' it."[30]

- *Small Group Instruction.* To better use the available technology, teachers must move from whole-class instruction toward smaller group projects and activities that are conducive to active, engaged learning and student interactions. This is not a shift all teachers warmly embrace. Smaller group work may mean that students learn different things at different times rather than an entire class learning the same material together. In many ways, this resembles the days before chalkboards and full-class instruction. Classrooms that effectively use technology evolve into cooperative rather than competitive social structures, and student assessment shifts from pencil-and-paper testing toward the evaluation of products and progress in meeting established criteria.[31]

Reflect on the relationship between constructivism and technology in the video resources on your CD-ROM.

The connection between technology and constructivism is not clear, but some researchers are beginning to understand elements of it. We know that teachers who have changed to a more constructivist approach in their classrooms are the same teachers who have used computers consistently and in meaningful ways in their classrooms. These teachers are more willing to discuss subjects in which they are not experts and tend to assign longer, more complex projects. It appears not that the technology makes teachers change but that the technology facilitates changes that teachers already wanted to make.[32]

■ *technology as facilitator of change*

Technology is not only a product of a given culture; it also shapes the culture that created it.
—Howard D. Mehlinger

However, change in education is rarely swift. Even highly motivated teachers who regularly used technology took substantial amounts of time (over three to five years) to become comfortable with new technology and able to fit it into their classroom goals.[33] With increasing pressure on schools to incorporate up-to-date technology and with other supporting factors present, such as sufficient funding and on-site technical support, we can expect to see changes in teachers' pedagogy as they become more comfortable with the power of technology.

■ *Project CHILD combines traditional and constructivist views of education*

Florida's Project CHILD (Computers Helping Instruction and Learning Development)* demonstrates some of the changes in common teaching practices and attitudes toward learning classrooms that help teachers effectively incorporate technology in teaching. Elementary-school teachers work together in teams of three, clustered by grade level (K–2 or 3–5). Each teacher focuses on one of three subject areas: reading, language arts, or math. For three hours each day, these teachers' classrooms are transformed into learning resource rooms for the teacher's subject-area focus. Students spend one hour per day in each of the three classrooms in their cluster. For the rest of the day, they are with one of the teachers whose classroom serves as their home base.

When students are in their math or language arts or reading resource room, they rotate among different activities, which include working at a computer station with three to six computers, working in a small group with the teacher at his or her station, and working at reading and writing stations. Through this rotation, students have access to computers every day in one subject or the other. Students keep a written "passport" that records progress and organizes their instruction as they move from classroom to classroom, working at different learning stations. This systematic approach ensures equitable computer time for all, and teachers can individualize instruction by examining students' passports and specifying where students begin working each day.

Reflect on the role of technology in teaching with the image in this section of your CD-ROM.

Project CHILD combines both traditional and constructivist views of instruction. While students are using their station time, teachers circulate to facilitate learning. In addition, teachers offer some traditional instruction when they pull out small groups for extra help or enrichment.

Project CHILD also aims to help teachers shift from being the single source of knowledge in their classroom to being a facilitator and coach. Children often work together to complete group projects and to have maximum computer time, learning from one another and the computer and other materials in each room.

■ *how computers are used as a key variable*

Even though the activities and assessments in Project CHILD differ from traditional schoolwork, students who participated in the program for a full three-year cycle scored better on standardized tests than their peers in conventional classrooms with similar computer-student ratios.[34] These results suggest that an important variable is not simply how many computers students have access to but how those computers are used.

*For more information, visit Project CHILD's web site at **http://www.ifsi.org/**.

■ *Professional Resources and Communication*

In the past decade, we have witnessed a boom in communications. Facsimile machines, cellular phones with web capabilities, satellite broadcasting, and powerful handheld computers have been shrinking our world. With these tools a teacher can communicate with colleagues worldwide, both quickly and cheaply.

■ *a less expensive technological modification*

■ Voice Mail   Technology's advantages are not confined to extremely expensive and complicated arrangements. For those schools and parents who do not yet have a powerful, efficient online connection, technology still provides ways to ease communication. The Bridge Project is a voice messaging system every teacher in a school can use to post a message on a voice "bulletin board" for his or her class. Teachers can leave a description of the week's activities as well as reminders for upcoming events. Parents can access this message twenty-four hours a day, seven days a week from any telephone. Parents can also leave a message for the teacher, or students can check homework assignments. In schools that use the Bridge Project, the number of daily teacher-parent contacts increased from three to fourteen per teacher in the project's first year.[35]

■ Email   Email is an excellent medium for teachers to use in sharing ideas, materials, and resources. Besides being fast and cheap, email can be sent with attachments, so correspondents can share anything from a word processing document to digital video files. It can also be sent to large groups of recipients as easily as to one, making it much more efficient than the telephone or mailings. Teachers can communicate with parents via email, and vice versa, without the disruption of ringing phones and answering machines. Within the school setting itself, email has streamlined the work environment, reduced staff meetings, and decreased the mounds of accumulated paper.

Reflect on the ways technology might help you with the image in this section of your CD-ROM.

■ *online teacher resources*

■ The Web   The Web connects teachers to professional organizations in their field and to vast databases of lesson plans and teaching materials throughout the world. The list of web sites at the end of this chapter is just a small sample of an incredibly large and growing resource. **Search engines** can help you find more information specific to your needs. In addition, news groups, described earlier, offer teachers an online source of resources and collegial communication.

■ *reducing teachers' isolation through technology*

Specific computer networks are also providing an innovative medium for professional growth and support of teachers, particularly new teachers. Welcoming Interns and Novices with Guidance and Support (WINGS) Online* is a publicly accessible electronic bulletin board that provides a problem solving community for new and student teachers in Texas. Monitored by experienced educators, teachers regularly ask telementors for advice, seek out research, pose dilemmas, and support each other. While not replacing in-person mentoring, the online community provides a limitless resource available anytime, anywhere to support teachers and build community.

■ *Management: Teacher Productivity Tools*

Teaching involves many complex tasks. Organizing learning activities, creating or gathering the materials needed, keeping records, managing conduct, and

*To learn more, visit WINGS Online (**http://emissary.ots.utexas.edu/wings/**).

Using ERIC

ERIC is a federally funded, national information system that provides access to a variety of services and products dealing with education-related issues. The ERIC database is the primary resource for locating research on teaching and learning. In addition, ERIC creates digests of research on important topics to help educators traverse the research landscape. ERIC is available to libraries on CD-ROM or to anyone with access to the Web at **http://www.eric.ed.gov/**.

AskERIC is a web-based question-answering service for teachers, library media specialists, administrators, and anyone else with questions about education. Just send an email message to **askeric@askeric.org**, and the AskERIC staff will draw on its extensive resources to answer your question, usually within forty-eight hours. You can also visit the web site mentioned above. In addition to these important services, ERIC offers hundreds of lesson plans, a virtual library, and links to many other educational services.

---

delivering instruction—all of these together add up to a big job. A teacher may have from 25 to 150 or more students every day, with attendance records to be kept and grades recorded for each one. Although no technology will take on all these tasks for teachers, tools are available to help with some of them.

software gradebooks save time

■ **Gradebooks**   A software gradebook, also referred to as an *electronic gradebook,* is a hybrid application of a spreadsheet and a database. The database functions keep records of student and parent information such as mailing addresses, phone numbers, locker numbers, book numbers, and other details. The spreadsheet functions calculate grades and provide the teacher with statistical information regarding assignments, tests, and performance of students over time. The computer's ability to handle these calculations and information retrieval tasks can save hours of work for teachers. It can also give teachers new ways to identify a student's strengths and weaknesses. Gradebook software will even allow the teacher to print charts of a student's academic performance over time (quarters or semesters) for the student or parent to inspect.

software to help teachers

■ **Other Teacher Productivity Tools**   Test generators and question bank software allow teachers to create a database of questions and then construct tests from them. The teacher can easily create two or three versions of the same test with the questions in a different order or with slightly different questions. This is particularly useful for pre- and post-assessments or for giving a different test to students absent on test day. IEP software helps manage the paperwork involved in the individualized programs required in special education. Time management tools, such as schedule or calendar software, can help teachers keep track of appointments and schedules. Grant-writing software can help teachers find alternative sources of funding and organize the process of applying for grants. As their size and price come down, some teachers are using handheld computers that allow grade input, schedule coordination, file sharing, organization of students' data, and web page downloading in a portable form. Tools such as these allow teachers to spend more time at the art of teaching and less time dealing with paperwork, organization, and materials management.

PAUSE AND REFLECT

❶ To what technologies should teachers have access?

❷ Do you envision yourself as a teacher who would be comfortable using technology in a constructivist way, such as Patricia Gonzalez did?

❸ What do you see as the pros and cons of such an approach?

How Are Computer Technologies Organized for Student Use?

Reflect on ways the Internet is changing education with the image on your CD-ROM.

Computer technologies generally operate in several different arrangements within the school setting, and it is useful to think of these arrangements across a continuum from concentrated to infused, as shown in Figure 6.1. When technology is *concentrated*, students are given intense exposure to computers from time to time. Technology that is integrated smoothly into the daily classroom experience is described as *infused*. Several common computer setups exist along this continuum.

■ Computer Labs

advantages of labs

Computer labs, which usually feature a number of computers in a single room, offer a concentrated arrangement in which all the students use computers at the same time. This setup is ideal for technology education—teaching about the computer or how to employ a particular application. A large display station for the teacher facilitates the demonstration of skills for more effective whole-class instruction. Forty-three percent of computers in American schools are found in computer labs and 48 percent are found in classrooms, according to one recent national survey.[36]

disadvantages of labs

However, most computer labs do not lend themselves to interdisciplinary or cooperative group projects because of a lack of open table space, but some teachers foster collaboration by having two chairs around one computer. Access to computer labs is another key factor in their use by teachers. If many classrooms share one computer facility, there may be little lab time for each class, and visits to the lab must always be planned. For these reasons, computer labs tend to foster technology education rather than what we might call education *with* technology, that is, education that uses technology to facilitate learning about other subjects.

■ Single-Computer Classrooms

productive uses for a single computer

In a slightly more infused arrangement, the single-computer classroom might have the computer on the teacher's desk or rolled into the room on a mobile cart. In the first case especially, the teacher can use it for record keeping and

Figure 6.1
Arrangements for Computer Technologies
One way to think about the different ways of arranging computer technologies within a school is to consider where each arrangement fits along a continuum, from concentrated to infused. If the arrangement is concentrated, students are exposed to computers in an intense way from time to time, whereas technology that is integrated smoothly into the daily classroom experience is considered infused.

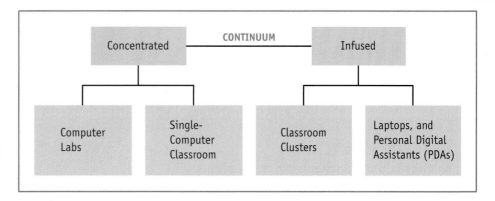

other administrative tasks. Thirty-six percent of teachers report having only one computer in their classroom.[37]

Although a single computer makes it difficult to use the technology for active instructional tasks, additional computers can sometimes be rolled into the classroom for lessons. Also, a display station can be attached to project the monitor's image on a large screen for classroom presentations and demonstrations. With software designed for the single-computer classroom, such as *Decisions, Decisions: Local Government,* discussed earlier in the chapter, the computer can even be used to facilitate cooperative groups. However, schools using this level of technology integration usually also have computer labs available for class use.

▦ *Classroom Clusters*

In a more infused situation, a cluster is usually a table or an area of a classroom where three to five computers are available for use at any time by the students in that class. Thirty-eight percent of teachers report having two to five computers in their classrooms.[38] Clusters provide convenient access to computer technologies for a variety of tasks. For example, a teacher might use two of the computers to allow cooperative groups access to cognitive and communication tools and the others as learning stations for specific subjects.

▪ *clusters are a flexible arrangement*

Providing a cluster of computers in each classroom generally requires more of an investment in technology than the other arrangements we have described. Whereas a computer lab of twenty-five computers may afford access for ten classrooms, clusters might require thirty to fifty computers. If a school can afford them, clusters offer a very flexible use of technology in the classroom setting. Teachers can plan to use them in instruction and can set up each computer to fit their needs. This arrangement genuinely fosters education *with* technology. It is not particularly good, however, for technology education, since not every student has access simultaneously.

▦ *Laptops and Handheld Computers*

Partnerships between business and education have made the dream of a portable computer for every student a reality in some places around the nation. In the fall of 1996, Microsoft began a Laptop Pilot Program at twenty-nine

POLICY MATTERS!

Web-Filtering Software: Censorship or Good Sense?

What's the Policy?

As more and more schools provide students with access to the World Wide Web, parents and teachers have become concerned about how to protect students from exposure to inappropriate web sites. As a result, many schools are adopting *acceptable-use policies (AUPs),** which are signed by teachers, students, and administrators and state the guidelines for the responsible use of computer technology.

Even with a strong acceptable use policy, some schools and school districts may not wish to rely on students alone to behave responsibly. These administrators also may choose to use web-filtering software.† This software disables access to web addresses that are known to be inappropriate, such as pornographic or hate sites. The software updates the filters daily by searching the Web for new inappropriate sites. Although not foolproof, web-filtering software is one way to monitor the burgeoning amount of information on the Web and to protect students from harmful information.

How Does It Affect Teachers?

When teachers assign students research projects using the Web, they need to realize that when web-filtering software is being used at school, the students may be unable to access certain sites that would be relevant to their research. On a day-to-day basis, teachers must be aware of the parameters set for the web-filtering software their schools use. Suppose, for example, that you are teaching a unit on AIDS and you have designed an activity in which students use the Web to search several sites to find up-to-date scientific research. All the sites work when you develop the idea at home, but at school, none of your students can access them. The reason is that your assignment is incompatible with the web-filtering software in use at your school. On the other hand, if your school does not use web-filtering software, and you assign your students to do a search on AIDS in class, they may come across inappropriate and/or dangerous information.

What Are the Pros of Web-Filtering Software?

From pornography to hate literature to directions on how to make a bomb, the Web is an unknown and unmonitored entity with the potential to cause extreme damage. The global nature and design of the Web make it almost impossible to enforce any code of moral or academic ethics.

Another problem is accuracy. No registry is required to publish a web page; anyone with ac-

---

laptops as the most infused arrangement

"pioneer" school sites across the United States. Participating students acquired laptop computers loaded with Microsoft Windows and Microsoft Office software to use regularly at home and at school. This arrangement facilitates deep, flexible use of technology by the students and encourages the teacher to assume the role of facilitator.[39] The laptop arrangement and the even more compact and affordable handheld computer, described earlier in the chapter, offer the most infused arrangement for a classroom and can provide seamless integration with the curriculum.

cess can create his or her own home page, and the information it contains is not necessarily subject to accountability. Students are quick to search, find, cut, and paste without bothering to evaluate the source and the content. This lack of quality control concerns many teachers and makes them hesitant to use the Web without "safety nets," such as web-filtering software, in place.

One additional consideration must be the school's liability. Some teachers and administrators worry that if a child encounters dangerous information and then uses that information to act unlawfully, the school could be held responsible. They prefer a restrictive web-filtering software and an AUP that errs on the side of restraint to protect the school from liability as opposed to the risks of allowing unrestricted access to all the information available.

What Are the Cons?

Some schools see problems with relying on web-filtering software: the filtering technology is not perfect, and schools that rely on it are more vulnerable if it fails. The use of filtering software also brings up censorship and First Amendment rights (see the chapter entitled "What Are the Ethical and Legal Issues Facing Teachers?" for more on this subject). Some teachers believe that even though the Web contains a great deal of inappropriate information, students should have unlimited access but be closely monitored. Teachers need to instruct their students in ways to evaluate

the authority of web sources‡, monitor students when they use technology, and enforce acceptable and responsible use. This strategy models trust and teaches proper researching skills instead of relying on an imperfect filter and withholding valuable information.

What Do You Think?

1. **In this scenario, if your school were reviewing its decision to use web-filtering software, how would you vote? Explain.**

2. **Would your decision on web-filtering software change if you knew that the software collected data on students' web-use habits for the company that created it?**

3. **How would you answer a parent who complains that her child came across pornographic information while researching the project you assigned?**

4. **How would you modify your lesson about online searching if a parent refused to sign his child's permission slip to use the Web at school?**

*For an example, visit: **http://www.jefferson.k12.ky.us/aup/policy.html**.

†Surf Control produces an array of filtering software. Available at: **http://www.surfcontrol.com/**; telephone: (800) 368-3366.

‡For some helpful questions to ask when evaluating a web site, visit: **http://www.library.jhu.edu/elp/useit/evaluate/**.

 Visit the web site to learn more about this policy issue.

PAUSE AND REFLECT

❶ Envision yourself teaching with each of these computer arrangements. What would you and your students be able to do in a computer lab? How would that be different if each of your students is able to use a Palm computer in school? How would your instruction change if you are assigned to a classroom with a single computer?

VOICES FROM THE CLASSROOM

Janet Muller teaches third grade at Duniway Elementary School in Portland, Oregon.

Infusing Technology into the Curriculum

Several years ago, I found myself charged with the daunting task of turning a group of wiggly third graders into sophisticated little techno-wizards. Four new computers were delivered to my classroom and the school district packed me off to a series of amazing classes. Unfortunately I never learned how I could effectively use four computers with 26 little children, and I often found myself pondering the value of a computer program based on sign-up sheets.

I began looking for a way to bring some serious technology into my room that would allow simultaneous student access to equipment. Soon, I stumbled onto the Palm Education Pioneer Program (PEP), an experimental online grant program that offered teachers a unique opportunity to design a classroom technology project using Palm handhelds. My proposal was chosen for funding and last fall we received 30 Palm IIIc color screen handhelds . . . and technology in Room 11 changed forever!

Each one of my third graders has his or her own Palm loaded with wonderful web sites, and when they arrive each morning, the students "hot-sync" to one of the four classroom computers to download updated information. Together, we read the *New York Times* and Reuters News Service each morning. Throughout the day students type their spelling words and check special web sites. They zoom through *Encarta* Spanish dictionaries, studying the definitions of unfamiliar Spanish words; take math, geography, and science quizzes; write collaborative stories; draw detailed maps; create animated illustrations; and play interactive critical thinking games.

After a year with the Palms, my students are as well informed about current events as their parents. The average spelling grade is 92% and my little kiddos draw maps you have to see to believe! But the most rewarding part of this entire project has been the remarkable technology proficiency these children have developed on their own. Putting a Palm in their hands has provided daily opportunities for problem solving, practicing, and experimentation.

My little third-graders WERE transformed into techno-wizards by virtue of opportunity. Rather than waiting for a seat at one of our desktop computers, they've been given an opportunity to take a handheld computer to their seat and use this amazing technology to shine at the important business of third grade.

 Visit the web site for more Voices from the Classroom.

What Are the Key Issues in Educational Technology?

You probably realize by now that many features of educational technology have given rise to serious debate among educators, policymakers, and the general public. To achieve the best use of available technology, schools need to reach some consensus on several key issues.

■ *Infrastructure and Budgeting*

 Visit the web site to link to more information about technology and budget issues.

Before technology can be used as an educational tool, schools must have in place the infrastructure to support it—that is, the basic facilities that make the technology usable. At the most fundamental level, the physical plants of American schools are often ill equipped to handle the demands of technology. Of course, a discussion of infrastructure problems immediately raises issues of money, both the initial costs of new technology and the yearly allowances that must be made in school budgets. This section offers a quick survey of infrastructure and budgetary issues and the ways in which they interrelate.

■ *inadequate power supplies*

Electrical Problems   One basic obstacle to technology integration has been inadequate power supplies. For many years, classrooms were designed with only one electrical outlet at the front of the room. A cluster of computers will not run safely from one outlet. Rewiring has cost both time and money as schools join the information age.

■ *expense of wiring*

Network Wiring   Network wiring has been another roadblock on the information superhighway. The Telecommunications Act of 1996 defined equal access to "universal service" to include electronic networking and provided a fund to help reduce the price of wiring each classroom to form a schoolwide network. This fund of $2.25 billion per year is used for local and long-distance phone charges, high-speed data lines, and web access in schools. Depending on how needy a school district is, discounts can be as high as 90 percent.[40] Much progress has been made in networking schools: by 1999, there was one instructional computer with an online connection for every nine students.[41] However, schools and officials in rural and isolated areas are realizing that connecting fiber-optic cable or other technology infrastructure is more difficult and expensive than they anticipated.[42]

■ *student-to-computer ratios improving*

Access   The ratio of students to computers has dramatically improved in K–12 schools in the last fifteen years, dropping from about 125 to 5. On average, five students share one computer.[43] This trend is encouraging, but significant gaps remain in terms of the quality of equipment. For example, approximately half of school computers are not capable of running sophisticated applications, processing large amounts of data, displaying graphics, or running several applications at once.[44] The challenge in education is not to simply get technological equipment into schools but to keep it up to date and usable in a daily classroom situation.

Technology Budgets   Although costs of personal computers have dropped considerably since they first entered schools, information technology is expensive, especially when it is implemented on the immense scale of public education. For example, state and local governments are spending $7 billion annually to equip schools with computers, networks, hardware, and software.[45] Schools struggling under financial pressure may choose to accept donations of technology equipment in return for access to student information. The accompanying box discusses these questionable practices in more detail.

■ *continued need for up-to-date equipment*

■ *budgets to include repair, maintenance costs*

Beyond the basic issue of providing the needed hardware, school administrators must plan for an ongoing technology budget that includes such items as repair costs. Maintaining a network, within a school or among schools, can be a time-consuming task requiring highly trained personnel. Although many such tasks can be contracted out to local businesses, this factor must be accounted for in yearly budgeting.

Commercial Influences in Schools: Where Do You Draw the Line?

Schools are faced with competing pressures: Industry demands technologically savvy students. Lawmakers demand tight budgets, which can limit technology purchases. Under these opposing forces, some schools have chosen corporate partnerships as the answer. Many corporations are willing to provide cash or free equipment to schools.

What do these businesses get in return? Businesses see vast potential revenue from the 13 million children and teens who will be online by 2005, and they want a way to capture those students' attention and money. Some companies, for example, offer schools free software in exchange for the rights to post online advertisements on school computers. These exchanges have proven controversial. Many parents and educators believe public schools should be commercial-free spaces where children grow and develop away from the pressures of advertising. Others feel that advertising is a small concession to make in exchange for the benefits gained. For more information on corporate sponsorships, see the box titled "Reading, Writing . . . and Purchasing?" in the chapter entitled "How Are Schools Governed, Influenced, and Financed?".

Issues of student privacy further complicate the dilemma. Some web-filtering software, which businesses have donated to schools, collect data on the demographic characteristics and surfing habits of groups of students, and the information is later sold to other businesses. Recent legislation requires school districts to inform parents if students' personal data is gathered for marketing purposes, and parents can choose for their child not to participate.

Where do you draw the line in protecting students? Is it sufficient to guard their personal information, or should students be shielded from the advertising of corporate interests as well?

Source: Amy Aidman, "Children's Online Privacy," *Educational Leadership* 58 (October 2000), pp. 46–47; *Protecting Children and Communities from Commercialism*. Available at: **http://www.commercialalert.org/n2h2/**.

specialists need to support teachers

■ **Support Personnel**   Besides repair personnel to keep the system running, teachers should have access to training and support personnel. Even the most advanced technologies are useless if teachers are not comfortable with their operation. Teachers who encounter technological difficulties may become discouraged and find it easier to avoid using technology altogether. Educational technology specialists who work on-site (in the school itself) are especially important. A technology specialist can act as a safety net for the integration of technology into teaching. Teachers may be more likely to take a risk and try something new if they know help is readily available.[46]

■ *Education of Teachers*

Because of the excitement and demands generated by new technology, pressures have risen to improve both the preparation of new teachers and the staff development options for in-service teachers.

■ **Teacher Preparation**   When you graduate, you can count on having to demonstrate your skills in technology. Twenty-six states currently require teachers to have technology training before being licensed to teach, and three states

■ *teachers' technology standards*

Visit the web site to link to more information about the INTASC standards.

require a technology test for prospective teachers.[47] However, by the end of the decade, new teachers will be held accountable for meeting performance standards. The development of these state requirements is guided by the Interstate New Teacher Assessment and Support Consortium (INTASC). **(Refer to the inside cover of this text for further coverage of INTASC's core standards in other chapters.)** One of INTASC's goals is for every teacher to use "knowledge of effective verbal, nonverbal, and media communication techniques to foster active inquiry, collaboration, and supportive interaction in the classroom."[48] Schools of education, much like elementary and secondary schools, are struggling with how to develop competent teachers who will meet these goals. Many instructors indicate that, even with the recent emphasis on computer literacy, instructional technology is not adequately modeled for future teachers.[49] Schools of education are continuing to rethink their programs and are gradually using modern technology to enhance what they offer. To this end, education students often develop electronic portfolios of their work, create computer-based assessments, and use digital video to capture and reflect on their student teaching.

■ *in-service and pre-service teachers learn from each other*

The University of Virginia's Curry School of Education operates the Technology Infusion Project (TIP), which pairs each preservice teacher enrolled in the Introduction to Classroom Computing course with an in-service teacher who has an interest in educational technologies. During their collaboration, the in-service teacher provides insight about curriculum and classroom practices while the preservice teacher shares the new skills he is learning, such as hypermedia applications or skills in telecomputing. As both teachers become more familiar with new technologies, they jointly explore instructional possibilities, culminating in a long-term project that they teach together in the classroom. Preservice teachers gain a valuable classroom perspective from a veteran in the field and ground their technology learning in classroom practice. Whereas technology workshops often intimidate in-service teachers, TIP's collaborative nature makes it a more comfortable experience.

■ *keeping up to date*

■ Staff Development   Some states are adding more stringent requirements for teachers to renew their licenses. Several states also offer incentives for teachers to develop technology skills that range from paying for classes to buying hardware and software. Nonetheless, teachers report that one of the greatest obstacles to their use of computers is lack of release time to learn how to use technology. In 1999, teachers received an average of thirty-two hours of training in technology use.[50]

Experts do not agree on exactly how training should be offered. Some believe it should be ongoing at teachers' convenience, whereas others advocate an intensive, off-site course with follow-up seminars to allow teachers a chance to learn with undivided attention. With the advent of widespread telecommunications networks, many professional development courses are now offered online.* Teachers who cannot be released during the school day can log on at night or during the summer to work through self-paced lessons. Accompanying discussion groups allow time for reflection.

---

*One example is Classroom Connect (**http://www.classroom.com**).

PAUSE AND REFLECT

① What skills in using media and technology do you think teachers should have?

② How can you prepare yourself to use technology in your classroom?

③ What are your concerns about using technology in the classroom?

④ What support systems do the teachers you know have for using technology in instruction? Whom do they ask when they have questions?

▧ *Parents*

▪ *parents and children learning together*

Technology can be a "hook" to get parents involved or a quick deterrent to send them running. Parents who are not familiar with technology may be intimidated by or fearful of their child's computer use. Technology can become an obstacle between you and your students' parents, but several initiatives are aimed at breaking down these barriers while also educating parents.

Since 1987, Indiana's Buddy Project has worked to increase student achievement using technology in "any time, anywhere" settings to extend the learning beyond the bounds of school.* The Buddy Project supplements existing home and community-based technology to ensure access for all. The project works to strengthen family involvement in education. For example, participating students in kindergarten through eighth grade take home a Buddy Backpack which is filled with themed activities to do with their families. Parents teach other parents, children teach parents, and children teach one another. The Buddy Project extends the child's learning opportunities beyond the classroom walls while creating a special opportunity for the family to become involved as well. With sensitive training, technology can "hook" parental interest in education. For example, one Indiana farming family was able to use their new technological skills to help turn around their family business.[51]

▧ *Equity*

▪ *the digital divide*

The U.S. government reports that urban households with incomes of $75,000 and higher are more than nine times as likely to have a computer at home than rural households at the lowest income levels, and more than twenty times as likely to have web access.[52] Students who use a computer at home have opportunities to develop skills and to explore technology's potential for themselves that are not available to students without those luxuries. Initiatives such as the Buddy Project help to equalize the technological playing field that income levels can divide. However, simple access is not the only barrier. One technology expert argues that students from poorer families are more likely to use computers for games whereas children from middle class families are more likely to use the computer for online research.[53]

Some critics argue, however, that programs like the Indiana Buddy Project are the exception, and current patterns of technology use in schools contribute to disparities in educational quality. At school, data indicate that poorer stu-

*To learn more, visit the Buddy Project web site (**http://www.buddyproject.org/**).

dents are at a disadvantage. While the presence of computers in schools in wealthier and poorer areas has almost equalized, the digital divide still exists in terms of quality of equipment and type of instruction. For example, underprivileged children are more likely to use computers in a rigid drill-and-practice format rather than in more flexible formats, such as doing online research, that build higher-level cognitive skills. In fact, schools with large percentages of low-income children are only about half as likely to have classroom web access as those with higher-income populations.[54] Besides the basic question of fairness, these inequalities will have implications when these students graduate and look for jobs without the computer skills of their more affluent peers.

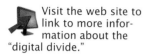 Visit the web site to link to more information about the "digital divide."

Technology access and use also divides along racial lines. For example, African American and Hispanic households lag behind the national average rate of computer ownership. Overall, about half of all American households have a computer, but only one-third of either African American or Hispanic households have one.[55] As computers become more commonplace in schools, teachers need to consider students' access to technology outside of school, particularly in assigning homework.

Significant improvement has occurred in rural areas, helping to close the digital divide. Even though connecting rural areas has been more expensive than anticipated, rural households with online access increased between December 1998 and 2000 by 75 percent, bringing rural households' online access close to the national average.[56]

■ *gender inequities*

Gender differences also have emerged from the use of technology in education. For example, in 2000 only 15 percent of high school seniors taking the Advanced Placement Computer Science exam[57] and 9 percent of the recipients of engineering-related bachelor's degrees were female.[58] Researchers argue that certain types of technologies aggravate the differences between boys and girls. For example, many commonly used applications value speed, aggression, and efficiency[59]—qualities that boys tend to display—whereas technology tends to be more interesting for girls when it's used for a relevant problem-solving exercise and not as an end in itself.[60] Although researchers may argue about whether these differences arise from natural differences between girls and boys or from cultural and social influences, there is little doubt that girls receive less exposure and training in technology during their school experience than boys. However, with the growth of telecollaboration in both education and business, and the move to a more integrated approach to technology in the curriculum, girls' skills may become more valued. Tasks that require versatility and collaboration may invite girls to participate.

■ *what teachers can do*

Teachers can do a lot to dispel inequities within their own classrooms. Students with little computer experience can be teamed with more experienced users. Classrooms and computer labs can be made available to students before and after school, and teachers can promote gender equity through modeling, attitude, and expectations. Technology need not become a wedge widening the gap between the "haves" and the "have-nots"; but without awareness of the problem, the potential for increased inequity is very real.

PAUSE AND REFLECT

❶ Where do you see evidence of the digital divide in the world outside of the K–12 classroom?

❷ How will the digital divide affect you and your classroom?

■ *Integration into the Curriculum*

We need to recognize that it is one thing to use technology in isolated classrooms and quite another to make technology a potent force in transforming an entire school or an entire education system.

—BARBARA MEANS

■ essential conditions

For computer technology to become a genuine part of school life, as it has in the business world, the tools of technology must be *integrated* into school behaviors. Integrating technology means bringing the tools of technology into daily learning and teaching activities, just as teachers already do with chalkboards and books. This is not an easy task. Much of this chapter has focused on how computer technologies can be used as tools for student learning, but we have also seen that many support systems must be in place.

What conditions must be present in a school "to create learning environments conducive to powerful uses of technology"?[61] Among other conditions, schools must have the following:

- Student-centered approaches to learning

- Access to contemporary technologies, software, and telecommunications networks

- Educators skilled in the use of the technology for learning

- Technical assistance for maintaining and using technology resources

- Ongoing financial support for sustained technology use

- Content standards and curriculum resources

- Community partners who provide expertise, support, and real-life interactions

- Vision with support and proactive leadership from the education system

- Assessment of the effectiveness of technology for learning

As this list* indicates, real change in education and technology cannot be the job of a lone teacher who is a whiz on the Web or a solo school board member who votes for new software. It must be a systemic change coming from a critical mass of individuals who are committed to the integration of education *with* technology.

A Final Word

One key issue that we have not fully addressed is whether all the "hype" about technology will simply go the way of the filmstrip. Are we spending billions of dollars on fancy hardware, remodeling schools to accommodate wireless networks, and asking veteran teachers to change their ways without reason? What do we lose when we incorporate technology into our teaching? With increased access to vast amounts of up-to-date information and powerful new technologies, are students learning "the basics" as well as they do in more traditional classrooms?

*International Society for Technology in Education, *National Educational Technology Standards— Connecting Curriculum and Technology* (telephone: 800-336-6191 [United States and Canada] or 541-302-3777 [international]; email: **cust_svc@iste.org**; **http://www.iste.org**. Copyright 2000. Reprinted with permission.

When "techno-reformers" talk about their grand plans, they have one purpose in mind: preparing future employees in a technology-driven work environment.[62] Teachers, on the other hand, have a broader focus: they want to develop healthy bonds with their students that will lead to intellectual growth. Teachers hope to develop responsible, educated citizens who have every opportunity open to them. When teachers see the rapidly changing world of technology in which machines sometimes break, certain applications take a long time to learn, and some programs are not flexible enough to meet their needs, they hesitate to take part in it.[63] While policymakers rush to move schools into the information age, it's important not to forget that teachers make up a crucial part of the integration question. In order to reach some consensus, the dialogue should begin not with the goals of technology, but with the goals of schooling. When agreement is found, educators should raise the question of how technology can help reach those goals.[64]

■ *technology is not the panacea*

Certainly new technologies are no panacea for the classroom, but they offer tools that can help change the classroom from a teacher-centered to a more cooperative and student-centered environment. Students can use technological devices as tools—not toys—in the same ways that they will likely use technology in their future lives. We believe that all teachers should have the opportunity to gain skill in educational technologies, and in particular we believe it would behoove new teachers to develop these skills in the context of their preservice work. Most important, we want you to consider how technology will affect your future classroom. Ask yourself where technology can enhance what you do and where it can allow you to innovate. If it is not accomplishing these goals, ask yourself why you are using it.[65]

■ *is technology worth it?*

KEY TERMS

assistive technology (196)
cognitive tools (182)
databases (190)
distance education (195)
drill-and-practice (186)

news group (194)
search engines (200)
simulation (191)
spreadsheet (193)
telecollaborate (189)

telecommunications (194)
tutorials (193)
virtual fieldtrips (192)
word processor (183)
World Wide Web (186)

FOR REFLECTION

❶ Do you think parents should be concerned about the role, or lack of it, that technological tools play in the education of their children?

❷ Should governments spend billions on technology for schools, or should the money be spent differently?

❸ What do you see as the goals of schooling? Are there ways you can use technology to reach those goals?

FOR FURTHER INFORMATION

PRINT RESOURCES

S. A. Armstrong and G. Lucas Educational Foundation, *Edutopia: Success Stories for Learning in the Digital Age* (San Francisco: Jossey-Bass, 2002). A collection of stories from innovative leaders in schools who are integrating technology in a meaningful way.

L. Cuban, *Oversold and Underused: Computers in Classrooms 1980–2000* (Cambridge, MA: Harvard University Press, 2001).

The author takes a critical and historical look at the use of technology in education.

R. C. Forcier and D. E. Descy, *The Computer as an Educational Tool: Productivity and Problem Solving*, 2nd ed. (Englewood Cliffs, NJ: Prentice Hall, 2001).

This is an introductory book in the use of computers as a tool in education.

J. M. Healy, *Failure to Connect: How Computers Affect Our Children's Minds—for Better and Worse* (New York: Simon and Schuster, 1998).

The author explains how computer use interacts with brain development at different ages.

R. Heinich, M. Molenda, J. D. Russell, and S. E. Smaldino, *Instructional Media and Technologies for Learning*, 7th ed. (Upper Saddle River, NJ: Prentice Hall, 2001).

Now in its seventh edition, this is one of the seminal books on the "how to" of using media in the classroom.

D. H. Jonassen, *Computers as Mindtools for Schools: Engaging Critical Thinking*, 2nd ed. (Englewood Cliffs, NJ: Prentice Hall, 1999).

Centering on the use of computer applications to foster constructivist, higher order thinking skills, this is a useful book for learning how to integrate "mindtools" into instruction.

C. D. Maddux, D. L. Johnson, and J. W. Willis, *Educational Computing: Learning with Tomorrow's Technologies*, 3d ed. (Needham Heights, MA: Allyn and Bacon, 2001).

This text combines history, theory, and practice to provide a strong base of knowledge for applying educational technologies in classroom instruction.

B. Means, W. Penuel, and C. Padilla, *The Connected School: Technology and Learning in High School* (New York: John Wiley and Sons, 2001).

Through case studies of six high schools that have pioneered the use of technology, this book comments on successes and challenges of integrating computers in schools.

J. W. Schofield and A. L. Davidson, *Bringing the Internet to School: Lessons from an Urban District* (New York: John Wiley and Sons, 2002).

This book discusses the findings of a five-year study of Internet use in schools.

WEB RESOURCES

In addition to these printed materials and the web sites listed within the chapter, the following list offers some educational web sites for you to look through. Remember, however, that these sites are only starting points. For specific information, use a search engine. Also, keep in mind that web addresses can change without warning. If your web browser cannot locate an address, one trick that sometimes works is to shorten the address to the next root level. For example, if **http://www.iste.org/Research/Background/Online.html** does not work, try **http://www.iste.org/**. If you still have trouble, try a web search engine and use some descriptive keywords.

International Society for Technology in Education (ISTE), *ISTE's Electronic Resources*. Available at: **http://www.iste.org/resources/index.shtml**.

A superb list of links that covers a wide range of issues including standards, digital divide, professional development, and technology integration.

ISTE, *Learning and Leading with Technology*. Available at: **http://www.iste.org/L&L/index.html**.

A monthly journal available online that offers great suggestions from teachers for teachers on how to use technology effectively in the K–12 classroom.

Kathy Schrock, *Guide for Educators*. Available at: **http://school.discovery.com/schrockguide/**.

A very well-organized list of useful links, with an especially helpful section categorized by subject area.

Edutopia Online. Available at: **http://www.glef.org**.

A rich resource of articles related to the future of public education, with a strong emphasis on technology.

Judi Harris, *Virtual Architecture Web Page*. Available at: **http://ccwf.cc.utexas.edu/~jbharris/Virtual-Architecture/**.

An excellent resource for teachers who want to explore telecollaborative projects.

Internet Resource for Special Children (IRSC), *disABILITY Links*. Available at: **http://www.irsc.org/disability.htm**.

A helpful site for information and resources about a wide range of disabilities and health conditions.

ERIC Clearinghouse on Information and Technology. Available at: **http://ericit.org**.

A searchable database of journal articles focused on educational technology. Of particular note is an ERIC Digest on the Field of Educational Technology, found at: **http://www.ed.gov/databases/ERIC_Digests/ed438807.html**.

What Are the Ethical and Legal Issues Facing Teachers?

Chapter Preview   This chapter aims to sharpen your sense of the ethical dimension of teaching and your understanding of the legal underpinnings of many aspects of school life. We examine several common ethical problems faced by teachers, along with legal issues and recent court rulings that have affected them.

This chapter emphasizes that:

- Ethics and the law are closely related, but they also differ.

- Ethical teaching has six specific characteristics.

- In addition to teaching's everyday ethical dimensions, teachers confront certain other, more complex ethical problems.

- Teachers need to understand fully how two basic legal terms, *due process* and *liability,* relate to their work.

- Broad areas of the law—from contracts to copyright, from self-defense to religion in the classroom—permeate school life.

- Students have rights under the law, such as the rights to due process and privacy, and teachers need to understand and respect these rights.

If each of us were the only person on the face of the earth, we could behave exactly as we chose. We would not have to worry about the rights or feelings of anyone else. We would be free of the constraints and demands imposed by others as we went about doing our own will. Quite obviously, though, this is simply not the case. Everyone who walks the earth is bound by real, if unseen, connections with his or her fellow humans. The English poet John Donne said it most succinctly: "No man is an island."

Our systems of ethics and laws are a major part of these invisible connecting fibers. Together they make civilized society in a neighborhood and coexistence on a planet possible. Ethics, as we say in the chapter entitled "What Are the Philosophical Foundations of American Education?", brings us into the realm of what is the right way to act. **Ethics** refers to a system or a code of morality embraced by a particular person or group. Law is related to, but different from, ethics. A **law** is a written rule that members of a given community must follow. The law is a system of such rules that governs the general conduct of a particular community's citizens.

ethics and the law

Laws and Our Ethics   Whereas ethics may be invisible obligations that we perceive, laws typically are statements that have been hammered out by the legitimate authority of a particular community, state, or nation and are used in court as standards by which to judge, and often penalize, the actual behavior of individuals. As a matter of fact, what someone might refer to as an unstated law is not a law at all but an ethical statement.

law as codified ethics

Laws, then, are concrete, made by people and usually written down for the public to see; ethics, on the other hand, consists of ideas that are less tangible and observable. Most of our laws are simply the codification of what we see as our moral or ethical obligations to one another. Sometimes, however, laws are unethical, such as the racial segregation laws that existed in this country only a few decades ago, and sometimes ethical obligations are not written into law, such as the ethical obligation to help the weak, the poor, and the sick.

The Teacher's Responsibility   What does all this have to do with teachers? First, it is the responsibility of teachers to convey to the young the fundamental moral message that we are all legally and ethically bound to one another. Much of this moral message is embedded in the content of our curricula, from our great stories to our history as a people. Second, a unique set of ethical relationships and legal obligations is embedded in teachers' work, and teachers, therefore, carry a special ethical and legal burden. This second issue is the subject of this chapter.

teachers' unique power

At the heart of the teacher's unique ethical and legal relationship with students is power. Like it or not, power resides in the "office" of teacher. Compared with a corporate executive or a military officer, it may not appear that a teacher has a great deal of power, but, in fact, the teacher has a special type of power.

If you wish to know who a man is, place him in authority.
—Yugoslav proverb

This power arises from the fact that the teacher has an impact on people when they are still at a very malleable stage. The teacher is in command of the classroom insofar as he or she has the responsibility for what goes on. Teachers evaluate their students. They not only "mark" them with tangible symbols that become part of students' official records; they also mark their minds and hearts. Many careers are open to you, but few offer such truly awe-inspiring power, and because of the potential for abuse of this power, there are codes of ethics to guide the teacher and a body of laws governing the work of teaching. Since ignorance of the law (and ethics) is no excuse, we urge you to take the material in this chapter quite seriously.

The Ethics of Teaching

Visit the web site to link to more information about ethics and teaching.

In a sense, individuals lose their "freedom" when they get married, and in a similar sense, people lose their freedom to do as they please when they become teachers. In both situations people make commitments, and ethical constraints come with these commitments. Constrained by ethics, the teacher is not always able to act in a manner that he or she finds most satisfying. For instance, the teacher cannot respond with sarcasm to a student's foolish or rude remark. Even though a child—sometimes even a very small child—can provoke a rush of anger, the teacher cannot act on that anger. In another, more positive sense, though, ethics are principles that call the teacher to higher modes of professional behavior. It is the ethical principles that teachers follow that mark the teacher's character and the social significance of the profession.

PAUSE AND REFLECT

1 When you think of some of your favorite teachers, can you recall in any ways you would say they exhibited ethical habits or principles?

2 What would you say is the greatest ethical obligation of a teacher?

CASE STUDY

The Characteristics of Ethical Teaching

case of Marilyn Henderson

Being an ethical teacher means having a rather special relationship with one's students and the other people with whom one works. Consider the following situation, as told to educator Kenneth Howe by a practicing teacher.

Marilyn Henderson is a fifth-grade language arts teacher at Willoughby Elementary in South Lake, a medium-size city with a population of roughly 150,000. Marilyn is troubled to learn that Connie Severns, a fifth-grade social studies teacher with whom Marilyn worked previously in another school in the South Lake system, will be transferred to Willoughby. Marilyn believes Connie to be incompetent and is uncomfortable with this knowledge, especially in light of the fact that her students will be moving through Connie's class. As Marilyn recalls, "Connie didn't teach anything; she couldn't teach anything." Others in the district share Marilyn's assessment of Connie as a teacher and apparently with good reason. Connie seems totally to lack control. Children cry and complain about the chaos, some steal things from her purse, and on one occasion, another teacher discovered a child chasing Connie around the room.

Marilyn had previously tried to do something about Connie's incompetence but met with little success. The teachers' union advised her that they would have to stand behind a tenured teacher, and the school administration claimed to have to follow procedures that could take years, according to Marilyn. At this point in time (before Connie's transfer), the principal of Willoughby called the affected teachers together. He, too, was concerned about Connie's transfer and proposed that they discreetly and surreptitiously "write things down" to build a case that they could use to have Connie fired. Marilyn is asked to be a part of this. What should she do?[1] ▪

This story provides just a peek at the teacher's ethically complex world. Howe suggests that in dealing with issues involving ethical judgment, we as teachers need to exhibit six characteristics: appreciation for moral deliberation, empathy, knowledge, reasoning, courage, and interpersonal skills.[2]

▪ **Appreciation for Moral Deliberation**   We need, first, to see an ethical dilemma such as Marilyn's as a situation characterized by conflicting and competing moral interests (Connie's need for a job, the students' need for a competent teacher, and the other teachers' need to be fair in what they say to and about Connie). We need to see the complex moral dimensions of the problem and appreciate that care must be taken to protect the rights of all parties.

▪ **Empathy**   *Empathy* is the ability to mentally "get inside the skin of another." We need to feel what the others in an ethically troublesome situation are thinking and feeling. In the case described, we would need to empathize with the principal who is inheriting a questionable teacher, the students and their parents, Connie, and Marilyn and the other teachers.

▪ **Knowledge**   One of the tools of a teacher who is able to deal effectively with ethical issues is raw knowledge. We need to remember the facts that will enable us to put an issue in context. What does Connie actually do in the classroom? What formal procedures are in place to deal with ineffective or incompetent teachers? We need to be able to formulate reasonable approaches to the problem and then, from experience, anticipate the consequences of each approach. In Marilyn's case, she needs to be able to think clearly about the alternatives—such as participating in the principal's questionable plan or, perhaps, directly confronting Connie—and she must think through, with some degree of accuracy, what the likely consequences of such action would be. This involves knowledge of the context in which she and Connie are working.

▪ **Reasoning**   To reason is to reflect systematically on an issue. When we reason about an issue, we move through it step by step and draw conclusions, or we may compare a particular event or action with some moral principle and come to some conclusion. For instance, Marilyn may hold as a moral principle that people should not deceive others and, further, that spying is deception. Through reasoning, she may come to the conclusion that what the principal has asked her to do is spying. Of course, this leaves Marilyn with another problem: how to tell her principal that his plan is unethical.

▪ **Courage**   To feel, to know, and to reason are not enough. To be ethical, we must act, and action sometimes takes courage. To be ethically correct often requires the willpower to act in what we perceive to be the right way rather than in the comfortable way. Frequently, when confronted with a seemingly no-win dilemma like Marilyn's, we tend to ignore it in the hope that it will simply go away. However, as the theologian Harvey Cox sees it, "Not to decide is to decide." Among other things, Marilyn will have to find a way to tell her principal

▪ "seeing" competing
interests

▪ feeling what others feel

▪ knowing all the facts

▪ thinking systematically

▪ confronting, not
evading, problems

that she simply cannot be a part of his secret reporting network. Besides courage, this will require tact.

acting with sensitivity

■ **Interpersonal Skills**   Acting on ethical principles demands sensitivity and courage. Therefore, teachers need the communications skills to deal sensitively with issues that demand great tact. They need to be able to call up the right words, with the right feeling and tone, and to address the issue at hand openly and honestly.

■ *Ethical Dilemmas in Teaching*

Although teachers spend most of their professional lives working with students in an instructional manner, sometimes ethical concerns break in and demand their attention. Recently, as teacher education students interviewed practicing teachers, they asked them to describe an ethical situation they had encountered in the last few years. The two cases that follow are based on those interviews.

As you read each case, take time to reflect carefully on it. As you work through these situations, keep in mind the six characteristics described by Kenneth Howe. Also, discuss these cases with other people. We often see much more in a situation involving ethics and recognize many other possible courses of action once we have talked to others about it.

C A S E   S T U D Y
A Big Deal or a Little Fudge?

Recently, drugs have plagued your community, and increasingly they are coming into the schools. You are a sixth-grade teacher, and there has been only sporadic evidence of drugs in your building. On the other hand, your principal has been making what seems to you a big deal out of very little in his crusade to stamp out drugs in "his" elementary school. He has threatened the student body, first-graders through sixth-graders, in a special assembly about what will happen to them if they are caught with drugs of any kind. Most of your in-service training time this year has been taken up with the subject of drugs. You are concerned about the misuse of drugs in our society. However, you, like most of the other teachers, find the principal's preoccupation with drugs overzealous and slightly laughable, and you are afraid of what will happen to the first offender he catches.

drugs in the classroom

Coming from lunch, you see Alan, one of your sixth-graders, showing two of his friends a plastic bag containing what appear to be three or four marijuana joints. Startled, but unsure that you have actually seen what he has, Alan shoves the bag into his pants pocket. You act as if nothing has happened and usher the boys into class. To gain time to think, you set the students to work on a composition.

Alan is a kid with a spotty record in the school. His family life is rumored to be rather chaotic, but he has behaved well in your class. You have never seen the slightest evidence that he has been high in school. Knowing Alan, you guess he got the dope from one of his brothers and brought it to school to impress his friends. On the other hand, you could be wrong, and the situation could be much more serious. One thing you are sure of is that if you report what you saw to the principal, as you are expected to, he will move in on Alan like a SWAT team. As you mull all this over, Alan and his friends are nervously watching you and anxiously looking back and forth at one another. Then, suddenly, Alan gets up, comes to your desk, and asks if he can go to the boys' room. What do you do? ■

C A S E   S T U D Y
Righting Wrongs?

Donald Mitchell is a veteran history teacher in your high school, and he has "ruled the roost" in the department for the past fifteen years. Many current and former advanced-placement (AP) and honors students adore him; they find him exceedingly challenging, and they claim that his teaching prepares them for the rigors of college.

Apart from his senior AP classes, Mr. Mitchell teaches two sections of American government to tenth-grade students. A number of the students in those two classes have individualized education programs (IEPs). He publicly claims skepticism about many of these students' learning disabilities, doing grudgingly what he has to do to comply with the IEPs. (Learn more about learning disabilities and IEPs in the chapter entitled "Who Are Today's Students in a Diverse Society?".)

You have often heard Mr. Mitchell complain about "lowering standards of educational excellence" when he sits with his cronies in the school lunchroom. He does not hesitate to announce to the others about what he sees wrong with the school administration, the student body, and on occasion, even faculty from other departments. His latest pet peeve is the "laxness" with which the English department teaches writing, so he designed a strict procedure for writing his history papers. You have often found Mr. Mitchell to be boorish, but you reasoned that his behavior and opinions are his own prerogative. After all, you think to yourself, his teaching approaches are really a matter of academic freedom.

One afternoon, one of your students comes to class visibly upset. Janelle is one of your more challenging students. She has had a few minor run-ins with the vice-principal, and she does not demonstrate much interest in academics. You often have been frustrated by what you see as her lack of motivation and effort. Privately, you ask her what is wrong. She tells you that she has just left Mr. Mitchell's class where she received a paper that was given a D−. You listen to her, reluctant to talk about the grading policies of another teacher. Yet, after calming down, the student tells you that it wasn't the grade itself that made her so upset, but how the teacher returned the papers. She claims that Mr. Mitchell stood at the front of the class stating that some of the students' papers followed the proper format. Others, he sneered, were so riddled with errors and so poorly written that the only use for any of them would be to line a kitty litter bin. He added that he designed his format so that some students would learn to write correctly, but that many of them apparently could not or would not even follow his simple format. With that statement, he scattered those papers on the floor. He passed the satisfactory papers to the rest of the students, and when the rest of the students, all inclusion students, were left without their papers, he glanced at them and said, "Well, go on. They're right there if you want them." And he pointed to the floor.

Janelle tells you that she waited until class was dismissed to pick up her paper from the floor. You excuse Janelle so that she can go to the girls' room, and then you ask to speak to another student who is in that same class. When you ask him, again privately, if anything unusual happened in his history class, the student replies it was a regular class. You're still curious, so you ask him how Mr. Mitchell returned the papers. The student looks at you quizzically and says, "How'd he return the papers? The same way you do. He walked around the room and handed them back to us."

You're very disturbed by the story Janelle told you, and you want to do something to intervene. Yet, the other student's report makes you hesitant.

academic freedom or spiteful behavior?

What if nothing unusual did occur? Making an enemy of Mr. Mitchell would not be the politically savvy thing to do, and Janelle, you know, can be difficult at times. Maybe she was just angry for some reason at the teacher and wanted to cause trouble, but what if that story was true? What should you do?

PAUSE AND REFLECT

1 Do these situations really involve ethics? Do they involve unfairness or a breach of ethical standards?

2 Are there complexities that cause ethical conflicts? If so, what are they?

3 What are the consequences of various courses of action?

4 Who needs to be considered as you try to decide on courses of action?

5 What, specifically, would you say or do?

The Everyday Ethics of Teaching

As we hope the preceding case studies make clear, serious ethical issues strongly influence the lives of teachers. Few teachers get very far into their careers without having to deal with situations like these. But these cases do not exhaust the ethical responsibilities of the teacher; everyday events that occur in the classroom and school life have an even greater ethical impact on students.

That government is best which governs least, because its people discipline themselves.

—THOMAS JEFFERSON

Although it is clear that parents have the primary responsibility for the ethical training of their children, schools do have an impact on the character and moral lives of students. Classrooms and schoolyards overflow with issues of right and wrong: a child submits a report that is downloaded from the Internet; a group of girls start a rumor that another girl is pregnant; a teacher continually picks on the same student. Events like these send strong ethical messages to students. How the teacher and the rest of the school respond to this ethical dimension of schooling is what we refer to as *the everyday ethics of teaching*. In particular, teachers ethically influence students in three ways: by example, by the classroom climate they create, and by the dialogue they establish.

■ *three ways to influence ethically*

First, the *personal example* provided by teachers includes the care and manner with which they do their work, how they treat students and others, and their use of examples from history and literature to enrich the ethical understandings of students.

Second, teachers can establish a beneficial *classroom climate* by creating an environment of safety and trust where students are free from fear and ridicule, where a spirit of cooperation and friendly competition prevails, and where students are working hard and feeling the satisfaction of learning.

Third, teachers can establish an *ethical dialogue* in their classrooms by discussing with students the core ethical values such as honesty, respect for others, and responsibility that come into play in the curriculum and the life of the school.

The everyday ethics of teaching, then, means *doing the job as it ought to be done*. It means realizing the preciousness of the minutes and hours that you spend with students and making sure they do not waste their time with you.

■ *Codes of Professional Ethics*

Teachers do not struggle alone when they face ethical issues. Besides their own understanding, reasoning, courage, and other qualities, they have the support of a professional group.* Professional groups, such as those of doctors, architects, and teachers, have special obligations to their clients. Because of their special knowledge and power, they have an ethical responsibility to those they serve.

To educate a man in mind and not in morals is to educate a menace to society.

—THEODORE ROOSEVELT

The way teachers do their work is regulated, then, both by their own ethical standards and by those of the teaching profession. Whereas some professions have formulated their own universal code of ethics (like the Hippocratic oath taken by all medical doctors), there are several published codes of ethics for teachers. The best known is the code of the National Education Association (NEA), which is reprinted in the box in this section. The American Federation of Teachers (AFT) has a "Bill of Rights" that deals with the ethical treatment teachers should receive. It contains what it refers to as *self-evident truths,* for example, "The right of teachers to be secure in their jobs, free from political influence or public clamor, shall be established by law. The right to teach is a property right, based upon the inalienable rights to life, liberty, and the pursuit of happiness."[3] A third example is the Boston University Educator's Affirmation, which is taken voluntarily in a special ceremony, typically in the junior year. More like the Hippocratic oath taken by physicians, this statement is a positive declaration of the high ideals and professional standards to which teachers commit themselves:

 Visit this chapter of the web site to link to the AFT "Bill of Rights."

■ *one school's code*

Boston University Educator's Affirmation

I dedicate myself to the life of an educator, to laying the living foundations upon which successor generations must continue to build their lives.

I dedicate myself to the advancement of learning, for I know that without it our successors will lack both the vision and the power to build well.

I dedicate myself to the cultivation of character, for I know that humanity cannot flourish without courage, compassion, honesty, and trust.

I dedicate myself to the advancement of my own learning and to the cultivation of my own character, for I know that I must bear witness in my own life to the ideals that I have dedicated myself to promote in others.

In the presence of this gathering, I bind myself to this affirmation.[4]

The Teacher and the Law

Once upon a time, teachers were like the kings and queens of small kingdoms. Their authority was wide, and their decisions were rarely questioned. Students who would not or could not do the work were "held back" or told not to come back. Students who did not conform to the teacher's standards of behavior were expelled. Students and their parents tended to view education as a special opportunity that put definite responsibilities on their shoulders. In fact, much of the legal authority of teachers was based on the principle of *in loco parentis,* or 'in the place of parents." In other words, it was generally agreed that teachers

---

*The extent to which teaching is or is not a profession is an important question and is the subject of the chapter entitled "What Does It Mean to Be a Professional?".

NEA Code of Ethics

Preamble

The educator, believing in the worth and dignity of each human being, recognizes the supreme importance of the pursuit of truth, devotion to excellence, and the nurture of democratic principles. Essential to these goals are the protection of freedom to learn and to teach and the guarantee of equal educational opportunity for all. The educator accepts the responsibility to adhere to the highest ethical standards.

The educator recognizes the magnitude of the responsibility inherent in the teaching process. The desire for the respect and confidence of one's colleagues, of students, of parents, and of the members of the community provides the incentive to attain and maintain the highest possible degree of ethical conduct. *The Code of Ethics of the Education Profession* indicates the aspiration of all educators and provides standards by which to judge conduct.

The remedies specified by the NEA and/or its affiliates for the violation of any provision of this Code shall be exclusive and no such provision shall be enforceable in any form other than one specifically designated by the NEA or its affiliates.

Principle I— Commitment to the Student

The educator strives to help each student realize his or her potential as a worthy and effective member of society. The educator therefore works to stimulate the spirit of inquiry, the acquisition of knowledge and understanding, and the thoughtful formulation of worthy goals.

In fulfillment of the obligation to the student, the educator—

1. Shall not unreasonably restrain the student from independent action in the pursuit of learning.

2. Shall not unreasonably deny the student access to varying points of view.

3. Shall not deliberately suppress or distort subject matter relevant to the student's progress.

4. Shall make reasonable effort to protect the student from conditions harmful to learning or to health and safety.

5. Shall not intentionally expose the student to embarrassment or disparagement.

6. Shall not on the basis of race, color, creed, sex, national origin, marital status, political or religious beliefs, family, social or cultural background, or sexual orientation, unfairly:
   a. Exclude any student from participation in any program;
   b. Deny benefits to any student;
   c. Grant any advantage to any student.

7. Shall not use professional relationships with students for private advantage.

8. Shall not disclose information about students obtained in the course of professional service, unless disclosure serves a compelling professional purpose or is required by law.

Principle II— Commitment to the Profession

The education profession is vested by the public with a trust and responsibility requiring the highest ideals of professional service.

In the belief that the quality of the services of the education profession directly influences the nation and its citizens, the educator shall exert every effort to raise professional standards, to promote a climate that encourages the exercise of professional judgment, to achieve conditions which attract persons worthy of the trust to careers in education, and to assist in preventing the practice of the profession by unqualified persons.

In fulfillment of the obligation to the profession, the educator—

1. Shall not in an application for a professional position deliberately make a false statement or fail to disclose a material fact related to competency and qualifications.

2. Shall not misrepresent his/her professional qualifications.

NEA Code of Ethics *(cont'd)*

3. Shall not assist entry into the profession of a person known to be unqualified in respect to character, education, or other relevant attribute.

4. Shall not knowingly make a false statement concerning the qualifications of a candidate for a professional position.

5. Shall not assist a noneducator in the unauthorized practice of teaching.

6. Shall not disclose information about colleagues obtained in the course of professional service unless disclosure serves a compelling professional purpose or is required by law.

7. Shall not knowingly make false or malicious statements about a colleague.

8. Shall not accept any gratuity, gift, or favor that might impair or appear to influence professional decisions or actions.

Source: From National Education Association, *Code of Ethics of the Education Profession*, adopted by the NEA Representative Assembly, 1985. Used by permission.

---

acted as parental figures while students were in their care. For that reason, teachers' leeway in treating students was fairly broad and they could make decisions about students, based on what they thought was in the best interest of the student or students. In the last few decades, however, the attitude toward schooling in our country has changed. The authority of the adults in general and teachers in particular has eroded noticeably, and students are often more fixated on their rights than on their responsibilities. There are many reasons for this change, but suffice it to say that we are a very litigious society. Our country has

■ *rise in litigation*

more lawyers per capita than any other nation in the world. And our increasing tendency to use the courts to settle differences and conflicts has had its impact on the work of the teacher. Teachers are often cautioned to remember that students are autonomous, with individual rights that continue to exist even when students pass through schoolhouse doors and are under the supervision of teachers. As a result, teachers are required to be much more deliberate and cautious in their dealings with students to prevent an infringement of students' rights than they were in earlier decades.

On the other hand, it can be argued that our new consciousness of the teacher's legal responsibilities and our heightened sense of students' rights have helped rid schools of dictatorial practices by teachers and administrators, the systematic denial of certain rights to students, and the abusive use of corporal punishment. The new presence of the law in educational matters is, like many changes, a mixed bag.

Woodrow Wilson once said, "The law that will work is merely the summing up in legislative form of the moral judgment that the community has already reached." Our laws, then, are our collective social judgments and decisions about what is fair. Laws differ from codes of ethics, though, because they apply to all the people, not to a particular group like doctors or teachers. Laws are public, whereas ethics can reflect one's private standards. And laws have judicial teeth, whereas codes of ethics do not. Rarely is a teacher suspended, or expelled, or even sanctioned by the teaching profession for violations of the NEA's Code

■ *law = collective judgment*

of Ethics.[5] However, teachers are regularly affected by the law and are occasionally brought to court.

■ *The Teacher and Due Process*

- A young junior high teacher, on a lark, changes his "image." He comes to school one Monday morning sporting a shaved head and a diamond stud earring. He is fired on Tuesday.

- A teacher gives a speech at a meeting of the local gay and lesbian alliance. The newspaper runs a story on the event, and the superintendent asks her to resign quietly.

- A business education teacher who has been teaching for three years has been visited by administrators only twice during that period. He loves teaching and was recently told by his principal that he was a "shoo-in for tenure." Instead of getting the expected letter from the superintendent outlining the upcoming tenure review process, he receives a dismissal notice claiming that his teaching is not up to the district's standards.

All three of these examples represent violations of the teachers' rights to due process. Due process is one of the most important principles embedded in our nation's laws. The essential meaning of **due process** in education is that fairness should be rendered and teachers' rights as individuals should not be violated. Many of the most influential court decisions concerning education, teachers, and the law concern fundamental issues of due process.

■ *due process = fairness*

Due process protections come directly from two amendments to our Constitution. The Fifth Amendment states that "no person shall . . . be deprived of life, liberty, or property, without due process of law." The Fourteenth Amendment adds, "nor shall any State deprive any person of life, liberty, or property, without due process of law."

The Fourteenth Amendment goes on to stipulate that no person should be denied "the equal protection of the law." Legal rulings related to due process in education often reflect the requirement that individuals be treated equally in their education or by school officials.

Two Types of Due Process   When judging the fairness of an action, there are two due process concerns. One, *substantive due process,* has to do with the issue itself. The other, *procedural due process,* concerns the fairness of the process followed. For example, if a teacher is fired because he wears a nose ring, this is an issue of substantive due process: Is this matter substantive enough in this particular circumstance to deny a teacher employment? What is a fair decision in this matter? Procedural due process would involve how the case is handled. Suppose the teacher, after hearing several rumors that the nose ring is irking the superintendent, gets a curt letter saying his "services are no longer needed." Is this process fair? Has the teacher had a fair chance to defend himself?

■ *substantive due process*

The precise meaning of procedural due process changes from state to state, but the Supreme Court decision in *Goldberg* v. *Kelly* (1970) indicated that "the minimum procedural safeguards . . . demanded by rudimentary due process" would include the following:

■ *procedural safeguards*

- The opportunity to be heard at a reasonable time and place

- Timely and adequate notice giving details of the reasons for the proposed suspension or dismissal

- An effective opportunity to defend oneself, including oral presentation of evidence and arguments

- An opportunity to confront and cross-examine witnesses

- The right to retain an attorney

- A decision resting solely on the legal rules and evidence adduced at the hearing

- A statement of the reasons for the determination and the evidence relied on

- An impartial decision maker[6]

Procedural due process exists so that individual teachers and students are protected from arbitrary actions against them. The principle of due process and these guidelines reach into many corners of the teacher's life, as we will see in the upcoming sections.

Some of the most fundamental legal issues have to do with the legalities of employment. When, for instance, is a teacher actually hired? How does a teacher know he or she has an actual teaching position? What does having tenure mean for a teacher?

Contracts, Tenure, and Dismissal

Teachers are not self-employed; they are employees of a school board or, in the case of a private school, of a board of trustees. As employees of a governing body, teachers must be familiar with and abide by the stipulations of the contract issued to them by the school board. If teachers do not fulfill the requirements of the contract, they are at risk of losing their jobs.

Reflect on contracts and collective bargaining with the image in this section of your CD-ROM.

Contracts to Teach   Imagine the following situation. You are a recent college graduate, newly licensed to teach, and you are actively interviewing for teaching positions. Your interview at the Long Meadow school district goes extremely well, and the superintendent tells you she would like you to join the faculty. She tells you that she is going to recommend your hiring to the school board, telling you that for all intents and purposes, you should consider that you have a teaching position, since the board usually votes to approve the superintendent's recommendations. You tell her that you would like to join the faculty, accepting her verbal offer.

Several weeks go by, and you hear nothing from the school district. In the meantime, you are invited to interview at the Centerville school district. When you interview there, you realize it is *the* ideal school district for you. The school administrators seem equally impressed with you, and in several days, the superintendent calls and offers you the position. Although you want to accept immediately, you ask the superintendent for a day to think over the offer. In fact, what you really want to do is find out your status at the Long Meadow school district. Do you really have a job there? If you accept the offer at Centerville, are you violating some legal obligations to the Long Meadow school district?

a contract . . . or not?

The simple answer is, it all depends on whether you have a legal contract for employment. A **contract** is a binding agreement between two or more persons or parties. It indicates the rights and responsibilities of each party to the agreement, and all teachers, new or old, sign a contract with their Board of Education or trustees. Contracts differ from district to district and state to state, but generally, contracts include the teacher's salary, course or teaching assignments or instructional areas, the maximum class size, length of school day and school year, and grievance procedures. A **grievance** is the formal expression of a complaint about an unsatisfactory working condition. Grievances typically concern disputes over working conditions; when a person files a grievance, he or she usually argues that the working condition was in violation of the teacher's contract. Additionally, contracts generally indicate if the local teachers' association or union is the official bargaining agent for teachers.

Contracts are for a set period of time. Most new teachers work on a contract that has to be renewed annually if the teacher is to stay on. Even teachers on tenure (to be discussed shortly) sign a yearly contract stipulating the terms of employment. Occasionally teachers work under a **continuing contract**, which states that its terms will remain in force until the teacher is given notice that the contract will be terminated on a particular date.

To be considered a legally enforceable document, a contract must do the following:

elements of legal contracts

1. Have a lawful subject matter

2. Represent a meeting of the minds of both parties

3. Include an exchange of something of value (called a *consideration*)

4. Be entered into by parties who are competent to do so

5. Be written in proper form (instead of in vague terms such as "pay the teacher what he or she is worth")

In addition, the school board must act officially to ratify a teacher's contract. Many people assume that contracts must be written. In fact, unless state law requires a written contract, an oral contract that includes all legal requirements can also be legally binding.[7]

So in the above scenario, unless all of the conditions were included in your discussion with the Long Meadow superintendent and the school board acted upon, or *ratified*, the superintendent's recommendation to hire you, you did not have a legally binding offer. Therefore, you could accept the Centerville offer without hesitation.

What if that scenario were altered slightly? What if you had signed a contract for the Long Meadow school district and then accepted the Centerville offer? In that instance, you could be held liable for **breach of contract.** A legal contract is binding on both sides—the school district's and the teacher's. If either party violates conditions of the contract, the contract itself is said to have been breached, and the other party can sue for damages.

breach of contract

When an injured party successfully sues the other party for breach of contract, the court may order that the contract be fulfilled, that the injured party receive monetary damages, or both. For instance, the district may have to rehire a fired teacher and pay damages, or a teacher who walks away from a job may have to pay the district's cost of finding a replacement. In addition, anytime a teacher breaches a contract, however, his or her professional reputation will likely be tarnished. So before you accept a position, you should study the contract carefully and ask about anything unclear to you. That contract will govern many of the important details of your life as a teacher.

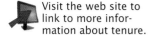 Visit the web site to link to more information about tenure.

Tenure   Imagine a few years have passed since you accepted the Centerville position. At what point are you granted **tenure,** or what some states call *continuing contract status*? New teachers are hired on a probationary period, often three years, so that the school district can ensure that the nontenured teacher can teach well enough to be granted permanent faculty status. State law determines when a teacher is eligible for tenure and outlines the requirements for earning tenure or continuing contract status. Some states require that the school board take some positive action to grant the teacher tenure status; in other states, the teacher automatically is granted tenure when he or she successfully completes the probationary period.

long-term rights

What does possessing tenure actually mean for a teacher? The word *tenure* comes from the Latin root "to hold," as in "hold that job." So if you become a tenured teacher in the Centerville school district, you are entitled to contract renewal every year. The general purpose of tenure was nicely stated by the Supreme Court of Pennsylvania in 1957: tenure helps to maintain "an adequate and competent teaching staff, free from political or arbitrary interference." In addition, tenure allows "capable and competent teachers" to feel secure and to perform their duties efficiently.[8] A school district needs to follow a stricter set of guidelines for disciplining or dismissing a tenured teacher than for teachers who have not yet earned tenure. Tenure guarantees your position as a teacher in the school district, but does *not* mean that you are guaranteed to have the exact same teaching assignment every year. A teacher can be reassigned to teach second grade after being a fourth grade teacher for years, or a school district can reassign a tenured teacher to another school in the district.

Dismissal   Occasionally teachers fail; they simply cannot handle the job. Or they make a big mistake, such as striking a child in anger. Occasionally, too, teachers have "philosophical differences" with administrators, sometimes further complicated by mild or severe cases of "personality conflict." These situations and many more may result in an attempt to dismiss a teacher. Dismissal procedures are covered by the laws in each state, and those procedures must follow due process.

special conditions

If a school district decides in the middle of a school year (and therefore in the middle of a contract) to dismiss an untenured teacher, the teacher always has a right to a full hearing and due process. On the other hand, if the district decides not to extend a second- or third-year contract to a new teacher, the situation is less clear. Although in some states an untenured teacher who is not being rehired can demand a hearing, in most states the school district does not have to justify its reasons for not rehiring a teacher on probationary status.

tenure as "property"

For tenured teachers, the legal situation is different. Tenure is protected under the Fourteenth Amendment and is considered part of the teacher's "property." Tenured teachers have the expectation that they will have continued employment, so that is considered a "property interest." In a sense, the tenured teacher has "earned" and "owns" the job, and he or she can be separated from it only under very special circumstances. In light of that fact, a teacher can call on the full protection of the law, as she or he would if someone were trying to take away a home or a car. To justify dismissal, the school district must prove that the tenured teacher has violated some provision of the tenure law. In most states, a tenured teacher can be dismissed only "for cause." States vary concerning what they consider due cause for dismissal, but most require a good reason that will withstand the scrutiny of the courts, such as sexually molesting a student, gross negligence, or gross incompetence. In some states, the law stipulates that a tenured teacher cannot be dismissed without being given opportunity to correct his or her deficiencies. In those instances, the courts usually determine what is "remediable," or faults that could be corrected by the teacher. So, if a teacher demonstrates poor classroom management, that can be seen as something correctable, and most courts would not allow a tenured teacher to be dismissed before he or she was warned about the management problems and given a chance to correct them. Certain actions, however, are so unprofessional that the damage is "irremediable." Being convicted of a crime or engaging in sexual relations with a student are considered irremediable.[9] In those instances, the school district is under no legal requirement to help the teacher correct his or her behavior and dismissal procedures can begin immediately.

■ *conduct unbecoming*

The most common reasons for dismissal include immorality, insubordination, incompetence, and "conduct unbecoming a teacher." The last reason is a fairly vague term that allows school districts to begin dismissal procedures for a teacher shown to violate the ethical principles governing the teaching profession. The broadness of the term, *conduct unbecoming a teacher,* allows schools some leeway in dismissing a teacher whose behavior is unethical, but may not be classified under the other more specific causes such as insubordination or incompetence. For example, sometimes "conduct unbecoming" means a teacher has used the classroom for purposes other than teaching. One teacher was dismissed because he used class time to advocate that the students, their families, and friends vote for a particular candidate running for superintendent of schools.[10] In another case, a teacher was dismissed for tampering with the school telephone system and eavesdropping on telephone conversations.

It is the responsibility of the courts to weigh the individual situation, to review the law on the subject, and to determine whether the case justifies dismissal.

■ *reductions for economic reasons*

Reduction in Force   In most instances, then, a tenured teacher can only be dismissed for wrong behavior or incompetent teaching. The one exception to that is if the school district needs to eliminate some teaching positions for economic reasons. Sometimes the courts allow schools to dismiss teachers as a result of curricular reorganization. For example, a school board might decide to drop its classical language department. Most commonly, however, reductions occur when the school district has a drop in student enrollment and does not need all the teachers that it employs, or experiences a budgetary shortfall that requires teacher dismissals. Under those conditions, a school district can lay off tenured teachers, and the decision about which tenured teachers to dismiss is usually made on the basis of seniority. Called **reduction in force,** or "riffing" in slang, it was common in the 1970s and 1980s, when student enrollments were shrinking, but riffing is rarely used today, except in the case of a district budget crisis.

CASE STUDY
The Teacher and Liability

Lori Spinelli, a middle-school Spanish teacher, often employed cooperative learning activities in her lessons so students would have more opportunities to practice speaking and listening to each other. Although the students worked together, Lori often circulated around the room to converse with each small group, using the week's vocabulary words in her brief conversations with them. One afternoon, while she was working with a small group in the front of the classroom, she heard a scream from the back. One of her students, Jared, was writhing in pain on the floor. He had tried to show his group members a certain dance move and had dislocated his shoulder. Later that afternoon, Lori replayed that class in her mind, feeling more and more dread, worrying and wondering about whether she would be held liable for Jared's injury. True, she had been in the classroom, but Lori realized that while she was talking to the group in the front of the room, her back had been turned to most of the students in the room, including Jared. What if Jared's parents held her and the school district liable for their son's injury? ▪

Liability means blame, as in, "The teacher can be held liable for the student's dislocated shoulder," and other accidents and mistakes—that is, the teacher behaved negligently or intentionally in a way that allowed the injury to happen.

▪ *areas of liability*

Teachers are responsible for ensuring the safety and well-being of their students in their own classrooms and work spaces and in the activities they oversee. This includes fieldtrips and after-school clubs and activities, such as band, sports, and play rehearsals. Teachers are also liable if they do nothing when they observe a student in some potentially dangerous act that eventually turns out to be harmful. Turning one's back on misbehavior in no way lessens this responsibility. Teachers can be held liable for acts of omission.

So Lori has good reason to be concerned. A court trying to determine if her supervision was adequate would focus on whether Lori could have reasonably prevented Jared from getting injured or whether his injury was something that could not have been reasonably anticipated by her.

▪ *a failure to supervise*

Two court cases help shed light on the extent of a teacher's liability. In one case (*Sheehan v. St. Peter's Catholic School*, 1971), an eighth-grader was injured when her teacher took a group of students outside to watch a baseball game, then went back inside the school. In the teacher's absence, a group of students began throwing pebbles at the spectators, and Margaret Sheehan was hit in the eye with a pebble, sustaining a serious eye injury. In that case, the court ruled that the school did not take reasonable precaution to prevent student injury. It is impossible, after all, for a teacher to monitor students if the teacher is inside while the students are outside. The teacher should have anticipated that in leaving the group of students alone, unsupervised, a dangerous situation could develop.

So does that mean, then, that teachers need to be directly observing students at all times? Does it mean that a teacher like Lori would be considered liable for her student's dislocated shoulder? Maybe not.

In another case concerning liability, teachers took a group of junior high and high school students to visit Chicago's Natural History Museum (*Mancha* v. *Field Museum of Natural History*, 1971). When the group arrived at the museum, the teachers allowed students to visit the exhibition halls on their own. One student, while in an exhibition hall apart from the teachers, was approached and then beaten up by a group of teenagers who did not attend the same school. In this case, the court ruled that the risk of student injury in a museum usually would be "minimal," so that it was an unreasonable expectation that teachers should have been able to foresee and prevent the student's beating. Furthermore, the court indicated that expecting teachers to supervise directly every student on the field trip would place such an unreasonable expectation on teachers that few would plan field trips or other educationally valuable activities for their students.[11]

▪ *can't supervise everywhere*

So, even though teachers are required to exercise prudence and foresight in their supervision of students, the courts expect *reasonable* prudence and foresight. Some student injuries are accidents or unforeseen injuries, and in those cases, the teacher is not held responsible.

▪ **Liability Precautions**   Indeed, when teachers can demonstrate they have taken reasonable precautions to prevent student injury, courts have not found

Certain school activities can be dangerous . . . and an area of potential teacher liability.
(© Sven Martson/The Image Works)

teachers liable for student injuries. To show that they have been "reasonably prudent," teachers need to be able to demonstrate that:

- They made a reasonable attempt to anticipate dangerous situations.

- They provided proper supervision.

- They took precautions.

- They established rules.

- They gave a warning to minimize the chances of students getting hurt.

Because teachers are vulnerable to legal suit, it is important that they be covered by some form of liability insurance. However, in recent years, many teachers have been scared into buying more insurance than they need or, more commonly, into buying insurance when they are already covered by school district insurance policies. Therefore, the new teacher should check on-the-job coverage with the district's personnel director before beginning work.

One area in which experts claim teachers are particularly at risk is automobile liability. Often teachers volunteer to take students in their own cars to a sports game or on a fieldtrip. Even if teachers have personal insurance, they often do not have enough to cover liability claims if a serious accident happens. Before taking students in a private car, the teacher needs to be sure that the district's insurance policy covers such cases or that his or her own policy is adequate.

To Lori Spinelli's great relief, no charges were brought against her. Lori had established an orderly classroom, and she was in the room when Jared was injured. Other students indicated that Ms. Spinelli had taught them rules of be-

■ *liability insurance*

■ *automobile liability*

havior and of courtesy, especially since they would often be working in small groups. Jared was, in general, a well-behaved student, so there would be no reason for Lori to expect that he would decide to jump up and show a dance move to his group members. Finally, her lesson for the class, presenting and practicing written dialogues for their partners, would not be considered a dangerous situation for students. The mere fact that her back was turned to Jared's group wouldn't be grounds to hold her liable. No teacher can face all of the students all of the time. Lori's established good teaching practices and her sound judgment demonstrated her competence. In another situation, in which just a few of those factors were different, a teacher may have been held responsible.

In all these issues of liability, it is important for the teacher to use good judgment. Accidents often "just happen," and there may be no liability. As noted earlier, if a school injury results in a legal suit, the courts will try to determine if the teacher was providing reasonable care and, in general, was acting in a prudent and careful manner.

■ Reporting Child Abuse

Visit the web site to link to more information about reporting child abuse.

In addition to preventing harm to students under their supervision, teachers also have a legal responsibility to safeguard students from abuse and neglect at the hands of their parents and other adults. Teachers in every state are required by law to report suspected child abuse or neglect. The laws vary somewhat from state to state, but they all include two or more of the following elements in their definition of abuse and neglect: physical injury, mental or emotional injury, and sexual molestation or exploitation.[12] If a teacher suspects that a student has experienced *any* of those injuries, the teacher *must* report her suspicions of child abuse and neglect to the appropriate authorities. Schools typically have detailed instructions in their faculty handbooks about how to report such suspicions. Additionally, principals or other administrators will often remind teachers of those procedures, so that all teachers understand explicitly the necessary reporting procedures.

A teacher does not have to be *certain* that a child is being abused before he or she makes a report to the principal. Child abuse is clearly one of those areas where it is better to act and be wrong. If a teacher has a reasonable cause to suspect that a child is being abused, that is sufficient grounds for making a report. To protect a teacher from reaction to an incorrect report or from the anger of an offending parent, the reporting is kept confidential. Further, teachers are granted immunity from accusations of slander or any possible libel suit. Without such protection, many teachers would hesitate to report their suspicions. (For a more detailed discussion of child abuse, see the chapter entitled "What Social Problems and Tension Points Affect Today's Students?".)

■ Self-Defense

Teachers must be vigilant about possible abuse of their students.
(© Bill Aron/PhotoEdit)

Schools are very crowded places, and they are crowded, by definition, with immature individuals. Thus, it is not at all surprising that conflicts erupt and teachers find themselves encountering hostile behavior. For instance, a teacher may have to break up a playground fight or stop some students from vandalizing another student's locker, or a student may strike a teacher in anger.

Self-defense is defined broadly here to take in all these situations. In the first two cases, fighting and vandalism, the teacher is expected to intercede in the interest of safety. In a fight, for instance, the teacher must act to stop the students from hurting one another. Strong words usually are effective, but sometimes the teacher must become physically involved. The operating principle here is "reasonable force." If a teacher uses reasonable force, and if, in the process of stopping the fight and separating the students, a student suffers an injury (say, a strained wrist or dislocated arm), the courts typically will find that the teacher is not liable. If the same injuries resulted from a fight the teacher did not act to stop, he or she may be held liable.

In more obvious cases of self-defense, a student threatens or actually strikes a teacher, and the principle of reasonable force applies here too. What constitutes reasonable force is generally a matter of common sense, but the heat of the moment can make good judgment difficult. In one case, a male seventh-grader who weighed 110 pounds struck a 220-pound coach. The coach grabbed the boy, lifted him off the ground, and threw him against a wall, breaking the child's back. When brought to court, the teacher-coach claimed self-defense. He lost—big time. Usually in the court's view, it is the teacher's responsibility to keep a level head.

> ■ *"reasonable force"*

■ **Assault and Battery**   A teacher's recourse against an abusive student is governed by assault and battery laws. In legal terms, *assault* has come to mean a threat to do harm. Threats should always be taken seriously and reported to the principal, but their legal status depends very much on the student's ability to carry through on the threat. An angry fourth-grader's threat to "do something terrible to you" does not have the same status as a high school junior's threat that he would like to blow up your classroom.

> ■ *assault*

Battery means a willful attack on another that results in harm. Being unintentionally knocked to the hall floor by a rushing student is not battery. (It may, however, call for some disciplinary action by the school.) Being intentionally pushed by a student or a parent is an entirely different matter and makes the pusher immediately liable.

> ■ *battery*

Incidents of assault or battery should be promptly reported and disciplinary action demanded or legal charges filed. Often teachers, particularly new teachers, are hesitant about making a fuss or turning offending students in to the proper school authorities. But verbal abuse and physical violence have no place in our elementary and secondary schools.

■ *Freedom of Expression*

One of the most treasured rights of American citizens is the freedom of expression. Freedom of expression includes symbolic expression and verbal or written expression. For teachers, freedom of expression also subsumes **academic freedom,** the freedom of a teacher to select course materials and to teach in a way he or she thinks fit. Before we go on, take a moment to consider your ideas about freedom of expression.

PAUSE AND REFLECT

❶ Is the freedom of expression limitless? Can a teacher say anything or teach anything, claiming it is his or her right to free expression?

❷ To what degree do you think that you, as a potential teacher, should have the right to select your own course materials or to provide information to students?

❸ Are there any instances in which you think a teacher's freedom of expression should be limited?

Until about thirty-five years ago, teachers who publicly criticized administrators' decisions or school board policies received little sympathy from judges. The attitude of the courts was that judges had no business interfering in the legitimate affairs of the schools. Things changed, though, as a result of Marvin Pickering.

Pickering's free speech case

Pickering, a high school English teacher, wrote a long and sarcastic letter in the local newspaper about his superintendent and school board. He accused them of, among other things, taking the local taxpayers "to the cleaners," making excessive expenditures on athletics, and forcing teachers to live in an atmosphere of totalitarianism. It was later shown that Pickering's information on a number of issues was wrong.

Pickering was fired. He sued for his job, and the original court verdicts upheld the firing.

Pickering's case was appealed before the U.S. Supreme Court in 1968. Because Pickering, an English teacher, made erroneous statements about athletic expenditures and those expenditures were matters of public record, the Court indicated that Pickering did not speak with any greater authority on the matter than any other taxpayer. The Court also found that his comments did not impede his proper performance in the classroom or otherwise interfere with the regular operation of the schools, so the judges reversed the lower courts' ruling and ordered Pickering reinstated and compensated.[13]

In effect, the Court said in the *Pickering* decision that society needs to balance the interests of a teacher, as a citizen commenting on issues of public concern, and the interests of the state, as the teacher's employer trying to promote smoothly running schools. So although the Court affirmed the teacher's right to free expression, it pointed out that this First Amendment protection is not an absolute right. A teacher cannot expect to say absolutely anything, then cry out for protection under "freedom of expression." As a U.S. Court of Appeals stated

Scoville v. Board of Education

in the 1970s *Scoville v. Board of Education* case, "Freedom of speech includes the right to criticize and protest school policies in a nondisruptive manner, but it does not include the use of 'fighting' words or the abuse of superiors with profane and vulgar speech."[14] In many possible situations, such as when teachers become disruptive forces in a school or make irresponsible statements, the courts will not support their expression of their views. For instance, in 1981 the courts ruled against a teacher who had claimed that the racially derogatory comments he made to his principal and assistant principal were constitutionally protected.[15]

The Supreme Court also ruled against teacher John Stroman (*Stroman v. Colleton County School District,* 1992) after he circulated a letter harshly critical of school administration. In it, he urged fellow faculty members to stage a "sick

Reprinted with special permission of King Features Syndicate.

out" to show the administrators just how unified the faculty was in their discontent. The Court, however, indicated that urging a "sick out" when individuals were healthy was an appeal for dishonest behavior and conduct unprofessional for teachers.[16]

Reflect on freedom of expression with the image in this section of your CD-ROM.

■ **Symbolic Expression**   Personal expression is not limited to spoken and written words. Dress styles, armbands, and buttons have been used in recent years to "make a statement." Typically the courts support teachers (and students) in these cases of free symbolic expression. A key issue here involves the potential of this type of expression to lead to "substantial disruption" within the school. A school might forbid such symbolic clothing as a teacher's Ku Klux Klan button in a high school with many African-American students or students' gang "colors" or jacket insignia if they provoke fighting. These judgments cannot, however, be a matter of a teacher's or an administrator's "taste." Bans on symbolic expression of one's views or preferences must be based on clear indications that the efficiency or safety of the school is endangered.

teaching controversial issues

■ **Academic Freedom**   A subcategory of freedom of expression, academic freedom, deals largely with issues in the classroom and the teachers' (and students') rights to discuss ideas and read material of their choosing. Academic freedom allows teachers to speak freely about their subject matter, to select reading assignments, to choose teaching methodologies based on their professional judgment. It is designed to allow experimentation with ideas and to foster an open spirit of inquiry. Academic freedom can meet with opposition when teachers want to discuss controversial or unpopular ideas such as sexual mores, gun control, or abortion. If such issues are a part of the school's curriculum, there is rarely a problem. But when a teacher "adds" them to the curriculum, he or she needs to make a reasonable case that they are relevant to the curriculum. Dismissal for teaching controversial issues may or may not be upheld by the courts. Teaching about volatile issues that may disrupt a particular school, such as homosexuality or the alleged characteristics of different races, is frowned on by the courts. So is teaching controversial material considered unsuitable for the age of the students. In addition, courts have not allowed teachers to use controversial teaching methods that are unsupported by professional opinion or prohibited by reasonable school policy.

Reflect on academic freedom with the image in this section of your CD-ROM.

Political issues, both local and national, are also points of tension. In the classroom, teachers may discuss current political controversies, but they must deal with them neutrally and in a balanced way. Away from work, advocating a particular cause or political party is fine, but a teacher may not behave as a partisan supporter in the classroom.

■ the Keefe *case*

Particular essays and books that contain sexually explicit material or even words that are offensive to certain members of a community have been a great source of legal controversy in schools. In one important case, *Keefe v. Geanakos* (1969), a Massachusetts English teacher, Robert Keefe, assigned his students an article from the well-respected *Atlantic Monthly* that contained offensive language. Keefe's assignment caused a storm, and he was eventually fired for refusing to agree not to assign the article again. Subsequently, he was reinstated by a circuit court decision because the offending language existed in a number of books already in the school library; because the school board had not notified him that such material was prohibited; and, finally, because that court believed the word in question was not all that shocking to the students. As the decision stated, "With the greatest respect to such parents, their sensibilities are not the full measure of what is proper education."[17]

■ the Parducci *case*

The Court ruled similarly in another often-cited case concerning academic freedom (*Parducci v. Rutland*, 1970). Marilyn Parducci, a high school English teacher, had assigned *Welcome to the Monkey House*, by Kurt Vonnegut, to her eleventh grade English class. Ms. Parducci was called down to the principal's office the next morning and was told not to teach that story in any of her classes. Parducci disagreed, contending that the short story had merit as a literary work, despite the principal's remark that it was "literary garbage." Parducci indicated to the principal and assistant superintendent that she would continue to teach her eleventh grade English class using whatever material she wanted and in whatever way she thought best. Parducci was fired from her job, with the explanation that she was "insubordinate" and the course reading had a "disruptive" effect on students. The Court found that the Vonnegut story was not inappropriate reading for eleventh-graders. The finding added that the short story was met with "apathy" by most of the students, so the reading itself could not have created an undue distraction.[18]

■ the not so Boring *case*

Absolute academic freedom at the K–12 level does not exist, however, and some court decisions rule against teachers' perceived academic freedom. A more recent case contrasts the rulings of the Keefe case and the Parducci case (*Boring v. Buncombe County Board of Education*, 1998). Margaret Boring chose the play *Independence* for her advanced acting class to perform in a statewide competition. Boring's class also presented excerpts of the play to an English class at the high school, but not before Ms. Boring requested that the English teacher collect parental permission slips from the students since the play contained mature subject matter. One of the parents complained about the play to the school principal; the school principal asked for a copy of the script and after reading the script, informed Boring that the class would not be allowed to perform that play at the state competition.

The teacher and parents of the actors met with the principal, requesting that he not cancel their performance. He agreed that they could perform the play, but only after certain portions were deleted. The students performed the play, with portions deleted, and won second place at the competition. At the end of that school year, the principal requested the transfer of Boring from that high school, citing "personal conflicts resulting from actions she initiated during the course of the school year."[19] Boring argued that her transfer was in "retaliation" for expression of unpopular views through the production of the play. It was thus a violation of her right to freedom of speech.

The Court ruled in the school board's favor. In the decision, the Court stated that this was nothing more than an ordinary employment dispute, not a matter of public concern. For that reason, the Court found that the dispute did not constitute protected speech. The Court also wrote that school administrators have a "legitimate pedagogical interest in the makeup of the curriculum of the school," and that the "school, not the teacher, has the right to fix the curriculum."[20]

Issues of academic freedom often generate a great deal of heat. When they reach the courts, the following considerations, among others, are brought to bear:

relevant considerations

1. The teacher's purpose

2. The educational relevance of the controversial publication

3. The age of the students involved

4. The quality of the disputed teaching material and its effects on the class.[21]

Those are critical guidelines to remember when one teaches.[22] Perhaps the most important point to remember is that academic freedom is limited: it cannot be used to protect the incompetent teacher or the indoctrinating zealot.

Copyright Laws

Good teachers are always on the hunt for effective teaching materials: a story that carries a special message, a poem that captures an idea with beauty and economy, an article that contains the latest information about an issue students are studying. Having found the "perfect" piece, it is difficult to resist the temptation simply to copy it and share it with the class, and the wide availability of photocopying equipment makes this practice all too easy.

justification for copyright laws

Printed matter, however, is the product of someone's labor, the same way a painting or a piece of furniture is. In the law, it is considered intellectual property. The creator or author has a legal right to receive a reward for his or her labor. Without such payment, few could afford to write books, plays, or articles. For this reason, first in 1909 and more recently in 1976, the U.S. Congress passed copyright laws to protect writers and publishers from the unauthorized use of their material.

Visit the web site to link to more information about copyright.

For teachers, the heart of the current copyright law is its **fair use** guidelines, which help specify what printed materials teachers may photocopy and under what conditions they may do so. The general principle behind fair use is "not to impair the value of the owner's copyright by diminishing the demand for that work, thereby reducing potential income for the owner."[23] In other words, if people simply copy print materials whenever they want, they will not buy the books, and publishers and authors will suffer. Some copying is allowed, of course, and it is important for teachers to know what they may and may not do.

fair use guidelines

Teachers may:

- Make a single copy for class preparation of a chapter from a book; a newspaper or magazine article, short story, essay, or poem; or a diagram, chart, picture, or cartoon from a book or magazine

POLICY MATTERS !

School Censorship

What's the Policy?

As information and ideas have increasingly permeated the world of children, the debate over censorship has heated up considerably. Policies about approval of teaching material or about "appropriate material" are rarely called censorship by district or school administrators, but they often forbid the use or display by students and teachers of certain books or academic materials.

Among the most common causes for invoking censorship policies are "the three Ss": swear words, Satanism, and sex. In Monroeville, N.J., a parent objected to a school copy of *Webster's Dictionary* because it contains sexually explicit definitions. It was removed. In Texas, schools have banned certain jewelry, clothing, and symbols, including the peace sign and Star of David, that some believe are associated with Satanism.

How Does It Affect Teachers?

New teachers, typically fresh from the freewheeling intellectual environment of the college campus, are often shocked to discover censorship in the schools. Often, too, they discover it the hard way: they are reprimanded when a school newspaper they are supervising contains an off-color joke or vulgar language; a children's book their college teachers were wild about turns up on the district's banned list; they are expected to confront students who have downloaded pornography or racist materials from the Internet during class. No one had told them about censorship, but it is nevertheless there.

Consequences for teachers who choose not to censor their activities or materials can be severe. Recently, for example, an experienced and highly respected journalism teacher was released from her role as advisor to the school newspaper. The school principal in particular was dissatisfied with the tone and much of the content of the school newspaper. Several of the journalism students and newspaper staffers were sure that their advisor-teacher was released because she supported them in writing such hard-hitting articles as an investigative piece on how easily teenagers can buy cigarettes in the town's local stores. They were convinced that replacing her is an act of censorship. The teacher lost her position, but has added a new term to the educational lexicon: happy talk journalism. It is useful, then, for a new teacher to inquire about any censorship issues before accepting a new assignment. But since even the word *censorship* sets people's teeth on edge, we recommend

- Make a copy for each of their students of a poem if it is fewer than 250 words and printed on not more than two pages; and one copy for each student of an article or short story if it is fewer than 2,500 words

  Teachers may not:

- Make copies of a work for their classes if another teacher in the same building already has copied that same material for his or her class
- Make copies of the same author's work more than once a semester or make copies from the same anthology, text, or periodical issue more than three times a semester
- Create a class anthology by copying material from several sources (a favorite trick of many teachers!)

that you inquire instead about policies dealing with "controversial material" or policies guiding the selection of "appropriate teaching materials."

What Are the Pros?

Many parents, community members, and even teachers firmly believe children and adolescents are not ready to be exposed to everything. Further, they believe the school board has the responsibility to put in place and monitor censorship policies designed to protect students from exposure to inappropriate material.

The late Albert Shanker, a legendary fighter for teachers' rights, nicely stated the larger issue behind such cases:

> There is a tension between a teacher's academic freedom and a community's right to prescribe an appropriate curriculum for its students, between a teacher's academic freedom and his responsibility not to indoctrinate his students, between the school board's right to set a curriculum and a parent's right to determine what is appropriate for his child . . . between a student's right to learn whatever he wants and the parent's right to shield his child from potentially harmful ideas.

What Are the Cons?

The limits on academic freedom and free speech that such policies impose may end up being too constricting. As a result, students and teachers might be forbidden to engage in potentially valuable learning experiences. Groups such as the American Association of University Professors have taken strong positions calling for more freedom in all classrooms, not just the college classroom. They report the growing threat of censorship at all levels of education and have called for teachers to be granted the professional right to select the material they believe is useful in promoting teaching and learning.

What Do You Think?

1. **Do you believe it is appropriate for precollegiate schools to have censorship rules?**
2. **What censorship issues, if any, came up during your years in elementary and secondary school?**
3. **What do you think is the most appropriate way to explore the censorship policies of a potential place of employment?**

 Visit the web site to learn more about this policy issue.

SOURCES

David Hill, "Defending Mrs. Halas," *Education Week,* March 10, 1999; "Schools Fend Off More Attempts at Censorship," *USA Today,* August 30, 1990, p. 1D.

Commission on Academic Freedom and Pre-College Education, *Liberty and Learning in the Schools* (Washington, DC: American Association of University Professors, 1986). NOTE: The Shanker statement is from p. 3 of this report.

- Make multiple copies of weekly newspapers or magazines specifically designed for classrooms, or of consumable materials, such as copyrighted games, exercises, and particularly worksheets from workbooks

- Charge more for legally permissible copies than it cost to copy them

These guidelines may seem overly restrictive and technical, but teachers actually have more liberal guidelines for copying than the average citizen does.

■ **Videotapes, Software, and the Internet** There is a great temptation for teachers to tape material "off the air" and to build tape libraries of material to use in instruction. Although this may be effective pedagogy, it may not be legal. Commercially produced videos are intellectual property and are also

special rules for TV tapes covered by our copyright laws. Copyrighted television programs (and most of them are copyrighted) can be kept for only forty-five days, after which they must be erased or taped over. Also, during the first ten days after the taping, the teacher may show the tape only twice: once for initial presentation and once when "instructional reinforcement" is called for. Finally, schools cannot routinely record material for potential later use by a teacher. It can be done only at a teacher's request.

The personal computer has helped to revolutionize American life, in general, and American education, in particular. In recent years, it has been possible to link up to vast worldwide networks of information through a telephone line or other cable. With these links, a world of information is at your fingertips. It is possible to copy information from government agencies, libraries, legal systems, and other schools with the touch of a button. For example, you may be tempted to copy a research report from an online news information service and make copies for all of the students in your class. Unless there are specific stipulations against such usage, this is acceptable practice. However, intellectual property rules are currently a big issue on the Internet and World Wide Web, and the law is still evolving. Many teachers find that their school's media specialist can help them keep up with changes in copyright laws regarding digital, as well as print and video, materials.

Computer software programs are not treated in the same way as text, video clips, or still pictures. Commercially sold software differs from material "taken off" the Internet. Software should not be passed around and copied. In some cases, the software publisher may allow the purchaser to make one backup copy of the software, but making any other copies is a violation of the copyright laws. Although all of this may seem like "overkill," it is important for teachers to follow the rules—not simply because it is the law, but because students will follow their example.

Lifestyle and the Teacher

■ *teachers and community values*

Teachers bring into their classrooms more than their minds and their lesson plans. They bring their attitudes and values. Elementary and secondary teachers traditionally have been considered extensions of the family in passing on to the young the community's positive values. In past generations, teachers who behaved in ways counter to the community's values were dismissed. Teachers were summarily fired for homosexuality, being pregnant and single, living with someone of the opposite sex, using illegal drugs, being publicly drunk, or committing a crime. However, the late 1960s saw a shift in the balance between the community's right to require certain standards of behavior and the rights of individuals to their own lifestyles and values. Although some areas are still legally quite uncertain, on many questions, judicial opinion (the way judges are tending to rule) is clear.

PAUSE AND REFLECT

❶ To what degree do you believe that a teacher's personal life should be truly private? Should what the teacher does on his or her own time always be protected by the law?

❷ Is the teacher completely free to live his or her life in whatever way he or she decides?

Personal Appearance: Hair, Clothes, and Weight

less leniency today

Although in the late 1960s and early 1970s the courts tended to rule in favor of teachers' rights to do what they wished with their hair, currently the courts are siding more often with school districts' rights to impose reasonable grooming codes for teachers. Teachers, according to the current view, do not have a *constitutional* right concerning their "style of plumage."[24]

The situation is similar for clothing. Courts are upholding districts' judgments on skirts that are considered too short, as well as the requirement (in some districts) that male teachers wear neckties. Courts are asserting that the First Amendment does not extend to "sartorial choice."

For health reasons, obesity may be its own punishment. However, does a school district have a right to fire a teacher because it decides she or he is too fat? A California school district released a forty-two-year-old female physical education teacher because, at 5 feet 7 inches and 225 pounds, the district felt she was "unfit for service." Her principal argued that she "did not serve as a model of health and vigor" and was restricted in her ability to perform on the trampoline, in gymnastics and modern dance, and in other aspects of the program.[25] Here, though, the court sided with the teacher, claiming that the district had not proved that her girth had impaired her performance.

Private Sexual Behavior

the Morrison *case*

In the past, sexual behavior was considered an area in which a community had a complete right to impose its standards on people selected to teach its children. Currently, however, the courts are increasingly viewing teachers' private sexual habits or preferences as separate from their public, professional lives as teachers. A landmark case involved Marc Morrison, who was fired after his former lover, another male teacher, reported their brief relationship to the superintendent. The school district believed it was on solid ground in dismissing Morrison, for several reasons. The district's representatives argued that California's law requiring teachers to be models of good conduct applied to the case, that teachers are required to impress on their charges "principles of morality," and, further, that homosexual behavior is contrary to the moral standards of the people of California.

private versus professional life

However, in 1969 the California Supreme Court ruled in Morrison's favor. It acknowledged that homosexuality is, for many people, an uncertain or controversial area of morality. But the court made an important distinction between a teacher's private life and his or her professional performance. Since there was no evidence that Morrison's sexual orientation had ever been part of his relationship with his students, or in any way affected the performance of his teaching duties, or, in fact, affected his relationship with his fellow teachers, he was reinstated.[26]

Similarly, cases involving pregnancy out of wedlock and unmarried couples living together are being settled in favor of the individual teacher. However, the conditions just cited are required. The behavior must not intrude into the classroom or seriously affect the teacher's professional performance.

Reflect on teachers' private lifestyles with the image in this section of your CD-ROM.

A teacher would, however, be misguided to think that his or her behavior after school hours is always protected under the law. A tenured California teacher was fired after she was arrested by an undercover policeman for engaging in sexual activity at a swingers' club. California state courts ruled that her behavior at this semi-public party showed "a total lack of concern for . . . decorum

TABLE 7.1   Selected Court Cases Dealing with Teachers' Rights and Responsibilities

Issue	Case	Ruling
A teacher's liability for student's injury	*Sheehan* v. *St. Peter's Catholic School* (1971)	A teacher is liable for student injuries (i.e., eye injury) if he or she leaves students unsupervised
	Mancha v. *Field Museum of Natural History* (1971)	A teacher is not liable for student injuries under unusual circumstances (i.e., fight in a museum) if he or she has taken appropriate precautions.
A teacher's right to free speech (such as criticizing the school authorities)	*Pickering* v. *Board of Education* (1968)	A teacher can criticize the operation of a school as long as this does not interfere with the normal running of the school.
	Scoville v. *Board of Education* (1970)	Freedom of speech does not include the use of "fighting words" or the abuse of superiors with profane and vulgar speech.
A teacher and academic freedom	*Keefe* v. *Geanakos* (1969)	A teacher may not be dismissed only for selecting reading assignments with offensive words.
A teacher and his or her private life	*Morrison* v. *State Board of Education* (California, 1969)	A teacher's sexual orientation is not grounds for revocation of licensure, particularly when it in no way affects the performance of professional tasks.

or preservation of her dignity and reputation" and that she demonstrated a serious lack of "normal prudence and good common sense."[27] Flaunting one's deviation from the community's standard tends to increase the chances that the courts will uphold dismissal. In all these cases, however, circumstances play a crucial role in the courts' final opinion.

■ *Conduct with Students*

■ *teacher held accountable*

Whereas the courts have become increasingly lenient on issues of private sexual behavior, the line is being held firm with regard to socially unacceptable behavior that spills over into the classroom. One sure way to lose one's teaching position is to make a sexual advance to a student. Usually one incident is enough to sustain a dismissal. The same goes for smoking marijuana, taking other drugs, public drinking to the point of drunkenness, or even using excessively obscene language in the presence of students. In this area, the teacher bears the full weight of the responsibility to be a role model.

Teachers should also realize that they can become "overinvolved" with students, even when no sexual impropriety has occurred. A fourth-grade teacher was dismissed from his job when he became so involved with one of his students that he sued the boy's mother for custody. The child had been allowed to live with the teacher for nine months, but when the mother wanted her son to return home, Drew Kerin, the teacher, sued for custody. The custody battle generated so much publicity that the district fired him. Kerin was found to have "exploited his position as a teacher" and that provided "just cause for termination."[28]

In general, then, except in matters of personal appearance, the courts are allowing teachers a good degree of freedom in their private and personal lifestyles as long as their choices and their behavior do not adversely affect their performance as teachers. Table 7.1 summarizes the court cases and rulings discussed in this and the previous sections.

Law, Religion, and the School

According to the First Amendment to the Constitution, "Congress shall make no law respecting an establishment of religion, or prohibiting the free exercise thereof." During the past two centuries, the American judicial system interpreted this amendment inconsistently with respect to the place of religion in public schools, a topic of high controversy and much public unrest in recent years. The controversy is not new: the role of religion has been a bone of contention since the beginning of public education in the United States.

Among the questions currently being asked are the following:

- What religious observances, if any, are permitted in public school classrooms?

- Is all prayer, public and private, illegal in our schools?

- Are extracurricular religious clubs allowed in public schools?

- May parents insist that schools provide alternative textbooks consistent with their religious beliefs?

▣ *Prayer and Scripture in the School*

Until the mid-twentieth century, religious observances, including Bible reading and prayers, were common in the public schools. In fact, Bible reading and the recitation of the Lord's Prayer were required by constitutions or by statutes in a number of states. In *Abington School District v. Schempp* (1963), however, the Supreme Court ruled both to be unconstitutional.

In a 1962 decision (*Engel v. Vitale*), the Court had already ruled against the recitation of a nondenominational prayer, holding that Bible reading and prayer violate both clauses of the First Amendment. The Court recognized that the schools involved did not compel a child to join in religious activities if his or her parents objected; nevertheless, the Court held that the social pressures exerted on pupils to participate were excessive. In essence, no distinction was believed to exist between voluntary and compulsory participation in religious activities.

The Court did note that the study of comparative religion, the history of religion, and the relationship of religion to civilization were not prohibited by this decision. It would also appear that, although the Bible may not be used to teach religion, it might, if objectively presented, be used in such areas of study as

Visit the web site to link to more information about religion and schools.

rulings against prayer

Reflect on religion and secular humanism in schools with the image in this section of your CD-ROM.

"Meeting at the flag" for morning prayer is a growing movement in our schools.
(© Rob Crandall/The Image Works)

history, civics, and literature. Indeed, most thoughtful people would agree that failure to be conversant with the Old and New Testaments makes understanding of Western history and literature impossible. In the same way, if a student set out to learn about Chinese culture and was not permitted to read Confucius, he or she would be doomed to a very limited understanding.

The Court has approved the right of public school pupils who so desire to say prayers and read scriptures of their choice in the morning before school starts or after the regular school day has ended. If prayers are said during lunch period, they must be silent.

■ *prayer at graduation*

In a more recent decision (*Lee* v. *Weisman*, 1992), the Court determined that the recitation of prayers at a public school function was unconstitutional. A principal of a public middle school, Robert Lee, had invited a rabbi to say a benediction and invocation at the middle school graduation exercises, instructing the rabbi to offer nonsectarian prayers. Student Deborah Weisman and her father filed a suit in court seeking a permanent injunction against including prayers in graduation ceremonies. The Court used the following facts to reach its decision: (1) public school officials direct the performance of formal religious exercises at graduation ceremonies, and (2) although such exercises do not require attendance, they are in a real sense obligatory for all students, even those who object. As a result, the Court upheld the decision of the lower court, ruling that it is unconstitutional to include clergy members who offer prayers as part of school graduation ceremonies.[29]

Teaching about religion is not the same as teaching someone to be religious. In our multicultural, multiethnic society, understanding another person's faith will foster tolerance and harmony, a goal common to all religions.

—MARGARET BARTLEY

What if the students themselves select the prayer or the person delivering the prayer at after-school events? In 2000, the Court also ruled that student-led, student-initiated prayer at football games violates the First Amendment, in part because

■ *student-led prayer at games*

attending school football games is mandatory for some students, such as athletes, cheerleaders, and band members and other students who might object to the prayers feel social pressure and/or genuine desire to participate in high school football.[30]

■ *Religious Clubs and Prayer Groups*

■ *religious extracurricular clubs*

Are extracurricular religious clubs legal in public schools? Court decisions provide no clear guidelines here. In at least one case, a district judge ruled in favor of such clubs based on students' right to free speech. But a U.S. Circuit Court of Appeals overturned the decision, maintaining that such clubs violated the First Amendment's "establishment of religion" clause. The U.S. Supreme Court did not clear the waters: the five-justice majority upheld the district court opinion on a technical point, but declined to comment on the constitutional issues raised.[31]

■ *after hours student prayer groups*

In yet another case, *Board of Education of Westside Community Schools v. Mergens* (1990), the courts ruled that extracurricular religious group meetings held on public school grounds did not necessarily violate the U.S. Constitution. The Court stated that if the school provides a limited public access for other noncurriculum student groups, then, under the Equal Access Act, a student religious group may also use the school building for its meetings. Under these circumstances, then, a student religious group meeting in the cafeteria after school does not violate the constitutional separation of church and state.[32]

Subsequent court rulings have maintained students' rights to use school facilities for religious club meetings, even if the club is directed by adults. The Supreme Court ruled that a school district could not prohibit the Good News Club, a private Christian organization for children 6 to 12 years old, from meeting in a school building after school hours. The Court stated that the school district had already adopted broad community access to its schools, and in doing so, had created an open forum. Prohibiting the club from meeting violated the club's First Amendment right of free speech (*Good News Club v. Milford Central School District,* 2001). A key point here is that teachers do not participate.

■ *Religion and Secular Humanism*

The many court cases dealing with prayer in school, extracurricular clubs, and the presence of the Bible in schools, as well as the publicity surrounding them, have had a chilling effect on teachers and administrators. Rather than get involved with what is clearly a controversial set of issues, many public educators have tended to discourage any expression or even mention of religious issues or topics. This, in turn, has caused a reaction from parents and others who think that by ignoring the religious dimension of life, the public schools create a distorted, and ultimately dangerous, view of humankind—a view labeled *secular humanism*. Secular humanism asserts the dignity of human beings, but ignores the idea of God and the spiritual.

■ *secular humanism issue*

Objecting to what they see as the prevailing secular humanism of the schools, some parents contend that such fundamental questions as, "What is a person's true nature?" can be treated in schools from every perspective except the religious view. They claim that this is not only intellectually unbalanced, but a danger to their children. Speaking to this issue, one legal scholar has written, "When government imposes the content of school, it becomes the same deadening agent of repression from which the framers of the Constitution sought to free themselves."[33] Many parents are voting not only with their pocketbooks, by turning down school budgets and tax requests for public schooling, but also with their feet, by walking away from the public school system. This trend has fueled a dramatic growth in religious schools and particularly in home schooling in recent years.

Specific objections to secular humanism in the schools have taken a number of forms. Two examples are the controversies over teaching about the origins of the human race and those over the use of certain textbooks.

■ **The Creationism Versus Evolution Controversy**   Major concern over the teaching of evolution dates to the famous 1925 Scopes trial in Tennessee in which a high school biology teacher, John Scopes, was accused of illegally teaching the theory of evolution. Although the trial came to national attention at the time (and again decades later with the award-winning play and film *Inherit the Wind,* based on that trial), no legal precedents were set. The issue returned to the public eye later in the century, when citizens asked for equal time for the biblical account of creation. In 1982, the Louisiana legislature passed the Balanced Treatment for Creation-Science and Evolution-Science Act, which quickly came to be known as the Balanced Treatment Act. The act defined *scientific creationism* as "the belief that the origins of the elements, the galaxy, the solar system, of life, of all the species of plants and animals, the origin of man, and the origin of all things and their processes and relationships were created ex nihilo (from nothing) and fixed by God."[34] In addition to requiring that scientific creationism be taught whenever evolution was taught, the act required the development of curriculum guides and research services for teaching creationism. On the other hand, the act provided none of these resources or protections for those teaching evolution.

After several challenges and lower court rulings, a case, *Edwards v. Aguillard,* reached the U.S. Supreme Court, which in 1987 ruled seven to two against the Balanced Treatment Act. According to the Court, the Balanced Treatment Act was, in fact, not balanced because its provisions favored the teaching of creationism over evolution. Further, the Court asserted, the Balanced Treatment Act was motivated by the legislature's desire to promote a particular religious viewpoint and thereby violated the Constitution's provision against the establishment of a state-sponsored religion. Despite the Court's arguments, few observers think this controversy has been settled. In 1999, the Kansas Board of Education voted on the state's standard and no longer required the teaching of evolution in public schools.[35] Within days, suits were filed challenging the decision. Despite the fact that 68 percent of Americans believe creationism should be taught in our schools,[36] it appears that the creationism-versus-evolution clash has become the battleground between those who believe the public schools have become antireligious and are promoting secularism and those opposed to the schools teaching a religious point of view.

■ **The Textbook Controversy**   Recent court cases have been launched by fundamentalist Christian parents who argue that texts used in their children's public school classes are anti-Christian and thus a violation of their children's constitutional rights. In a 1986 Tennessee case, a U.S. district judge agreed that students' constitutional rights were violated when they were expelled after they refused to read certain texts. However, the following year a U.S. Court of Appeals reversed the decision of the lower court and ruled that the texts in question did not promote or require a person to accept any religion.[37]

■ *Balanced Treatment Act*

■ *Tennessee case*

Shortly after, another challenge to the public schools' choice of textbooks was made in Alabama by fundamentalist parents, students, and teachers. Forty-four textbooks used in history, social studies, and home economics courses were cited as advancing secular humanism. In this case (*Smith v. Board of School Commissioners of Mobile County*), the courts followed a pattern similar to that of the Tennessee case just described. Initially, the district court ruled that secular humanism is a religion and that some of the textbooks in question did discriminate against theistic religion. On appeal, this decision was reversed, and the court ruled that the textbooks promoted neither secularism nor any other religion.[38]

◼ *Guidelines for Religious Neutrality*

Table 7.2 summarizes the court rulings on religion and the public schools. Yet with all the cases taken together, teachers may very well remain confused about what they can and cannot do. Thankfully, some attempts have been made to establish guidelines for the teacher and the school.

Thomas McDaniel recommends a *religious neutrality principle* in the classroom and offers the following four guidelines for putting it into practice:

◼ *suggested guidelines*

1. Students may not be required to salute the flag or to stand for the flag salute if this conflicts with their religious beliefs.

2. Bible reading, even without comment, may not be practiced in a public school when the intent is to promote worship.

3. Prayer is an act of worship and as such cannot be a regular part of opening exercises or other aspects of the regular school day.

4. Worship services, such as prayer and Bible reading, are not constitutional even if voluntary rather than compulsory. Consensus, majority vote, or excusing objectors from class or participation does not make these practices legal.[39]

This principle of religious neutrality does not mean, however, that the public school must ignore religion. On the contrary, teachers in public schools are free to study the history and contributions (pro and con) of individual religions with their students, to have them read the Bible as literature, and, in general, to expose students to our culture's religious heritage. When teachers cross the line into advocating a particular religion or involving students in prayer, they become vulnerable to legal action.

A few years ago, as debate over such issues continued, the White House asked the Department of Education to issue a directive on religion in the public schools. The resulting guidelines are an attempt to find a new common ground between religious expression and religious freedom and, further, to correct the perception (or the fact) that schools are hostile to religion. Among the specific points listed in the guidelines are the following:

◼ *White House guidelines*

• Public schools should not interfere with or intrude on a family's religious beliefs.

• Public education should be respectful of religion, should be open to appropriate religious expression, and should teach about religion because it is so very much a part of our nation's history.

• Advocacy of religion by teachers and administrators has no place in public education.

TABLE 7.2   Selected U.S. Court Cases Dealing with Religion and the Schools

Issue	Case	Ruling
Teaching evolution and/or creationism		
Teaching evolution in public schools	*Scopes* v. *State of Tennessee* (1925)	The court upheld the state law permitting the teaching of evolution as an explanation of the origins of the universe.
Balancing the teaching of creationism and evolution in public school curricula	*Edwards* v. *Aguillard* (1987)	Schools teaching the biblical explanation of creation violate the Constitution's provision against teaching a particular religious viewpoint.
Public schooling, prayer, and the Bible		
The inclusion of Bible reading and prayer	*Engel* v. *Vitale* (1962)	Bible reading and teacher-led prayer in schools are in violation of the First Amendment; because of the social pressures involved, there is no difference between voluntary and compulsory prayer in school. However, private prayer and Bible reading are protected.
	Abington School District v. *Schempp* (1963)	Reading the Bible and reciting the Lord's Prayer in public schools are in violation of the First and Fourteenth Amendments; however, the Bible may be studied for historical, cultural, or other general educational purposes.
Reciting nondenominational prayers at public school ceremonies	*Lee* v. *Weisman* (1992)	It is unconstitutional to include adult-led prayers at public school ceremonies because all students are virtually obligated to attend ceremonies like graduations, even those students who object to the practice.
Students reciting nondenominational prayer at extracurricular events	*Santa Fe Independent School District* v. *Doe* (2000)	Schools cannot allow student-led prayer at extracurricular events (e.g., sporting events) because attendance is not completely voluntary.
Public schools and extracurricular religious groups	*Board of Education of Westside Community Schools* v. *Mergens* (1990)	If a public school allows a limited public forum for other extracurricular groups, the Equal Access Act indicates that extracurricular religious groups may meet in public school buildings without violating the Constitution.
Extracurricular religious clubs meeting on public school property		

- Students' religious clubs and groups are entitled to hold meetings, to have common prayer, to read scriptures, and to have their meetings publicized through school bulletin boards, newspapers, and public address systems.

- Although school-sponsored prayer should not be permitted, it is appropriate to begin the school day with a moment of silence.[40]

Although this directive from the Department of Education has been well received by many parents and educators, it has not yet been tested in the courts. Nor does it address all of the conflicting issues surrounding religion in public schools.

PAUSE AND REFLECT

① Do you believe that the textbooks you used as a student, or that you have seen in your fieldwork, promote secular humanism? What can you do, as a teacher, if your assigned curriculum materials seem to you to promote or denigrate a particular religious viewpoint?

② Do you believe that controversies about religion in the schools will have a chilling effect on your own willingness as a teacher to have students read religious literature or study the contributions of religions?

Students and the Law

Many of the most important legal issues that affect the lives of teachers relate directly to students and their rights. Students, particularly public school students, have a special status under the law. In this section, we will touch on a few of the more significant and current student-related issues that can affect the teacher.

The Student and Due Process

As described earlier in this chapter, the courts for many years used the legal principle of ***in loco parentis*** in cases involving students. Teachers following this principle are expected to treat their students in a caring and informal manner instead of in the formal and legalistic manner that governs relationships "out in the world." By the same reasoning, since we do not require due process in the home, for a long time it was not valued in the schools.

Gradually, though, in court cases such as *Tinker*[41] and others described in upcoming sections, the *in loco parentis* principle has eroded, and the courts have come to appreciate that students often need to be protected from the arbitrary use of authority. As a direct result, many schools have developed clear statements governing procedures for expulsion, suspension, student privacy, freedom of speech and publication, and various breaches of discipline. Informing students of the rules, procedures, and consequences of violations in these areas is a major step toward providing due process rights. Still, the most important aspect of due process is the spirit of fair and evenhanded justice with which teachers respond to the daily events of the classroom.

more explicit rules today

In terms of disciplinary matters relating to students, schools can operate on a continuum with regard to student due process. For trivial matters or emergencies, schools may act without due process. For matters that may result in a short suspension (one or two days) or some entry on the student's record, schools must use some measure of due process, and for disciplinary matters that may result in a long-term suspension or expulsion, schools must demonstrate careful due process.[42]

Suspension and Expulsion

Ever since schools began, individual students have had difficulty following the rules and staying out of trouble. In recent decades, as schools have tried harder to keep older youth from dropping out, and as drugs and violence have increased in society as a whole, problems have escalated. One of the most dramatic and horrible examples is the massacre that happened at Columbine High School in Colorado in the spring of 1999.

rising discipline problems

Educators need to keep in mind that some students, having been compelled to stay in school, find little to capture their imaginations and to motivate them. For these students, school continues to be a place of failure and frustration, and trouble is often close behind. Some of the more common forms of school infractions today are stealing; vandalizing school property or someone's private property; bringing a weapon to school; possessing, using, or selling drugs or alcohol; fighting (or encouraging others to fight); and repeatedly disobeying the reasonable directives of teachers and other school personnel.[43]

power of suspension or expulsion

School districts are not powerless in the face of these kinds of disciplinary breaches. For the good of maintaining a safe and effective academic environment, schools have three alternatives: in-school suspension, out-of-school suspension, and expulsion. Typically, in-school suspension is for minor offenses and is brief in duration. Out-of-school suspension and expulsion are, of course, more serious and for a longer period, with expulsion meaning complete separation from the school. This school district power must be wielded in a manner that ensures that students' constitutional rights to due process are protected. And it is here, in the administration of suspension and expulsion, that school administrators in particular have become entangled in the courts.

Lopez suspension case

■ **Major Court Cases**   One of the most important cases was *Goss* v. *Lopez*,[43] a 1975 suspension case involving Dwight Lopez, a high school sophomore from Columbus, Ohio. Lopez was suspended for ten days for allegedly becoming involved in a cafeteria disturbance. This suspension occurred without a hearing and without any prior notification. Although a suspension of this length and without a hearing or prior notice was in accord with the Ohio statutes, a suit was filed stating that Lopez's constitutional rights had been violated because there was no notice or hearing. The case went to the U.S. Supreme Court, which ruled in favor of Lopez on the grounds that students facing suspension from a public school have property and liberty interests and therefore are protected by due process. In addition, the Court stated that "longer suspensions (longer than ten days) or expulsions for the remainder of the school term, or permanently, may require more formal procedures."

violation of PL 94–142

In a 1988 case with some similar elements, *Honig* v. *Doe,* the Court ruled against California school officials.[45] A school district had suspended indefinitely two emotionally disturbed students on the grounds that they were dangerous, and the Court ruled that this suspension was a violation of PL 94–142 (later called the Individuals with Disabilities Education Act (IDEA)), which allows school authorities to suspend dangerous students with disabilities only for a maximum of ten days. Longer suspensions require either the permission of parents or the consent of a federal judge.

test of zero-tolerance rules

Because of the fear of school violence, exacerbated by the Columbine school tragedy, a number of school districts have adopted a **zero-tolerance policy** toward weapons or school fights. Court cases involving "zero tolerance" have yet to be heard by the Supreme Court; however, lower courts have already heard cases in which zero-tolerance policies have played a part. A recent court case in Illinois highlights zero tolerance, as well as the volatile issue of racial profiling (*Fuller* v. *Decatur Public School Board of Education School District 61,* 2000).[46] The school district, in accordance with its zero-tolerance policy on fighting, expelled a group of students for two years for starting a fight in the bleachers at a home football game. The fight, from all accounts, including a videotape, was brief but violent; seven spectators were injured. The students argued that the expulsion was because of racial profiling; they were unfairly singled out, they argued, because they were stereotyped as gang members. Further, they argued that because no guns, knives, or drugs were involved, their behavior did not merit an expulsion. The Court ruled that the students failed to present any evidence that their expulsion was in any way based on their race.[47] So, although that court case found no evidence of racial profiling in the school's application of its zero-tolerance policy, it seems likely that future cases will involve both issues in school disciplinary actions.

Zero-tolerance policies, while hailed by many as tools to bring greater order and discipline to our schools, are not without their detractors. In recent years there have been a number of highly publicized incidents, such as the suspension of a third grader for bringing a butter knife to school, that have made this policy rather controversial, which only proves that no school policy can substitute for an educator's common sense.

Visit the web site to link to more information about zero tolerance policies.

Pregnancy, Parenthood, and Marriage   As mentioned earlier, not many years ago, unmarried teachers who became pregnant were routinely dismissed from their teaching positions. Additionally, once a student was discovered to be either married, pregnant, or both, she was dismissed. With regard to students, this policy of dismissal was standard procedure until relatively recently. Pregnant students were considered to be morally corrupting influences on other students, and their presence in school was seen as legitimizing premature sexual activity and early marriage. Although many people still hold these views, the courts have tended in recent years to see such dismissals as discriminatory to young women and a denial of their rights to an education.* The result is that most school districts make arrangements for the education of pregnant students. Nevertheless, vexing issues keep coming up, such as, "Should a quite pregnant cheerleader be allowed to continue cheering?"

rights of pregnant students

Guidelines for Educators   Overall, in recent years, the pendulum of judicial decisions seems to be moving away from an emphasis on student rights and back in favor of the authority of the schools.[48] Nevertheless, when dealing with matters that might lead to suspension or expulsion, teachers and administrators should follow these guidelines:

useful guidelines

- *Documentation.* First, before suspension and expulsion can take place, students must be notified (either in writing or orally) of the nature of their offense and what the intended punishment is.

- *Explanation.* Second, the school must give the students a clear explanation of the evidence on which the disciplinary charges rest.

- *Opportunity to defend oneself.* Third, the school must give the students an opportunity to refute the charges before a fair and impartial individual with decision-making authority.

---

*Title IX of the Education Amendments (1972), which addresses issues of prohibiting sexual discrimination in any education program receiving federal funds, is the basis for most court decisions supporting a pregnant young woman's right to stay in school.

Corporal Punishment

Visit the web site to link to more information about corporal punishment.

Although few educational theorists living today advocate it, corporal, or physical, punishment is alive and well in American schools. The Supreme Court has regularly refused to rule on corporal punishment, leaving the issue up to the states. The trend among the states is clearly in favor of banning it. In 1979 only two states had banned corporal punishment in public schools, but currently twenty-seven states prohibit it.[49] A number of other states currently have legislation pending that would abolish corporal punishment. Still, many states leave the decision up to local school districts. Approximately 50 percent of students attend school in districts that do not allow corporal punishment.[50]

limits on corporal punishment

What does this situation mean for teachers from a legal point of view? First, they must know the rules of their state and school district. Second, they must be aware that the courts have ruled that corporal punishment can be administered only under certain conditions. Thus, teachers must be sure they are using only "moderate" and "reasonable" corporal punishment and using it only to establish discipline. A teacher who severely punishes a child, especially if any permanent disability or disfigurement results, is highly liable to suit. Also, punishment cannot be administered out of spite, revenge, or anger. In ruling on cases of excessive corporal punishment, the courts scrutinize the teacher's state of mind and motivation. The instruments of corporal punishment and where it can be administered are also matters of concern to the courts. Fists are totally inappropriate; so are switches and canes. Blows must not strike parts of the body where the risk of injury is high. Also, the punishment must be in scale with the crime—no whipping for whispering, for instance. Apparently the days of the principal's dictum, "The beatings will continue until the morale improves," are over.

Corporal punishment, of course, also entails important ethical considerations. Is it better to paddle a schoolyard bully and keep him in school or have legal hearings and separate him from the possibility of further education? One large problem with corporal punishment is that a ruler on the palm provokes terror in one student, but is all but meaningless for the next student. On the other hand, noncorporal punishment, such as the prolonged separation of an offending student from classmates, may cause true psychic pain for some children. The entire area of dealing with disruptive and offending students needs careful thought and even more careful actions.

Search and Seizure

Many students, even students of junior high and elementary ages, possess and sell illegal drugs. Schools have drug problems because American youth culture is inundated with images of drug use, and drugs are only one problem relating to search and seizure. Despite the risks of suspension or expulsion resulting from many schools' zero-tolerance policies, students also bring alcohol, pornography, and even dangerous weapons to school. As a result, school administrators may be urged to step up their searches of students for possession of drugs, alcohol, weapons, or other illegal items.

locker search rules

A student's locker may be searched by an appropriate school official, usually an administrator, *if there are reasonable grounds* to suspect that the locker contains something illegal or dangerous. The New York State courts have gone further in stating that "not only have the school authorities the right to inspect, but the right becomes a duty when suspicion arises that something of an illegal nature may be secreted there."[51] On the other hand, courts have found that it violates students' rights under the Fourth Amendment and is therefore illegal for school personnel to systematically spot-check lockers in hunts for drugs, weapons, or other illicit materials. Students' rights are even more closely protected when it comes to clothing and body searches.

probable cause

Reasonableness and Probable Cause   In the world outside school, one of the basic conditions for any kind of search of a person or possessions is "probable cause"—that is, that those in authority, need to have a substantial reason for believing that the person is in possession of something illegal. Yet because schools are specifically designed for the education and supervision of minors, courts have often allowed schools to use greater latitude in their searches. These decisions have been in keeping with the principle of *in loco parentis,* that schools act in place of the parents during the school day. Schools may only need to demonstrate a "reasonable suspicion" that a student was in possession of an illegal substance, rather than demonstrating the "probable cause" that law enforcement officials would need to demonstrate under similar circumstances.[52]

criterion of "reasonableness"

The importance of *reasonableness* in cases of search and seizure is shown by the 1985 U.S. Supreme Court case *New Jersey* v. *T.L.O.*[53] A teacher found two high school girls smoking in the bathroom and immediately brought them to the assistant vice principal's office. One girl admitted to smoking, but the second denied not only smoking on this occasion, but even being a smoker. The administrator asked the second student to come to his office, where he opened her purse and discovered a pack of cigarettes, cigarette-rolling papers, marijuana, a pipe, empty plastic bags, a wad of bills, and a list of "people who owe me money." Enter the police. The student was turned over to the juvenile court, where she was judged to be delinquent. She appealed on the basis that the search of her purse had violated her constitutional rights and therefore the evidence against her had been obtained illegally.

Find the full text of the *New Jersey* v. *T.L.O* decision in the text resources of your CD-ROM.

The case went to the U.S. Supreme Court, and the student lost. The Court stated, "The legality of a search of a student should depend simply on the reasonableness, under all the circumstances, of the search." Reasonableness appears to be determined, first, by whether or not the search has been initiated by a "reasonable" suspicion. Having seen rolling papers, it was reasonable to look for marijuana, since the two are so often closely related. The second criterion of reasonableness is that its scope and conduct must be "reasonably" related to the circumstances that gave rise to the search. Further, school officials must take into consideration the age and gender of the student and the nature of the offense.

The distinction between "reasonable suspicion" and "probable cause" is a fine line that is not always crystal clear. The prudent guideline for schools in their searches, though, is that any invasive search (body searches, for example) would require "probable cause," whereas less invasive searches (student lockers) would not require as rigorous a standard. In those cases, a "reasonable suspicion" would suffice. Mistakes here, particularly in the case of unwarranted strip searches, can be not only painfully embarrassing to the students, but also very expensive for the school district.

custodial responsibility versus rights

Finally, the police do not have the same *custodial relationship*—the same kind of responsibility toward students—that school officials do. Therefore, as a general rule, police need a warrant and the consent of school officials to search individual students or their lockers.

PAUSE AND REFLECT

1 If school authorities hear rumors that there are drugs in students' lockers, do you believe it is correct for them to search students' lockers without their permission?

▨ **Drug Tests as Searches**   Most people have heard of potential employees or Olympic athletes taking tests to see if they have any illegal drugs in their systems. Can schools decide to administer such kinds of drug testing for those who go out for sports teams?

In the late 1980s, the Vernonia School District of Oregon noted a surge in students' use of drugs. Athletes, in particular, were leaders in this drug culture. So the school decided to institute random urinalysis to spot check for drug use among the athletes. All students who signed up for a team were required to provide their own and their parents' written consent for testing.

In 1991, a seventh-grader, James Acton, signed up to play football, but was denied participation on the team because he and his parents refused to provide the test consent forms. The family sued, claiming that the drug testing was an invasion of student privacy and an illegal search. The case eventually was decided in the Supreme Court, which ruled in favor of the Vernonia School District. The justices took into consideration several of the district's arguments, including observations that athletes participate in any number of activities, from "suiting up" in the locker room to preseason physical exams, that reasonably decrease their expectations of privacy, and that the drug test was relatively unobtrusive. The Court also considered the severity of the need, based on the widespread student drug use, and ruled that the policy was reasonable and constitutional. In its ruling, however, the Court cautioned against assuming that suspicionless drug testing would be constitutional in all other situations. The Court indicated that in this case, the most salient factor was that the school district was enacting its governmental responsibilities in monitoring and supervising schoolchildren entrusted to its care.[54] In 2002, the Court significantly broadened its ruling to include not just athletes, but all students engaged in "competitive" extracurricular activities, be they football or debating. The ruling reaffirmed and stressed the school's "custodial responsibility." Because search and seizure touches upon such fundamental American rights, schools will probably always need to be vigilant about how school policies and practices align with constitutional rights.

Freedom of Speech

The right to say what we want, where we want, is the cornerstone of a free society, and as such it is near and dear to Americans. Justice William O. Douglas stated, "Restriction of free thought and free speech is the most dangerous of all subversions. It is the one un-American act that could most easily defeat us."[55] Despite our courts vigilant protection of this right, however, it is not an absolute right. The great Supreme Court Justice Oliver Wendell Holmes wrote that freedom of speech does not give a person the right to yell "Fire!" in a crowded theater or to knowingly and maliciously say or write lies that damage the reputation of another. In schools, freedom of expression must be balanced with the school's responsibility to maintain a safe and orderly environment and to protect people's feelings and reputations.

▨ *limits of free speech*

VOICES FROM THE CLASSROOM

Rob Famularo has been a sixth-grade teacher at Brookside Middle School in Allendale, New Jersey, for seven years.

Dress Codes

In my very first year as a teacher, I quickly realized the numerous and varied job responsibilities that undoubtedly come with the profession. On any given day a teacher may be asked to be a coach, friend, counselor, helping-hand, disciplinarian, or facilitator, to name just a few. What I did not realize quite so quickly, however, was the number of important decisions I would make on a regular basis. Many of these decisions carry moral, ethical, or legal implications. Consider, for example, the decisions involved in enforcing my public school's dress code.

Although the United States Supreme Court has stated that students relinquish some of their First Amendment rights in school, teachers nonetheless often struggle with the legal and ethical ramifications of controlling student dress and deeming what is "appropriate or inappropriate" attire for school. There are, of course, lots of theoretical, legal, and ethical questions surrounding dress

codes, such as, "Is it the responsibility of a public school to determine what attire is appropriate dress for school?", "Can a school still make this determination even if a parent objects or disagrees?", and " How can a teacher make an objective and consistent decision for every student?" These questions, which contain deep moral, legal, and ethical significance, are worthy of thoughtful reflection and consideration by anyone entering the teaching profession.

The situation becomes quite real, however, when the administration sets a specific dress code that I am expected to enforce when students enter my classroom first period in the morning. Can (or should) I tell a female high school student that her skirt is too short or that her shorts are more appropriate for the beach, rather than for school? Or should I simply turn a blind eye to the situation, saving both the girl and me the embarrassment? Am I really doing my job by ignoring the situation? This is when teachers get the chance to truly define their own personal meanings for what seem like abstract legal and ethical questions.

 Visit the web site for more Voices from the Classroom.

Students' First Amendment Rights   During the 1960s and early 1970s, many social protests and antiwar demonstrations spilled over into the schools, particularly the high schools. In one case, *Tinker* v. *Des Moines Independent Community School District* (1969), students who had been suspended for wearing antiwar arm bands took the issue to court, claiming that the school had interfered with their right to freedom of expression. The Supreme Court ruled in favor of the students, stating that their black arm bands were a form of symbolic speech in protest of the Vietnam War and should not be prohibited. A key point in this affirmation of students' First Amendment rights was the passive and nondisruptive nature of the students' protest. According to the Court, there was no evidence that the wearing of arm bands would "materially and substantially interfere with the requirements of appropriate discipline in the operation of the schools."[56]

A Shift in Legal Direction: Restricting Student Speech   During the 1970s and 1980s, the *Tinker* case was often cited, but the tide of court opinion in favor of student rights to free speech soon began to recede. In the 1986 case of *Bethel School District No. 403* v. *Fraser,*[57] Matthew Fraser, a high school student

■ *Tinker case—symbolic protest*

Find the full text of the *Tinker* v. *Des Moines Independent Community Schools* decision in the text resources of your CD-ROM.

■ *Fraser case— lewd speech*

Reflect on censorship of student speech with the image in this section of your CD-ROM.

in Bethel, Wash., nominated another student for vice president of the student government in a formal speech at an assembly before 600 students. Despite the warning of two teachers, Fraser built his speech on an elaborate, graphic, and explicit sexual metaphor comparing the nominee to a sexual organ. The court records of this case fail to tell us the outcome of the election, but Matthew Fraser got the ax. He was suspended for three days and removed from the list of candidates to speak at graduation. Fraser sued and won initially, but when the case went to the Supreme Court, he lost by a seven-to-two decision. The Court affirmed the school's right to "establish standards of civic and mature conduct" and to enforce them.

School Newspapers and Freedom of the Press   School newspapers have long been the arena for struggles over freedom of speech and freedom of the press. Often the very best efforts to make the paper "vital" and "relevant" draw the newspaper staff into controversies. This is what happened at Hazelwood East High School in the spring of 1983.[58] Attempting to make their paper, *The Spectrum,* speak more directly to the real issues confronting their fellow students, the staff submitted two controversial articles, one dealing with the personal accounts of three Hazelwood students who had become pregnant and the other focusing on divorce and its effect on students.

Hazelwood/Kuhlmeier case—school newspapers

In line with standard practice, the advisor and teacher of the journalism class that produced the paper passed the issue on to the principal for his approval. The principal eliminated the two pages containing the offending stories and sent the other four pages to the printer. In response, Kathy Kuhlmeier and the six other journalism students sued, contending that their freedom of speech rights had been violated. Eventually, in 1988, the Supreme Court ruled in favor of the school district. Although dissenting justices complained about the potential for "thought control" and the "denuding of high school students of much of the First Amendment protection that Tinker in itself prescribed," the majority supported the principal's actions as legal and responsible. As stated in the majority opinion:

students' rights lose ground

> A school may in its capacity as publisher of a school newspaper or producer of a school newspaper or producer of a school play disassociate itself not only from speech that would substantially interfere with its work or impinge on the rights of other students but also from speech that is, for example, ungrammatical, poorly written, inadequately researched, biased, prejudiced, vulgar or profane, or unsuitable for immature audiences. . . . A school need not tolerate student speech that is inconsistent with its basic educational mission even though the government could not censor similar speech outside the school.[59]

Implications of the Court Cases   Taken together, the three cases we have just discussed—*Tinker/Des Moines, Bethel/Fraser,* and *Hazelwood/Kuhlmeier*—suggest that freedom of speech and expression in schools is hardly absolute. Students may be punished for offensive or disruptive speech or publications. Schools, then, are something like Justice Holmes's crowded theaters, and the students' freedom of speech is somewhat limited. Students can and should express themselves, but in an orderly and nonviolent way. And the school has the right and responsibility to be certain that language is not used to hurt or scandalize the students in their charge.

■ *problems with the Internet*

One cutting-edge freedom of speech issue involves use of the Internet. As discussed in the chapter entitled "What Should Teachers Know About Technology and Its Impact on Schools?", the Internet can be a marvelous educational tool, opening up infinite intellectual resources to students. However, it can also expose students to written and visual pornography, obscenity through email, and chatroom predators. Many school districts have been struggling to respond to these dangers without unduly restricting students' exploration. Among the responses currently in place are orientation programs on appropriate use of the Internet, more careful supervision of computer stations, and special software designed to block forbidden sites. Many districts have or are developing **acceptable use policies** designed to provide rules of the road for students using this technology.

■ *Sexual Harassment*

Visit this chapter of the web site to link to more information about sexual harassment.

As discussed in the chapter on "What Social Problems and Tension Points Affect Today's Students?", a recent American Association of University Women (AAUW) study, entitled *Hostile Hallways*, reports that 81 percent of American students acknowledged that they were the subjects of sexual harassment at some time during their school lives. However, only 11 percent reported the incident to a teacher. The most common offenses were sexual jokes, gestures, and comments, followed by sexual touching, grabbing, and intentionally brushing up against another person in a sexual way. Whereas most of the offenses were student to student, a quarter of the girls and one-tenth of the boys reported being harassed by a school employee.

■ *sexual harassment*

Since the study first appeared, schools have attempted to address this abuse, focusing in particular on student-to-student harassment. The study's definition of **sexual harassment** is "unwanted and unwelcome sexual behavior which interferes with your life."[60] However, what constitutes sexual harassment in a particular situation can be a thorny issue. For instance, in the fall of 1996, a North Carolina school suspended a *six-year-old* boy who had kissed a female classmate on the cheek for sexual harassment. On the other hand, many readers may know of serious and frightening harassment incidents from their own school experience. One such incident was the subject of a Supreme Court ruling in *Davis* v. *Monroe County Board of Education.*[61]

When LaShonda Davis was in fifth grade in Forsyth, Georgia, her harassment nightmare began. A fellow student began groping her, grinding up against her, and declaring that he was "going to get in bed with her." The girl and her parents made repeated complaints to her teacher and the school principal. After five months, the teacher finally agreed to move the boy's desk to the other side of the room. But the sexual taunting and lewd overtures continued, until finally the family sought legal counsel. Six years after the initial incident, and with much legal work, the suit finally made its way to the Supreme Court. The Court, in a controversial five-to-four decision, ruled for the Davises and against the school district.

What has made this case legally controversial is the perceived danger of our courts being flooded with cases ranging from innocuous flirtations to true, hardcore harassment. Further, judges worry that the budgets of school districts will be drained by the legal expenses involved in fighting frivolous suits. However, in the prevailing opinion, the *Davis* decision stresses that school districts are liable only if they were "deliberately indifferent" to information about "severe, pervasive, and objectively offensive" harassment among students.[62] It appears that

TABLE 7.3 Selected Court Cases Related to Students' Rights

Issue	Case	Ruling
Students' right to free speech		
Students' right to make a symbolic protest	*Tinker* v. *Des Moines Independent Community School District* (1969)	Students have the right to symbolic protest, if that protest does not interfere with the school's operation.
Students' right to use lewd language for a school speech	*Bethel School District No. 403* v. *Fraser* (1986)	Schools have the right to establish and enforce standards of civic conduct.
Student newspapers and freedom of the press	*Hazelwood School District* v. *Kuhlmeier* (1988)	Because public schools are not public forums, school officials have the right not to publish student articles that may violate the sensibilities of other students.
Students' right to education		
Disabled students with behavior problems	*Honig* v. *Doe* (1988)	Dangerous students with disabilities may not be suspended for more than 10 days without parental consent or permission of a federal judge.
Students' school suspension for fighting at a game	*Fuller* v. *Decatur Public School Board of Education School District 61* (2000)	School's policy of zero tolerance for fighting was upheld by courts.
Students' right to freedom from sexual harassment	*Davis* v. *Monroe County Board of Education* (1999)	School held liable if it ignores excessive sexual harassment of one student by another student.
Students' right to due process		
Students' right to notification and hearing before a suspension	*Goss* v. *Lopez* (1975)	Schools violate students' constitutional right to due process if they suspend students without a hearing.
Students' rights regarding search and seizure		
Students' protection from school searches of personal items	*New Jersey* v. *T.L.O.* (1985)	Schools can search students' lockers and other private items if there is reasonable cause.

while the Court has come to the defense of harassed students, the criteria for what actually constitutes an offense have been set quite high. Nevertheless, the problem of sexual harassment in our schools is out of the closet, and schools, which formerly have taken this issue casually, are now working to respond. Table 7.3 summarizes the *Davis* case, along with other major students' rights cases discussed in preceding sections.

▪ *Records and Students' Right to Privacy*

In this information age, most of us probably have a history tucked away on computer disks. For students, the history may consist of school records, various test scores, and ratings by teachers on everything from citizenship to punctuality.

Teachers and other staff members judge a student's character and potential, and others use those judgments to decide whether the student should go to this school or get that job. Certainly we need some system of exchanging information about one another; otherwise, we would hire only our friends or attend only those schools where enough people knew us to vouch for us. However, the kind of information in school records may be very imperfect, and the danger that it will be misinterpreted or fall into the wrong hands is great.

Find the full text of the Family Educational Rights and Privacy Act in the text resources of your CD-ROM.

In the early 1970s, a series of situations came to light in which information was poorly used or parents and students were denied access to records (for example, when a diagnosis was used to justify sending a child to a class for students with mental retardation). In response, the U.S. Congress passed the Family Educational Rights and Privacy Act in 1974. The act, also known as the **Buckley amendment,** outlines who may and who may not see a student's record and under what conditions. A clear winner from this legislation is parents, who previously were kept from many of the officially recorded judgments that affected their children's futures. The amendment states that federal funds will be denied to a school if it prevents parents from exercising the right to inspect and review their children's educational records. Parents must receive an explanation or interpretation of the records if they so request.

■ *the Buckley amendment*

■ *the downside of Buckley*

However, the Buckley amendment does not give parents the right to see a teacher's or an administrator's unofficial records. For instance, a teacher's private diary of a class's progress or private notes about a particular child may not be inspected without the teacher's consent.

Although the Buckley amendment has undoubtedly reduced the potential for abuse of information, it has had a somewhat chilling effect on teachers' and others' willingness to be candid in their judgments when writing student recommendations for jobs or colleges. Because students may elect to see a teacher's letter of recommendation, some teachers choose to play it safe and write a vague, general letter that lacks discriminating judgments, pro or con, about the student. In effect, some faculty members and other recommenders have adopted the attitude, "Well, if a student doesn't trust me enough to let me write a confidential recommendation, I'll simply write an adequate, safe recommendation."

Nevertheless, the Buckley amendment's impact, in our view, has been positive. In the past, many students lost opportunities for higher education and desirable jobs because of inaccurate statements in recommendations or in their school records. One professor reported to us an incident that occurred in his school in 1975, shortly after the Buckley amendment came into being: "Our counselors at the junior high school where I taught were 'purging' the records of subjective comments with black markers. In one student's permanent record folder, a *Playboy* magazine fell out. It seems a grade school teacher took it from Carl and included it in his permanent record because she wanted future teachers to know 'what kind of kid Carl really was.'"

Despite the fact that the Buckley amendment is well over twenty-five years old, the implications for what constitutes a violation of students' right to privacy concerning his or her educational records are not always apparent. That fact was made all too clear in the fall of 2001, when the Supreme Court agreed to hear a case involving student rights to privacy.

An Oklahoma mother, Kristja Falvo, brought suit against the Owasso Independent School District for violating the Family Educational Rights and Privacy Act. Her son's classroom teacher asked the students to grade each other's quizzes and call out the grades so the teacher could record them. The mother argued that such a practice violated her son's right to privacy because the practice publicly disclosed educational information about him. Ms. Falvo was especially concerned that this practice would have a detrimental effect on his learning. In a 2002 decision, the Supreme Court ruled in favor of the school district, stating that peer grading is not in violation of the Buckley Amendment.

A Final Word

This chapter has been the beginning of what we hope will be your ongoing probe of the important role that two related issues, ethics and law, play in the life of the teacher. Together these issues permeate the school environment. Whereas ethical issues may raise timeless questions, some laws continually change, and even now the courts may be giving a different complexion to some of the decisions cited in this chapter. Also, the chapter has touched on many issues only lightly and has omitted others because of lack of space. We urge you to move on from this introduction to investigate further the work of the teacher in its larger ethical and legal framework.

KEY TERMS

academic freedom (233)
acceptable use policy (257)
breach of contract (227)
Buckley amendment (259)
continuing contract (227)
contract (226)

due process (225)
ethics (216)
fair use (237)
grievance (226)
in loco parentis (249)
law (216)

liability (230)
reduction in force (RIF) (229)
sexual harassment (257)
tenure (227)
zero-tolerance policy (250)

FOR REFLECTION

❶ Can you remember examples of the "everyday ethics" of teaching shown by the teachers you had in elementary and secondary schools? Can you remember examples in which your teachers' ethical behavior was questionable?

❷ Do you believe tenure practices are justified and lead to better schools? Why or why not?

❸ What do you think about the current controversies over the place of religion in public schools? Of prayer? Of the Bible and other religious works?

❹ Teachers are expected to be people of good character and role models to students. What are the limits of this expectation? What are some points at which the rights of the school district end and the rights of the teacher begin?

FOR FURTHER INFORMATION

PRINT RESOURCES

Jane Edwards, *Opposing Censorship in the Public Schools: Religion, Morality and Literature* (Mahwah, NJ: Erlbaum Associates, 1998).

This book summarizes a number of the debates surrounding censorship and reports on several controversies related to specific works of literature.

Louis Fischer, David Schimmel, and Cynthia Kelly, *Teachers and the Law,* 5th ed. (New York: Longman, 1999).

This book, written by scholars who are lawyers and professors of education, bridges the worlds of the courts and the classroom with great detail and clarity.

Michael W. LaMorte, *School Law: Cases and Concepts,* 6th ed. (Boston: Allyn and Bacon, 1999).

This current text covers both key legal opinions and dissenting opinions, and adds valuable commentary and explanation.

Kenneth Strike and Jonas Soltis, *The Ethics of Teaching,* 3rd ed. (New York: Teachers College Press, 1998).

This short book is an excellent source for ways to approach the topic of ethics in teaching. It contains a number of practice cases.

2000 Deskbook Encyclopedia of American School Law (Rosemont, MN: Data Research, 2000).

This excellent annual reference book is an easily accessible source on the current law and legal issues surrounding all aspects of public and private education.

Perry Zirkel, "De Jure" column in *Phi Delta Kappan* (Bloomington, IN: Phi Beta Kappa International, Inc).

This recurring magazine column reports on important issues of school law and provides an excellent way to follow recent developments.

WEB RESOURCES

Acceptable Use Policies: A Handbook. Available at: **http://www.pen.k12.va.us/VDOE/technology/ AUP/home.shtml**.

This handbook, available on the Internet, is produced by the Virginia Department of Education and is a rich source of information on using the Internet in schools and developing acceptable use policies.

The Missouri Department of Elementary and Secondary Education Updates. Available at: **http://www.dese. state.mo.us/schoollaw**.

This excellent web site is a goldmine of information on an array of court cases, from school prayer to student-on-student sexual harassment. (Keep in mind, however, that rulings may, in some cases, apply only to the state of Missouri.)

The Legal Information Institute's Supreme Court Collection. Available at: **http://www.law.cornell.edu.supct**.

This web site gives you access to the most important Supreme Court school-related decisions.

The Emory University School of Law. Available at: **http://www.law.emory.edu**.

This web site provides easy access to both Supreme Court and state court rulings on current and past school related rulings.

Part Three

Foundations and the Future

J ust as the subjects of anatomy and chemistry are essential to the practice of medicine, certain areas of organized knowledge are essential to the practice of education. These areas, called the *foundations of education,* provide the intellectual underpinnings of educational practice. This section covers several of these key areas: school governance, finance, philosophy, and history. Truly professional teachers ground their daily practice in the wisdom gleaned from these foundational areas. This section concludes with a chapter on recent movements for educational reform, in which all the foundational components come to bear in the effort to improve our schools.

What Are the Philosophical Foundations of American Education?

Chapter Preview This chapter examines the role of philosophy, a key foundational discipline in the work of the teacher. First, we describe philosophy; then we discuss four different philosophies and analyze their applications to the classroom.

This chapter emphasizes that:

- Philosophical knowledge has a fundamental role in clarifying questions of education.

- Philosophical thought has distinct characteristics which contribute to the way we know the world. Four branches of philosophy—metaphysics, epistemology, axiology, and logic—relate rather directly to the work of the teacher.

- Four philosophies of education—perennialism, essentialism, romanticism, and progressivism—have many practical implications for the classroom teacher.

- Psychological theories, particularly constructivism, influence modern educational thought.

- Teachers need to have a philosophy to guide their practice. Many develop eclectic personal philosophies that incorporate elements of several major philosophical views.

- Discovering your personal philosophy is a lifelong process, but it should begin now.

A medical student who wants intensely to be a surgeon, has marvelous hands, and displays a high level of technical skill, but does not know how the body functions or what constitutes health can hardly be called a doctor.

An aspirant to the ministry who loves to work with people and possesses a marvelous gift of speaking, but has no opinion about humanity's relationship to God or about the purpose of religion can hardly be suited for religious ministry.

And a person who has a great desire to be with young people, wants to live the life of a teacher, and possesses great technical skill, but lacks purpose and direction is hardly a teacher.

These three individuals are like wind-up toys, moving along blindly without a plan or an intellectual compass. And although this image may be somewhat dramatic, there *are* people who prepare for professions without getting to the core meaning of what those professions are all about. Such directionless behavior can cause problems in any occupation or profession, but particularly in teaching. What kind of a teacher can someone be who lacks a view of what people are and a vision of what they can become? Who cannot clearly define right and wrong in human behavior? Who doesn't recognize what is important and what is unimportant or can't distinguish clear thinking from sloppy thinking? The person who would take on the responsibility for educating the young without having seriously wrestled with these questions is, to say the least, dangerous, for he or she is going against the very grain of what it means to be a teacher. In fact, it is safe to say that such a person is not a teacher, but a technician.

■ *philosophy as foundation*

This chapter introduces you to philosophy, one of the foundational subjects in education, which, along with history and psychology (and, to some degree, economics, political science, sociology, anthropology, and the law), forms the intellectual underpinning on which the practice of education rests. The study of philosophy helps the teacher systematically to reflect on issues that are central to education, including such basic concepts as *learning, teaching, being educated, knowledge,* and *the good life.*

What Is Philosophy?

■ *love of wisdom*

The word **philosophy** is made up of two root words: "love" (*philo*) and "wisdom" (*sophos*). In its most basic sense, then, philosophy is the *love of wisdom.* Although not all people love wisdom in the same way or to the same degree, all humans are questioning beings—seekers of answers. As children, we are preoccupied with such lofty questions as, "How do I get fewer veggies and more dessert?" Then we progress to such questions as, "How does the teacher always know to call on me when I don't have the answers?", and "What do I need to do to get a decent grade in geometry?" Ultimately, we may move to more fundamental levels of questioning: "Who am I?", "What is the purpose of life, and what am I doing here?", "What does it mean to be a really good person?"

Visit this chapter of the web site to link to more information about the nature of philosophy.

■ *Fundamental Questions of Existence*

Until about one hundred years ago, most people relied on religion and philosophy for answers to such fundamental questions. Whereas religion is said to represent the revealed word of God, philosophy represents a human attempt to sort out by reason the fundamental questions of existence. Many of the great thinkers of Western civilization—Plato, Aristotle, St. Thomas Aquinas, René Descartes, Jean-Jacques Rousseau, Immanuel Kant, Friedrich Nietzsche, John Locke, John Stuart Mill, William James, Alfred North Whitehead, and John Dewey—have been philosophers. Because education has always been a central human concern, philosophers have thought and written a great deal about education and the questions surrounding it.

> *The real object of education is to have a man in the condition of continually asking questions.*
>
> —Bishop Creighton

Only a few people in our society are professional philosophers who earn their daily bread (usually a rather meager fare) by pursuing answers to the fundamental questions of life. However, all of us who wrestle with such questions as "Who am I?" and "What am I doing with my life?" are engaged in philosophical activity. Although there is a distinction between the few professional philosophers and the great number of us who are amateurs, the questions we ask and the answers we glean usually have a major impact on the practical affairs of our lives and on how we choose to spend our life force.

■ *impact of philosophy on our lives*

■ Sources of Our Philosophy

The very practical decision of whether to become a teacher, a real estate broker, or a professional bungee jumper almost always has its roots in a person's philosophy of life. In developing a philosophy, we draw on many influences: our experiences in life, our religious views, and our reading of literature, history, and current events. A major difference between professionals and amateurs, however, lies in the precision of their methods.

■ *factors that influence our philosophies*

Philosophy is an extremely pure and abstract science. Philosophers work with neither test tubes nor white rats, use neither telescopes nor microscopes, and do not fly off to remote societies to observe the natives. The method or process of philosophers is questioning and reasoning; their product is *thought*.

■ The Philosopher's Method and Language

■ *concern with meanings of words*

Basically, philosophers are concerned with the meanings of things and how to interpret those meanings. Therefore, they have an intense interest in the real meanings of words. Although some philosophical discussion and writing involves technical language, it generally uses "plain language," the ordinary language of people. However, philosophers try to be extremely clear and careful about their use of terms. They do not want their ultimate goal (meaning) to be lost in a thicket of fuzzy language.

Although philosophy appears to deal with simple issues in simple language, behind the philosophers' questions are raging debates about profound issues that can have far-reaching implications. For example, the question, "What is a human?" leads to other questions, such as "When, if ever, can a fetus be aborted?" and "What rights do severely disabled persons have?" Or "Should humans clone humans?"

" How do you expect me to learn anything when you're the one who keeps asking all the questions?"

Reprinted by permission from *Phi Delta Kappan*.

PAUSE AND REFLECT

Before you go much further in this chapter, you should clarify where you stand today. What are your answers to these philosophical questions:

1 What are the fundamental life questions to which you are seeking answers?

2 What is or are the ends or goals of an education?

3 Should a school lay out what is to be learned, or should the students have a large say in what and how they learn?

The Terrain of Philosophy

▪ *four branches of philosophy*

Philosophy covers a large amount of intellectual turf. The terrain of philosophy is divided into several areas, including four that are particularly important to the teacher: metaphysics, epistemology, axiology, and logic. These four branches of philosophy are central to the educative process and, in fact, speak directly to the work of the teacher.

▪ Metaphysics

▪ *what is real?*

Metaphysics involves the attempt to explain the nature of the real world, or the nature of existence. Metaphysics attempts to answer the question "What is real?" without relying on revealed religion, such as the Bible. Further, the metaphysician characteristically believes that it is not possible to address fundamental matters such as the nature of a human being or of the universe, simply by collecting data and formulating statistically significant generalizations. From most metaphysical perspectives, the true nature of a person cannot be captured by measuring or counting alone. A person is more than the sum of his or her height and weight, IQ (intelligence quotient) and SAT scores, and other "vital" statistics.

In probing the nature of reality, the metaphysician asks a whole array of questions: "Does life have meaning?", "Are human beings free or totally determined?", "Is there a purpose to life?", "Is there a set of enduring principles that guide the operation of the universe?", "Can these principles be known?", and "Is there such a thing as stability, or is our world ever-changing?"

▪ *teachers take metaphysical stands*

▪ **Metaphysics and the Curriculum**   These abstract questions are ones that the educator cannot dismiss. Ultimately, the purpose of education is to explain reality to the young. The curriculum and how we teach it represent one statement of what that reality is. Although teachers may not actually be metaphysicians, they do take a stand on metaphysical questions. If a teacher decides to teach because he or she believes the most important thing in the universe is a human mind, that a career decision is driven by a metaphysical view: the importance of an individual person. The people on school boards also take stands on metaphysical issues. For example, whether a particular school system makes a major investment in educating individuals with severe mental disabilities or emphasizes vocational education depends very much on someone's decision about the nature of the person and the place of work in a person's life.

▦ *Epistemology*

Epistemology deals with questions regarding knowledge and knowing. The epistemologist, seeking the true nature of knowing, asks such questions as "What is true knowledge (as opposed to false ideas)?" and "Is truth elusive, always changing and always dependent on the truth seeker's particulars of time, place, and angle of vision?" Some people, whom we call *skeptics,* question our capacity to ever really know the truths of existence. And some, whom we call *agnostics,* are convinced there are no "truths" and that seeking knowledge of ultimate realities is an empty hope.

Epistemology deals not only with the nature of truth but also with the ways in which we can know reality. Questions, such as "How do we come to know the truth?" and "What are the sources for gaining knowledge?", are part of the conversation. There are a variety of ways by which we can know, and each of these ways has its advocates and detractors. Among the ways of knowing are by divine revelation, by authority, through personal intuition, from our own five senses, from our own powers of reasoning, and through experimentation.

■ *what is truth?*

■ *how do we acquire knowledge?*

■ **Teaching and Ways of Knowing**   Questions concerning knowledge and knowing are, almost by definition, of great concern to the teacher. The epistemological question "How do you know this or that?" goes to the heart of teaching methodology. If a teacher wants her students to have a concept of democracy, how does she proceed? Does she explain the characteristics of different forms of government, such as monarchy and oligarchy, and then the characteristics of democracy? Or does she take a more hands-on approach and have the students do a role-playing exercise during which one student is appointed class dictator and the rest must obey the student-dictator's orders? The student who has only read about democracy "knows" it in an *epistemologically* different way than a student who has been bullied and harassed for several days by a teacher-appointed dictator.

It is becoming increasingly clear, in fact, that individuals differ in their preferred methods of learning. As discussed more fully in the chapter on "Who Are Today's Students in a Diverse Society?", much of the teacher's work is helping the student find the most effective way of coming to know (or gaining new knowledge).

In some instances, the teacher may find that some people—for example, parents and community members—may have strong opinions regarding these epistemological questions. Many people have strong beliefs about the true origin of humankind and how one knows it. This issue is sometimes called the *creationist controversy,* and it rests on a sharp and fundamental argument over the questions "Who are we?" and "How did we get here?" One faction insists that the public schools should present the evidence of our origin that is given in the Book of Genesis, which we know by divine revelation. Others insist that the way to know the origin of the human race is through the scientific theory of evolution, grounded in the interpretation of artifactual evidence. So behind this ongoing educational controversy is a fundamental question of epistemology.

■ *impact on teaching methods*

■ *creationist controversy*

🖳 Reflect on the terrain of educational philosophy with the image in this section of your CD-ROM.

▦ *Axiology*

Axiology focuses on the nature of values. As human beings, we quite naturally search for the correct and most effective way to live. In doing so, we engage

what values should we pursue?

questions of values. Of course, when different people look at life, they often come up with very different sets of values. For instance, *hedonists* believe in seeking pleasure and living for the moment. On the other hand, *stoics* have an austere way of looking at life and seek to be unaffected by pleasure or pain. Many people regard values from a religious perspective, asserting that unless humanity and the rest of the natural world were originally created by God, existence as we know it is just the meaningless coming together of cosmic dust and debris. In this view, the only genuine values derive from God.

Most people would agree with Socrates that schools have a dual responsibility: to make people smart and to make them good. To the degree that teachers accept the second function, they are grappling with an axiological issue. In fact, teachers are intimately involved with questions of moral values. Young people are seeking ways to live lives that are worthwhile, and teachers traditionally have been expected to help students establish moral values both as individuals and as contributing members of society. (See the chapters entitled "How Should Education Be Reformed?" and "What Are the Ethical and Legal Issues Facing Teachers?" for more discussion of this issue.) Moral values such as honesty, respect for other people, and fairness are necessary if we are to live together in harmony. Despite a large core of values on which a majority of people agree, such as respecting others and avoiding violence in settling disputes, other value issues separate people. Sexual behavior, capital punishment, gun control, and abortion are examples of contemporary social issues that involve a wide range of viewpoints about what is right.

teachers and moral values

Ethics and Aesthetics   Axiology has two subtopics: ethics and aesthetics. **Ethics** takes us into the realm of values that relate to "good" and "bad" behavior, examining morality and rules of conduct. At one time, teaching children how to deal with issues of good/bad and right/wrong was the primary purpose of schooling. In recent decades the pendulum has swung the other way, and schools have been more concerned with factual knowledge and skills than with ethical knowledge. There are, however, many signs that schools are being called back to help children deal with ethical issues.[1]

issues of right and wrong

The subject of ethics not only teaches us how we can intellectually ascertain the "right" thing to do, but also is often used to help us establish a particular set of standards, such as a code of ethics. In the chapter entitled "What Are the Ethical and Legal Issues Facing Teachers?", we give particular attention to these issues.

The second subtopic of axiology, **aesthetics,** deals with questions of values regarding beauty and art. Many discussions about the value of a particular film, book, or work of art are attempts to come to some aesthetic judgment on the value of the work. Whether a person "has good taste" is an example of a common aesthetic judgment.

issues of beauty

Logic

Logic is the branch of philosophy that deals with reasoning. One of the fundamental qualities that distinguishes human beings from animals is that humans can *think*. Logic focuses on reasoning and modes of arguing that bring us to valid conclusions. The pursuit of logic is an attempt to think clearly and avoid vagueness and contradictions. Certain rules of logic have been identified, and they constitute the core of this branch of philosophy.

the human ability to think

LEADERS IN EDUCATION
SOCRATES (469–399 B.C.)

The ancient Greek philosopher Socrates was condemned to death for supposedly corrupting the youth of Athens. Today we know him primarily through the written "dialogues" of his student Plato. How much Plato's portrayal resembled the actual man is open to debate. Nevertheless, the Socrates of Plato's dialogues has had a deep and lasting influence on both philosophy and education, giving us such common terms as *Socratic teaching, Socratic questioning,* and the *Socratic method.* The following passage explains some of the basic tenets of Socrates' approach.

Socrates expressly denied that he was a teacher in the commonly accepted sense of that term. What he meant by this—at least in part—was that he was not a sophist, a professional pedagogue who, for a fee, would endeavor to transmit some knowledge that he possessed to someone who lacked it. Not only did Socrates charge no fees, he claimed not to have command of any such knowledge.

The learning that Socrates was concerned with simply didn't fit the information-transmission model of education implicit in the Athenian public mind and the teaching profession. Neither did his pioneering focus on virtue and wisdom square well with the popular attachment to honor, fame, and wealth. As he tries to explain at one point to Anytus in Plato's dialogue *Meno,* "[W]e are inquiring whether the good men of today and of the past knew how to pass on to another the virtue they themselves possessed, or whether a man cannot pass it on or receive it from another." Since it was clear that wisdom and virtue could not simply be passed on from one person to another, Socrates sought an alternative way of conceptualizing how such excellences of mind and character were acquired. What was the teacher's role in that acquisition, if not simply being a supplier?

As an alternative to the receiving-knowledge-from-another model, Socrates proposed that learning was "recollection"—that is, a process akin to dredging up knowledge from one's own resources. "Teaching" on this model he later compared to acting as a "midwife"—assisting in the birth of knowledge *in* another person rather than serving as a supplier of it *to* another person. This was to be accomplished in conversation, mostly by skillful questioning and cross-examination ("Socratic teaching," "Socratic questioning," and "Socratic method").

Socrates admitted to behaving like a "gadfly" in this dialectical pursuit of truth, goading people into serious thinking about human living. And he also confessed to acting like a benumbing "sting ray" or "torpedo fish," referring to his ability to render people tongue-tied about matters that they thought they already knew perfectly well—but actually didn't. Not until people felt the sting of not really knowing about life's important matters could they be prompted to inquire into them seriously.

 Visit the web site for more information about Socrates.

Source: Reprinted by permission of Steven S. Tigner.

■ *reasoning from general to particular*

■ **Deductive Reasoning** A primary task of the schools is to help children think clearly and communicate logically. Two types of reasoning are commonly taught in schools: deductive and inductive. In **deductive reasoning,** the teacher presents a general proposition and then illustrates it with a series of particulars. The most highly developed form of this approach is the classic method of the syllogism. In a *syllogism,* one makes two statements, and a third statement, a conclusion, is *deduced* or drawn from them. For instance:

All human beings are mortal.

I am a human being.

Therefore, I am mortal.

In deductive reasoning, such as in this example, the general proposition, an abstract concept, is followed by a factual statement, which in turn leads to a new factual statement and the creation of new knowledge, at least for the learner.

As another example, imagine that in October, Mrs. Wells, a fifth-grade teacher, writes on the board:

All trees that shed their leaves at the end of a growing season are deciduous trees.

As a two-week project, Mrs. Wells asks her class to observe and record data about the trees that surround their school. For two weeks, the students observe the three dozen maple trees shedding their leaves during the fall. The teacher then writes her earlier sentence on the board again:

All trees that shed their leaves at the end of a growing season are deciduous trees.

And, using their observational data (and a little intellectual nudging from Mrs. Wells), the students complete the syllogism:

Maple trees shed their leaves at the end of the growing season.

Therefore, maple trees are deciduous.

Then the students try to identify other types of trees that fit the deciduous classification.

Much of what a teacher does in school is helping children both acquire the intellectual habits of deductive thinking and expand their storehouse of knowledge through this process.

■ *reasoning from particular to general*

■ **Inductive Reasoning** **Inductive reasoning** works in the opposite fashion. The teacher sets forth particulars, from which a general proposition is derived or *induced.* For instance, the teacher may wish to lead the students to the discovery that water is essential to plant growth. He gives each child two similar plants (a different type, from weeds to flowers, for each child) and then has each student daily feed one plant with water and leave the other plant without water. After ten days the teacher has the students report the condition of their plants, and from all of these individual reports he leads the students to generalize about the necessity of water to plant life. In fact, they have derived or induced their answer.

■ *need for both types of reasoning*

While the two forms of reasoning are opposite, both are essential to logical thought and, therefore, need to be developed in learners. Effective teachers design a variety of learning activities, some of which, like the tree example above, help students think deductively, and others, like the plant example, focus on inductive reasoning.

Logic, however, is not confined to inductive and deductive reasoning. To think logically means to think clearly, in many different ways. Teachers need logic in many aspects of their work, from trying to understand the behavior of a child who seems to have an erratic learning pattern to developing tests that accurately measure what has been taught in a course. Most of all, teachers need to model this clear, logical thinking for students.

Overall, the four branches of philosophy—metaphysics, epistemology, axiology, and logic—address some of the major concerns of the teacher. The answers they suggest to the teacher and the implications they have for actual classroom practice are areas to which we now turn.

PAUSE AND REFLECT

❶ Which of these four branches of philosophy do you think is of greatest importance to you as a future teacher?

Schools of Educational Philosophy

Visit the web site to link to more information about schools of educational philosophy.

Answers to the philosophical questions that pepper the preceding section have almost infinite variety. Over the years, however, certain answers by particular philosophers have received more attention and allegiance than others. These more enduring sets of answers or world views represent schools of philosophy. Some started with the early Greek philosophers and have grown and developed through the centuries. Other schools of thought are more recent and offer fresh, new formulations to ultimate questions.

In this section, we describe four philosophies that have had a major impact on American education and demonstrate the variety of ways in which teaching and learning can be conceived. It is important to keep in mind, however, that many important philosophies relevant to education, such as neo-Thomism and classical Eastern thought, or existentialism, are not included here. In addition, there are major educational ideas that do not quite qualify as "philosophies," but are having a big impact on schools.

■ *four philosophies influential in American education*

The four philosophies we have selected for this chapter are perennialism, essentialism, romanticism, and progressivism. Behind these very daunting words are very different ideas of what people are, how we should live our lives, and how we should conduct the education of children. We have selected these philosophies, not because they are our pick of the "Top Four Philosophical Hits," but because of the level of influence each viewpoint has had on American educational thought and practice. We have grouped these philosophies as *subject-centered* or *child-centered*. For each of these philosophies, we present first a brief explanation of its origins and the core ideas it embodies, the implications for teaching and learning, and then a "personal point of view" by a teacher (fictitious) who is committed to that particular philosophy. We have tried to show that these positions are not just windy abstractions or the preoccupations of ivory tower thinkers; rather, they shape what people teach and how they teach it.

■ Subject-Centered Philosophies

The first two schools of philosophy, perennialism and essentialism, stress the importance of subject matter knowledge in education. Both schools of thought show a strong allegiance to the curriculum and both argue that well-educated students should possess a defined body of knowledge.

■ **Perennialism**   **Perennialism,** derived primarily from the writings of Plato, views truth and nature, in particular, human nature, as constant, objective, and

■ *truth is unchanging*

unchanging. Beneath the superficial differences from one century or decade to the next, the rules that govern the world and the characteristics that make up human nature stay the same. The purpose of life, according to Plato, was the search for these constant and changeless truths, which reside in the nature of things. This search was achieved through the Socratic dialogue or dialectic, a process in which ideas are debated in a back-and-forth discussion until some recognizable clarity (the light) was reached. Essential to undertaking such a pursuit was mental discipline and rational thought processes.

The function of education is to teach one to think intensively and to think critically. Intelligence plus character—that is the goal of true education.
—MARTIN LUTHER KING, JR.

Education is crucial to perennialists because it develops a person's mental discipline and rationality, which are necessary to the search for truths that will help humans avoid being dominated by the instinctual or animal-like side of human nature

Perennialism in the School   For the perennialist, the purpose of education is to find the changeless "truth," which is best revealed in the enduring classics of Western culture. Classical thought, then, should be emphasized as a subject matter in schools. Perennialists believe that schools should teach disciplined knowledge through the traditional subjects of history, language, mathematics, science, and the arts. Perennialists place particular emphasis on literature and the humanities because these subjects provide the greatest insight into the human condition. Although this view of the curriculum is evident in many areas of education, in its most complete form it is known as the *Great Books approach,* developed by Robert Maynard Hutchins, who was president and chancellor at the University of Chicago throughout the 1930s and 1940s and the recently deceased Mortimer

Reflect on perennialism and Great books approaches with the image in this section of your CD-ROM.

Adler, a professor at the University of Chicago during the same time period. The Great Books, which constitute a shelf of volumes stretching from Homer's *Iliad* to Albert Einstein's *On the Electrodynamics of Moving Bodies,* are a perennialist's ideal curriculum.

The object of education is to prepare the young to educate themselves throughout their lives.
—ROBERT MAYNARD HUTCHINS

For perennialists, the development of the intellect is best achieved through a teacher-directed instructional approach in the early years of schooling. Socratic dialogue is then used to help mature learners question and examine their beliefs in order to move closer to the truth.

Since the early 1990s, a controversy has arisen over the content of perennialist literature, history, and philosophy courses. Scholars and students have criti-

■ *controversy about Eurocentrism*

cized colleges and high schools for promoting a "Eurocentric" view of knowledge and culture, one that ignores the contributions of all but "dead, white, male writers and thinkers." They urge a more inclusive curriculum, one that gives greater attention to women, minorities, and Eastern, African, and Hispanic cultures. Whereas some take this movement as a direct attack on the perennialist curriculum, others see it as a natural and useful extension of the perennialists' search for the best of the world's wisdom. One perennialist friend of ours, who welcomes this new approach, suggested, "Sure, students should know about Islamic literature and Eastern philosophy, but they should first get to know their own neighborhood, Western culture."

The Paideia Proposal   For the perennialist, then, immersion in these great works helps students reach the perennialist's goal, which is a state of human excellence that the ancients called *paideia*. This is a state not only of enlightenment but also of goodness. As such, it is a goal that perennialists believe all humans should seek.

approach of the Paideia Group

In the 1980s, Mortimer Adler and a group of educators breathed new life into perennialism with the publication of *The Paideia Proposal* and then a series of supporting books.[2] *The Paideia Proposal* presents this educational philosophy not as an austere, joyless curriculum, but as an exciting, involving intellectual and aesthetic journey. Several of the Paideia Group who worked with Adler in formulating this plan are both minority group members and superintendents of big-city school districts serving a large population of poor and minority students. Much of the appeal of *The Paideia Proposal* is that it asserts that *all* children, not just the gifted or the privileged children of the rich, should have this classical education. Members of the Paideia Group see it as providing both quality and equality in education. Nevertheless, interest in *The Paideia Proposal* has faded somewhat in recent years, another curricular movement has attracted the interest of educators with perennialist leanings.

Education as Preparation for Life

disciplined book learning prepares for life

Education, then, is of great importance to perennialists, but it is an education that is rigorous and demanding. Perennialists hold that education is preparation for life, and should therefore not attempt to imitate life or be lifelike. Students should engage in a rigorous examination of the classics in order to discover the timeless wisdom embodied therein, rather than focusing on knowledge that might seem personally meaningful.

In summary, the perennialists' view is that one learns through disciplined study of the great works and ideas of the past. It is a view that leans heavily on the authority of the collected wisdom of the past and looks to traditional thought to guide us in the present. As such, the curriculum is structured and clearly defined. Further, perennialists see education as protecting and conserving the best thought from the past. In this sense, the perennialist favors a very traditional or conservative ("conservative" as in *conserving* the best of the past) view of education. The following case study presents the point of view of a more or less typical perennialist teacher.

CASE STUDY

A Perennialist Teacher

I came into education twenty-five years ago for two reasons. First, I was bothered by what I thought was all the nonsense in the curriculum and by all the time my friends and I wasted in school. We were allowed to take whatever courses we wanted, the majority of which were

electives as wasted time

electives which seemed to be little more than the teacher's hobby. There were so many discussions—discussions that seemed to go nowhere and seemed only vaguely to touch on the supposed content of the course. I often felt as if we were simply sharing our ignorance. My second reason for becoming a teacher is a more positive one. I am convinced that our society, our culture, has great ideas,

them. For one thing, essentialists do not focus as intently on "truths" as do perennialists. They are less concerned with the classics as being the primary repository of worthwhile knowledge. They search for what will help a person live a productive life today, and if the current realities strongly suggest that students need to graduate from high school with computer literacy, the essentialist will find a place for this training in the curriculum. In this regard, essentialists are very practical. Whereas the perennialist will hold fast to the Great Books, the essentialist will make more room for scientific, technical, and even vocational emphases in the curriculum. Essentialists see themselves as valuing the past but not being captured by it.

beyond the classics

The philosophy behind the Core Knowledge program (discussed in the chapter entitled "What Is Taught?"), which speaks out in detail about what students from kindergarten to eighth grade should know, is probably best categorized as essentialist. Based on the book, *Cultural Literacy*, by E. D. Hirsch, Jr., this content-rich curriculum stresses academics and learning of specific knowledge. While its emphasis on important ideas and great works of the past makes it attractive to perennialists, the curriculum's focus on current literature and emphasis on science point more to its alignment with the essentialist movement. Currently the Core Knowledge curriculum is being used in more than 600 schools.

Core Knowledge program

Visit the web site to link to more information about Core Knowledge.

> *The ability to think straight, some knowledge of the past, some vision of the future, some skill to do useful service, some urge to fit that service into the well-being of the community—these are the most vital things education must try to produce.*
>
> —VIRGINIA CROCHERON GILDERSLEEVE

Essentialist Goals and Practices   For essentialists, the aim of education is to teach the young the essentials they need to live well in the modern world. To realize this goal, schools should focus on the established disciplines, which are the "containers" of organized knowledge. The elementary years should concentrate on the basics such as the "three Rs." These and other foundational tools are needed to gain access to the disciplined knowledge with which one begins to come in contact in high school.

Although there is some debate about what is "essential" in the curriculum, essentialists believe this is not a debate to which children can contribute fruitfully. Therefore, the role of the student is simply that of learner. The individual child's interests, motivations, and psychological states are not given much attention. Nor do essentialists hold fast to what they would call a "romantic" view of children as being naturally good. They see the students not as evil, but as deficient and needing discipline and pressure to keep learning. School is viewed as a place where children come to learn what they need to know. Teachers are not guides, but authorities. The student's job is to listen and learn. Given the imperfect state of the students, the teacher must be ingenious in finding ways to engage their imaginations and minds.

student as learner, teacher as authority

One notable essentialist was James Bryan Conant, a Harvard professor and president for much of the first half of the twentieth century. Concerned about disparities in the knowledge and skills that different high school students brought with them to college, Conant argued for standardization of college requirements for high school students. He was also influential in the establishment of the SAT as a measure of essential knowledge a potential college student needs to possess.

Reflect on essentialism with the image in this section of your CD-ROM.

The "Back-to-Basics" movement of the 1980s was also an essentialist-driven reaction to schooling in the 1960s and 1970s, during which core academic studies took a back seat to individual self-fulfillment and social equity. The following case study offers the perspective of a representative essentialist teacher.

CASE STUDY
An Essentialist Teacher

In my view, the world is filled with real problems, and the young people who leave school have to be ready to take up the challenge of life and solve those problems. So for me, the watchword in education is *usefulness*. I think everything that is taught has to pass the test of whether or not it is useful. My job as a teacher is to find out what is useful and then to make sure the students learn it.

■ *stress on usefulness*

I believe that school should be relevant to the young. However, my view of what is relevant is very different from the views of lots of other people. For me, relevance is not what is personally "meaningful" or a "do-your-own-thing" approach. What is relevant is what helps the individual live well and what benefits humanity. For that we need to look very carefully at the past and sort out the most valuable learning. That is what should be taught and what should be learned. I find the back-to-the-classics approach quite valuable. However, most advocates go too far in concentrating on classics. They also stress the humanities and the arts a little too much and tend to underplay science and technology. If children are going to function in today's world, and if our world is going to solve all the problems it's confronted with, we have to give more attention to science and technology than we have in the past. But clearly the past is the place to begin our search for the relevant curriculum.

■ *selecting learning from the past*

It's not the most pleasing or satisfying image, but I think the concept of the student as an empty jug is the most accurate one. Certainly kids come to school with lots of knowledge and lots of interests. However, the job of school is to teach them what they don't know and to teach these things in a systematic and organized way. It's not to fill their minds with isolated fragments of information but to fill them with systematic knowledge. They need tools to learn, and, as they get older, they need human insights and skills that come from the disciplines.

Given that there is so much to learn, an emphasis on student "interests" and "projects" and "problem solving" is quite wasteful. There is plenty of time for that outside of school or when school is over. Inside the school, the teachers are the authorities, and the students are there to learn what they don't know. The environment should be task oriented and disciplined. It doesn't have to be oppressive or unjust or any of that. I tell my students that learning is not necessarily going to be fun, but that at the end of the year they will have a great sense of accomplishment. I'd take accomplishment over fun anytime. By and large, most students do too. ■

■ *task orientation and discipline*

PAUSE AND REFLECT

❶ What knowledge do you believe will be essential for the students you teach to learn in order to be effective members of their society?

■ *Child-Centered Philosophies*

In contrast to perennialism and essentialism, the next two schools of philosophy, romanticism and progressivism, look first to the learner rather than the curriculum. Both consider the development of the learner to be the main purpose of education. A well-educated person does not necessarily have a definite body of knowledge; rather, a well-educated person is able to function well in society and life.

■ *condemnation of society*

■ **Romanticism**   **Romanticism,** or naturalism, is based on the writings of Jean Jacques Rousseau, an eighteenth century Swiss-French philosopher. In a condemnation of society and the educational system of the time, Rousseau wrote *Emile,* a novel that details Rousseau's ideas about education through the example of a fictional young boy, Emile.

Visit the web site to link to more information about Rousseau and *Emile.*

The Education of Emile   Rousseau believed that children are born good and pure, but once exposed to the evils of society, they become corrupted. To keep children good, they need to be isolated from society for as long as possible. Rousseau describes a serene, yet well-controlled bucolic environment for the ideal education of Emile; he is to be educated by a private tutor at the country manor where he lives. Emile's education begins with his exploration of the world of nature surrounding him. From his observations, he may ask questions about the natural world that the tutor answers. There are no formal lessons, no books to read or facts to memorize, no specific curriculum to learn. Emile decides what he learns about and when. As Emile matures, the tutor helps him develop rational thinking skills, but Emile continues to decide the topics of study. When Emile is around fifteen, he is slowly introduced to certain social situations until he is deemed "ready" by his tutor to resist the evils of society and live a productive life in the social world. By the time he is twenty, Emile is ready to take a mate and make a life for himself.

■ *purpose is self-fulfillment*

A sense of curiosity is nature's original school of education.

—SMILEY BLANTON

■ *guided by child's curiosity*

Implications for Education   Unlike the perennialists and essentialists who highlight the importance of educating the individual for society, the romantics consider the individual more important than the needs of society. For the romantics, the purpose of education is individual self-fulfillment, which means that education must help the students develop physically, intellectually, socially, and morally (usually in that order).

Romantics believe that education is a natural process, one that grows out of children's innate curiosity. This curiosity is most obvious during the "why?" phase of young childhood, when nearly every utterance out of the child's mouth is another question: "Why is the dog barking?", "Why is the boy sad?", or "Why is the bird blue?" (Parents often want to ask in return, "Why do you ask so many questions!".) Romantics argue that we must let children's interests and curiosity drive their learning. The teacher's job is to respond to the children's questions as they arise and not to impose the learning of subjects that are not of interest to the child. The learner's responsibility is to maintain his or her natural curiosity and desire to learn. Because learning is guided by student interests, there is no set or common curriculum of study for the romantics. Some students may be interested in kayaking while others want to study photography and still others may be fascinated by how a DVD player works. As students pursue their own areas of study, the approach to teaching and learning also becomes individualized. Much of the learning is self-directed and self-guided by the students, with teachers serving as sources of information or resources to help the students satisfy their curiosity rather than as taskmasters or authorities on knowledge.

Reflect on romanticism with the image in this section of your CD-ROM.

Romanticism has been especially influential in the early childhood and elementary grades. Many early childhood educators, including such pioneers as Maria Montessori, Frederick Froebel, and Johann Pestalozzi, basically agreed with Rousseau's ideas about humans' innate curiosity and using the child's inter-

■ influence on early childhood education

■ Link to these schools from this chapter of the web site.

ests to define the curriculum. Although none proposed as radical a school setting as Rousseau's pastoral manor, they did adopt some of Rousseau's other ideas about education, such as providing young children with extensive opportunities to manipulate wooden blocks and clay and other real materials.

Today, schools like Summerhill in Suffolk, England (**http://www.s-hill. demon.co.uk/index.htm**), and the Sudbury Valley School in Framingham, Mass., (**http://www.sudval.org/svs/startup.html**), embody many of the beliefs of the romantics. At these schools, there are no set curricula, no formal classes, and no tests. Students decide what they want to study and in some cases are also expected to take responsibility for their learning.

CASE STUDY

A Romantic Teacher

■ wonder turned off by school

Have you ever seen the thrill on a young child's face when he or she figures out how to make something work? What about their wonder as they ask another question about why there are rainbows or thunder and lightning? I see these young children, and then I look at some of the students in school today. Their faces are filled with so much dread or disinterest or boredom that I get disheartened. What happened to that enthusiasm, that excitement for learning, I wonder? That schools, which should be places of learning, can turn students off to learning so strongly is the reason I became a teacher. I want my classroom to be a place where students can explore their interests and satisfy their curiosities. I can't make them learn information if it's not something they're interested in.

In my classroom, students decide what they want to study and I help them find the resources. Sometimes we get books from the library, or find web sites on the Internet. The Internet has been a wonderful resource for my students. Some of them have been able to have online conversations with professionals in fields like aerospace engineering and bioengineering. Sometimes, I set up face-to-face meetings with professionals in a particular field. Last week, we had a computer programmer in to talk to a couple of students who were interested in learning more about writing code. It's so exciting to see students enthusiastic about what they are learning.

Kids' views are often just as valid as the teachers'. The best teachers are the ones that know that.

—MORLEY SAFER, TV JOURNALIST

I am aware of the criticism about this approach to learning; students have big holes in their knowledge, they don't learn "the hard stuff," they can't pass standardized tests. My students may not do very well on standardized tests (what do they *really* measure, anyway?), but they do learn the hard stuff! I mean, computer programming, aerospace engineering, and bioengineering? Those are not easy topics to understand. It may be that my students don't know a lot of facts in the standardized subjects, but they know well what they learn because they have selected these topics themselves. They *want* to learn about them, so they do. ■

■ Reflect on the place of romanticism in the classroom with the image in this section of your CD-ROM.

PAUSE AND REFLECT

❶ How would teachers in public schools, who are held accountable for students' mastery of curriculum standards, be able to follow a romantic philosophy of letting student interest guide the curriculum?

LEADERS IN EDUCATION
JOHN DEWEY (1859–1952)

John Dewey, the founder of instrumentalism, is widely considered the single most influential figure in the history of American educational thought. At the same time, his ideas and beliefs have been frequently misunderstood and misinterpreted, leading to the misapplication of his theories.

Dewey grew up in Vermont, where he attended public schools and the University of Vermont. As a graduate student in philosophy at Johns Hopkins University, he was deeply influenced by the ideas of Charles S. Pierce and William James, founders of pragmatist philosophy. Dewey recognized the implications for education of Pierce's argument that ideas, or propositions, have worth only if they make a difference in future thoughts or actions. Calling his own philosophy *instrumentalism* to emphasize the principle that ideas are instruments, Dewey argued that philosophy and education both involve the practical, experimental attempt to improve the human condition.

Dewey denounced the public school's classical curriculum in the nineteenth century as totally unsuited to the demands of newly industrialized society of the United States. He claimed that the schools were divorced from life and that they failed to teach children how to *use* knowledge. Defining education as a "continuous reconstruction of experience," Dewey said that schools should teach children not what to think but how to think. In his 1916 *Democracy and Education,* Dewey claimed that the schools offered students as future citizens no preparation for the responsibility of citizenship in a democracy. Dewey called for schools to provide a concentrated study of democratic processes and to reflect those processes in the organization of school life, going as far as advocating that students be given the power to make decisions affecting life in the school in a democratic way. Participation in life, rather than preparation for it, he considered the watchword of an effective education.

In 1896, Dewey established the University Laboratory School, an elementary school at the University of Chicago. It was experimental in two senses: in its use of experiment and inquiry as the method by which the children learned and in its role as a laboratory for the transformation of the schools. The activities and occupations of adult life served as the core of the curriculum and the model teaching method. Children began by studying and imitating simple domestic and industrial tasks. In later years they studied the historical development of industry, invention, group living, and nature. Dewey wrote that we must "make each one of our schools an embryonic community life, active with types of occupations that reflect the life of the larger society and permeated with the spirit of art, history, and science."

The late 1920s to the early 1940s, the era of progressive education, saw a massive attempt to implement Dewey's ideas, but the rigid (and often inaccurate) manner in which they were interpreted led to remarkable extravagances in some progressive schools. For instance, some educators considered it useless to teach geography because maps changed so rapidly. The role of subject matter was gradually played down in progressive schools, replaced by a stress on method and process. The rationale was that it was more important to produce a "good citizen" than a person who was "educated" in the classical sense. Well into his nineties, Dewey fought vehemently against these corruptions of his views.

The centrality of John Dewey's thought to American education has waxed and waned over the years. Traditionally more popular in universities than in actual classroom practice, Dewey is often invoked by people attempting to make the schools more humanistic and the curriculum more relevant to the current world. Whether in favor or out, John Dewey represents the United States' most distinctive contribution to educational thought.

 Visit the web site for more information about John Dewey.

■ **Progressivism**   **Progressivism** is a relatively young philosophy of education. It came to prominence in the 1920s, growing out of the progressive political and social movement of the time. It drew from some of the ideas of Rousseau and from the work of John Dewey, the most influential educational philosopher of the twentieth century (see the "Leaders in Education" box in this section).

■ *nature is always changing*

Progressivism views nature as being in flux, as ever changing. Therefore, knowledge must continually be redefined and rediscovered to keep up with that change. Whereas other philosophies see the mind as a jug to be filled with truth, or as a muscle that needs to be exercised and conditioned, the progressive views the mind as a problem solver. Like the romantic, the progressive believes that people are naturally exploring, inquiring entities. When faced with an obstacle, they will try to find a way to overcome it. When faced with a question, they will try to find an answer. For the progressive, education aims to develop this problem-solving ability.

Progressive Education   Progressive educators believe that the place to begin an education is with the student rather than with the subject matter. The teacher identifies what the student's interests and concerns are and tries to shape problems around them. The student's motivation to solve the problem is the key and posing problems based on student interests helps heighten their motivation. The teacher then helps the student develop strategies to solve the problems posed.

■ *student's concerns most important*

The teacher's task is not to implant facts but to place the subject to be learned in front of the learner and, through sympathy, emotion, imagination, and patience, to awaken in the learner the restless drive for answers and insights which enlarge the personal life and give it meaning.
—NATHAN M. PUSSEY, PRESIDENT, HARVARD

Students should start with simple study projects and gradually learn more systematic ways to investigate until they finally master a variety of problem-solving strategies. Rather than being a presenter of knowledge or a taskmaster, the teacher is an intellectual guide, a *facilitator* in the problem-solving process. Students are encouraged to be imaginative and resourceful in solving problems. They are directed to a variety of methods, from reading books and studying the traditional disciplines to performing experiments and analyzing data.

Method is of great importance to the progressive. On the other hand, knowledge—formal, traditional knowledge—is not given the same honored place. For the progressive, there is really no special, sacrosanct knowledge or subject matter which students must learn. The value of knowledge resides in its ability to solve human problems.

Regarding the school curriculum, progressives believe that a student can learn problem-solving skills from electronics just as easily as from Latin, from agronomy just as well as from geometry. The focus for progressive educators is teaching students *how* to think rather than *what* to think. Progressive teachers often use traditional subject matter, but they use it differently from the way it is used in a traditional classroom. Because the problems students are trying to solve are of paramount importance, the subjects contribute primarily through providing contexts for problems students must solve. Subject matter knowledge may also provide information that leads to solutions. The focus for progressive educators is teaching students *how* to think rather than *what* to think. It is the process, not the product, which is of greater importance. Although both romantic and progressive educators start with the student's interests, progressives have more structure behind their teaching and they have goals for their students, to which we turn now.

Reflect on progressivism with the image in this section of your CD-ROM.

POLICY MATTERS!

Standards: High Academic Achievement or Test-Driven Classrooms?

What's the Policy?

Back in January 1996, then president Bill Clinton spoke to the nation in these words: "I challenge every community, every school, and every state to adopt national standards of excellence, to measure whether schools are meeting those standards and to hold them accountable for results."[4] A movement in the 1980s and 1990s to establish national standards had failed. However, many states have since developed and adopted their own sets of standards for what students should know and be able to do. However, national standards, or at least national testing, may be experiencing a resurgence. President George W. Bush has made education a priority of his administration and, in 2001, Congress adopted legislation that would require school districts that receive federal funding (nearly all public schools in the United States) to test all students in grades 4, 8, and 12.

How Does It Affect Teachers?

Standards are something of an educational double-edged sword. On the one hand, standards provide clarity. Teachers and students know what they are trying to accomplish, and therefore they can focus instruction and attention on achieving those standards (for instance, "At the end of second grade, students will be able to read at X level of proficiency; at the completion of tenth grade, students will have attained Y level of mathematical proficiency").

On the other hand, the focus of instruction often narrows, not to the larger concepts behind the standards but to the tests that claim to measure the standards. Scores on these tests become the criteria for students'—and, yes, the teacher's—success or failure. Given that fact of life, teachers may tend to rely on that infamous educational methodology, teaching-to-the-test.

What Are the Pros?

Supporters of educational standards have positive goals. The *standards movement,* as it is called, is driven by the desire of parents and other taxpayers to have the well-educated young adults of the United States help it to maintain its position in the world.

The School as Training Ground for Democracy   Unlike the romantic educator who may see society as a negative influence on the student, the progressive sees society as an integral aspect of the student's life. Progressives view schools as small societies in themselves, places where students are learning as they live life, not simply preparing for life. This gives the progressive school a unique atmosphere, different from a perennialist storehouse of wisdom or a place with the clearly defined roles and authority structures of the essentialists.

■ *school as a democracy*

Progressive educators believe the school should be democratic in structure so that children can learn to live well in a democracy and become good citizens. They emphasize group activity and group problem solving so that students learn to work with others and help others. This is one reason many teachers who describe themselves as progressive educators are enthusiastic about cooperative learning strategies such as those discussed in the chapter on "What Is Taught?".

Education makes people easy to lead, but difficult to drive; easy to govern, but impossible to enslave.

—HENRY BROOKS ADAMS

Implicit in the progressive approach is the belief that children must not only learn to solve their own problems, but also

Also, educators and others naturally desire to have clear targets and to know how well we are doing. Further, the standards movement has been energized by widely published reports of international studies of student achievement, studies that show American students' performance ranging from poor to mediocre.

What Are the Cons?

Philosophical disagreements seem to underlie many of the key objections to the use of standards. Standards, with their emphasis on mastering specific bodies of knowledge that experts believe students should know, appear to emanate from perennialist or essentialist concepts of education. Perhaps because of these emphases, standards seem to work against teachers committed to progressive or constructivist methods of teaching. As discussed earlier, when teachers are under pressure to make sure their students meet standards of achievement, creative methods such as cooperative learning and projects often go by the board. Direct instruction becomes the rule, followed by much drill and practice. This may help to accomplish high test scores, but these short-term achievements may make education dull, uninspiring, and ultimately counterproductive. In other words, a legitimate public desire for better education may be fostering quite questionable educational practice with little or no long-term gains.

What Do You Think?

1. What other arguments can you think of to support the standards movement in schools? To oppose the standards movement?

2. Can you think of some effective ways to measure students' problem-solving abilities or the development of their own sense of meaning?

3. How does your philosophy of education influence your views on academic standards?

4. Critics argue that standardized tests measure only factual bits of knowledge rather than deep conceptual knowledge. What should be the measure of student knowledge?

 Visit the web site to learn more about this policy issue.

help to solve those of their neighbors. For progressives, one of the main purposes of education is to make society better, which requires people working together to solve problems. It is not uncommon for the problem-solving activities of the progressive school to spill out into the community, and involve students in issues like ecology and poverty. In this way, students learn an important principle of progressive education: knowledge should be used to redesign or improve the world.

One notable progressive educator was William Heard Kilpatrick (1871–1965), who was a professor of philosophy of education at Columbia University in New York. He was a follower of many of Dewey's ideas about education, but differed on the importance of subject matter in a child's educational experience. Rejecting formal curriculum study, he developed the project method of education in which students work in groups on a topic of interest to them. He believed that students learn only what is of interest to them so that they should be the ones to determine topics of study. He also helped to found Bennington College in Vermont, which still embodies the progressive philosophy.

Both progressive and essentialist educators claim their particular approach is the true American philosophy of education. One can make a case that they both are, but each reflects different aspects of the American personality. Progressivism represents our antiauthoritarian, experimental, and visionary side; essentialism speaks to our more practical, structured, and task-oriented side. In recent years, many of the tensions and public debates in American education can be traced to struggles between these two philosophies of education. Clearly, though, essentialist educators gained ground on progressive educators in the 1980s and 1990s. Concerns over the country's global economic competitiveness and the perceived "softness" of our schools have created a receptive climate for essentialist views.

To judge your own sympathy for the progressive approach, see what you think of the following representative statement by a progressive educator.

CASE STUDY

A Progressive Educator

I'm a progressive educator and proud of it. I'm not ducking that label just because it is unpopular in many quarters these days, usually among people who don't really understand what it is. Quite honestly, for the life of me, I cannot understand how a teacher can be anything *but* a progressive educator.

I'm dedicated to a few simple and, I believe, obvious principles. For one thing, children come into the world with a very plastic nature, capable of being molded one way or another. We should therefore work to surround them with activities and opportunities that bring them in contact with good things. Also, by their nature, children are curious. Instead of rejecting their curiosities, I believe we should build on them. Schools should be exciting, involving places where students are caught up in interesting activities.

■ *children molded by environment*

I think that I'm a progressive educator because I have looked at my own experiences. I know I learn best when I'm trying to solve a puzzle or a problem that really interests me. And somehow I've always been able to get much more interested in how we're going to solve the problems of our own society than in the affairs of the Athenians and Spartans. I can get much more involved in a research problem about which DVD player gives the best value for the dollar than about some dry economic problem presented to me by a teacher. And I really don't think I'm different from the overwhelming majority of students.

■ *learning through direct experience*

I see many of my fellow teachers spending all their energy damming up student curiosity and imposing work on their students. And then the teachers wonder why they themselves are so tired or burned out. I'm sure it's quite tiring to try to convert children into file cabinets and to stuff facts into their heads all day.

One of the things that sets me apart is that I'm not so hung up as others are on what I call the "talky" curriculum. I am convinced that students learn most effectively by *doing,* by experiencing events and then reflecting on and making meaning out of what they have experienced. I think more science is learned on a nature walk than from the same time spent reading a textbook or hearing teacher explanations. I think students learn more abstract principles, such as democracy, from trying to set up and maintain a democratic society in their classroom than from a lot of learned lectures and dusty prose on the subject. I'm trying to get to their hearts and their heads. The traditional approach gets to neither place.

■ *focus on current and future problems*

To me, life is a matter of solving problems. New times have new problems and demand new knowledge. I don't want my students to be ready for life in the eighteenth century. I want them to be effective, functioning, curious citizens of the twenty-first century. They are going to need to be able to develop solutions to fit new and unique problems. Although much knowledge is important, they need to realize that knowledge is only today's tentative explanation of how things work. Much of what we know now is incorrect and will have to be replaced.

It's not that I think that ideas and content and the traditional subjects are worthless. Far from it. I teach much of the same material as other teachers. However, I get there by a different route. I let the issues and problems emerge and then give the students a chance to get answers and to solve problems. And, as they quickly learn, they have to know a great deal to solve some of the problems. Often they get themselves involved with some very advanced material. The only difference is that now they want to. Now they have the energy. And, boy, once they get going, do they have energy! No, it doesn't always work. I have students who coast, and I've had projects that failed. But I'd put my track record against those of my more traditional colleagues any day. ■

PAUSE AND REFLECT

1 Did any of your teachers take a progressive approach to teaching? If so, how did you, as a student, respond? Do you believe your students would respond well if you chose to implement a progressive approach?

The Influence of Psychological Theories

Since early in the twentieth century, educational practice has been greatly influenced by the discipline of psychology. Psychology, the scientific study of the mind and human behavior, was a natural influence on the work of teachers, particularly with its focus on how we learn. Over the years, various schools of psychology have emerged, often having roots in particular philosophies. Some of these psychological theories have had a great deal to say to educators. Two in particular have had an impact on our schools: behaviorism and cognitive psychology.

■ *Behaviorism: Conditioning Students or Setting Them Free?*

The psychological theory of behavior modification or **behaviorism** is an educational approach that emerged directly from the pioneering research of the late B. F. Skinner (1904–1990), who himself was influenced by the social efficiency movement in education of the 1920s and 1930s. Skinner developed the theory called operant conditioning, which viewed learning as the learner's response to various stimuli (for example, sounds, words, or people) present in the environment. Subscribing to the view that humans learn to act in specific ways based on the response they receive for their actions (generally reward or punishment), the behaviorist teacher believes that learners need incentives, both positive and negative, as motivators to learn. The curriculum is organized in sequenced, discrete segments. Behaviorist teachers will often use objective tests made up

■ *learning by rewards and punishments*

Visit the web site to link to more information about behaviorism.

predominantly of multiple-choice questions to measure how well students have learned the curriculum and to give prompt feedback to students. In some behaviorist classrooms, students are expected to practice a specific skill until they show a certain level of mastery of the skill. In planning for teaching, the behaviorist (1) uses clear objectives, spelled out in terms of the behaviors to be learned; (2) establishes a learning environment, which will positively reinforce desired behaviors and eliminate undesirable behaviors; and (3) closely monitors and gives the learner feedback on progress until the goal is achieved. Because the same behaviors and knowledge are desirable for all students, standardization of the curriculum and of measuring progress is important.

In the 1960s and 1970s, many educators made behaviorism their dominant, organizing educational theory. However, this education movement was criticized for being teacher dominated and causing teachers to treat students as passive objects to be conditioned. Nevertheless, behaviorism remains a dominant theoretical presence, particularly in the areas of special education and classroom discipline. Many teachers rely on behavior modification practices to get students to be quiet when they see or hear the teacher's signal or to do their best work to get a reward sticker.

Critics argue that a behaviorist teacher exercises too much control over students' learning and focuses on the learning of facts rather than deep conceptual knowledge. In response, behaviorist teachers insist that their goal is to eventually put control of learning in their students' hands once they have learned to respond appropriately to the teacher's prompts.

Cognitive Psychology: Students as Makers of Meaning?

Over the past twenty years, researchers in both medicine and psychology have been investigating the human brain to find out more about its role in human learning and memory. Cognitive psychologists, drawing heavily on the trail-blazing research of Swiss psychologist Jean Piaget (1896–1980), as well as that of the Russian psychologist Lev Vygotsky (1896–1934), and the American psychologist Jerome Bruner (1915–), have discovered a great deal about how people learn to think and solve problems. Their discoveries have led to the development of new theories about learning and cognition that have tremendous implications for how teachers teach. One increasingly popular theory derived from the research findings is that in order for new information to be internalized by the learner, it must be integrated into the learner's pre-existing knowledge base. This process of integration is referred to as **constructivism**.

knowledge constructed

the individual as meaning maker

According to this theory, knowledge cannot be *transmitted* directly from the teacher to the learner, but is *constructed by the learner* and, later, *reconstructed* as new information becomes available. Instead of seeing students as partially full vessels waiting to be filled, teachers should view them as actively engaged in making meaning. Teachers, therefore, need to create learning situations where students can build their own knowledge rather than having students sit and listen to the teachers' lectures. Constructivism has become so influential in education in recent years that we give it particular attention here.

Constructivists view individuals as having an aversion to disorder. They believe that we are all continually trying to sort things out, to find clues and patterns amid our impressions that will help us to make sense of the world around us. When we encounter something new, say, a strange sound in the night, we im-

Visit the web site to link to more information about constructivism.

mediately attempt to fit it into the patterns or structures we already possess (for example, "That's the midnight whistle of the Ole Ninety-Eight headin' down to New Orleans"). But sometimes we encounter new information which leads (or forces) us to realize that our knowledge base as it is currently "constructed" is incorrect or outdated ("Uh-oh! The railroad retired that train two years ago!"). We may respond in a number of ways: we search for new input from our senses, seeking either to reconstruct the knowledge base, developing different patterns and structures so that the information "fits" ("Maybe that noise was from the hot water boiler and it's about to explode," or "Maybe that creepy guy from the apartment down below is on my fire escape," or "Maybe I shouldn't read Stephen King novels before going to bed!"). In some instances, we may be so convinced of our knowledge base that we refuse to make allowances for the new information. ("No, I'm sure that it was a train whistle. They must have put that train back in service.") Students follow the same patterns as they try to make sense of new information they encounter in school.

Cognitive psychologists also suggest that we organize our knowledge in ways that allow us easy access to knowledge we use regularly. These cognitive structures, which are called *schemas* or *schemata,* change constantly and continually as new information is taken in, hypotheses are developed, and theories are tested. These processes of hypothesis development and testing can be done independently or in interaction with others. Thus, real learning for constructivists involves moving from the Trivial Pursuit or Jeopardy type of factual or declarative knowledge to applicable knowledge—in other words, from "knowing what"

According to constructivists, active involvement in learning helps student build their own knowledge.
(© Elizabeth Crews)

VOICES FROM THE CLASSROOM

Susan Dougherty writes about her career as a fourth-grade teacher at Bayberry School in Watchung, New Jersey.

Constructivist Philosophy

As I began my career in education I held firm one belief about students: they must be active participants in the classroom. Twelve years later, I hold that same basic belief but have refined what it means for a learner to be active.

Early in my career *active* meant that my students would not sit in rows and spend the day doing seatwork. My first position as a kindergarten teacher quickly revealed that I might strive for something greater than physical activity. Of course, kindergarten students are active—try and keep them from being anything but active! I came to recognize that while active bodies can be important, what I really wanted was to engage the minds of my students.

As I taught students at many elementary levels, I learned to ask probing questions that re-

quired my students to consider their learning carefully. How do you know to add these two numbers? What kind of person do you think the main character of this story is? How would you explain why oil floats on water to someone who didn't understand? While my students were often physically active, acting out scenes from a novel we were reading, experimenting with magnets or prisms, or using pattern blocks to build models of math problems, they also spent time physically inert, but inwardly engaged in active thought.

Soon, however, I was not satisfied with simply engaging the minds of my students. I wanted to reach their hearts. I wanted to awaken a passion for learning within each student. How might a teacher encourage the awakening of such passion? One key, I think, is to allow and encourage the students to ask and seek the answers to their own questions. In this way, students' minds and hearts become active, leading them on a lifelong journey of inquiry and self-motivated learning.

 Visit the web site for more Voices from the Classroom.

---

to "knowing how." To do this, learners must develop cognitive learning strategies for particular kinds of learning tasks; that is, they have to learn how to think through or go about solving problems.

■ Implications of Constructivism for Teachers in the Classroom

■ active learners

The constructivist teacher does four things: (1) actively involves students in real situations, (2) activates students' prior knowledge before presenting new information, (3) uses questions to provoke students' thoughts, and (4) structures learning experiences so that new information is presented in readily accessible forms. At heart, the constructivist teacher behaves more like a coach. Such a teacher is interested primarily in helping the child engage problems and issues, search below the surface, try out various possible solutions or explanations, and finally construct meaning from these experiences. Constructivist classrooms are active places with many opportunities for discovery and experimentation, often a heavy use of cooperative learning, and teachers who are fellow learners rather than fact givers and drill masters.

Critics of constructivism claim that its qualities of student-centered and self-constructed learning have led to declines in both academic achievement and classroom discipline. If this is true, it represents a poor application of constructivist principles, which are making their way into our classrooms. In contrast, we believe that constructivism is the linchpin to truly learning to learn, a key component to the school reform programs discussed in the chapter entitled "How Should Education Be Reformed?".

Your Philosophy of Education

At this point, you may well be confused and possibly discouraged. To expect to be able to understand and evaluate critically every aspect of each philosophy is to expect of yourself what few professional philosophers are able to do. What you have just finished reading is a précis of some of the major ideas of Western civilization (see Table 8.1 for a summary). Some of these ideas have been around for centuries, and some are the fruits of twentieth-century thinkers.

Selecting the philosophy by which you will live and by which you will guide your professional activities takes much more investment of time, thought, and energy than reading our short chapter.

Some teachers, like the teacher-philosophers in this chapter, settle on one philosophical view, and that view structures all of their work. Other teachers lean strongly toward a particular philosophy, even if they may not be fully conscious of their position or be able to give it a proper philosophical label. Typically they have a particular view of the learner, of how the learner should be approached, and of what is most worth knowing.

However, few teachers are philosophical purists. Some teachers, recognizing that they draw ideas from various philosophies, label themselves *eclectics*. But what does it really mean to be an eclectic in contemporary education?

PAUSE AND REFLECT

1 It is perhaps unfair of us to ask you so soon after having read descriptions of different philosophies and theories of education, but, right now, which one holds the great intellectual appeal to you? Which one holds the least appeal? And, "why" to both questions?

■ *Eclecticism: Not an Excuse for Sloppy Thinking*

Eclecticism embodies the idea that truth can be found anywhere and therefore people should select from various doctrines, systems, and sources. The eclectic teacher selects what he or she believes to be the most attractive features of several philosophies. For example, the teacher might take from romanticism the innate curiosity of the learner and from essentialism a curricular viewpoint dominated by the criterion of usefulness.*

■ *the lazy kind of eclecticism*

Eclecticism is quite popular, but often for the wrong reasons. It sometimes appears as the easy way out of philosophical uncertainty, just taking what you please from the philosophical cafeteria of ideas. ("Let's see now: I think I'll begin with a light salad of romantic individuality and follow that up with a main course of progressive problem-solving projects, but with some hearty perennialist classics as side dishes. And, oh, yes—let's finish with a popular and tasty dessert of essentialist vocational training.") One problem with this approach is the possibility of inconsistency. To take one's view of society from the romantic, who gives primacy to individual freedom, and one's teaching methodology from the progressivist,

*In the process of writing this chapter, we discovered that we are really traditional but progressive essentialists who are searching for a Great Books Club to join.

TABLE 8.1   Four Philosophies and Their Applications to Education

	Perennialism	Essentialism	Romanticism	Progressivism
Metaphysics: What is real? Does it have meaning?	The meaning of life is the search for unchanging truth found in the collective wisdom of Western culture.	What is relevant is what helps an individual live well and what benefits humanity.	Reality is stable; the meaning of life is derived primarily through self-development away from society.	Reality is in flux and ever-changing, so meaning is in the context of the individual, who is a "problem solver."
Epistemology: Knowledge and knowing—what is truth?	Truth and knowledge are changeless, revealed through guided reflection and in classics of Western culture.	Truth exists in the classics *and* modern science. Students must learn process *and* content. Knowledge is gained through the interaction of experiences and rational thought.	Knowledge is gained through sensory experiences and interaction with one's environment.	Knowledge is gained via individual experience: Truth is individually defined so that emphasis is on learning *how* to learn.
Axiology: Values, ethics, aesthetics	Changeless. Determined by the very nature of reality.	Determined by the natural order of things. Values exist in the best of culture.	Determined by the individual.	Determined by each individual in interaction with his or her culture, based on the shared values of the community or culture.
Logic: How we think, deductive and inductive	Rationality, especially deductive thought, is developed by studying classics and through the Socratic dialectic.	Rationality is best developed through interplay of deductive and inductive thinking.	Primarily inductive thought since learning starts with experiences and moves to hypotheses.	Emphasis is on inductive thinking and problem solving.
Purpose of Education/Schooling	Educate the intellect; develop in learner rational thought and an understanding of the truths of humankind.	Prepare students to be productive, contributing members of society.	Make learner strong (physically, intellectually, morally) to resist the evils of society.	Helps students become good citizens familiar with the workings of democracy and with good problem-solving skills.
The Teacher	Teacher is expert of content knowledge. Passes on to next generation the accumulated wisdom of the past.	Teacher is expert of content knowledge. Teaches essential knowledge. Maintains task-oriented focus.	Teacher responds to learner's requests for knowledge; does not initiate learning in learner.	Teacher is facilitator of student learning; provides resources for students' problem-solving abilities. Develops students' problem-solving abilities. Helps children do what they want to do.

TABLE 8.1   Four Philosophies and Their Applications to Education *(cont'd)*

	Perennialism	**Essentialism**	**Romanticism**	**Progressivism**
Teaching Strategies	Cultivates rational powers through contact with the culture's best and through imitation. For older students, Socratic dialogue is key to uncovering truths found in classics.	Avoids methodological frills and soft pedagogy and concentrates on sound, proven instructional methods.	Creates productive learning environment for learner; individualized approach to learning, depending on student interests.	Stimulates students to plan and carry out activities and research projects using group processes and democratic procedures.
The Child	Is there to learn what is taught.	Is there to listen and learn.	Is naturally good and must be protected from the evils of society.	Learns by doing and by discovering.
Curriculum	In younger grades, focus on basic skills to develop mental discipline and rational thought processes. Older learners study materials reflecting universal and recurring themes through which the truths of humanity can be revealed.	Strong emphasis on basic skills in elementary schools and on disciplined knowledge and scholastic achievement in secondary schools.	Dependent on the interests of the learner. No set curriculum, no specific skills to be acquired.	Centered on student's interest in real problems and interdisciplinary solution seeking.

Source: Adapted from a table suggested by James Hotchkiss. Used by permission of James Hotchkiss.

who stresses group membership and democratic process, is liable to make everyone confused. Selecting eclecticism cannot be an excuse for lazy thinking.

■ *eclecticism as a real teaching strategy*

On the other hand, most teachers feel quite free and justified in borrowing teaching methodologies and strategies that are associated with various philosophies of education. The ardent perennialist teacher may choose to involve his or her sixth-grade students in a "hands-on" project constructing a large topographical map of Odysseus's ten-year journey to his home after the fall of Troy. Conversely, the free-spirited romantic teacher may insist that each student memorize and be able to recite fifty lines of *The Odyssey*. Although this type of eclecticism may, in a narrow sense, seem philosophically inconsistent, at its root is the recognition that no philosophy of education is able to dictate the ideal methodology or learning strategies for all situations or all students trying to learn all subject matter. Related to this is the growing realization, discussed in the chapter entitled "Who Are Today's Students in a Diverse Society?", that different students possess a great range of learning styles and that what works with one student may flop with another. In sum, eclecticism can be a serious philosophical position, and eclecticism in the selection of teaching strategies is quite justified. But, again, the choice to be "eclectic" should not be a substitute for sloppy thought.

Identifying Your Own Philosophical Leanings

Think of your favorite teacher from elementary or secondary school, or a teacher you have admired during your teacher education. On a separate piece of paper, list some of that teacher's practices that you admire most. Include instructional techniques, classroom management strategies, ways of relating to the students—anything you think helped that person be an effective teacher.

Now, on the same piece of paper, write the philosophical outlook that you think may have underlain each practice you admired. This will take some reflection, and you may well find that no single philosophy matches all the teaching characteristics you listed. Use whatever philosophical labels seem most appropriate.

After completing both tasks, what general conclusions can you draw about the philosophy of this teacher you admire? Does your teacher reflect the tenets of a single educational philosophy discussed in this chapter? Or does she or he take an eclectic approach, drawing on different philosophical traditions? Are there ways in which this teacher is too unique to fit any category?

As a final step, reflect on what this tells you about your own philosophical leanings. If you hold this teacher in high regard, presumably you share at least some of his or her philosophical convictions. Is there anything that surprises you about the philosophical beliefs you have deduced? Do they suggest that you are more traditional or more progressive than you supposed? More child-centered or subject-matter-centered? More nicely balanced, or just more muddled? What aspects of your own philosophical base do you need to think about further and clarify?

■ *Philosophy and Liberal Education*

We are not suggesting that you sit yourself down, think through all these issues, and come up with a tight set of philosophical answers that will last the rest of your lifetime. Rather, we hope that we have focused—or refocused—your attention on some of life's most critical questions and on some issues that are at the very core of teaching.

■ *opportunities to develop your philosophy*

One purpose of the general education component of teacher education programs (that is, the courses in the arts and sciences required of the prospective teacher) is to provide a chance for future teachers to think through these fundamental questions of human existence. A primary purpose of the college curriculum is to present the student with a spectrum of society's best thinkers and their attempts to understand their own existence. On the other hand, the infamous college bull sessions may be where the real philosophical inquiry goes on; they are frequently thinly veiled discussions of what really counts in life and what one should try to do with one's life. In effect, then, both the formal apparatus of college and its curriculum and the informal opportunities to meet, talk, and test your ideas with a variety of people should help you discover where you stand on some of these essential human questions.

A Final Word

As we said at the beginning of this chapter, the teacher who will be more than a technician has an obligation to take philosophical issues and questions seriously. Teachers owe it to themselves and to their students to understand where they are going and why they are going there. On the other hand, teachers owe it to themselves to make sure that the schools they work in are hospitable—and certainly not hostile—to their own philosophies of education. It is important, therefore, that you be ready both to discuss your own philosophy of education with prospective employers and to inquire about the district's or school's philosophy. However, do not expect those interviewing you to be able to define their schools precisely according to the particular philosophies described in this chapter. Although educators live out a philosophy of education, we are not always able easily to capture it in words.

KEY TERMS

aesthetics (268)
axiology (267)
behaviorism (285)
constructivism (286)
deductive reasoning (270)

epistemology (267)
essentialism (274)
ethics (268)
inductive reasoning (270)
logic (268)

metaphysics (266)
perennialism (272)
philosophy (264)
progressivism (281)
romanticism (278)

FOR REFLECTION

At the present time, what beliefs do you have about the following: the role of the teacher, the nature of the learner, the nature of the curriculum, how people learn best? Thinking about these topics will help you to begin to formulate your philosophy of education.

1 What role, if any, does religion play in your philosophy of education?

2 Why do you think that superintendents and principals often ask teaching candidates about their philosophy of education?

3 And now, a really hard question: If you are leaning toward eclecticism, in what areas of teaching and learning would you draw on the various philosophies presented?

FOR FURTHER INFORMATION

PRINT RESOURCES

Gary D. Fenstermacher and Jonas F. Soltis. *Approaches to Teaching* (New York: Teachers College Press, 1986).

This slim volume shows how two philosophers can unpack the term *teaching* and explain what is behind several different approaches to instruction.

Jostein Gaarder, *Sophie's World: A Novel About the History of Philosophy* (New York: Farrar, Straus and Giroux, 1994).

This interesting and innovative book is an excellent introduction to philosophy and the history of ideas.

The writer is clearly a marvelous teacher, plus a most engaging writer.

Gerald Gutek, *Historical and Philosophical Foundations of Education: A Biographical Introduction,* 3d ed. (Upper Saddle River, NJ: Prentice-Hall/Merrill, 2000).

This textbook is a comprehensive and up-to-date account of the competing schools of educational philosophy and their application to schooling. It provides thumbnail sketches of key figures and leads the reader in investigating their thought.

WEB RESOURCES

American Philosophical Association (APA). Available at: **http://www.oxy.edu/apa/apa.html**.

This excellent web site provides basic information and reference material on many branches and schools of philosophy.

Larry Shaw, *Five Educational Philosophies*. Available at: **http://edweb.sdsu.edu/people/LShaw/F95syll/ philos/phintro.html**.

This web site, developed by Professor Larry Shaw, is an excellent description of the key ideas competing for dominance in American education.

Materials on the Philosophy of Education. Available at: **http://commhum.mccneb.edu/PHILOS/ phileduc.htm**.

This site is a fine collection of further readings, including original sources, on the major philosophies of education.

What Is the History of American Education?

Chapter Preview   To understand our present educational system, its successes and failures, and the problems it still faces, we must look to our past. There we can identify the forces that have affected and continue to affect the development of American education. This chapter reviews the history of schooling and education in the United States, pointing out six important themes and examining the contributions that significant men and women have made.

This chapter emphasizes that:

- Education in colonial America was originally religious in orientation but differed in form according to geographical area. Schooling in colonial America was not universal; it was primarily for white males.

- During the nineteenth century, influenced by the ideas of Thomas Jefferson and Benjamin Franklin and led by such reformers as Horace Mann, free public education became a reality. Common schools at the elementary level were tax supported and open to all children; the purpose was to cultivate a sense of American identity and loyalty.

- The nineteenth century also saw the development of public high schools that were designed to prepare young people, within a single institution, for either vocations or college; this goal of providing comprehensive educational opportunities was unique to American education.

- Private education has always played an important role in America, particularly in our nation's early days. Even today, about 11 percent of elementary and secondary school-age children attend private schools. Most private schools have a religious affiliation and thus offer alternatives to the public schools' secular emphasis.

- Equal educational opportunities for minorities and women have not always existed in America. Ethnic groups such as African Americans, Hispanic Americans, Native Americans, and Asian Americans, as well as women, have had to fight uphill battles to gain educational rights and treatment equal to those given to white males.

Rare is the college student who feels a burning urgency to answer the question, "What is the history of American education?" Unless you are a history buff, you will probably ask yourself, "Why do I need to know this stuff? How will it help me do a better job in the classroom?" In truth, knowing something about the history of American education probably will not directly affect your classroom practices. So why should you study this aspect of education?

why study educational history?

First, understanding American educational history will give you a sense of perspective. As educators, we are sometimes accused of being faddist, which implies that we blindly follow each new approach or idea, thinking it is the greatest thing since sliced bread. On the other hand, we are sometimes accused of reinventing the wheel, spending a great deal of energy discovering something that has been in the educational literature for years or was a significant part of the education program of a different culture.

Second, although studying the history of American education will not give you answers to the immediate problems you are likely to face in your classes, it will enable you to better understand the culture and context in which you will work. It will help you obtain the "big picture" of why things operate as they do in today's schools.

Finally, studying the history of education will help you appreciate its truly noble heritage. Schools have been a progressive instrument in the lives of most people who have attended them. They have freed people from superstition and false information and have given them new skills, positive values, and world-expanding visions of what each individual, as well as what we as a people, can become. Some of the greatest people who have walked the earth—Socrates, Jesus, Gandhi, among others—saw themselves essentially as teachers. Teachers, then, are part of an old, progressive, and inspirational human endeavor. Knowing our educational history and gaining a historical perspective will help you live up to and extend this tradition.

Themes in American Education

Reading this book, surrounded by college classmates and friends, may seem a natural step in your educational career. Kindergarten or nursery school led to elementary school, then to middle school or junior high school, then to high school, and now college. You may have taken this progression for granted, assuming that's the way things have always been.

Actually, you are enjoying a level of education that was available only to the elite of earlier generations. You are already close to the top of an educational pyramid for which the foundation was laid almost 350 years ago. The growth of the pyramid has been shaped and energized by six major themes in American educational history:

six major themes

1. *Local control.* Originating in New England during colonial times, the concept of local control of schools spread during the nineteenth century with the common school district system. Because of a fear of a strong federal government, the framers of the U.S. Constitution made no reference to education. As a result, state governments assumed the role of educational authorities and then delegated substantial powers to local school boards. Not until the mid-twentieth century did the federal government really become involved in educational matters.

2. *Universal education.* Education for all children has been a developing theme in American education. In the colonial period, education was reserved for a small minority, mainly white males. During the nineteenth and twentieth centuries, children from various groups previously omitted from educational opportunity (girls, minorities, immigrants, people with disabilities) gained access to elementary and secondary education. Today, a college education is generally available to all who actively seek it.

3. *Public education.* In the colonial period, education was generally private and primarily for the middle and upper classes. Nationhood brought not only the spread of publicly supported education but, by the early twentieth century, compulsory education as well. Nevertheless, private education remains a small but important part of the overall educational system.

4. *Comprehensive education.* The basic abilities to read, write, and do arithmetic were once sufficient to prepare most children for their adult roles in society. However, the growth of urban, industrial life in America during the nineteenth and early twentieth centuries also demanded that people be educated for work. The result was the comprehensive public high school, which includes both training for trades and preparation for college.

5. *Secular education.* In earliest colonial times, the purpose of education was religious training. Beginning in the eighteenth century and progressing through the twentieth, the function of American education became increasingly secular, concerned with producing socially responsible citizens. Religious study has remained mainly in the private sector.

6. *Changing ideas of the basics.* Literacy and classical learning were the main goals of colonial education, whereas practical skills for a pragmatic, democratic society were the aims of the nineteenth-century schools. Technical and scientific literacy were added to the basics in the computer- and space-age late twentieth century.

Many contemporary educational issues have their roots in these six themes, which continue to shape the character of American schooling and education. Consider these examples of current issues:

- *Local control.* What should be the role of the federal government regarding education? Should national goals, standards, curriculum, and assessment for elementary and secondary schools be implemented?

- *Universal education.* How can we ensure the quality of education regardless of whether students live in wealthy or poor school districts?

- *Public education.* Should private and religious schools receive public tax support?

- *Comprehensive education.* Should the schools require all students, vocational and college prep, to follow a common curriculum?

- *Secular education.* How should public schools treat the presence of religion in American society and world culture?

- *Changing ideas of the basics.* Is technological literacy a new "basic" of education, and, if so, how will schools finance programs that train students to use new technologies?

These are just a few of the issues facing today's policymakers. As you read the rest of this chapter, look for links between historical forces and the key topics and debates in contemporary education. This chapter's tour through history is not a dead-end journey into the past. What happened in earlier generations has had a great impact on the schooling you received and the system you will enter as a teacher.

PAUSE AND REFLECT

1 Why is it important for teachers to know the history of American education? How might you use such knowledge?

Elementary Education

Colonial Origins

Link to more information about colonial schooling at the web site.

In the 1600s, some girls received elementary instruction, but formal colonial education was mainly for boys, particularly those of the middle and upper classes. Both girls and boys might have had some preliminary training in the *four Rs*—reading, 'riting, 'rithmetic, and religion—at home. Sometimes, for a small fee, a housewife offered to take in children, to whom she would teach a little reading and writing, basic prayers, and religious beliefs. In these **dame schools,** girls also learned some basic household skills such as cooking and sewing. The dame schools often provided all the formal education some children, especially girls, ever received.

apprenticeships

Throughout the colonies, poor children were often apprenticed or indentured to local tradesmen or housewives. Apprenticeships lasted three to ten years, generally ending around age twenty-one for boys and eighteen for girls. During that time, an apprentice would learn the basic skills of a trade and might also be taught basic reading and writing and perhaps arithmetic as part of the contractual agreement.

Although the lines were not drawn hard and fast, the three geographic regions of the colonies—New England, the South, and the Middle Colonies—developed different types of educational systems, which were shaped by each region's particular settlement patterns.

New England Town and District Schools   In New England, the Puritans believed it was important that everyone be able to read the Bible and interpret its teachings. As early as 1642, Massachusetts passed a law requiring parents to educate their children. That law was strengthened in 1647 by the famous **Old Deluder Satan Act.** Because Satan assuredly would try to keep people from understanding the Scriptures, it was important that all children be taught how to read. Therefore, every town of fifty or more families was obligated to pay

town schools

a man to teach reading and writing. With these schools, known as **town schools,** New England set the precedent that if parents would not or could not educate their children, the government was obligated to take on that responsibility.

moving schools

When settlers spread out, seeking better farmland, the town schools began to disappear. What emerged in their place was the so-called *moving school,* a schoolmaster who traveled from village to village, holding sessions in each place for several months before moving on. One can imagine how much actual learning occurred under such circumstances!

district schools

Discontent with this system of education led to the development of the **district school.** By this scheme, a township was divided into districts, each having its own school and master and funded by the town treasury. The theme of local control of schooling developed in these various kinds of schools. The district school system soon entrenched itself in New England because it was inexpensive to finance and gave some measure of schooling to every child. Laws made attendance compulsory, but they were not very strongly enforced.

Some towns allowed girls to have one or two hours of instruction between 5:00 and 7:00 AM, when boys were not using the school building. For the most part, however, girls had no access to the town elementary schools until after the American Revolution,[1] and if few girls went to school in the towns, even fewer did so in the outlying districts. The theme of universal education, which would include girls, was not to develop until the next century.

The town and district schools were unlike today's schools in many respects. The schools were usually crude, one-room buildings housing twenty or thirty students. The interiors typically were colorless and cold. Heating was such a problem that students usually had to provide firewood.

Foolishness is bound up on the heart of the child; but the rod of correction shall drive it from him.

—*NEW ENGLAND PRIMER*

New England Primer

Students entered school around age six or seven and stayed in school for only three or four years. They learned their ABCs, numerals, and the Lord's Prayer from a *hornbook,* which consisted of a page that was laminated with a transparent material made from boiled-down cows' horns and then attached to a flat piece of wood. Having learned the basics, students graduated to the **New England Primer,** an illustrated book composed of religious texts and other readings. Although there were other primers and catechisms, the *New England Primer* was the most famous and remained the basic school text for at least one hundred years after the first edition of 1690.

dreary atmosphere

The learning atmosphere was repressive and grim. Students were under orders to keep quiet and do their work, and learning was characterized by an emphasis on memorization. Group instruction was almost unheard of; each child worked independently, one on ABCs, another on spelling, and another on the catechism. Class recitation was nonexistent. Instead, the master, sitting on a pulpit at the front of the room, called students up to recite to him one at a time.

If students did well, they were praised and given a new task. If they did poorly, they were criticized harshly and often given a rap across the knuckles or on the seat of the pants. It was believed that if children did not pay attention, that was simply a sign of how easily the devil could distract them from the path of righteousness. Such views continued to serve as a justification for severe classroom discipline throughout the first 250 years of American history.

Education in the South Conditions in the South were quite different from those in New England. Many upper-class Englishmen emigrated to the South, where they established large estates. As opposed to the more centralized conditions in New England, the great distances between southern settlements encouraged plantation owners to educate their children with private tutors, who were often local ministers or itinerant scholars. In addition, most southern

private tutors

settlers were members of the Anglican church and did not share the Puritan belief that everyone had a religious obligation to learn to read.

In the towns of the South, schools were established by governmental authority, but their administration was usually delegated to a group or corporation, which could collect tuition, own property, hire and fire teachers, and decide curriculum content. As in England, education of the poor and orphans was often undertaken by the Anglican church or by religious groups such as the Society for the Propagation of the Gospel in Foreign Parts. The lack of concern for general education of the entire community caused public education in the South to lag behind that in other sections of the country for many generations.

■ **Education in the Middle Colonies**   Unlike Puritan New England and the Anglican Southern Colonies, the Middle Colonies were composed of various religious and ethnic groups. Quakers, Catholics, Mennonites, Huguenots, Baptists, and others each wished to train their children in their respective faiths; Dutch, German, and Swedish settlers also wanted a separate education for their children. As a result, **private venture schools,** which were licensed by the civil government but not protected or financed by it, flourished, and the use of public funds to educate everyone's children did not become customary.

■ *private venture schools*

In these private schools, parents paid the teacher directly on a contractual basis. The instructor managed the school and curriculum, accepting or rejecting students as desired. The denominational schools in the Middle Colonies shared the New England concern for proper religious training as a primary goal, but they also began early to offer, in addition to the basics, practical subjects such as bookkeeping or navigation.

▒ *The Common School*

■ *emerging idea of common school*

Before the American Revolution, the term **common school** referred to schools that provided education for the average person, but it was not necessarily at public expense or available to all.

Even in colonial New England, it was the students' parents who had to pay for the schooling. In the first blush of the new republic, however, conditions began to favor **universal education,** the idea that some sort of elementary education should be provided free, at public expense and under public control, for everyone who could not afford or did not want private schooling. Even though the Constitution had relegated control of education to the states, the impetus for such public schooling came from the federal government, in particular as a result of the enactment of the **Northwest Ordinances** of 1785 and 1787. Concerned with the sale of public lands in the Northwest Territory (from present-day Ohio to Minnesota), Congress passed the Northwest Ordinance of 1785. Every township was divided into thirty-six sections, of which one was set aside for the maintenance of public schools. In the Ordinance of 1787, Congress reaffirmed that "religion, morality, and knowledge, being necessary to good government and the happiness of mankind, schools and the means of education shall forever be encouraged."[2]

■ *Northwest Ordinances*

■ **Arguments for the Common School**   After the American Revolution, it was recognized that a democratic government would be only as strong as the people's ability to make intelligent choices, which in turn depended on a basic education for all. It was also argued that education was a natural right, just like the very rights for which the Revolution had been fought. During this period,

LEADERS IN EDUCATION
NOAH WEBSTER (1758–1843)

Although best remembered today for his *American Dictionary of the English Language,* first published in 1828, Noah Webster was best known in the nineteenth century for his *American Spelling Book* (also known as the *Blue-Backed Speller*). This small, blue-backed booklet appeared in 1783 and became the most widely used schoolbook during the early nineteenth century.

A native of Connecticut and a graduate of Yale University, Webster was a lawyer, schoolmaster, politician, and writer. His intellectual interests were extremely broad. He wrote a paper on epidemic and pestilential diseases, edited John Wingate's historical journal, wrote several scientific treatises, discoursed on banking and insurance, and, along the way, mastered twenty-six languages, including Sanskrit!

An intensely patriotic individual, Webster believed that America had to shed its British influence and develop its own sense of cultural identity and unity. The best way to do this, he believed, was to reshape English language and literature to reflect the unique American culture. The creation of an American language would bind the people together and help produce a strong sense of nationalism. His dictionary contained the first-time appearance of such American words as *plantation, hickory, presidential,* and *pecan.*

Webster knew that if Americans were to develop a sense of national identity and pride, the process should start at an early age. Accordingly, he wrote his blue-backed *American Spelling Book,* one of the most successful books ever written. Roughly 100 million copies were printed, and it is estimated that more than a billion readers used the book—a record surpassed only by the Bible. The *American Spelling Book* was often the only book schoolchildren had because it served as a combination primer, reader, and speller. The book contained many moral stories and lessons, as well as word lists and guides to pronunciation. Webster must be credited with the fact that Americans differ from the British in writing *color* instead of *colour* and *center* instead of *centre.* Not only did he set the style for American spelling, but he made it the liveliest subject in the classroom. Spelling bees and other spelling games brightened up otherwise typically dull instruction.

Known as the "schoolmaster of the republic," Noah Webster campaigned for free schools for both boys and girls in which children could learn the virtues of liberty, just laws, patriotism, hard work, and morality. He was an educational statesman whose work, more than anyone else's, helped create a sense of American language and national culture.

 Visit the web site for more information about Noah Webster.

> *If a nation expects to be ignorant and free, in a state of civilization, it expects what never was and will never be.*
> —THOMAS JEFFERSON

Benjamin Franklin and Thomas Jefferson suggested educational plans, as did other leaders of the Revolution.

The early period of independence saw an increased concern with citizenship and nationhood. A system of common schooling would strengthen unity. An influx of immigrants in the 1840s and 1850s, following a period of upheaval in Europe, further stimulated demand for an educational system that would serve to "Americanize" the waves of foreigners and keep society stable.

In contrast to European social structure, class membership in America was rather fluid: wealth and social status in this country depended less on the social class into which a person was born. Universal education, one of the key themes of American education, was thus seen by the newly evolving working class as a means of equalizing economic and social opportunities. As a result, another reason given for spreading educational opportunity was that better-educated people would increase productivity and enhance everyone's prosperity while diminishing crime and reducing poverty.

Whereas the *New England Primer* reflected the religious orientation of much colonial education, the textbooks of the nineteenth century began a trend toward secular education (another of the six major themes in the history of American education), emphasizing morality and Americanism. No other book was more popular than the six-volume series of **McGuffey Readers,** which sold more than 100 million copies between 1836 and 1906. Besides training students in (American) English language and grammar, these texts introduced poetry and the writings of statesmen, politicians, moralists, and religious leaders. "They assumed the Fatherhood of God, the brotherhood of man, the wickedness of war, crime, and inhumanity, and above all, they buttressed the concept of the sacredness of property and bulwarked the position of the middle class in society."[3]

Although at this time universal education was meant only for whites, the same arguments advanced by its advocates were used later to extend universal education to include racial and ethnic minorities and children with disabilities, to name just a few groups that have been denied equal educational opportunities. The desegregation efforts of the 1950s and 1960s were based on these very arguments. (For further discussion of the issue of equal educational opportunity, see the chapter entitled "What Social Problems and Tension Points Affect Today's Students?".)

Arguments Against the Common School As proper as these thoughts may sound to the modern ear, they often encountered opposition. The arguments against the public common school were based on economics as much as on educational or political principles: why should one family pay for the education of another's children? Many people believed that schooling, especially for the poor, should be the responsibility of religious groups. Still others thought that a free public school would gradually weaken or dilute the particular culture or religion that they had sought to establish in America. If ethnic groups mingled together, what would be the fate of each group's native culture and language? Similar concerns are reflected in the current controversies about multicultural and bilingual education, discussed in the chapter entitled "Who Are Today's Students in a Diverse Society?".

And what was to be done about religious study? The ability of different religious groups to exist together in one school, as in democracy itself, demanded that no one religious group be favored over another. Although there were many competing proposals, the common schools finally settled on the teaching of basic moral values such as honesty and sincerity, as a substitute for direct religious instruction. As described in the chapter entitled "What Are the Ethical and Legal Issues Facing Teachers?", the same issues remain with us today.

Victory of the Common School Between 1820 and 1920, the establishment of common schools made steady progress around the country. By the middle of the nineteenth century and certainly by the end of the Civil War, thanks in large part to the efforts of Horace Mann and other common school advocates, the ideal of universal elementary education was generally acknowledged,

McGuffey Readers

Reflect on the influence of the common school with the image in this section of your CD-ROM.

who pays for universal education?

what about religious study?

LEADERS IN EDUCATION
HORACE MANN (1796–1859)

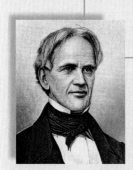

Horace Mann was the radical educational reformer of his day. Although trained as a lawyer, he became eminently successful as an educator and a politician. Asked why he had exchanged the practice of law for education, he answered that "the interests of a client are small compared with the interests of the next generation."

Born in Franklin, Mass., Mann received only the most rudimentary schooling until he was fifteen. Most of his education was self-acquired, a fact that profoundly influenced his philosophy of education. He studied hard to be admitted to Brown University, where he became a brilliant student. In 1827, Mann was elected to the Massachusetts House of Representatives, and a luminous political career lay ahead of him, but he became committed instead to education and to the use of political methods to bring about educational reform.

Mann made it his aim to abolish the cruel floggings that were then routine in the public schools. Schoolmasters believed it their duty to drive the "devil" out of their students, and many of them administered from ten to twenty floggings a day. Most schoolkeepers believed flogging to be an aid to learning. Not only were students treated cruelly, but attendance at school was itself a punishment. Schools were often little better than hovels: the lighting was poor, and many buildings were unsanitary and unsafe. Mann criticized corporal punishment and inadequate facilities in public speeches, lectures, and letters, and lobbied for reform in the state legislature and in Congress.

Horace Mann strongly believed in the ideals of the common school and championed its cause throughout his career. He saw education as a tool of liberation by which the poor could raise themselves, African Americans could become emancipated, and children with disabilities could adjust to their handicaps. After all, Mann reasoned, education had brought him fame and position. Thus, more than 150 years ago, the idea of social mobility through education was born in America.

For education to be as powerful a force as Mann envisioned it, he thought the school term must be lengthened and teachers' salaries raised. To make learning more relevant and enjoyable, he helped introduce new textbooks designed to illustrate the relationship between knowledge and the practical problems of society. Mann organized libraries in many schools, making books readily available to students. He believed less in the formal curriculum than in individual learning—undoubtedly because of his own self-education.

Mann was responsible for the establishment of the Massachusetts Board of Education and for the founding in 1839 of the first public *normal school* (a two-year school chiefly for the training of elementary teachers) in Lexington, Mass. Although the normal school opened with only three students, the concept spread and was widely imitated throughout the country. Mann was intensely interested in teacher training, and he believed teachers should be intellectual, moral, and cultural models for their communities.

Many of Mann's ideas were controversial, but he was most violently denounced for his position on religion in the schools. Although a religious man, he believed religious training belonged outside the schools, which should be run by the state. Because of his views, Mann was attacked from many Boston pulpits.

Mann was regarded as a dreamer and a visionary by many of his colleagues. When he took over the presidency of Antioch College in 1852, it opened its doors to all races and religious sects, and admitted women on an equal basis with men, some educators predicted that these measures would promote the collapse of higher education. Were he alive today, Mann might still be fighting for ideas he espoused more than a century ago, because many people have yet to accept these ideas.

 Visit the web site for more information about Horace Mann.

TABLE 9.1   Types of Elementary Schooling

Type of School	Location	Time Period	Purpose
Dame school	Most of the colonies	Seventeenth century	Private school held in housewives' home; taught basic reading, spelling, and religious doctrines
Town school	New England	Seventeenth and part of eighteenth century	Locally controlled institution, public but not free; simple curriculum of reading, writing, catechism, and arithmetic
Moving school	New England	Eighteenth century	Provided schooling for communities spread out over wide areas; an itinerant teacher moved from village to village
District school	Primarily New England	Mid-eighteenth to mid-nineteenth century	Replaced town and moving schools; public but not free; each district hired its own schoolmaster, again with emphasis on basic skills
Private tutoring	Primarily the South	Seventeenth to early nineteenth century	For children of the wealthy
Private venture school	Primarily Middle Colonies, but widespread	Eighteenth and nineteenth centuries	Private schools, offering whatever subjects the schoolmaster chose and parents wanted for their children
Common school	New England, Middle Colonies, and the South at first; now universal	1830 to present	Provided free, public, locally controlled elementary schooling; curriculum emphasized basic skills, moral education, and citizenship
Kindergarten	Widespread	1855 to present	Emphasized play and constructive activities as preparation for elementary school

The Common School is the greatest discovery ever made by man.

—Horace Mann

■ *public school enrollment burgeons*

if not universally practiced. By 1930, eleven states and the District of Columbia had passed compulsory attendance laws in addition to making common schools generally available.

As a result, between the Civil War and World War I, the number of students in schools grew enormously. In 1870, 57 percent of children between five and eighteen years old were enrolled in some form of schooling. By 1918, more than 75 percent of that age range were enrolled.[4] In 1870, average attendance was forty-five days a year; in 1918, it was more than ninety days. Thus, the hundred years between 1820 and 1920 saw extraordinary growth in the commitment to free, publicly supported, universal education. (See Table 9.1 for a summary of the different types of elementary schooling during our history.)

PAUSE AND REFLECT

❶ Why did the educational development of colonial America differ among the New England, Middle, and Southern Colonies? In what ways were the educational systems different? Can you see similarities to any of the colonial systems in today's schools?

> **2** How are the arguments for and against common schools reflected in today's controversies about using vouchers to pay for private or religious schooling?

Other Developments in Elementary Education

Link to more information about European influences on American education at the web site.

European Influences   From Europe came new ideas about education. One of the most far-reaching experiments was the **kindergarten,** or "children's garden," where pleasant children's activities such as songs and stories were used to lay a foundation before formal education began. Friedrich Froebel of Germany developed the first kindergarten in 1837. The first American experiments were actually made before the Civil War, but in 1873 a public school kindergarten was established in St. Louis, and the idea spread rapidly. Elizabeth Peabody brought Froebel's ideas to the United States and was influential in instituting early childhood education in our country.

Pestalozzi

European influence also resulted in greater emphasis on the interests of the child in elementary education (see Table 9.2). Johann Pestalozzi modeled his educational doctrines in a Swiss experimental school at the beginning of the nineteenth century. Pestalozzi attempted to educate the heads, hearts, and hands of his pupils, relying on attitudes of acceptance and love of the individual student to reach large numbers of poor and handicapped children. Among his instructional techniques were *object lessons,* lessons that focused on actual objects and pictures. He also emphasized learning through sense perceptions and sequencing of learning experiences from the known to the unknown.

Herbart

German educator Johann Friedrich Herbart, influenced by Pestalozzi's thinking, stressed that the primary purpose of education was moral development. Herbart also established a highly structured mode of teaching that strongly influenced American teachers during the early part of the twentieth century.

Montessori

European thinkers, and American educators influenced by them, believed students could learn best by direct experience, by using their senses and relating new learning to their previous knowledge. As a result, some schools incorporated more physical activity and manual training in their curricula. This innovation was designed not to train technical workers but to complement and round out traditional intellectual instruction. Maria Montessori (profiled in the chapter entitled "What Social Problems and Tension Points Affect Today's Students?") was particularly influential in developing a curriculum that emphasized learning through the senses for young children.

The thoughts of Froebel, Pestalozzi, Herbart, and Montessori, among others, entered American education through their influence on issues of curriculum and instruction. The emphasis on the child's interest and experience, advocated by the progressive educators (described in this chapter and in the chapter entitled "What Are the Philosophical Foundations of American Education?") and still strong in American elementary education, owes much to these European thinkers.

Curriculum Changes   During the colonial period, it was hardly necessary for one to know anything beyond the four Rs unless one was wealthy and wanted to go on to college. In the early and mid-nineteenth century, the common school curriculum simply expanded on the colonial curriculum. The primary concern, however, was less with religious training and more with obtaining functional

less religious training

TABLE 9.2   Major European Educational Thinkers

Name	Dates	Major Contributions
John Comenius (Czech)	1592–1670	Emphasized sensory experience in learning Materials and instruction should be based on developmental stages of child growth Developed textbooks that were among the first to contain illustrations Stressed that schools should be joyful and pleasant places Believed we acquire knowledge of world through our senses
John Locke (English)	1632–1704	Believed we acquire knowledge of world through our senses Pioneer of the inductive, or scientific, method Recommended utilitarian and practical learning in a slow, gradual process
Johann Pestalozzi (Swiss)	1747–1827	Stressed the importance of children learning through their senses and concrete situations Advocated love and unconditional acceptance of children; schools should be like warm and loving homes
Johann Herbart (German)	1776–1841	Believed the chief aim of education was moral development Developed the concept of curriculum correlation—each subject should be taught so it relates to other subjects Believed history, geography, and literature were core subjects Developed Herbartian method of instruction: (1) preparation; (2) presentation; (3) association; (4) systematization; and (5) application
Friedrich Froebel (German)	1782–1852	Introduced the kindergarten, or "children's garden," whose goal was the cultivation of the child's self-development, self-activity, and socialization Believed the teacher should be a model of human dignity and cultural values Songs, stories, and games stimulated the child's imagination and transmitted the culture
Maria Montessori (Italian)	1870–1952	Established preschools run on the principle of allowing children freedom within a carefully designed environment Curriculum focused on three types of experiences: practical, sensory, and formal studies Created learning materials designed to develop sensory and muscular coordination Required considerable training of teachers to implement the structured curriculum

knowledge for life after school. Subjects such as spelling, geography, history, and government were added because they were considered important for good citizenship. Natural science, physical training, and mechanical drawing were also included to provide a complete, well-rounded education. The movement toward comprehensive education is one of the key themes of the history of American education.

▪ **Consolidation**   Although the one-room school had served well in the days of the frontier, as areas developed, it became clear that the smaller, poorer districts could not provide the educational opportunities available in larger, wealthier ones. As a result, the early 1900s saw a period of consolidation of smaller

▪ *merging of districts*   school districts into larger, unified systems. In 1910, more than half the states allowed such unification. By the 1920s, the growth of industry and the invention of the automobile (and the school bus) had helped consolidate the large number of one-room schools around the country into centrally located, modern facilities that could serve larger areas better than the old district schools.

The Progressive Education Association

The Progressive Education Association   John Dewey (who is discussed more fully in the "What Are the Philosophical Foundations of American Education?" chapter) and other educators tried to create new, experimental, child-centered schools in the early 1900s. In 1919, the establishment of the Progressive Education Association was a formalized attempt to reform education according to the following principles:

progressive principles

1. The child should have freedom to develop naturally.

2. Natural interest is the best motive for work.

3. The teacher is a guide, not a taskmaster.

4. A student's development must be measured scientifically, not just by grades.

5. Students' general health and physical development require attention.

6. The school and the home must work together to meet children's needs.

7. The progressive school should be a leader in trying new educational ideas.[5]

Reflect on the progressive school movement with the image in this section of your CD-ROM.

The progressive school movement eventually went in several different directions. Some educators argued for letting children be free to do whatever they wanted; others tried to make the school into a community center for recreation, adult education, and even social reform. Critics ranged from traditionalist advocates of the subject-centered curriculum to some progressives, like Dewey himself, who argued that the ties between society and the child would be broken if children were granted total freedom to do whatever they wanted.

influence of progressives

The 1940s brought a rather conservative reaction to the progressivism of the previous generation. However, it is good to remember that many ideas we take for granted now—such as teaching through student projects, fieldtrips, and non-lecture methods of instruction—were hotly debated innovations that were introduced by progressive educators.

Since World War II

Since World War II   After World War II, the role of the United States in world affairs increased tremendously, thus broadening the scope of educational objectives. The use of the single textbook was supplemented by a great variety of learning resources. Other major developments in elementary education included the rapid increase in kindergartens and an emphasis on providing special

special education receives attention

educational programs for children with disabilities. Between 1948 and 1953, the number of schools offering special education services increased by 83 percent, and enrollments in kindergartens in public schools increased from 595,000 in 1939–40 to 1,474,000 in 1953–54.[6]

new curriculum projects

A number of national curriculum projects were developed and implemented in the elementary schools during the 1950s and 1960s. In response to the Soviet launch of the space satellite *Sputnik*, many of the projects emphasized mathematics, science, and social studies.

education of gifted and disadvantaged

Also during this period two types of students received major attention from elementary school educators: the gifted and the disadvantaged. Gifted students received attention because of our nation's concern over the Cold War with the

Soviet Union and our perceived need to produce scientific breakthroughs to ensure our military superiority over the Soviets. As the movement for civil and human rights gained momentum, more and more curriculum reform movements also focused on the "culturally disadvantaged" child. In response to judicial decisions and protests by minority groups, the federal government advanced significant financial aid to change schools to better address the needs of these children. Compensatory education programs, such as Head Start and Title I of the Elementary and Secondary Education Act, improved the learning of disadvantaged children. (See the chapter entitled "How Are Schools Governed, Influenced, and Financed?" for more details on compensatory education programs.)

As achievement test and Scholastic Aptitude Test (SAT) scores declined during the 1970s, many parents, politicians, and educators argued that the schools had tried to accomplish too much and had lost sight of their basic purposes. A return to the basics seemed to be the cry of the late 1970s and early 1980s. Today academic rigor continues to be emphasized, but more programs have been developed to meet the needs of students who are at risk for dropping out.

back to the basics

Although a public elementary school education is now available universally, the issues of what constitutes a proper education—how comprehensive it should be, how secular it should remain, and how basic learning should be defined—are far from resolved. The changing nature of what constitutes the basics of education has been another one of the key themes of the history of American education.

Secondary Education

Link to more information about the history of high school at the web site.

Today's *public comprehensive high school* has evolved from earlier forms of secondary education that included colonial *grammar schools* designed to either prepare students for college or for particular careers and private *academies*, popular throughout the nineteenth century. Table 9.3 summarizes four types of secondary school, together with the modern junior high and middle school.

Early Forms

Latin Grammar Schools   In the colonial period, all secondary education—that is, all education beyond the elementary level—served the sole purpose of training for entrance to college. The earliest secondary institution was the **Latin grammar school,** whose name gradually came to mean "college preparatory school." The term *prep school* still carries that classical connotation today.

emphasis on classical education

A boy entered a Latin grammar school around age seven or eight and spent the next seven years learning Latin texts written by ancient Romans or medieval scholars. Much work was memorized, and over three or four years the student learned composition and writing of Latin verses. Following this, the student studied Greek, moving in the final year to classical Greek writers and the New Testament. He also might have given some attention to the study of the Hebrew language.

The first Latin grammar school in the colonies is generally considered to have been established in 1635 in Boston. It was public and open to boys of all social classes. The Old Deluder Satan Act of 1647, which required communities of fifty or more families to establish elementary schools, also required

TABLE 9.3 Types of Secondary Schooling

Type of School	Location	Time Period	Purpose
Latin grammar schools	New England, Middle Colonies; a few in the South	Seventeenth and eighteenth centuries	Emphasized Latin and classical studies; designed to prepare young men for college
English grammar schools	Middle Colonies, New England; a few in the South	Eighteenth century	Private secondary schools designed to provide practical rather than college preparatory studies
Academies	Middle Colonies, New England; a few in the South	Eighteenth and nineteenth centuries	Private secondary schools designed to prepare young people for business and life; emphasized a practical curriculum, but gradually shifted back to college preparation
High schools	New England, Middle Colonies at first; now universal	1821 to present	Provided public secondary schooling; combined functions of Latin grammar schools and academies (college preparation and preparation for life and business)
Junior high schools	First in California and Ohio; now universal	1909 to present	Designed to provide students in grades 7–9 with better preparation for high school
Middle schools	Universal	1950 to present	Designed to meet the unique needs of preadolescents, usually grades 6–8; an alternative to junior high schools

communities of one hundred or more families to establish Latin schools. At first, Latin grammar schools were found primarily in New England; a bit later they were instituted in the Middle Colonies. Wealthy families in the South generally either hired tutors or sent their sons back to England for college preparation.

■ **Alternative Forms of College Preparation**   During the colonial period, many students, especially in the South, received their secondary education from tutors or at private venture schools, which were more common in the Middle Colonies. Instruction provided by a single schoolmaster obviously lacked variety

corporate schools

and dependability. Gradually, corporate schools were developed; these institutions were governed by a board of trustees or directors and were able to continue as a corporate endeavor beyond the tenure of any particular teacher.

English Grammar Schools   The growth of middle-class businesses in the 1700s led to the demand for a secondary education that would provide practical instruction in everything from navigation and engineering to bookkeeping and foreign languages. Thus there arose private **English grammar schools,** which catered to the growing number of students who needed more than elementary instruction but were not interested in preparing for college. Classes were offered

commercial subjects

at various times and places, sometimes to both girls and boys. Commercial rather than religious subjects were taught. Some subjects, such as music, art, and dancing, were actually not practical but were meant to train students for socializing in polite company.

Secondary Education for Females   In the 1700s, private venture English grammar schools were more flexible than the Latin grammar schools and, as a result, were the first secondary institutions to accept female students. Depending on the sophistication of the particular school and the preferences of its clientele, girls typically studied the three Rs (reading, 'riting, 'rithmetic), geography, and French, but they also sometimes learned English grammar, history, and Latin. Some practical vocational subjects such as bookkeeping were occasionally taught along with such traditional and socially accepted skills as art and instrumental music.

greater opportunities for girls

Because of the somewhat larger number of private venture schools in the Middle Colonies, girls who lived there probably had greater educational opportunity than girls elsewhere. Quaker leaders, including William Penn and French-born Anthony Benezet, were concerned with and supported the education of several deprived groups, such as African Americans and Native Americans—and women.

In the South, the daughters of wealthy landowners could receive traditional instruction in the various arts and letters, such as music, dancing, and French, which would give them the social skills appropriate for the lady of a household. By the end of the colonial period, separate class-based education tracks were developed for girls similar to those for boys in the English or Latin grammar schools.

The Academy

A new type of secondary school grew up during the second half of the eighteenth century. The **academy** was an attempt to combine Latin and English grammar schools through separate Latin and English departments within one school. Academies were unlike the Latin grammar schools in that the primary language of the academy was English; they were unlike the English grammar schools in that they included classical subjects in the curriculum. Gradually the academy took the place of both types of school.

Growth of Academies   The number of private academies grew rapidly after the American Revolution in response to the growing need for practical business training. Around 1850, about 6,000 academies were in operation.[7] Compared with the Latin grammar schools, the academies included instruction for a larger age range, which on the low end overlapped the curriculum of the

The availability of women teachers at low salaries during the late nineteenth century helped keep education costs down but, at the same time, contributed to the low salary problem that is still with us today.
(© Corbis/The National Archives)

■ *emphasis on practical studies*

common schools and on the upper end sometimes provided instruction that was as extensive as that of colleges. Although academies first focused on practical, useful studies rather than on college preparatory courses, over the years the emphasis shifted back to the classical languages and curriculum. Because they were private institutions, the academies were also at greater liberty to accept girls.

■ *surge in education for females*

■ **Female Academies**   The real surge of development in education for girls and young women came in the first half of the 1800s with the growth of academies and seminaries that were established especially for young women. Female academies were established by Emma Willard in Troy, New York (1821); by Catharine Beecher in Hartford, Connecticut (1828); and by Mary Lyon in South Hadley, Massachusetts (1837). A secondary education acquired at one of these institutions was often the highest level of education women would ever receive. Eventually, some of these academies themselves became colleges.

The female academies had to buck the established tradition against formal education for women, who in many quarters were still considered intellectually inferior to men. The schools compromised somewhat by offering courses related to home economics in addition to more classical subjects.

■ *practical skills and teacher preparation*

In practical terms, the leaders of the women's education movement were committed to two goals. One was to produce women who could handle the domestic chores and challenges of wives and mothers intelligently and wisely so as to "become companions rather than satellites of their husbands."[8] The curriculum of female academies therefore was designed to include subjects similar, but not identical, to those at men's institutions. Domestic skills were presented as practical applications of the more abstract traditional subjects. The other goal of women's education was to prepare women as teachers.

The Public High School

Although the private academies reflected the democratic independence of the middle class, their tuition and fees effectively cut out participation by the poorer working class. In the years following the American Revolution, the growing demand for free public elementary education understandably provided a basis on which to argue for free secondary education. Such schooling at public expense was the educational system most appropriate for democracy, it was argued, and the only system that could maintain democracy.

■ *early public high schools*

In 1821, Boston created the first public English high school; a second one, for girls, was established in 1826. The number of public high schools throughout the states increased slowly but steadily as an extension of the common school system. Unlike the academies, high schools were governed by the public rather than by private school boards. Although by no means universally accepted, the argument for free public high schools was a logical one, based on the inequality of providing elementary schools for all and secondary schools only for those who could afford tuition.

> *The ladder was there, "from the gutter to the university," and for those stalwart enough to ascend it, the schools were a boon and a path out of poverty.*
>
> —Diane Ravitch

Opponents of the idea of public high schools did not dispute the need for common elementary schools. They did argue, though, that secondary school was a luxury and was not within the domain of the taxing authorities. In 1874, however, in the famous **Kalamazoo case** (*Stuart and Others v. School District No. 1 of the Village of Kalamazoo and Others*), the Michigan courts ruled that the school district could tax the public to support both high schools and elementary schools. This court case set the precedent for financing public high schools.

Debate Over the Secondary Curriculum   In the late nineteenth century, debate shifted from whether public secondary schools should be supported to what the content of the curriculum should be. Guidelines for the curriculum were derived largely from the goals expressed for the schools. One goal was to reduce social tensions and strengthen the democratic form of government by bringing together all social classes and ethnic groups.

■ *multiple purposes*

Another goal was to provide better preparation for Americans to participate, on graduation, in the full range of industrial occupations. In addition, the high schools were to offer specialized vocational and technical training. At the beginning of the 1800s, the appeal of the academies had been to provide training in studies that prepared students for a practical livelihood and not necessarily for college. By the 1840s the same goal was being demanded of public high schools. Seen in retrospect, the academies were really a link between the earlier grammar school and the later high school. High schools were supposed to provide both a terminal educational experience for most students and a bridge to higher education for those who were capable and chose to pursue further studies.

■ Reflect on the history of secondary education with the image in this section of your CD-ROM.

The Comprehensive High School   To meet these varied purposes, the secondary curriculum shifted considerably between the Civil War and World War I. The basic mathematics courses in arithmetic, geometry, and algebra tended to be taught in a more commercial and practical context. American literature began to compete with English literature, and commercial English was added to the study of literary English. The classical languages continued to give way to modern foreign languages. In the sciences, physiology, chemistry, physics, botany, and astronomy were joined by meteorology, zoology, forestry, agriculture, and geology. Physical education was added to the curriculum. In social studies, the number of courses in American history grew, although European history continued to be central. Civics and citizenship were added to history. Moral philosophy fell away completely and was replaced by purely commercial courses such as typing, stenography, commercial law, home economics, industrial arts, and man-

■ *a more diverse curriculum*

■ Reflect on the issue of tracking with the image on this section of your CD-ROM.

Figure 9.1

Enrollment in Public Elementary and Secondary Schools by Level, 1869–70 to 1999, with Projections to 2011

Sources: Thomas D. Snyder, *120 Years of American Education: A Statistical Portrait* (Washington, DC: U.S. Department of Education, National Center for Education Statistics, 1993), p. 26; Debra E. Gerald and William J. Hussar, *Projections of Education Statistics to 2011* (Washington, DC: U.S. Department of Education, National Center for Education Statistics, 2001), Table 2, p. 13.

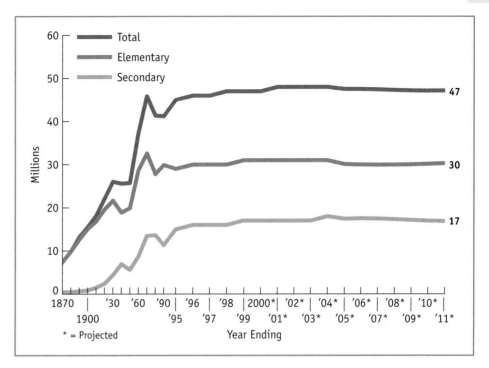

ual training.[9] The result was the institution known today as the **public comprehensive high school,** which embodies the notion of comprehensive education, another of the key themes of American education.

During the twentieth century, public comprehensive high schools continued to spread. Between 1890 and 2000, the number of students in public high schools increased as a percentage of all students attending public school, from 1.6 percent to 35 percent.[10] This increase is shown graphically in Figure 9.1.

Growth of Junior High and Middle Schools

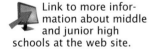 Link to more information about middle and junior high schools at the web site.

For some time, educators debated the best way to divide grade levels for elementary and secondary training. The main question was when to stop teaching basic skills and start teaching content: Should there be eight elementary grades and four of secondary school, or six elementary and six secondary, or some other arrangement?

In an attempt to resolve these issues, educators began to experiment with various ways to reorganize the grades. Finally, in the school year 1909–10, in both Columbus, Ohio, and Berkeley, Calif., a separate program was established for the intermediate grades seven, eight, and nine. The new grouping was called

■ *first junior high schools*

junior high school. By 1926, more than 800 school systems had a six-three-three organization, and that pattern became the dominant one.[11]

Since the 1960s, however, the system of five elementary—three intermediate—four secondary grades has become increasingly popular, with a **middle school** for grades six, seven, and eight rather than a junior high school. Advocates argue

■ *arguments for middle schools*

that middle schools have significant advantages over junior high schools. For one thing, they offer a unique environment where ten- to thirteen-year-olds are free to grow up at their own rates and where attention is focused on the needs of this age group rather than on mimicking the high school's emphasis on academic and sports competition, as is often the case with junior high schools.

Because of the earlier onset of puberty in today's children, sixth-graders may be better served in a school designed for early adolescents in grades six, seven, and eight than in an elementary school. Additionally, giving the ninth grade, which is still considered the first year in the college entrance sequence, to the high school frees middle schools to try new programs and new approaches without having to make them specifically applicable to college preparation.

■ emphasis on personal growth

Since the middle 1980s, there has been a deepening national commitment to the improvement of the education of early adolescents, with a strong emphasis on personal growth and development. To encourage this kind of personal growth, middle schools often use interdisciplinary team teaching, block scheduling, advisory homerooms, and exploratory activities and courses.

■ criticisms of middle schools

However, many education officials have become concerned about what they see as a lack of emphasis on academics in the middle school. The Third International Mathematics and Science Study (TIMSS), discussed in the chapter on "What Is Taught?", revealed that while American fourth-graders outperform their counterparts in mathematics in all but seven other nations, by the time they reach eighth grade, pupils in twenty other nations do better than U.S. students. As a result of TIMSS and other standardized testing, some critics see the middle schools as having gone "soft," overemphasizing self-esteem building at the expense of academic rigor. These critics see the middle school curriculum as being unfocused, repetitive, and unchallenging. Some critics argue for doing away with middle schools and going to a K–8 elementary school and a 9–12 high school; others want to maintain the middle school but increase its academic focus. In the past, many states permitted teachers with either elementary or secondary teaching licenses to teach in middle school, but more of them are upping the academic coursework required of elementary school teachers who want to teach in middle schools in an effort to refocus the middle school curriculum on academic subject matter. A number of states have broadened the licensure eligibility of secondary teachers to allow them to teach as low as the sixth grade. Thirty-three states also offer teacher licenses specifically for middle school that focus on both adolescent development and academic subject-matter preparation.[12]

■ how different are they?

Middle schools continue to increase in proportion to junior highs. By the beginning of the twenty-first century, middle schools outnumbered junior high schools by about four to one.[13] One researcher concludes, however, that despite the policy talk and incremental changes in curriculum, organization, and instruction, most middle schools, especially those in the cities, still resemble the junior high schools they were designed to replace.[14] These resemblances include departmentalization, teachers teaching separate subjects, teacher-centered instruction, students grouped by ability, and little interdisciplinary teaching. Although many schools exhibit the desired characteristics of a middle school, they are still not the majority.

■ *Secondary Education Today*

Look at the pictures of the two secondary classrooms on the next page, one taken in the late 1800s and one from today. In what ways are they similar? How are they different? The most remarkable observation made about secondary education today is how little it has changed over the last one hundred years. There have been changes, of course, but they have been small relative to the changes that have occurred in American living patterns, values, technologies, and careers. The curriculum revolves around subjects that are taught by specialists and are not very different from the subjects offered in schools during World War I.

The reason lies in the basic structure of the high school. Its organizing framework, developed in the nineteenth century, persists today across all regions of the country. High schools are complicated organizations, requiring considerable orchestration to work efficiently. A change in one part of the system means that other parts must also change. As a result, relatively little change occurs. The chapter entitled "How Should Education Be Reformed?" examines recent efforts at structural or system-wide reform.

■ *high school structure resists change*

PAUSE AND REFLECT

1 What made the development of the American secondary school so unique in the history of the world?

2 How would you structure the educational sequence from elementary to secondary school? Why?

Private Education

Private schools have always been part of American education. For more than 150 years, until the growth of the common school movement in the early 1800s, most education in America was private. Historically, private schools have served three major purposes, providing (1) instruction for various religious denominations, (2) an exclusive education for the wealthy, and (3) an alternative for any group that finds the available forms of education unsatisfactory.

Since the middle of the nineteenth century, by far the largest private school enrollments have been in parochial schools run by the Roman Catholic church. The earliest Catholic schools existed primarily in the Spanish-speaking Southwest and in French-speaking Louisiana. After 1840, however, Irish and Italian immigration increased the support of Catholic institutions in the North and East. The total number of Catholic schools grew from about 100 in 1840 to about 3,000 in the 1880s, to 8,000 in 1920, and to more than 13,000 in the early 1960s. From that point through the early 1980s, however, many Catholic schools closed. Today, the number of Catholic schools has stabilized at slightly less than 8,200.[15]

■ *Catholic school growth*

Link to more information about private schools at the web site.

■ *discrimination against private schools*

■ *still an important alternative*

In terms of enrollment, Catholic schools now have a total student membership of about 2.5 million, compared with an estimated 1.87 million students in other religious schools and an estimated 842,000 in nonsectarian private schools.[16] There are more than 27,000 private schools with a total enrollment of about 5.3 million, or about 11 percent of all students in U.S. schools.[17] The chapter entitled "What Are Your Job Options in Education?" offers more information about teaching opportunities in private schools.

The steady reduction in the percentage of private school students in the nineteenth and early twentieth centuries was not only a sign of public school strength; it also reflected outright discrimination and pressure against those who wanted to be "different." An extreme case followed World War I, when Nebraska passed a law prohibiting the teaching of German in either public or private schools. However, in 1922, the U.S. Supreme Court ruled that a state could not interfere with the prerogative of parents to educate their children as they see fit—in this case, at a private school that taught the German language—simply on the grounds of desiring to "foster a more homogeneous people with American ideals."[18] When, in 1925, an Oregon law required all children to attend public school, a Roman Catholic school and another private school successfully challenged the law on the grounds that their Fourteenth Amendment rights were being threatened. In a landmark decision in *Pierce v. The Society of Sisters*, the Court overturned the Oregon law, holding that the act "unreasonably interferes with the liberty of parents and guardians to direct the upbringing and education of children under their control."[19] As a consequence of this decision, nonpublic schools survived efforts to eliminate them.

But if public schools have clearly become the principal mode of education in America, it is also significant that private education has remained an important alternative for about 10 percent of the population. This fact reflects a paradox. On the one hand, from the early days, private schools have represented the freedom of immigrant groups to pursue life in America and to educate their children as they choose. That privilege was essential to the young democracy and still represents a basic freedom of choice in America. On the other hand, some argue that private education supports a caste system that is, in principle, not democratic. The very existence of private forms of education can be viewed as an implied criticism either of the quality of public education or of its availability on equal terms to all comers, irrespective of class, religion, or race. As discussed in detail in the chapter entitled "What Social Problems and Tension Points Affect Today's Students?", this issue has gained in importance as school voucher plans expand to include private and religious school options.

PAUSE AND REFLECT

❶ Do you believe the role of private education is likely to increase or decrease in the upcoming years? Why?

Education of Minorities

The picture of American education that we have drawn up to now has been quite rosy because the educational achievements of this country over the past 350 years are indeed impressive. There is, however, a less pleasant side to the picture. The history of education provides insight into people's values in general, and the educational experience of minorities tends to reflect how a society relates to them. The somewhat idealized image of the melting pot begins to break down when we look at the experience of nonwhite groups.

Ethnic minorities such as African Americans, Hispanic Americans, Native Americans, and Asian Americans traditionally have not been given equal educational opportunity in America. Not until the late nineteenth century, for example, did the federal government make any serious effort to provide education for Native Americans. American society is still suffering today from the effects of educational neglect of various minority groups.

As we begin discussing the education of minorities, it is important to note that members of a minority group are often discussed as though they were a homogeneous subgroup of Americans. However, the terms *African Americans, Asian Americans, Hispanic Americans,* and *Native Americans* actually encompass many ethnic, national, and linguistic groups. Although it is convenient to use these broader terms, we should not forget that within each subgroup great diversity exists.

■ *minorities excluded from equal educational opportunities*

Learn more about education of minority students in the video resources on your CD-ROM.

■ *Education of African Americans*

Link to more information about the education of African Americans at the web site.

■ **Before the Civil War** As is true of colonial education generally, the earliest motivation to educate African Americans was religious. In New England, as early as 1717, the Reverend Cotton Mather started an evening school for slaves. In the South, the first attempts to educate African Americans were carried out by clergy, particularly English representatives of the Society for the Propagation of the Gospel in Foreign Parts. To dubious slave owners, ministers defended the education of slaves not only as a religious duty to save their souls but also because conversion to Christianity, it was believed, would make them more docile.[20]

■ *schools for free African Americans in the North*

In the North, schools were established for free African Americans. In 1731, Anthony Benezet, a French-born Quaker, started a school for slave and free African-American children in Philadelphia. In 1774, another school was begun by Benjamin Franklin, as president of the Abolitionist Society. In 1787, an African Free School was established in New York City with an enrollment of forty students, which grew to more than five hundred by 1820. The city provided funds in 1824 and took over the school in 1834, thus providing education for African Americans before many white children were receiving it.

Yet conditions were not all bright in the North. In 1833, Prudence Crandall, a white schoolmistress in Canterbury, Conn., began to take in African-American girls. The villagers boycotted the school, threw manure into its well, and tried to burn it down. Finally, a mob broke the windows, and the school was closed.[21]

Prejudices, it is well known, are most difficult to eradicate from the heart whose soil has never been loosened or fertilized by education; they grow there, firm as weeds among stones.

—CHARLOTTE BRONTË (FROM *JANE EYRE*)

■ *education for African Americans prohibited in the South*

In the South, following slave rebellions in the early 1800s, states gradually prohibited altogether the teaching of African American children, whether slave or free. Some slaves were taught to read by favorably disposed masters. However, slave owners generally reasoned that reading would lead to thinking, and thinking would lead to the desire for freedom. As the Civil War approached, abolitionist agitation often came from the few liberal colleges, such as Oberlin College in Ohio and Bowdoin in Maine, that allowed the enrollment of African American students.

The Late Nineteenth Century   In the period following the Civil War, the seeds for the education of African Americans that had been sown before the war slowly began to sprout. During the period of Reconstruction, from 1865 into the 1870s, the federal government, through the Freedmen's Bureau and, in the former Confederacy, an occupying army, attempted to promote African-American voting registration and schooling. Help also came from private and religious philanthropies in the North. Because it was hoped that whites also would benefit from these endeavors, schooling was advocated for the general public as well. Yet the common school movement was weakest in the South, and at first, most whites there refused to participate not only in integrated schools, but also in segregated schools, both of which they believed the northern carpetbaggers were forcing on them.

efforts to promote education

By the end of Reconstruction, southern whites began to allow the existence of separate schools for African Americans. African American enrollment in the schools, which had been only 2 percent of the school-age children in 1850, was 10 percent by 1870 and 35 percent by 1890, although it dropped somewhat after that during a period of severe repression by the new white state governments.[22] During this period, "Jim Crow" laws were passed separating African Americans from whites in all areas of life.

separate schools in South

Into these conditions, a young African-American teacher named Booker T. Washington (1856–1915) was called to start an African-American normal school in Tuskegee, Ala., in 1881. Originally named the Tuskegee Normal School for Colored Teachers, it was later renamed the Tuskegee Institute. There, Washington found only a few students, no buildings or classrooms, and a hostile white community. Washington, who had been born a slave, realized that the traditional curriculum of the classics would neither prepare his students to help other African Americans learn nor help ameliorate the tensions with the white community. Believing strongly in the idea of learning by doing, Washington instructed his students to build the school themselves. In this process, they learned practical skills, grew produce that could be sold to the white community, and in general showed the whites that African-American people could be productive members of society. Booker T. Washington gradually came to be considered the outstanding African-American leader of the time by the white establishment.

Booker T. Washington

Tuskegee Institute— practical education

But a growing number of young African Americans who, unlike Washington, had not been born into slavery believed that Washington's conciliatory policy of training for menial positions in white society would not benefit African-American people in the long run. They believed that practical training is necessary, but there must also be an intellectually sound and academically rich program of study for the "talented tenth" of the student body, who would form the African-American intellectual leadership. This was the view of W. E. B. Du Bois (1868–1963), an African-American intellectual and scholar who held a doctorate from Harvard.

Reflect on Washington and DuBois's influences with the image in this section of your CD-ROM.

Education must not simply teach work—it must teach life.

—*W. E. B. Du Bois*

In 1862, the U.S. Congress passed the **Morrill Act.** This legislation granted each state a minimum of 30,000 acres of federal land with the proviso that the income from the rent or sale of these lands must be used to establish colleges for the study of agriculture and mechanical arts. A total of 6 million acres of federal land were donated to the states. The resulting land-grant institutions, such as the University of Illinois, Texas A & M, and Michigan State University, became the great multipurpose state universities that now enroll hundreds of thousands of students from all segments of society.

The Tuskegee Normal School was established in 1881 by Booker T. Washington.

(© Corbis/Library of Congress)

second Morrill Act

In 1890, Congress enacted a second Morrill Act that increased the endowment of land to the original land-grant colleges but forbade the granting of money to a college with an admission policy that discriminated against nonwhites unless a separate facility for African Americans existed nearby. This second Morrill Act thus provided federal support to states to create "separate but equal" colleges for African Americans. As a result of this legislation, a number of so-called **1890 institutions** were created for the higher education of African Americans. Many of these historically African American colleges such as Florida A & M and North Carolina A & T still exist today, but as integrated institutions.

1890 institutions

"separate but equal"

In 1896, in the case of **Plessy v. Ferguson,** the Supreme Court upheld the constitutionality of "separate but equal" accommodations for African Americans. Although the ruling originally referred to seating in a railroad car, it was quickly extended to the schools. The practical significance of this ruling was to add federal sanction to the legal separation of African-American schoolchildren from white children, most notably in the South, for almost the next sixty years.

southern African American schools impoverished

■ The Twentieth Century   The fact that southern schools for African Americans were not equal to those for whites is woefully clear from looking at financial expenditures alone. In 1912, the southern states, as a group, paid white teachers slightly more than $10 per white child in school but paid African-American teachers less than $3 per African-American child. In the 1930s, in ten southern states, African-American children made up 34 percent of the school population but received only 3 percent of the funds available for school transportation. Discrimination also existed in the distribution of federal funds, particularly in vocational education, the largest and most important educational program subsidized by the federal government.[23]

de jure *segregation*
de facto *segregation*

Most northern states did not have **de jure school segregation,** or *segregation by law,* but the crowding of African Americans into isolated neighborhoods often resulted in **de facto** segregation—that is, segregation resulting primarily from residential patterns. Furthermore, large numbers of southern African-American children who migrated with their parents to northern cities often had to be demoted because they had not mastered the same amount of material as their northern counterparts. Generally, even in the North, African-American teachers taught African-American children.

however, some gains

Although these conditions continued in varying degrees through the 1940s, some gains were nevertheless achieved. The average daily attendance of African-American children increased and approached that of white students. The salaries of African-American teachers also increased, reducing the economic gap between African-American and white teachers with equal training.

In the late 1940s, the National Association for the Advancement of Colored People (NAACP) began taking cases to the courts. Beginning with universities rather than elementary schools, the NAACP succeeded in having the courts rule that various law school facilities for African Americans were clearly unequal to those for whites.

Read *Brown* v. *Board of Education* in the text resources on your CD-ROM.

The stage was then set for the precedent-shattering case of **Brown v. Board of Education of Topeka** (1954), in which the Supreme Court ruled that separate educational facilities are inherently unequal and that laws requiring white and nonwhite students to go to different schools were illegal. The Court concluded that *de jure* school segregation violated the Fourteenth Amendment of the Constitution. Early desegregation efforts therefore were aimed at eliminating *de jure* segregation.

Desegregation Efforts   Throughout the 1960s and into the 1970s, many school systems, often in response to specific court orders, also attempted to reduce or eliminate *de facto* school segregation. As a result, many school districts underwent desegregation efforts. What have been the results of these efforts?

desegregation results

Several researchers have concluded that desegregated schools have accomplished more than mere educational reform—that is, African-American students who attended integrated schools experienced desegregation in several aspects of adult life, including attending predominantly white colleges and universities, working in desegregated settings, and living in desegregated neighborhoods.[24]

Busing   Although these long-range findings are quite positive, desegregation efforts have had some negative results. One major problem has concerned busing. Busing students to desegregated schools was one of the most inflammatory issues in education in the 1970s and 1980s. Emotions on the topic often ran very high—so high, in fact, that white parents sometimes slashed bus tires, burned buses, and physically prevented buses from running to avoid having their children bused to other schools.[25]

court-ordered busing

The federal court system was the prime mover in ordering school districts to employ busing in the desegregation process. For example, the U.S. Supreme Court, in *Swann v. Charlotte-Mecklenberg* (1971), concluded that the need to hasten desegregation was great, and busing was deemed an appropriate measure provided the distance of travel was not so great as to risk the health of the children or impinge significantly on the educational process.

VOICES FROM THE CLASSROOM

Mary Reese is retired and lives in Charlottesville, Virginia. She was an elementary school teacher for eleven years before becoming a principal. She later served as assistant superintendent of schools in Charlottesville, Virginia, and associate director of the American Association of School Administrators.

Teaching in Segregated Schools

College diploma and job contract in hand, I headed to my first teaching job in a small, rural, segregated school. The advice, help, and insights provided by the experienced principal and teachers that first year convinced me that teaching was indeed a good career choice. It mattered not that the "new" books they were excited about receiving turned out to be the "used" books from the white school, and that the children had to walk fairly long distances to get to school because there was no bus transportation provided for them. The belief that a new school year meant a new opportunity to help children created an unbelievable aura of new beginnings.

I later became a teacher in a segregated school in a large urban school district—a school serving students from three public housing units. Again, "new" books, except for newly adopted state textbooks, included used books from other schools. School repairs, if made at all, were taken care of after the needs of the white schools had been attended to.

One of the most powerful insights from both of these experiences was how important the teacher was to the life of the students and the community in which they lived. I taught more than the basic academic skills to students. I assumed the role of family social worker, financial advisor, and any other roles necessary to help students and their parents believe that the school was there for them. I had to convince the student and parent that getting a good education was the key to a better future. I took it as my responsibility to help them learn that segregation was only a barrier if we let it become one.

I became the principal of that urban school after ten years of teaching in it. Shortly thereafter, the school was integrated, and we became a mix of low-income black, and middle-class white students. It was bittersweet to see much of the maintenance work that had been requested and never done, suddenly being taken care of without my having to submit work order requests. It was humiliating to have white parents come and give the woodwork and cafeteria equipment "the white-glove treatment." But it was as equally rewarding to know that their fears would be unfounded because of my belief that the school should be a clean and safe place for any student and staff member assigned there. Because we already had excellent teachers, a strong academic program, and a belief in and requirement of strong parental involvement, integration proceeded more smoothly than in some of the other schools.

 Visit the web site for more Voices from the Classroom.

■ *mixed success*

Busing to achieve desegregation has had mixed success. One of the most successful busing plans began in Berkeley, Calif., in 1968, and standardized test scores indicated that white, African-American, and Asian-American students all made better progress after desegregation.[26] On the other hand, in many other communities, attempts to desegregate the schools by busing met with tremendous community resistance.

Big-City Desegregation   A major obstacle to desegregating big-city public schools is that the minority percentage of inner-city populations has increased dramatically during the past several decades. In part, this has been the result of "white flight," an exodus of white students whose parents have chosen to move to the suburbs or place their children in private schools. (However, not only whites are fleeing the city schools; middle-class African Americans are also leaving to give their children a chance to be educated in better schools.) Today, cities such as New York, Los Angeles, Chicago, Detroit, Atlanta, Houston, and Dallas have school minority enrollments approaching 90 percent.[27] How can schools in major cities be desegregated when the percentage of racial minority students is growing and the percentage of white students is decreasing?

metropolitan-area strategies

One solution would be to take the emerging residential segregation as given—minority cities and white suburbs—and attempt to overcome its effects on school segregation with metropolitan area–wide school desegregation. In this approach, children would be bused over the entire metropolitan area. However, the Supreme Court has ruled that this approach is justified only if racially discriminating acts of either state or local officials are judged to have occurred in the creation of either predominantly white or African-American school districts.

decline of busing

During the 1980s, court-ordered busing was no longer the preferred method for integrating the schools. Busing, of course, was never an end in itself. It was only one means of integrating society, and polls indicate that even opponents of involuntary busing agree that our society needs to be integrated.

Supreme Court reverses direction

Several Supreme Court decisions during the 1990s dramatically reversed school desegregation plans ordered by lower courts, thus eliminating much of the pressure to desegregate schools. In these rulings, the Court declared that (1) school districts could be released from lower-court desegregation oversight if the school district had complied in good faith with the lower court's decree and eliminated, to the extent practicable, vestiges of segregation in student and staff assignments, transportation, facilities, and extracurricular activities; (2) federal desegregation decrees were never intended to be perpetual, and the day-to-day operations of schools should be returned to local officials as soon as possible; and (3) desegregation decrees cannot eliminate differences in student performance caused by poverty, poor family structure, and other socioeconomic factors, so once the lingering effects of legally enforced segregation are eliminated, school districts may run schools that happen to be all black or all white. In essence, the Court has said that there are practical limits to what a federal court can do to remedy prior discrimination, and once school districts have corrected initial racial imbalances, they are not required to remedy subsequent imbalances caused by demographic changes. Today the principal cause of segregated schools is not legal action but the choices of individuals whose housing patterns segregate our society and our schools. As long as these patterns persist, desegregation of the schools will continue to be problematic.

segregation increasing

Recent Developments   Following the developments of the 1980s and 1990s, evidence suggests that resegregation of African Americans is now fast approaching the levels before 1970.[28] This is particularly true in large urban centers, as was discussed earlier. Although many political and educational leaders remain committed to desegregated schools, others are questioning whether integration is an idea whose time has passed. In many communities, these leaders, typically members of minority groups, call for shifting the emphasis from integrating schools to improving the quality of one-race neighborhood schools. They have lost faith that desegregation is the answer to better schools.

O P E N
TO
D E B A T E

Desegregation

▶ **JIM:** I'm very disappointed at the decisions of the Supreme Court and the executive branch of the federal government to back off continued desegregation efforts in our nation's schools. Now, more than ever, we need to create "one nation," which is virtually impossible in a segregated society and segregated schools.

▶ **KEVIN:** I think our government went as far as it could to desegregate schools, including ill-conceived and enormously expensive busing plans. It's a policy that no longer works. We no longer have *de jure* segregation, the government did away with that. What we now have is *de facto* segregation, and it's not the government's job to force integration if people don't want to live side by side.

▶ **JIM:** If black and white children don't go to school together, how in the world will they learn to trust one another and work together in society? If housing patterns don't bring them together, then it should be the responsibility of the government to bring them together in schools.

▶ **KEVIN:** I disagree. And the real issue is social class segregation, not race. Parents, black and white, want their children to have good educations and, if they can, they move to communities they believe can provide their children with good schools. The problem, then, is the schools serving those who don't have the financial resources and can't move. And here it's the poor quality of instruction. If we worried less about segregation and social engineering schemes and more about providing poor and minority kids with a quality education, the issue of integrated schools would be less important. As long as kids are achieving at high levels, who cares whether they attend racially integrated schools?

▶ **JIM:** I care, and so do a lot of other people. In one Public Agenda poll, eight out of ten African-American parents thought it was important for the schools their children attended to be racially integrated, and seven out of ten white parents agreed. Schools teach children lots of things besides what's covered on standardized tests.

▶ **KEVIN:** Well, that same poll indicated that three-quarters of African-American parents thought that quality teaching had been neglected while pursuing integration. What black and white parents want are schools where their children will be safe, have qualified teachers, learn to read and do math, and have a real chance to improve their lot in life. If all our children were provided with a quality education and had a chance to participate in the American dream, this issue of forcing integrated schools would disappear in a flash.

JIM: I think that's short-sighted thinking. Yes, attention to safe schools and academic matters are very important for all children, but so are experiences with children of different races. If these kids don't get these experiences in school, where will they get them?

Visit the web site for more information about this debate topic.

These supporters of resegregation argue that it demeans African-American children to believe that they can only learn when sitting next to white children in desegregated schools. Some also think that resegregation will protect African-American culture from the gradual eradication that would occur in an integrated setting. Further, they argue, resegregation would relieve African Americans of the disproportionate burden they have carried under most desegregation arrangements. Supporters of desegregation counter with the argument that most parents are mainly interested in good schools for their own children, not for the children of others. Accordingly, they say, whites will only support African-American students who happen to be in school with their own children. If African-American children are to benefit educationally, they need to attend school with white children. Otherwise, resegregation forces poor, largely African-American school districts in low-tax-base cities to continue their losing struggle to find educational money that they don't have. As one advocate for desegregation says, ". . . blacks who favor resegregation are doing whites the great favor of relieving both their guilty consciences and their pocket books."[29]

> *Segregation was wrong when it was forced by white people, and I believe it is still wrong when it is requested by black people.*
> —CORETTA SCOTT KING

desegregation does not always lead to integration

Desegregation Versus Integration   Another point needs to be made before closing this discussion: desegregation does not necessarily lead to integration. True integration is a very human process that can occur only after desegregation has gone into effect. It happens when people from different racial and ethnic backgrounds learn to be comfortable with one another and to get along together. It means ending racial prejudice and respecting ethnic differences. Anyone who has spent time in racially mixed schools, especially high schools, knows that African-American and white students who attend the same school can still be extremely distant from each other. Just bringing together students from different racial groups, social classes, and neighborhood backgrounds will not automatically lead to friendship, understanding, and appreciation of one another. As long as our society remains segregated, efforts to integrate our schools are likely to produce tension, at least in the short run. Integrating individuals with increasingly diverse racial, cultural, and linguistic backgrounds remains one of the great challenges to schools and society.

Reflect on desegregation with the image in this section of your CD-ROM.

PAUSE AND REFLECT

① Where do you stand on the issue of *de facto* resegregation of urban schools? What, if anything, should be done about it?

❷ In what ways did desegregation of American schools work, and in what ways has it not?

▧ *Education of Native Americans*

As early as 1622, in an ominous forecast of future policies, one colonist wrote back to England that it was easier to conquer the Indians than to civilize them.[30] The education of Native Americans received less public attention than that of African Americans because Native Americans were considered an impediment to westward expansion, they were far from major population centers, and their dealings were largely with the federal government.

▧ *education for religious purposes*

Initially the education of Native Americans, like that of African Americans, had a religious purpose. Once they had been put on reservations, the Native Americans received schooling from missionaries, who attempted to "civilize" them through the three Rs and, of course, the fourth one—religion. In the 1890s, these missionary schools were gradually replaced by government boarding schools, which tried to assimilate Native Americans by prohibiting them from speaking their native language and teaching them skills associated with white society, such as farming and mechanical skills for boys and domestic chores for girls. Little emphasis was placed on academics. The elimination of Native American languages and culture was considered an important strategy in the efforts to assimilate Native Americans.

My son, Wind Wolf, is not an empty glass coming into your class to be filled. He is a full basket coming into a different environment and society with something special to share. Please let him share his knowledge, heritage, and culture with you and his peers.

—ROBERT LAKE

The people who had been Native Americans for 20,000 years finally became American citizens in 1924. However, that did not mean they controlled their own education. The federal government, through the Bureau of Indian Affairs (BIA),

At the beginning of the twentieth century, special schools for Native Americans, such as the Carlisle Indian School in Carlisle, Pennsylvania, taught basic skills, such as mending clothes, to students.

(© Corbis/Bettmann)

Link to more information about the education of Native Americans at the web site.

directed the education of Native Americans until the mid-1970s. During this time Native American participation was virtually ignored, as was acknowledgment of their culture in their educational programs.

By 1965, Native Americans had begun to demand control of their schools, and a few demonstration sites for such tribal schools were funded. These schools were able to include much of the native culture in their curricula, but they were still financially dependent on the federal government, which meant limited instructional materials and lower-paid teachers than in many public schools.

federal legislation

Between 1972 and 1975, Congress enacted three bills that affected Native-American education and self-determination. These bills encouraged the establishment of community-run schools, offered grants to develop culturally relevant and bilingual curriculum materials, placed the Office of Indian Education under the U.S. Office of Education (now the Department of Education), and established an advisory council made up of Native Americans. The BIA is still actively involved in educational matters, but now in a supportive rather than directive capacity. The federal government has shifted much responsibility for educating Native Americans from the BIA and tribal schools to public schools. The BIA runs 171 schools, primarily located in Arizona, New Mexico, North Dakota, and South Dakota. About two-thirds of the schools are operated by Indian tribes or tribal organizations under grants or contracts with the BIA.[31] The schools serve 4,700 students—fewer than 10 percent of all American Indian students enrolled in K–12 schools in the United States. The other 90 percent of Native American students in grades K–12 attend public schools. This trend may have helped reduce the isolation of Native-American students. However, because Native-American community involvement in public education is slight, the move toward public schooling has resulted in a loss of the limited control Native Americans had begun to exercise over the education their children receive.

majority attendance in public schools

remaining problems

Today the education of the Native-American population in the United States, about 500,000 students, is still plagued by poverty, parental alcoholism, underachievement, absenteeism, overage students, and a high dropout rate of 39 percent.[32] Native-American students drop out of school more than any other racial group. Many Native Americans believe that a culturally appropriate curriculum is needed to overcome these deficiencies and reduce the cultural discontinuities between home and school. Only a small percentage of Native-American students have teachers from their same tribe; most of their teachers are white females. One evaluation of Native-American schools concluded that they should integrate their programs into a whole-school, standards-based reform effort and increase the participation of the Native-American community. A 1998 presidential order on educational opportunities for American Indians and Alaska Natives established an interagency task force to develop a coordinated federal response to help these students, including establishing a research agenda and supporting pilot programs to improve technical assistance.[33]

Education of Hispanic Americans

As with Native Americans, the first contact Spanish-speaking people had with the United States was often a result of annexation and warfare. Although they have lived in the continental United States for more than 400 years, Hispanic people came into substantial contact with Anglo-Americans about 200 years ago, and almost from the beginning, there was a cultural clash. Hispanic children first attended religious mission schools, which were gradually replaced by secular public schools. In the process, the Spanish language and Hispanic culture were subjected to a type of discrimination that was perhaps less blatant than that against African Americans but just as pervasive. The common school of the nineteenth and twentieth centuries, although it opened educational and social opportunities in Anglo America, often sealed off those opportunities for Hispanic Americans. Hispanic children tended to receive lower scores than Anglo-American children on English-language intelligence quotient (IQ) tests, which not only were written in a language that was not their own, but also reflected white middle-class values. Thus, an image of Hispanic children's intellectual inferiority was reinforced.

■ *discrimination against Hispanics*

Since the 1940s, the courts have acknowledged that *de facto* segregation exists between Anglo-American and Hispanic schoolchildren and have required corrective integration plans. The 1965 Elementary and Secondary Education Act provided new support to the education of Hispanics, as it did to the education of Native Americans. Another response has been the establishment of bilingual education programs to provide instruction in the native tongue at the same time students learn English. As a result, students can enter the English-language curriculum at the appropriate age levels for their grades. However, as mentioned in the chapter entitled "Who Are Today's Students in a Diverse Society?", bilingual education programs are being denounced and replaced with English immersion programs in such states as California and Arizona.

■ *bilingual education*

Although significant progress has been made, there is still much concern about the education of Hispanics in the United States. For example, the high school completion rate for Hispanics ages twenty-five to twenty-nine is only 62 percent, compared with 93 and 89 percent for Anglo-Americans and African Americans, respectively. About 14 percent of Hispanics have earned bachelor's degrees, compared with 36 and 17 percent for Anglo-Americans and African Americans, respectively.[34] Furthermore, reading and mathematics proficiencies are significantly lower for the Hispanic population in comparison with the Anglo-American population. The public schools have not served these students well, and the cost in human and economic terms is enormous.

■ *high dropout rates, low academic achievement*

Hispanic youth represent the fastest-growing segment of the U.S. population, and Hispanics now account for more than a quarter of all new entrants into the labor force. Fourteen percent of all students enrolled in grades K–12 are Hispanic, and 25 percent of Hispanic students speak only Spanish at home. Further, Hispanic students who speak mostly Spanish at home have parents who have less education than those who speak mostly English at home. Only 49 percent of Hispanic students who speak mostly Spanish at home had parents with a high school education or higher, compared with 83 percent who spoke mostly English at home.[35] Children whose parents have not completed high school, and who do not speak English, are less likely to receive at home the background skills and knowledge to begin school successfully. Schools need to develop programs to address the needs of these students, particularly those with limited English proficiency. As demographers project higher and higher percentages of Hispanic students enrolled in public schools in the twenty-first century, the schools' response to these students' needs will have important consequences for society. Without increased educational attainment, Hispanic Americans will be relegated to low-skill jobs and locked in the lowest socioeconomic brackets, with negative consequences for all Americans.

Education of Asian Americans

diverse groups of Asian Americans

The diversity of Asian Americans is evident from the historical beginnings of different groups of Asian Americans in the United States, and it persists in educational issues today. The three largest groups of Asian Americans are the Chinese, Filipinos, and Japanese.

discrimination against Asian Americans

Discrimination against early Asian Americans was rampant, especially in the West, where most Asian Americans settled. Although immigrants from China, the Philippines, and Japan often entered the United States to fill the need for hard labor jobs, whites resented the competition for employment. Exclusionary laws limiting immigration of these groups were passed in the late 1800s and early 1900s.

School segregation of Chinese-American children in California lasted until at least 1946. Japanese-American children in California were forced to attend segregated schools up until World War II. With the outbreak of World War II, anti-Asian hostility subsided somewhat for immigrants of Chinese, Filipino, and Korean descent. However, the "yellow peril," perceived as emanating from Japanese Americans, resulted in the imprisonment in detention camps of more than 110,000 Japanese Americans, most of whom were American-born citizens.

recent Asian immigration

With the end of World War II, discrimination against Asian Americans began to subside. Naturalization rights were extended to resident Asian aliens. With the postwar expansion of the American economy, many Asian Americans benefited from greater job opportunities. Previous immigration restrictions were lifted in 1965, and the influx of Asian immigrants greatly increased. Since the U.S. withdrawal from Vietnam in 1975, enormous numbers of Indochinese immigrants have come to the United States and entered our school systems. The adaptation of more recent Asian immigrants has varied because of a range of educational levels and previous socioeconomic circumstances. Asian and Pacific Islanders currently constitute about 4 percent of all students enrolled in public elementary and secondary schools, and this figure is expected to continue to rise for the foreseeable future. Current census estimates indicate that Asian and Pacific Islanders number roughly 11.3 million, or about 4 percent of the U.S. population. It is projected that by the year 2020, this group will reach about 20 million, or 6 percent of the U.S. population.[36]

With the higher educational achievement and income levels of some Asian Americans, this group has often been touted as a "model minority" that has overcome discrimination through hard work, perseverance, and industriousness.

stereotype misleading

However, this rosy stereotype is misleading and at times has contributed to misconceptions and complacency in meeting the educational needs and concerns of Asian-American students.

language difficulties

Many recent Asian-American immigrants to the United States have little or no knowledge of the English language. This creates formidable language and cultural barriers for students entering the U.S. education system, and may lead to serious family-school discontinuities, alienation from school, and dropout problems. The Supreme Court established in *Lau* v. *Nichols* (1974) that schools must offer students sufficient special instruction to be afforded equal educational opportunity. (See the chapter on "Who Are Today's Students in a Diverse Society?" for more on *Lau* v. *Nichols*.) There is a pressing need for adequate language instruction for this subgroup of Asian Americans, and as immigration continues to increase, this need will likely grow in our school systems.

impediments to parental involvement

Parental and community involvement of Asian Americans in the education process also needs to be fostered. Parents of Asian-American students are often noted as being concerned with their children's education. However, because of the respect traditionally given educators, they are hesitant to intervene when they are dissatisfied with their children's educational progress. Another deterrent to parental participation is the fact that a much higher proportion of Asian-American families have two parents employed, a situation that makes attendance at traditional teacher conferences or parent-teacher organization (PTO) meetings difficult. Many communities are making efforts to organize and voice the needs of Asian-American students.

As the number of Asian-American students continues to grow, it will become increasingly important for teachers and administrators to be knowledgeable of and sensitive to the special problems and needs of Asian-American students and their families. To serve these students adequately in our schools, it is particularly important to keep in mind that Asian Americans are a changing and complex group whose achievement, aspirations, and learning styles should not be stereotyped.

 Link to more information about the education of Asian Americans at the web site.

PAUSE AND REFLECT

1. In what ways were the histories of the education of minority groups and women similar and different?

2. Limited English proficiency seems to be a major problem in increasing educational attainment for several minority groups. What ideas do you have about how this problem should be addressed?

A Final Word

At the beginning of this chapter, we identified six major themes that have shaped the history of American education and schooling: local control, universal education, public education, comprehensive education, secular education, and changing ideas of the basics. If you think back over the issues raised in earlier chapters of this text, you can see the effect of these themes on contemporary education. For example, the universal and public nature of the educational system strikes at the issue of equal educational opportunity and questions of school finance and governance. Current controversies over the content of education—questions about the secular or sacred nature of the curriculum, debate about the need for standards of learning, and efforts to provide excellence in education without sacrificing equality of opportunity—relate to the concepts of secular, universal, and comprehensive education and the definition of what is "basic." Thus, these six themes continue to play themselves out in our evolving educational system. Table 9.4 lists important dates and events in American education, many of which relate to these six themes.

TABLE 9.4   Key Events and Curriculum Trends in American Education

Time Period	Key Educational and National Events	Educational Trends/ Emphases and Characteristics of Curriculum	Dominant Educational Philosophies
1620– Revolutionary War	1635—Establishment of the Boston Latin grammar school 1647—Massachusetts Old Deluder Satan Act 1687–90—First edition of the *New England Primer*	Education limited by sex and socioeconomic class. Curriculum emphasized religious training (Bible), moral development, reading, writing, and arithmetic basics.	Perennialism
1770s–1820s	1775–83— Revolutionary War 1783—Noah Webster publishes *American Spelling Book* 1785, 1787—Northwest Ordinances 1788—U.S. Constitution ratified	Education emphasized literacy to make democracy work. Curriculum emphases included moral development, either practical education for career or university education.	Perennialism
1820s–80s	1821—First U.S. public high school 1821—Emma Willard establishes first school for women's higher education 1839—First U.S. public normal school, Lexington, Mass. 1860—First U.S. English-language kindergarten 1861–65—Civil War 1862—First Morrill Act establishes land-grant institutions	Education used to promote "melting pot" assimilation of immigrants and minorities. Curriculum emphases included basic tools of literacy, conservative moral values (*McGuffey Readers*), cultivation of American identity.	Perennialism
1880s–1950s	1890—Second Morrill Act calls for nondiscrimination in college admissions or "separate but equal" institutions 1914–18—World War I 1896—U.S. Supreme Court *Plessy* v. *Ferguson* case establishes separate schools for whites and blacks 1930s—Great Depression 1939–45—World War II 1944—GI Bill funds higher education for veterans	Child-centered curriculum became popular, emphasizing activities and experiences rather than verbal and literacy skills, cooperative rather than individual learning activities, citizenship, and self-adjustment.	Progressivism Romanticism

TABLE 9.4 Key Events and Curriculum Trends in American Education *(cont'd)*

Time Period	Key Educational and National Events	Educational Trends/ Emphases and Characteristics of Curriculum	Dominant Educational Philosophies
1950s–1970s	1954—U.S. Supreme Court case *Brown* v. *Board of Education* requires desegregation of schools 1957—Soviet Union launches *Sputnik* 1965—Elementary and Secondary Education Act 1971—U.S. Supreme Court case *Swann* v. *Charlotte-Mecklenberg* rules busing may be used for desegregation 1972—Title IX 1975—Education for All Handicapped Children Act (Public Law 94-142) 1979—Department of Education established	Curriculum emphases in the 1950s and 1960s included structure of the discipline and the discovery method of teaching, teaching gifted and talented students. Emphases in the 1970s on mainstreaming, multicultural education, career education, and a flexible curriculum with many electives.	Essentialism
1980s		Educational reform; reports issued leading to back-to-basics movement, core curriculum, stronger academic requirements. Inclusion and multicultural education grew.	Essentialism Perennialism
1990s	1990—Americans with Disabilities Act 1990—Individuals with Disabilities Education Act	Growing teacher shortage National Education Association (NEA) and American Federation of Teachers (AFT) merger talks fail Growing standards movement leads to high stakes testing. Strong technology emphasis. Growing rejection of bilingual education.	Essentialism
2000 and beyond	2002—Leave No Child Behind Act (reauthorization of Elementary and Secondary Education Act)		Essentialism

KEY TERMS

academy (310)

Brown v. *Board of Education of Topeka* (320)

common school (300)

dame school (298)

de facto [school] segregation (320)

de jure school segregation (320)

district school (299)

1890 institutions (319)

English grammar school (310)

junior high school (313)

Kalamazoo case (312)

kindergarten (305)

Latin grammar school (308)

McGuffey Readers (302)

middle school (313)

Morrill Act (318)

New England Primer (299)

Northwest Ordinances (300)

Old Deluder Satan Act (298)

Plessy v. *Ferguson* (319)

private venture school (300)

public comprehensive high school (313)

town school (298)

universal education (300)

FOR REFLECTION

1 Why is it important for teachers to know the history of American education? How might you use such knowledge?

2 How did the moral lessons you were taught in school compare with those taught in earlier American schools?

FOR FURTHER INFORMATION

PRINT RESOURCES

Larry Cuban, *How Teachers Taught: Constancy and Change in American Classrooms, 1880–1990,* 2nd ed. (New York: Teachers College Press, 1993).

This text is a historical examination of instructional practices in American classrooms.

Gary Orfield, Susan Eaton, and the Harvard Project on School Desegregation, *Dismantling Desegregation: The Quiet Reversal of Brown* v. *Board of Education* (New York: New Press, 1996).

This text explores how the desegregation efforts of the 1960s and 1970s are being reversed, particularly by Supreme Court rulings. The authors contend that our nation is making a serious mistake in doing so.

Teresa L. McCarty, *A Place to be Navajo* (Mahwah, NJ: Lawrence Erlbaum Associates, 2001).

An ethnographic account of the Rough Rock, Ariz., People's School, the first American Indian community-controlled school. Rough Rock was the first to teach in the native language and to produce a body of quality children's literature by and about Navajo people.

Joel Spring, *The American School, 1642-2000,* 10th ed. (New York: McGraw-Hill, 2002).

This book focuses on the social, political, and ideological forces that have shaped the evolution of schooling in America from colonial times to the present.

David B. Tyack and Larry Cuban, *Tinkering Toward Utopia: A Century of Public School Reform* (Cam-

bridge, MA: Harvard University Press, 1995).

This important book on school reforms in the United States argues that utopian policy talk about school reform usually has involved only incremental policy action: "tinkering with the system."

Wayne J. Urban and Jennings L. Wagoner, *American Education: A History,* 2nd ed. (New York: McGraw-Hill, 2000).

This book is a relatively brief overview of American education, written by well-known scholars.

WEB RESOURCES

"Lessons of a Century," *Education Week,* January 27, 1999–December 15, 1999. Available at: **http://www.edweek.org.**

Ten monthly installments examining aspects of the educational landscape of twentieth-century America, including the people, trends, historical milestones, enduring controversies, political conflicts, and socioeconomic forces that shaped education.

Library of Congress. Available at: **http://www.loc.gov.**

Users of this site will find easy access to THOMAS (legislative information), the Library of Congress catalog, and much more. Particularly relevant for the history of American education is the "Learning Page," which provides information on using materials in the American Memory historical collections, as well as lesson plans and links to related web pages.

How Are Schools Governed, Influenced, and Financed?

Chapter Preview   Few beginning teachers are concerned about issues related to school governance and finance. The topic seems remote to them; it is something administrators and representatives of teacher organizations care about, but it does not seem particularly vital for beginning teachers concerned with learning how to survive in the classroom. We feel differently; we believe beginning teachers must have some understanding of the way schools and school systems operate because they will be affected personally by governance and financial decisions. Not understanding how these decisions are made and how they might affect you as a teacher will reduce your effectiveness as a professional.

This chapter emphasizes that:

- Legal responsibility for school governance belongs to the state. Traditionally, however, policy decisions and administration have been delegated to local school boards.

- In addition to local school boards and state governments, many other groups exercise some measure of influence on educational decisions, either through legal authority or through less formal means. These other groups include professional education organizations, parents, teachers, the business community, the designers of standardized tests, the federal government, and the courts.

- Court rulings in some states have shifted the responsibility for public school financing from dependence on local property taxes to greater reliance on state support.

How would you explain the fact that:

- A very popular high school teacher was not given tenure?

- The sex education program being planned in your hometown was never implemented?

- A textbook with a fresh approach to the curriculum was removed from circulation after a year, even though the teachers favored its use?

- A coalition of superintendents from poor school districts in your state sued the state government for increased financial support?

- Legislators in New York State banned schools from subscribing to Channel One, a free television news service for school-age children?

It is quite likely that at least one of these questions applies to your local school district or state. They all reflect the struggle for governance, control, and influence over the public schools. This chapter explores how the American educational system is organized, governed, and financed. Although there are legal authorities for the schools and organizations established to exercise this authority, the educational system is strongly influenced by interest groups that do not appear on any organizational chart. We first examine the legal governing authority that exists in most states and then discuss special-interest groups that influence educational policy. Then we look at how the American educational system is financed and how disparities between rich and poor school districts are generating strong challenges to current financing policies.

Who Legally Governs Public Education?

In most countries, the public schools are a branch of the central government, federally financed and administered and highly uniform in curricula and procedures. In the United States, however, responsibility for the public schools has evolved as a state function as a result of the Tenth Amendment to the U.S. Constitution, which reserves all powers to the states that are not specifically designated to the federal government. Each of the fifty states has legal responsibility for the operation and administration of public schools within its own boundaries. In most aspects of public education (we will discuss certain exceptions later), the authority of federal, county, and city education agencies is subject to the will of the state authorities.

education as a state function

Although legal responsibility for school governance belongs to the states, policy decisions and administration have usually been delegated to local school boards, which exist because Americans have come to insist on control of schools at the local level (Figure 10.1). Recently, however, states have been reasserting their policymaking prerogatives.

state versus local control

State Offices and Administrators

At the state level, educational services can be influenced by a variety of actors, from the governor through the many employees of the state's department of education.

The Governor and the State Legislature   Policy analysts agree that the state legislatures are the most influential actors in establishing educational policy because they make the laws that govern and affect education within their states. In recent years, because of the high profile of educational issues, legislatures' interest in educational policy has increased, particularly in the areas of school finance and establishing standards for student academic achievement. Like legislatures, the governor's office has the power to affect educational policy but often chooses to do so only on limited issues. Many governors, however, have played more prominent roles, beginning with the educational reforms of the 1980s. Former president Bill Clinton and his education secretary, Richard Riley, for example, became nationally visible as governors through their educational leadership in Arkansas and South Carolina, respectively. President George W. Bush likewise pushed his education agenda as governor of Texas.

governors play leadership role

On financial issues, the roles of governor and legislature are especially obvious. Governors propose and legislatures act on budgets that contain funding for

Figure 10.1
Organizational Structure of a Typical State School System

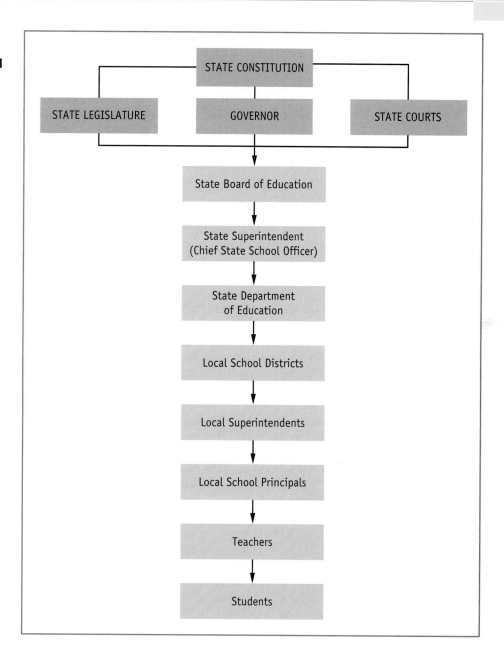

■ *the "Golden Rule"*

school districts. This is, as one wag has stated, the "Golden Rule: Whoever has the gold makes the rules." When state economies are strong, more tax revenues are available to invest in public education, as occurred during the mid- and late 1990s. However, when recessions occur, state governments, facing a loss of tax revenues, cut back on their educational commitments and initiatives, forcing school districts to cut budgets. In either scenario, governors and state legislatures have tremendous influence over educational policy and expenditures.

■ **The State Board of Education** The state's legal responsibility for public education requires it to establish an organizational framework within which the local school districts can function. The result is the establishment of a **state board of education** to exercise general control and supervision of schools

Link to more information about state board of education at the web site.

policymaking function

within the state. The state board of education is the state's educational policymaking body for elementary and secondary schools. It typically sets goals and priorities for education in the state; formulates education policy and curricular offerings, including establishing academic standards and their assessment; establishes and enforces rules and regulations for the operation of educational programs; represents the public in matters regarding the governance of education; reports to the public on accomplishments and needs; and makes recommendations to the governor and/or state legislature for the improvement of education. The state board of education also establishes and enforces minimum standards for the operation of all phases of elementary and secondary education from the state to the local school system level.

selection of members

The procedure for selecting state board members varies from state to state. In most states, members are appointed by the governor, but in about one-third of the states, members are elected by popular vote. The number of members on a state board of education varies from state to state, but a board of nine to fifteen members is typical.

The Chief State School Officer   The executive officer of the state board of education, the **chief state school officer,** usually is responsible to the state board of education for the administration of public education. (The actual titles for this position, which vary from state to state, include *superintendent of education, commissioner of education, secretary of the state board of education,* and others.)

duties of chief state school officer

The responsibilities normally involve serving as the chief administrator of the state department of education (see below) and the state board of education, recommending improvements in educational legislation, arranging studies and creating task forces to identify problems and propose solutions, and reporting on the status of education within the state to the governor, legislature, state board of education, and the public. This officer exercises little direct administrative authority over local educational officials, but his or her indirect influence is widely felt at the local level. In thirteen states the officer is elected by the voters, is appointed by the governor in twelve states, and is appointed by the state board of education in twenty-four states.

The State Department of Education   The **state department of education** (sometimes called the *state department of public instruction*) usually operates under the direction of the state board of education and is administered by the chief state school officer. The state department of education is responsible for carrying out the policies of the state board of education and the laws passed by the state legislature. It consists of a large bureaucracy of officials, often numbering in the hundreds.

influence of state departments

Originally organized to provide statistical reports, state departments of education have grown in size, power, and influence. Their primary responsibilities usually include administering and distributing state and federal funds, licensing teachers and other educational personnel, providing schools with technical assistance in improving curriculum and teaching, providing educational data and analyses, providing administration for special programs, accrediting college and university educational licensure programs, evaluating existing programs, and issuing reports. Most schools, school districts, and colleges of education are strongly affected by the policies and actions of these state departments. School and college personnel, including public school teachers, serve on advisory committees and task forces to assist the chief state school officer and the state department of education in their decision-making processes.

■ *The Local School District*

To facilitate local control of education, the state creates local school districts for the purpose of carrying out education in conformity with state policy. The school district is thus a unit of the state government and is usually distinct from the local municipal government.

■ Link to more information about school boards at the web site.

■ The Local School Board The policymaking body of the school district is the **local school board,** which represents the citizens of the district in setting up a school program, hiring school personnel to operate the schools, determining organizational and administrative policy, and evaluating the results of the program and the performance of personnel. Many school boards are empowered to raise money through taxes. Although school board members are usually elected by the citizens of the local district, they are officially state officers (not simply local representatives), and they must follow the guidelines and policies

■ *board members are state officers*

In the first place, God made idiots. That was for practice. Then he made school boards.

—Mark Twain

established by the legislature, the state board of education, and the state department of education. The tension between states' efforts to regulate educational policy and local districts' desire to determine their own policies has increased as states have taken the initiative in the recent educational reform movement.

Methods of selecting school board members are usually prescribed by state law. About 96 percent of the school boards are elected by popular vote, and the remainder are appointed, often by the local mayor or city council.

■ *school boards lack diversity*

What does the composite profile of school board members look like? As Table 10.1 indicates, the majority of today's school board members are male, white, and between ages forty-one and sixty—demographic characteristics that have changed little in recent years.[1] However, the proportion of women serving on boards has increased from 12 to around 39 percent since 1972. Representation of minorities continues to be small. At least 83 percent of members have annual family incomes over $50,000. Two-thirds of them have at least bachelor's degrees. Most are professionals, managers, or business owners, have children in public school, and consider themselves to be conservative. These figures indicate that in many ways, school board members are not typical of the public they serve. Whether or how this atypical aspect influences their values and decisions is not known. Can you think of any ways in which it might?

■ Reflect on the composition of school boards with the image in this section of your CD-ROM.

■ The Superintendent of Schools The **superintendent of schools,** a professional educator selected by the local school board to act as its executive officer and as the educational leader and administrator of the school district, is undeniably the most powerful officer in the local school organization. Since the school board consists of laypeople who are usually not education experts, it often delegates many of its responsibilities to the superintendent and staff.

■ *duties of superintendent*

Gathering and providing information to the local school board so it can make informed decisions is one of the superintendent's most important functions. Additionally, the superintendent must recruit, select, place, and promote personnel. Often, too, the superintendent plans the budget and supervises the maintenance, construction, and renovation of buildings.

Decisions about how to improve educational opportunities, including all aspects of curriculum and instruction, may originate with the superintendent. The superintendent generally has responsibility for maintaining harmonious relations with the community by communicating the mission of the schools to the public and marshaling support for district programs.

TABLE 10.1   Profile of School Board Members

Characteristic	Percentage
Gender	
Male	61
Female	39
Ethnic background	
Black	8
White	86
Hispanic	4
Other	2
Age:	
Under 30	0.5
30–39	5.4
40–49	40.1
50–59	33.8
60 or older	20.3
Family income	
Under $50,000	17
$50,000–$74,999	24
$75,000–$99,999	22
$100,000–$149,999	21
More than $150,000	16

Note: Because of rounding, some totals may not add up to 100 percent.

> *But one thing about today's superintendent is almost a given . . . he must indeed be a political animal.*
>
> —ARTHUR BLUMBERG

Theoretically, the superintendent's role is administrative and executive—he or she (only 13 percent of the nation's superintendents are female) keeps the schools functioning, whereas the local school board of education retains policymaking responsibilities. In practice, however, the superintendent has become the major policymaker in the school district.

Superintendents Versus Local School Boards   The way a school board and superintendent operate together to control a school district depends on their relationship. According to independent observers, this relationship often is one of conflict.

■ *conflict*

One observer, Larry Cuban, asserts that "conflict is—and always has been—the essence of the superintendency."[2] One measure of conflict between superintendents and school boards is the turnover rate: how often superintendents change their jobs. The average tenure for superintendents in urban districts is slightly less than 5 years, and the national average among all superintendents is just under 6 years.[3]

■ *high turnover rate often indicative of conflict*

Cuban describes the conflict between the superintendent and the school board, or between the superintendent and local private groups, as one of seem-

A principal's leadership style and values set the tone for the way a school functions.

(© Michael Newman/PhotoEdit)

responsibilities of principal

Reflect on the role of the principal with the image in this section of your CD-ROM.

shortage of principals predicted

ing competitors seeking to achieve their goals at the expense of the other participants. Cuban maintains that the issues over which boards and administrators disagree may change as a result of shifting political concerns, changes in school funding or demography, or constantly changing coalitions of teachers or local constituencies. But the relationship remains one of conflict regardless of particular issues. Although school boards hire and fire them, superintendents are expected to lead the board. If they fail to do so, board members are likely to act independently, often with disastrous consequences.

School boards and superintendents search constantly for local constituencies to provide the funding and support for school programs, and with every school board election, new points of view may be brought to the governance of the district. Superintendents must weather these changes in points of view and the emerging coalitions resulting from board member turnover. Sympathies with the schools' mission may be in a constant state of flux, requiring superintendents to exercise coalition-building skills. Their survival as non-elected public officials rests on their ability to mobilize support and manage conflict.

■ **The School Principal**   For the schools within a school district, the superintendent and the local school board of education select professional educators to serve as principals. High schools and middle schools may have a staff of administrators to assist the principal, including assistant or vice principals with specific responsibilities for discipline or curriculum and instruction. At the elementary level, on the other hand, principals may be responsible for more than one school building or may serve part-time as teachers. Whatever the pattern of administrative assignments, those who act as principals are generally considered to be a part of the administrative organization, directly accountable to the superintendent and the local school board of education. (See Table 10.2 for a profile of school administrators.)

As administrators, principals usually interview prospective faculty members and make faculty assignments, supervise and evaluate staff members, schedule students and classes, manage school budgets, administer district discipline policies, and procure and dispense supplies. The tasks are many; to list them all would be impossible. Historically, the role of the principal has included management, supervision, and inspection duties. Most importantly, principals are expected to function as instructional leaders for their schools. In a number of states, principals and their teachers are being held accountable for increasing student learning on statewide assessments of achievement.

Effective principals serve as instructional leaders by promoting a productive working and learning environment. They do so by understanding the mission of the school, communicating it to the staff and students, and rewarding excellent performance. They also represent the school to parents and the community. Involving parents and community members in the school's activities and securing their support for these activities is an important function of the principal.

Researchers are predicting a shortage of principals during the first decade of the new millennium. The shortage exists in all types of schools—rural, urban,

TABLE 10.2   Profile of School Administrators (in Percentages)

	Superintendents	High School Principals	Junior High and Middle School Principals	Elementary School Principals
Sex				
Male	86.8	78.8	66.8	44.8
Female	13.2	21.2	33.2	55.2
Ethnic background				
White	94.9	85.9	83.0	80.8
African American	2.2	8.4	10.5	12.0
Hispanic American	1.4	3.8	5.1	5.8
Asian American	0.2	0.9	0.7	0.7
Native American	0.8	1.1	0.8	0.7
Other	0.5	0.7	—	0.6
Highest degree earned				
Bachelor's	0.3	1.4	1.8	1.8
Master's	32.2	54.8	55.5	53.9
Professional Diploma	22.0	31.6	33.6	34.6
Doctorate	45.3	12.1	9.1	9.7
Salary (12 month)	$118,496	$83,367	$77,382	$72,587

Note: Because of rounding, some totals may not add up to 100 percent.

Sources: "Salaries and Wages for Professional and Support Personnel in Public Schools, 2000–2001" Arlington, VA: Educational Research Service, 2001, pp. 20–21. U.S. Department of Education, National Center for Education Statistics, Schools and Staffing Survey, 1999–2000 "Public School Principal Survey," "Public Charter School Principal Survey." Parts of this table compiled 07/30/02 by Thuy Dam, National Education Data Resource Center, Request 944315. Thomas E. Glass, Lars Bjork, C. Cryss Brunner, *The Study of the American Superintendecy 2000*, Arlington, VA: American Association of School Administrators, 2000, pp. 17, 128.

and suburban—and at all levels, elementary through high school. Why the anticipated shortage? The number one reason is that teachers who might want to become principals believe that principals don't get paid enough for the responsibilities they must shoulder. Also, unlike teachers, in most states, principals do not have tenure as administrators. Other reasons include the belief that the job is too stressful and time consuming and the perceived difficulty in satisfying the demands of statewide assessments, parents, and the community.[4]

PAUSE AND REFLECT

1 From what you have read about the role of the superintendent, what impressions have you formed about the power of the superintendent and the constraints on that power?

2 One of the authors of this textbook believes that the hardest job in public education is that of a high school principal. Do you agree or disagree and what reasons do you have for your position?

3 In your opinion, should chief state school officers be elected or appointed? What reasons do you have for your position? What arguments can you muster for the opposite opinion?

Who Influences American Public Education?

It is not our intention in this chapter to examine in detail the authority and power that enable various groups to influence certain aspects of public education. However, a brief look at the interplay of influence exercised by professional education organizations, parents, business, standardized testing, the courts, and the federal government yields some fascinating insights into how decisions about public education are actually made.

■ *Professional Education Organizations*

Among the most influential forces on the schools are professional education organizations, in particular the National Education Association (NEA) and the American Federation of Teachers (AFT).

In recent years, the role of teachers' organizations in determining educational policy has greatly increased. At the national level, the NEA and the AFT exert considerable influence on educational policy and legislation. Moreover, the state affiliates of the NEA and AFT are among the most effective lobbying groups in their respective states. (See the chapter entitled "What Does It Mean to Be a Professional?" for more on these two teacher organizations.) State politicians pay attention to these teacher organizations because of their power and influence. The NEA and AFT affiliates have well-articulated positions on selected issues, represent thousands of teachers who can be mobilized to vote for or against particular legislators, and spend considerable amounts of money to make their positions known. At the local level—largely as a result of collective bargaining techniques, including work stoppages or the threat of them—teacher organizations have won more and more power over educational policy.

■ teacher organizations are powerful

Today many local teacher organizations, including NEA and AFT affiliates, have won recognition as the official bargaining representatives of their members. Teacher organizations are also demanding that issues previously considered the prerogatives of local school boards and superintendents be subject to collective bargaining. Among these issues are teacher and paraprofessional salaries, clerical and secretarial assistance, curriculum development, fringe benefits, in-service training, class size, textbook selection, and even the appointment of department heads and other school administrators.

Reflect on site-based decision making at charter schools with the image in this section of your CD-ROM.

Teachers' efforts to negotiate their teaching role and its conditions have not always been welcomed by local school boards and superintendents. However, one recent reform effort to improve schools, **site-based decision making,** has tended to increase teachers' power. The idea behind site-based decision making is that most changes need to occur at the school level, and therefore many administrative and budget decisions should be made at that level, with teachers becoming involved in the decisions that affect them and their students. Site-based decision making transfers much of the budget and decision making from the central school district administration to the individual school level. As a result of such reform efforts, teachers are gaining more authority over important school decisions.

■ site-based decision making

> *Just as war is too important to be left to the generals, education is too important to be left to the educators.*
>
> —PAUL WOODRING

■ *Parents*

■ *parental influence*

Ask educators who has the most influence in determining whether children succeed in school, and they will almost always say, *parents.* Parents are their children's first and primary teachers and the only ones who follow a child's progress from year to year. As the two major forces for educating and socializing children in society, parents and teachers should be natural allies. Too often, however, a wide chasm separates them. Some teachers fear that parents will interfere in their classrooms; others feel pressed for time and don't want to spend the extra effort to communicate with and effectively involve parents. Some parents seem too consumed with the problems of work and raising a family to become involved in schools, whereas others actively participate in various school functions. Research is clear that without effective parental involvement in the schools, most students will not succeed academically. In a national survey of school superintendents, 68 percent identified a lack of parental involvement as the biggest roadblock to student achievement.[5]

Family support and emphasis on the value of education are extremely important influences on a child's success in school.
(© Joan Clifford/Index Stock)

The Parent-Teacher Association (PTA) is a loosely-knit national organization with 6.5 million members and more than 26,000 local units. The local

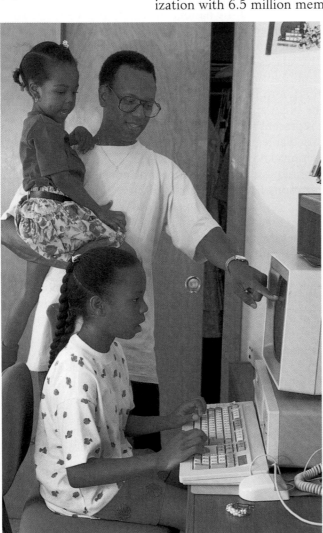

parent-teacher group, sometimes called the **parent-teacher organization (PTO),** may or may not be affiliated with the national PTA. Local groups devise their own organizations and activities to fit the needs of the local school community. Generally, they serve as a communications link between parents and the formal school organization, with teachers usually acting as representatives of the schools.

Formally, the school system ordinarily operates by means of down-the-line communications, from the superintendent to the principal, to the teacher, and then to the parents. Typically, school systems are less receptive to up-the-line communications from parents or teachers to administrators. But when the formal hierarchy does not respond to up-the-line communications in a satisfactory manner, parents and school officials can resort to an informal communications system in an attempt to get a better response.

An instance of informal communications occurred when the energetic principal of a New Haven, Connecticut, school in a low-income neighborhood galvanized the PTO in a campaign for a new school to replace the old one. When the city administration raised obstacles, the principal called together the PTO members and other neighborhood leaders to ask their support for the construction of a new school. Within twenty-four hours, they were exerting pressure on the city school board and the administration. Needless to say, the school was built.

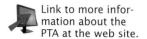
Link to more information about the PTA at the web site.

Most PTOs, however, are comparatively impotent in achieving educational aims. Educational reformers are concerned about the ineffectiveness of parent groups, because they know that reforms will last only if parents are actively involved in the work of their schools. Some states have actually passed legislation mandating that schools involve parents in school governance and in the education of the students.

ways to improve parental involvement

Many strategies can be used to increase parental involvement and improve the partnership between parents and teachers. These strategies include frequent parent-teacher conferences; homework hotlines on which parents can telephone the school to find out about homework assignments or communicate with teachers; workshops for parents that address a variety of topics; school volunteer programs; and school councils on which parents, teachers, and administrators discuss school policies and practices. Teachers and school administrators must be trained to overcome barriers to effective parental involvement and to create school environments where parents of all races, ethnicities, and social classes feel welcome.

> *A parent is the most important teacher a child ever has.*
> —JOAN BECK

Business

Throughout American history, concern about the quality of U.S. public education and its ability to produce workers with the knowledge and skills that business needs has prompted partnerships between educators and business executives. In particular, during the 1980s and 1990s, the business community was at the forefront of efforts to restructure public education. Business leaders have been substantially involved in almost every educational reform report. As a result, they have become both the strongest critics and the staunchest advocates for public education. The chief executive officers of such major corporations as Procter & Gamble, Xerox, Apple Computer, Eastman Kodak, Coca-Cola, IBM, RJR Nabisco, and many others have demanded and pushed for educational reforms in state capitals, the halls of Congress, and the White House. More than 100,000 business-school partnerships have been formed since 1983, and business has donated hundreds of millions of dollars to improve elementary and secondary schools. One major effort on the part of business to influence school reform is the Business Coalition for Educational Reform (BCER), a group of 13 national business organizations and more than 1300 local and state coalitions. The BCER supports efforts to raise academic standards for all students and to ensure that standards reflect the knowledge and skill needed for workplace success.[6] Further information on school restructuring efforts appears in the chapter entitled "How Should Education Be Reformed?".

business plays leading role in reform

education/economy link

Why should the business community show such interest? The initiatives to improve the quality of American education go beyond altruistic impulses. One source estimates that the education market represents potential revenue of $600 billion for corporate interests. With that kind of money involved, businesses would certainly like to make their presence known.[7] In addition, like the nation's governors, many business leaders are convinced that education reform is essential to the health of the American economy. Competition from Asian and European manufacturers in world markets, a massive U.S. trade deficit, and industry's perception that entry-level workers lack proper job skills have focused attention on educating the American work force. In fact, U.S. companies spend billions of dollars annually on remedial education for their workers.

Reading, Writing, . . . and Purchasing?

Students are a captive audience in public schools, and they have enormous purchasing power. Elementary-age children have about $15 billion per year to spend, and they influence another $160 billion of spending by their parents. Teenagers spend about $57 billion of their own money yearly. Commercial businesses pitch their wares to these children and youth in schools through a variety of marketing techniques. Here are a few examples from the Center for Commercial-Free Public Education:

- In Springboro, Ohio, one real estate agent created "ReMax Night" at the local high school, distributing free T-shirts and party balloons with the Re-Max logo on them.

- In Colorado Springs, Colorado, 7-Up and Burger King advertise on the sides of school buses.

- Clairol distributes free bags of shampoo to students as they leave school, along with surveys asking whether they had "a good or bad hair day."

- A Nike program asks young people to devote a week of classroom time to learning the life cycle of a Nike shoe. The curriculum fails to address the sweatshop portion of the manufacturing process.

- A Texas school roof features a Dr. Pepper logo that is visible from planes flying overhead.

- Dow Chemical's *Chem-TV* and *Chemapalooza* videos feature teenagers dancing and singing about the wonderful world of chemicals.

What other examples of commercialism can you think of that might affect students in public schools? Are you concerned about this trend? Why or why not?

Sources: Alex Molnar and Jennifer Morales, "Commercialism@ Schools," *Educational Leadership* (October 2000), pp. 39–44; Henry A. Giroux, "Education Incorporated?" *Educational Leadership*, 56, no. 2 (October 1998), p. 16; "A Word from Our Sponsor," *Virginia Journal of Education* (November 1998), p. 13.

business intrusion?

Reflect on school-business relationships with the image in this section of your CD-ROM.

Not everyone sees business involvement in education as totally positive. Some express concern that financial support from business will lead to business intrusion—that schools may be unduly shaped to meet business needs. Another concern centers on business's provision of free curriculum and instructional materials for teachers. Critics argue that corporate handouts are not just supplementary gifts but sophisticated marketing tools containing subtle and not-so-subtle messages to support the corporation's biases and promote brand identification and product loyalty. Some people cynically view business's push for the expanded use of technology in schools as an attempt to create a new market for computers and other educational technology.

Channel One controversy

Among the most controversial business ventures is Channel One, a commercial service that delivers ten minutes of high-quality news programming directly to public school classrooms free of cost in exchange for two minutes of advertising. A school that subscribes to the twelve-minute newscast receives a satellite dish, two videocassette recorders, a television set for every classroom in the building, and schoolwide cabling to hook it all together. By 2001 about 12,000 middle schools and high schools had signed on, reaching an estimated 8 million students, about 40 percent of the nation's twelve- to eighteen-year-olds.[8] Many educators have attacked the concept as gross commercialism and a dangerous precedent. One state superintendent, an opponent of Channel One,

The classroom is . . . a place in which the claims of various political, social, and economic interests are negotiated. The classroom is both a symbol and a product of deadly serious cultural bargaining.

—NEIL POSTMAN

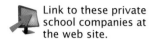

Link to these private school companies at the web site.

▨ *privatization*

▨ *cooperation or exploitation?*

▨ *increase of standardized testing*

states, "The problem is, they want us to sell access to our kids' minds, and we have no right, morally or ethically, to do that."[9] Supporters argue that the program rouses students' interest in current events, especially since many teenagers don't read newspapers. In addition, supporters argue, the equipment provided by Channel One enables schools to take advantage of other cable offerings, such as the Discovery Channel, Cable News Network, C-Span, and the Learning Channel. Are the advantages worth the cost? What do you think?

▨ **Privatization Efforts**   Another way business influences education is through the recent movement toward private management of public schools that has occurred in some urban areas. Private corporations such as the Edison Schools, TesseracT Group (formerly known as Educational Alternatives, Inc.), Advantage Schools, and Sylvan Learning, Inc., have contracted with some school districts to provide specific educational services, to operate schools whose students have been performing poorly on academic tests, or to begin new schools with promising designs. One private consulting firm that has tracked the rise of the education industry estimates that about 10 percent of the charter schools operating by the end of the twentieth century were managed by for-profit companies.[10] Advocates of this **privatization** movement argue that private corporations can operate these schools more effectively and less expensively. Opponents, especially teachers' unions, claim that schools operated under a profit motive may shortchange students' welfare in order to make money. They do this, the critics claim, by hiring inexperienced teachers, using unlicensed staff, and eliminating high-cost special education programs. To date, private management of public schools has often led to cleaner buildings, greater access to computers, and more individualized instruction, but the verdict is still out on whether they lead to academic improvement.

There is no question that the role of the business community in educational affairs has greatly expanded since the mid-1980s, and most people see this trend as positive. Businesses and corporations, with a vested stake in the outcomes of public education, will undoubtedly continue to be major players in the reform of our educational system. The challenge for educators will be to walk the line between partnerships and cooperation on the one hand and exploitation for commercial purposes on the other.

Standardized Testing

As programs for school improvement proliferated in the 1980s, the trend to assess the quality of schools and teachers by using standardized tests also grew in influence. Many states now require high school students to perform well on tests of general academic competence as a prerequisite for graduation, and almost all states require local public school districts to test students at some point(s) between grades one and twelve. The 2002 reauthorization of the Elementary and Secondary Education Act ("No Child Left Behind") requires states to test students each year between grades 3 and 8 if they wish to receive federal funds associated with this federal legislation. (This act is discussed in more detail later in the chapter.) Forty-five states require aspiring teachers to pass a state-prescribed, standardized test before entering a teacher education program and/or before being licensed to teach.[11]

■ *overemphasis on testing?*

Many educators and parents express grave concerns about what they think is an overemphasis on testing. Measuring school excellence by standardized tests poses a danger arising from the limited and simplistic nature of the tests. Evaluation experts warn that tests external to the schools can be limiting if schools pattern their curricula to conform to the content of the tests. Schools may fail to teach what is difficult to test. In some instances, the content and actual form of a test have become the curriculum itself as weeks of classroom drill have centered on previous versions of tests.

Reflect on authentic assessment with the image in this section of your CD-ROM.

Others worry that standardized tests overemphasize technical information and underemphasize educators' professional judgments about the worthiness of a school's programs. With a national call to stress more problem solving, critical thinking, and writing skills, educators see a contradiction in using standardized tests that don't measure these outcomes. They are calling for more *authentic assessment*—that is, using such things as actual specimens or examples of students' work to determine educational achievement.

■ *standards movement*

Currently, there is a strong movement in the United States for each state to create standards for student achievement linked to some form of assessment. More and more, policymakers believe that student achievement will not increase markedly until high standards are set and quality work by all students is expected and rewarded. Current standardized tests are seen as reflecting only minimum standards and as being insufficient to measure high learning outcomes. As individual states develop assessment tests that measure what students are expected to learn, the reliance on national standardized tests that are not coordinated with local and state curricula is likely to diminish.

PAUSE AND REFLECT

1 Did the schools you attended work in partnership with business and industry? Did your education prepare you for further education and entry into the work force? What, in your opinion, is an appropriate relationship between business and schools?

2 In your opinion, are the schools doing too much, the right amount, or too little testing of students? Why do you say this?

3 What do you think of Channel One? Do the benefits outweigh the drawbacks? Support your position.

■ *The Federal Government*

Although the federal government does not have formal authority over education, the judicial and executive branches of the government exercise considerable influence over schools in the country through court rulings and the activities of the U.S. Department of Education.

■ *strong court influence*

The Federal Courts   The history of education has been shaped by important court decisions on the duties and responsibilities of school officials in such areas as school desegregation, religion in the schools, student rights, and, particularly at the state level, school finance. The U.S. Supreme Court has played a particularly important role in changing educational policy in this country. Because its rulings have altered or reduced the power of state and local educational authorities, some of the Court's decisions have generated deep resentment among those who abhor this "federal intrusion" into states' rights. Other people

POLICY MATTERS!

Who Should Be Accountable for Getting Results?

What's the Policy?

As a condition for spending more money on elementary and secondary education, legislatures and state boards of education are increasingly demanding that educators be accountable for achieving results. No longer content to measure quality schooling by its inputs (school facilities, dollars spent, teacher-pupil ratios, number of books in school libraries, and educators' salaries, for example), policymakers in a number of states are insisting that educators get results, and results are narrowly construed as increased student achievement test scores. In many areas, school report cards are publicized to inform communities about how well their schools are performing in terms of test scores.

How Does It Affect Teachers?

Some states are implementing steps to reward educators whose schools produce more student learning than expected and punish those whose schools fail to meet the accepted standard. For example, in Virginia, by year 2006, 70 percent of the students in each school must successfully pass the statewide assessments of student learning for the school to maintain its accreditation. In other states, educators are being given pay bonuses if the students in their schools exceed expectations.

What Are the Pros?

Advocates of accountability argue that input measures are at best indirect and that the true test of a school's effectiveness is how well its students learn the knowledge and skills it is attempting to teach. They contend that only by looking at the results of students' schooling, as measured by student test scores, can we ascertain the worth of schools.

What Are the Cons?

Many educators are concerned about using test scores for accountability purposes. Should the quality of a school be judged on the basis of a single criterion, test scores? Should all schools be judged on the basis of the same test even if they differ dramatically in terms of the resources available and the challenges faced by the children they serve? Schools serving poorer communities face many more challenges in educating their students than do schools located in wealthier areas. Scores on these standardized tests may reflect the socioeconomic status of the communities served more than they indicate the quality of the schools.

What Do You Think?

1. **Do you think states should publicly issue school report cards that reflect how well students in a given school performed on statewide assessments of learning standards? What are the advantages and disadvantages of doing so?**

2. **Can each educator's contribution to a child's learning be determined and distinguished from that of other educators? If so, how?**

3. **How should other important learning outcomes for which schools are responsible, such as good citizenship, be taken into account in determining a school's effectiveness? Or should they?**

 Visit the web site to learn more about this policy issue.

applaud the Court's decisions as steps to make American education more responsive to broad democratic principles. The Court has issued rulings affecting such important educational policies as desegregation, public aid to private schools, rights of people with disabilities, gender equity, and sexual harassment. It recently upheld the constitutionality of the controversial Cleveland voucher

Federal legislation and federal court decisions have significantly affected education, including the education of children with such disabilities as deafness.

(© Will Hart/PhotoEdit)

plan. (See the chapter entitled "What Social Problems and Tension Points Affect Today's Students?" for a discussion of vouchers and public funding for private and religious schools.)

However, the courts alone, as powerful as they are, cannot do everything. Often judicial rulings need to be supported by federal administrative and legislative action. In the famous 1954 case of *Brown v. Board of Education of Topeka,* (discussed in more detail in the chapter on "What Is the History of American Education?"), the U.S. Supreme Court ruled that the doctrine of "separate but equal" had no place in public education. But how was this momentous judgment to be implemented? The Court declared that "all deliberate speed" should be employed to abolish the dual school system for African Americans and whites, but no judicial guidelines were developed to steer the process. As a result, for a decade, almost no changes occurred until the 1960s, when a combination of new congressional laws on civil rights and education and strong enforcement of desegregation by President Lyndon Johnson's administration took place. See the chapter entitled "What Are the Ethical and Legal Issues Facing Teachers?" for a more detailed discussion of the impact of Supreme Court decisions on American education.

■ *enforcement necessary*

Read *Brown v. Board of Education* in the text resources on your CD-ROM.

Link to the Department of Education from the web site.

■ **The U.S. Department of Education**   The Department of Education is a significant part of the federal government, with cabinet-level status and a discretionary budget of about $49 billion in fiscal year 2002. The department administers a variety of programs passed by Congress, including programs concerned with elementary and secondary education, postsecondary education, educational research and development, vocational and adult education, special education, and civil rights. It also administers funds devoted to the collection of educational statistics. In addition, billions of additional federal dollars for education are administered by other federal agencies, such as the Department of Health and Human Services, the National Science Foundation, and the Department of Defense.

■ *fluctuating federal involvement*

The federal government's level of involvement in education often fluctuates depending on whether Republicans or Democrats control the White House and Congress and on the particular ideology professed by the party in power. Republicans generally have sought to decrease the involvement of the federal government in education, even advocating abolition of the U.S. Department of Education, whereas Democrats tend to be more supportive of both the department and federal efforts to improve education. However, under President George W. Bush, the federal government's share of costs for elementary and secondary education have increased from 7 percent to almost 8 percent by 2002. As we'll see in the next section of this chapter, much of this money has been allocated for the raising of standards and for accountability measures.

PAUSE AND REFLECT

1 What other groups, besides those listed, influence education?

How Are Schools Financed?

The total amount of money available to a school district for education is the sum of locally raised revenues, state aid, federal aid, and miscellaneous revenues. During much of the country's history, most of the money used to support public elementary and secondary schools came from local revenue sources, primarily the property tax. But from the late 1970s to the present, for the first time in American history, the states' share of support for public education exceeded the local share (Figure 10.2). Increased state revenues have helped offset the decreases in local funding of the schools. Currently state governments contribute about 50 percent, local governments offer about 42 percent, and the federal government provides almost 8 percent toward the financing of public schools.[12]

■ *funding percentages vary*

The percentage of revenue received from federal, state, and local sources varies considerably from state to state. Federal contributions for public education

Figure 10.2
Percentage of Revenues Received from Federal, State, and Local Sources for Public Elementary and Secondary Schools

Sources: *Rankings and Estimates: Estimates of School Statistics 2002* (Washington, D.C.: National Education Association, 2002), p. 81.

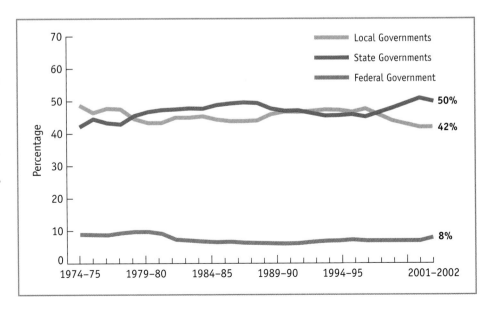

Where Does the United States Stand on Education Funding?

Many politicians, arguing against the need for increased spending on education, assert that the United States already spends more on public education than do most comparable countries but gets worse results. "Money is not the answer," they claim.

We can shed some light on the debate by comparing U.S. educational spending with that of some other countries. To allow for differences in size of the economies, we can consider public spending on education as a percentage of gross domestic product (GDP), the total value of a country's output. The United States spends 3.74 percent of its GDP on elementary and secondary education, roughly the average of the twenty-five industrialized countries sampled. Countries that spend more than the United States include Norway (4.4), Denmark (4.3), Sweden (4.5), Switzerland (4.5), France (4.4), and Portugal (4.2). Countries spending less than the United States include Japan (3.0), Ireland (3.3), Mexico (3.5), and the Netherlands (3.1). Surprisingly, Japan ranks below the United States, spending 3.0 percent.

Such figures indicate that the United States devotes the same percentage of its resources to elementary and secondary education as the average of other industrialized nations. However, the United States might be expected to spend proportionally more than other countries because of certain characteristics of our school system and society. Our decentralized school system is more expensive than the single, centrally administered system that characterizes many of the other industrialized nations. Our population is more diverse than most countries', thus presenting unique educational challenges, and the very high number of U.S. children living in poverty creates additional demands for schools. Also, the United States, compared with the other countries, spends a much greater percentage of its public education funds (17 percent) on special education services. Given these factors, our percentage of GDP spent on elementary and secondary education does not seem extravagant.

Sources: Organization of Economic Cooperation and Development, *Education at a Glance 2001*. Available at: **http://www1.oecd.org/els/education/ei/eag/list.htm**; Richard Rothstein with Karen Hawley Miles, *Where's the Money Gone?* (Washington, DC: Economic Policy Institute, 1995), p. 8.

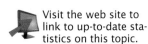 Visit the web site to link to up-to-date statistics on this topic.

range from a high of 14 percent for Mississippi to a low of less than 4 percent for New Hampshire and New Jersey. Local contributions to revenues range from a high of almost 85 percent for New Hampshire to a low of less than 1 percent for Hawaii, which has a statewide school district. Other than Hawaii, which gets 89 percent of its school funding from the state, the state receiving the highest proportion of revenues from state sources is New Mexico, at 72 percent, and the lowest is New Hampshire, at 9 percent.[13] Let's look in more detail at state and local spending and funding patterns.

■ *School Spending*

■ *rising expenditures per pupil*

Figure 10.3 shows the upward trend in average expenditure per pupil in daily attendance. The nationwide average stood at $7,079 per pupil for 2000–2001.[14] From state to state, however, the per-pupil expenditures vary widely (Figure 10.4), ranging from more than $13,078 per pupil each year to $4,374. The reason for these differences is primarily economic. A state's ability to pay for education depends on the income level of its residents and corporations. In general, the southern states fund education at lower levels than the northern states. As a result of lower funding, are students who live in some of the Sunbelt states be-

Figure 10.3
Expenditures per Pupil

Source: Data in current dollars from *Projections of Education Statistics to 2011* (Washington, DC: U.S. Department of Education, National Center for Education Statistics, 2001), Table 34, p. 89.

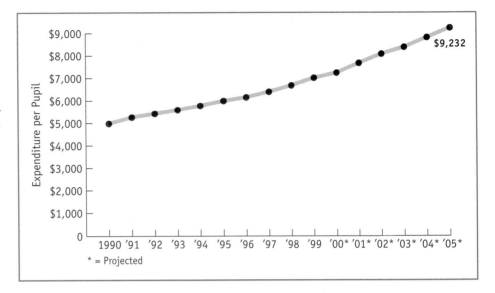

ing deprived of a quality education? The connection between funding and excellence of education is often disputed, but a group of researchers from the University of Chicago, after reanalyzing thirty-two studies on this issue, concluded that higher per-pupil expenditures, better teacher salaries, more educated and experienced teachers, and smaller class and school sizes—all directly a result of higher funding—are strongly related to improved student learning.[15]

■ *State and Local Funding*

How is money raised to pay for educational expenditures, and by what systems of taxation? State revenue systems are as diverse as school finance plans and

© Steve Breen/Asbury Park Press 1997. Reprinted by permission of Copley News Service.

Figure 10.4
Average Expenditure per Pupil, by State, 2001–02, Based on Fall Enrollment

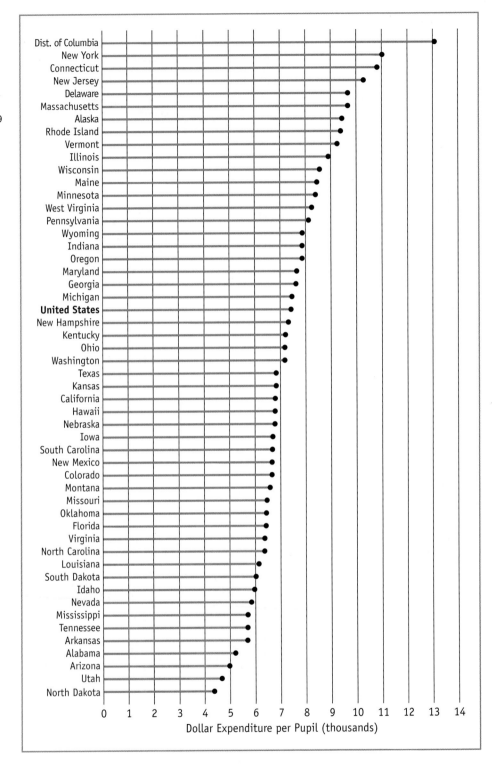

VOICES FROM THE CLASSROOM

Vidya Bhat graduated from the University of Virginia in 2001, and at the time of this writing is a first-year teacher in the New York City public schools.

Funding Differences Between School Districts

I am a second-grade teacher in New York City, and as a first-year teacher, I find that my expectations of teaching and the realities that I experience are worlds apart.

In September, I imagined a bright cheery classroom filled with beautiful students, as well as a plethora of books, paper, and other necessary educational supplies. Instead, I received an overcrowded classroom, barren of any sort of teaching materials. Much to my chagrin, my situation still remains the same, and it is now April. Although I have some curriculum materials for math, I still do not possess any textbooks for science, social studies, or language arts. More importantly, I have very little quality children's literature to spark my students' interest in reading.

I, like the majority of the teachers in my school, purchase everything from loose-leaf paper to chalk. Because my school does not permit the faculty to use the office's one and only copy machine, I have to pay for all of my own photocopies. While it is a known fact that no one goes into teaching for the money, it is surely disheartening to think that my administration believes it to be okay that teachers have to forgo parts of their salaries toward getting the basics for their classrooms.

The "reason" why I do not have books or supplies, as explained to me by a school staff developer, is simply that there were no school aides hired to unpack and distribute the books and supplies that reside in the supply room. Now, I cannot tell you how many times I have tried to get into that supply room! However, my attempts have been completely unsuccessful. The staff developer further explained that according to our union, teachers and administrators cannot unpack and distribute supplies because it isn't part of our contract, and theoretically, it would be taking away a position from a school aide that would potentially be hired to do that job.

On the bright side, I have a wonderful group of students who are eager to learn. I truly believe in the power of the self-fulfilling prophecy, which is why I do not let my teaching situation depress me. I need to maintain my fresh and positive outlook on the profession so I can make sure that I give my students all the tools they need to succeed. When my older colleagues tell me that I should circulate my résumé in elementary schools outside New York City, I often think about what it would be like to teach in the suburbs. More money, more supplies, more support . . . seems like a teacher's dream. Then I come back to reality and remember my students, who have a classroom with very few books and supplies, and then it finally dawns on me. If all the young teachers leave the urban schools flocking to the comforts of the suburbs, then who will teach New York City's kids?

 Visit the web site for more Voices from the Classroom.

■ *sources of revenue*

reflect the socioeconomic makeup, the political climate, and the educational needs of each state. State governments use a combination of sales, personal income, corporate income, and excise taxes to generate revenues. Some states fund their schools partly with income from state-run lotteries. Local governments, in contrast, rely primarily on the property tax for income. Most states require the citizens in a school district to vote either on the property tax rate to support education or on the school budget itself.

■ *Michigan reform*

In an unprecedented move, in 1993 the Michigan legislature voted to eliminate local property taxes as a source of revenue for the public schools. Many observers called the action *bold,* whereas others termed it *reckless.* What made the action so controversial was the fact that the Michigan legislature at that time lacked an alternative funding system to replace the $6.3 billion in local property tax funds for schools. State leaders planned to use the self-inflicted crisis to dramatically recast the existing school finance system, which left great gaps in spending power between wealthy and poor school districts. By 1994, the voters of Michigan had voted to increase the state sales tax by 50 percent and raise taxes on cigarettes to replace the greatly reduced property tax, thus permitting the state to reallocate state resources to poorer school districts. Other states have followed the Michigan example of less reliance on local property taxes.

■ *unequal funding*

Why would districts want to rely less heavily on property taxes? Many knowledgeable educators and politicians argue that one of the greatest causes of unequal educational opportunity is the method used to finance school systems. Because of local districts' heavy reliance on property taxes, districts where property values are high generate much more money to finance their schools than districts where property values are low. Within the same state, for example, the average amount of money spent per child in one district may be more than three times the amount spent in a nearby district. Such spending differentials result in great educational disparities, as measured by pupil-teacher ratios, training and experience of staff, and availability of facilities, equipment, and counseling services.

■ *School Finance Reform and the Courts*

As a result of numerous court decisions, efforts to equalize the disparities in funding within states have shifted some of the responsibility for funding from local school districts to the state level. In 1971, pupils and their parents filed a class action suit, *Serrano* v. *Priest,* against California state and county officials concerned with financing public schools. The suit charged that the state's school-financing scheme was unconstitutional. The Supreme Court of California supported the parents' claim that the quality of a child's education must not be a function of wealth other than the wealth of the state as a whole. The court also held that the California system of financing schools on the basis of local property taxes violated the Fourteenth Amendment to the U.S. Constitution, which provides equal protection of the law for all citizens.

■ *Serrano* v. Priest

In 1973, however, the Supreme Court of the United States, by a five-to-four vote, reversed a similar decision (known as the *Rodriguez* case) involving the school finance system of the state of Texas. The Court found that the U.S. Constitution was not violated because the right to an education is not guaranteed explicitly or implicitly by the Constitution. Although *federal* law had not been violated, the Court did indicate that the finding should not be interpreted as a victory for the status quo. In effect, issues of inequity in school finance were returned to the province of the state courts and legislatures. Many state constitutions, unlike the U.S. Constitution, contain equal protection clauses that can be interpreted to include education as a protected right.

■ *equality as state concern*

Since the *Rodriguez* case, other state courts have ruled that their school financing systems violate their state constitutions. In those states where the finance system has been ruled unconstitutional, the issue has centered on inadequacies in the level of educational opportunities offered to children in the poorer school districts. The courts in those states examined whether the poor children were receiving a sufficient education as required by the state constitution and as measured by contemporary education standards or by comparisons with the best or highest-spending districts. In contrast, in states where the system of school finance was upheld, the courts usually interpreted their state constitutions as guaranteeing only a basic minimum level of funding.[16] As a result of court challenges, more than twenty states have reformed their school finance laws since 1973.

pressures for equality

Reflect on equitable school funding with the image in this section of your CD-ROM.

Educators, parents, and public officials are greatly concerned that the quality of a child's education should not depend on whether the child lives in a school district with high property values. Many of these concerned citizens are urging that state governments become responsible for raising educational revenue and distributing the full costs of local schools to the school districts. The school districts would continue to be in charge of the operation of the local schools but would no longer carry the burden of raising needed money.

PAUSE AND REFLECT

1 Of the methods of school financing discussed in this chapter (local property taxes, state financing through statewide taxes, and state-run lotteries), which do you believe is most equitable? Why?

2 Do you believe state governments should redistribute money from rich to poor school districts through state taxing power? Why or why not?

Federal Funding

Although the federal government typically provides much less money for public schools than do state or local governments, federal funds are strategically important and have a far greater impact than their proportion of school funding would suggest.

categorical aid

Funding in the Past Much of federal aid to education traditionally has been in the form of **categorical grants**—that is, the money must be spent for designated purposes (or categories) that are stated generally in the legislation and more precisely by the federal agency administering the funds. As a result, the federal government has been able to influence school districts and institutions that have accepted or sought its aid. For example, to qualify for federal funds to improve its reading program, a school district would have to conform to the guidelines and restrictions accompanying the money. Many financially stricken school districts have been grateful for additional funds, regardless of the regulations they carry.

strong funding, 1960–80

During the period from 1960 to 1980, federal education programs thrived. The federal government's share of elementary and secondary school revenues increased from 4.4 to 9.8 percent during this period.[17] Congressional acts provided money to colleges, cities, states, and agencies to finance a wide variety of projects, including construction of buildings and other educational facilities; improvement of instruction or administration; development of educational personnel, including teachers and paraprofessionals, particularly for high-poverty areas; provision of loans for prospective teachers; and funding for educational research.

During President Reagan's administration (1981–89), categorical grant programs were largely replaced by block grants to state and local education agencies. **Block grants** are sums of money that come with only minimal federal restrictions and are transferred from the federal government to the state governments as a block of money rather than by categories. Moreover, the Reagan administration successfully held the line on federal expenditures for education. These changes reflected the belief of President Reagan, and of many other Republicans, that the federal government should play a reduced role in educational policymaking. In fact, the federal government's share of support for public education fell from 9.8 percent in 1980 to 6.1 percent in 1990, but by 2002 had climbed back to slightly less than 8 percent (see Figure 10.2). Today the federal government employs both categorical and block grant programs.

■ *block grants*

■ *federal role increases with "No Child Left Behind" Act*

■ **"No Child Left Behind" Act of 2001**   In 2002, President Bush signed into law the revised Elementary and Secondary Education Act (ESEA), also known as the "No Child Left Behind" Act of 2001. The act is the main federal law on K–12 education, and the revision greatly increases the federal role in education by putting into place requirements that will reach into virtually every public school in the country. It calls for required statewide reading and mathematics tests every year in grades 3–8 beginning in the 2005–2006 school year, a "highly qualified" teacher in every classroom, and demonstrable progress toward academic proficiency within 12 years by all their students in every state and school district. The law also puts pressure on school districts to turn around low-performing schools with a series of consequences for schools that persistently fail to improve. The law was accompanied by the largest dollar increase ever in federal education aid, more than 6.7 billion additional dollars for fiscal year 2002. (See the boxed insert on the next page for more details on the provisions of this act.)

■ *mixed reactions to "No Child Left Behind" Act*

Reactions of educators around the country to the "No Child Left Behind" Act have been mixed. Although greatly appreciating the increased funding for public education, some of the provisions of the act bothered many educators, particularly the increased emphasis on testing and the lack of attention to increased spending for special education. As one school district superintendent stated: "I have the same concern you're probably going to hear from a lot of educators: this mad rush for testing. . . . It's such a narrow band of information that they're going to use to make crucial judgments."[18]

Others are concerned because ESEA fails to provide funds for special education services that schools are required by federal law to provide. As one superintendent stated, "Probably the best thing that the federal government could do right now is fund the additional $5 million in special education costs that my district has to pay each year as a result of federal mandates on special education."[19]

■ *urban school districts will benefit from Title I*

Educators from urban school districts expressed enthusiasm for how federal aid is distributed under the Title I program for disadvantaged students—the largest ESEA program (see more on Title I in the following section). The act provides extra funding for school districts with high concentrations of poor children, and urban areas are estimated to see increases of at least 30 percent in Title I aid. High poverty rural areas will also see significant gains.

■ **Compensatory Education**   Although the federal government provides money for a variety of educational programs, its most significant efforts have been to address the needs of children from high-poverty areas who are at risk for

"No Child Left Behind" Act Key Provisions

On January 8, 2002, President George W. Bush signed into law the No Child Left Behind Act of 2001 (NCLB). This new law contains the most sweeping changes to the Elementary and Secondary Education Act (ESEA) since it was enacted in 1965. It changes the federal government's role in K–12 education by asking America's schools to describe their success in terms of what each student accomplishes. The act contains the President's four basic education reform principles: stronger accountability for results, increased flexibility and local control, expanded options for parents, and an emphasis on teaching methods that have been proven to work. Major provisions of the law include the following areas.

Annual Testing

By the 2005–06 school year, states must begin administering annual, statewide assessments in reading and mathematics to students in grades 3–8. States may select and design their own assessments, but the tests must be aligned with state academic standards. By 2007–08, states must administer science assessments once during each of the three levels of schooling: elementary, middle, and high school. Test results must include individual student scores and be reported by race, income, and other categories to measure not just overall trends, but also gaps between, and progress of, various subgroups.

Academic Improvement

States must set a minimum performance threshold and, within 12 years, all students must attain this level of proficiency. Each state must raise the level of proficiency gradually, but in equal increments over time, leading to 100 percent proficiency. If a school fails to make adequate progress for two consecutive years, the school will receive technical assistance from the district and must provide public school choice to the students. If inadequate progress continues, then more drastic consequences ensue, including possible reconstitution of the school.

Teacher and Paraprofessional Qualifications

All teachers hired under Title I, beginning in fall 2002, must be "highly qualified," which means that a teacher has been licensed (including alternative routes) and has demonstrated a high level of competence in the subjects that he or she teaches. By the end of the 2005–06 school year, every public school teacher must be "highly qualified."

 Read the *No Child Left Behind Act* in the text resources of your CD-ROM.

Source: "An ESEA Primer," *Education Week*, January 9, 2002, pp. 28–29.

---

educational failure. **Compensatory education** is an approach to creating more equal educational opportunities for disadvantaged children. In particular, compensatory education attempts to overcome a student's learning problems by incorporating extra education into the regular school program or, to keep such problems from developing, by providing students with appropriate preschool programs. The most famous preschool initiative is **Head Start,** a federal program that aims to improve the learning skills, social skills, and health status of poor children so that they can begin schooling on an equal basis with their more advantaged peers. For the 2002 fiscal year, the federal government budgeted more than $6.5 billion for Head Start programs. Since its inception in 1965, Head Start has served over 20 million children.[20]

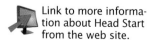 Link to more information about Head Start from the web site.

Head Start programs target children who are "at risk" of school failure by intervening in their early years to improve their skills.

(© Syracuse Newspapers/Gary Walts/The Image Works)

■ *varieties of programs*

Compensatory programs come in many forms. Some help parents learn how to interact more effectively with their babies and young children in the areas of cognitive and psychosocial development. Some programs like Head Start emphasize early intervention and target children who are "at risk" for later school failure. Other compensatory programs target older children and focus on basic skill instruction, tutoring, or remediation in a variety of academic areas. Dropout prevention programs, job training, and adult literacy instruction are all attempts to help older individuals improve the quality of their lives through education and to help prevent the cycle of educational disadvantage from being passed down through generations.

Link to more information about Title I from the web site.

Title I   As described earlier in this section, the **Elementary and Secondary Education Act (ESEA)** authorized the federal government's single largest investment in elementary and secondary education. Compensatory education was formalized in Title I of the original ESEA in 1965. Congress continues to strongly support Title I because the money reaches almost every school district and thus provides jobs and services in every congressional district. Few members of Congress will vote against providing these benefits to their districts. **Title I** was designed to do two things: (1) deliver federal funds to local school districts and schools for the education of students from low-income families and (2) supplement the educational services provided to low-achieving students in those districts. Subsequent reauthorizations of ESEA have changed the rules for

■ *Title I requirements*

schools that receive Title I funds. To receive money, states and school districts must submit a state improvement plan that includes the adoption of challenging content standards and aligned assessments for Title I students. Schools are now allowed to use their Title I funds on a schoolwide basis rather than only for the poorest students, and they can combine money from multiple federal programs. However, school districts must now rank their schools based on their percent-

Success for All

One compensatory education program that is quite successful is the Success for All program developed by the Center for Research on Effective Schooling for Disadvantaged Students at Johns Hopkins University. The Success for All program restructures the elementary school with one goal in mind: to ensure that all students perform at grade level in reading, writing, and mathematics by the end of third grade.

Success for All schools offer a half-day of preschool and a full day of kindergarten, both focused on providing a developmentally appropriate learning experience for children. The curriculum emphasizes the development and use of language and balances academic readiness with music, art, and movement activities. The program also implements the center's research findings on one-to-one tutoring, regrouping for reading, family support teams, frequent assessments of learning with immediate help on problems, and the use of an effective reading program. Two social workers and one parent liaison work full time in the schools to provide parenting education and to encourage parents to support their children's efforts.

The program also includes tutors for children in grades K–3. Each tutor is a certified, experienced teacher or paraprofessional who works one-on-one with eleven students per day. First-graders get priority for tutoring.

Evaluation results have been outstanding, much higher than for any other intervention strategy ever tried with at-risk students. Starting with one Baltimore school in 1987, the Success for All program had spread to more than 1,800 schools in 48 states, serving more than 1 million students by 2002, and it has produced dramatic gains in students' reading proficiency. Almost all Success for All programs are in high-poverty, Title I schools. Early programs were more expensive than regular instruction, but that situation seems to have changed. By restructuring elementary schools and reconfiguring the uses of Title I money, special education, and other funds to emphasize prevention and early intervention rather than remediation, the administrators have brought costs in Success for All schools in line with those of other schools that have access to these resources.

The major lesson learned, say Robert Slavin and his colleagues, is that disadvantaged children can routinely achieve substantially greater success in schools that are neither exceptional nor extraordinary. Rather than having to depend on the outstanding principal or charismatic teacher to ensure success, every child, regardless of background, has an excellent opportunity to succeed in school.

In spite of its success in teaching students to read, many teachers don't like the program because it tells them exactly what to do throughout their lessons. In essence, they are asked to follow a fast-paced script written by the Success for All researchers. For some teachers, this process seems contrary to their beliefs about the importance of paying attention to the learning style of each child and varying their instruction accordingly.

 Link to Success for All from the web site.

Sources: Robert Slavin, "Success for All." In *Encyclopedia of Education*, 2nd ed., ed. James W. Guthrie (New York: Macmillan Reference, U.S.A., 2003); Robert E. Slavin and Nancy A. Madden (Eds.), *Success for All: Research and Reform in Elementary Education* (Mahwah, N.J.: Lawrence Erlbaum Associates, 2001); Success for All brochure produced by the Success for All Program, Johns Hopkins University, Baltimore; Jay Mathews, "As Schools Shop for Success, Teachers Rethink Role," *The Washington Post*, June 21, 1999, pp. A1, A8.

ages of poor students and distribute Title I funds accordingly, with the poorest schools receiving the most money per pupil. As mentioned above, the "No Child Left Behind" Act of 2001 will boost Title I funding for school districts with high concentrations of poor children by changing the funding formula.

Between 1965 and 2002, Title I provided about $150 billion for educational services in almost all of the nation's school districts. Title I now provides more than $10 billion each year on behalf of more than 12.5 million children in

47,700 schools and is the largest federal investment in our public schools. Of the 12.5 million Title I students, about two-thirds are enrolled in grades one through six. Hispanic-American students make up 29 percent; African-American students, 29 percent; Asian-American students, 3 percent; Native-American students, 2 percent, and white students, 35 percent of those receiving Title I support. Title I grants serve about 1.5 million preschool and kindergarten children; 167,000 private school children; some 100,000 students identified as homeless; and about 2 million students with limited English proficiency.[21] In spite of what seems like an enormous amount of money, only about 50 percent of all eligible children receive services from Title I funds. Because Title I has never been funded at a high enough level to meet the needs of low-income schools and because its resources are widely dispersed, even the recent funding increases have not checked the growing educational crisis in low-income areas.

■ *insufficient funding*

■ *evaluations mixed*

Evaluations and Controversies   Evaluations of Title I programs and Head Start have been mixed. The earliest hopes—that compensatory education would increase student IQ scores and scholastic achievement—have not realized significant results. However, long-range studies that have followed students from preschool to age nineteen, like the study of students in the very successful Perry Preschool Program in Ypsilanti, Michigan, provide other indicators of program success. Effective early childhood programs may result in fewer special education placements, more high school graduations, lower teen pregnancy rates, increased employment and earnings, fewer crimes committed, and greater commitment to marriage.[22] *Early intervention*—beginning the program early in the child's life—may provide the key to success in compensatory education programs.

■ *early intervention a key*

■ *Title I reforms called for*

Critics of Title I see little point in strengthening programs that they believe have failed to meet their original goals. Proponents of compensatory education programs argue that, considering the enormity of the problem, expenditures thus far are a mere drop in the bucket. They also argue that a simultaneous attack must be made on external factors that contribute to low achievement, such as poor housing, family instability, and low income. Some argue that instead of spending the money to hire teachers and aides to provide remedial services, programs they maintain haven't worked effectively, schools receiving Title I money should incorporate proven school improvement models, such as Success for All (see the box on the previous page) or James Comer's School Development Program model (see the chapter entitled "Who Are Today's Students in a Diverse Society?").

Proponents can also point to recent gains in achievement. A 1999 national assessment of Title I showed that Title I schools were making positive gains in reading and mathematics. The report concluded that Title I schools are benefiting from improved resource targeting, improving alignment of curriculum with standards, and a more cohesive school program through greater use of school-wide goals and clarification of parent roles. Although the performance of students in high-poverty schools is improving, they remain much further behind their peers in meeting basic standards of performance in both reading and mathematics. The report urges that schools continue to focus on standards for learning, align the curriculum with the standards, reduce instructional reliance on paraprofessionals, and strengthen parent involvement.[23]

Both sides acknowledge that not all programs are equally effective. The best programs achieve desired results, whereas the less effective programs do not seem to have lasting effects on student performance.

A Final Word

What is the outlook for the future? The long period of economic prosperity during the mid- and late 1990s left the federal government with unanticipated surplus tax revenues. As a result, federal contributions to education increased, including new programs designed to prepare teachers to use technology effectively. However, the economic recession of 2001 has reduced federal revenues so continued increases in education spending will be harder to achieve in the near run. Even with the recent increase in federal money for education, the main action for education reform will continue to be in the states' arenas. The federal government's role in education is likely to be that of an active but minor partner.

▪ *states will remain key funders*

KEY TERMS

block grants (356)

categorical grants (355)

chief state school officer (336)

compensatory education (357)

Elementary and Secondary Education Act (ESEA) (358)

Head Start (357)

local school board (337)

parent-teacher organization (PTO) (342)

privatization (345)

site-based decision making (341)

state board of education (335)

state department of education (336)

superintendent of schools (337)

Title I (358)

FOR REFLECTION

❶ The National Education Association and the National Association of Secondary School Principals make this statement about successful secondary schools: "In good secondary schools, the principal and teachers develop and maintain a variety of cooperative links with the community. Family and community involvement and support complement the efforts of the school." Describe some of the cooperative links you would suggest at either the elementary or secondary level.

❷ What role do you think the federal government should play in compensating for educational disadvantages as a result of poverty?

FOR FURTHER INFORMATION

PRINT RESOURCES

Vern Brimley, Jr., and Rulon R. Garfield. *Financing Education in a Climate of Change,* 8th ed. (Boston: Allyn and Bacon, 2002).

This comprehensive text examines how schools are financed in this country, the role of the federal government, and significant court cases affecting school finance.

Susan Moore Johnson, *Leading to Change: The Challenge of the New Superintendency* (San Francisco: Jossey-Bass, 1996).

In this text, the author studies twelve superintendents, their models of leadership, and how contexts influence their behavior.

Jonathan Kozol, *Savage Inequalities: Children in America's Schools* (New York: HarperPerennial, 1992).

National Book Award winner Jonathan Kozol presents his shocking account of the American educational system in this best-selling book.

Frederick M. Wirt and Michael W. Kirst, *The Political Dynamics of American Education* (Berkeley, CA: McCutchan, 1997).

This text presents an analysis of the politics of education by two leaders in the field.

WEB RESOURCES

U.S. Department of Education. Available at: **http://www.ed.gov**.

This home page will keep you abreast of educational initiatives of the federal government. Clicking on the National Center for Education Statistics link (under Programs and Services) will give you access to many government publications and statistics on education. For information on Head Start, use **http://www2.acf.dhhs.gov/programs/hsb/**.

National Education Association. Available at: **http://www.nea.org**.

The NEA web site offers many resources, including an annual report on Rankings and Estimates that features many statistics on the states, including average teacher salaries, per pupil expenditures by state, per capita expenditure on education, and many other interesting statistics. To find the report, go to the Search function and enter "Rankings and Estimates."

Education Commission of the States. Available at: **http://www.ecs.org**.

The Education Commission of the States (ECS) is an interstate compact created in 1965 to improve public education by facilitating the exchange of information, ideas, and experiences among state policymakers and education leaders. ECS produces many policy papers on education issues affecting state policymakers. Go to "Education Issues" and select a particular issue for a review of what's known about the issue. Issues are far ranging, including charter schools, child abuse, brain research, technology, desegregation, and early childhood, among others.

How Should Education Be Reformed?

Chapter Preview This chapter gives you a concentrated look at the educational reform movement. For more than twenty years, politicians and educators have been working vigorously on the latest attempt to alter the course of American elementary and secondary education. Though results have been mixed to date, certain patterns and key educational ideas are evident.

This chapter emphasizes that:

- Reform has been a part of American education for the past one hundred years.

- The current educational reform movement is being fueled by a widespread belief that our schools are not educating students adequately for the demands of our current time, let alone the future.

- Although most people agree that schools should educate students to be good citizens, workers, and people, differing educational philosophies and beliefs about purposes of schooling lead to a variety of different approaches to schooling.

- Some key educational ideas *ought* to be at the heart of this current reform movement.

- Responsibility for school reform resides primarily with state educational agencies, with significant contributions from the federal government, national associations, and local educational agencies.

- Teachers are the crucial element in meaningful reform.

It has been said that trying to change our schools is like trying to change a flat tire on a speeding car—something that needs to be done but is nearly impossible to achieve. For nearly one hundred years, attempts have been made to bring about change in American schools, with mixed results. Many of these reform efforts have been fueled by philosophical debates as to what the purpose of schools should be (see the chapter entitled "What Is a School and What Is It For?"). For example, in the early 1900s, with the development of factories, which were seen as a more efficient way of producing goods, some people argued that *students* could be more efficiently educated if schools looked and functioned more like factories. They also thought that students would become better adult workers if their schools were more like factories. Opponents (including John Dewey, who is profiled in the chapter entitled "What Are the Philosophical Foundations of American Education?") thought that schools should educate students to be good thinkers and citizens who, as adults, would work to bring about a better, more equitable society.

The most influential recent movement to bring about change in our schools grew out of a 1983 report by the National Commission on Excellence in Education entitled, *A Nation At Risk*. In clear and forceful language, the Commission described what it called a "rising tide of mediocrity" in the schools and demanded that it be stemmed through a greater focus on the academic achievement of students. In the twenty years since this report was released, some progress has been made toward reforming schools. How much more can or must be made is open to debate. Some educators argue that much more still needs to be done to improve our schools, since the reforms implemented to date have not led to many gains in student outcomes. Others disagree, stating that our schools are a great social achievement in that we educate more children to higher levels than any other society in the world. Citing the generous amounts of money Americans spend on the education of their young (in 2000, elementary and secondary education funding represented 3.74 percent of the U.S. gross domestic product), they argue that dropout rates are as low as they have ever been.[1] They are encouraged by good news such as significant gains reported among African-American and Hispanic students in mathematics during the early 1990s and gains in high school completion rates among African Americans, which now nearly equal those of white, non-Hispanics.[2]

Other skeptics believe that the schools, particularly the public schools, are incapable of being reformed. They argue that schools, as institutions, are deeply resistant to change and that unlike corporations, whose effectiveness can be judged by bottom-line profits or losses, the effectiveness of schools is all but impossible to measure, in part because their purposes remain multiple. Without a single, clear definition of a well-educated person, schools cannot agree on how to reform themselves.

Still others oppose all these efforts at change, arguing that childhood is childhood and that school should provide continuity and stability in a society in constant flux. Schools fulfill this specific function well and therefore do not need to be reformed. In short, these defenders of the schools ask, "If it ain't broke, why fix it?" Nevertheless, those in favor of serious school reform vastly outnumber these voices of caution and opposition.

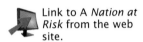

Link to A *Nation at Risk* from the web site.

■ *debate about need for reform*

PAUSE AND REFLECT

❶ What do you believe are the most compelling reasons to reform American schools?

② What current strengths of our schools could be weakened by the current reform trends?

■ *major motivations for reform*

To receive a proper education is the source and root of all goodness.

—PLUTARCH

One educator captured the views of many when he wrote that a good school respects and keeps in balance the need "to educate the 'three people' in each individual: the citizen, the worker, and the private person."[3] Using this breakdown, we can categorize the major motivations to reform our educational system as follows:

To develop a democratic citizen, the following must be done:

- There are dramatic differences between the schools serving the children of the rich and those serving the children of the poor.

- Disturbingly high percentages of students know nothing about our democratic traditions and how our government functions.

- There is little understanding of the world and the global role and responsibility of the United States.

To develop the good worker:

- Our way of life and our individual standard of living are closely linked to our nation's ability to maintain its economic leadership, a leadership that is seriously threatened by the comparatively low level of knowledge and skills demonstrated by the graduates of our schools in mathematics, science, and vocational education.

- The world of work is rapidly being transformed, and schools are not keeping pace. As Americans cope with an information age, many of our schools are still trapped in a horse-and-buggy approach to teaching and learning.

To develop the good person:

- Our children seem to be failing to develop a "moral compass" and the personal habits of responsibility, diligence, kindness, and courage that are associated with mature adulthood.

- Too many students are concerned with personal gain and individual rights rather than the well-being of their community and society.

Keeping in mind these three goals (which are also the three purposes of schooling we discussed in the chapter entitled "What Is a School and What Is It For?") as a basis for reform, we now turn to how our schools ought to be reformed.

PAUSE AND REFLECT

❶ Before addressing the *what* and *how* issues of school reform, we should consider the question of *ought:* What *ought* to be the nature of this reform? Take a moment now and reflect on your own education. Drawing on what you see as the primary purpose of schooling, make a short list of current aspects of schooling that you believe need to be reformed. Your answer should be driven by a view of what we want our schools to achieve, including a set of goals and a realistic plan. (It is crucial for a builder to have goals and a plan before starting a project.)

What Ought to Be the Elements of Educational Reform?

■ A Call for Excellence

■ *the call to excellence*

Underlying all the experimental programs, curriculum innovation, and other efforts for school improvement is the commitment to *excellence*. From the Sputnik crisis in the late 1950s to the 1983 report by The National Commission on Excellence in Education to the present, excellence has been the rallying cry and the focus of educational reform. Teachers are challenged to ignite in their students a desire to excel in all aspects of school life. A particular concern for educational reformers is that the performance of American students surpass that of students from other countries such as Japan and Germany. Many educational policy makers insist that American competitiveness will suffer if our students do not excel in all areas of study.

Nearly everyone will agree that we want our students to excel and achieve outstanding results. The more difficult question is how to achieve these results. A number of elements have been advanced as essential for achieving excellence and true and lasting educational reform: high standards, accountability, active learning, assessment accountability, a sense of community, a focus on lifelong learning, character education, and teacher development.

■ High Standards

The reform movement we are witnessing is characterized by the belief that all students can reach high standards. Students must adopt a serious task

STONE SOUP © 1999 Jan Eliot. Reprinted with permission of Universal Press Syndicate. All rights reserved.

LEADERS IN EDUCATION
MARVA COLLINS

Marva Collins is a star, an educational celebrity, if you will. She and her work have been the focus of two *60 Minutes* programs; an award-winning film, *The Marva Collins Story,* featuring Cicely Tyson; and literally hundreds of magazine and newspaper stories. In the 1980s, she was asked by President Reagan to be Secretary of Education but refused in order to stay with the school she founded. She has been the recipient of the prestigious Jefferson Award for Great Public Service Benefiting the Disadvantaged. Forty-two universities have conferred honorary doctoral degrees on this one very passionate teacher.

Marva Knight was born in Monroeville, Ala., in 1936, in the days of school segregation. Her all-black school had few books and she, like other black children in her town, was not permitted to use the public library. Nevertheless, her father, a businessman, infused in Marva a strong desire for learning and a quest for personal excellence. She attended Clark College in Atlanta and after graduation returned to Alabama to teach. After two years, she moved to Chicago, obtained a teaching position in the city's public schools, and married Clarence Collins.

The 1960s and 1970s were troubled times in the Chicago public schools, but Marva earned the reputation of a hard-driving, no-nonsense teacher who "got results." She set high standards for her poor, largely black, inner-city classes and used what were considered unorthodox teaching methods. She insisted that her students read a great deal, often assigning challenging classic texts such as Shakespeare and Chaucer. Memorization was a methodological mainstay in her classes. She worked hard to make learning an adventure where the enthusiasm and hard work of both teacher and students paid off. But, most of all, she was adamant that her students would not and could not fail. Her motto was and still is, "Children do not fail. We, as a society, fail them."

After fourteen years, Marva grew discouraged with what she was able to do within the public school system. She was also unhappy with the education her daughter and son were receiving in a prestigious private school. In 1975, with the full support of her husband and $5,000 she withdrew from her teachers' retirement fund, she opened her own school on the second floor of her home: the Westside Preparatory School (WPS). Her school began with her two children and four other neighborhood youngsters. One of these children was physically disabled and another was considered borderline retarded. At the end of their first year at WPS, each child scored at least five grades higher than he or she had the previous year.

Word spread throughout the community and the next September, WPS had twenty students, mostly students who had been failing in the public schools. What Marva Collins was able to do with these students and also get them to do soon caught the attention of parents and other educators. The school expanded and Marva trained new staff members. Her mix of phonics, classics, memorization, study of foreign languages, critical thinking, and reading aloud drew critics, but the students kept coming and the scores kept rising.

When visitors came to WPS to see how she did it, they found teachers without desks, continually on the move. Her theory is that a teacher in motion is there to help students when they make mistakes and to keep discipline problems from emerging. Teachers inspire students with the vision of their personal success. Perhaps reflecting her father's business sense, Marva and her teachers tell students to make "daily deposits" into their personal accounts of knowledge and skills so that every child can become a winner and never have to go through life faced with "insufficient funds." Also, at the beginning of each year, both students and teachers take time to write out mission statements of what they commit to achieve during the year. These mission statements are living documents, consulted regularly.

Through her notoriety, writings, and lecturing around the world, this energetic, passionate woman has enriched educational practice, brought success to thousands, and changed the lives of hundreds of thousands. She has summed up her mission with this quote: "Once children learn how to learn, nothing is going to narrow their mind. The essence of teaching is to make learning contagious, to have one idea spark another."

 Visit the web site for more information about Marva Collins.

orientation toward their studies and show mastery of content that is measured through rigorous tests.

In the past, teachers were encouraged to focus first on raising students' self-esteem through positive reinforcement and gentle coaching. In a high-standards environment, self-esteem is seen as the direct by-product of student achievement. Instead of *giving* self-esteem to students, the teacher sets up learning situations so that students can be successful and *earn* it. One elementary school captures the twin themes of setting high standards and earning self-esteem by challenging its students with the motto "Your best today. Better tomorrow."

earning self-esteem

Helping children achieve high standards is a challenge for the teacher, too. It requires that teachers understand individual students by knowing their weaknesses and strengths, interests, and talents. It demands that teachers not only know their subject matter but also know how to engage students of many different abilities, interest levels, and learning styles.

Reflect on standards-based education with the image in this section of your CD-ROM.

▇ *Accountability*

Teachers and schools that set high standards need to find some way of determining if the standards are being met. Some form of accountability is usually required. During the 1970s and 1980s, a major motivation behind the accountability movement was declining test scores. As is discussed later in this chapter, schools across the country began using standardized achievement tests and so-called *minimum competency tests* to see how they were doing compared with other schools. On the basis of these test scores, the performances of school districts, their teachers, and their students were judged; programs were added or dropped and individuals rewarded or punished. The pressure to boost test scores was intense, and many teachers quite naturally responded by emphasizing in their instruction the knowledge and skills that were being tested. In effect, teachers began **teaching to the test.** What was tested became what was taught.

minimum competency tests

Link to more information about accountability and assessment from the web site.

As instruction narrowed to concentrate more and more on the basics, student scores seemed to improve and state after state reported that their students were scoring above the national average on the standardized tests given. At this point, in state after state and in community after community, what has been called the "Lake Wobegon effect" (named after a fictional town portrayed by public radio humorist Garrison Keillor, a place where "all the children were above average") occurred. Each community interpreted its test results to mean that its children were above average. On closer examination, however, educators and policy makers interpreted the results to mean that the children were becoming overly familiar with the test questions and were able to score well on the tests. Others interpreted the results to mean that the standardized tests being used were inappropriate or invalid. A common complaint was that the multiple-choice tests assessed lower-level thinking skills instead of the higher-order ones for which educators and business leaders were calling.

■ *new type of assessment demanded*

Educators and the business community began to call for schools to emphasize critical thinking skills and problem-solving abilities, qualities that are difficult to measure through multiple-choice and other objective tests. Some educators called for a different type of assessment, one that would directly measure real student performance on important tasks. For example, if we want to know how well students can write, we can examine samples of their writing. Or if we want to know how well students understand scientific concepts and can carry out scientific processes, we can ask them to conduct an actual experiment. In other words, the assessment would actually measure what we wanted students to be able to do rather than relying on them to choose the correct response on a multiple-choice test item. This type of assessment is known as **authentic** or **performance assessment.** Advocates claim that authentic assessment involves performance tests that get closer to how students apply knowledge rather than how they store it in their minds.

> *We must put knowledge directly in the hands of teachers and seek accountability that will focus attention on "doing the right things" rather than on "doing things right."*
>
> —LINDA DARLING-HAMMOND

■ *portfolios*

One method of authentic assessment involves having students collect their work over time and assemble it to create **portfolios.** These portfolios might showcase students' best work, much like an artist's portfolio. In other instances, the work in the portfolio is representative of work done throughout the semester, showing students' growth over time. In either case, these portfolios can be evaluated by students and teachers to determine learning progress.[4] In many parts of the country, in fact, student teachers assemble portfolios of their own work to show their professional skills when they apply for employment. (See the chapter entitled, "What Are Your Job Options in Education?" for more on teaching portfolios.)

■ *unresolved issues*

Authentic assessment is not without its critics and unresolved issues. Whether performance assessments can satisfy the validity requirement (answering the question, "Is this a true measure of what I want to assess?") and the reliability requirement ("Will this test yield a similar result when administered at different times and under different circumstances?") has yet to be determined. Cost is also a major concern. Evaluating writing samples or judging students' success in conducting a scientific experiment is much more time consuming, and therefore more costly, than machine scoring a multiple-choice exam. Standards of judgment present another difficulty. Even if testers use rubrics that specify criteria and standards of assessment, the subjectivity of the human evaluator is an important consideration. In addition, questions about how to judge excellence, originality, and creativity in art and writing, let alone math or science, remain. Though many questions remain, the case of Vermont is a good illustration of the unresolved issues of portfolio assessment. In the early 1990s, the state of Vermont began a statewide portfolio assessment program for all students at all grade levels. After a few years of implementation, the program had to be suspended because it was proving to be too costly, too time consuming, and with too much variation in the scores. Whatever form of assessment is used, any educational reform needs to include some way of knowing if students are in fact meeting the standards set and becoming the well-educated individuals that society wants.

Active Learning: The Constructivist's Approach

There is an old saying that all teachers know well: "You can lead a horse to water, but you can't make it drink." Similarly, you can have a child in a classroom, but you can't make him or her learn. Pouring information into students or forcing them to do workbooks or problem sheets won't always do it. Nor will the great majority of students learn if simply allowed to wander through a library or laboratory on their own. Something must happen in learners before they learn. Curiosity? A problem that they want or need to solve? And then, with the direct or indirect help of the teacher, the student "constructs" knowledge from the information available to him or her.

humans as active makers of meaning

Reflect on constructivism with the image in this section of your CD-ROM.

Constructivism is a theory of knowledge acquisition built on the idea that the learner interacts with new information to "construct" meaning from it. (See the chapters entitled "What Should Teachers Know About Technology and Its Impact on Schools?" and "What Are the Philosophical Foundations of American Education?" for more on constructivism.) Constructivism provides a frame of reference for organizing classroom practices so that students learn in all content areas.[5] Contrary to educational practices in which learners passively receive information, the constructivist approach requires that learners actively interact with the information, building on their prior knowledge, attitudes, and values. As learners encounter new information or experiences, they ask themselves, "What makes sense here? What happens when I do this or change that?" In this **active learning** process, learners build and add to their understanding of concepts, rules, and strategies through direct, hands-on experimentation.

How does constructivism embody the call for excellence of educational reform? First, a primary ingredient of the constructivist approach is a learner taking responsibility for his or her own learning. The teacher and the school play important supporting roles, but the initiative of the learner is essential. Students can achieve excellence only if they take responsibility for their learning.

characteristics of constructivist classrooms

Constructivist classrooms foster experiential, inquiry-based learning in an atmosphere of intellectual play. Teachers in these classrooms ask challenging, open-ended questions and allow for much wait-time. In short, constructivism incorporates much of what has been written about in this text, including inductive teaching, student-teacher interaction, cooperative learning, multi- and interdisciplinary teaching, and extensive use of new technologies.

Although constructivism is only one learning theory, it can be a powerful approach to teaching and learning. It can bridge the gap between teacher-centered drill or rote learning on the one hand and excessively abstract learning on the other. An ancient Chinese proverb captures well the essence of constructivism: "Tell me and I forget. Show me and I will remember. Make me do it and I learn."

A Sense of Community

urban sanctuaries

"Small is beautiful" has been the slogan for many social activists over the last two decades. Social scientists studying adolescents in our cities found what they labeled *urban sanctuaries,* neighborhood organizations that attracted and served inner-city youth, particularly those who were disaffected and drifting toward gangs. These urban sanctuaries had "family-like environments in which individuals are valued and rules of membership are clear. Their activities offer opportunities for active participation and present challenges that result in accomplishments. They are youth driven and sensitive to youth's everyday realities.

A boy shares his artwork and a poem about his brother with some classmates.
(© Nancy Sheehan/PhotoEdit)

They assume that youth are a resource to be developed, not a problem to solve."[6] These messages, however, are just beginning to gain a foothold in American education.

Recent years have brought a growing realization that the largest of our schools, although more efficient and cost-effective, can have some destructive side effects. The schools have an aura of impersonality that results in the disengagement of many students. It is common to hear such statements as "I'm lost here," "No one really knows me and no one cares," or "I'm just a name in someone's gradebook." Though these criticisms are directed most often at high schools, they hold for many of our junior high and middle schools and even some elementary schools. Clearly, the larger our schools get and the greater the number of classmates and adults with whom students must interact, the more students disengage, and disengaged students cannot achieve excellence.

Recent studies have found not only a decline in student engagement, and therefore in academic achievement, in large schools but also a decline in faculty morale and an increase in faculty absenteeism.[7] Further, large schools are often equally overwhelming for parents, who tend to remain at a distance and therefore uninvolved in their children's school life.

■ *disengagement of students*

■ **Schools-Within-Schools**   School-as-community advocates believe that any school whose principal does not know the names of all the students is too big. Reformers such as James Comer of New Haven's School Development Project and Theodore Sizer, founder and chair emeritus of the Coalition of Essential Schools, argue that a sense of community is essential to the development of an

POLICY MATTERS!

Class Size: Is Less Always Better?

What's the Policy?

A major achievement of our schools during the twentieth century was reducing class size from fifty and sixty students early in the century to a national average of twenty-two today. However, reducing class size even further has been, is, and will continue to be on the reform agenda of the American schools. For example, in 1996, the state of California, as part of a massive movement to fix its ailing schools, initiated its Class Size Reduction Program, a well-intentioned and expensive effort to reduce class size to twenty in kindergarten through third grade. Other states, such as Texas, Nevada, Indiana, Tennessee, and Virginia, have also instituted class size reduction initiatives.

How Does It Affect Teachers?

Almost every teacher and administrator we know would enjoy having smaller classes. Teachers with fewer students are often able to spend more time on instruction and less time hassling with the discipline problems that seem to naturally accompany large groups of young people. Fewer students also means less time tending to "administrivia." Teachers have the chance to get to know each student and teach each one in ways that meet his or her individual needs.

What Are the Pros?

There is widespread agreement that public school classes are too large and reducing the student-teacher ratio will substantially improve student outcomes. Fewer students means more attention to each one so that students can achieve better results. Surely a fourth-grade teacher with seventeen children can know and meet the needs of his class better than one with twenty-five. Surely an algebra teacher with 85 students can zero in on her students better than one with 150 or 160 students. Much of educational theory seems to suggest that increased individual attention can help students with special needs, students at risk for dropping out, students who are not achieving as much as they could—in fact, just about all students.

What Are the Cons?

A key problem for those who wish to make classes smaller is money. Teachers' salaries represent the bulk of most school districts' budgets, and any significant reduction in class size would be extremely expensive. For instance, lowering the

"houses" of students

academic environment. In these reform projects, new schools are purposely kept small, and existing large schools are broken up into "houses" of 100 to 400 students. The number of teachers with whom the students interact is similarly reduced, and these houses function as **schools-within-schools.** Because students and teachers stay in the same house for several years, they are able to establish stronger and deeper relationships. Each student is a *known* person rather than a name on a class roster.

One obvious advantage of the house plan is that it allows teachers to plan together and to bring to bear their different perceptions of a child who is having difficulties. In addition, these smaller, more intimate school environments provide a more stable emotional climate for students. Faculty advisors have better knowledge of and more exposure to students and can offer them more help in dealing with students' problems or challenges. In this smaller setting, advocates argue, students are much more likely to achieve the standards of excellence set for them.

pupil-teacher ratio from 20 to 19 in a school district with 100 teachers would mean hiring five new teachers and increasing the school budget by approximately 4 percent or paying for the five teachers by making cuts in the sports program, the computer lab, or the counseling services. But if reducing class size improves student achievement, wouldn't it be worth it? This takes us to the scientific reason for resistance to this reform.

Few educational questions have been more frequently studied than the relationship between class size and student achievement. Several well-executed studies have found that small class size does have a positive effect at the lower elementary grades. The conclusion of a review of more than 300 individual studies, however, was that, in elementary and secondary schools overall, most of the studies suggested that either the fewer educators per student (yes, larger classes!) the better or that the achievement gains made in smaller classes were trivial.

The explanation for such unexpected research results lies in the answer to the following question: "Would you rather have your child in a twenty-seven-student class with a skillful, experienced teacher or in a fifteen-student class with an inexperienced teacher with an emergency certificate?" During California's late 1990s class reduction push, for example, thousands of people accepted appointments and entered the newly created reduced-size classrooms on emergency teaching certificates. Only then did they learn that an emergency certificate does not make a person a teacher. California's effort to improve early elementary education through reducing class size has been widely judged a failure. However, with intensive professional development for emergency certificate teachers, student academic performance has shown progress in recent years.

What Do You Think?

1. **How many students would be in your ideal classroom? Why?**
2. **Do you think that if qualified teachers could be found for smaller classrooms, research results on student achievement would show greater gains for students in small classes?**
3. **Do you believe there are any other reasons besides academic achievement that small classes would be better than large ones?**

 Visit the web site to learn more about this policy issue.

SOURCES: Debra Viadero, "Small Classes: Popular, But Still Unknown," *Education Week*, February 18, 1998; Reducing Class Size, What Do We Know? March 1999. Available at: **http://www.ed.gov/pubs/ReducingClass/Class_size. html#research.**

PAUSE AND REFLECT

1 Reflecting back on your own recent schooling, did the schools you attended have this sense of community? Does the college or university you are attending have this sense? What could be done to give it more of a sense of community?

Lifelong Learning

need for learning throughout life

In our global, rapidly evolving social and economic environment, people need more than an education. They must also be capable of continuous learning. The jobs we perform and the tasks we must accomplish today will likely differ ten years from now. Therefore, schools must attend to the habits of mind and skills that will keep people learning throughout their lives, making them **lifelong learners**. Not only must students become good learners, but in order to be lifelong learners, they also need to be enthusiastic learners. In other words, students must know *how* to learn, and they must *want* to learn.

■ **Tools for Learning**   The human brain is a glorious instrument capable of enormous feats of creativity, from writing symphonies to making scientific breakthroughs. The average brain can store and manipulate more information, by several hundred times, than the largest computers. But the brain has its drawbacks. It loses or "misfiles" information. Numerous and assorted messages enter it through the eyes, ears, and other senses and somehow get lost. When we want to remember an idea, it often is simply "not there," or somehow the information received gets modified so that when we take the exam, we are sure there are two quarts in a gallon and four pints in a quart. Thus, although the brain is humankind's treasure, it is hardly perfect. And to work well, the brain must be trained and well-maintained.

■ *training the brain*

By *trained*, we mean we have to teach people how to use their brains effectively. Most likely the majority of our readers have been urged a time or two by parents and teachers to "Use your brains!" Our meaning is both an extension of that request and a more specialized suggestion. We are urging that we give our brains more power through the use of new tools. In the same manner that reading extends the power of the brain by giving it access to vast amounts of important information, other tools can make the brain more efficient and better able to take in, interpret, process, store, and retrieve information. *Well-maintained* means we continue to make use of these important tools long after we have left the hallowed hallways of schools.

■ *tools for learning*

A fresh focus on the skills of learning can and ought to be a major part of school reform. Of course, we must attend to the three Rs. We are not suggesting that we give a lower priority to subject matter. Rather, to make knowledge (that is, intellectual capital) more useful, students need to learn how to learn. As teachers, we must give our students the necessary **tools for learning:** advanced reading, remembering, recording, researching, test taking, analyzing, and creating. These are the tools that can help students excel, not just in school, but later, in the workplace and in life, in general.

■ *Reclaiming Character Education*

■ Link to more information about character education from the web site.

The calls for excellence in education are not limited to just academic achievement. Many reformers have also been concerned about excellence of character, and much of the dissatisfaction with schools that has fueled recent educational reform efforts comes from parents and community leaders who believe the schools have not done enough to affect positively the character and ethical values of students. Many reformers are convinced that failure to address these needs of students lies at the heart of the schools' problems. A "good student" has come to mean someone who does well on tests and achieves academically rather than someone who is a good person and who demonstrates characteristics such as responsibility, consideration for others, self-discipline, and the ability to

■ *definition of character education*

work hard. In order to achieve excellence in student achievement, serious school reform must address the issue of **character education,** which we define as the effort to help the young acquire a *moral compass*—that is, a sense of right and wrong and the enduring habits necessary to live a good life. Character education, then, involves helping the child *to know the good, love the good, and do the good.*[8]

Formal education is the playing field on which society vies over values.

—THEODORE SIZER

A Sample of the Tools for Learning

Here is a list of some of the skills, or what we are calling the Tools for Learning, that we believe ought to be taught to all students:

- *Various methods for remembering important information.* This largely involves teaching people how not to forget: how to move information from the fleeting short-term memory to the more enduring long-term memory.

- *Two or three methods of taking notes and saving important information.* Definite skills are associated with capturing what another person is saying, and students should systematically learn these skills.

- *Study reading.* One practices study reading when the material is complex and contains information one wants to remember later. It is quite different from reading a novel or reading a telephone book. It is a set of skills that is at the heart of academic success, as well as success in many jobs.

- *Preparing for different kinds of tests.* Schools should show students how to study for different types of tests, such as objective and essay tests, and how to deal with test anxiety in various situations. Because examinations and tests do not end with graduation,

schools should teach students how to cope with and master these challenges.

- *Doing research.* Students need to learn how to get answers to questions by using libraries, the Internet, expert sources, and data-gathering resources of all kinds. In essence, these are the skills of finding and accessing different data sources and using the information to solve a problem.

- *Thinking through a problem in a systematic way.* Instead of jumping to conclusions or relying on how they feel about an issue, students should learn how to think critically.

- *Generating creative ideas.* Much of life in and out of school requires new solutions or imaginative resolutions. Students need to learn techniques for generating novel and creative ideas individually, as well as group-oriented techniques such as brainstorming.

- *Getting the academic job done.* Students need to know how to set goals, develop a work plan, monitor their own behavior, bring a task to successful closure, and gradually become more successful at academic learning. This is important not simply to succeed in school, but because the modern workplace demands these academic skills.

◼ *objections to character education*

Arguments Pro and Con Some people argue that the public school has no role in character development and moral education because these are rooted in deeply held religious world views. As such, they are out of bounds to the public school, which should concentrate on cognitive skills exclusively, skills such as reading, writing, and application of the scientific method.[9] These people claim that if parents want attention paid to moral values, they should put their children in private schools.

◼ *whose values?*

Others question character education by asking, "*Whose* values should the public schools teach?" In a nation of diverse cultural backgrounds, a nation committed to freedom of thought and expression, is there any one set of values that can be taught without infringing on someone's deeply cherished beliefs? One answer to this objection is that the tax-supported public schools can teach the civic virtues that are necessary for life in a democratic society, such as respect for the rights of others, courage, tolerance, kindness, and concern for the underdog. Another way to approach the answer is to look at a few of the sights we might encounter while walking around some schools, as described in the following paragraph.

A counselor is calling a student's home about apparently excused absences, only to find that the parent's letters have been forged. A young boy is in the principal's office for threatening his teacher with a knife. Three students are separated from their class after hurling racial epithets at a fourth. A girl is complaining that her locker has been broken into and all her belongings stolen. A small group of boys are huddling in a corner, shielding an exchange of money for drug packets. In the playground, two girls grab a third and punch her in the stomach for flirting with the wrong boy.[10]

Schools that tolerate such behavior not only are failing to address the character education needs of their students but also have become places where the intellectual goals of schooling are impaired. In addition, such schools win little support from the general public, the people who pay for public education.

Reflect on character education with the image in this section of your CD-ROM.

We believe that most educators know it is impossible to educate students in a moral vacuum. The process of schooling necessarily affects the way children think about issues of right and wrong. Further, the overwhelming majority of Americans, regardless of religion, class, or racial background, support certain moral values such as respect, persistence, a thirst for justice, honesty, responsibility in our dealings with one another, consideration, compassion, persistence at hard tasks, and courage in the face of adversity.[11] We believe that few people would not wholeheartedly support the schools' vigorous advocacy of these virtues. Teachers and schools can positively influence the development of desirable habits and character formation in numerous ways, but two in particular are worthy of note: using the curriculum and involving students in service activities.

wide support for certain values

■ **Character in the Curriculum**   One major approach is to teach more directly and more vigorously the positive moral values that are embedded in our culture. Our history and literature are permeated with value issues and moral lessons from the past. Instead of simply having students study the facts of a historical period or read a story to build vocabulary or appreciate style, the teacher can confront them with ethical issues and moral lessons that are integral to the subject matter. Instead of merely teaching scientific methodologies and findings, the teacher can have students examine the implications of applied science, such as genetic manipulation. They will see that the use of science and technologies, such as nuclear energy, fossil fuels, and high-speed computers, is not neutral but has ethical implications. As teachers, we must see the content of our curriculum as the carrier of our moral heritage and work to engage our students in that moral heritage.

moral issues in subject-matter disciplines

■ **Service Learning**   Knowing about justice, compassion, and courage is one thing; making them a part of one's life and practicing them diligently is another. Students need real opportunities to practice these virtues. As many reformers realize, schools can create opportunities for students, from the early grades on, to help one another and the adults in the school building. As students get older, they can be given more and more responsibility for working with and caring for younger students. In the later stages of high school, groups of students can take on projects in the larger community, such as helping a parent whose child has a disability or assisting with an exercise class at a senior citizens' center. Likewise, individual students can provide companionship to elderly shut-ins or peer counseling to troubled youngsters. The emphasis in such programs is not merely on the study of virtues but also on virtues in action.

VOICES FROM THE CLASSROOM

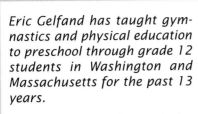

Eric Gelfand has taught gymnastics and physical education to preschool through grade 12 students in Washington and Massachusetts for the past 13 years.

I can remember one of the members of my gymnastics team getting very upset about not winning. Tyler was 11 years old and anything less than first place resulted in distress, inability to concentrate, and a feeling of failure. His reaction was stronger than others, but many on our team shared the sentiment: self-esteem and success depended on winning. I decided to initiate a discussion of our definitions of winning with the entire team.

In this discussion we discovered that our definition of winning was based on beating others and factors over which we had no control, like the score that the judge would give us. The new definition of winning that we developed focused on giving our best effort in each moment. We also decided to concentrate only on factors that we could control, such as improving our focus and technique, supporting each other, learning from our competitors, and regulating our thoughts and emotions. We decided if we did these things, then we had each won.

Tyler's feelings of self-esteem and success slowly began to change, but not the first time we talked about it, or the tenth time I reminded him to refocus on our new goals, or even on the fiftieth time that he made himself feel good by remembering that he had done his best. Through the efforts of the entire team over a period of three to four years, Tyler arrived at a place where winning meant something very personal and attainable at all times. This evolution meant valuing respect, persistence, temperance, and compassion for ourselves and others above all else. These virtues slowly became habits, which slowly became a part of our character and who we are today. It was incredibly hard to keep ourselves focused on this goal when our society values a very different definition of winning.

In reading this chapter, you will learn that school reform depends on the efforts of individual teachers to help our children become good workers and citizens. What do you think the definition of "winning" is in academics? If the current definition is not attainable by all of your students, how can you change the system or work within it to make every child successful? I believe that the key is to value the building of character as much as achievement within a discipline. It's simple; it just takes a few years of relentless hard work and compassion.

 Visit the web site for more Voices from the Classroom.

■ *move toward social service*

Service learning programs are growing rapidly in our schools. A recent survey by the National Council for the Social Studies (NCSS) shows that 83 percent of U.S. high schools offered service learning opportunities in 1999, up from 27 percent in 1984.[12] An important feature of the much-acclaimed Central Park East, the junior-senior high school in New York City's Harlem, is the requirement that each student perform two hours of service every week. The service can be performed in school by, for example, setting up a science laboratory for an experiment, checking out books at the library's circulation desk, or serving food in the school's cafeteria. In the local community, students do a variety of tasks, such as acting as a guide in one of the city's museums or delivering food to shut-ins.[13]

Several states are considering making a certain number of hours of community service a requisite for high school graduation. In 1993, Maryland became the first state to make service an actual requirement. Currently, Maryland high school students are required to perform seventy-five hours of service before they

Character education in action!

(© R. Hutchings/PhotoEdit)

can graduate. We believe schools must succeed in this mission for students' sake and also because a strong program of character education makes teaching a much more satisfying profession.

Professional Development

example of U.S. industry

In the 1980s and 1990s, American business and industry dramatically reformed themselves after decades of inefficiency and loss of markets to their global competitors. The result has been a tremendous growth in national prosperity. An important key to this recovery has been a major investment of time and money in the education and advanced training of the American worker. Individuals from the corporate boardroom to the factory floor learned new ways of doing their work. Today, continuing education is a staple in the American workplace.

Along those lines, educational reformers argue that in order to have better-educated students, we need to make sure that our teachers are "excellent." To that end, many state departments of education have required teachers to continue their education after their initial teacher preparation. Also, virtually all school districts have salary incentives for advanced training such as college courses, degrees, and workshops.

an array of activities

Initially called *in-service education,* the effort to extend the education of teachers is usually referred to as **staff development,** or more recently **professional development.** As such, the term covers an array of activities, including on-site school- or district-sponsored workshops where teachers come together to learn new skills such as searching the Internet, integrating technology into the curriculum, inquiry-based science instruction, writing across the curriculum, or new classroom management strategies; college or university courses and programs, often leading to advanced degrees in specialized areas such as reading, special education, or guidance counseling; and training experiences provided by textbook companies introducing their new curricula to the school. To this list we would add items such as distance learning courses on using technology in the classroom, a teacher-organized book club on women in fiction, an adult education course on yoga and meditation, writing case studies of educational problems or issues that other teachers can use, mentoring new teachers, and a sabbatical year to study the history of Native Americans. The boundaries of what constitutes professional development are often debated, but we believe the essential attribute is that it aids the teacher in becoming a better teacher.

For many practicing teachers, professional development activities often conjure up memories of trudging off to after-school gatherings where they are lectured to by strangers on topics that hold little interest or relevance for many or to state-mandated required courses or workshops that they take in order to renew their licenses. These efforts are at best, minimal, and at worst, the major stumbling block to true educational reform. Although a school district that hires a teacher and a state that licenses a teacher have the right to require a teacher's continuing education, such a top-down approach is not likely to serve the needs of children in this new century. For educational reform to truly take hold, several changes like the following are needed:

four needed changes

1. Schools should be conceived of as **learning communities,** in which everyone—adults and children alike—is always learning.

2. Teachers, specialists, and administrators must see their continuing educational growth as an integral part of their workday.

3. The definition of *professional development* should be broadened to take into account whatever contributes to making an educator more effective.

4. Although teachers must be willing to devote their time and energy to staff development, the cost should be borne by the school district or the state.

characteristics of effective professional development

Effective professional development does the following for teachers:

- Focuses on teachers as central to student learning, yet includes all members of the school community

- Focuses on individual, collegial, and organizational improvement

- Respects and nurtures the intellectual and leadership capacity of teachers, principals, and others in the school community

- Reflects the best available research and practice in teaching, learning, and leadership

- Enables teachers to develop further expertise in subject content, teaching strategies, uses of technologies, and other essential elements of teaching to high standards

- Promotes continuous inquiry and improvement of schools

- Is planned collaboratively by those who will participate in and facilitate that development

- Requires substantial time and resources

- Is driven by a coherent long-term plan

- Is evaluated ultimately on the basis of its effects on teacher instruction and student learning, and uses this assessment to guide subsequent professional development efforts

Mortimer Adler, the force behind the Paideia Proposal mentioned in the chapter entitled "What Are the Philosophical Foundations of American Education?", once said, "The teacher who has stopped learning is a deadening influence rather than a help to students being initiated into the ways of learning."[14]

Educational reform expert Michael Fullan suggests that teachers seeking to improve themselves are characterized by four attitudes: they accept that it is possible to improve; they are ready to be self-critical; they recognize better practice than their own; and, most importantly, they are willing to learn what they have to learn to do what needs to be done.[15] In our view, a teacher who is not engaged in learning activities because of lack of opportunity or lack of personal incentive is stunting his or her own career and is a barrier to the educational reform we need.

We now turn to actual reform initiatives, many of which involve one or more of the elements we have described. As in any other type of reform, certain ideas and principles get attention, while others are ignored or lose ground. As you read about the reforms that have been implemented, compare them in your mind both to what you think ought to be done and to what we have been suggesting here.

PAUSE AND REFLECT

1 Which of the reforms above are you most in favor of? About which do you have doubts? If we made you Czar of American Education, are there any mentioned reforms you would make and why?

Current Reform Initiatives

message of A Nation at Risk

Most educators agree that the current reform effort started with the 1983 federal report, *A Nation at Risk.* This strongly worded report declared that our nation was in serious danger and that our schools had left the nation vulnerable to our military and economic competitors. The report called for longer school days, more homework and effort on the part of students, tougher grading policies, more testing, and more demanding textbooks. It arrived at a time of particularly widespread dissatisfaction with the public schools. Just two years before the report's release, a *Newsweek* poll revealed that nearly half (47 percent) of the American public believed the schools were doing a "poor" or only a "fair" job.[16] The remainder of the 1980s saw a blizzard of national and state reports, most hitting many of the same themes, and all calling for massive change. The 1990s was a period of intense development of curricular, programmatic, and pedagogic initiatives aimed at bringing about change in schools and better student performance. Several different groups at the national, state, and local levels created proposals for reform. What have been the results?

Children are the messages we will send to a time we will never see.

—NEIL POSTMAN

National-Level Reform Efforts

As we discussed in the chapter entitled "How Are Schools Governed, Influenced, and Financed?", the U.S. federal government has a limited role in education. Compared with other modern nations, ours is a highly decentralized

TABLE 11.1   Goals 2000: The National Education Goals

Goal 1	By the year 2000, all children in America will start school ready to learn.
Goal 2	By the year 2000, the high school graduation rate will increase to at least 90 percent.
Goal 3	By the year 2000, all students will leave grades 4, 8, and 12 having demonstrated competency over challenging subject matter including English, mathematics, science, foreign languages, civics and government, economics, arts, history, and geography; and every school in America will ensure that all students learn to use their minds well, so they may be prepared for responsible citizenship, further learning, and productive employment in our Nation's modern economy.
Goal 4	By the year 2000, the Nation's teaching force will have access to programs for the continued improvement of their professional skills and the opportunity to acquire the knowledge and skills needed to instruct and prepare all American students for the next century.
Goal 5	By the year 2000, United States students will be first in the world in mathematics and science achievement.
Goal 6	By the year 2000, every adult American will be literate and will possess the knowledge and skills necessary to compete in a global economy and exercise the rights and responsibilities of citizenship.
Goal 7	By the year 2000, every school in the United States will be free of drugs, violence, and the unauthorized presence of firearms and alcohol and will offer a disciplined environment conducive to learning.
Goal 8	By the year 2000, every school will promote partnerships that will increase parental involvement and participation in promoting the social, emotional, and academic growth of children.

Sources: Goals 2000: Educate America Act (March 31, 1994); *The National Education Goals* (Washington, DC: U.S. Department of Education, 1994).

system with most of the decision making and financial support coming from the state and local governments. The national government can command attention, however. Once *A Nation at Risk* had focused the nation's attention on education, President Reagan and his secretary of education, William Bennett, pursued a *bully-pulpit* strategy—that is, the White House staff began using the president's office to call people's attention to the plight of our schools and to advocate change. Since then, education has remained at the forefront of the national agenda and has had a prime place in every presidential candidate's platform in the past twenty years.

■ **National Education Goals for the Year 2000**   Nowhere has the bully-pulpit strategy been more evident than in the much-heralded Education Summit held in 1989. Then-president George H. Bush and the state governors together committed themselves and their offices to school reform, later adopting a list of goals (shown in Table 11.1) to be reached by the year 2000. A leading figure at the summit was the then-governor of Arkansas, Bill Clinton, who spoke for many when he said, "Not only are we to develop strategies to achieve them [the goals], but we stand here before you and tell you we expect to be held personally accountable for the progress we make in moving this country to a brighter future."[17] Few were surprised when, as president, Clinton reaffirmed

■ *Goals 2000*

Read the National Educational Goals in the text resources on your CD-ROM.

his commitment to these **National Education Goals,** which were adopted into law as the *Goals 2000: Educate America Act.* However, now that year 2000 has come and gone and we have not achieved these benchmark indicators of progress, we hear less and less about Goals 2000. This is not to say that education draws less attention than before. On the contrary, education continues to be the object of much discussion and reform efforts at the federal level.

Read the *No Child Left Behind Act* in the text resources of your CD-ROM.

In his first year in office, President George W. Bush, declaring education reform as the "cornerstone" of his administration, proposed a new plan for American education. Called "No Child Left Behind," the president's plan, signed into law in 2002, is based on four elements of educational reform: accountability, local control and flexibility, expanded parental choice, and doing what works.[18] (See the chapter entitled "How Are Schools Governed, Influenced, and Financed?" for details about the No Child Left Behind Act.)

■ **National Standards**   Because of the decentralized nature of U.S. education, each state educational agency (SEA) has the authority to decide what students in that state learn. For many years, these SEAs delegated curricular authority to the local educational agencies (LEAs) so that each school district could decide the most appropriate course of study for its students. Critics complain that these practices lead to too much variation in what students were learning, raising concerns about both the quality of education received and equality of educational opportunity. These concerns led to a drive for national standards or a national curriculum. E. D. Hirsch Jr., who popularized the concept of "cultural literacy," presents the equality argument, insisting that a national curriculum is needed because so many students move around from state to state and school to school. With a national curriculum, relocated students would be able to integrate easily into their new school environment, with no time lost academically. Hirsch points to facts such as these: one-fifth of all Americans relocate every year; one-sixth of all third-graders attend at least three different schools between first and third grades; and a typical inner-city school has a 50 percent student turnover between September and May.[19] Others make the quality argument by citing the educational excellence attained by France, Germany, and Japan, all countries with national standards and national exams. These proponents insist that a national curriculum will ensure that all students in the United States receive a high-quality education, no matter where they attend school.

■ *advocates of a national curriculum*

■ *the critics*

Other educators, however, strongly oppose national standards and an accompanying curriculum and testing program, fearing an educational power grab by the federal government. In their view, the idea of Washington bureaucrats, instead of locally accountable individuals, answering the questions "What should our children know?" and "How well should they know it?" seems both educationally flawed and politically dangerous. Opponents also believe that in a large nation with so many racial and ethnic groups and so many regional traditions, a national curriculum would trample cultural diversity and promote a bland sterility. Further, many are convinced that a national curriculum would put disadvantaged students at an even greater disadvantage.

■ *the compromise: voluntary standards*

So far, Congress has consistently resisted the establishment of a mandatory national curriculum and national subject-matter examinations, although the No Child Left Behind Act will create a national requirement that states test their students' achievement in key subjects every year. In sum, the outlook seems to be as follows: national influence, yes; national control, no; obligatory national testing, probably not in the near future.

Instead of federally mandated standards, **national curricular standards** have been developed by discipline-specific national groups of scholars and educators as part of larger attempts to bring about curricular reform. These curricular reform projects identify not just *what* students all over the United States should learn at each grade level, but in some cases, *how* students should be taught.

One such effort, *Project 2061* (sponsored by the American Association for the Advancement of Science), was discussed in some detail in the chapter entitled "What Is Taught?". Others include *Becoming a Nation of Readers* (sponsored by the Commission on Reading) and *Science/Technology/Society (S/T/S)* (sponsored by the National Science Foundation). The National Writing Project, a professional development project for teachers, promotes a process approach to composition and works with 130,000 teachers in forty-nine states to help teach students become better writers. Likewise, the National Council of Teachers of Mathematics developed new curriculum and evaluation standards that stress students not just *knowing* how to do mathematics but being able to explain what they're *doing* as well. The University of Chicago School Mathematics Project (UCSMP) has created a K–12 curriculum which emphasizes reading, problem-solving, everyday applications, and the use of new technologies The Algebra Project, which was developed by Bob Moses in Cambridge, Mass., is a national mathematics project designed to help low-income students and students of color be successful in acquiring the requisite math skills needed in the Information Age. In addition to these efforts, national projects are currently under way in all the major subject-matter areas, including history, geography, and the arts— many of which have already published content and teaching standards in their respective disciplines.

Reflect on national standards with the image in this section of your CD-ROM.

These various curriculum reform projects have in common a partnership among scholars in the discipline, teacher educators, and classroom teachers. Ideas and suggestions flow across lines that were once rigid. University academics observe in elementary and secondary classrooms, and, back on the campus, elementary and secondary school teachers instruct scholars on the realities of teaching their subjects to a wide variety of youthful students.

Some state educational agencies have found these standards to be of use as they develop statewide curriculum guides and state-mandated tests (we will discuss these under State Educational Reform later in the chapter).

■ **National Voluntary Networks**   One of the most interesting recent educational developments is the appearance of networks of schools and school districts. Among these loose, voluntary alliances are two mentioned earlier: the Coalition of Essential Schools begun by Theodore Sizer and the network of schools modeled after James Comer's New Haven School Development Project. Others include John Goodlad's National Network for Educational Reform, Robert Slavin's Success for All Schools, Henry Levin's Accelerated Schools, and a newly established network called Schools of Character, formed by the Character Education Partnership. Schools in these networks commit themselves to a common educational ideal or set of ideals rather than a prescribed course of study or approach to teaching and learning. For instance, the schools in the Coalition of Essential Schools try to put into practice the Ten Common Principles, among which are the following:

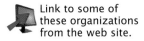

Link to some of these organizations from the web site.

- Helping adolescents use their minds well

- Teaching for the mastery of essential skills and acceleration in certain areas of knowledge

- Recognizing the student as worker rather than the teacher as deliverer of information

- Provoking students to learn how to learn

- Reflecting values of trust, decency, tolerance, and generosity in the tone of the school

- Expecting much from students without threatening them[20]

summary of current situation

Implications of National-Level Reform Efforts   Overall, two things are clear about education reforms at the national level. First, we are in the middle of a strong push toward national influence on education, and with President George W. Bush's education plan, the push may get stronger. Second, there has been a strong response from the states to improve their curricular standards and to hold local school districts accountable for these standards by imposing statewide testing with high-stakes consequences (graduation-dependent testing). The days of strong local control over schools in America may be waning.

State Educational Reform

state task forces and commissions

As education became more and more of a national issue, reform also became a hot political topic from the state house to the mayor's office. Statewide task forces were formed by governors, state legislatures, and state boards of education, and a large number were formed by citizens' groups and foundations. Some states had several at the same time. Numerous local school districts established their own blue-ribbon commissions to respond to what was increasingly called *the school crisis.* As the late Ernest Boyer said, "You could draw a 'Keystone Cops' image here of people charging off in different directions and bumping into each other and, in some instances, having a conflict with one another. There is no overall sense of where the problem is and how we should work together to get there."[21] There was, however, one common theme: the **call to excellence.**

> *The politics of education is complex and ever changing. At various times and places it can appear to be an asset or a liability. But it is real. Only through understanding and making proper use of politics can education be improved.*
>
> —WENDELL PIERCE

Throughout both American industry and education, mediocrity was the dominant criticism and excellence became the rallying cry of the reformers. Many of these recent state and local task force reports have *excellence* or *quality* in their titles. Because these task forces and reports were sponsored by state governmental agencies or well-connected citizens' groups, their recommendations were quickly turned into legislative proposals for school reform.

Common Elements in State Reforms   The "search for excellence," at the state level then, came down to specific proposals for change. The most widely adopted state reforms are described in the following sections.

more courses in core subjects required

An Increase in Graduation Requirements   Instead of one or two years of English and history, states began requiring three and four years in core subjects. For academic high school diplomas, science and advanced mathematics courses were required. The idea of "social promotion," moving students through the grades to stay with their own age groups, independently of their performance, came under great pressure and has been eliminated in many places, especially with the advent of mandated tests for graduation (see the section on standards-based education). The U.S Department of Education reports that the average number of academic credits earned in high school increased from 15 in 1983 to 18 in 1999. Even more significant are the gains in academic credits earned by African-American and Latino populations (17.2 and 17.7, respectively). In addition, 15 percent of high school students are now taking advanced math courses and 7 percent are taking physics courses, up from 5 percent and 5 percent, respectively, in 1983.[22]

■ more time in school

More Academic Learning Time   In the minds of many educators, the short school day and the long, academically fallow period between June and September are major causes of the poor performance of American students. Recent research confirms that in nine out of ten instances, students achieve more when they spend more time in class.[23] School days, which in many locales were only five-and-a-half to six hours, were lengthened to six-and-a-half to seven hours. The school year, which in many states was between 170 and 175 days or fewer, has been lengthened to 180 days or more in thirty-four states.[24] Though many of the reform reports recommended that our schools follow the example of Japan (240 days) and Germany (216 to 240 days),[25] no states and relatively few school districts have taken such a major step in lengthening the school year. One reason is that lengthening the amount of schooling is extremely costly.

Even with the lengthening of the school day and year, student academic performance did not improve as much as desired. A second reform initiative focused on the standard 48-minute high school class period as a contributor to students' mediocre performance, and proposed longer periods to allow for a more sustained academic study of a given subject. As discussed in the chapter on "What Is Taught?", *block scheduling*, while having many different iterations, essentially allows for longer periods during the school day so that students can spend more time engaged in learning in a given discipline.

In some states, the idea of **year-round education** has attracted the attention of educators. In most year-round schools, students go to school the same number of days as in traditional schools, but the school days are more evenly distributed throughout the school year. The most popular schedule is referred to as "45-15." Students attend school for forty-five days, then have fifteen days vacation. In the summer, students have six weeks vacation instead of the usual eight to ten weeks. According to the National Association for Year-Round Education, as of 2002, more than 3,000 public schools in forty-one states, as well as many private schools, had adopted some kind of a year-round schedule.[26] Proponents insist that the shorter summer break helps students retain information better. They also cite the cost savings for school districts that can house more students without adding new buildings. Critics of year-round education cite the strain such a schedule places on school finances when upgrades such as air conditioning are needed. They are also concerned about disrupting established family life patterns and summer opportunities for teachers' professional development.

Standards-Based Education   Taking the lead from the national movements for standardized courses of study, many states have begun to mandate the course of study for all public school students in their states. Proponents of standards-based education argue that, just as businesses have to meet certain quality standards of production, schools should also be held to certain standards in the education of students. By clearly and precisely identifying what students at each grade level are expected to know, state policymakers can more easily determine the quality and effectiveness of the schools throughout the state. Critics argue that similar reform efforts have already been tried and failed. They also express concern about possible *standardization* of education, which often ignores the individual learning needs of the students.[27]

Link to more information about state content standards from the web site.

Presently, forty-nine states have adopted curriculum or content standards specifying the material that all students in that state are expected to know and at what grade level they should know it. In many cases, these state standards are drawn from the voluntary national standards. (See the chapter entitled "What Is Taught?" for examples of content standards.) In order to make certain that the effort and monies going into their reform efforts are paying off, state legislatures are demanding *accountability*, generally in the form of state-mandated assessments. The result has been a huge growth in interest in testing and assessment. In the 1970s, relatively few states had a statewide testing program, a system that assessed whether students met the state's curriculum or content standards. But by 2002, as a result of the new testing movement, forty-nine states had such programs.[28]

increase in statewide tests

> *Ideas move fast when their time comes.*
>
> —CAROLYN HEILBRUN

The movement for statewide testing has been a mixed blessing. The statewide tests have been used as educational "report cards" to allow policymakers and the public to see how the schools in different districts are doing.[29] From this information, state educational policymakers can provide financial assistance for the underperforming school districts. But, as was stated in the section on teaching to the test earlier in this chapter, many believe the demand for testing and accountability has increased measure-driven instruction. Although there has been a call for authentic assessment, progress toward it appears to have stalled in recent years with the growing popularity of state-mandated measures of accountability and a return to "teaching to the tests."

SES and high-stakes tests

A second concern revolves around the "high-stakes" nature of the tests. In many states (with the urging and backing of federal policymakers), students must pass a state-mandated test to receive their high school diplomas. Emerging data show that students from lower socioeconomic communities are failing such tests at higher rates than students from higher socioeconomic communities. Some critics suggest high-stakes tests will lead to even greater socioeconomic disparity as failing students will be unable to attend college or get anything but a low-paying job.

Higher Expectations for Teachers   One of the major state-driven reform efforts of the 1980s and 1990s was the move to improve the quality of America's teaching force. Three initiatives in particular were notable: teacher competency testing, stiffening requirements for entering teacher education, and career ladder programs.

testing teachers

The first initiative, **teacher competency testing,** was not new, but it underwent massive growth during the last two decades of the twentieth century. Currently forty-three states have some form of teacher testing, typically taking place when candidates are leaving their teacher education programs or before they receive state licensure.[30] One vexing issue that has plagued the movement for teacher competency testing has been finding an appropriate and valid standard to which all teacher candidates should be held. In some states, the cut-off scores that have often been established are so low as to make them meaningless. In effect, teachers are supposed to demonstrate their proficiency by jumping over a hurdle, but the hurdle has been so low as to be meaningless. In other states, the standard is considered too arbitrary, dissuading teachers from seeking licensure in those states.

Reflect on teacher testing with the image in this section of your CD-ROM.

Increased graduation requirements and calls for more testing are part of many states' educational reforms.
(© Bob Daemmrich/Stock Boston)

■ *changes in teacher education*

Link to the NCTAF from the web site.

The second initiative had to do with teacher education. Legislatures across the country have been making changes in the licensure requirements for teaching and in the process of approval for universities and colleges that prepare teachers. In general, the call has been for an increase in liberal education (for instance, the elimination of education as a major in favor of an academic subject such as mathematics or English) and for fewer and better education courses. In recent years, all but two states have raised admission standards for teacher education programs, reevaluated teacher education programs, or developed unified course requirements for students in such programs.[31] Also, several states, such as Connecticut, have established loan programs for college students who wish to prepare for careers in teaching.

Some of the most constructive criticisms have come from the profession itself. The National Commission on Teaching and America's Future (NCTAF) published two reports, *What Matters Most* (1996) and *Doing What Matters Most* (1997), in which it offered the nation a blueprint to guide the reform of teacher education. The Commission recommended reform in five key areas:

- Setting professional standards for teachers that are linked to new student standards

- Ensuring high-quality teacher preparation and professional development

- Improving teacher recruitment and hiring practices

- Rewarding teacher knowledge and skill

- Designing schools that are organized for student and teacher success

To date, the NCTAF had partnered with nineteen states to help them implement reforms that will enhance the quality of teaching in those states. Although some progress has been made in the first two areas, less success has been made in the last three areas.

changes in the career ladder

The third initiative involved **career ladders.** Critics have long complained about the "flatness" of the career structure in teaching. The criticism goes something like this: "Beginners have too much responsibility at the beginning of their careers and too little opportunity to make the most of their abilities once they really learn to teach. The only way to get promoted in education is to be promoted *away from students,* to become a department chair, curriculum coordinator, or administrator." With the encouragement of state legislatures, a variety of teacher specialty programs, such as master teacher programs, differentiated staffing, and mentoring programs for new teachers, have appeared on the scene. Typically, these programs give experienced teachers new roles, new responsibilities, and usually new rewards. Although these innovations have had somewhat limited adoption, the assumption that "a teacher is a teacher is a teacher" has been dispelled, and new roles, such as mentor teacher and team leader, have been opened to teachers who want new challenges but also want to stay in the classroom, close to students.

Higher Salaries for Teachers   A key problem revealed by the blizzard of reports published in the 1980s and 1990s was the weak reward system for teachers. Career ladders and other schemes, which expand and enrich the teacher's role, are one way to reward teachers, but more was needed if teaching was to become an attractive professional option for talented students. Salaries were an

rising salaries

obvious target. During the 1980s, the average teacher salary increased at a rate twice that of inflation. Since then, average salaries have generally kept pace with inflation. In some states, dramatic increases in teacher salaries were legislated by the state or local governments. From 1982–83 to 1988–89, the average teacher salary increased by 98 percent in Connecticut, 75 percent in Vermont, 55 percent in Virginia, 53 percent in South Carolina, and 50 percent in California.[32]

Visit the web site to link to up-to-date statistics on this topic.

Closely linked to this change has been a substantial move to make teaching more attractive by increasing the starting salaries of teachers. In the late 1980s, beginning teachers earned $12,000 to $13,000. By 2001, the national average for beginning teachers was almost $29,000. In fact, a number of school districts around the country have established starting salaries of $30,000 and above. A more recent phenomenon has been the offering of signing bonuses to teachers, especially in certain hard-to-fill disciplines such as math, sciences, and foreign languages. The signing bonuses may be state- or district-funded and in some cases, may be as much as $20,000.

performance pay

All across the country the lock-step pay scale by which teachers were rewarded only by years of service and number of courses taken has been altered to allow for **performance pay (pay-for-performance),** a form of recognition and reward for acquiring new knowledge or skills, or for increasing student achievement. A five-year pilot program has been implemented recently in Colorado. The success of the program will soon be made known.

School Choice   As you have read about in other chapters, there are many different groups who are concerned about the quality of education that students receive (see the chapter entitled "How Are Schools Governed, Influenced, and Financed?"). Some of these groups think that the education of our young is too

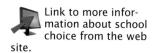 Link to more information about school choice from the web site.

■ *broadening schooling options*

■ *shortage of local funding for reform*

■ *shifting power to state level*

■ *ideas emerge at local level*

important a responsibility to leave to the public schools. Others argue that the only way to bring about better quality is to increase competition among and between schools. These beliefs have served as the impetus for different attempts to reform the structure and organization of public schools in the United States. These include charter schools and educational vouchers, which give parents more choices for the education of their children. (See the chapter entitled "What Social Problems and Tension Points Affect Today's Students?".)

Although there has been a good deal of commonality among the reform movements from state to state, a few states have distinguished themselves for their energetic and innovative responses to the call to excellence. Among those states are Kentucky, South Carolina, Connecticut, and, in particular, California.

■ *Local-Level School Reform*

Former Speaker of the U.S. House of Representatives, the late Tip O'Neill, was fond of saying, "All politics are local." The same is true of education. Children are educated at their local schools, not at the state capitol or in Washington, D.C. Though some school reform efforts such as the Coalition of Essential Schools Project are national in scope, they are implemented in local schools under the supervision of a school district.

At present, however, the great majority of changes being made in schools are coming at the direction of the various states' departments of education, and educational funds are often linked to how faithfully and quickly a school district implements the desired reform mandates.

Locally initiated reform efforts, although in no way stopped, have slowed down, partly because of a shortage of local funds. Growing competition for fixed amounts of municipal tax dollars—from police and fire departments to agencies serving the poor and the elderly—and competing thoughts on the primary purpose of public education have made it difficult to secure monies for new, locally supported reform efforts.

Because state funds are often given out or withheld on the basis of compliance with state-level directives, local school boards may be left with limited decision-making authority. The Kentucky Educational Reform Act is a case in point. Through this plan, the state-level judges, legislators, and education officials are telling the local Kentucky schools how they must change. What we are witnessing is a classic shift in power, with the statehouse dictating more and more not just what should be taught but how it should be taught.

Though the center of gravity may be elsewhere, the local school district is deeply involved in the current reform movement. Furthermore, the overwhelming percentage of reform ideas that have made their way onto the agendas of national and state reform groups existed first at the local level. They became statewide or national because they succeeded first at the local level. In the future, more innovative ideas such as block scheduling, year-round education, single-sex schools, school uniforms, and site-based decision making, will continue to come up from our local schools.

PAUSE AND REFLECT

❶ Looking back on your own elementary and secondary schoolings, can you recall any locally initiated innovations, unique projects, or experimental programs?

Letter from a Homeschooling Mother for *Those Who Can, Teach*

Homeschooling these days offers every child an opportunity for a world-class education. It doesn't cost much, and it is adaptable to many circumstances and individuals.

By having personally tailored curricula and individual attention, home-schooled students' time is rarely wasted. My children have their formal lessons during the morning hours, but in some way, the schooling never stops. Besides the basics, my second grader has studied Ancient Greek history this year, along with American history, and is getting a leg up on languages by being introduced to Greek and Latin vocabulary. (On a standardized test, she amused the researcher by identifying the figure of a person behind bars as Socrates in prison.) My preschooler son is working through reading lessons, memorizing poetry, and otherwise engaging in creative activities.

During the afternoons, the kids read and follow their own interests. My seven-year-old has charted the birds that come to our yard. She's learning how to knit and sew (thanks to a family friend, who is better at it than I am). My five-year-old son climbs trees and examines bugs. They work out elaborate fantasies about knights and princesses, pioneer families, and discovered elves. They build forts and press flowers.

For homeschooling parents, offering each child (not just the brightest) the opportunity to become passionate about ideas is worth the sacrifice of having their children under their supervision for most of the day. Students develop the habit of learning, so they don't always have to depend on an instructor. They come to know what it means to master bodies of knowledge and how to reason. They can progress at their own rate. The advanced student is not held back, and made to repeat exercises he has already learned. The slower student does not miss building foundational skills because other students are ready to move on. Where the student has weaknesses, he receives extra help. Where there are strengths, he has the opportunity to soar. As a teacher I am able to teach them a time-tested curriculum so the child is spared trendy new subjects that may not be around in ten years.

Perhaps understandably, parents of homeschooled kids are often asked, "What about socialization?" It is true that homeschooled children do not spend their days in a classroom filled with 22 peers, and are thus deprived of this particular group experience. Yet this freedom from the bustling crowd can be an advantage. The children learn to cooperate with other children of all ages, primarily and significantly their siblings, but friends and peers in sports and other activities, too.

Homeschooling support networks are well developed and very diversified. Most days, tennis, violin, and ballet classes and trips to the library get us out of the house. My son plays in a city t-ball league. They participate in plays with their local homeschool support group. They also have more time with grandparents, neighbors, and other members of the community. And, of course, their friends come over to play. With all this, the children divide their time between other children and the adult world. This is why these students are so strikingly comfortable around people of all ages.

I believe I, and many other parents, can serve my children and society best by educating them in our home. And, besides the impressive progress they are making, I am enjoying it immensely.

Hilary Tucker is a mother of three children and lives in Auburn, Alabama.

■ *growth in homeschooling*

One very local school reform that has gained greater popularity in the past twenty years is the homeschooling movement. Parents, dissatisfied with the education their children receive in the local public schools, decide to educate their children themselves, most often in their homes (see box above). The U.S. Department of Education estimates that there are 850,000 children being homeschooled. Reasons for homeschooling vary all the way from concerns about the

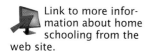

Link to more information about home schooling from the web site.

moral climate in public schools or religious objections to the curriculum to the absence of particular courses of study. In all cases, however, parents strongly believe that they can provide a better education for their children than the public schools can. Regulations for home schooling vary from state to state. In some states, parents have to submit an educational plan for their homeschooled children; in other states, they merely inform the school and/or the state education agency of their intention to home school their children.

The Current State of School Reform

piecemeal reform

Although we clearly have a new set of educational reform priorities, goals, and expectations, few schools have experienced sweeping changes as a result of educational reform. Some have made fundamental changes in the way they engage children and in what they teach. Most have adopted pieces of reform such as a new districtwide mathematics curriculum, a computer lab, or a career ladder for teachers. Some states have pushed through serious changes that affect the great majority of their schools, but they are the rarities. The school experience of the first-grader or the high school senior is in many ways pretty much the same today as it was in 1983, when the current reform era began.

American education is not like an individual who, after a few life failures, looks in the mirror and says, "That's it; I'm going to get my act together starting today," and from that moment on is a "new" person. American education is a giant institution, involving 15,000 centers of decision making (school boards), well over 55 million people (students, teachers, and administrators), and influences from many quarters of society. And most important, like any institution, it has a standard operating procedure (SOP). Everyone starting a school year in September (except for the newcomers, the kindergartners) has a clear set of expectations about what school ought to be like. Without this, chaos would result. But because of these expectations, altering the course of schooling is quite a demanding task.

Perhaps a better parallel than an individual trying to change the course of his or her life is a large luxury liner plowing through the ocean. Someone convinces the captain that dangerous icebergs lie ahead. The captain first has to be assured that the reports are reasonable, next decide where the safe water is, and then turn the wheel. But because of its size and momentum, the ship may need miles to truly change course. This is where we believe American schools are today. They have heard the message; they have committed to change course and avoid the hazards; they have begun to turn the wheel. Whether the ship actually turns and misses the dangers, we must wait to see.

A Final Word

teachers at the center

Clearly it is the teacher who stands at the center of true school reform. It is the teacher who actually delivers educational services, who creates or fails to create an environment for learning, and who either knows or does not know how to engage students in their own pursuit of excellence. Since 1983, Americans have seen their industries "reengineered" and "restructured," making them much more competitive in the global marketplace. Educational researchers are now suggesting that schools follow the example of outstanding private-sector firms, guiding their reform efforts by the following five principles:

■ *principles from private sector*

- Ensure that all front-line workers, or teachers, understand the problem in the same way

- Design jobs so that all front-line workers have both incentives and opportunities to contribute to solutions

- Provide all front-line workers with the training needed to pursue solutions effectively

- Measure progress on a regular basis

- Persevere and learn from mistakes; there are no magic bullets

The final decisions about educational reform are, by necessity, made by teachers. Although it is discouraging (and even threatening) to know that we have not yet achieved our goal of reforming our schools, we Americans are often at our best when challenged. And clearly school reform is part of the unfinished business of America and the American teacher. A job of critical importance to all of us awaits you.

KEY TERMS

active learning (370)

authentic (performance) assessment (369)

call to excellence (384)

career ladders (388)

character education (374)

constructivism (370)

learning communities (379)

lifelong learners (373)

national curricular standards (383)

National Education Goals (382)

performance pay (pay-for-performance) (388)

portfolios (369)

schools-within-schools (372)

teacher competency testing (386)

teaching to the test (368)

tools for learning (374)

year-round education (385)

FOR REFLECTION

1 Are any of the reform initiatives described in this chapter evident in your local schools?

2 Which of the reform efforts described in the chapter most interests you? Why?

3 If monies for schooling continue to be tight, which educational reforms will be most weakened? Which will be least weakened?

4 What do you believe teachers should do to take a more active role in the reform process?

FOR FURTHER INFORMATION
PRINT RESOURCES

Gordon Cawelti, *Portraits of Six Benchmark Schools: Diverse Approaches to Improving Student Achievement* (Alexandria, VA: Association for Supervision and Curriculum Development, 1999).

This well-written report offers portraits of excellent public schools with high standards, multiple changes, strong leadership, collaborative teams, and committed teachers—in other words, reform success stories.

Kevin Ryan and Karen Bohlin, *Building Character in Schools: Practical Ways to Bring Moral Instruction to Life* (San Francisco: Jossey-Bass, 1999).

This book offers teachers both a theory and a set of practical steps to infuse their teaching with our core moral values. In addition, the book has many practical lists and materials to promote character in classrooms and schools.

Theodore Sizer and Nancy Sizer, *The Children Are Watching* (Boston: Beacon Press, 1999).

This short book by two veterans of the school reform wars focuses on the personal side of the reform effort. The Sizers describe schools and students the way they currently are and then suggest ways teachers need to respond.

WEB RESOURCES

Andy Carvin. *EdWeb: Exploring Technology and School Reform*. Available at: **http://edweb.cnidr.org**.

This book is devoted to school reform, the spread of educational technology, and the interconnections between these two trends. It includes information on such topics as school choice, accountability, school restructuring, and the Coalition of Essential Schools.

ASCD SmartBriefs. Available at: **http://www. ASCD.org**.

SmartBriefs is a free educational news service that can be received through email. It contains news, commentary, and educational resources.

The Educational Gadfly. Available at: **http://www. edexcellence.net**.

A different slant on the educational news and policy developments, you can sign up for *The Gadfly*, weekly bulletin of policy news, book reviews, and lively commentary by Chester E. Finn.

Part Four

The Teaching Profession

This section deals with both practical and theoretical questions: Will there be job openings in teaching? How do you go about obtaining a teaching position? What kind of salary can you expect to make? What does it mean to be a professional teacher? Why teach?

It is anticipated that during the next ten years, more than 2 million new teachers will have to be hired to offset rising student enrollment and replace departing teachers. Yet finding the teaching position in the school that is right for you can be a complex and challenging prospect. This section explores the teaching profession: what it is and how to become part of it.

What Are Your Job Options in Education?

Chapter Preview This chapter provides you with information regarding the availability of teaching positions in elementary, middle, and secondary schools. It also explores other career opportunities both within and outside the educational field. Study the information carefully and discuss it with your instructors and your career planning and placement office. Your program of study may offer more job options than you have realized.

This chapter emphasizes that:

- Many factors influence the availability of teaching jobs. At the present time, some teaching fields face a severe shortage, while in other fields the supply and demand seem balanced.

- Teacher salaries have made some gains in recent years, with the average salary of classroom teachers in 2001–2002 being over $44,499 and the average salary of *beginning* teachers in 2000–2001 being just under $29,000. However, salaries vary tremendously from state to state and from school district to school district.

- Certain job-hunting strategies will increase your chances of locating the right job for you. You may have to spend considerable time and energy preparing materials for your job search.

- Licensure requirements differ from state to state for both general and specialized areas of teaching.

- A wide variety of careers are available to people trained as teachers. Should you be unable to secure a teaching position or wish to change careers after you have taught, the skills you have acquired in teacher education can be transferred to related occupational areas.

- No matter what the job market may be at a particular moment, there has never been a surplus of good teachers. Better-prepared teachers will find it easier to gain employment and will improve the teaching profession and its public image.

WANTED: Men and women with the wisdom of Solomon, the patience of Job, and the nerves of David before Goliath. Needed to prepare the next generation for productive citizenship in the twenty-first century, often under adverse conditions. Applicants must be willing to fill in gaps left by unfit, absent, or working parents; satisfy demands of local bureaucrats and state politicians; impart healthy self-esteem; and, oh, by the way, teach content!

Hours: 50 to 60 hours per week
Pay: Growing respectable
Reward: The luxury of always knowing that you are doing something significant with your life

This fictitious ad contains many messages about the roles that teachers play. It also highlights the fact that there is a serious need for skilled new teachers in our nation's schools. As you have thought about teaching as a career, you have probably wondered whether you will be able to obtain a teaching position when you graduate. Although we would like to answer this question for you personally, we obviously cannot. We can, however, provide you with information that may help you increase your chances of obtaining the kind of teaching position you are seeking.

Will There Be Job Openings in Education?

■ *Factors Influencing Teacher Supply and Demand*

Teaching is a large occupation, representing 4 percent of the entire civilian work force. There are more than twice as many K–12 teachers as registered nurses

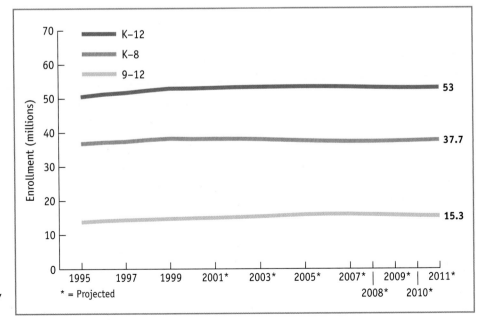

FIGURE 12.1
Enrollment in Public and Private Schools (in millions)

Source: William J. Hussar and Debra E. Gerald, *Projections of Education Statistics to 2011* (Washington, DC: National Center for Education Statistics, 2001), p. 12. Available at: **http://nces.ed.gov/pubs98/pj2008/p98t01.html**.

FIGURE 12.2
Classroom Teachers in Public and Private Schools (in thousands)

Source: William J. Hussar and Debra E. Gerald, *Projections of Education Statistics to 2011* (Washington, DC: National Center for Education Statistics, 2001), p. 79.

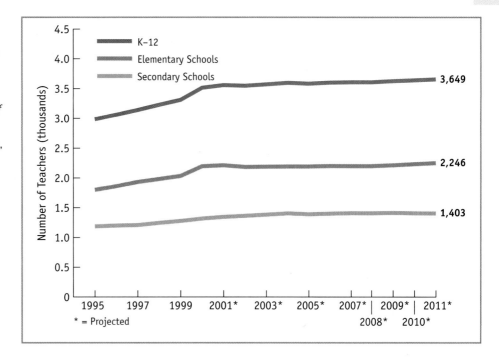

and five times as many teachers as either lawyers or professors.[1] With a teaching work force of this size, many jobs exist. In fact, many people believe there will be a shortage of teachers in the near future. However, estimates of shortages are based on rapidly changing situations influenced by unpredictable factors. The following sections discuss a number of these factors.

rising student enrollments

Student Enrollment in Schools   Obviously, when more students are enrolled in schools, more teachers are needed. The good news is that enrollments in public and private schools reached 53.3 million students in 2002, eclipsing the previous record set in the 1970s, and are projected to stay about the same until 2011. Enrollments in secondary schools will increase over this period while those in elementary schools will decline somewhat. However, enrollments in different geographical regions of the United States are following different patterns. Student enrollments are increasing in the western part of the United States and declining in the northeastern states. The number of classroom teachers is expected to increase from 3.5 million in 2002 to 3.65 million by 2011, with the number of secondary school teachers increasing at a faster rate than the number of elementary school teachers[2] (Figures 12.1 and 12.2).

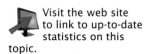 Visit the web site to link to up-to-date statistics on this topic.

Class Sizes   During the 1980s and 1990s, the demand for new teachers was boosted by declining class sizes, especially in California. In 1996, California provided more than $750 million to cut class sizes in grades K–3 from as many as 30 students to 20, requiring an estimated total of 26,000 additional primary school teachers.[3]

Nationally, current class sizes now hover around 21 students per teacher in the public elementary schools and slightly more than 23 students per teacher in public secondary schools. Class sizes in private schools are slightly smaller

stable class sizes

than in public schools, averaging a bit more than 20 students per class for both elementary and secondary schools.[4] However, the changes in class sizes during the next few years are expected to be small, and they will not likely affect the demand for new teachers in any significant fashion.

many teachers elect not to teach

Enrollment in Teacher Education Programs   Across the nation, about 200,000 teachers are prepared each year; however, only about 60 percent of those prepared to teach actually enter the classroom. And of these, 30 to 50 percent leave teaching within the first five years.[5] Thus, an adequate number of teachers are prepared to meet the demand, but because so many choose not to teach or to stop teaching after a few years, the supply doesn't match the demand for new teachers.

Link to more information about geographical teacher needs from the web site.

Geographical Location   Location significantly influences the teaching job market. Some communities have far more applicants than available teaching positions. University towns, for example, usually have a great surplus of teachers. Although large urban areas historically have had more teachers available than they needed, they are now experiencing significant teacher shortages. One study examined the nation's largest urban school districts and found that almost all of them had an urgent need for teachers in at least one high need area, such as special education.[6] Rural America traditionally has had difficulty attracting and holding onto teachers because of lower salaries and a more sedate lifestyle than that sought by many young teachers. There are not enough qualified teachers who are willing to teach in urban and rural schools, particularly those serving low-income students or students of color.

jobs available in Sunbelt and Midwest states

Generally speaking, teacher vacancies are greatest in the West (California, Arizona, Nevada, Hawaii, and Utah); the Great Plains/Midwest (the Dakotas, Minnesota, Iowa, Nebraska, and Missouri); and the south and south central states. There are fewer vacancies and/or more competition in the Great Lakes states (Wisconsin, Michigan, Illinois, Indiana, and Ohio) and the Middle Atlantic states (Delaware, District of Columbia, Maryland, New Jersey, New York, and Pennsylvania).[7]

Teachers tend to be more "place bound" than many other professionals— that is, because of family commitments or the importance of geographical location, many teachers seeking jobs are reluctant to stray far from home. So even though teaching jobs may be available in Las Vegas (which they are!), teachers from the Northeast, for example, may not want to relocate to Nevada.

job availability depends on teaching field

Subject Matter and Grade Levels Taught   Teachers are not interchangeable units. They are prepared for different specialties (for example, special education, elementary education, art, or high school social studies), and the job market in each of these subfields is different. Moreover, the job market for specific subfields may change often. It is unwise, therefore, to decide whether to become an English teacher because you have heard that today there is generally either a surplus or a shortage of such teachers. There have been and continue to be chronic teacher shortages in certain subjects, including speech pathology;

fields with teacher shortages

special education (all areas); bilingual education; audiology; mathematics; science (physics, chemistry, earth and physical science, biology); English as a second language; technology education; and languages (particularly Spanish). As of 2002, no teaching fields were considered to have a surplus of teachers.[8] In

There is a demand for male teachers at the elementary school level, where they compose less than 12 percent of the teaching force.
(© Frank Siteman / PhotoEdit)

▪ *shortage of minority and male teachers*

addition to looking for teachers in the subjects just listed, schools are seeking increased numbers of minorities and males. Because 73 percent of all teachers are female, schools want to increase the number of males in the teaching force, especially at the elementary school level, where less than 12 percent of the nation's 1.3 million public school teachers are men.[9]

▪ *aging teacher work force*

▪ Retiring Teachers, Teacher Turnover, and Returning Teachers

An estimated 2.2 million new teachers will be needed during the next ten years. One factor that bodes well for the long-term job outlook is that teachers, like much of the rest of the American work force, are getting older. More than one-quarter of teachers are at least 50 years old, and nearly half will retire over the next decade.[10]

Another factor influencing job availability concerns the percentage of eligible teachers who elect not to teach or those who leave teaching after a few years. As mentioned earlier, 40 percent of those prepared to teach elect not to enter teaching, and of the 60 percent who do teach, 30 to 50 percent leave teaching within the first five years. Sadly, the brightest novice teachers, as measured by their college-entrance exams, were the most likely to leave. Factors influencing the high turnover included poor working

Teaching was the hardest work I had ever done, and it remains the hardest work I have done to date.

—ANN RICHARDS

(FORMER GOVERNOR OF TEXAS)

conditions, dissatisfaction with student discipline, lack of mentoring, and unhappiness with the school environment.[11]

What is difficult to estimate is the number of licensed teachers, currently not teaching, who might re-enter the teaching force if jobs are readily available. When teacher shortages have been predicted in the past, these returning teachers have filled the anticipated shortages. Whether this pattern will continue remains to be seen. Teachers licensed through alternative routes (alternative licensure is discussed later) have thus far made up only a small percentage of the available pool of teachers, but that situation could change if states promote these programs more vigorously.

■ *job availability affected by economy*

Economic Conditions   In spite of the positive long-term outlook for teaching positions in times of economic hardship, school districts may find it necessary to reduce the size of their teaching forces to balance budgets. During the 1990–91 recession and, to a lesser extent, the 2001 recession, school districts in a number of states found it necessary to issue reduction-in-force notices (RIFs)—to teachers, informing them that they were in danger of not being rehired for the following fall. Although painful in the short run, such layoffs will probably be only temporary and will have little overall effect on the long-term demand for new teachers. RIF notices do show, however, that the demand for teachers is greatly influenced by school district budgets, which in turn are affected by the health of the state and local economies.

■ *demand for teachers promising*

Summary   What, then, are the job prospects for the future? The situation is very promising, because the number of classroom teachers in elementary and secondary schools is projected to stay at a high level at least until 2011, primarily because of teacher retirements and teachers who leave the field. Recruitment of teachers recently has become so competitive that many districts are offering incentives to qualified teachers, including paying bonuses ranging from $1,500 to $20,000, closing costs or reduced mortgage rates on home purchases, and relocation expenses. Some states are even considering offering state income tax breaks for teachers. However, if the supply of qualified teachers doesn't keep up with the demand, states and local school districts may, as they have in the past, increase class size, hire less-than-qualified personnel, and assign teachers trained in one field to teach in an understaffed field. However, the 2002 Leave No Child Behind Act requires all states to ensure that by the 2005–06 school year, every public school teacher must be "highly qualified," which means that the teacher has been licensed by the state and has demonstrated a high level of competence in the subjects that he or she teaches. (See the chapter entitled "How Are Schools Governed, Influenced, and Financed?" for more on this legislation.)

■ *federal legislation requiring "qualified" teachers*

Keep in mind, too, that demographic projections and supply-and-demand forecasting are not only hard to apply but also very inexact and short-lived. With difficulty, forecasters try to take into account factors such as retirement rates, supplies of former teachers re-entering the field, and programs that may attract individuals from nonteaching fields into the profession. What seems to be true for a particular geographic area, a particular teaching field, or a particular year may be out of date at the moment you are reading it.

■ *obtain recent information*

Therefore, you ought to make every effort to get the most up-to-the-minute information possible about teacher supply and demand. You should consider such information carefully before making a choice about a career in education and, in particular, about a specific subfield within education. This is especially true for people who are unable to wait for openings in their areas of teaching interest or unable to relocate. Sources of data with which to begin your search are your school's career counseling office, the department chairperson's or dean's office, and your state department of education. Also, see the listing of useful references at the end of this chapter.

The bottom line is that demand for teachers is high and is expected to continue to be high in the coming years, and there has never been a surplus of good teachers in any field.

■ The Severe Shortage of Minority Teachers

One of the greatest teacher supply-and-demand problems concerns minority teachers. At a time when the minority school-age population is increasing rapidly, the number of minority teachers is decreasing. The shortage is severe now and appears likely to become worse.

■ *fewer minority teachers*

As you saw in the chapter entitled "Who Are Today's Students in a Diverse Society?", enrollments of students from minority groups are increasing and currently are estimated to be 37 percent. Teaching staffs, on the other hand, are becoming more and more white. Almost 91 percent of public school teachers are white, 7 percent are African American, and only 2 percent come from other minority groups, including Hispanic American, Asian American or Pacific Islander, and Native American or Native Alaskan.[12] Most minority teachers are located in central cities rather than in suburban or rural areas. During most of the 1990s, the graduation rates of minority students from teacher education were lower than their percentage distribution in the teaching force. Although minority enrollment in teacher education has been increasing in recent years, the need is still acute.

This shortage of minority teachers is problematic for several reasons. First, the growing number of minority children deserve to have positive minority role models who can help guide them in a world still plagued by racism. Second, white children also need to have minority teachers as positive role models to help them overcome the effects of stereotyping and racism. Third, it is important for our country's well-being to have a teaching staff that reflects the diversity of racial and ethnic backgrounds in our country's population.

[Emma Belle Sweet] taught me many things. . . . But nothing could be so important to me and of such enduring quality as her simple, human act of figuratively leading me gently by the hand to a sense of self-respect, dignity, and worth.
—RALPH BUNCHE (AN AFRICAN-AMERICAN AND 1950 NOBEL PEACE PRIZE WINNER)

■ *factors affecting shortage of minority teachers*

The shortage of minority teachers exists for a number of reasons. Before desegregation efforts, nearly one-half of African-American professional workers were teachers. When schools desegregated in the 1960s and 1970s, resulting in the consolidation of formerly all-black and all-white schools, thousands of African-American teachers were dismissed. Today, other professions that pay more and have higher status are actively recruiting minority college students. Another causal factor has been the increasing use of competency tests at either the beginning or the end of teacher education programs. Minority college students traditionally have not performed as well on standardized tests as white college students. As a consequence, many minority teaching candidates are either failing to pass these tests or are being discouraged from even considering teaching as a career.

The shortage of minority teachers deprives both white and minority students of positive role models.
(© Chip Henderson/Stone/Getty Images)

What can be done to address this problem? Teaching salaries must continue to improve if teaching is to compete with other professions for well-qualified candidates. Assistance programs to help minority candidates perform well on competency tests have been effective in a number of universities and need to be expanded to other colleges. Active recruitment programs for minority candidates must be developed and implemented, and they must reach down into the middle and high schools to encourage minority students to consider teaching as a career. Scholarship and loan-forgiveness programs are needed for students who want to teach but cannot afford college. And the American public must communicate, in a variety of ways, that it values teachers and the work they do.

■ *Employers Besides the Public Schools*

■ Department of Defense schools

■ **U.S. Government**   A large employer of teachers is the U.S. government. The Department of Defense operates 224 elementary and secondary schools in seven states, Puerto Rico, Guam, and fourteen countries around the world, making it the twenty-second largest school district in the United States. These schools enroll approximately 106,000 students and employ about 9,000 educational personnel.* Salaries are comparable to those in the United States, but

*For more information on applying for a job with the Department of Defense overseas schools, write the U.S. Department of Defense, Office of Dependents Schools, Personnel Center, 4040 North Fairfax Drive, Arlington, VA 22203-1635 or call the office at (703)696-3068.

VOICES FROM THE CLASSROOM

Karen Irving has taught chemistry and other science disciplines at the secondary and college levels for 19 years, including six years of public high school teaching and six years of private high school teaching.

Teaching in Public Versus Private Schools

I loved the pulse of my urban high school with its creative and energetic faculty. With three other chemistry teachers in our school of just under 2000 students, we never lacked ideas or opinions about how to best help our students succeed. Sometimes we struggled to match our equipment availability to our classroom plans, but we always benefited from the sharing of experiences and expertise.

In addition to a large and diverse faculty, my urban high school boasted a large and diverse student population. However, with just three to four hours of planning time per week and 130 to 150 students in five sections, as well as science fair projects, science teams, and other extracurricular responsibilities, little time remained in my schedule to offer extra help to my students.

After six years of public high school teaching, I accepted a science teaching position at an independent, college preparatory, girls' school. Because my teaching assignment at the private school included 60 to 65 students in four sections, the amount of time during the school day to plan lessons and work with students (eight hours per week) doubled from what I was used to in the public setting. In addition, because the weekly school schedule included time for faculty meetings and student clubs during the school day, teachers and students shared free time before and after school for help sessions, make-up work, and additional student enrichment. Other conditions were different, too. More parents returned teacher telephone calls, provided necessary home support for learning, made arrangements for students to attend help sessions, attended school functions, and generally worked together with school personnel to ensure that their children received a quality education.

If I had the chance to create an ideal high school environment, I would blend elements of both public and private schools. Ideal High would boast a diverse, creative, and energetic faculty and student population with small classes and sufficient time for teachers to plan and deliver quality lessons. Each student would have the opportunity to reach his or her full potential. Parents, administrators, teachers, and students at Ideal High would share a common vision of an educational community of disciplined effort and academic achievement.

 Visit the web site for more Voices from the Classroom.

preference is given to applicants who have at least one year of successful full-time employment as a professional educator.[13]

■ **Private Schools** Although much of the data presented in this chapter refer to public elementary and secondary schools, private education is a highly significant part of the American educational system. There are more than 26,000 private schools with an enrollment of more than 6 million preschool, elementary, and secondary school students and a staff of 413,000 teachers. About 11 percent of the children in elementary or secondary schools attend a private school, with the overwhelming majority attending religion-affiliated schools. Projections are that over 500,000 new teachers will be needed in private schools over the next decade.[14]

■ *private schools a significant employer*

■ salaries less in private schools

Because private schools employ about 12 percent of all elementary and secondary teachers, they obviously offer an employment opportunity for new teachers. Many teachers who work in religion-affiliated schools do so because of religious motives. These teachers are often willing to work for less money than their public school counterparts, and as a result, the average teacher salary in private schools is about 25 percent lower than that in public schools. In many cases, lower salaries tend to be offset by favorable working conditions. Compared with public schools, private schools have fewer disciplinary problems, stricter discipline, smaller classes, fewer students using drugs, students who are absent less often, parents who are more supportive, more assigned homework, and more time spent in instruction in the central academic subjects. Although private school teachers tend to work about two more hours per week than their public school counterparts, they believe they have more influence over important school policies.[15] Thus, for many individuals, teaching in a private school is an attractive alternative to teaching in the public schools. Recently, however, private schools are finding that they are losing instructors to the public schools. Pay raises and benefits, signing bonuses, and smaller classes have combined to make teaching in the public schools more attractive, particularly as various states relax their licensure requirements, making it easier for private school teachers to move to public schools. Many private schools are responding by raising tuitions to pay for increased teacher salaries. Helpful references for finding teaching jobs in nonpublic schools are provided at the end of this chapter.

PAUSE AND REFLECT

1 What are the present and projected teacher supplies in the field that currently interests you? In the geographic area you desire?

2 Are you willing to leave your current location to find a teaching position? Are you willing to teach in an urban school? A rural school? A private school?

■ *What Are Teachers Paid?*

We might answer this question by saying, "Not nearly enough." No one ever went into teaching because of the lure of big money. As we note in the "Why Teach?" chapter, most of the rewards for teaching are personal rather than monetary. Most of teachers' satisfactions come from being of service to others and helping students learn. That does not mean, however, that you have to be a pauper to enjoy the satisfactions that come from teaching. Salaries are a legitimate concern for a prospective teacher; after all, everyone must have sufficient income to meet the costs of living. You will have to decide whether the salary you are likely to make as a classroom teacher will allow you to establish the lifestyle you want. This section will give you some objective facts with which to make your decision.

■ average teacher salaries

The 2001–02 average salary of classroom teachers in the United States is estimated to be about $44,600.[16] Figure 12.3 shows the rise in average salaries since the 1990s, and Table 12.1 shows how salaries vary by state and region. The Average Salary column in the table represents the average for *all* public elementary and secondary school teachers, and the Beginning Salary column indicates the average for *first-year* teachers. For teachers in their first year, the average pay across the nation as a whole was just under $29,000 in 2000–2001, ranging from a low of $20,675 (North Dakota) to a high of $36,293 (Alaska).[17]

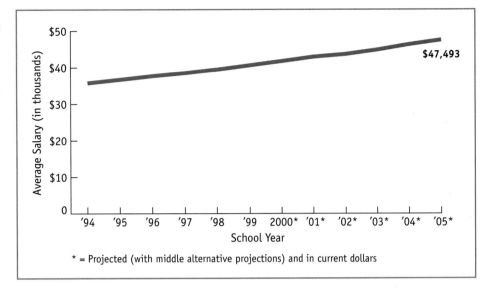

FIGURE 12.3
Average Public School Teacher Salaries

Source: William J. Hussar and Debra E. Gerald, *Projections of Education Statistics to 2011* (Washington, DC: National Center for Education Statistics, 2001), p. 90.

Most public school salary schedules are usually determined by two factors: years of teaching experience and amount of education, usually expressed in terms of college credit-hours or advanced degrees. Thus, the longer you teach and the more college education you receive, the more money you will make (see Table 12.2 on the web site for an example of a school district salary schedule). In addition, some states and school districts have used various forms of merit or **performance pay (pay-for-performance) plans** to reward teachers for exceptional teaching, acquiring new skills needed by the school, achieving national board certification, raising student test scores, or assuming more professional responsibilities. (See the chapter entitled "What Does It Mean to Be a Professional?" for more on national board certification.)

salary schedules

As you can see from Table 12.1, salaries vary considerably from state to state. Each school district determines what it will pay its teachers, with many states setting a minimum base salary below which the school district cannot go. Generally, the large and middle-size school districts pay better than the small ones, and urban and suburban school districts pay better than rural ones. Many school districts offer extra pay for special duties such as directing the band or coaching athletic teams. Some offer summer teaching or curriculum development jobs. Most states and school districts provide public school teachers with a number of fringe benefits, including sick leave, health and life insurance programs, and retirement benefits. When applying for a teaching position, be sure to ask about these benefits.

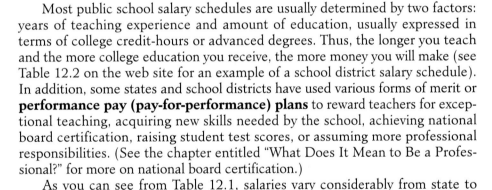 See an example of a salary schedule at the web site.

fringe benefits

How Do You Obtain a Teaching Position?

The job market is very encouraging for beginning teachers, but regardless of how great the demand for teachers is or how effective you may be as a teacher, school district personnel are not likely to walk up to you and offer you a job

TABLE 12.1 Average and Beginning Teacher Salaries, by State and Region

State	Average Salary ($) (2001–2002)	Beginning Salary ($) (2000–2001)	State	Average Salary ($) (2001–2002)	Beginning Salary ($) (2000–2001)
New England			**Southeast**		
Connecticut	53,551	32,203	Georgia	44,073	31,314
Rhode Island	49,758*	29,265	North Carolina	41,991	29,786
Massachusetts	49,054	26,290	Virginia	41,262*	28,139
New Hampshire	38,911*	25,020	Alabama	39,268*	28,649
Vermont	39,240	26,152	South Carolina	38,943*	26,314
Maine	37,300	23,689	Florida	39,275	25,786
Mideast			Tennessee	38,554	28,074
New Jersey	51,186	30,937	Kentucky	37,847	25,027
New York	53,081	32,772	West Virginia	36,751	24,889
Pennsylvania	50,599	31,127	Louisiana	34,505*	26,124
Delaware	48,363	32,281	Arkansas	37,140*	24,469
Washington, D.C.	47,049	31,889	Mississippi	32,800*	23,292
Maryland	46,200	30,321	**Rocky Mountains**		
Great Lakes			Colorado	40,222*	26,479
Michigan	52,037*	29,401	Wyoming	37,841	24,651
Illinois	50,000	31,222	Idaho	37,482*	23,386
Ohio	44,029	24,895	Utah	37,414*	24,553
Indiana	44,195	27,311	Montana	34,379*	21,728
Wisconsin	42,232	26,232	**Far West**		
Great Plains			California	53,870*	33,121
Minnesota	43,330*	27,003	Alaska	49,418	36,293
Iowa	38,230	26,058	Oregon	46,039	27,903
Missouri	37,904	27,173	Washington	43,474	27,284
Kansas	36,673	26,010	Hawaii	42,615	29,204
Nebraska	36,236	24,353	Nevada	41,524*	29,413
North Dakota	31,709*	20,675	U.S. Average	44,449	28,986
South Dakota	31,295	22,457			
Southwest					
Texas	39,232	29,823			
Arizona	39,973	26,801			
New Mexico	36,440	25,999			
Oklahoma	34,744	27,016			

*estimated

Sources: Average salaries from "Ranking Estimates of the States and Estimates of School Statistics 2002," Update Fall 2002 (Washington, DC: National Education Association, 2002), available at: **http:www.nea.org/edstats/reupdate02.html**. Beginning salaries from F. Howard Nelson, *Survey and Analysis of Salary Trends, 1998, 2001*. Table I-8, p. 8. Copyright © 1998, 2001. Reprinted with permission from American Federation of Teachers.

unless you have taken a number of steps that we will outline in this section. We will suggest several courses of action that will greatly increase your chances of finding the best teaching job for you.

■ *Campaign Actively*

■ *develop a plan*

First, you must be determined to campaign actively for a teaching position. Draw up a plan, in writing, of how you will proceed. Don't wait for happenstance. You might get lucky and land a job on your first try, but why take a passive attitude when you can do much to increase your chances of obtaining satisfying employment? For example, try attending job fairs sponsored by various colleges, universities, or school districts.

The great aim of education is not knowledge but action.

—HERBERT SPENCER

Job seekers often make two common mistakes.[18] One is to try one strategy, wait for results (positive or negative), then try something else. What you should do is pursue many avenues or strategies simultaneously. The second common error is to block oneself out at the wrong stage in the process. Some teachers only halfheartedly write for information or never complete the application form. Others withdraw their applications prematurely. Remember, you can always say "no" to a job offered to you, but you can never say "yes" to one that has not been offered. Keep your options open.

■ *Prepare Materials*

■ *prepare a good résumé*

Next, you need to get certain materials ready. These include your résumé, cover letter, credentials, and transcripts. Your résumé allows you to present yourself the way you want to be presented to prospective employers. Its purpose is to help you get an interview with school district officials. You should make several copies of your résumé.

Many sources are available to help you write your résumé. The office of career planning and placement at your college or university is a good place to start. These offices often run workshops on résumé writing and frequently have samples of well-written résumés for you to examine. The American Association for Employment in Education (AAEE) annual *Job Search Handbook for Educators* listed in the For Further Information section at the end of the chapter is an excellent source on how to write résumés and on other job search strategies.

■ *teaching portfolios*

Find more information about assembling a teaching portfolio from the web site.

Another set of materials that more and more teachers are using to help them obtain jobs is called a **teaching portfolio.** Just as artists, actors, architects, and journalists use portfolios to display the products of their work, so can teachers. A teaching portfolio can include an organized collection of such items as research papers, letters of commendation or recommendation, pupil evaluations, teaching units, and videocassettes of lessons you have taught. There is no set format; you are limited only by your common sense and your own imagination. Remember, the purpose of the portfolio is to market yourself effectively, so don't be modest. A properly constructed portfolio will say much more about you than your résumé ever can. Many beginning teachers are constructing electronic portfolios either as web sites or on disk. The advantage of an electronic portfolio is that it is easily accessible by potential employers and can be changed or added to as needed. Electronic teaching portfolios are also being used to demonstrate that prospective teachers have achieved standards—such as the INTASC (Interstate New Teacher Assessment and Support Consortium) standards—required for state licensure. The National Board for Professional Teaching Standards (discussed in the chapter entitled "What Does It Mean to Be a Professional?") has advocated teaching portfolios as a means of assessing a teacher's work for national certification. (See the AAEE *Job Search Handbook for Educators* for specific recommendations on portfolio construction.)

cover letters

The cover letters you write to prospective school districts should be addressed individually. The letters may all have the same or similar content, but the recipients should not feel they are receiving a standard letter. And, incidentally, be sure to ask for an interview. That's why you are writing the letter.

establish your credential file

Almost all school districts require credentials, or the whole package from your college recommending you for licensure. Be sure to check with the career planning and placement office about how to establish your **credential file** and what should go into it. Typically this file will include letters of recommendation, a copy of your transcript, and a résumé. Career planning and placement office personnel will help you assemble this file, and they will send copies of your file to school districts on your request. You should start on the file early in your program so you will have time to accumulate the required materials. Letters of recommendation should be recent, and they should come from those who are familiar with your teaching, academic knowledge, and character. Be certain to include letters from your university supervisor and your cooperating teacher in whose classroom you did your student or internship teaching. Be familiar with

Buckley amendment

the Family Educational Rights and Privacy Act, also known as the Buckley amendment, which affords you certain kinds of legal protection regarding what goes into your file.*

Reproduce unofficial copies of your official transcript. Many applications require that transcripts accompany them. Because colleges charge several dollars per transcript, you can save money by reproducing the transcript yourself. Most school districts will accept unofficial transcripts (those sent from you rather than directly from the college) for the initial screening process. If you receive a job offer, you will then have to provide the school district with an official copy.

▣ *Develop Interview Skills*

prepare for interviews

The success of your personal interview with the school district representative is one of the most important determinants of whether you get hired, so be prepared. Try to anticipate the kinds of questions that might be asked (see the box on the following page for some sample questions). Try role playing with a friend who plays the role of the interviewer while you play the candidate. Audiotape your "interview" so the two of you can criticize it.

empathy for children important

One survey indicated that the major factor school officials look for is whether the candidate has empathy for children. Be prepared to show your empathy, not by saying you have it but through the examples you give from your own experience. You should also ask those who write letters of recommendation for you to emphasize this aspect.

Remember, *you* are also interviewing the school district or specific school. You should look for a good fit between you and your style of teaching and what the school or district expects from you. Don't be so eager to get any position

---

*A copy of this law appears in the Federal Register 53, no. 69 (April 11, 1998), pp. 11942–11949. It can also be obtained by writing the U.S. Government Printing Office, Washington, D.C. 20402.

Typical Questions Asked During Job Interviews

Most interviews follow a simple question-and-answer routine. Your ability to communicate effectively with a stranger in a stressful situation is critical. Being prepared is the best way to avoid a disorganized answer. Sometimes the interviewer plays "devil's advocate," disagreeing with a position you articulate to see if you will back down from it in deference to an authority figure. You should be aware of this possibility; be prepared to assess your position straightforwardly, and then stand behind it. Avoid "waffling." Your success in interviewing depends on how convincingly you can convey your ability to teach.

Interviews are often subjective, so your enthusiasm, self-confidence, eagerness, and believability will affect the outcome of your interview. Be sincere and mean what you say. First impressions are important, so dress conservatively. At the conclusion of the interview, restate any important points you want to emphasize. Ask the interviewer for a business card and ask when the selection decision will be made. Send the interviewer a thank-you note; courtesy can make a difference.

Questions you may be asked include the following:

Motivation/Experience/Education

- Tell us about yourself.

- Why do you want to teach?

- Why do you want to work in our school district?

- What grade levels or subjects are you most interested in teaching?

- What do you consider to be your strongest attributes as a teacher? Weaknesses?

- What was your biggest problem in student teaching? How did you resolve it?

- How would you work with students who perform below grade level, especially those from poverty backgrounds?

Teaching Skills

- What is your philosophy of education?

- What are the most important learning outcomes you want your students to achieve?

- What skills and experience do you have in employing cooperative learning strategies or computers for instructional purposes?

- How can you motivate unmotivated learners?

- How would you involve parents to help students learn?

- How do you individualize your teaching?

- What is your grading philosophy?

Classroom Management

- What ideas do you have regarding maintaining classroom control?

- What rules for students would you establish in your classroom?

- How would you enforce these rules?

- Describe the most difficult student discipline situation you have faced and how you handled it.

Professional Responsibilities

- How do you plan to keep growing as a professional?

- What professional journals do you read?

- What added school responsibilities are you willing to accept?

Hypothetical Questions

- What would you do if you caught a student cheating?

- If money were unlimited, how would you improve education?

- How would you handle a student who refused to do the work you assigned?

During a job interview, you will answer many questions. But to gain the information that will help you choose among the jobs offered to you, you will also need to *ask* questions. Remember, you are interviewing the prospective employer, too. Before you accept a position, you will need to know about the following:

Instructional Assignment

- Characteristics of the school district and student population

- Curriculum and resources available

- Typical class size

- Salary and benefits (medical and dental coverage and retirement)

- District's expectations and reimbursement policies for professional development

- Orientation or support services available for beginning teachers

These are just a few suggestions. For additional information on interview questions, see "Interview Questions to Answer and Ask," *2002 Job Search Handbook for Educators* (Columbus, OH: American Association for Employment in Education, 2002), p. 25.

that you ignore the issue of fit. As charter schools continue to develop (see the chapter entitled "What Social Problems and Tension Points Affect Today's Students?"), new teachers will have more options to choose from in terms of work climate, educational philosophy, and learning goals. Also consider whether you will have access to an induction program and a mentor teacher. Research shows that having a good mentor teacher increases the likelihood of your success as a teacher. Secondary teachers should also ask whether the number of class preparations is reduced for beginning teachers. Having only one or two types of classes to prepare for makes the first year of teaching much easier than having to make three or four preparations for different courses.

■ *Determine Job Availability*

use your college placement center

Your next major task is to find out what jobs are available and where. Several strategies are possible. Your college's career planning and placement office receives hundreds of notifications of position vacancies. Contact that office often to see if there are any vacancies that might interest you. Another source may be the teacher employment office operated by the state department of education. About one-third of the states run such offices, and you can register with them for free or for a slight charge. These offices send registered candidates a listing of openings in their specialty area for both state and out-of-state vacancies.

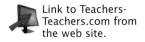
Link to Teachers-Teachers.com from the web site.

personal contacts important

There are also private organizations that keep current nationwide teacher vacancy lists and will try to match your qualifications with those vacancies either for free or for a nominal fee. One such organization is Teachers-Teachers.com (available at: **http://www.teachers-teachers.com**). This free service to prospective teachers allows them to post their résumé online, which can be accessed by thousands of schools seeking teachers. (See the For Further Information section at the end of the chapter for more information on this web site.) Personal contacts too are often very effective in securing a position. Don't hesitate to call friends and acquaintances who might be able to help you obtain interviews. They probably can't get you a job, but they may be aware of vacancies and know whom you should contact. Contacting specific school districts directly is another way to determine what positions are available. Call, write, or visit the personnel office of the school districts in which you are interested. This will ensure that you get current information directly from the school district. Alternatively, use the World Wide Web to see if the school districts that interest you have home pages. If they do, they may very well list their job openings on their pages. Again, the AAEE *Job Search Handbook for Educators* lists and discusses a number of Internet sources with teaching and other educational job opportunities. We have cited a few of these sources at the end of the chapter.

■ *Gain Experience Through Substitute Teaching*

■ *advantages of substitute teaching*

Many education students develop valuable experience, earn some money, and establish an entrance into a school district by serving as substitute teachers. Some universities even offer coursework in becoming an effective substitute. Besides giving you the opportunity to refine your teaching skills, substitute teaching can provide a competitive advantage in the job market. Some school districts are apt to hire full-time teachers from their substitute ranks if the substitutes have done a good job. After all, school officials would rather hire a known teacher in whom they have confidence than take a chance on a new teacher whom they don't know. If you're interested in being a substitute teacher, visit the district personnel office to find out the requirements and attend substitute-teacher training sessions if they are offered.

PAUSE AND REFLECT

1 What ways can you think of to increase your chances of being hired when you are ready to teach?

2 Are the average teacher salaries reported in this chapter about what you expected? How do the salaries in your geographic area compare with the national average?

How Do You Become Licensed?

■ *state license required to teach*

All fifty states and the District of Columbia require public elementary and secondary school teachers to be licensed to teach by the department of education in the state in which they work. The terms *licensure* and *certification* are often confused or misused. **Licensure** is the official recognition by a state governmental agency that an individual meets state requirements, whereas **certification** is the process by which the profession grants special recognition to an individual who has met certain qualifications specified by the profession. Often, however, the term *certification,* as in, "I'm going to get my certification to teach," is used when *licensure* is meant. This usage is a carryover from earlier times. Today some states continue to use *certification* as a synonym for *licensure,* but in this book, we have tried to distinguish the terms.

■ *Traditional Licensure Programs*

Link to state certification offices from the web site.

Traditionally, to qualify for licensure, a teacher has had to complete an approved teacher education program. Besides conferring a bachelor's degree, which provides the necessary liberal arts background, teacher education programs fulfill the state requirement that prospective teachers take certain education courses or demonstrate certain competencies.

Since the mid-1980s, many states have increased the requirements for licensure, adding test requirements such as the PRAXIS examinations (teacher competency exams developed by the Educational Testing Service) or, in some cases, state-developed minimum competency tests of basic skills. Often prospective teachers are examined on their content-area knowledge. Increasingly, competency testing is being used to screen candidates for licensure. In addition, some states require U.S. citizenship; some, criminal background checks; some, an oath of allegiance; and several, a health certificate. And some local school districts may require teacher applicants to take written examinations or meet other to be hired.

Because the requirements for licensure differ from state to state, you should become aware of the requirements for the state in which you will seek employment. Someone in your placement office or your school of education most likely will be able to acquaint you with licensure requirements. Your education library probably contains books that list the licensure requirements for all the states. Should you not be successful there, you can call or write directly to the teacher licensure office in the states in which you are interested. A directory of state teacher licensure offices in the United States appears as an appendix at the end of this book. A number of states have reciprocal agreements to accept one another's licenses as valid. If you move from one state to another, you may want to check whether your teaching license is accepted by the state to which you are moving.

Besides the basic licenses for teaching at the elementary and secondary levels, many states require different licenses, or *endorsements,* for such specialization areas as special education, bilingual education, and kindergarten. If, as you gain experience, you want to move out of teaching into a supervisory, administrative, or counseling position, you will need a special license.

If at all possible, you would be wise to become licensed or endorsed in more than one teaching area. Adding a second field of licensure will make you more attractive to prospective employers, particularly in smaller school districts, which have less flexibility to hire specialists who teach in only one area. If you are going to be an elementary school teacher, having an additional license or endorsement in reading, special education, early childhood education, or bilingual education would be very worthwhile. Another way to increase your appeal to prospective employers would be to take a major or minor in mathematics, one of the sciences, or instructional technology. Elementary school teachers with expertise in these areas are in short supply. If you are going to teach at the secondary level, you can broaden your appeal by being licensed to teach in two or more subject fields. For example, if you are a Spanish major, minor in French; if you are a chemistry major, minor in physics or mathematics. Any doubling up of teaching fields will work to your advantage.

In summary, individual states use licensure requirements to assure the public that the teachers teaching the youth of our society have been adequately prepared. Licensure requirements should present you with little difficulty as long as the teacher education institution you attend meets the general regulations of the state department of education and as long as you maintain contact with the college official responsible for coordinating the education program with the state licensure requirements. But in many states, the traditional route to

> *To those bright young people who want to enter the profession that has been so good to many of us— education—I say, "Good choice!" My advice to them is not "You're too smart to be a teacher," but rather, "You're too smart not to be one."*
>
> —JAMES R. DELISLE

Being happy in your work will make you a more effective teacher.
(© Michael Newman/PhotoEdit)

> *I am teaching. . . . It's kind of like having a love affair with a rhinoceros.*
> —ANNE SEXTON

work on which one wants to spend one's life. Nevertheless, a whopping 30 to 50 percent of teachers leave the profession within the first five years,[5] presumably many of them first-year teachers. But statistics do not determine personal fate. It is our strongest belief that many of the problems and issues that are behind teachers leaving the field are preventable through planning and a few resolutions.

▇ *Begin Now*

▪ *start to work on yourself* First, start now to prepare for the predictable events and problems of the initial year. Make a systematic study of your strengths and weaknesses, with an eye toward using your strengths in the classroom and gradually eliminating your trouble areas. For instance, if you have an especially good reading voice, plan to capitalize on it as a teacher. Students from preschool through college love to be read to. On the other hand, if you are painfully self-conscious and shy, develop a plan to overcome this shortcoming. Don't try to defeat your shyness with big, dramatic gestures, such as trying out for the lead in the college play. Take an incremental approach, using small steps. Plan to speak to someone standing in line next to you whom you don't know; volunteer answers in class. With problematic areas like this, but also with your strengths, seek the advice and help of trusted friends, family, and teachers. Realize that your shyness may never completely go away, but you will gradually feel more and more comfortable speaking and working with people if you push yourself to make small advances regularly. You may surprise yourself—remember Joan Kinney above.

▇ *Keep a Teaching Journal*

A **teaching journal** can be any notebook that is large enough to hold your teaching thoughts and suggestions. Or, if you prefer working at a keyboard, a computer file can serve the same purpose. Although some teachers started such books in grade school when they first decided to teach, the beginning of one's formal preparation as a teacher is a very good time to begin a journal.

benefits of a journal

A teaching journal can be used to record all the useful ideas and strategies you discover, saving them for the time when you are actually teaching. It can include teaching skills learned in lectures or observed in the field, such as how to grade papers effectively or how to give students evaluative feedback on in-class presentations. In addition, it could include methods of disciplining in different situations, easy and efficient ways to take attendance, ways to present particularly difficult concepts, things to do when students get restless or overexcited, and sources of good curricular materials.

Having such a journal serves two functions. First, the teaching journal is a constant reminder that you are preparing to be actually in charge of your own classroom (a fact that often is not in sharp focus for preservice teachers). Second, the journal can be a lifesaver when you are struggling during the first year. A typical journal entry might look like this:

Tuesday, October 7

Ninth-Grade English

Began the introductory lesson on Shakespeare and the Globe Theater today. The biographical info went over only minimally well. Brian and Mark loudly wanted to know why they needed to know when he was born and died and what difference it made. Some of the other kids looked bored as I went into my spiel, and I realized I was probably lecturing too much.

Next time I should review my information that I present, and figure out what's important for them to know and what's extraneous. Just because I'm fascinated with it doesn't mean that it's all appropriate or necessary for a ninth-grader's introduction to Shakespeare. Also, maybe some sort of question-answer sheet about Shakespeare would work better and get more involvement from the kids.

On the bright side, they all seemed to love the Globe Theater model. They really liked the way it opened, showing the cross-section with all the various stage areas. Brian and Mark were among the most interested in the model. The kids also seemed to be able to follow along on their photocopied drawing of the Globe. Jon and Elizabeth (who usually aren't impressed with anything) told me that it was "pretty cool." The next time, maybe I'll start with the theater and allow more time for them to explore it.

Besides offering professional advantages, the teaching journal can be a valuable personal record. One twenty-year teaching veteran in Massachusetts has kept a journal about his teaching experiences throughout his career. He finds that it has "captured the moment," recording what he was thinking and experiencing as he taught throughout the years.

An alternative form of this idea is to develop a card file of "teaching tips," either with index cards or in a similar computerized format. This file of tips can provide quick, easy reference for planning or problem solving.

Keeping a journal is one of the chief characteristics of the *reflective practitioner,* a goal and ideal we have stressed throughout this book.

The Proper Frame of Mind

cultivating humility

It is important to have the right frame of mind during your first year of teaching—that is, someone who is untested and who has a great deal to learn. Humility is a virtue that has been all but drowned out in our modern, "We're Number One" culture. Zen masters and teachers of the spiritual life urge the beginner to assume an attitude of submissiveness before what is to be learned. Not weakness, but humility. Many new teachers strive hard to *avoid* humiliation, not realizing that a humble person cannot be humiliated. Instead of assuming a false confidence, one can acknowledge that there is much to learn and open oneself up to that learning.

Making use of this suggestion is somewhat tricky. The humble frame of mind we are urging is one of alertness and quiet observation of your new context, expecting difficulties of some sort but being quietly confident that solutions will come. By all means, it does *not* mean becoming a doormat. In a way, the new teacher should be like a good apprentice: working hard, eyes open, asking questions, and being eager to learn everything possible about the craft.

An aspect of having a proper frame of mind is understanding the social and economic context within which your new school exists. Schools vary immensely depending on their social, ethical, religious, and economic make-up. (You will find background information in the chapters entitled "What Is a School and What Is It For?" and "How Are Schools Governed, Influenced, and Financed?".) Study your new community and ask questions, so you are not blindsided by attitudes and behaviors that previously you have never encountered.

Find a Mentor

values of mentor

A first-year teacher can have no greater gift than a good **mentor,** an experienced teacher who is willing to act as a guide and confidant through the first year. Besides all of the information and tips that a mentor can give you, a good mentor is an interpreter-guide on what is essentially foreign turf. A mentor can tell you which pieces of paper from the principal's office need to be responded to immediately, who has the formal power and who has the real power, what the administrators emphasize most in teacher evaluations, and which teachers are most willing to share ideas and which ones are not. Perhaps even more important, a mentor is a friend. (Remember Catherine Foley and Joan Silver above.)

Seventy percent of teachers who have been mentored claim that the experience significantly improved their teaching. On the other hand, only one in five teachers reports having received such guidance.[6] However, in recent years many school districts have developed special arrangements to help beginning teachers. Some have special induction programs, some have mentor programs, and some have both. In situations where there is no induction program or a mentor is not assigned, we nevertheless urge you to make finding a mentor a high priority.

Make Your Students' Parents Your Allies

We suggest that all teachers, but particularly new teachers, take a very proactive, positive approach to parents. Instead of having them get to know you indirectly through the often distorting eyes and mouths of their children ("My new teacher, Miss Sniddly, hates me. And besides, she can't teach. How come I got stuck with a new teacher?"), help them get to know you and what you will be doing with their children this school year.

What Can the New Teacher Expect?

Well, in California, You Can Expect $5,000 Worth of Help!

If you are worried about being isolated in your classroom with twenty-three third-graders who can't seem to fit into that terrific reading center program your cooperating teacher demonstrated so well for you during your student teaching, never fear. There is help on the way—at least if you are going to teach in California, Kentucky, Mississippi, Wisconsin, and several other states, plus a number of school systems, that have made a major commitment to the induction of new professionals.

For twenty years, California has been a leader in professional teacher induction programs. Our most populous state expects to hire more than a quarter million teachers in the next five years to teach its 6 million students. To launch them on their new careers, California has a statewide mentor program (with an annual budget of $80 million) and a new Beginning Teacher Support and Assessment Program (annual budget of $75 million). These programs are targeted at first- and second-year teachers and are closely geared toward helping new teachers to help their students reach the newly adopted statewide student achievement standards. Underlying these programs are two building blocks: the development of a common language about teaching between new and veteran teachers and a common set of thirty-five scales to describe teaching, aptly called *Descriptions of Practice*. These scales are quite specific and observable, and therefore form the basis for down-to-earth discussions of how to improve classroom teaching.

As you can see from the numerous references and suggestions throughout this chapter, we strongly believe that your fellow teachers, your new colleagues, can be a tremendous source for your growth and development as a professional. In fact, they can be a goldmine of tricks of the trade on issues such as how to get students' attention and keep it, how to use your new school's personal computers when you've been trained on Apple Macintosh computers (or vice versa), how to lead a discussion and actually take it somewhere, how to organize your classroom for effective learning, and how to get those three girls in the back to stop giggling and passing notes. Although your own initiative in getting to know your fellow teachers is important, the advent of programs for new teachers is good news indeed. More than just tea and sympathy (or a stapler and an aspirin), these new programs hold the promise of dramatically altering the rocky roller-coaster life of first-year teachers.

Source: Margaret Olebe, Amy Jackson, and Charlotte Danielson, "Investing in Beginning Teachers—The California Model," *Educational Leadership* 56, no. 8 (May 1999), pp. 41–44b.

establish communication with parents

One way to do this is to prepare a short statement to be carried home and signed, introducing yourself to parents and outlining your major goals for the year. Stress that you and they are in a partnership to help their child have a productive year. Further, let them know how to get in touch with you and that you are looking forward to meeting them. Tell them the date for Back-to-School Night and that you are looking forward to meeting them. One new first-grade teacher we heard about sent a letter with a snapshot of herself to her first-graders and their parents once she received her class list in the summer. She wrote a little about herself, told them some of the things they would do during the coming school year, and (for the parents) explained her approach to teaching. Besides being exciting for the students, this technique helped the new teacher start the year (and, more importantly, finish the year) with her students' parents as strong allies.

A second suggestion is that once you have established disciplinary and homework policies, a copy should be sent home for parental sign-off.

Third, on the first day, get the home, work, and mobile telephone numbers of each student's parent or parents. The fact that you possess these valuable bits of information will not go unnoticed by your students.

Fourth, it is a good idea to call all parents early in the fall. In particular, call the parent(s) as soon as a student appears to be falling behind, tuning out, or misbehaving: "Mrs. Tate, this is Philip's teacher. Philip's performance has begun to slip. What can we do to get him back on track?" "Mr. Fisher, this is Kathleen's teacher. Kathleen just won't stop talking in class. It is interfering with other students and keeping her from doing the work she is capable of. What can we do to make this the good year we all want for Kathleen?" The key word in dealing with parents is *we,* as in "What can *we* do?" Phone calls should be made and brief notes sent home for positive reasons as well. Such a "good news" call can make a parent's month!

Finally, if problems persist, insist on a parent visit. (Conversations such as, "We need to work together to get little Adolph involved in his schoolwork," are helpful for everyone involved.) There is no surer way to get children's attention than to have them realize they are the reason their parents had to leave work early to come to school. And although this is an upsetting bother for many parents, it is usually worth it because of the positive effect it can have on their child's school experience.

◼ Take Evaluation Seriously

The news that they are to be evaluated by their principal or some other administrator is often a surprise to novice teachers. Even more shocking is the revelation that the related evaluation reports are sometimes the cause of not being rehired.

Typically, it is a major job responsibility of principals and other district administrative personnel to visit systematically and evaluate the performance of new teachers. Depending on the district and the conscientiousness of the administrator, this can take place anywhere from once to a dozen times during the first year. Usually, though, there are three or four evaluative visits, followed up closely by feedback conferences during which the administrator goes over his or her observations. Together these evaluative visits play an important part in the school district's decision to rehire the teacher or terminate his or her employment.

It is important, then, for new teachers to understand thoroughly how their work will be evaluated. Before you accept a teaching position, be clear about how and when your work will be evaluated. Most school districts have an official evaluation and feedback form, and you should know this well. Check out the department of education's web site in your state to see how new teachers are evaluated. If the school or district's evaluator gives you advance notification of a visit, prepare for the occasion. Find out from your mentor teacher what the administrator really stresses in teaching. And do your best. If the evaluator raises issues or makes suggestions for improvement, take them seriously. You do not necessarily have to agree, but you should not casually ignore the issues. In most cases the comments are legitimate, and the new teacher should strive to repair or strengthen the area that was criticized.

◼ Take Care of Yourself

One of the greatest surprises of full-time, fully responsible teaching, as opposed to student teaching, is how tiring it is. Teaching is physically, mentally, and

Reflect on how you will work with students' families with the image in this section of your CD-ROM.

▪ *preparing for and responding to feedback*

Kevin and Jim's Seven Additional Rules for Surviving the First Year of Teaching

(Or Seven Compelling Reasons Why Future Teachers Should Not Try to Resell This Book to the Evil Used-Book Buyers)*

1. *When in doubt, think.* Instead of simply fretting about problems or panicking, use your best tool: your mind. Reflect. Problem solve. Try to identify the problem, possible solutions, and what seems best, and then act and judge whether that option helped the situation.

2. *Don't look for love in the classroom.* Maybe respect, but not love. Don't even expect to be appreciated—that may not come from your students for ten or twenty years.

3. *Deal with your authority problems before entering the classroom.* Come to terms with the fact that you will be responsible for maintaining an orderly and civil environment and think about how you will accomplish this feat.

4. *If you are not organized, get organized.* Coping with the planbooks, student papers, office memos, attendance records, grades, report cards, and so on, requires much more organization than many beginners have practiced.

5. *Love thy school secretary and custodians.* Many beginners fail to realize how important the school secretary and custodians are in enabling teachers to do an effective job and in the "informal communication network" of the school.

6. *Focus on learning.* Many beginners fail to concentrate on making sure their students really learn something and thus have feelings of accomplishment. Students will put up with a great deal of "beginning teacheritis" if they sense they are learning.

7. *Don't—we repeat, don't—get married two weeks before the start of your first teaching job.* For reasons unknown to the authors, each year, thousands of new college graduates decide to jump at the same time into two of life's most difficult undertakings: beginning a career and starting what they hope will be a lifelong relationship.

*The authors promise that if you follow these seven rules faithfully, you will survive the first year of teaching. You may even like it! On the other hand, if you do not survive the year, return the unused portion of the book to your instructor for a refund.

■ *physical health*

The love of nurturing and observing growth in others is essential to sustaining a life of teaching. This implies that no matter what you teach or how you present yourself to your students, you have to be on the learner's side and to believe that they can and will grow during the time that you are together.

—HERBERT KOHL

emotionally draining, particularly until one gets conditioned to it—that is, until one gets into "teaching shape." This is true for many jobs. The stress and strain of new employment wear newcomers down and set them up for colds, flu, and other mild ailments. The problem is compounded in teaching because it is such an "in your face" occupation (referring to all those coughing, sniffling, and wheezing faces you encounter every day). A classroom is a magnificent germ factory, with viruses claiming new victims regularly. The teacher who is exhausted, run down, and staying up late reworking lesson plans and correcting papers is a prime target for whatever is circulating in the environment.

The stress and strain of a new teaching position also can cause mild depression. In their first year, few teachers live up to their own expectations. Often new teachers are away from their regular support system of family and friends. Having not yet

mental health

established realistic standards, they really don't know if they are succeeding or failing. A bad class or even one resistant or disrespectful student can emotionally unseat them. To counter this vulnerability to sickness of body and spirit, new teachers need to give special attention to their health. When you feel yourself becoming overstressed or burnt out, take deliberate steps. Reduce stress directly by trying to solve key problems that are bothering you and look for ways to relieve stress indirectly as well. Plan a weekend away, take vitamins, or join an aerobics class. Instead of getting overtired and run down, beginners need to take special pains to get enough rest, eat well, and get adequate exercise.

A Final Word

Much of this chapter has dealt with the trials of being a new teacher. Nevertheless, most new teachers have a great sense of accomplishment and are proud of themselves at the end of their first year. They have learned an enormous amount in nine or ten months. Along with the trials, teaching has its pleasures and bright moments, making it a rewarding and fulfilling occupation for most. English novelist Joyce Cary has written that human joy comes not from the great events but from the little, everyday things, like a good cup of tea. The joys and satisfactions of teaching can lie in mundane happenings and small surprises. As a teacher, you may find joy in the following:

- Experiencing those electric moments when you can *feel* the children thinking and *see* them making new connections

- Watching two lonely kids, whom you brought together, walk down the hall side by side, now friends

- Getting your planbook back from the supervisor with the comment, "These are *excellent* lessons"

- Finding in your box, on a rainy Friday afternoon, a note written in a childish scrawl, "You are my most favorite teacher. Guess who?"

- Shopping downtown and meeting one of your students, who proudly introduces you to her mother as "my teacher," and being able to tell by the mother's response that you are respected in their household

- Having a former student call to tell you that he has a problem and needs your advice

- Chaperoning a dance and having what you thought was your most hostile student happily introduce his girlfriend to you

- Hearing in the teachers' lunchroom that your supervisor called you "a real professional"

- Being observed by the principal and having your students make you look terrific

- Surviving until June, being bone-tired but proud of what you and your kids have been able to do

- Cleaning out your desk on the last day of school after the kids have been dismissed and finding a box of candy with a card signed by the whole class

- Realizing—be it daily, weekly, or monthly—that what you are doing with your life *really does make a difference*

KEY TERMS

culture shock (424)   social distance (438)
mentor (449)   teaching journal (447)

FOR REFLECTION

1 Can you remember any beginning teachers you have had who fit the scenarios described in this chapter or got into similar situations?

2 How do you explain the different attitudes toward students of teachers in training and first-year teachers?

3 If you were to begin teaching tomorrow and were free to evaluate your students in any way you chose (or not to evaluate at all), what would you do?

4 What do you expect to be the major problems you will encounter as a beginning teacher?

5 What can you do now to begin solving those problems?

FOR FURTHER INFORMATION

PRINT RESOURCES

Esme Raji Codell, *Educating Esme: Diary of a Teacher's First Year* (Chapel Hill, NC: Algonquin Books, 1999).
This book is the account of a new fifth-grade teacher in a Chicago inner-city school. Hip, imaginative, and irreverent, the book takes the reader through the teacher's triumphs and travails with students and a particularly dense administrator.

Richard D. Kellough, *Surviving the First Year of Teaching: Guidelines for Success* (Columbus, OH: Merrill/Prentice Hall, 1999).
Designed specifically as a survival guide for beginners, this manual is filled with practical tips from first lessons to conducting conferences with parents.

"Supporting New Teachers," *Educational Leadership* [special issue] 56, no. 8 (May 1999).
This special issue has several articles focusing on the plight of first-year teachers and how schools can help them get over their initial difficulties.

Harry K. Wong and Rosemary T. Wong, *The First Days of School: How to Be an Effective Teacher* (Sunview, CA: Harry Wong Publishing, 1998).
This highly acclaimed handbook abounds with tips and strategies to help the new teacher get a strong start through motivation and minimizing discipline and the other problems that plague new teachers.

Erma S. Hershman and Dyan M. McDonald, *The Survival Kit for New Teachers: A User-Friendly Handbook*, 2nd ed. (Garland, TX: ITPA, 2001).
The title says it all. Although this book focuses largely on elementary classrooms, the authors have another 2001 book with a similar title except this is for "new secondary teachers."

WEB RESOURCES

EZ School. Available at: **http://www.EZSchool.com**.
This web site, associated with Amazon.com, is a treasure of resources for the new teacher. It is filled with good ideas, teaching plans for a range of subject matter, and worksheets.

What to Expect Your First Year of Teaching. Available at: **http://www.ed.gov/pubs/FirstYear/index.html**.
This web site is an excellent resource for beginning teachers. It combines many of the practical tips and much of the advice in this chapter with several resources helpful to beginning teachers.

What Does It Mean to Be a Professional?

Chapter Preview   In this chapter, we focus on the teacher as a professional—that is, as a member of an occupational group. We will see how this rather abstract concept of *professionalism* affects the daily life of the classroom teacher. In effect, we put the role of the individual teacher in the larger context of being a member of a profession.

This chapter emphasizes that:

- Teachers can become involved in different types of situations and conflicts in which they will need counsel or support.

- Teachers have become more powerful in recent years, but they don't have the same kinds of power that members of some other professions have.

- The question of whether teaching is a profession can be judged by reference to specific criteria. Furthermore, cases can be made both for and against teaching being a profession.

- There are levels of professionalism and the National Board for Professional Teaching Standards and its standards for certification may have a substantial effect on teachers.

- The National Education Association and the American Federation of Teachers, the most influential teacher organizations, have quite different origins and are competing for the support of classroom teachers.

- The teaching profession is still defining itself and much depends on its capacity to maintain the public's trust. Current educational demands require the teacher to be a continuous learner. Teachers can continue their professional growth in various ways.

The essence of a career in teaching is close, hands-on work with the young. When people think about becoming teachers, their thoughts and daydreams usually revolve around working with students. Rarely do they bother with hypothetical issues beyond the scope of the classroom. This is both natural and appropriate because the teacher's success or failure depends on his or her effectiveness with students. Nevertheless, there is much more to being a teacher than this. Teachers work within a system that exposes them to pressures from many quarters. Prospective teachers are often somewhat naive about the pressures and forces that will affect them, and naiveté can be dangerous, both in making a career decision and in making a successful career.

■ *teaching within a system*

To help you see this point, we would like you to indulge in a set of daydreams for a few moments. We will offer you a few brief scenarios, and after reading each one, you should reflect on how you might react. As you read each scenario, imagine yourself teaching in that ideal classroom you carry around in your head. Assume that you appear to be doing a fine job. You are really enjoying it. Your students are making nice progress. They seem to be interested in their work. A few parents have indicated that although they were initially worried that their precious child was to have a new (in other words, *untested*) teacher, they are thrilled with the child's progress in your class. So, things are going very well, until . . .

> *The only way to keep our kids foolproof is to keep them away from fools.*
>
> —WILL ROGERS

■ *target of pressure groups*

1. You get a special-delivery letter from a group called Patriotic American Parents (PAP). You have heard they are very active in your area and are especially interested in schools. Their letter informs you that their lawyer is preparing a case against you for using books that are on their disapproved list. (You didn't know there was such a list, but sure enough, there is, and you have been using books from it!) They claim they have evidence that you are waging a subtle but nevertheless vicious war against the cause of justice and liberty and have succeeded in temporarily deflecting the minds of some of your students from the truth. Furthermore, they want to know why you display the United Nations flag and why there are no pictures of past presidents on your classroom walls. Finally, you are said to recite the Pledge of Allegiance in a much too hasty fashion, which is clearly a sign of your disrespect for your country. This is the first you have heard of these charges or even of the Patriots' interest in you. You think of yourself as patriotic and are shocked by the letter. They have requested that you respond in writing by next week or they will begin legal proceedings.

■ *the invisible contract*

2. In late January, the superintendent, who holds a conference with each new teacher, told you she thought you were doing a fine job and that she wanted you to return next year. In passing, she remarked that she would be getting a contract to you in the spring. Toward the end of April, you got a little nervous and called her. You spoke to her executive secretary, who said not to worry, that you were on the list, and that a contract would be coming before long. You stopped worrying. Today is the last day of school, and you find a very nice personal note from the principal in your school mailbox. He thanks you for your fine work during the year and says he is sorry you will not be back next year. You call the superintendent's office. She is in conference, and her executive secretary says they are not renewing your contract. She cannot remember speaking to you in April. She knows nothing about the case. She

does know, however, that the Board of Education has put on a lot of pressure for cuts in next year's personnel budget. She ends by telling you, "You must be very disappointed, dear. I know how you feel."

conflict with colleagues

3. You noticed something peculiar when you sat down at the faculty dining table one lunch hour. Conversations stopped, and you had the distinct impression your colleagues had been talking about you. A few days later, an older teacher stopped you in the hall after school and said, "I don't want to butt in, but you really are upsetting Mrs. Hilary and Mr. Alexandra." Mrs. H. and Mr. A. have the classrooms on either side of yours. Apparently they claim your class makes so much noise that they can't get anything done. Both are very traditional in their approach to education, whereas you believe in a more activity-oriented approach. Although your class is rather noisy occasionally, it is never chaotic, and its noise is usually a by-product of the students' involvement in the task. Twice Mr. Alexandra has sent messengers with notes asking that your class be quieter. You have always complied. You hardly know either teacher. You have never really talked to Mr. Alexandra except to say hello. Mrs. Hilary, with whom you've chatted, prides herself on being a strict disciplinarian. What she means, you have inferred, is that she is able to keep the children quiet. You know Mr. Alexandra is chummy with Mrs. Hilary. You go to the vice-principal, who seems to know all about the case, but only from the Hilary-Alexandra angle. Inexplicably, the vice-principal gets quite angry and claims that until you came along, the faculty got along beautifully. Furthermore, you are being very unprofessional in making complaints against experienced teachers. You feel as if you are trapped in a bad dream.

These horror stories, of course, are not everyday occurrences. Also, keep in mind that entrance into any profession has its trials. These accounts are intended to help you realize that you can be an effective teacher and still have trouble keeping your job. What is the common theme running through each of these anecdotes? You, the teacher, were succeeding in your work with children, but forces outside the classroom began to impinge on you. PAP wanted to make a target case of you. The school system bureaucracy was ready to put you on the unemployed rolls. Two of your colleagues damaged your reputation with the faculty and administration. Other than that, it was a super year.

Although you may feel confident that you could handle some of these situations, it is doubtful that you could cope with all such cases that might arise. In some instances you would be powerless to respond effectively to your adversaries, and you might end up a helpless victim of circumstance. Fortunately, a teacher is not alone. Like people in many other occupational groups, teachers have organizations that protect them from such indignities and injustices. These organizations function on several levels, from the local to the national, and usually their very existence keeps situations like those described from occurring. When they do occur, these organizations are there to support the teacher, even though seniority usually rules. At least, that is the way they should work.

organizational support

It is important to realize that in becoming a teacher, you are not just committing yourself to work with children. You are joining an occupational group composed of other individuals with similar responsibilities, concerns, and pressures whose help you may need and who, in turn, will need your help.

LEADERS IN EDUCATION
KAY TOLIVER

"I'm a teacher. What else would I do?" Kay Toliver asks.

Kay Toliver teaches at P.S. 72 in Spanish Harlem, where she has been instilling a love of knowledge in middle school students for more than twenty-five years. Toliver teaches on the cutting edge of mathematics, stressing thinking and application over computation, and weaving history and art through class discussions into the study of mathematics. Because many of her students come from poor, unstable backgrounds and have poor language skills, she emphasizes writing, reading, and research. Her students must always be prepared to explain their solutions orally, in complete and clear sentences. They are required to keep daily journals, in which they write about what they have learned in class, ideas about how to apply the concepts they study, or simply observations about the class or the teacher. Toliver believes that the students' ability to express themselves in well-written English must be acquired hand-in-hand with mathematical discovery. In addition to enhancing writing skills, the journals allow the teacher to gain a glimpse of her students' confusions in mathematics. "A teacher can stand in front of the class and think she's giving a great lesson. But that's not always the truth," she explains.

Kay Toliver's influence is spreading beyond her classroom to videos. In 1995, she was featured in a Peabody award–winning public television special, "Good Morning Miss Toliver." Also, with Jaime Escalante, Toliver contributed to "Interactions: Real Math—Real Careers," a multimedia tool that connects prealgebra math principles to real life in scenarios featuring career professionals. Along with Escalante, Toliver sees the way to future jobs through mathematics, especially for students from the inner city.

In addition to the mathematical tools, P.S. 72 children use computers. Toliver feels her students must be technologically competitive. With money she received from one of her many awards, the Presidential Award for Excellence in Science and Mathematics Teaching, she purchased software and computers for her school's computer lab.

Toliver has seen many students who have been exposed to drugs or crime, or both. Frequently, one parent is gone, or a child may be in foster care. Too often a sibling is in jail, and the students' peers are dealing with everyday street life in East Harlem. But having grown up in the South Bronx and East Harlem, she is well acquainted with the world of her students. As a result, discipline is not a problem in Toliver's class. Students understand she is serious and works hard to make math interesting. "We don't need different methods to teach so-called disadvantaged children. We just need teachers who are dedicated and who believe their students can succeed," she says. A teacher friend, Cathy Hess Wright, has said of her, "Ms. Toliver is a teachers' teacher. She knows how to reach inside the souls of the students and make them see that the power to succeed is within each of them. In a time when many young people feel that society has labeled them as failures, Ms. Toliver's message comes through clearly as one of hope, discipline, and motivation."

Kay Toliver hopes some of her students will share her love of teaching and become teachers themselves. Recently, after she had appeared on a television special, five students told her they wanted to become teachers. She had become a real-life role model after the television appearance. She likes being recognized for her work, but mainly she finds rewards in the changes brought to the lives of her students by mathematics.

"Becoming a teacher was the fulfillment of a childhood dream," says Ms. Toliver. "My parents always stressed that education was the key to a better life. By becoming a teacher, I hoped to inspire African-American and Hispanic youths to realize their own dreams. I wanted to give something back to the communities I grew up in."

Learn more about Kay Toliver's approach at: **http://www.nationalmathtrail.org/ ktmathtrail.html**.

 Visit the web site for more information about Kay Toliver.

Source: "Inspiring Young Minds: Kay Toliver," by Arwen Larson, *TECHNOS Quarterly*, Winter 1993, Vol. 2, No. 4. Used by permission.

The Status of Teaching: A Profession or Not?

The question "Is teaching a profession?" probably arouses little interest in many of our readers. Most people thinking about a career in teaching are more interested in whether it will be a personally rewarding way to spend their time than in whether it is a true profession. Will teaching bring me personal satisfactions? Will it provide an outlet for my talents and energies? Will I be effective with kids? These questions are, we suspect, closer to your skin. Nevertheless, the question of professionalism and the related issues are important to teachers and influence the quality of education teachers provide for children. They will also affect the quality of your life as a teacher. So what actually is a profession?

■ *professionalism a key question*

A **profession** is more than a group of individuals all engaged in the same line of work. Professions have a more or less recognizable set of characteristics that distinguish them from nonprofessions.[1] As you read the following list of characteristics, check whether you think teaching qualifies on each premise:

■ *does teaching qualify?*

yes ❏ *no* ❏

1. A profession renders a unique, definite, and essential service to society. Only the people in the particular profession render the service; for instance, only lawyers practice law. The service rendered must be considered so important that it is available to all the people in a society.

yes ❏ *no* ❏

2. A profession relies on intellectual skills in the performance of its service. This does not mean that physical actions and skills are not needed; rather, the emphasis in carrying on the work is on intellectual skills and techniques.

yes ❏ *no* ❏

3. A profession entails a long period of specialized training. Because professional work requires special intellectual skills, it requires specialized intellectual training. General education such as that represented by a bachelor's degree is valued but is not considered adequate. The specialized training must cover a substantial period and not be obtained in cram courses or correspondence schools.

yes ❏ *no* ❏

4. Both individual members of the profession and the professional group enjoy a considerable degree of autonomy and decision-making authority. Professional groups regulate their own activities rather than having outsiders set

policies and enforce adherence to standards. Whereas factory workers have very limited decision-making power and are closely supervised in the performance of their work, professionals are expected to make most of their own decisions and be free of close supervision by supervisors.

yes ❑ *no* ❑

5. A profession requires its members to accept personal responsibility for their actions and decisions and, in general, for their performance. Because the professional's service is usually related to the client's human welfare, this responsibility is an especially serious one.

yes ❑ *no* ❑

6. A profession emphasizes the services rendered by its practitioners more than their financial rewards. Although the personal motives of any individual professional are not necessarily any higher than any other worker's, the professional group's public emphasis is on service.

yes ❑ *no* ❑

7. A profession is self-governing and responsible for policing its own ranks. This means there are professional groups that perform a number of activities aimed at keeping the quality of their services high and looking out for the social and economic well-being of the professional members. Also, these self-governing organizations set standards of admission and exclusion for the profession.

yes ❑ *no* ❑

8. A profession has a code of ethics that sets out the acceptable standards of conduct for its members.

These characteristics, then, are the major requirements of a profession. Few professions satisfy all of them fully. However, the list does serve as a benchmark by which occupational groups can measure themselves and direct their development if they wish to enjoy professional status. With this in mind, let's look at the arguments for and against teaching as a profession.

■ *The Case* Against *Teaching as a Profession*

The roots of teaching as an occupation go back to ancient Greece, where slaves called *paidagogos,* or pedagogues, taught children to read and write and helped them memorize passages of poetic history. Despite this long history, however, a careful look at current practices reveals that teaching does not qualify as a profession.

■ teaching not a unique service

A Child's Many Teachers   If education is a teacher's unique function, the teacher certainly has a great deal of competition. Children today learn a tremendous amount from media offerings, including *Sesame Street,* public affairs specials, MTV, and *Sports Illustrated.* The nonteacher-educators include parents, ministers, older friends, neighbors, employers, best friends, coaches, scout leaders, playground and camp counselors, and grandparents. The world is bursting with teachers, and those who hold forth in school buildings have only a small piece of the action.

■ training not rigorous

Limited Training   Although teaching has intellectual and theoretical foundations, it requires a rather short period of specialized training (considerably less than some of the skilled trades), and entrance into the occupation is not especially competitive, particularly on intellectual grounds. If it is a profession, it

Sometimes a teacher's best work is done outside the classroom.
(© Tony Freeman/PhotoEdit)

is one largely composed of college graduates with a wide range of academic abilities, levels of commitment, and motivations for becoming teachers.

What office is there which involves more responsibility, which requires more qualifications, and which ought, therefore, to be more honorable than that of teaching?

—HARRIET MARTINEAU

■ **Constraints on Autonomy**   Although there is a good deal of talk about teachers' autonomy and decision-making power (and teachers have come a long way since the early days of the country, as described in the box on Rules and Duties for Teachers), in today's classrooms, autonomy and decision-making power still exist at a very low level. Teachers are at the second rung from the bottom (superior only to students) of the local hierarchy commanded by the local board of education. Unlike lawyers and doctors, who can reject clients, teachers have students assigned to them. They also have a supervisor: their principal, lead teacher, or department head. They teach a curriculum and are responsible for their students' meeting content standards that have been chosen or developed largely by others.

If their supervisors do not like the results, teachers are only rarely protected by their professional group from being fired (or, more gently, "not rehired") by the local school board. Teachers do not formally evaluate other teachers; administrators do that. Moreover, most of the important decisions that affect teachers' daily lives, even those that bear directly on the standards of their own profession, are made by nonteachers (administrators and citizen school board members). Although teachers are beginning to get more involved in teacher preparation programs and are acquiring some say in the licensing and certification of teachers, laypeople and bureaucrats still wield a great deal of decision-making power. Some teachers, like factory workers, even have to punch a time clock (or, more genteelly, they "sign in" and "sign out"). In sum, they have very little to say about what goes on in their "shop."

■ *little decision-making power*

Rules and Duties for Teachers in the Nineteenth Century

- Teachers will fill the lamps and clean the chimney each day.

- Each teacher will bring a bucket of water and a scuttle of coal for the day's session.

- Make your pens carefully. You may whittle nibs to the individual tastes of the pupils.

- Men teachers may take one evening each week for courting purposes, or two evenings a week if they go to church regularly.

- Women teachers who marry or engage in improper conduct will be dismissed.

- Every teacher should lay aside from each day's pay a goodly sum of his earnings. He should use his savings during his retirement years so that he will not be a burden to society.

- Any teacher who smokes, uses liquor in any form, visits pool halls or public halls, or gets shaved at a barber shop, will give good reasons for people to suspect his worth, intentions, and honesty.

- The teacher who performs his labor faithfully and without fault for five years will be given an increase of twenty-five cents per week in his pay.

From the rules and duties for teachers teaching in an 1872 Missouri school district.

little accountability

Responsibility for Their Profession Teachers rarely lose their jobs because Johnnie can't read or Samantha failed calculus. After a teacher achieves tenure, it takes some form of gross negligence, clear incompetence, or serious sexual offense for him or her to be fired. As professionals, teachers do very little policing of their own ranks. Their professional organizations are just like other self-serving organizations, whether composed of teamsters or autoworkers—that is, the primary energies of teacher associations and unions go to their own survival and growth. Secondarily, they attempt to protect their members, increase their salaries, and expand their benefits.

little involvement

Most teachers, in fact, are minimally involved in professional organizations and their activities. Except when the organization calls a strike—a somewhat contradictory activity for a "profession" supposedly dedicated to serving children—teachers generally just pay their dues. Most teachers claim they are too busy to take an active role in professional affairs. This lack of real involvement in professional activities may stem from the fact that so many teachers have second jobs, either as homemakers or in the labor market. They are unenthusiastic about working for higher standards because one of the first sacrifices to professionalism would be their second job.

Job Security and Salary In reality, teachers work in circumstances very different from those of other professionals. Like other public servants, they are hired rather than operating as independent agents. They are on a fixed salary schedule and are protected by tenure laws rather than independently having to find a market for their services. In effect, teaching is a low-paying, relatively high-security job rather than a high-paying, low-security profession. Seniority as a teacher appears to be more important than competence. Talk about professionalism may be personally satisfying to teachers, but it does not conform to the reality of the teacher's occupational life.

■ *The Case* for *Teaching as a Profession*

The very nobility of the teacher's work is evidence in favor of its status as a profession. Society has entrusted teachers with its most important responsibility: the education of its young. Throughout history, many great thinkers have acknowledged how crucial the work of the teacher is to the fulfillment of personal and national goals. And, as this realization has spread in recent decades, opportunities and rewards for the teacher have continued to improve.

Reflect on the professionalism of teaching with the image in this section of your CD-ROM.

■ *service above and beyond the call of duty*

■ **Teachers' Commitment to Service**   Service to others is at the very heart of what it means to be a professional. Teachers make large material sacrifices to serve children. The overwhelming percentages of people who teach could find work that, in material terms, is much more rewarding. Many could command large salaries in business or more lucrative professions. According to a recent survey, teachers even spend an average of $589 of their own money on school supplies and instructional materials each year to make up for the limited budgets in their own schools.[2] This is truly service above and beyond the call of duty!

You have not done enough, you have never done enough, as long as it is still possible that you have something of value to contribute.

—DAG HAMMARSKJÖLD

■ *teach difficult skills*

■ **The Teacher's Unique Skills**   Although children learn from many people—from parents to television personalities—teachers are the specialists who pass on to the young the key skills necessary to participate effectively in the culture. They aid the young in acquiring the most difficult, if not the most important, skills—those that involve thinking and manipulating ideas. Neither reading nor geometry is often learned on the street. Although teachers do not undergo a particularly lengthy period of specialized training, they are in a sense continually educating themselves. Teachers are expected (and, in most states, required by law) to upgrade their teaching skills and knowledge periodically.

■ *have a domain of control*

■ **The Teacher's Autonomy**   Teachers have an immense area of personal control. They normally determine the method of instruction. They decide which aspects of the curriculum they will highlight and which they will cover quickly. The limits on their creativity in the classroom are few or nonexistent. After the initial few years of teaching, they are seldom observed and evaluated. Teachers' classrooms are their castles.

If teachers believe they do not have enough autonomy or do not agree with their administrators, they are free to move to another school. However, a teacher's autonomy is accompanied by a responsibility to teach effectively. Like other professionals, teachers must be able to justify the manner in which they render their social services, whether it is grading or disciplinary actions. Teachers take responsibility for their actions and, like other professionals, are open to criticisms of their performance.

PAUSE AND REFLECT

❶ Where do you stand on the question, "Is teaching a profession?" To you, what are the best arguments for and against the professional status of teaching?

▓ A Third Possibility: An Evolving Profession

Like most other complex questions, our query about whether teaching is a profession cannot be answered satisfactorily with simple pro-and-con arguments such as those just offered. Also, teachers differ so much in the conditions under which they work, and they possess such varying degrees of knowledge, commitment, and expertise that it is difficult to come up with a definitive answer. In some schools, teachers fulfill many of the criteria of professionals. In other schools, they seem to function as clerks and technicians.

In certain ways teaching clearly is eligible for professional status, and in certain other ways, it deviates sharply from accepted canons of professionalism. On the one hand, teachers provide an intellectual service to the community. They undergo specialized training to master the theoretical basis of their work. Ethical standards guide their work with students. On the other hand, they too often function like many other lower level white-collar workers and civil servants. Too often seniority and job security are the rules rather than excellence and independence. Like many other occupational groups that are considered professional, at this moment in history, teachers only partially qualify.

▓ *teaching as an evolving profession*

Another way to look at the issue (and one we favor) is to think of teaching as an *evolving profession*—that is, it is in the process of becoming a full profession. What will determine whether teaching becomes a full-fledged profession during your lifetime? Among the factors are the trends toward greater self-determination, better preparation, and recognizing excellence in teaching.

▓ **Greater Self-Determination**   It may be true that a teacher lacks the autonomy of, say, a small-town lawyer. Yet every profession has limits on its autonomy. For example, today, more and more doctors and dentists are employed by health maintenance organizations (HMOs) and are forming unions to protect their rights. The crucial point, though, is the direction in which teaching is moving.

▓ *need more self-determination*

To make teaching a full profession, teachers must take on a larger role in the governing of their career affairs. Whereas the direction of education and the schools should be in the hands of many groups (parents, community leaders, students, and teachers), control over the teaching profession per se should be largely in the hands of teachers. Up to now, the great majority of teachers have taken the attitude, "Let George do it," allowing others to make the major decisions about who should teach, how teachers should be trained, and under what conditions they should render their services. This situation will not substantially change until teachers take a major role in making it change.

▓ **Better Preparation**   To make teaching a full profession, teachers must also demand better preparation requirements. As long as the public believes that any college graduate with a smattering of education courses can walk in off the street and do a teacher's job, people will not treat teachers as professionals. As described in the chapter entitled "What Are Your Job Options in Education?", this dangerous perception may even worsen if, due to teacher shortages, states then issue "emergency licenses" to individuals without any professional training at all! We are definitely not suggesting that teachers should adopt artificial trappings, like a doctor's smock or a general's uniform, to appear more distinctive and impressive. Rather, teachers must appear better because they *are* better. Like architects and surgeons, teachers must know their

> *To erect fine buildings and to seek to meet the needs and abilities of all individuals who desire to avail themselves of the opportunities so generously offered without providing teachers with qualifications commensurate with the ideal is a sham.*
>
> —I. L. KANDELL

work, and it must be imbued with a sense of high purpose. When that happens, the public will decide whether teachers should be treated as professionals.

Recognizing Excellence in Teaching　We need to realize that not all of the 3 million plus people working in the American schools are interested in and, in some cases, capable of measuring up to the standards of professionalism discussed earlier. At present, what we are calling (and, incidentally, will continue to call) the *teaching profession* is a mixed bag, with a great many transients "just passing through," a great many rather uncommitted teachers, and a great many truly excellent, dedicated career teachers.

More than thirty years ago, an educator captured what we believe to be the essence of the professional teacher in the following statement:

> Let us define a career teacher as one who plans to, and actually does, make a life occupation of teaching; one who is philosophically, emotionally, and spiritually committed, who is never satisfied with what he does and how well he's doing it, and who fully intends to keep on growing for the rest of his life.[3]

recognizing the best

This educator went on to estimate that only about one out of four practicing teachers fits his definition. And herein lies the difficulty: until the great majority of teachers qualify by this educator's definition or until there is a qualitative re-grouping of those presently identified as "teachers," teaching will not truly be called a profession.

Levels of Professionalism

What people (yourself included) think of the professional status of teaching is clearly important. However, it is dwarfed in importance compared with how you will live out your professional life and how you *will be* as a teacher. One way to think about this is to conceive of teaching as having three levels, or three ways that teachers go about their work.[4] Level One is the *imitative-maintenance* teacher, Level Two is the *meditative* teacher, and Level Three is the *generative-creative* teacher.

three levels of professional behavior

The Level One Teacher　Individuals functioning at Level One are essentially going through the motions prescribed by someone else in a rather mechanical fashion. They tend to be preoccupied by classroom discipline and keeping students busy. They may be successful at getting students *through* their lessons and examinations, but they are somewhat robotic in their narrowly following preset patterns, patterns set out in curriculum guides or textbooks. Level One teachers find security in *teaching to the test* and in what are pejoratively called *teacher-proof materials,* rigid instructional materials that step-by-step guide the teachers' actions. Although not in itself a problem, this *imitative-maintenance* approach doesn't allow the teacher to respond to the unique needs of students or to the special circumstances that continually arise in a classroom. This kind of unimaginative teaching makes teaching more of a technical occupation than a profession.

going through the motions

The Level Two Teacher　As the label, *meditative,* implies, teachers at Level Two mentally reflect on what they are doing in a classroom, but their reflection lies within a narrow range. They have an awareness of the uniqueness of their

limited reflection

The Level Three teacher finds creative ways to meet the individual needs of students.

(© Elizabeth Crews)

classroom and their students, and they go beyond their rigid curricular guides and materials, but their adaptations are few and more like tinkering around the instructional edges. They may, for example, deviate from the prescribed instructional guide but not very far. Level Two teachers may vary their instructional patterns to fit certain classroom events—that is, the obvious boredom of students—or they may bring in supplemental materials. However, they are hardly innovative.

■ *creative and effective teachers*

■ **The Level Three Teacher**   There is a large jump to the *generative-creative* level. These teachers focus on their individual students, and they take a wide view of knowledge. They attend to their curricular guides and the prescribed materials, but those materials are launching pads rather than targets of their instruction. Their classrooms are characterized by a great variety of instructional approaches and problem-centered materials. They play off the interests and talents of their students but not in a casual or pandering way. Their expectations for students are high and transcend required tests and examinations. They approach instruction as diagnosticians, seeking the best ways to engage students in their own mental growth. They do not simply transmit knowledge, but they create. They create in students a desire to learn and they create classroom environments where individual students become self-directed learners.

Few new teachers burst on the educational scene as Level Three *generative-creative* teachers. Many start at Level Two or attain it quickly. It is important, though, to have an understanding of your current behavior and to work toward this highest level. The very embracing of the goal will put you on the road to full professionalism.

■ *National Board of Professional Teaching Standards*

Currently a move is afoot to recognize and provide greater support to superior (or Level Three) teachers and to strengthen the claim of professionalism for the

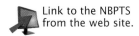

Link to the NBPTS from the web site.

career of teaching in the process. The National Board for Professional Teaching Standards (**www.nbpts.org**) aims to play a leading role in this effort.

The lack of recognizable high standards has discouraged some potentially outstanding people from entering teaching and has lowered the level of aspiration of others. High standards tend to focus people's attention and harness their energies. For example, in long-distance running, the four-minute mile was long considered the unbreakable barrier. For years and years, sports commentators pontificated that it was beyond the capacities of humans to run a mile in four minutes or less. Then, in 1957, Roger Bannister, a relatively obscure medical student, broke the magic barrier. A new standard was set, and runners reset their sights. The following year, *thirty-seven* runners broke that "unbreakable barrier." Today, breaking the four-minute barrier is commonplace. The reason is that a new standard has been set and people have risen to it in great numbers. The **National Board for Professional Teaching Standards (NBPTS)** is trying to perform a similar function for the teaching profession.

■ *standards stimulate achievement*

Formed in 1987, the NBPTS established standards for teaching practice and has developed a series of board certification assessments based on these standards. Board advocates believe that these standards allow teachers to gain a highly regarded, professional credential like that available to physicians, accountants, architects, and other professionals.

■ **Core Propositions and Characteristics**   The NBPTS is dedicated to and directed by five core propositions:

■ *five core propositions*

1. Teachers know the subjects they teach and how to teach these subjects to students.

2. Teachers are committed to their students and their learning.

3. Teachers are responsible for managing and monitoring student learning.

4. Teachers think systematically about their practice and learn from experience.

5. Teachers are members of a learning community.[5]

In addition, the organization has five distinguishing characteristics:

■ *five distinguishing characteristics*

1. The NBPTS is for experienced teachers or teachers with a baccalaureate or an advanced degree who have graduated from an accredited college or university and have at least three years of teaching experience.

2. "Taking the boards" is completely voluntary. It is not intended to be a condition of work, like state licensure, but an achievement testifying to an individual teacher's attainment of a high level of professionalism.

3. "Taking the boards" involves submitting oneself to a set of examinations and assessments in particular areas or subject matters such as early childhood, English language arts, and physical education and health. Currently, board certification is offered in twenty-six different teaching fields, and there are plans for adding more.

4. These assessments are not typical paper-and-pencil tests. Teaching, by its very nature, is a mixture of thought and action and is not measured well by traditional "sit-down" testing. Among the means of assessment are videotapes of one's teaching and an evaluation of one's professional portfolio. Such a portfolio might include examples of students' work, sample lesson plans, and other items that the teacher believes will support his or her

candidacy. Candidates do, however, take examinations to assure depth of knowledge in their field.

5. The primary control of the NBPTS is in the hands of a sixty-three–person board of directors. Although administrators, teacher educators, and the general public are represented on the NBPTS, two-thirds of the board members are teachers—a further step toward achieving professionalism in teaching.

advantages of the NBPTS

Advantages to Board Certification   NBPTS certification means a salary bonus for those teachers so designated. The amount varies by state, but can be as much as $5,000 a year for the length of the ten-year certification. Board certification also means that school boards have a recognizable basis on which to award merit pay other than arbitrary and impressionistic criteria such as, "Her children do well on tests," or "He seems to work long hours and is popular with the brightest students." As of 2002, just over 23,900 teachers in forty-nine states had achieved board certification.[6] Besides raising salaries, board certification offers a number of other advantages. Teachers who have achieved NBPTS certification are professionally more portable, or able to move more freely across state lines. Also, this effort should stimulate research on what constitutes superior teaching. And it should trigger more attention to this research-based knowledge within teacher education and throughout the teaching force. Most of all, it should contribute to the essential but difficult mission of creating a system of recognition for highly skilled and dedicated professionals.

arguments against the NBPTS

Criticisms of NBPTS   The NBPTS, however, is not without critics. Some educators claim that there is no solid knowledge base in teaching (as opposed to medicine or architecture) on which to ground the board's assessments. Others see the NBPTS as a public relations move to enhance the status and salaries of teachers with artificial trappings ("Fillmore got himself board certified, but we all know he couldn't teach a duck!"). Still others, suspicious that the NBPTS is controlled by its majority of teacher members, see it becoming a vehicle primarily to serve the economic interests of teachers and to insulate them further from their "clients" (the students and their parents). Finally, some continue to caution a wait-and-see attitude, acknowledging the strengths in the idea of a board, but are waiting to see if board-certified teachers really do bring about more student learning than noncertified teachers.

Reflect on NBPTS certification with the image in this section of your CD-ROM.

As we will see in the next section, the two largest professional organizations, the **National Education Association (NEA)** and the **American Federation of Teachers (AFT),** have been involved in promoting NBPTS certification, as well as performing other important functions.

What Every New Teacher Should Possess: The Interstate New Teacher Assessment and Support Consortium Standards

In the same year that the NBPTS began its work, the Council of Chief State School Officers (CCSSO) began a parallel work, but one that focuses on what prospective teachers ought to know and be able to do in order to attain initial teaching licenses in their states. This effort, which is gathering great support as of late, is to lay out standards for a common core of teaching skills and knowl-

POLICY MATTERS!

A Two-Tiered Profession?

What's the Policy?

For years, competition has been a hallmark of most occupations and careers—except for teaching. If anything, careers in teaching have been characterized by a lack of competition. In fact, most teachers believe cooperation among teachers is important and shun any competitive model that might destroy that cooperation. With the advent of the NBPTS, however, a new and controversial element of competition has emerged.

How Does It Affect Teachers?

The NBPTS began certifying in 1995, so it is safe to say that this type of advanced certification is still somewhat in its infancy. Varying degrees of interest and enthusiasm exist for this innovative staffing designation among different states and school districts. Besides the substantial prestige associated with being board certified, those teachers who achieve this distinction receive salary increases, job flexibility and mobility, and increased opportunities for leadership within the profession. And, of course, those who don't, won't.

What Are the Pros?

Some are convinced that an element of competition, which features recognition and extra compensation for outstanding performance, is needed to attract talented new teachers to the field—and keep them there. Traditionally, a teacher's salary has depended on degrees earned and years of service rather than competence. If a teacher wanted recognition in education, he or she had to move out of the classroom into administration or college teaching.

What Are the Cons?

The overriding question concerning any new program is, "Will it improve the education we provide for our children?" In the case of national board certification, there are a host of other policy questions as well, including the following:

- Who will pay the $2,300 examination fee?

- How will districts foot the bill for salary increases and benefits for certified teachers?

- Will board-certified teachers be assigned to the students in greatest need or to the most advanced and gifted? Or will they decide whom they teach?

- Will this new distinction enhance the career of teaching, making it more attractive, or will it bring into teaching a poisoning division of first team/second team, a new antagonism between the teacher ranks of haves and have-nots?

What Do You Think?

1. **In your school experience, have the truly outstanding teachers been adequately recognized and rewarded?**

2. **Other than those mentioned above, what do you see as the advantages and disadvantages of a two-tiered teaching profession?**

 Visit the web site to learn more about this policy issue.

first tier of skills

edge for all beginning teachers and standards for teachers in specific subject matter areas and levels of schooling. The CCSSO formed the Interstate New Teacher Assessment and Support Consortium (INTASC) and has been working with the NBPTS to create model standards for "board-compatible" teacher licensing. The INTASC standards are, in effect, the "first tier" of skills and knowledge, which all new teachers should possess. The idea behind these standards is not only to have new teachers across the country possess a common

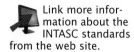

Link more information about the INTASC standards from the web site.

core of professional abilities, but also to lay the foundation for a seamless transition to acquiring the NBPTS certification later on.

Currently, thirty-nine states are working together to develop and implement the INTASC standards, and a few states are piloting the standards as part of their initial licensing process. The ten INTASC standards for all beginning teachers are listed on the inside covers of your book. For more information on INTASC and the standards, go to **http://www.ccsso.org/intascst.html**.

PAUSE AND REFLECT

❶ What are you doing now to ensure that you meet the INTASC standards as a beginning teacher?

❷ Does the idea of working toward board certification appeal to you? Why or why not?

Professional Associations

Like other occupational groups such as doctors and teamsters, teachers have associations that protect their interests and attempt to improve their lot. For example, teacher salaries (which are the major cost of schooling) and other educational expenses come out of the taxpayers' pockets. Tax revenues are used for many purposes and are heavily competed for by groups attempting to fight crime and delinquency, to increase aid to the elderly and the poor, and so on.

■ *the need for an advocate*   In the rough-and-tumble of a democracy, teachers need someone or something to look out for their interests and the interests of the recipients of their services: children. This is the avowed function of many teachers' associations.

In addition, the protection of teachers' rights and improvement in their rewards and working conditions will not just happen. There is an old saying: "Nobody gives you nothin' for nothin'." The advances teachers make will occur largely as a result of their hard work and readiness to stand up for what they believe.

■ *two competing alternatives*   Our primary focus in this section is on the large umbrella organizations of teachers, the NEA and the AFT, because these have the most immediate and sustaining effects on the lives of teachers. In 2002, more than 70 percent of all public school teachers reported belonging to the NEA. The AFT represents slightly fewer than 25 percent. These two large associations claim to represent teachers to the federal, state, and local governments; to educational authorities at the state and local levels; and, finally, to the general public. It is important to know something about them, because if you become a teacher, they will claim to be speaking for *you*. In fact, many new teachers report being asked to join a professional association their first day on the job.

As you read the following pages, be aware that the NEA and the AFT are and have been in a struggle for the hearts, minds, and membership dues of teachers for four decades. Further, each is concerned about putting its case before and gaining the support of future teachers. Bob Chase, president of the NEA, and the late Albert Shanker, former president of the AFT, each agreed to write a special letter to the readers of this book, and we urge you to read these inserts. In addition, there is a short insert about one of the newer, smaller professional associations, the American Association of Educators, which is taking a very different approach than the major professional organizations of teachers.

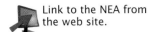
Link to the NEA from the web site.

The National Education Association

Founded in 1857, the NEA (available at: **http://www.nea.org**) today is a complex institution that operates on the national, state, and local school district levels and serves a diverse clientele of rural, suburban, and urban teachers. The bulk of its 2.6 million or more members are classroom teachers, but also included are teacher aides, administrators, professors, retired educators, and college students preparing to become teachers. In addition, the NEA has some 13,520 local affiliates in some 80 percent of the nation's school districts.[7]

▪ *a range of support services*

Services to Members
The NEA offers its members a wide range of services, from an extensive array of publications to research on issues such as comparative salary scales and the attitudes of teachers on various topics. In addition, its UniServ program has some 1,500 professionals in the field working with teachers, ready to give local teachers help in such specialized areas as collective bargaining. In addition to these support services, a number of special services are available to members, such as travel programs, insurance policies, mutual fund programs, and book club programs. Also, the NEA (as does the AFT) comes to the aid of teachers, like those in the vignettes that began this chapter, whose legal rights are being violated or who are being treated shoddily or unethically.

The NEA and Political Issues
Since the NEA's inception, its goal has been "to elevate the character and advance the interests of the profession of teaching and to promote the cause of education in the United States." In advancing this goal, it regularly comes out against issues such as competency testing of teachers. On the other hand, since 1987, the NEA has supported the NBPTS and has long been a champion of small class sizes and special programs for linguistic and ethnic groups within schools.[8]

▪ *NEA as a political force*

Further, it has taken forceful positions on such issues as public monies for private schools and various voucher plans. (The NEA is opposed to supporting private schools with public funds or vouchers, even though 22 percent of its members send their own children to private schools.)

> *If one is going to change things, one has to make a fuss and catch the eye of the world.*
> —ELIZABETH JANEWAY

In recent years, the primary focus of the NEA's work is on practicing public school teachers. To do this, the NEA has increasingly devoted its attention to political action at the local, state, and national levels. In 1976, the NEA for the first time formally backed a presidential candidate (Jimmy Carter), and since then, it has consistently backed Democratic candidates for national and most state offices.

The NEA has become a strong political player for various reasons. One political commentator referred to teachers as "bright, articulate, and reasonably well informed, making them naturals for political activism."[9] Also, teachers have the best record of any occupational group in registering to vote—well over 70 percent.[10]

▪ *a power on the national scene*

Further, the NEA is big, having recently passed the teamsters in membership. Its sheer size and presence in many congressional districts, not to mention its substantial political war chest, give it great clout in Washington, D.C.

The NEA's relatively recent alignment with one political party is not without risks. Former Secretary of Education William Bennett, accusing the NEA of political bias, called the organization, "the absolute heart and center of the Democratic Party."[11] Republicans frequently criticize the NEA as a lobbying group that is more interested in the welfare of teachers than in the education of children.

Those Who Can, Teach

Bob Chase, Former President, National Education Association (NEA)

Alfred Nobel wanted his prizes given to those who, during the preceding year, "shall have conferred the greatest benefit on mankind," with at least one going to the person who "shall have done the most or the best work for fraternity between nations, for the abolition or reduction of standing armies, and for the holding and promotion of peace congresses."

Teaching is one of the most rewarding and noble professions in the world, and one of the most beneficial to mankind. However, I don't believe that during the 101-year history of the Nobel Peace Prize has the award been given to a teacher. But it has gone to their former students.

Though often unappreciated and underpaid, teachers motivate, inspire, and cultivate the minds of children to reach their highest potential. As a teacher and president of the 2.6 million-member National Education Association, I say with great pride, "Those who *can,* teach."

Qualified teachers are second only to parents in the impact they have on a child's life. No matter what profession our children choose, or if they are one day awarded a Nobel Peace Prize, a caring teacher made a difference in their lives. A teacher committed to providing every student who enters the classroom with a quality education. By their deeds, teachers touch the future.

But this dedication is hard earned. Each day teachers are confronted with new problems that are challenging. A teacher's intellect, heart, and even his/her sense of humor are tested.

But the millions of individuals who have chosen education as their lifelong career believe that no challenge is too great. There is nothing more rewarding than to see the light of comprehension in a child's eyes when he/she understands what is being taught. Educators are the ones who ensure that "no child is left behind," and no school fails.

Those who can, teach! For many years, professional development programs for teachers were haphazard. Today's teachers are required to continuously sharpen their professional skills, improve their practice, and keep abreast of the latest advances in knowledge or technology. Teachers attend classes, workshops, and seminars to become more proficient in their subject areas and to improve their teaching techniques. Some have completed, or are in the process of completing, the very rigorous national certification program.

We know that parents are a student's first teacher, and that parental involvement is imperative for academic success of students. But sometimes parents are not involved in the child's school or the learning process. The teacher becomes the parent figure for those students—their friend, supporter, and motivator. But educators know that a child achieves at a much higher level when parents participate in school activities and their child's education. So, teachers are trying new ways to encourage parents to become an integral part of their child's education. These include visiting the homes of their students and meeting with parents outside of the traditional parent-teacher coference twice a year. A harmonious home/school relationship results in an excellent education experience for the child.

Teachers are also some of the most powerful advocates for children in the world. They research and review political records so that parents and colleagues know which candidates are most concerned about quality education and the well-being of children.

Through collective bargaining, teachers work to secure reduced class size, quality education programs, up-to-date resources and technology equipment, better working conditions, and improved salaries.

Yes, teachers are powerful advocates for children and quality public education. And frequently, they are asked to defend their stand on some of these issues. So, teachers become ambassadors of education and defenders of the rights of children and education employees.

It takes a very special person to become an educator. Teaching is much more than standing in front of a classroom and filling children's minds with knowledge. Teaching is an all-day, every day, and every week-in and week-out commitment. Teaching is the triumph of hope over hopelessness, intelligence over inhumanity.

For those reasons, those who *can,* teach, continue to teach, and remain steadfast in their efforts to improve student achievement, and ensure that students have a safe and violence-free environment in which to learn. Teachers make a difference in the lives of their students, in their schools, in their communities, and in their world. Teachers are indeed qualified candidates for Alfred Nobel's Peace Prize!

From Bob Chase, "Those Who Can, Teach." Reprinted by permission of the National Education Association.

Further, the NEA does not always reflect the political views of its members because teachers as a whole do not have deep attachments to either the political left or the political right. It has been reported that the teaching profession "has almost as many Republicans and independent members as Democrats. In other words, about two-thirds of its members have differed in their party preference."[12]

■ The American Federation of Teachers

The AFT's membership is approximately one-third the size of the NEA's, but it represents teachers in key urban areas across the country. Currently it bargains for teachers in New York City, Chicago, Philadelphia, Cleveland, Pittsburgh, Kansas City, St. Louis, Detroit, Boston, Houston, Dallas, Atlanta, and Washington, D.C.[13] Through recruiting of paraprofessionals and other school-related workers, the AFT has gained more than 28,000 members each year since 1985.[14]

I ask for philosophy from my union and it gives me politics, partisanship and public relations. Teachers learn to be pragmatists or they don't survive. Underneath their veneer of practicality, they are dreamers. Truck drivers and longshoremen might not need a philosophical guiding light from their union leaders, but teachers do. Teachers yearn for commitment, for caring and for conscience.

—SUSAN OHANIAN

The AFT's leadership is very clear about placing the organization squarely within the American labor movement. The AFT itself is affiliated with the American Federation of Labor and Congress of Industrial Organizations (AFL-CIO), which has a membership of more than 14 million. Much of the AFT's growth in the last three decades has been due to success in introducing the collective bargaining process in the annual salary negotiations of teachers. The AFT's aggressive techniques, including strikes and the threat of strikes, are credited with substantial salary increases for teachers and with forcing the NEA into more militant tactics.

■ *the feisty alternative*

■ The AFT's Stance on Issues   Although the AFT is noted for its hard bargaining on bread-and-butter issues such as salaries and benefits, it has also been a defender of academic freedom and greater participation in decision making by teachers. On the down side, the shrinking student enrollments in some of our major cities, which are the AFT's real power base, have preoccupied the organization and sapped its energies. In spite of the fact that the AFT opposes many of the same issues as the NEA, such as vouchers, and shares with it only qualified support for charter schools, the AFT has a more progressive reputation, owing largely to the efforts of its long-time leader Albert Shanker, who died in 1997. Once seen by many as the champion of raw "teacher power" and as concerned only with the good of teachers, Shanker became a strong advocate of educational

■ *the AFT's recent agenda*

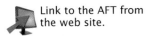 Link to the AFT from the web site.

The Role of a Professional Union

Albert Shanker, Former President, American Federation of Teachers

Is a professional union a contradiction in terms? Can teachers be both union members and professionals? And what does the term *professional* mean when it is used about teachers? These have been, and still are, defining questions for the AFT.

When I started teaching, in the days before teachers had achieved collective bargaining, the word *professional* was typically used as a club. Whenever a teacher stepped out of line—whether by criticizing something the principal had said or protesting an unfair assignment or failing to pick up a piece of paper from the classroom floor—he was likely to be told, "That's not professional!" The phrase seldom had anything to do with a teacher's exercising professional judgment or conforming to professional standards. It was used to make teachers obey orders that went against their sense of sound educational practice and, often, their common sense. Professionalism in this meaning of the word was not a standard but a threat used by administrators: Do this, don't say that, or else.

In those days, many teachers were also victims of their own definition of professionalism. They believed it was somehow unworthy and undignified (unprofessional) for teachers to try to improve their salaries and working conditions through organizing and political action. Teachers often told me that their parents, who were union members, had worked hard so their children could be professionals, so what kind of professional joins a union? This professionalism was not professionalism at all. It was the willingness of teachers to sacrifice their own self-interest and dignity (and the interests of their students) in order to maintain a false feeling of superiority.

The basic argument for unionism and collective bargaining is as true today as it was then. School systems are organizations, many of them quite large, and individual employees are likely to be powerless in such organizations. They can be heard and have some power to change things only if they are organized and act collectively. How did teachers feel about

themselves when school boards, superintendents, and principals could assign teachers to whatever duties they chose without consulting or even notifying the teachers? Some would be assigned to be "floaters" in a school and had to teach in a different classroom each hour. A few would always get the most violent classes while favored colleagues always got the best and easiest assignments. Certainly these teachers did not feel like professionals—hired hands were probably more like it.

The spread of collective bargaining has not made everything perfect, of course. Some people even blame the growth of teacher unions for the problems in our schools and the difficulty we are having in getting school reform. But if that were so, schools would be much better in states where there is no collective bargaining (like Mississippi or Texas) than in states where it exists (like New York or Connecticut), and that is plainly not the case.

Critics have often said that a teacher union can't really be interested in educational issues and the union's involvement in discussions of reform is just a ploy for getting bigger salary increases. But from the earliest years of collective bargaining, issues of educational quality have been part of AFT's agenda. At first, we were told that a union had to stick to bread-and-butter issues—that things pertaining to school improvement could not be part of the collective bargaining process. But teachers do not enter the profession because they demand big salaries; they enter it largely for the intrinsic satisfaction derived from doing a good job for their students, and they want to use their collective power to make schools work better for kids. Over the years, while seeking better pay and working conditions for teachers, we have also fought to increase the scope of bargaining, and educational issues now make up a large part of any contract.

In recent years, AFT has taken the lead in supporting the NBPTS, an effort to put teaching on a similar footing with other professions by setting standards of excellence and recognizing teachers who meet the standards. The union has also spoken out on school reform issues, sometimes to the extent that rank-and-file members have wondered whether this outspokenness about the need for reform would backfire and cost jobs. AFT's position is that if schools are not working well, we need to understand why and propose ways of fixing the problems. Otherwise, students and teachers both suffer, and the entire system is in danger of failing in the long run.

What are our plans for the years ahead? The push to professionalize teaching needs to continue and go hand in hand with unceasing efforts to improve the schools for all our students. At the same time, we need to continue dealing with the bread-and-butter issues that have always been important to our members. Can we do all this? We think so. We have never been stronger or more convinced that the future of public education depends on what our professional union does.

Source: "The Role of a Professional Union," by Albert Shanker, Reprinted by permission from American Federation of Teachers.

---

reform in his later years. He lobbied both his organization and the public in support of many reform efforts such as the NBPTS, certain kinds of merit pay, higher minimum standards for teachers, and longer and more intense teacher education In contrast, the NEA has only recently come to support many of these reform efforts.

rumors of merger

A Possible Merger?   For twenty-five years or more, the leaders of both the NEA and the AFT (along with many members of the press) have been discussing merging the two groups into one organization-union that would represent the entire teaching force. The advantages of one giant organization have attracted many people. It has been suggested that political strength in national elections and the ability to call a nationwide school shutdown would give teachers enormous power. Also, the two organizations spend much of their resources competing with each other to represent teachers in contract talks with local school systems, resources that could be used to improve education and the professionalism of teachers. Although unification would do much to solidify the power of teachers to affect change, internal organizational issues and jealousies have kept the NEA and AFT apart. In the summer of 2001, the two organizations stopped fighting and signed the "NEAFT Partnership" agreement, launching "an ongoing effort by the two groups to collaborate in projects ranging from education conferences to political and legal campaigns."[15] Although hardly a marriage, this agreement appears to be somewhere between "going steady" and deciding to get engaged.

PAUSE AND REFLECT

❶ Once you are established as a teacher, does the idea of becoming active in one of these two professional organizations or unions appeal to you personally? If so, what is the attraction?

Other Professional Associations

In addition to the NEA and AFT, there are many other educational organizations. Each supports certain constituents and serves their special interests. Table 14.1 offers a sample of these groups. The ones listed under the heading Specialized Associations of Teachers are primarily for teachers of a particular subject

Reformers in the Ranks: The Association of American Educators

Formed in 1994, the Association of American Educators (AAE) represents a fresh approach for teachers who are dissatisfied with the two major professional groups. In its first six years, it gained 33,000 teacher members in all fifty states. Although not anti-union, the AAE is opposed to many of the stands of the NEA and AFT, such as teacher strikes, opposition to voucher plans, and affirmative action for racial balance, and it is built on a few principles:

1. To encourage and support teachers who embrace certain views on education in America, such as the view that our schools should aim to improve a young person's character as well as his or her intellect.

2. To keep the governance of the organization in the hands of practicing teachers. Currently, more than half the AAE's board of directors is composed of classroom teachers who have won national teacher-of-the-year awards.

3. To keep the focus on educational issues and to stay out of politics. In contrast to the $500 to $700 combined annual local, state, and national dues charged by the major organizations, the AAE dues are a mere $125, and much of that goes for liability insurance.

This lean and mean organization does not offer its members all of the supportive services of its larger rivals. It is, however, turning out to be an alternative for those who are tired of paying hefty dues and who disagree particularly with the political stands and social views of the larger organizations. For more information, call (800) 704-7799.

---

matter or area within the life of the school. Under the second heading, Nationwide Special-Interest Groups in Education, are more broad-based organizations that typically include members of the public, administrators, people from higher education, and teachers. Through journals, in-service training, or professional development institutes, as well as conferences and conventions, these organizations play an important part in keeping teachers informed about research and developments in their fields. It is here where much of the teacher's professional activity goes on. We urge you to consider joining the association closest to your interests.

■ *Student NEA*

There are also professional associations dedicated specifically to future teachers. The largest of these is the Student National Education Association (SNEA), formerly called Future Teachers of America, which has some 55,000 members. As a branch of the NEA, the SNEA offers you many of the benefits of NEA membership, such as liability insurance when members student teach, access to the NEA's research files, and subscriptions to its regular publications, *The NEA Handbook* and *Today's Education.*

■ *education's honorary societies*

Three other professional groups are open to prospective teachers: the honor societies of Pi Lambda Theta, Phi Delta Kappa, and Kappa Delta Pi. These associations are international in scope but typically organize around chapters on university or college campuses. They have regular meetings on recent developments in the field, such as constructivist approaches to learning, brain research, and character education. These organizations provide an excellent opportunity for students to meet other education students in a nonclassroom setting and particularly to meet practicing teachers and administrators in a professional but informal setting. If membership in such honorary associations interests you, we suggest first that you speak to one of your education professors about which, if any, of the organizations are on your campus and how you can learn about them; sec-

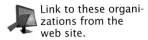

Link to these organizations from the web site.

TABLE 14.1 Nationwide Organizations of Interest to Teachers

Specialized Associations of Teachers

Council for Exceptional Children **(http://www.cec.sped.org)**
National Science Teachers Association **(http://www.nsta.org)**
National Council of Teachers of English **(http://www.ncte.org)**
National Council for the Social Studies **(http://www.ncss.org)**
National Association for Music Education **(http://www.menc.org)**
National Association for the Education of Young Children
(http://www.naeyc.org)
Association of Career and Technical Education **(http://www.acteonline.org)**
International Reading Association **(http://www.reading.org)**
National Council of Teachers of Mathematics **(http://www.nctm.org)**
American Council on the Teaching of Foreign Language **(http://www.actfl.org/)**
National Art Education Association **(http://www.naea-reston.org)**
American Alliance for Health, Physical Education, Recreation and Dance
(http://www.aahperd.org)
Association for Education Communications and Technology
(http://www.aect.org)

Nationwide Special-Interest Groups in Education

National School Boards Association **(http://www.nsba.org)**
American Association of School Administrators **(http://www.aasa.org/)**
Association for Supervision and Curriculum Development **(http://www.ascd.org)**
American Educational Research Association **(http://www.aera.net)**
Council of Chief State School Officers **(http://www.ccsso.org)**
Association of Teacher Educators **(http://www.siu.edu/departments/coe/ate)**
American Association of Colleges for Teacher Education **(http://www.aacte.org)**

ond, you can call, write, or email the headquarters of these organizations to obtain general information and to learn whether there are chapters on your campus. It is not unheard of for beginning education students to initiate new chapters.

▦ *Professionalism at the Crossroads*

Although for a century teachers have had professional organizations with which they could affiliate, only in the last forty years have they employed aggressive trade union tactics. In recent decades, the term *professionalism* frequently has been equated with "teacher power" and with teachers' capacity to close down schools through strikes and work stoppages. The power of teachers to shut down schools affects not only children's education, but also an entire community's economic health, from the immediate effects on working fathers and mothers to longer-term effects on the community's desirability as a place to live and raise children. Further, the growing alliances between the two major teachers' organizations, the NEA and the AFT, and the Democratic party have tinged teacher professionalism with a troubling political gloss.

Professionalism can also be a cover for quite self-serving ends. Occasionally teachers use their "professional status" as a barrier against criticism by children

Sometimes teachers take to the streets but with decreasing frequency.
(© Bob Daemmrich)

and parents ("How dare you question what I have done? I am a professional!"). Further, in the interest of protecting and expanding the rights of its members, a professional group can be quite insensitive to the needs and rights of the client group. For instance, insisting on tenure rights for all teachers who have taught for three years or more makes it difficult to get rid of those teachers who turn out to be genuinely incompetent. In the big cities, basing eligibility for transfer to more congenial schools on seniority may be robbing the most difficult schools of exactly the experienced teacher talent they need. Behind the jargon of professionalism, then, one often finds naked self-interest that can do harm to the teachers' clients—children.

■ *behind the jargon*

■ *Wanted: A New Professionalism*

In recent years, while teachers adopted a labor-management stance (with the "management" being their administrators and the local school board), American industry has seen a decline in aggressive trade unionism. In its place a new, cooperative spirit has brought about a revival of many of our industries. As we discuss in the chapter entitled "How Should Education Be Reformed?", following slogans of "excellence" and "re-engineering," workers and management have changed the economic landscape. We see the beginnings of a similar revival in the "educational excellence" movement and the "restructuring" efforts currently sweeping through our schools. In our view, the issue of teacher professionalism is very much wrapped up in these broader school reform efforts. Whether teachers are treated as professionals will depend on the bottom line: the performance of our schools. To promote that performance, teachers need to begin with a personal commitment to excellence. Your satisfaction as a teacher and your impact on students will be strongly influenced by the effect of this next topic on your career.

Your Own Professional Development

At one time, it was considered adequate for a teacher to obtain an undergraduate education and a teaching license and then have no further training. However, forces both inside and outside the teaching profession have since adopted the stance that the teacher must be a continuous learner. Many states have legislated continuing education for teachers. In fact, in more than one-half of the states, it is no longer possible to gain permanent licensure. More and more states are requiring teachers to keep up with developments in their fields or specific areas of education.

Central to this drive for the continuing education of teachers, or **professional development,** as it is often called, is the growth of new knowledge and the demand for new skills. A dramatic example is the rising interest in technological literacy. As American society has become increasingly dependent on electronic information services, the needs and advantages of being comfortable and competent with computers, the Internet, CD-ROMs, videodiscs, and networking have become clear. Therefore, elementary and secondary schools and colleges are rushing to provide students with this new competence. And to keep up with the rapidly widening "information superhighway," teachers, like their students, need to become continuous learners.

Link more information about professional development from the web site.

▨ *Types of Continuous Learning Opportunities*

Education must not any longer be confined to the young. The young must not look forward to its completion; the old must not look back on it as an accompaniment of immaturity. For all people, education must be made to seem a requirement of human life as long as that endures.

—Isaac Asimov

▨ *self-renewal through study*

▨ **Independent Study**   One aim of education is to develop the ability to engage in independent study. *Independent study* is jargon for being able to "go it alone." Although this approach is much discussed among educators, students seem to get little actual practice in choosing and systematically investigating their own areas of interest. Independent study, though, is one of the most important means for continual self-renewal available to you as a teacher. Teachers are confronted daily with things they do not understand about children and knowledge and human learning:

- Is there anything in this discussion about learning styles and how I can apply it in my classroom?

- What does the new brain research suggest about teaching X and Y?

- What are the fundamental skills of composition that children should know?

- How can I help my students use history for their own benefit?

Such questions are daily grist for the teacher's independent study mill. Of course, your study should not be confined to professional problems. Your own personal interests may lead into such areas as organic gardening, physical fitness, classic movies, the politics of colonial America, the humanizing of the corporate state, or harnessing the media. Not by professional problems alone doth the teacher live!

▨ *forming study groups*

▨ **Group Study**   Group study is another common form of continuous learning for the teacher. It often takes the form of committee work. When a problem

Good colleagues make professional growth a pleasure.
(© Robin Sachs/PhotoEdit)

arises in the school for which there is no apparent solution, a group of people takes on itself the task of exploring the problem with a view toward recommending an enlightened course of action. In recent years, to obtain opinions from outside the school, teachers and administrators have begun inviting community residents to these study groups. Typical issues these groups might take on are curricular alternatives, avoiding bullying on the playground, an analysis of the unused education resources in the community, a writing across the curriculum program, and the potential benefits and costs of using paraprofessionals in a high school.

graduate courses

Graduate Study   A third way for you to continue to learn is to take courses or to work toward an advanced degree. Most colleges and universities offer courses suitable for and interesting to teachers. Special and regular courses are offered in the evening, on weekends, and during the summer vacation. Many universities are now offering computer-based distance-learning courses, which enable teachers (and others) to do advanced study without leaving their homes. These courses and degree programs not only allow teachers to gain a deeper understanding of their work but also make it possible for some teachers to train for other jobs in education, such as guidance counseling, administration, or college teaching.

programs sponsored by district

In-Service Programs   A fourth opportunity you will have to grow and learn is to attend an in-service program or a professional development program sponsored by the school or school district. In-service programs are often targeted at school- or districtwide problems or issues. For instance, if students in a particular school are getting unsatisfactory grades on standardized achievement tests, the district may choose to provide special in-service training for the faculty, or the district may decide to switch to a new, supposedly better mathematics program, a change that will also require special training for the faculty. In-service training often takes place weekly or monthly, before or after school. Also,

VOICES FROM THE CLASSROOM

Theresa Madison teaches Grade 10 Language Arts at Brighton High School in Brighton, Massachusetts.

Professionalism

Before I began teaching I had a certain vision of what the world of teachers would be like. I prepared myself for hearing a lot of "when you've been around as long as I have" and "when you get to be my age you'll understand." I felt a sort of pre-embarrassment for all the mistakes I would probably make before I "got it." To me, the profession presented itself as a kind of hierarchy where the big cheese of the school would offer condescending advice and rolled eyes at my rookie mishaps.

Now, only six months into the experience, I am happy to say that my fears were quite wrong. Not too long ago, I went to visit a colleague of mine, Jane, in her classroom during one of her planning periods. She's been a teacher for about six or seven years and at our school for only three. About a minute or two into our conversation, I noticed that the door that adjoined her room with Mrs. Conner's room was open and students were moving between the two. Soon Mrs. Conner herself came bustling in and out of Jane's room, looking for glue sticks and getting a clarification about some graphic organizer.

After asking what was going on, I made a concerted effort to hide my surprise. Jane was asked to take on a smaller class load this year and to spend the remaining time as a literacy coach. She told me that the job included sitting in on classes for a week or so and then working one-on-one with that particular teacher to experiment with different instructional practices and techniques. But Mrs. Conner? She had been teaching for 30 years. This was a woman who had a way with students, parents, and other teachers that I wished I could bottle and sell. It was one thing to smile and nod at staff meetings when younger teachers spoke but to invite a teacher with far fewer years on the job into your classroom was quite a different scenario.

I could only describe the feeling as humbling. Nobody, it seemed, was out to get me, or laugh at my naiveté. The more I began to look around, the more I noticed that many of my colleagues were "age blind." The task at hand was to educate students, and if someone had a better way of doing things or if some workshop came along that could benefit a teacher's practice, then many of these educators were up for another learning experience. I had always heard that teachers were learners for life, but I wasn't sure how many of them bought that old cliché. As it turns out, seeking more for our students and our own practice is not considered a sign of weakness or a stigma by all of those scary veterans; it's simply part of being a professional.

 Visit the web site for more Voices from the Classroom.

---

special days are sometimes set aside on which school is canceled or students are dismissed early so teachers can participate in in-service training.

■ **Supervision** A fifth form of continuous learning comes through supervision. During a teacher's early years in the profession, school districts provide professional advice that amounts to one-on-one help. For instance, if you are a new high school teacher, your department head may observe your classes regularly and discuss the observations with you, or if you are an elementary school teacher, your building principal or lead teacher may make regular visits and follow them with feedback sessions. Although supervision can sometimes be quite threatening, particularly to nontenured teachers, it offers an opportunity to obtain valuable insight and information about your teaching techniques and skills.

■ *observation and feedback*

The more we know, the more we want to know; when we know enough, we know how much we don't know.

—CAROL ORLOCK

■ *mentoring*

■ **Mentoring**   In recent years, many school districts around the country have instituted mentoring programs whereby more experienced teachers are assigned to assist beginners. (Mentoring is discussed in more detail in the chapter entitled "What Can the New Teacher Expect?".) Along with special training, the mentors may receive a reduction in teaching responsibilities, a salary increase, or both. **Mentoring** programs formalize and make more systematic a time-honored process in which an experienced teacher takes a rookie under his or her wing, helping the beginner make the theory-into-practice transition and serving as a nonjudgmental colleague.

■ **Systematic Reflection on Practice**   Teaching can become a matter of routine, sometimes mindless routine. This condition is enormously dangerous to a teacher's development. Even more important than engaging in the activities we have discussed is developing the habit of reflecting on one's practice. If teachers, new or old, are to improve, they need to make systematic reflection on what is happening in their classrooms a regular part of their professional lives. In the "spaces" in their lives—the time between classes, driving home, or working out at the gym—they need to be asking themselves questions like the following:

Reflect on your professional development with the image in this section of your CD-ROM.

- What went right in class today?

- What didn't work?

- What can I do to get my uninvolved students more engaged?

- Are there other ways of presenting this material that will connect with students who have different learning styles?

■ *reflection is essential*

This may explain why we have sprinkled throughout each chapter opportunities for you to "Pause and Reflect." We are convinced that the true key to sustained development as a professional is the probing habit of reflection and commitment to growth as a teacher.

A Final Word

■ *the teacher as both object and artist*

So to all of you who teach, hats off. Yours is an invaluable profession, a calling sure and high and noble, a model we cannot live without if we expect to remain strong and free. Don't quit. Don't even slack off. If ever we needed you, we need you today.

—CHARLES SWINDOLL

Becoming a teacher may be compared with sculpting a work of art from a piece of stone. The difference is that the teacher is both the sculptor and the stone. The teacher begins with a vision of what he or she wants to be and then sets to work transforming the vision into a reality. The process requires an understanding of the material with which one is working—the self—and of the tools one can use. It also requires a vision of what one needs to become. Finally, it takes long hours of chipping away and then smoothing the surfaces. To be a teacher, particularly a teacher who is continuously moving forward, is a lifelong commitment to be an artist.

KEY TERMS

American Federation of Teachers (AFT) (468)

mentoring (482)

National Board for Professional Teaching Standards (NBPTS) (467)

National Education Association (NEA) (468)

profession (459)

professional development (479)

FOR REFLECTION

❶ Do you think it is important for teachers to devote themselves to becoming professionals? If so, what must they do? Are you willing to do it? How do you feel about the description of the "career teacher" in the "Recognizing Excellence in Teaching" section of this chapter? Do teachers need a professional organization? What essential functions does such a group perform?

❷ At this moment, what seems to you to be the most important issues with which teachers should concern themselves? Increased power? Higher salaries? Better training? Something else? Be prepared to defend your choice. What can you do to help bring about the changes you consider most important?

❸ Do you believe it is right for teachers to strike? Why or why not?

❹ Which of the ideas for lifelong professional development described in this chapter appeal to you most?

FOR FURTHER INFORMATION

PRINT RESOURCES

Linda Darling-Hammond, "Teachers and Teaching: Signs of a Changing Profession." In *The Handbook of Research on Teacher Education,* ed. Robert Houston (New York: Macmillan, 1991), pp. 267–290.

This article summarizes much recent research on various factors and trends affecting the teaching profession, from the demographic composition of the teaching force to supply-and-demand factors.

Gerald Grant and Christine Murray, *Teaching in America: The Slow Revolution* (Cambridge, MA: Harvard University Press, 1999).

This book traces the progress of two groups, college professors and precollegiate teachers, pointing out the similarities and differences in the evolution of professions. Drawing lessons from the development of the professorate, the authors point out the steps teachers need to take to continue their progress.

Dan C. Lortie, *Schoolteacher: A Sociological Study* (Chicago: University of Chicago Press, 1975).

This classic book presents a sociological view of the ethos of the teaching profession, that pattern of orientations and sentiments that are peculiar to teachers.

National Education Association, *Status of the American Public School Teacher: 1995–96* (Washington, DC: National Education Association, 1996).

This report is one in a series of studies conducted every four years. It contains a massive amount of information on who teachers are, what is on their minds, and the conditions of their work. Information on the 2000 report was not available when this book went to press, but you can contact NEA directly at the address above.

Eugene F. Provenzo and Gary McCloskey, *Schoolteachers and Schooling: Ethoses in Conflict* (Norwood, NJ: Ablex, 1996).

This short book gives a thoughtful and detailed picture of how teaching has changed in the last third of the twentieth century and the forces at play in a teacher's life.

Public Agenda, *A Sense of Calling: Who Teaches and Why,* 2000.

An encouraging and current report on new teachers' attitudes about their chosen profession, their satisfactions, and their concerns. In addition, the report also deals with the perceptions of administrators of new teachers and their performance.

WEB RESOURCES

American Federation of Teachers. Available at: **http://www.aft.org**.

The AFT's web site provides information on the organization and its programs, commentary on current issues, and links to other interesting web pages. Contact the American Federation of Teachers, 555 New Jersey Avenue, NW, Washington, DC 20001.

National Education Association. Available at: **http://www.nea.org**.

This web site offers a great deal of information about the NEA and its programs. Contact the National Education Association, 1201 16th Street, NW, Washington, DC 20036, (202) 822-7200, FAX: (202) 822-7292.

Why Teach?

Chapter Preview This chapter's purpose is to help you answer a fundamental question: Why become a teacher?

This chapter also emphasizes that:

- A great variety of motivations lead people to select teaching as their occupation, and often the same person has more than one reason for choosing teaching.

- Teaching, like other occupations, often attracts people because of the rewards it offers them. The rewards of teaching can be divided into extrinsic and intrinsic rewards.

- In deciding whether to become a teacher, you can draw on a number of sources of useful experiences, including actual encounters with teachers and children, vicarious classroom experiences, guidance from friends and acquaintances in the profession, and most importantly, your own personal reflections.

If you teach, it is quite likely that by the end of your second year of teaching you will have had both of the following experiences:

1. Someone at a party or some other social gathering will ask you what you do and how you like teaching. Soon the person will tell you that he or she has always wanted to be a teacher and regrets having become a stockbroker/ bookkeeper/sales representative/flight attendant/disc jockey, and that he or she may still give it all up and become a teacher.

2. You will get to know an experienced teacher who confides in you that he or she deeply regrets having become a teacher. While in college, the person felt definitely cut out for teaching and actually enjoyed it in the beginning. But gradually, he or she became fed up with the whole thing—bratty kids, pushy administrators, the same old faces in the teachers' lounge, the instant-expert parents, the overemphasis on standards and high-stakes testing. Now the person feels trapped in teaching and sees no way to get out.

The purpose of this chapter is to keep you from becoming "the other person" in either of these two situations. It is to help you make a well-thought-out decision about what to do with your life, particularly if you are one of those still undecided about becoming a teacher.

Motivations for Teaching

scrutiny of teachers

The education of America's children regularly tops the list of the public's social concerns. Particularly now in the first decade of the twenty-first century, our educational system is receiving major attention from social critics and politicians. Because of this high priority, our teaching force—present and near future—is receiving a good deal of scrutiny. Americans are relying on our teachers to instruct, guide, inspire, motivate, and occasionally prod our children to learn and to learn more than ever before. Amid the cries for increased standards and high-stakes testing are assertions that new teachers are disgruntled and dissatisfied with the work. Critics suggest that teaching now appeals to too many young people with few skills and little drive, lured to teaching only by the security of regular pay raises and summers off. Is there any truth to these opinions?

Motivations of Current Teachers

today's teachers felt a true calling

An in-depth study, conducted in 2000 with 664 public school teachers and 250 private teachers, all having taught for five or fewer years, paints a picture of how today's newest teachers feel about their work. The researchers aptly titled their report *A Sense of Calling: Who Teaches and Why,* and concluded "most new teachers are highly motivated professionals who bring a strong sense of commitment and high morale to their work."[1] They see themselves as talented and dedicated professionals. Reflecting the title of the report, 86 percent of the new teachers affirmed that only those "with a true sense of calling" should teach.[2] Nine out of ten claim that the teaching profession demands a high level of energy and effort, requiring more talent and hard work than many other professions. The teachers in this study continually commented on the need for enthusiasm to do the job well. An overwhelming 98 percent described other new teachers with whom they

Figure 15.1
What Superintendents and Principals Say About Our New Teachers

Source: Public Agenda, A Sense of Calling: Who Teaches and Why (New York: The Public Agenda, 2000), p. 13.

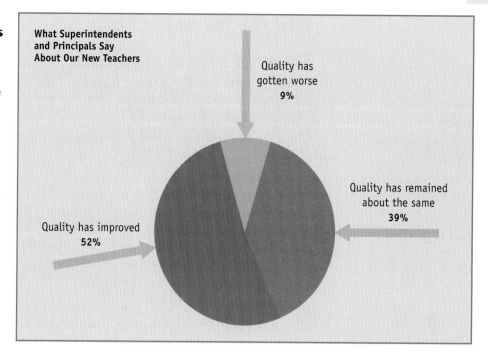

What Superintendents and Principals Say About Our New Teachers

Quality has gotten worse
9%

Quality has remained about the same
39%

Quality has improved
52%

vo·ca·tion n. 2. An inclination, as if in response to a summons, to undertake a certain kind of work.

—AMERICAN HERITAGE DICTIONARY

■ strong commitment

The best prize life offers is the chance to work hard at work worth doing.

—THEODORE ROOSEVELT

work as sharing in their sense of commitment and enthusiasm.[3] Their principals and superintendents have a similar high regard for them, with a stunning 98 percent agreeing with the descriptions of their new teachers as "motivated" and "energetic."[4] As Figure 15.1 shows, rumors that the quality of new teachers has deteriorated are hardly born out by those who do the hiring. We suspect that there are few professions where workers have such high regard for newcomers.

But why do these teachers teach? The study reveals some surprisingly consistent answers (Table 15.1). Nearly all of these new teachers (96 percent) reported that teaching is the work they love to do. Four out of five claim that they would choose teaching again if starting over. Three out of four insist that, "teaching is a lifelong choice," and two out of three report that they get a lot of satisfaction out of teaching. Contrary to the rumor that many simply drift into teaching, a mere 12 percent say, that they "fell into teaching by chance." All but a handful have extremely altruistic attitudes about their work, telling the researchers that teaching offers them an opportunity for "contributing to society." For some, teaching is clearly a *short-term career*. One in five indicated that they would probably change careers at some point. However, this figure contrasts sharply with the 50 percent of young college graduates in other fields who say that they expect to change careers at least once.[5]

Judging from this study, it seems that new teachers show a remarkable certainty that they made the right choice in pursuing a teaching career. It also appears that the majority of today's new teachers have taken the time to reflect on whether teaching is the right career choice for them. But what about you and your personal decision?

TABLE 15.1   Why Teachers Teach

What Teachers Say	Percentage Who Say It
Teaching is work they love to do	96
They would choosing teaching again if starting over	80
Teaching is a lifelong choice	75
They get a lot of satisfaction out of teaching	68
They fell into teaching by chance	12

■ *Examining Your Own Motives for Teaching*

Centuries ago, Francis Bacon told us "knowledge is power." Much earlier, Socrates (one of civilization's great teachers, about whom you read in the chapter entitled "What Are the Philosophical Foundations of American Education?") recognized the enormous power of self-knowledge when he urged, "Know thyself." Understanding one's motives in something as important as a career choice is crucial to good decision making. A superficial motivation to teach can, and frequently does, lead to failure and disappointment. For instance, you may admire and want to emulate a former teacher. And you may, out of respect for this person, decide to teach without ever analyzing whether you have the ability, skills, attitudes, or drive to do so. Or you may think it is admirable to like and help children. But in the process of actually working with, say, sixth-graders, you may discover that you can't stand sixth-graders or that you are not even particularly interested in children.

■ *understand your real motives*

Clarifying your motives then helps you identify your strengths as a person and as a prospective teacher and to cope with your shortcomings. Someone whose desire to teach grows out of a passion for art history has to know how to guard against hostility toward students who don't share that love of art. More than a few frustrated teachers have been heard to mutter, "Those ungrateful little whiners aren't worthy of Shakespeare" (or French infinitives, or the wonders of the protoplasmic process, or the niceties of quadratic equations). In any event, we have written this chapter—and, indeed, the entire book—in the hope that you will use it to gain a greater understanding of how you and a career in education might fit together.

■ *make a list*

In the chapter entitled "What Is a School and What Is It For?", we asked you to write down what you believed were your motives for considering becoming a teacher. Before having you review your list, we would like you again to take a moment to write down, on the blank lines that follow, what you now feel are your motives for wanting to be a teacher. If you are still not completely sure whether you want to be a teacher (this probably applies to many readers), list your motives both for and against becoming a teacher. Compare your list to the one you made for the chapter entitled "What Is a School and What Is It For?". Have you noticed any changes? If you were uncertain back then, have you seen any factor shift from your list of motives *for* becoming a teacher to your list of reasons *against* teaching, or vice versa? We hope that you have seen a change. Our goal in writing this book, as we have said, is to provide you with the information that you need to see how well a teaching career will fit into your life.

Incidentally, you may wish to save the list for future reference. You may notice even more changes. More than a few readers have discovered that their motives for teaching have shifted dramatically as their teacher preparation and classroom experiences have unfolded.

We use the plural, *motives,* for a particular reason. Most of us have mixed motives, some altruistic and some personal, regarding what is important to us. Our motives often conflict, and sometimes they are incompatible. In any event, one motive is rarely enough to explain a choice as complex as the career in which we plan to spend a large part of our lives.

Why Become a Teacher?

Motives for	Motives against

Having answered the question "What are my motives for wanting to become a teacher?" (and we surely hope you have), here are a few examples you might check against your own list:

can you find yourself among these?

- I really like the idea of having a positive influence on twenty-five (or 150) kids every day.

- I can't think of anything else to do with my major.

- Teaching seems to be a fairly secure, low-risk occupation with many attractive benefits and lots of vacation time.

- I always loved history/mathematics/science/literature, and teaching seems to be a career that will allow me to work with a subject matter that I love.

- I can't imagine anything more important to do with my life than helping children with disabilities learn to cope with, and even overcome, their barriers.

- The instruction I had in school was incredibly bad, and I want to correct that situation.

 Explore motivations for teaching with the video resources on your CD-ROM.

- My parents would really be pleased and proud if I were a teacher.

- Quite simply, I love children.

- I enjoy being in charge and being able to influence students.

- I really don't know what else I could do. I know about teaching, and I think I could do it.

- I'm concerned that society is falling apart, and I want to look out for the kids.

- One of my students might become a famous painter, or the president of a major foundation, or who knows what. It would be great to have a strong impact on just one significant life.

- I really want to become a principal/coach/guidance counselor/college professor/educational researcher, and teaching seems to be the way one has to start.

- I have strong religious beliefs and see teaching as a good and useful way to live my life. Education seems as if it's going to be the action field of the future, and I want to be part of it.

- Businesses are increasingly interested in training and educating their employees, and I want a career as a private-sector educator working in corporate America.

- I have always felt I have a calling, a vocation, to be a teacher.

The Rewards of Teaching

As we have seen, an individual's response to the "Why teach?" question can run the gamut from "What's in it for me?" to "How can I help others?" Moreover, at different times and in different moods, our individual motivations may be quite different. As social psychologist Peter Drucker quipped, "We know nothing about motivation. All we can do is write books about it." On the other hand, the motivational *factors*—those qualities that reside within teaching—are clearer and relatively constant. Researchers have identified a set of occupational rewards that can help us sort out both the attractive and unattractive qualities of a career in teaching.[6] The two broad categories of rewards are extrinsic and intrinsic rewards. **Extrinsic rewards** are the public, external attractions of an occupation, such as money, prestige, and power. The **intrinsic rewards** of an occupation are the internal psychic or spiritual satisfactions one receives from one's work, such as a personal sense of accomplishment or an enjoyment of the work itself. It will undoubtedly be no surprise to the reader that teaching is somewhat out of balance, receiving generally high marks on one set of rewards and low marks on the other.

■ *categories of rewards*

■ Extrinsic Rewards

Teaching has rarely been cited for its abundance of extrinsic rewards. Although it offers more extrinsic rewards than occupations such as law enforcement and coal mining, when compared with other professions, teaching ranks low in extrinsic compensations.

■ **Salaries** As you saw in the chapter entitled "What Are Your Job Options in Education?", teachers' salaries, as well as benefits such as retirement plans and health care, have improved substantially in recent years, and there are encouraging signs that steady gains can be expected. Nevertheless, compared with salaries in occupational fields with similar educational requirements (for example, a college degree and specialized training), teachers' salaries do not fare well. Whereas salaries in some professions usually begin low and then increase significantly, salaries for teachers may rise only modestly over the course of an entire teaching career. However, the importance of salary, like the whole issue of monetary needs, varies enormously from one individual to the next. And, again, as

To hear lessons and control restless children six hours a day through thirty-six weeks in a year is wretched drudgery, but to train and develop human minds and characters is the most inspiring work in the world.

—Ellen Hyde,

to the graduating class of the Framington Normal School in 1886

■ *modest salaries*
■ *variable status*

you saw in the chapter entitled "What Are Your Job Options in Education?", teachers' salaries vary significantly from one geographical location to the next.

At 22, I graduated Phi Beta Kappa. I had choices at my fingertips: law school, grad school . . . corporate America, here I come! Adults swelled their chests in pride. My peers practiced the "on my way to a Lexus" shuffle. Then the question: "And what are your plans after graduation?" Answer: "I'm moving to New York to teach elementary school in the South Bronx." As a 23-year-old teacher with sore feet and 28 incredible kids, my explanation reminds me of a song. I had a choice to sit it out or dance. I chose to dance.

—THALIA THEODORE, WASHINGTON POST
(DEC. 2, 2001), P. F1

■ *power over others' lives*

■ **Status**   *Status* refers to one's position in a group—that is, where one stands in relation to others. Whereas the status of a doctor or a beggar is rather clear, the status of a teacher is more difficult to discern. To young parents entrusting their child to the schools, the status of the teacher is quite high. To the same parents twelve or fifteen years later, on hearing that their child wants to become a teacher, the status may have diminished. However, our nation's current commitment to reform our educational system is having a positive effect on the status of teaching. A recent public survey asked which of eight professions (e.g., physician, lawyer, nurse, and journalist, among others) "provides the most important benefit to society." Respondents put teaching first, by close to a four to one margin over physicians (62 percent versus 17 percent). This is a significant change, since in a closely comparable poll in 1988, only 35 percent of respondents put teaching first.[7]

■ **Power**   The same recent survey made it quite clear that the public sees the quality of teachers as the greatest influence on student learning.[8] Anyone who claims that teachers do not have power has forgotten what it was like to go to school without having done the assigned homework and to sit in fear of being called on by Mrs. Gotcha. Any individual who can make another's day or ruin another's year has power. The power of the teacher is not a dollars-and-cents power, like that possessed by a corporate chief executive officer. And although power is not usually seen as one of the rewards of teaching, it nevertheless is a quality that "resides in the office." Yet, as sociologist Dan Lortie has observed, "Teachers are not supposed to *enjoy* exercising power per se."[9]

■ **Work Schedule**   There is an old joke about a student in an education course being stumped on an exam by the question, "What are the three best things about teaching?" Finally, in desperation, he writes "June, July, and August." Compared with other workers, teachers spend much less time at their work sites. Ignoring what teachers do at home by way of preparing lessons, correcting papers, and checking homework, we can say they work six or seven hours a day for fewer than half the days of the year. Compared with those in the power and status occupations, such as corporate finance or medicine, teachers have

This fifth-grade teacher is making reading books fun.
(© Paul Conklin)

■ *flexibility and personal control over time*

less demanding work schedules. Also, teachers have much more flexibility and personal control over how they use their time. For many men and women for whom family life is a top priority, the time close to home and the summer vacations are major pluses for a career in teaching. Teachers' work schedules therefore are one extrinsic reward that carries a great deal of weight.

■ *Intrinsic Rewards*

Extrinsic rewards, such as company stock options or yearly bonuses, are quite tangible. Intrinsic rewards are, by their very nature, in the eye of the beholder. What is one person's intrinsic reward, such as taking a busload of students on an overnight fieldtrip to the state capital, is another's living nightmare. However, the most satisfied teachers are usually those attracted to its intrinsic rewards.

■ **Students**   The attraction of working with students has long been one of the strongest rewards perceived by teachers. The daily contacts, the conversations and exchanges, and even the struggles to motivate a student are a deep source of satisfaction for many teachers. Seeing children learn, grow, and develop—seeing them able to do things that they were unable to do at the beginning of the

■ *the joy of helping others*

school year—is a genuinely fulfilling experience. Being important to others satisfies profound human needs for most of us, and teachers know about and appreciate this potential to affect the lives of others. When educational researchers Mihaly Csikszentmihalyi and Jane McCormack asked teenagers to tell who or what had influenced them to become the kinds of people they are, 58 percent (almost three out of five) mentioned teachers.[10]

Our goal is not so much the imparting of knowledge as the unveiling and developing of spiritual energy.

—Maria Montessori

This reward is particularly meaningful to elementary school teachers, who spend so much time with the same group of fifteen to thirty children. Secondary school teachers, who focus on a particular subject matter and see as many as 150 students in a day, identify working with students as an important attraction but not always to the same degree as their elementary school counterparts do.

■ **Performance of a Significant Social Service**   In the award-winning film about early Renaissance England, *A Man for All Seasons,* Sir Thomas More says to Richard Rich, the man who eventually betrayed him, but who at the time was seeking a cushy job at court, "Why not be a teacher, Rich? You'd be a fine teacher. Perhaps a great one." Disappointed, Rich replies, "And if I were, who would know it?" More then says, "You . . . your pupils . . . your friends . . . God—not a bad public, that." To many teachers, the greatest satisfaction derived from teaching is the sense that they are doing important work for the common good. This realization buoys them up and helps them tolerate the less attractive aspects of teaching. Whereas workers in government and business are aware, in an abstract sense, that they are contributing to the social good, teachers have daily flesh-and-blood testaments to the importance of their service directly in front of them. As Figure 15.2 shows, members of the general public seem to agree that teaching provides valuable benefits for society. In our own classes, we see more and more college students not only seriously considering teaching as a career but also selecting teaching specifically because they see it as a way to pay back the country and to fulfill other service-related goals. For many teachers, the deeper motive behind the performance of important service for others is a religious one. They see teaching as a way to serve God through being of service to the young.

■ *contribution to society*

A man of humanity is one who, in seeking to establish himself, finds a foothold for others and who, desiring attainment for himself, helps others to attain.

—*Confucius*

■ **Stimulation and Support from Fellow Teachers**   When describing the work of teaching, researchers often report on the sense of isolation many teachers

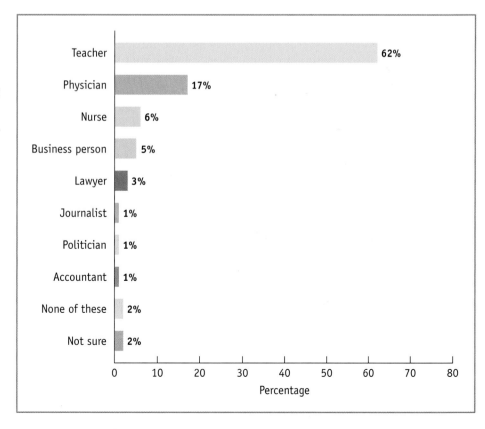

Figure 15.2
Profession That Provides the Most Benefit to Society
Source: From David Haselkorn and Louis Harris, "The Essential Profession: A National Survey of Public Attitudes Toward Teaching, Educational Opportunity, and School Reform." Reprinted with permission of Recruiting New Teachers, Inc.

TABLE 15.2   Is Teaching Satisfying?

How important is it to you that a job have each of the following characteristics?

	Percentage of New Teachers Responding	
	"Absolutely Essential"	"My Current Teaching Position Has It"
Involves work you love to do	83	96
Allows enough time to be with family	81	79
Contributes to society and helps others	72	97
Provides the supervision and support you need	64	78
Has job security	60	84
Gives the sense that you are respected and appreciated	59	66
Has good opportunities for advancement	33	59
Pays well	30	31

collegiality

experience.[11] Nevertheless, for many teachers, their contacts and interactions with colleagues are an important intrinsic reward. Teachers enjoy the shoptalk and camaraderie that is a natural part of school life. Because teachers are not always rewarded for their individual job performance or for their expertise, feelings of competition are less prevalent than among occupational groups such as salespeople or lawyers, who must establish and hold a clientele. Teachers know they are part of a cooperative venture.

teaching as pleasurable activity

■ **The Work of Teaching**   For many teachers, the process of teaching is a meaningful reward in itself. Whether it is explaining an idea, working with small groups, or designing instructional units, the actual work is highly gratifying. Like a pianist moving through a favorite sonata or a lawyer cross-examining a witness, teachers often draw their deepest satisfactions in and from the act of applying their craft. Of course, teachers vary in which activities they find rewarding. Some draw their rewards from establishing a nurturing, cooperative environment, some from unraveling complicated problems for students, and some from seeing students work and learn independently. For these teachers, all else pales before their fulfillment in simply doing the work of a teacher.

I believe the impulse to teach is fundamentally altruistic and represents a desire to share what you value and to empower others. I am not talking about the job of teaching so much as the calling to teach. Most teachers I know have felt that calling at some time in their lives.

—HERBERT KOHL

■ *Rewards in Perspective*

Around the world, teachers' intrinsic motives appear to be quite comparable. For example, consider the answers given by new teachers across the United States in the research study described earlier in the chapter, *A Sense of Calling*. Researchers asked these new teachers, "Is teaching satisfying?" and specifically how important it was to them that the work have certain characteristics. Table 15.2 summaries their responses.

Whether one is teaching in Chicago or Krakow, the inner rewards are very similar to those described by this group of new teachers, but this is not so with the extrinsic rewards. Different countries reward teachers in vastly differing ways. In several European and Asian countries, teachers enjoy a great deal of status and attractive salaries relative to other occupations. Typically, this occurs in countries that recognize that an investment in education reaps substantial economic benefits.

Reflect further on your motivations for teaching with the image in this section of your CD-ROM.

The issue of intrinsic and extrinsic rewards is captured by the story of a television reporter filming a documentary on the work of the late Mother Teresa and her community of nuns in the slums of Calcutta, India. After filming a young American nun cleaning the running sores, filth, and infections covering the body of a dying beggar, the reporter looked down at the nun and declared, "I wouldn't do that for a million dollars!" Without taking her eyes off the dying patient, the young nun replied, "Neither would I." One of the great intrinsic benefits of a career in teaching—and one not shared by the vast number of other occupations—is the certainty that your work with the young is profoundly important. But be they extrinsic or intrinsic, the rewards we seek are expressions of our personal values.

PAUSE AND REFLECT

1 Which of the extrinsic rewards discussed above applies to you most? Which of the intrinsic rewards?

2 As you have probed your own motives for considering teaching, what have you learned about yourself?

Sources of Useful Experience

One of the major educational insights applied to schooling in recent years concerns individual differences. There is a new appreciation for the unique learning styles and often the unique learning problems of children and youth. As a result, the "one-true-way" approach to education is gradually slipping by the boards. The same insight about individual differences applies to making an intelligent career choice. Because people learn in such diverse ways and differ so much in what they already know and need to learn, we can give only sketchy guidelines here. We recognize four categories of experience that may help you answer the question, "Should I teach?"

◼ *Real Encounters*

romantic images versus real children

People who plan to be teachers should test their commitment to teaching by putting themselves in actual school situations. As much as possible, students of teaching should observe in schools and participate in various activities that give them **real encounters** with children and adolescents. Many teaching candidates avoid actual contact with the young until they begin student teaching, only to find that young people are much different from the romantic images they have manufactured. "Those nasty little fifth-graders are so disgustingly . . . human!" one shocked student teacher said. Frequently, too, teaching candidates limit their encounters to typical elementary and secondary school students. They do not consider teaching children with mental or physical disabilities or even becoming a specialist such as a reading teacher. As a result of their past experiences, they have been exposed to only a narrow segment of the opportunities and challenges of teaching.

■ ways to get your educational feet wet

Increasingly, school districts are using college students as teacher aides and assistant teachers, both during the regular school year and in summer school. And a large number of teacher education programs have cooperative arrangements with schools that give college students opportunities to play various roles within the school, usually as part of their coursework in teacher education. As we mention in the chapter entitled "What Are Your Job Options in Education?", we particularly urge prospective teachers to take the opportunity resulting from the current teacher shortage and become substitute teachers. Although the work is demanding, there is much that will be learned from it. Besides the valuable experience and the money earned, these substitute teaching stints often lead to regular teaching positions in the future. School districts typically are more interested in hiring someone whom they have had a chance to see in action than strangers who they only know from résumés and references.

> *Those who educate children well are more to be honored than they who produce them; for these only gave them life, those the art of living well.*
>
> —ARISTOTLE

If your schedule doesn't permit substitute teaching, many schools also gratefully accept part-time volunteer help from education students. Schools, however, do not exhaust the opportunities. There is much to be said for nonschool contact with children, such as camp counseling, playground work, after-school recreation projects, work in orphanages and settlement houses, and youth-related church work. Other possibilities include coaching a team or sponsoring a club. The opportunities are many. The important thing is to get your feet wet—to get the feel of working with children in a helping relationship.

Link more information about real-life opportunities from the web site.

■ *Vicarious Experiences*

Not all learning has to take place in the school of hard knocks. In fact, civilization itself requires that we be able to capitalize on the experiences of others.

Real-world experience with children can help you make an informed decision about teaching as a career.
(© Elizabeth Crews)

■ *the teacher in fiction and film*

Artists and other talented people can make others' experiences accessible to us for enjoyment, edification, or both. Great fictional classics such as *Good-bye, Mr. Chips,* by James Hilton, and *The Corn Is Green,* by Emlyn Williams, portray teachers and schools, as do somewhat more contemporary novels such as Bel Kaufman's *Up the Down Staircase* and Evan Hunter's *Blackboard Jungle.* (All four of these books have been made into films.) There have also been some fine nonfiction accounts of teaching; among the best are Tracy Kidder's *Among Schoolchildren,* Samuel G. Freedman's *Small Victories,* and Esmé Raji Codell's *Educating Esmé* (all are cited in the For Further Information section at the end of this chapter.

Reflect on media portrayals of teachers with the image in this section of your CD-ROM.

Films, such as *The Emperor's Club, Mr. Holland's Opus, October Sky, Dangerous Minds, Dead Poet's Society,* and *Stand and Deliver,* as well as some television shows such as *Boston Public,* are other sources of **vicarious experiences** that help us both relive our own experiences in school and see it in a different light. However, that light is often distorting. Leslie Swetnam has reported on how the media, particularly film and television, twist the public's image of the teacher. Swetnam states, "Problems arise from the misrepresentation of who teaches, where they teach, how they teach, and what demands are placed on teachers, thereby creating an alarming distortion with consequences serious enough to warrant the concern of all educational professionals."[12] Her analysis of the most popular media presentations of teachers and schools shows that they overrepresent male teachers, secondary schools, minority teachers, and urban schools. Other distortions are that classes are small; teaching typically means the adult is talking (often with the skill of a stand-up comedian!) and, when the class finally gets around to it, learning is fun, fun, fun.[13]

Then there is a relatively recent genre of films, such as *The Breakfast Club, Election, Sugar and Spice,* and hoards of others, that present teachers as perverts and sadists. The less said about those films, the better. However, if approached with a critical eye, all these media images of teaching can prepare us for certain aspects of school life. We need to remember, however, that books, films, and television tend to portray school life at its extremes, featuring heightened situations well beyond the typical experiences of most teachers. The drama of teaching, on the other hand, is quiet, long term, and terribly real.

■ *Guidance*

■ *advice from others*

Another aid is the advice and counsel gained from those who know you. Besides parents and friends (who occasionally are too close to you to be objective), you can consult former teachers, career placement counselors, and your college professors. Your professors of education can be particularly helpful, because they usually are familiar with the realities of teaching. You should be somewhat cautious here, however. First, choose people who know you well rather than those who have seen you just at your better moments. Second, do not expect a comprehensive computer printout of hard data with a firm decision at the bottom line. If you get a few glimpses of insight from the person whose advice you are seeking, be satisfied. Third, be cautious, since many people are compulsive advice givers. People often generalize on the basis of too little knowledge, and they are sometimes just plain wrong. Receive advice openly, but follow it cautiously.

■ *Reflection*

■ *taking time out to think*

The most important aspect of the real school encounters, guidance, and vicarious experiences you collect is that they provide you with data for reflection. As

VOICES FROM THE CLASSROOM

Elida Laski taught kindergarten for three years in Chula Vista, California, and is now a literacy coach for three early learning centers in the Boston public school system.

Are You Born with It?

In my second year of teaching, a colleague told me, "Good teachers are born, not made, and you were born with *it*." After four years of teaching, I still wonder about this comment. What is that *it*, that certain something that distinguishes excellent teachers? Do you have to be born with that certain something in order to be a good teacher? If you are born with *it*, do you always know that teaching is the profession for you? Is it true that some people are just not made for teaching, or can anyone learn what it takes? How do you know if you are meant to be a teacher?

I never intended to be a teacher. In fact, it was not until my senior year of college that, as a frustrated pre-med student, I entertained the idea of teaching and took two education courses. Immediately, I knew that teaching was for me! I had done very well in the pre-med track, but I never felt invested in what I was studying. Education courses required just as much, if not more, time and thought, and they were exciting in a way pre-med had never been. Education offered me the academic rigor of the sciences but also appealed to my heart.

Teaching demands systematic thought and reflection in order to deliver the instruction and analyze situations. It requires a solid understanding of content and pedagogy to be critical of new trends and develop curriculum. However, I believe it is instincts that humanize teaching—the gut feeling of what will work or not, the sense of how to connect with each child, the ability to juggle ten things at once and be fired up rather than stressed out, and so much more. Being in the classroom is still an adrenaline rush. I put in twelve-hour days without thinking twice. I cannot go to a store, museum, or park without thinking how I might apply what I see to my classroom. The joy of teaching, itself, drives me. That, I think, is the *it*. Whether you can learn *it* or have to be born with *it*, I still cannot say.

 Visit the web site for more Voices from the Classroom.

we have emphasized throughout this book, by **reflection** we simply mean the process of thinking about your experiences and their implications for you. People are often so busy experiencing things, or getting ready to experience them, that they fail truly to reflect on what they have done in a manner that will ensure that they get the most from the experience.

We cannot stress this point about reflection enough. It goes to the very heart of why we have written this book. Both of us are convinced that many people make sloppy decisions about becoming teachers. Often, they have not asked some of the fundamental questions about themselves and about schools. This is precisely why we have organized this book around a series of questions such as "Why teach?" and "What is a school and what is it for?"

Consider the importance of reflection with the image in this section of your CD-ROM.

PAUSE AND REFLECT

❶ Are you really and truly using all the resources available to you to help you make a conscious and clear decision about your future career? What can you do to enhance your chances of making a good career decision?

Case Studies in the Motivation to Teach

This section offers two case studies that illustrate common motives for going into teaching. Each case study is followed by a set of questions and a comment. The cases are intended as examples of how particular abstract motives take shape in teachers' lives. You may want to discuss the cases and the accompanying questions with other people. The shared experience of reading the cases and responding to the questions should help you probe and understand your own motivations. Finally, the cases and accompanying comments raise important issues about the nature of teaching.

CASE STUDY

The Desire to Teach a Particular Subject

Julia Tucker had been a star science student since junior high school. She received a partial scholarship to study chemistry in college and earned high marks in everything connected with science. She also derived a good deal of personal satisfaction from quietly showing her mostly male teachers and fellow students that a female could excel at science. When she graduated from college, she was heavily recruited by a chemical engineering firm. She immediately fell in love with her job. It took a little longer (two years), but she fell even more in love with Nicholas, a chemist, who was working on the same project. They got married, and a year and a day later, Justin was born. Julia was back at work in six weeks. Both Nicholas and she hoped to have four children, but it didn't work out that way. There was no second pregnancy.

Julia was disappointed, but she took it philosophically. After all, she had a wonderful job, a loving husband, and a son who was the joy of her life. Everything was fine until Justin went off to middle school and began taking science courses. Julia couldn't wait to help him with his science homework. She stayed up late reading his science textbooks. She found all sorts of excuses to talk to his teachers about science education. She found herself daydreaming at work about how to teach various scientific concepts to children. And she was also quietly

a midlife career switch

losing interest in the highly specialized type of chemistry she was doing. So, after a great deal of soul searching and several late-night conversations with Nicholas, she quit her job and went back to school to get a teaching license in chemistry.

That was more than a year ago. Now Julia has a job, but hardly the job she fantasized about in her old lab or the teaching position for which she prepared. To her surprise, the only available position (other than ones that would force her to move the family) was at the elementary level, as a fifth-grade teacher. The school superintendent realized that Julia would be a real asset to his school district, but he did not have an opening in the high school for two more years, when the chemistry teacher was scheduled to retire. So he presented Julia with a proposition: take some methods courses over the summer (at district expense), become a fifth-grade teacher for two years, help establish a new elementary science curriculum, and be the coordinator of the annual science fair. At first, Julia was quite wary about this possibility. She thought it would mean throwing away a good deal of her specialized knowledge and risking failure as an elementary

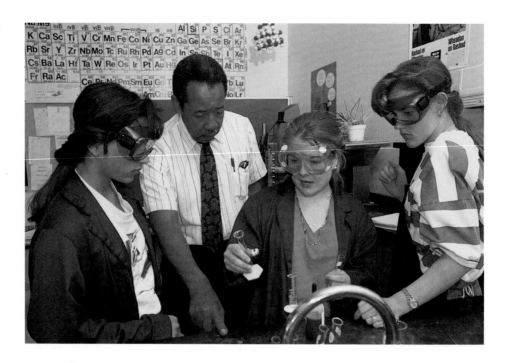

A chemistry teacher helps students with titrations.
(© Bob Daemmrich/Stock Boston)

school teacher, even though it would be for only two years. But after talking it over with Nicholas and getting great support from her son, she reluctantly agreed.

And then a funny thing happened. During the summer, as Julia took the methods courses and prepared herself for her fifth-graders, she became more and more enthused about teaching children who she believed were "just becoming interested in the outer world." Once she started working with her fifth-grade students, she was hooked. They were so alive, so responsive, and so hungry to know about the world. What a challenge! Thoughts of ever becoming a chemistry teacher took a back seat to the elementary classroom.

Now, in November, however, Julia has misgivings. There is a flatness in her class that worries her. Much of the September curiosity has turned into an early case of the midwinter blahs. Moreover, her supervisor has conducted the first formal observation of Julia's teaching, and she is curious about the supervisor's opinion.

"So, Suzanne," Julia says at their postobservation conference. "How did I do? You were writing up such a storm, I thought you would need another notebook!"

"Oh, I hope you didn't find that distracting. I probably should have warned you that I would be scribbling away."

"No, that's fine. I'm just curious to know how I did."

"I'd much rather hear what *you* think, Julia. How do you think the class went?"

"Well, I think pretty much as usual. They were a little quieter, perhaps because you were in there, but in general, that was an average class."

"I did notice it being quiet, Julia. How do you feel about that?"

"As a matter of fact, I'm confused by it. Since September, the decibel level has been steadily falling in all my classes, but particularly when we are doing science. I couldn't get them to shut up in September. They ate up everything I presented, especially science. They just seem to have lost interest."

"From what I just saw, and from what I have observed passing by your door these weeks, I'd agree. Interest looks low."

"Suzanne, I've really worked to find topics that will interest them. I built a whole unit on pollution last month with writing assignments and mathematics worked in. They said they were interested in heredity, so next month, we're going to do family histories with interviews and collections of family facts and artifacts. They were all excited about this in September, but now I'm stumped. What is the matter?"

"Quite honestly, Julia, I had a feeling that this would happen."

"What do you mean?"

"Well, when you came to interview last June, we were thrilled at the possibility of getting someone so knowledgeable and so experienced, and particularly someone who loves science so much. But those same qualities made us hesitant, too."

"I'm not getting you, Suzanne. I know we were all concerned that I didn't have traditional preparation for elementary teaching. You're not saying I know too much and I like science too much, are you?"

■ *sometimes love for a subject gets in the way*

"Yes and no. No, you don't know too much. And your love of science is a terrific asset. But, at the same time, these qualities are keeping you from being the potentially fine teacher you can become. Julia, let me be honest with you. You are drowning these kids with information—and not just in science. It seems to me that you're doing all the work. What worked so well for you during your student teaching, with high school juniors and seniors, just doesn't work with these elementary school wigglers."

I love to learn in order that I might teach; and I get no joy from learning anything if I alone am to know about it.

—SENECA

"Honestly, Suzanne, I'm not giving them high school material. This work is within their range. I don't mean to sound defensive, but really. . . ."

"Julia, think 'romance.'"

"Romance? I thought you told me to do health and human sexuality in the spring!"

"No, no. Romance. Like in 'the romance of science' and 'the romance of writing.' Do you remember telling us during your interview how you fell in love—your words, Julia—fell in love with science in the fifth grade when you had to do a project for the science fair? Well, what I think you ought to do is a little time traveling and think about what caused *your* romance with science. Was it a fascinating question? An unsolved problem? The excitement of maybe solving a problem the adults couldn't? Or was it a teacher pumping facts and theories into you?"

"Uh-oh. I think the dawn is breaking. I've been so busy talking at them and trying to teach them some basic information."

"Right. You've been so busy telling them about what you love that you forgot romance. You forgot that romance is a two-way street. It's a classic mistake of rookie teachers, even ancient ones like you. Sometimes you can get away with it in high schools, but not with these wigglers. Not with elementary schools."

"So what do I do now?"

"Well, let me put aside these notes, and let's see if you and I can put a little romance into the rest of the week's lessons."

"A little pedagogical seduction! Suzanne, I think you found the key!"

PAUSE AND REFLECT

1. How would you characterize Julia's motivation to teach?

2. What sorts of things do you think her students were thinking and feeling about her classes?

3. Julia is clearly an outstanding resource to the school. What, however, are her liabilities?

4. What clues should Julia have been picking up?

5. What are some things Julia might do to stimulate romance for science in her students?

■ *Comment*

Love for a particular subject matter or content is an important and commendable motive for teaching. A major purpose of school is to pass on to the young the best of society's knowledge. Another important purpose is to develop in young people basic skills, especially a love for learning. A teacher who has a passion to convey subject matter is often quite effective at both of these goals. We probably all have had teachers whose excitement and enthusiasm for their subject were contagious. Such teachers often drive students very hard, but they are frequently the ones who make the greatest impact on us.

■ *a balanced approach to subject matter*

But carrying love for a particular subject to an extreme can cause trouble. Neither Julia's motive nor her problem is uncommon. Real learning is usually built on students' interest. This interest in or love of learning can be blunted when the lover (the teacher) is too overpowering or too insistent. The great teacher, like the great lover, knows how to draw out another's interest and help students "fall in love."

There is another danger for the teacher who is "blinded" by love of a subject. This teacher may be so busy teaching what she or he enjoys that the rest of the curriculum gets shortchanged. For example, the English teacher who loves interpreting literature often finds it easy to avoid slugging it out with grammar, punctuation, and other essential writing skills. The elementary school teacher who loves science, like Julia, may fail to give the other subjects their due. Although this tendency to focus on what we know and love and to avoid what we do not know or like is understandable, it is also irresponsible. It is unfair both to the students and to later teachers, who will expect students to have a command over the avoided or neglected content.

■ *covering all subjects responsibly*

Teachers who are strongly motivated by the desire to teach a particular subject matter need to be somewhat cross-eyed. While keeping one eye on what they want to teach, they need to keep the other eye on the students and their day-to-day progress and needs.

CASE STUDY
The Desire to Aid in the Renewal of Society

Fred Harvey was in his late thirties. His disposition was so pleasant, and a smile came so readily to his face, that one of the other teachers in the large metropolitan high school referred to him as "everybody's Dad." Fred had a remarkable ability to remain relaxed when everyone else was tense, and he often broke up emotionally charged situations with an appropriate quip or humorous question.

Each year, Fred asked to teach the Curriculum II freshman history class. Of course, his request was always granted because the Curriculum II classes were considered the dumping ground for slow students and students who had given up. Some of the other teachers regarded the Curriculum II classes as "punishment." Year after year, Fred worked happily with students nobody else really wanted.

Fred's freshman history class was one of the most active in the whole school. He took his students beyond the walls of the school on expeditions to day court, the police station, and jail and through industrial plants in the area, and most years, he sneaked them into a baseball game. Yet his classes were not characterized by fun and games. The students worked very hard on long and involved homework assignments, intricate discussions of problems, and demanding tests.

One year, Fred invited another teacher to speak to the class on shipbuilding in the eighteenth century. The talk went well, and after the session the other teacher, Todd Vincent, commented to Fred that the discussion following his talk had been very different from what he had anticipated; the questions were thoughtful and displayed observation of detail that the guest speaker had not expected from a "bunch of Curriculum IIs."

Fred laughed. "You know, Todd," he said, "they amaze me, too, sometimes. Most of these kids really have behavior problems, not intellectual ones. If you looked at their case histories, you'd find that the majority of them were 'dropped through the ranks.'"

"What do you mean?" asked Todd.

"I mean that they were in regular classes a good bit of their scholastic lives. But when they became problems in class, their teachers decided that the cause of their poor behavior was that the work was too hard for them. So most of the children in this class really represent the rebels, the nonconformists, the 'antisocials.' These are the kids who some teachers claim 'won't go along with the system.' They're the kids about whom many teachers say, 'I don't care if they learn history as long as they become good citizens.'"

"Yes, but you must admit that very few of them will go to college. Most Curriculum IIs just drop out," said Todd.

"Maybe you're missing my point," said Fred. "I guess I'm saying that people can't be 'good citizens' unless they are contributing members of society, and that they should contribute something they think is worth contributing. If they can't get the basic tools that make a person productive, how can they be good citizens? It's a lot more than getting jobs or making decent livings. As a matter of fact, I feel these kids are much more capable than the kids we send to the university."

"In what sense?"

"In the sense that they are the least accepting of society as it exists now," replied Fred. "If you talked to some of them for an hour or so, you'd find that they really feel the school is hypocritical in many ways, and they aren't afraid to point out the hypocrisies. They'll tell you, for instance, that there are two sets of rules in the school, two sets of discipline procedures, two sets of privileges, and all the rest."

"But I hear the same thing from my 'honors' classes," Todd protested. "Those kids know about the double standard, too. They often tell me that an honors student here can get away with anything from cutting class to smoking in the john."

"You've got me wrong again, Todd. What these kids are saying is not that we expect too much of them but that we expect too little. For instance, if a kid dropped from an A to a C in your honors history course, what would happen?"

the danger of low expectations

double standards in schools

"The kid would probably go in and see the counselor, by request."

Fred replied, "That's right. When a kid everyone believes is bound for college does poorly, bells go off and people get concerned. They try to help the kid take a look at what's wrong. If one of these students goes from a C to an F, though, everyone says, 'Well, what more do you expect? The kid's only a Curriculum II and doesn't have the ability to sustain a C.' And they get all the inexperienced teachers and martinets in the school. Oh, they know that if they become real problems, they'll get counseling and possibly even better teaching. But that isn't their complaint. They know that the system isn't out to punish them. They know the system would rather they just float along and not bother anyone. That's the double standard in this school: those who are cared about and those who aren't. That's what these kids will tell you."

The role of the teacher remains the highest calling of a free people. To the teacher, America entrusts her most precious resource, her children; and asks that they be prepared, in all their glorious diversity, to face the rigors of individual participation in a democratic society.

—SHIRLEY HUFSTEDLER

■ *answering students' needs*

"You know," said Todd, "you're not just talking about the Curriculum II classes. I think the same thing is generally true of Curriculum I classes. It seems that a kid who's really bright gets a lot of attention, and so does the kid who is really slow, but it's that kid in the middle. . . ."

"Right," said Fred. "The kids in this class are the bottom of that middle group in terms of the concern they arouse from the system. And they know it. Yet, as you saw today, they are capable. We owe them a decent set of expectations. I've maintained high expectations for the kids. I would prefer to slightly overmatch them intellectually than undermatch them, because no development is possible when you're being undermatched constantly."

"Don't they complain about being pushed too hard?" asked Todd.

"Oh, sure! There's always a good deal of moaning, particularly in the early weeks, until they realize I don't dance to that tune. Pretty soon they settle in and decide to go along with the program. But then they realize that they are actually learning. At that point, they're hooked. They're mine, and I wouldn't trade teaching them for anything!"

"Well, Fred, this has been most instructive. I came to teach and I ended up learning."

"Me too. That's what keeps me going. And Todd, please come back next semester."

PAUSE AND REFLECT

❶ How is Fred's commitment to social renewal specifically shown in his classroom teaching?

❷ According to Fred, what is the criterion for assignment to Curriculum II classes in his school? Was this true of your high school?

❸ What is the double standard of which Todd Vincent spoke, and how do you explain it? What is the double standard of which Fred spoke, and how do you explain it? Did either of these double standards exist in your school?

❹ How do Fred's expectations for his students differ from those of most teachers you have known? In what other ways is he different from most of the teachers you have known?

JAIME ESCALANTE (B. 1930)

It is early in the fall term at Garfield High School in East Los Angeles, once a crime-ridden school filled with low achievers but now famous for outstanding calculus students. It is the morning after the second game of the World Series, and, as he enters the class, the teacher, known as *el professor,* shouts out his first question: "Who won the game?" After a pause, the students begin to chant enthusiastically, "Dodgers! Dodgers!" Having captured their attention, Jaime Escalante moves to the math lesson. Slapping a baseball into his mitt, he says, "As X approaches A, F of X is the trajectory. Could be a curve ball." And they are off—teacher and fifty-nine students—on a journey into the mysteries of calculus.

Jaime Escalante, the son of an elementary school teacher, was born in La Paz, Bolivia, and began his own teaching career before age twenty. While he was a high school math and physics teacher, his students began to accumulate prizes, and soon, he gained national recognition. Still in his twenties, he organized the first Bolivian national symposium of physics and math teachers. In 1963, amid growing social strife in Bolivia, Escalante, now married with two sons, decided to take his wife and young family to the United States.

The next ten years were years of adjustment and struggle, years when Escalante learned English, went back to college, and worked as a busboy and a cook. When he finally graduated, he took a job in the fast-growing computer industry and studied for the California Teaching Certificate in his free time. When the news came that he had passed the test and would be assigned to a run-down, troubled high school in the *barrio,* Escalante turned his back on a substantially larger paycheck and headed for Garfield High School.

When the school's accreditation was threatened because of its students' low academic performance and high dropout rate, Escalante made his move. Supported by reform-minded administrators, he began setting high standards and making serious demands on students. They were not allowed into his class unless they proved that they had done their homework. He skillfully used the time-honored carrot-and-stick approach. The carrot was college and the world of opportunities higher education opened up for them. The stick was his constant challenging of them: "You *burros* have math in your blood! Our Mayan ancestors were the first to develop the concept of zero!"

Jaime Escalante, the subject of the Academy Award–nominated film *Stand and Deliver,* later taught at Hiram Johnson High School in Sacramento, Calif. He has received numerous awards and has hosted the PBS series, *FUTURES with Jaime Escalante,* produced by the Foundation for Advancements in Science and Education. But he is more than the man who has helped hundreds of Mexican-American children discover self-discipline and learning and the enormous self-pride that comes with those accomplishments. Escalante is a tide turner. He has set an idea in motion, the idea that the poor and immigrant children in our country are capable of great intellectual feats. He has shown how remedial, slowed-down education can be replaced by demanding, accelerated education. "My skills are really to motivate these kids, to make them learn, to give them *ganas—* the desire to do something—to make them believe they can learn." He has always been clear about why he taught: his love of young people and his love of his subject. Although he has recently retired from active teaching, Escalante remains a clear and forceful spokesman for quality education, especially for minority children. Believing it handicaps rather than helps Latino students, he has taken a strong position against extensive bilingual education. Instead he urges a demanding education that will give minority students the knowledge and skills they need to compete in a demanding world. His educational views are captured in his famous motto, "Determination + Discipline + Hard Work = Way to Success."

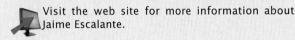
Visit the web site for more information about Jaime Escalante.

⑤ What do you think were Todd's major misconceptions as a teacher?

⑥ What does Fred see as the role of academic disciplines in education? If you had to, how would you argue against his position?

■ *Comment*

In addition to the serious injustice of underchallenging many of our students, Fred was reacting against the perversion of an important idea: teaching good citizenship. In Fred's school, as in many others, the idea of teaching good citizenship has been badly distorted.

During the 1930s, in a reform started by the American educator and philosopher John Dewey, many schools adopted the policy of awarding a grade for citizenship. Dewey and many of his followers envisioned training for citizenship as a process of working out in class actual problems that arise in a democracy. They saw the schools as an appropriate place to teach students about democratic decisions and to give them low-risk but real practice in such decision making in a context where mistakes were not "for keeps."

As sometimes happens with reforms, educational and otherwise, the processes the reformers introduced to the classroom degenerated into empty forms. Good citizenship came to mean docility, doing what one is told. Students could earn "good citizenship" grades by "playing the game" and not bothering anyone. Citizenship became a code word among teachers. A teacher who was given a class of "low achievers" or "discipline problems" was sometimes told, "Don't worry about the academics with these children. Just make them good citizens." Parents were told that their child wasn't a very good student but was "an excellent citizen." This meant that even though he or she didn't learn anything, the child did without question everything that students were supposed to do.

■ *misuse of citizenship grade*

The use of a citizenship grade as a conduct mark is an absolute travesty of the system Dewey and the reformers designed, for in reality good citizens are not docile sheep who can be "conned" with impunity. The long-term effect of the misinterpretation of citizenship as conformity and docility has been to discredit it as an appropriate goal for schooling. Yet, in Fred's case, we see a person consciously attempting to develop educated citizens. Fred's visits to courthouses, legislative sessions, and factories, as well as the classroom study of major social problems, are very much in keeping with what Dewey—and, indeed, Thomas Jefferson and James Madison—had in mind when they spoke of educating for freedom. ■

A Final Word

When we were racking our brains for a title for this book, someone reminded us of the nasty comment George Bernard Shaw, the late-nineteenth-century Irish playwright, made about teachers: "Those who can, do. Those who can't, teach." While possibly true then (which we doubt), it certainly is false now. In recent decades, the importance of education for the well-being of individuals *and* society became clearer. Much of America's power and prosperity resulted from our deep commitment to education. And teachers have been the keys to our educational achievements. One thing is crystal clear to thoughtful observers: we need even better schools and better teachers. Shaw was dead wrong. *Those who can, teach.*

Still, though, selecting a career is a personal decision and involves answering many questions, such as "Will I be happy?", "Will this career provide me with a satisfying lifestyle?", "Will I be up to the challenge, and will I find the work satisfying?", and "Will I grow in the experience?" People who are considering teaching as a life's work should grapple with these questions that surround the motives for choice. But they also need to scrutinize other, deeper motives.

■ *teaching, a vocation*

Teaching, like nursing, the ministry, and social work, is a service occupation. More correctly, teaching is a vocation. People are called to it. Built into teaching is the idea of contributing to the lives of others. For many people, the root of their decision to teach is deeper than a love of subject matter or an attraction to the life of a teacher. Many men and women select teaching for reasons that are, at heart, religious or humanitarian. In effect, they have a touch of the American follower of Mother Teresa in Calcutta. We suspect that teachers who are truly satisfied are people whose choice has been grounded in this deeper motivation. And although such religiously or humanistically based reasons for teaching are a private matter, it is a matter that each of us needs to explore very carefully. Of all the questions in this book, "Why teach?" is ultimately the most important one. How you answer this question will determine not only whether or not you will teach but what you will actually *accomplish* as a teacher.

KEY TERMS

extrinsic rewards (490) real encounters (495) vicarious experiences (497)

intrinsic rewards (490) reflection (498)

FOR REFLECTION

❶ What questions about your own motivation for teaching has this chapter raised?

❷ In your experience, did your teachers ever speak to you directly about their reasons for teaching? Did some teachers "tell" you by their actions what their motives for teaching were? Can you give an example?

❸ If you are currently planning to teach, what events in your life have helped you discover why you want to teach?

❹ Review the list of motives for teaching in the section of this chapter called "Examining Your Own Motives for Teaching." Put an *E* before those expressing an extrinsic motive, an *I* before those reflecting an intrinsic motive, and a *U* for "uncertain."

❺ Do you think of teaching as a calling? As a social service? If you do, why? If not, why not?

❻ Have you acquired the *habit of reflection* that is so necessary to make the most of your preparation to be a teacher?

PRINT RESOURCES

Esmé Raji Codell, *Educating Esmé: Diary of a Teacher's First Year* (Chapel Hill, NC: Algonquin Books, 1999).

This book is an inspiring, irreverent, and hilarious diary of a teacher's first year. All this and it is a wonderful read.

Marva Collins and Civia Tamarkin, *Marva Collins' Way* (Los Angeles: Tarcher, 1982).

This book takes the reader inside the world of one of America's most inspiring and controversial teachers. Marva Collins describes her method of educating the children others forgot.

Pat Conroy, *The Water Is Wide* (New York: Bantam Books, 1994).

This is a thinly veiled account of the author's first years of teaching on a small island off the coast of South Carolina. It is a moving account of how, through his efforts to transform the lives of poor children and their families, the teacher transformed himself. The book has been made into a highly acclaimed film, *Conrac*.

Samuel G. Freedman, *Small Victories* (New York: Harper and Row, 1990).

This book chronicles life in a New York City high school in the late 1980s. It depicts the highs and lows of teaching in urban schools and vividly describes the major problems affecting life in these schools.

P. R. Kane, ed., *My First Year as a Teacher* (New York: Penguin Books, 1991).

This book is a collection of accounts by twenty-five teachers of their first year in teaching. The teachers describe their struggles and triumphs as they grappled with their new profession.

Tracy Kidder, *Among Schoolchildren* (Boston: Houghton Mifflin, 1989).

The author spent the entire school year observing a fifth-grade teacher and produced a rich and fascinating account of a teacher's year. The book shows how one teacher shaped and moved the lives of her students.

Jay Mathews, *Escalante: The Best Teacher in America* (New York: Holt, 1990).

This is the biography of Jaime Escalante, who is profiled in this chapter and is the subject of the film *Stand and Deliver*. Escalante wins over his students, largely urban Hispanics, with a combination of challenges to pride, demands of dedicated hard work, and demonstrated love.

Endnotes

Chapter 1

1. Jacques Barzun, *Begin Here: The Forgotten Conditions of Teaching and Learning* (Chicago: University of Chicago Press, 1991), pp. 4, 14.
2. Thomas Jefferson, "A Bill for the More General Diffusion of Knowledge," in *Public and Private Papers,* ed. Tom Wicker (New York: Vintage Books/Library of America, 1990), p. 39.
3. Jean Anyon, "Ghetto Schooling: A Political Economy of Urban Reform." In *Exploring Education: An Introduction to the Foundations of Education,* 2d ed., ed. A. Sadovnik, P. Cookson, and S. Semel (Boston: Allyn & Bacon, 2001), p. 53.
4. Emile Durkheim, "Education; Its Nature and Role." In *Exploring Sociocultural Themes in Education,* 2d ed., ed. J. Strouse (Columbus, OH: Merrill Prentice Hall, 2001), p. 57.
5. Jean Anyon, "Social Class and School Knowledge." In *Exploring Sociocultural Themes in Education,* 2d ed., ed. J. Strouse (Columbus, OH: Merrill Prentice Hall, 2001), p. 131.
6. Jay Mathews, *Class Struggle* (New York: Times Books, 1998).
7. Elliot Eisner, *The Educational Imagination: On the Design and Evaluation of School Programs,* 3d ed. (Belmont, CA: Wadsworth, 1976).
8. Mike Rose, *Possible Lives* (New York: Penguin, 1995).
9. James Shaver and William Strong, *Facing Value Decisions: Rationale Building for Teachers* (Belmont, CA: Wadsworth, 1976).
10. Among the leading spokesmen for this position are Michael Apple and Henry Giroux. See Michael Apple, *Education and Power,* 2d ed. (New York: Routledge, 1995); Henry Giroux, "Critical Pedagogy: Cultural Politics and the Discourse of Experience," *Journal of Education* 67, no. 2 (1987), pp. 23–41.
11. Paulo Freire, *The Pedagogy of the Oppressed* (New York: Herder and Herder, 1970).
12. Philip W. Jackson, *Life in Classrooms* (New York: Teachers College Press, 1990).
13. Ibid., p. 16.
14. Joyce Epstein, "What Matters in the Middle Grades—Grade Span or Practices?" *Phi Delta Kappan* 71 (February, 1990), pp. 438–444.
15. Ibid., p. 438.
16. Ernest L. Boyer, *High School: A Report on Secondary Education in America* (New York: Harper and Row, 1983).
17. Henry J. Becker, "Curriculum and Instruction in Middle-Grade Schools," *Phi Delta Kappan* 71 (February, 1990), pp. 450–457.
18. James McPartland, "Staffing Decisions in the Middle School Grades: Balancing Quality Instruction and Teacher/Student Relations," *Phi Delta Kappan* 712 (February, 1990), p. 466.
19. Ibid., p. 468.
20. Ernest L. Boyer, *High School: A Report on Secondary Education in America* (New York: Harper and Row, 1983).
21. Ibid., pp. 21–22.
22. Larry Cuban, *How Teachers Taught: Constancy and Change in American Classrooms 1890–1980* (New York: Longman, 1984).
23. Ernest L. Boyer, *High School: A Report on Secondary Education in America* (New York: Harper and Row, 1983), pp. 141–143.
24. Op. cit.
25. Ibid., p. 57.
26. Ibid., p. 79.
27. Arthur G. Powell, Eleanor Farrar, and David K. Cohen, *The Shopping Mall High School: Winners and Losers in the Educational Marketplace* (Boston: Houghton Mifflin, 1985).
28. Ibid., p. 36.
29. Ibid., p. 173.
30. Laurence D. Brown, "A New Metaphor for U.S. High Schools Provides Fresh and Powerful Insights," *Phi Delta Kappan* 67 (May, 1986), p. 685.
31. "Seeking Change in High Schools," *Education Week* 28 (February 28, 1996), pp. 1, 9.
32. In preparing this section, we have drawn on the following studies: W. B. Brookover, *Effective Secondary Schools* (Philadelphia: Research for Better Schools, 1981); R. Edmonds, "Effective Schools for the Urban Poor," *Educational Leadership* 32 (1979), pp. 15–17; M. Rutter et al., *Fifteen Thousand Hours* (Cambridge: Harvard University Press, 1979); J. Stallings and G. Mohlman, *School Policy, Leadership Style, Teacher Change and Student Behavior in Eight Secondary Schools* (Mountain View, CA: Stalling Teaching and Learning Institute for the National Institute of Education, 1981); R. Blum, *Effective Schooling Practices: A Research Synthesis* (Portland, OR: Northwest Regional Education Laboratory, April 1984); H. J. Walberg, "Productive Teaching and Instruction: Assessing the Knowledge Base," *Phi Delta Kappan* 71 (February, 1990), pp. 470–478; T. Toch, *In the Name of Excellence* (New York: Oxford University Press, 1991); and Richard J. Murname and Frank Levy, "What General Motors Can Teach U.S. Schools About the Proper Role of Markets in Education Reform," *Phi Delta Kappan* 78 (October, 1996), pp. 113–116.
33. David C. Berliner, "Effective Classroom Teaching: The Necessary but Not Sufficient Condition for Developing Exemplary Schools." In *Research on Exemplary Schools,* ed. Gilbert R. Austin and Herbert Garber (Orlando, FL: Academic Press, 1985), pp. 127–54. Copyright 1985.
34. Edward A. Wynne, "Looking at Good Schools," *Phi Delta Kappan* 62 (January 1981): 377–381.
35. John W. Gardner, "Fall of the Twentieth Century," *Chicago Sun-Times,* June 16, 1968.

Chapter 2

1. National Clearinghouse for Bilingual Education, 2000, *Summary Report of the Survey of the States' Limited English Proficient Students and Available Educational Programs and Services, 1997–98.* Available at: **http://www.ncbe.gwu.edu/ncbepubs/seareports/97-98/part1.htm.**
2. Ibid.
3. Catherine Minicucci, Paul Berman, Barry McLaughlin, Beverly McLeod, Beryl Nelson, and Kate Woodworth, "School Reform and Student Diversity," *Phi Delta Kappan* 77 (September 1995), p. 77.
4. U.S. Bureau of the Census, *Resident Population of the United States: Estimates, by Sex, Race, and Hispanic Origin, with Median Age* (Internet Release Date: December 2000). Available at: **http://www.census.gov/population/estimates/nation/intfile3-1.txt**); National Center for Education Statistics, *Condition of Education 2000* (Washington, DC: The Center, 2000), p. 9.
5. Harold Hodgkinson, "American Education: The Good, the Bad, and the Task," *Phi Delta Kappan* 74 (April 1993), p. 620.
6. Geneva Gay, *Culturally Responsive Teaching: Theory, Research, and Practice* (New York: Teachers College Press, 2000); Gloria Ladson-Billings, *Crossing Over to Canaan: The Journey of New Teachers in Diverse Classrooms* (San Francisco: Jossey-Bass, 2001).
7. William Glasser, *The Quality School* (New York: Harper and Row, 1990).
8. Howard Gardner, *Frames of Mind* (New York: Basic Books, 1985); Howard Gardner, *Multiple Intelligences: The Theory in Practice* (New York: Basic Books, 1993).
9. Kathy Checkley, "The First Seven . . . and the Eighth," *Educational Leadership* 55 (September 1997), p. 12.
10. Harvey Silver, Richard Strong, and Matthew Perini (1997), "Integrating Learning Styles and Multiple Intelligences," *Educational Leadership* 55, pp. 22–23. Reprinted with permission of the Association for Supervision and Curriculum Development. Copyright © 1997 by ASCD. All rights reserved.
11. 23rd Annual Report to Congress on the Implementation of the Individuals with Disabilities Education Act, p. II-20. Available at: **http://www.ed.gov/offices/OSERS/OSEP/Products/OSEP2001AnlRpt/PDF/Chapter-2.pdf.**
12. "Final Fiscal 2001 and Fiscal 2002 Appropriations," *Education Week* (January 30, 2002), p. 26.
13. Sarah Wernick, "Hard Times for Educating the Highly Gifted Child," *New York Times,* May 30, 1990, p. B8.
14. Christine E. Sleeter, "Curriculum Controversies in Multicultural Education." In *Issues in Curriculum: A Selection of Chapters from Past NSSE Yearbooks, Ninety-eighth Yearbook of the National Society for the Study of Education,* ed. Margaret J. Early and Kenneth J. Rehage (Chicago: University of Chicago Press, 1999), p. 261.
15. M. Donald Thomas, "The Limits of Pluralism," *Phi Delta Kappan* 62 (April 1981), pp. 589, 591–592.
16. James A. Banks, "Multicultural Education: Characteristics and Goals." In *Multicultural Education: Issues and Perspectives,* 3d ed., ed. James A. Banks and Cherry A. McGee Banks (Boston: Allyn and Bacon, 1997), p. 7.

17. [414 U.S. 563, 571]. Available at: **http://caselaw.lp.findlaw.com/scripts/getcase.pl?court=US&vol=414&invol=563.**
18. Russell Gersten and John Woodward, "A Case for Structured Immersion," *Educational Leadership* 43 (September 1985), p. 75.
19. Raul Yzaguirre, "What's Wrong with Bilingual Education?" *Education Week,* August 5, 1998, pp. 46, 72.
20. Richard Rothstein with Karen Hawley Miles, *Where's the Money Gone?* (Washington, DC: Economic Policy Institute, 1995), p. 8.
21. Joetta L. Sack, "Pressure Building for 'Full' Federal Funding of IDEA," *Education Week,* March 14, 2001, p. 32.
22. "Some Thoughts on Assistive Technology Devices and Services," *The Special Educator* 8, no. 2 (September 22, 1992), pp. 17–19.
23. The Appalachia Educational Laboratory, *The Link* 14, no. 1 (Spring/Summer 1995), p. 21.
24. *The 2000 State of the States Gifted and Talented Education Report* (Oklahoma City, OK: Council of State Directors of Programs for the Gifted, 2000), pp. 3, 28–32.
25. *National Excellence: A Case for Developing America's Talent* (Washington, DC: U.S. Department of Education, Office of Research and Improvement, October 1993), p. 17.
26. Harriet Tyson, "A Load Off the Teachers' Backs: Coordinated School Health Programs," *Phi Delta Kappan* (January 1999), pp. K1–K8.
27. As cited in Lisbeth Schorr, *Within Our Reach* (New York: Doubleday, 1988), p. 5.
28. Thomas D. Snyder and Charlene M. Hoffman, *The Digest of Education Statistics 2001* (Washington, D.C.: National Center for Education Statistics, 2002), p. 79.

Chapter 3

1. Lisbeth Bamberger Schorr, "Effective Programs for Children Growing Up in Concentrated Poverty." In *Children in Poverty,* ed. A.C. Huston (Cambridge, UK: University of Cambridge Press, 1991), pp. 261–262.
2. *Kids Count Data Book 1999* (Baltimore: Annie E. Casey Foundation, 1999), pp. 6, 10.
3. Harold L. Hodgkinson, *The Same Client: The Demographics of Education and Service Delivery Systems* (Washington, DC: Institute for Educational Leadership, 1989), p. 3.
4. Federal Interagency Forum on Child and Family Statistics, *America's Children: Key National Indicators of Well-Being, 2001* (Washington, DC: U.S. Government Printing Office, 2001), p. 6.
5. Ibid.
6. U.S. Bureau of the Census, Current Population Reports, P60-213, *Money Income in the United States: 2000* (Washington, DC: U.S. Government Printing Office, 2000), Table A. Available at: **http://www.census.gov/prod/2001pubs/p60-213.pdf.**
7. Federal Interagency Forum on Child and Family Statistics, *America's Children* (Washington, DC: U.S. Department of Health and Human Services, 2001), p. 16.
8. Ibid.
9. U.S. Bureau of the Census, *Current Population Reports,* P60-200, *Historical Income Tables—Families: Share of Aggregate Income Received by Each Fifth and Top 5*

Percent of Families (All Races): 1947 to 2001 (Washington, DC: U.S. Bureau of the Census, 2002), Table F-2. Available at: **http://www.census.gov/hhes/income/histinc/ f02.html**.

10. Bernadette D. Proctor and Joseph Dalaker, U.S. Bureau of the Census, *Poverty in the United States: 2000* (Washington, DC: U.S. Government Printing Office, 2002). Available at: **http://www.census.gov/prod/2002pubs/ p60-219.pdf**.

11. Ibid.

12. Ibid.

13. *Kids Count Data Book 2001* (Baltimore: Annie E. Casey Foundation, 2001), p. 19.

14. Ralph da Costa Nunez and Kate Collignon, "Creating a Community of Learning for Homeless Children," *Educational Leadership* 55, no. 2 (October 1997), p. 56.

15. Yvonne Rafferty, "Meeting the Educational Needs of Homeless Children," *Educational Leadership* (January 1998), p. 49.

16. Federal Interagency Forum on Child and Family Statistics (Washington, DC: U.S. Department of Health and Human Services, 2001), p. 96.

17. *When Teens Have Sex: Issues and Trends* (Baltimore: Annie E. Casey Foundation, 1999), p. 8.

18. *Kids Count Data Book 2001* (Baltimore: Annie E. Casey Foundation, 2001, p. 16.

19. *National Clearinghouse on Child Abuse and Neglect Information.* Available at: **http://www.acf.dhhs.gov/programs/ cb/publications/cm99/high.htm**.

20. Cynthia Crosson Tower, *The Role of Educators in the Prevention and Treatment of Child Abuse and Neglect* (Washington, DC: National Center on Child Abuse and Neglect, 1992), pp. 22–27. Available at: **http:// www.calib.com/nccanch/pubs/educator/index.htm**.

21. Lloyd D. Johnston, Patrick M. O'Malley, and Jerald G. Bachman, *Monitoring the Future: National Results on Adolescent Drug Use, Overview of Key Findings 2001*, NIH Publication No. 02-5105 (Bethesda, Maryland: National Institute on Drug Abuse, 2001), p. 5. Available at: **http://monitoringthefuture.org/pubs/monographs/ overview2001.pdf**.

22. Ibid., Table 2.

23. "U.S.A. Suicide: 1997 and 1999 Official Final Data" (Washington, DC: American Association of Suicidology, 1999), available at: **http://www.suicidology.org/ suicide_statistics97.htm** and **http://www.suicidology.org/ index.html**; Jessica Portner, "Complex Set of Ills Spurs Rising Teen Suicide Rate," *Education Week*, April 22, 2000. Available at: **http://www.edweek.org/ew/ ewstory.cfm?slug=31problems.h19**.

24. Deborah Burnett Strother, "Suicide Among the Young," *Phi Delta Kappan* 67 (June 1986), p. 759.

25. Darcia Harris Bowman, "Federal Study Stresses Warning Signs of School Violence," *Education Week*, December 12, 2001, p. 12.

26. *Indicators of School Crime and Safety, 2001* (Washington, DC: National Center for Education Statistics, 2001), Table 15.1, p. 80.

27. Laura Sessions Stepp, "Cliques or Gangs?" *The Washington Post*, January 4, 1996, p. C5.

28. Michael D. Shear and Jacqueline L. Salmon, "An Education in Taunting," *The Washington Post*, May 2, 1999, p. C1.

29. R. Craig Sautter, "Standing Up to Violence," *Phi Delta Kappan* 76 (January 1995), p. K8.

30. Phillip Kaufman, Martha Naomi Alt, and Christopher Chapman, *Dropout Rates in the United States: 2000* (Washington, DC: National Center for Education Statistics, 2001). Available at: **http://nces.ed.gov/ pubs2002/droppub_2001/**.

31. Ibid.

32. Marvin Lazerson, "Access, Outcomes, and Educational Opportunity," *Education Week*, January 27, 1999, p. 46.

33. *Education Week on the Web*, "Choice." Available at: **http:// www.edweek.com/context/topics/issuespage.cfm?id=43**.

34. *Magnet Schools of America*, available at: **http:// www.magnet.edu/index.html**; Susan Black, "The Pull of Magnets," *The American School Board Journal* (September 1996), p. 35; Peter Schmidt, "Magnets' Efficacy as Desegregation Tool Questioned," *Education Week*, February 2, 1994, p. 17.

35. "Developing Magnet Programs," *Education Digest* 54 (February 1989), pp. 22–24. (Condensed from *Research in Brief*, September 1988, published by U.S. Department of Education Office of Educational Research and Improvement, Washington, DC.)

36. Caroline Hendric, "Magnets' Value in Desegregating Schools Is Found to Be Limited," *Education Week*, November 13, 1996, pp. 1, 27.

37. Black, "The Pull of Magnets," p. 36.

38. Ibid.

39. The Center for Education Reform. Available at: **http://www.edreform.com/pubs/chglance.htm**.

40. Joetta L. Sack, "Ed. Department Finds Charters Spur Existing Schools to Improve," *Education Week*, June 20, 2001, p. 32.

41. Thomas D. Snyder, Charlene M. Hoffman, and Claire M. Geddes, *Digest of Education Statistics 1998* (Washington, DC: National Center for Education Statistics, 1999), p. 35.

42. Mark Walsh, "RAND Study Balances the Debate on School Choice," *Education Week*, December 15, 2001, p. 1.

43. *How Schools Shortchange Girls* (Washington, DC: American Association of University Women, 1992).

44. *Gender Gaps: Where Schools Still Fail Our Children: Executive Summary* (Washington, D.C.: American Association of University Women, 1998). Available at: **http://www.aauw.org/2000/GGES.pdf**.

45. Myra Sadker, David Sadker, and Susan Klein, "The Issue of Gender in Elementary and Secondary Education," in *Review of Research in Education* 17, ed. Gerald Grant (Washington, DC: American Educational Research Association, 1991), pp. 269–334.

46. Myra Sadker and David Sadker, *Failing at Fairness: How America's Schools Cheat Girls* (New York: Charles Scribner's Sons, 1994), p. 44.

47. Michelle Galley, "Boys to Men," *Education Week* (January 23, 2002), pp. 26–29.

48. "The Educational Progress of Women," findings from *The Condition of Education, 1995* (Washington, DC: U.S. Department of Education, National Center for Education Statistics, 1995), p. 1.

49. *Hostile Hallways: Bullying, Teasing, and Sexual Harassment in School* (Washington, DC: American Association of University Women, 2001).

50. Mark Walsh, "Harassment Ruling Poses Challenges," *Education Week,* June 2, 1999, pp. 1, 22.

51. Lena Sun, "Gay Students Get Little Help with Harassment," *The Washington Post,* July 20, 1998, p. A8.

52. *When Teens Have Sex: Issues and Trends: KIDS COUNT Special Report* (Baltimore: Annie E. Casey Foundation, 1998), p. 14.

53. Ibid., p. 14.

54. Ibid., p. 9.

55. Ibid., p. 14.

56. *The Surgeon General's Call To Action To Promote Sexual Health And Responsible Sexual Behavior,* July 9, 2001. Available at: **http://www.surgeongeneral.gov/library/sexualhealth/call.htm.**

57. Ceci Connolly, "Abstinence Moves to the Head of the Class," *The Washington Post,* April 24, 2002, p. A3.

Chapter 4

1. Catherine Cornbleth, "Hidden Curriculum." In *Encyclopedia of Education,* 2d ed., ed. James W. Guthrie (New York: Macmillan Reference USA, 2003), in press.

2. Elliot W. Eisner, *The Educational Imagination,* 3d ed. (Upper Saddle River, NJ: Prentice Hall, 2001), pp. 87–97.

3. Karin Chenoweth, "Reading Wars, Take 2," *The Washington Post Magazine,* May 16, 1999, p. 17.

4. Jay Mathews, "Study Faults Computers' Use in Math Education," *The Washington Post,* September 30, 1998, p. A3.

5. *Science for All Americans* (Washington, DC: American Association for the Advancement of Science, 1989).

6. Arthur W. Foshay, "Knowledge and the Structure of the Disciplines." In *The Nature of Knowledge: Implications for the Education of Teachers,* ed. William A. Jenkins (Milwaukee: University of Wisconsin Press, 1961).

7. National Council for the Social Studies, *Expectations of Excellence: Curriculum Standards for Social Studies* (Washington, D.C.: The Council, 1994).

8. *Foreign Language Instruction in the United States: A National Survey of Elementary and Secondary Schools* (Washington, DC: Center for Applied Linguistics, 1997). Available at: **http://www.cal.org/pubs/results.html.**

9. Secretary's Commission on Achieving Necessary Skills, *What Work Requires of Schools* (Washington, DC: U.S. Department of Labor, 1991).

10. Tom Loveless, *How Well Are American Students Learning?* (Washington, DC: The Brookings Institution, 2001).

11. NAEP 2000 Reading Assessment, *The Nation's Report Card.* Available at: **http://nces.ed.gov/nationsreportcard/reading/results/achieve.asp.**

12. Yupin Bae, Susan Choy, Claire Geddes, Jennifer Sable, and Thomas Snyder, *Trends in Educational Equity of Girls and Women* (Washington, DC: U.S. Department of Education, National Center for Education Statistics, 2000), p. 4.

13. NAEP 2001 U.S. History Major Results, *The Nation's Report Card.* Available at: **http://nces.ed.gov/nationsreportcard/ushistory/results/.**

14. The National Institute on Educational Governance, Finance, Policymaking, and Management and Consortium for Policy Research in Education, *Policy Brief: What the Third International Mathematics and Science Study (TIMSS) Means for Systematic School Improvement* (Washington, DC: U.S. Government Printing Office, 1998), p. 3.

15. Robert B. Schwartz, "Lesson from TIMSS," *Hands On* (Cambridge, MA: TERC, Spring 1998).

16. William Schmidt, "Are There Surprises in the TIMSS Twelfth Grade Results?" *TIMSS United States, Report No. 8* (East Lansing, MI: United States National Research Center [TIMSS], April 1998), p. 4.

17. *Splintered Vision: An Investigation of U.S. Mathematics and Science Education, Executive Summary* (East Lansing, MI: U.S. National Research Center for the Third International Mathematics and Science Study, 1996), pp. 5–9.

18. National Education Commission, *Prisoners of Time: A Report of the National Education Commission on Time and Learning* (Washington, DC: U.S. Government Printing Office, 1994), p. 23.

19. Gerald W. Bracey, "Tinkering with TIMSS," *Phi Delta Kappan* 80, no. 1 (September 1998), pp. 32–36.

20. Larry Cuban, *How Teachers Taught: Constancy and Change in American Classrooms, 1890–1980* (New York: Longman, 1984).

21. Robin Rogarty, "Ten Ways to Integrate Curriculum," *Educational Leadership* 49, no. 2 (October 1991), p. 61.

22. Robert E. Slavin, *Cooperative Learning,* 2d ed. (Boston: Allyn and Bacon, 1995), pp. 3–4.

23. Ibid., pp. 14–70.

24. Joyce L. Epstein, "What Matters in the Middle Grades—Grade Span or Practices?" *Phi Delta Kappan* 71 (February 1990), pp. 438–444.

25. Scott Willis and Larry Mann, "Differentiating Instruction," *Curriculum Update,* Association for Supervision and Curriculum Development, Winter 2000, p. 2.

26. *Prisoners of Time,* pp. 10, 31, 34.

27. Meg Sommerfield, "More and More Schools Putting Block Scheduling to Test of Time," *Education Week,* May 22, 1996, pp. 1, 14.

28. E. D. Hirsch, Jr., *Cultural Literacy* (Boston: Houghton Mifflin, 1987).

29. Debra Viadero, "On the Wrong Track," *Teacher Magazine* (January 1999), pp. 22–23.

30. Dominic Brewer, Daniel Rees, and Laura Argys, "Detracking America's Schools: The Reform Without Cost?" *Phi Delta Kappan* 77 (November 1995), pp. 210–212+.

Chapter 5

1. Charlotte Danielson, *Enhancing Professional Practice: A Framework for Teaching* (Alexandria, VA: Association for Supervision and Curriculum Development, 1996).

2. David Ryans, *Characteristics of Teachers* (Washington, DC: American Council on Education, 1960).

3. J. W. Getzels and P. W. Jackson, "The Teacher's Personality and Characteristics." In *Handbook of Research on Teaching,* ed. N. L. Gage (Chicago: Rand McNally, 1963), p. 574.

4. Gloria Ladson-Billings, *The Dreamkeepers: Successful Teachers of African-American Children* (San Francisco: Jossey-Bass, 1994), p. 34.

5. Thomas L. Good and Jere E. Brophy, *Looking in Classrooms,* 8th ed. (New York: Longman, 2000), pp. 95–96; Gloria Ladson-Billings, "What We Can Learn from Multicultural Education Research," *Educational Leadership* (May 1994), pp. 22–26.

6. Good and Brophy, *Looking in Classrooms,* p. 88.

7. Ibid., p. 79.

8. Lee S. Shulman, "Knowledge and Teaching: Foundations of the New Reform," *Harvard Educational Review* 57 (February 1987), p. 8.

9. C. Argyris and D. A. Schon, *Theory in Practice: Increasing Professional Effectiveness* (San Francisco: Jossey-Bass, 1974), pp. 3–19.

10. B. O. Smith et al., *Teachers for the Real World* (Washington, DC: American Association of Colleges for Teacher Education, 1969), p. 44.

11. Richard Kindsvatter, William Wilen, and Margaret Ishler, *Dynamics of Effective Teaching* (White Plains, NY: Longman, 1996), pp. 2–3.

12. Wilford A. Weber, "Classroom Management." In *Classroom Teaching Skills,* 7th ed., ed. J. M. Cooper (Boston: Houghton Mifflin, 2003), p. 227.

13. David C. Berliner, "Effective Classroom Teaching: The Necessary but Not Sufficient Condition for Developing Exemplary Schools." In *Research on Exemplary Schools,* ed. Gilbert R. Austin and Herbert Garber (Orlando, FL: Academic Press, 1985), pp. 136–138.

14. Jacob S. Kounin, *Discipline and Group Management in Classrooms* (New York: Holt, 1970).

15. Alfie Kohn, "Beyond Discipline," *Education Week,* November 20, 1996, pp. 37, 48.

16. Good and Brophy, *Looking in Classrooms,* pp. 394–395.

17. Ibid., pp. 393–395.

18. Ibid., pp. 389–395; William W. Wilen and Ambrose A. Clegg, Jr., "Effective Questions and Questioning: A Research Review," *Theory and Research in Social Education* (Spring 1986), pp. 153–161.

19. Greta Morine-Dershimer, "Instructional Planning." In *Classroom Teaching Skills,* 7th ed., ed. J. M. Cooper (Boston: Houghton Mifflin, 2003), p. 26.

20. Ibid.

21. Mardell Raney, "*Technos* Interview with Jonathan Kozol," *Technos* 7, no. 3 (Fall 1998), p. 10.

Chapter 6

1. This example is loosely based on a class at Ligon Middle School in Raleigh, NC. Available at: **http://www.ncsu.edu/midlink/gis/hazardous_waste.htm**.

2. Marsha Alibrandi, "GIS as a Tool in Interdisciplinary Environmental Studies: Student, Teacher, and Community Perspectives," *Meridian* 1, no. 2 (June 1998). Available at: **http://www2.ncsu.edu/unity/lockers/project/meridian/jun98/feat2-3/feat2-3.html**.

3. David A. Dockterman, "A Teacher's Tools," *Instructor* 100, no. 5 (January 1991), pp. 58–61.

4. Gene White, "From Magic Lanterns to Microcomputers: The Evolution of the Visual Aid in the English Classroom," *English Journal* 73, no. 3 (March 1984), p. 59.

5. Paul Saettler, *The Evolution of American Educational Technology* (Englewood, CO: Libraries Unlimited, Inc., 1990), p. 98.

6. United States Department of Commerce, *The Emerging Digital Economy II* (Washington, DC: U.S. Government Printing Office, 1999). Available at: **http://www.esa.doc.gov/508/esa/pdf/EDE2report.pdf**.

7. Ray Kurzweil, *The Age of Spiritual Machines: When Computers Exceed Human Intelligence* (New York: Viking, 1999).

8. David H. Jonassen, *Computers in the Classroom: Mindtools for Critical Thinking* (Englewood Cliffs, NJ: Prentice Hall, 1996), p. 3. The concept of a computer application as a cognitive tool follows from the idea that "learning is a consequence of thinking"; see David Perkins, *Smart Schools: Better Thinking and Learning for Every Child* (New York: Free Press, 1992), p. 8.

9. David H. Jonassen, Chad Carr, and Hsiu-Ping Yueh, "Computers as Mindtools for Engaging Learners in Critical Thinking," *TechTrends* 43 (March 1998), pp. 24–32.

10. Cleborne D. Maddux, D. LaMont Johnson, and Jerry W. Willis, *Educational Computing: Learning with Tomorrow's Technologies* (Boston: Allyn and Bacon, 1992), pp. 204–205.

11. Matthew Maurer, "Supporting Language and Literacy Development with Technology," in *Leadership in Instructional Technology,* ed. Matthew Maurer and George Steven Davidson (Upper Saddle River, NJ: Merrill, 1998), p. 79.

12. Ibid., p. 76.

13. Andrew Trotter, "Teaching the Basics: Beyond Drill and Practice," *Technology Counts '98* in *Education Week* (October 1, 1998), pp. 25–27. Available at: **http://www.edweek.org/sreports/tc98/cs/cs1.htm**.

14. Diann Boehm, "I Lost My Tooth!" *Learning and Leading with Technology* 24 (April 1997), pp. 17–19.

15. Dennis M. Adams and Mary Hamm, *Collaborative Inquiry in Science, Math, and Technology* (Portsmouth, NH: Heinemann, 1998), p. 99.

16. Jennifer Underdah, Joycelyn Palacio-Cayetano, and Ron Stevens, "Practice Makes Perfect: Assessing and Enhancing Knowledge and Problem-Solving Skills with IMMEX Software," *Learning and Leading with Technology* 28, no. 7 (April 2001), pp. 26–31.

17. Paul G. Geisert and Mynga K. Futrell, *Teachers, Computers, and Curriculum: Microcomputers in the Classroom,* 2d ed. (Needham Heights, MA: Allyn and Bacon, 1995), pp. 119–124.

18. Jonassen, Carr, and Yueh, *Computers in the Classroom,* pp. 49–59.

19. Candy Beal and Cheryl Mason, "Virtual Fieldtripping: No Permission Notes Needed. Creating a Middle School Classroom Without Walls," *Meridian* 2, no. 1 (January 1999). Available at: **http://www.ncsu.edu/meridian/jan99/vfieldtrip/index.html**.

20. Hollylynne Stohl Drier, Kara M. Dawson, and Joe Garafalo, "Not Your Typical Math Class," *Educational Leadership* 56 (February 1999), p. 21.

21. David Perkins, Gavriel Salomon, and Tamar Globerson, "Partners in Cognition: Extending Human Intelligence with Intelligent Technologies," *Educational Researcher* 20, no. 3 (1991), pp. 2–9.

22. National Council of Teachers of Mathematics, *Principles and Standards for School Mathematics* (Reston, VA: The National Council of Teachers of Mathematics, 2000), p. 24. Available at: **http://standards.nctm.org/document/chapter2/techn.htm**.

23. Ann M. Farrell, "Teaching and Learning Behaviors in Technology-Oriented Precalculus Classrooms," Ph.D. dissertation, Ohio State University, *Dissertation Abstracts International* 51 (1990), p. 100A.

24. Peter West, "Support Pilot Distance-Learning Projects, Congress Urged," *Education Week,* March 17, 1993, p. 16.

25. U.S. Congress, Office of Technology Assessment, *Teachers and Technology: Making the Connection,* OTA-EHR-616 (Washington, DC: U.S. Government Printing Office, April 1995), p. 1103.

26. Mary Seegers, "Special Technological Possibilities for Students with Special Needs," *Learning and Leading with Technology* 29 (November 2001), pp. 32–39.

27. North Carolina Department of Public Instruction, *Assessment Brief: North Carolina Tests of Proficiency Graduation Requirements,* 7 (January 23, 2001). Available at: **http://www.ncpublicschools.org/accountability/testing/briefs/computerskills/**.

28. National Educational Technology Standards for Students (**http://cnets.iste.org/**).

29. Mary Ann Zehr, "Preparing Students for a Digital World," *Technology Counts '98,* in *Education Week* (October 1, 1998), pp. 33–35. Available at: **http://www.edweek.org/sreports/tc98/cs/cs3.htm**.

30. Thomas C. Reeves, "Technology in Teacher Education: From Electronic Tutor to Cognitive Tool," *Action in Teacher Education* 17, no. 4 (1996), p. 74.

31. Bagley and Hunter, "Restructuring, Constructivism, and Technology," pp. 684–689.

32. Henry Jay Becker and Jason Ravitz, "The Influence of Computer and Internet Use on Teachers' Pedagogical Practices and Perceptions," *Journal of Research on Computing in Education* 31, no. 4 (Summer 1999), pp. 356–384.

33. U.S. Congress, Office of Technology Assessment, *Teachers and Technology: Making the Connection,* OTA-EHR-616 (Washington, DC: U.S. Government Printing Office, April 1995), p. 41.

34. Sarah M. Butzin, "Using Instructional Technology in Transformed Learning Environments: An Evaluation of Project CHILD (Computers Helping Instruction and Learning Development)," *Journal of Research on Technology in Education* 33 (Summer 2001).

35. Bess Keller, "Forging the Home-School Connection: For More Information, Press 1. . . ," *Technology Counts '98,* in *Education Week* (October 1, 1998), pp. 49–51. Available at: **http://www.edweek.org/sreports/tc98/cs/cs7.htm**.

36. Ronald E. Anderson and Amy Ronnkvist, "The Presence of Computers in American Schools," *Teaching, Learning and Computing: A National Survey* (1998). Available at: **http://www.crito.uci.edu/tlc/findings/computers_in_american_schools/**.

37. U.S. Department of Education. National Center for Education Statistics, *Teachers' Tools for the 21st Century: A Report on Teachers' Use of Technology.* NCES 2000-102 (Washington, DC: 2000). Available at: **http://nces.ed.gov/pubs2000/2000102A.pdf**.

38. Ibid.

39. Rockman et al., "A More Complex Picture: Laptop Use and Impact in the Context of Changing Home and School Access" (San Francisco, 2000). Available at: **http://rockman.com/projects/laptop/laptop3exec.htm**.

40. Andrew Trotter, "FCC's E-Rate Proposal Would 'Spread the Wealth,'" *Education Week,* May 9, 2001.

41. C. Williams. *Internet Access in Public Schools 1994–1999* (NCES 2000-086). U.S. Department of Education. Washington, DC: National Center for Education Statistics.

42. Mary Ann Zehr, "Rural Connections," *Technology Counts 2001,* in *Education Week* (May 10, 2001). Available at: **http://www.edweek.org/sreports/tc01/tc2001_default.html**.

43. Robert C. Johnston, "Money Matters," *Technology Counts 2001,* in *Education Week* (May 10, 2001). Available at: **http://www.edweek.org/sreports/tc01/tc2001_default.html**.

44. Lori Meyer, "New Challenges: Overview of the State Data Tables," *Technology Counts 2001,* in *Education Week* (May 10, 2001). Available at: **http://www.edweek.org/sreports/tc01/tc2001_default.html**.

45. "U.S. Schools Lack E-learning Policies," *Education Week,* October 24, 2001. Available at: **http://www.edweek.org/ew/newstory.cfm?slug=08tech.h21**.

46. Lin Foa, Richard Schwab, and Michael Johnson, "Upgrading School Technology: 'Support the Zealots' and Other Pointers for Entering a Strange New Land," *Education Week,* May 1, 1996, p. 52.

47. Lori Meyer, "New Challenges: Overview of the State Data Tables," *Technology Counts 2001,* in *Education Week* (May 10, 2001). Available at: **http://www.edweek.org/sreports/tc01/tc2001_default.html**.

48. Interstate New Teacher Assessment and Support Consortium, *Model Standards for Beginning Teacher Licensing and Development: A Resource for State Dialogue* (1992). Available at: **http://www.ccsso.org/intascst.html**.

49. Sara Armstrong, "The Right Stuff: Curry Graduates Leave College Prepared to Teach" (September 1, 2001). Available at: **http://www.glef.org**.

50. U.S. Department of Education. National Center for Education Statistics, *Teachers' Tools for the 21st Century: A Report on Teachers' Use of Technology.* NCES 2000-102 (Washington, DC: 2000). Available at: **http://nces.ed.gov/pubs2000/2000102A.pdf**.

51. Rockman et al., "Beyond Buddy: The Sustained Influence of the Buddy System Project" (San Francisco: 1998). Available at: **http://rockman.com/projects/buddy/Bey.Buddy98.pdf**.

52. U.S. Department of Commerce, *Falling through the Net: Executive Summary* (Washington, DC: 1999). Available at: **http://www.ntia.doc.gov/ntiahome/fttn99/execsummary.html**.

53. Robert C. Johnston, "Money Matters," *Technology Counts 2001,* in *Education Week* (May 10, 2001). Available at: **http://www.edweek.org/sreports/tc01/tc2001_default.html**.

54. Ibid.

55. U.S. Department of Commerce, *Falling through the Net: Executive Summary* (Washington, DC: 2000). Available at: **http://www.ntia.doc.gov/ntiahome/digitaldivide/execsumfttn00.htm**.

56. Ibid.
57. John Gehring, "Not Enough Girls," *Technology Counts 2001,* in *Education Week* (May 10, 2001). Available at: **http://www.edweek.org/sreports/tc01/tc2001_default.html**.
58. AAUW Educational Foundation Commission on Technology, Gender, and Teacher Education, *Tech-Savvy: Educating Girls in the New Computer Age* (Washington, DC: American Association of University Women Educational Foundation, 2000). Available at: **http://www.aauw.org/2000/techsavvy.html**.
59. Cornelia Brunner, Dorothy Bennett, and Margaret Honey, "Technology, Gender, and Education: Defining the Problem," paper prepared for the AAUW Commission on Gender, Technology, and Teacher Education, October 1998.
60. Cornelia Brunner, "Opening Technology to Girls," *Electronic Learning* 16, No. 4 (February 1997), p. 55.
61. From *National Educational Technology Standards: Connecting Curriculum and Technology.* Copyright © 2000, ISTE (the International Society for Technology in Education), 800.336.6191 (U.S. and Canada) or 541.302.3777 (International), cust_svc@iste.org, **www.iste.org**. Reprinted with permission.
62. Larry Cuban, "High-Tech Schools and Low-Tech Teaching," *Education Week 16* (May 21, 1997).
63. Larry Cuban, "Techno-Reformers and Classroom Teachers," *Education Week* 16 (October 9, 1996).
64. Judy Salpeter, "What Does Research Say about Technology's Impact on Education: Interview with Larry Cuban," *Technology and Learning* (June, 2000). Available at: **http://www.techlearning.com/db_area/archives/TL/062000/archives/cuban.html**.
65. Judi Harris, *Virtual Architecture: Designing and Directing Curriculum-Based Telecomputing* (Eugene, OR: International Society for Technology in Education, 1998).

Chapter 7

1. From Kenneth R. Howe, "A Conceptual Basis for Ethics in Teacher Education," *Journal of Teacher Education* 37 (May/June 1996), p. 6. Reprinted with permission.
2. Ibid, p. 6.
3. American Federation of Teachers, *Bill of Rights* (Washington, DC: AFT, n.d.).
4. Steven Tigner, *Educator's Affirmation* (Boston and Toledo, OH: Boston University and University of Toledo, 1989). Reprinted by permission of Steven Tigner.
5. John Martin Rich, "The Role of Professional Ethics in Teacher Education," *Journal of the Association of Teacher Educators* 7 (Fall 1985), p. 22.
6. *U.S.L. Week 4223,* March 24, 1970, quoted in Louis Fischer and David Schimmel, *The Rights of Students and Teachers* (New York: Harper and Row, 1982), p. 323. Much of this chapter is drawn from the material presented in this excellent and highly readable book and also from Louis Fischer, David Schimmel, and Cynthia Kelly, *Teachers and the Law,* 4th ed. (1995) and 5th ed. (1998) (New York: Addison-Wesley Longman, 1998).
7. Louis Fischer, David Schimmel, and Cynthia Kelly, *Teachers and the Law,* 5th ed. (New York: Addison-Wesley Longman, 1998), p. 20.
8. *Smith v. School District of the Township of Darby,* quoted in Fischer, Schimmel, and Kelly, *Teachers and the Law,* p. 31
9. Ibid., p. 38.
10. Ibid., p. 47.
11. Ibid., pp. 76–77.
12. Ibid., p. 101.
13. *Pickering v. Board of Education,* 225 N.E. 2d 1 (1967); 391 U.S. 563 (1968).
14. *Scoville v. Board of Education,* 425 F. 2d 10 (7th Cir. 1970).
15. *Anderson v. Evans,* 660 F. 2d 153 (6th Cir. 1981).
16. *Stroman v. Colleton County School District,* 981 F. 2d 152 (4th Cir. 1992).
17. Fischer, Schimmel, Kelly, *Teachers and the Law,* 5th ed., p. 166.
18. Mark G. Yudof, David L. Kirp, Betsy Levin and Rachel F. Moran, *Educational Policy and the Law,* 4th ed. (Belmont, CA: West/Thomson Learning), pp. 255–256.
19. Ibid., p. 256.
20. Ibid., p. 257.
21. Fischer, Schimmel, Kelly, *Teachers and the Law,* 4th ed., p. 169.
22. Fischer, Schimmel, Kelly, *Teachers and the Law,* 5th ed., p. 169.
23. Thomas R. McDaniel, "The Teacher's Ten Commandments: School Law in the Classroom," *Phi Delta Kappan 60* no. 10 (June 1979), 707.
24. Fischer, Schimmel, Kelly, *Teachers and the Law,* 5th ed., p. 451.
25. Ibid., p. 324.
26. Ibid., pp. 297–298.
27. Ibid., p. 307.
28. Ibid., p. 306.
29. Perry A. Zirkel, "A Bedeviling Message from Providence," *Phi Delta Kappan 74,* no. 2 (October 1992), pp. 183–184.
30. *Santa Fe Independent School District v. Department of Education* (99–62) 168 F. 3d 806.
31. Benjamin Senor, "Even After the Supreme Court Ruling, We're Still in the Dark about Religion Clubs at School," *American School Board Journal* 173 (August 1986), p. 17.
32. Cheryl D. Mills, "Important Education-Related U.S. Supreme Court Decisions." In *Challenges and Achievements of American Education,* ed. Cordon Cawalti (Alexandria, VA: Association for Supervision and Curriculum Development, 1993), p. 192.
33. Stephen Arons, "Separation of School and State," *Education Week,* November 17, 1984, p. 24.
34. Thomas J. Flygare, "Supreme Court Strikes Down Louisiana Creationism Act," *Phi Delta Kappan 69,* no. 1 (September 1987), pp. 77–79.
35. Associated Press, "Science Standard Debates in Kansas," August 11, 1999.
36. "ABC Nightly News," August 25, 1999.
37. *Mozert v. Hawkins County Board of Education,* U.S. Dist. Ct. (E.D. Tenn.) 647 F Supp. 1194 (1987).
38. *Smith v. Board of School Commissioners of Mobile County* no. 87–7216 (11th Cir., 26 September 1987).
39. Thomas R. McDaniel, "The Teacher's Ten Commandments: School Law in the Classroom," *Phi Delta Kappan 60,* no. 10 (June 1979), 703. Reprinted with permission.
40. Richard Riley, Secretary of Education, and Walter Dellinger, Assistant Attorney General, *White House press release,* July 12, 1995, pp. 2–4.

41. *Tinker v. Des Moines Independent Community School District,* 393 U.S. 503 (1969).

42. Fischer, Schimmel, Kelly, *Teachers and the Law,* 5th ed., p. 271.

43. M.M. McCarthy and N.H. Cambron-McCabe, *Public School Law: Teachers and Students' Rights,* 3rd ed. (Boston: Allyn and Bacon, 1992).

44. *Goss v. Lopez,* 95 S.Ct. 729 (1975).

45. *Honig v. Doe,* 108 S.Ct. 592, 605 (1988).

46. *Fuller v. Decatur Public School Board of Education School District 61,* 78 F. Supp. 2d 812 (C.D. Ill. 2000).

47. Yudof, Kirp, Levin and Moran, *Educational Policy and the Law,* p. 525.

48. See, for instance, *Newsome v. Batavia Local School District,* 842 F. 2d 920 (6th Cir. 1988).

49. Thomas R. McDaniel, "The Teacher's Ten Commandments: School Law in the Classroom" (revised edition). In *Kaleidoscope,* 10th ed., ed. Kevin Ryan and James M. Cooper (Boston: Houghton Mifflin, 2004).

50. Temple University Center for the Study of Corporal Punishment and Alternative in the School, cited in John Johannsen, Harold W. Collins, and James A. Johnson, *American Education,* 6th ed. (Dubuque, IA: Wm. C. Brown, 1990), p. 71.

51. Fischer, Schimmel, and Kelly, *Teachers and the Law,* 4th ed., p. 268.

52. Fischer, Schimmel, and Kelly, *Teachers and the Law,* 5th ed., p. 279.

53. *New Jersey v. T.L.O.,* 105 S. Ct. 733 (1985).

54. *Vernonia School District 47J v. Acton,* 115 S.Ct. 2386 (1995) as reported in Yudof, Kirp, Levin and Moran, *Educational Policy and the Law,* pp. 317–320.

55. American Library Association's Censorship and Challenges web site. Available at: **http://www.ala.org/alaorg/oif/censors.html#links**.

56. *Tinker v. Des Moines Independent Communty School District.*

57. *Bethel School District no. 403. v. Fraser,* 106 S. Ct. 3159 (1986).

58. *Hazlewood School District v. Kuhlmeier,* 56 U.S.L.W. 4079, 4082 (12 January 1988).

59. Ibid.

60. American Association of University Women, *Hostile Hallways: The AAUW Survey on Sexual Harassment in America's Schools* (New York: Louis Harris Associations, 1993), p. 6.

61. *Davis v. Monroe County Board of Education,* 119 S. Ct. 1661 (1999).

62. Ibid.

63. *Owasso Independent School District v. Falvo,* 534 S. Ct. 00-1073.

Chapter 8

1. In a recent national survey of deans and department chairpersons of education schools and departments, 91.4 percent "agreed" or "strongly agreed" with the statement, "There exists a set of core values/virtues upon which most Americans agree, regardless of race, creed, class or culture, which can and should be taught in schools." See Emily Nelsen Jones, Kevin Ryan, and Karen E. Bohlin, *Teachers as Educators of Character: Are the Nation's Schools of Education Coming Up Short?* (Washington, DC: Character Education Partnership, 1999), p. 7; Association of Supervision and Curriculum Development, *Moral Education in the Life of the School* (Alexandria, VA: ASCD, 1989). Both President Clinton and Bush have called for greater emphasis on character education in our schools.

2. Mortimer J. Adler, *The Paideia Proposal: An Educational Manifesto* (New York: Macmillan, 1982); *Paideia Problems and Possibilities* (New York: Macmillan, 1983).

3. Lynn Olson, "Kudos for Core Knowledge," *Education Week,* March 17, 1999, p. 44.

4. *Education Week,* January 31, 1996, p. 21.

Chapter 9

1. Willystine Goodsell, *Pioneers of Women's Education in the United States* (New York: AMS Press, 1970/1931), p. 5.

2. R. Freeman Butts and Lawrence A. Cremin, *A History of Education in American Culture* (New York: Holt, 1953), p. 245.

3. Charles W. Coulter and Richard S. Rimanoczy, *A Layman's Guide to Educational Theory* (New York: Van Nostrand, 1955), p. 130.

4. Butts and Cremin, *A History of Education in American Culture,* p. 408.

5. John D. Pulliam, *History of Education in America,* 3d ed. (Columbus, OH: Merrill, 1982), pp. 157–159.

6. Gene D. Shepherd and William B. Ragan, *Modern Elementary Curriculum,* 6th ed. (New York: Holt, 1982), p. 440.

7. Butts and Cremin, *A History of Education in American Culture,* p. 260.

8. Merle Curti, *The Social Ideas of American Educators,* 2d ed. (Totowa, NJ: Littlefield, Adams, 1959), p. 183.

9. Butts and Cremin, *A History of Education in American Culture,* p. 443.

10. Thomas D. Snyder, *120 Years of American Education: A Statistical Portrait* (Washington, DC: U.S. Department of Education, National Center for Education Statistics, 1993), pp. 36–37; Debra E. Gerald and William J. Hussar, *Projections of Education Statistics to 2011* (Washington, D.C.: National Center for Education Statistics, 2001), p. 13.

11. William T. Gruhn and Harl R. Douglass, *The Modern Junior High School,* 3d ed. (New York: Ronald Press, 1971), pp. 46–53.

12. "Teachers Train for Tough Years," *USA Today,* October 6, 1998, p. D1.

13. Thomas D. Snyder and Charlene M. Hoffman, *Digest of Education Statistics 2001* (Washington, DC: U.S. Department of Education, National Center for Education Statistics, 2002), p.120.

14. Larry Cuban, "What Happens to Reforms That Last? The Case of the Junior High School," *American Educational Research Journal* 29, no. 2 (Summer 1992), p. 246.

15. Thomas D. Snyder and Charlene M. Hoffman, *Digest of Education Statistics 2001* (Washington, DC: U.S. Department of Education, National Center for Education Statistics, 2002), p. 73; Jeanne Ponessa, "Catholic School Enrollment Continues to Increase," *Education Week,* April 17, 1996, p. 5.

16. *School and Staffing Survey, 1999–2000* (Washington, DC: National Center for Education Statistics, 2002), p. 47. Available at: **http://nces.ed.gov/pubs2002/2002313.pdf**.
17. Ibid.
18. Herbert M. Kliebard, *Religion and Education in America: A Documentary History* (Scranton, PA: International Textbook, 1969), p. 119.
19. *The Religious Freedom Page*. Available at: **http://religiousfreedom.lib.virginia.edu/court/pier_v_soci.html**.
20. Earle H. West, *The Black American and Education* (Columbus, OH: Merrill, 1972), pp. 7–8.
21. Eric Lincoln and Milton Meltzer, *A Pictorial History of the Negro in America*, 3d ed. (New York: Crown, 1968), pp. 108–109.
22. *Historical Statistics of the United States, Colonial Times to 1970*, vol. I, Table Series H 433–441 (Washington, DC: U.S. Government Printing Office, 1975), p. 370.
23. Franklin Frazier, *The Negro in the United States*, rev. ed. (New York: Macmillan, 1957), pp. 427, 432–436, 438.
24. Gary Orfield, Susan E. Eaton, and the Harvard Project on School Desegregation, *Dismantling Desegregation* (New York: The New Press, 1996), pp. 105–106; Jomills Henry Braddock II, Robert L. Crain, and James M. Mc-Partland, "A Long-Term View of School Desegregation: Some Recent Studies of Graduates as Adults," *Phi Delta Kappan* 66 (December 1984), pp. 259–264.
25. Anthony Lukas, *Common Ground* (New York: Knopf, 1985), a Pulitzer Prize–winning description of desegregation efforts in Boston, Massachusetts.
26. Howard Ozmon and Sam Craver, *Busing: A Moral Issue* (Bloomington, IN: Phi Delta Kappa Educational Foundation, 1972), pp. 33–34.
27. Snyder and Hoffman, *Digest of Education Statistics 2000*, pp. 97–105.
28. Ethan Bronner, "After 45 Years, Resegregation Emerges in Schools, Study Finds," *The New York Times National*, June 13, 1999, p. 31.
29. Richard M. Merelman, "Dis-Integrating American Public Schools," *Education Week*, February 6, 2002, p. 37.
30. R. Freeman Butts, *The Education of the West: A Formative Chapter in the History of Civilization* (New York: McGraw-Hill, 1973), p. 279.
31. Mary Ann Zehr, "GAO: Student Achievement Lagging At Bureau of Indian Affairs Schools," *Education Week*, November 7, 2001, p. 12.
32. Lynn Schnaiberg, "Presidential Order on Indian Education Calls for Comprehensive Federal Policy," *Education Week*, September 9, 1998, p. 35.
33. "The Educational Excellence For All Children Act of 1999," *Education Week*, June 9, 1999, p. 47.
34. U.S. Department of Education, National Center for Education Statistics, *The Condition of Education 2000*, NCES 2000-062, Washington, DC: U.S. Government Printing Office, 2000, p. 56.
35. Ibid., p. 11.
36. Snyder and Hoffman, *Digest of Education Statistics, 2001*, p. 58; U.S. Census Bureau, *National Population Projections*. Available at: **http://www.census.gov/population/www/projections/natsum-T5.html**.

Chapter 10

1. Frederick M. Hess, "School Boards at the Dawn of the 21st Century," a report prepared for the National School Boards Association (Charlottesville, VA: University of Virginia, 2002).
2. Larry Cuban, "Conflict and Leadership in the Superintendency," *Phi Delta Kappan* 67 (September 1985), p. 28. See also Arthur Blumberg with Phyllis Blumberg, *The School Superintendent: Living with Conflict* (New York: Teachers College Press, 1985), p. 32, and Susan Moore Johnson, *Leading to Change: The Challenge of the New Superintendency* (San Francisco: Jossey-Bass, 1996), pp. 77–78.
3. Rhea R. Borja, "Study: Urban School Chiefs' Tenure is 4.6 Years," *Education Week*, February 6, 2002, p. 5.
4. "Education Vital Signs," *American School Board Journal* 185, no. 12 (December 1998), p. A14.
5. Ibid., p. A13.
6. Business Coalition for Education Reform. Available at: **http://www.bcer.org/**.
7. Henry A. Giroux, "Education Incorporated?" *Educational Leadership* 56, no. 2 (October 1998), p. 13.
8. Andrew Trotter, "Channel One Drops Cash-Incentive Plan Aimed at Teachers," *Education Week*, September 12, 2001, p. 17.
9. Thomas Moore with Nancy Linon, "The Selling of Our Schools," *U.S. News & World Report*, November 6, 1989, p. 40.
10. Education Week. Available at: **http://www.edweek.com/context/topics/issuespage**.
11. Eric Hirsch, Julia E. Koppich, and Michael S. Knapp, "Revisiting What States are Doing to Improve the Quality of Teaching: An Update on Patterns and Trends" (Seattle: Center for the Study of Teaching and Policy, University of Washington, February 2001), p. 16.
12. National Education Association, *Estimates of School Statistics 2001* (Washington, D.C.: National Education Association, 2001); Joletta L. Sack, "Federal Spending Burst Nudges Up Uncle Sam's Share," *Education Week*, February 13, 2002, p. 30.
13. Thomas D. Snyder and Charlene M. Hoffman, *Digest of Education Statistics 2001* (Washington, D.C.: U.S. Department of Education, National Center for Education Statistics, 2001). Available at: **http://nces.ed.gov/pubs2002/2002130b.pdf**.
14. "Education Vital Signs," *American School Board Journal* 188, no. 12 (December 2001), p. 49.
15. Rob Greenwald, Larry V. Hedges, and Richard D. Laine, "The Effect of School Resources on Student Achievement," *Review of Educational Research* (Fall 1996), pp. 361–396.
16. Deborah A. Verstegen, "Financing the New Adequacy: Towards New Models of State Education Finance Systems That Support Standards Based Reform," *Journal of Education Finance* 27 (Winter 2002), pp. 749–782.
17. Thomas D. Snyder, Charlene M. Hoffman, and Claire M. Geddes, *Digest of Education Statistics 1998* (Washington, DC: U.S. Department of Education, National Center for Education Statistics, 1998), p. 169.

18. Erik W. Robelen, "ESEA to Boost Federal Role In Education," *Education Week*, January 9, 2002, p. 28.
19. Ibid, p. 29.
20. U.S. Department of Health and Human Services. Available at: **http://www2.acf.dhhs.gov/programs/hsb/about/fact2001.htm**.
21. U.S. Department of Education. Available at: **http://www.ed.gov/offices/OUS/PES/ed_for_disadvantaged.html#factsheet**.
22. Deborah L. Cohen, "Perry Preschool Graduates Show Dramatic New Social Gains at 27," *Education Week*, April 21, 1993, pp. 1, 16–17; Lawrence J. Schweinhart et al., "The Promise of Early Childhood Education," *Phi Delta Kappan* 66 (April 1985), pp. 548–553.
23. The Longitudinal Evaluation of School Change and Performance (LESCP) in Title I Schools. Available at: **http://www.ed.gov/offices/OUS/PES/esed/lescp_vol1.doc**.

Chapter 11

1. Jon W. Wiles, *Promoting Changes in School* (New York: Scholastic, 1993), pp. 1–2.
2. John Gehring, "College and Minorities," *Education Week*, October 3, 2001. Available at: **http://www.edweek.org/ew/newstory.cfm?slug=05colleg.h21**.
3. Conway Dorsett, "Multicultural Education: Why We Need·It and Why We Worry About It," *Network News and Views* 121, no. 3 (March 1993), p. 31.
4. Quoted in Theodore Sizer and Nancy Fauste Sizer, *The Students Are Watching* (Boston: Beacon Press, 1999), p. 6.
5. For further information on portfolios and authentic assessment see Susan Black, "Portfolio Assessment," *The Executive Educator* (February 1993), pp. 28–31.
6. Milbrey W. McLaughlin, Merita A. Irby, and Juliet Langman, *Urban Sanctuaries: Neighborhood Organizations in the Lives and Futures of Inner-City Youth* (San Francisco: Jossey-Bass, 1994), p. 216.
7. Anthony Bryk and Yeow Meng Thum, "The Effects of High School Organization on Dropping Out," unpublished paper, University of Chicago, 1988, pp. 54–68. See also Anthony Bryk and Mary Erina Driscoll, "An Empirical Investigation of the School as a Community," unpublished paper, University of Chicago, 1988, pp. 54–63.
8. Kevin Ryan and Thomas Lickona, eds., *Character Development in Schools and Beyond* (Washington, DC: Council for Research on Values and Philosophy, 1987), pp. 21–26.
9. See Chapter 5, "Against Moral Education, in Barry Chazan, *Contemporary Approaches to Moral Education* (New York: Teacher College Press, 1985).
10. William Damon, quoted by Amitai Etzioni, *The Spirit of Community* (New York: Crown, 1993), pp. 100–101.
11. "Values Education: Time for Greater Emphasis!" *Phi Delta Kappan* 75, no. 2 (October 1993), p. 145.
12. Thomas Toch, *In the Name of Excellence* (New York: Oxford University Press, 1991), p. 260.
13. Julie Blair, "Kellogg Begins Program to Boost Service Learning," *Education Week*, May 26, 1999.
14. Mortimer Adler, *The Paideia Proposal: An Educational Manifesto* (New York: Macmillan, 1982), p. 59.

15. Quoted by Mark Edwards in "Turbo-Charging Professional Development," *The School Administrator* (December 1998), p. 36.
16. Toch, *In the Name of Excellence*, p. 9.
17. Editors of *Education Week*, "From Risk to Renewal," p. 4.
18. The No Child Left Behind Act of 2001 Reauthorization of the Elementary and Secondary Education Act Policies and Legislation. Available at: **http://www.whitehouse.gov/news/reports/no-child-left-behind.html**.
19. E.D. Hirsch, as quoted by Sara Mosle, *The New York Times Book Review*, September 29, 1996, p. 15.
20. Theodore Sizer, *Horace School: Redesigning the American High School* (Boston: Houghton Mifflin, 1992), pp. 207–208.
21. Quoted by the editors of *Education Week*, "From Risk to Renewal," p. 187.
22. Available at: **nces.ed.gov/nationsreportcard/science/trends.asp**.
23. Herbert Walberg, *U.S. News and World Report*, January 11, 1993, p. 60.
24. *Digest of Education Statistics 1998* (Washington DC: U.S. Department of Education, National Center for Education Statistics, 1999), p. 167.
25. Editors of *Education Week*, "From Risk to Renewal," p. 102.
26. National Association for Year-Round Education. Available at: **http://www.nayre.org**.
27. Robert Marzano and John Kendall, "The Fall and Rise of Standards-Based Education," National Association of State Boards of Education Issues in Brief (1998).
28. Eric Hirsch, Julia E. Koppich, and Michael S. Knapp, "Revisiting What States are Doing to Improve the Quality of Teaching: An Update on Patterns and Trends" (Seattle: Center for the Study of Teaching and Policy, University of Washington, 2001), p. 13.
29. Toch, *In the Name of Excellence*, p. 158.
30. Toch, *In the Name of Excellence*, p. 164.
31. Toch, *In the Name of Excellence*, p. 186.
32. Richard J. Murname and Frank Levy, "What General Motors Can Teach U.S. Schools About the Proper Role of Markets in Education Reform," *Phi Delta Kappan* 78, no. 2 (October 1996), p. 14.

Chapter 12

1. Richard M. Ingersoll, "Teacher Turnover, Teacher Shortages, and the Organization of Schools" (Seattle: Center for the Study of Teaching and Policy, University of Washington, 2001), p. 14.
2. William J. Hussar and Debra E. Gerald, *Projections of Education Statistics to 2011* (Washington, DC: National Center for Education Statistics, 2001), pp. 13, 79.
3. Ann Bradley, "Class-Size Cuts Set Off Hiring Spree in Calif.," *Education Week*, September 4, 1996, pp. 1, 29.
4. Kerry J. Gruber, Susan D. Wiley, Stephen D. Broughman, Gregory A. Strizek, Marisa Burian-Fitzgerald, *School and Staffing Survey 1999–2000* (Washington, DC: U.S. Department of Education, National Center for Education Statistics, 2002), p. 3.
5. Eric Hirsch, Julia E. Koppich, and Michael S. Knapp, "Revisiting What States are Doing to Improve the Quality of Teaching: An Update on Patterns and Trends" (Seattle: Center for the Study of Teaching and Policy, University of Washington, 2001), p. 19.

6. *Recruiting New Teachers.* Available at: **http://www.rnt.org/facts/index/html.**

7. *The 2002 Job Search Handbook for Educators* (Columbus, OH: American Association for Employment in Education, 2002), pp. 7–9.

8. Ibid, p. 9.

9. David Hill, "Odd Man Out," *Education Week,* September 11, 1996, p. 30.

10. Hirsch et al., p. 19.

11. *Quality Counts 2000: Who Should Teach?* Fourth annual edition of *Education Week's* 50-state report card on public education, January 13, 2000. Available at: **http://www.edweek._org/sreports/qc00/.**

12. Thomas D. Snyder and Charlene M. Hoffman, *Digest of Education Statistics 2001* (Washington, DC: National Center for Education Statistics, 2001), p. 81.

13. *Department of Defense Education Activity.* Available at: **http://www.odedodea.edu/communications/dodeafacts2002.htm.**

14. Hussar and Gerald, *Projections of Education Statistics to 2011,* Tables 1 and 32; Catherine Gewertz, "Teacher Need Hits Private Schools Hard," *Education Week,* May 23, 2001, pp. 1, 18.

15. Thomas M. Smith et al., *The Condition of Education 1996* (Washington, DC: U.S. Department of Education, National Center for Education Statistics, 1996), p. 34; James Coleman, T. Hoffer, and S. Kilgore, *Public and Private Schools,* Report to the National Center for Education Statistics, 1981.

16. *Rankings and Estimates* (Washington, D.C.: National Education Association, 2002), p. 78.

17. F. Howard Nelson, Rachel Drown, and Jewell C. Gould, "Survey and Analysis of Teacher Salary Trends 2000" (Washington, D.C.: American Federation of Teachers, 2001), p. 8.

18. Most of the ideas in this section are taken from John William Zehring, "How to Get Another Teaching Job and What to Do If You Can't," *Learning* 6 (February 1978), pp. 44, 46–51.

19. C. Emily Feistritzer, Alternative Routes for Certifying Teachers Escalate to Meet Multiple Demands (Washington, DC: National Center for Education Information, 2002). Available at: **http://www.ncei.com.**

20. J. Shen, "Has the Alternative Certification Policy Materialized Its Promise? A Comparison of Traditionally and Alternatively Certified Teachers in Public Schools," *Educational Evaluation and Policy Analyses* 19 (1997), pp. 276–283.

21. C. Emily Feistritzer, *Alternative Routes for Certifying Teachers Escalate to Meet Multiple Demands.*

22. *Occupational Outlook Handbook, 2002–03 Edition* (Washington, DC: U.S. Department of Labor, 2002). Available at: **http://www.bls.gov/oco/.**

Chapter 13

1. *Education Week* (March 17, 1999), p. 1.

2. Estelle Fuchs, *Teachers Talk: Voices from Inside City Schools* (Garden City, NY: Doubleday, 1969), p. 21.

3. T. M. Wildman and J. A. Niles, "Reflective Teachers: Tensions Between Abstractions and Realities," *Journal of Teacher Education* 38, no. 10, 1987, pp. 25–31.

4. From Gary Cornog, "To Care or Not to Care," in *Don't Smile Until Christmas: Accounts of the First Year of Teaching,* edited by Kevin Ryan (Chicago: University of Chicago Press, 1970), pp. 18–19. Copyright © 1970. Reprinted by permission of Kevin Ryan.

5. *What to Expect Your First Year of Teaching.* Available at: **http://www.ed.gov/pubs/FirstYear/ch6.html.**

6. "Teacher Quality: A Report on the Preparation and Qualifications of Public School Teachers" (Washington, DC: U.S. Department of Education, 1999).

Chapter 14

1. Myron Lieberman, *Education as a Profession* (Englewood Cliffs, NJ: Prentice-Hall, 1956).

2. "Paying a big price to boost learning," *Sacramento Bee* (December 29, 2001), p. B1.

3. Walter Boggs, quoted at 1963–64 convention of the National Commission on Teacher Education and Professional Standards. Myron Brenton, *What's Happened to Teachers?* (New York: Coward-McCann, 1970), p. 242.

4. *National Board of Professional Teaching Standards.* Available at: **http://www.nbpts.org.**

5. Ibid.

6. Kathleen Kennedy Manzo and Bess Keller, "National Board Honors," *Education Week* (December 11, 2002), p. 9.

7. National Education Association. Available at: **http://www.nea.org.**

8. Ibid.

9. Steven Chauffman, "The NEA Seizes Power: The Teachers' Coup," *The New Republic,* October 11, 1980, pp. 9–11.

10. Stanley Elam, "The National Education Association: Political Powerhouse or Paper Tiger," *Phi Delta Kappan* 63 (November 1981), pp. 169–174.

11. Peter Brim Low and Leslie Spencer, "The National Extortion Association?" *Forbes,* June 7, 1993. Available at: **http://www.familypolicy.com/book/chapter03.html.**

12. "NEA: Does It Still Speak for Teachers?" *Teachers in Focus* (April 1994), p. 4.

13. American Federation of Teachers, "Letter from Bella Rosenberg, Assistant to the President," January 18, 1991.

14. American Federation of Teachers. Available at: **http://www.aft.org.**

15. Jeff Archer, "NEA Agrees to New Alliance With AFT," *Education Week* (July 11, 2001). Available at: **http://www.edweek.ora/ew/ewstory.cfm?slug-42neamerge_web.h20.**

Chapter 15

1. *A Sense of Calling: Who Teaches and Why.* Public Agenda (2000), p. 36.

2. Ibid., p. 10.

3. Ibid.

4. Ibid., p. 12.

5. Ibid.

6. Sharon Feiman-Nemser and Robert E. Floden, "The Culture of Teaching," in *The Handbook of Research on Teaching,* 3d ed., ed. Merlin C. Witrock (New York: Macmillan, 1986), pp. 510–511.

7. David Haselkorn and Louis Harris, *The Essential Profession: A National Survey of Public Attitudes Toward Teaching, Educational Opportunity and School Reform* (Belmont, MA: Recruiting New Teachers, Inc., 1998), p. 2.

8. Ibid., p. 13.

9. Dan Lortie, *Schoolteacher* (Chicago: University of Chicago Press, 1975), p. 102.

10. Mihaly Csikszentmihalyi and Jane McCormack, "The Influence of Teachers," *Phi Delta Kappan* 67, no. 6 (February 1986), pp. 415–419. The article is reprinted in this text's companion volume of readings: *Kaleidoscope: Readings in Education,* 10th ed., ed. Kevin Ryan and James M. Cooper (Boston: Houghton Mifflin, 2004).

11. John Goodlad, *A Place Called School* (New York: McGraw-Hill, 1984); Judith W. Little, "The Persistence of Privacy," *Teachers College Record* (Summer 1990), pp. 509–536.

12. Leslie A. Swetnam, "Media Distortion of the Teacher Image," *The ClearingHouse* (September/October 1992), p. 30.

13. Ibid., pp. 30–32.

Appendix

Directory of U.S. State Teacher Licensure Offices

A teaching license is valid only in the state for which it is issued, and licensure and testing requirements are never static. If you are planning to move to another state, you should contact that state's licensure office, as listed below. Because the web sites for these offices often change, if you experience difficulty reaching any one of them, you can link to any state agency by going to **http://www.ccsso.org** and clicking on the state education agencies bar.

When you write or call the state licensure office, indicate the type of license you are receiving from your current state and which national tests you have taken, and ask for application materials and procedures for obtaining licensure in the new state. Another source of information about licensure requirements will be the actual districts to which you apply.

Alabama
Department of Education
Division of Instructional Service
5108 Gordon Persons Building
50 North Ripley Street
Montgomery 36130-2101,
    334-229-4271
www.alsde.edu/html/home.asp

Alaska
Department of Education
Teacher Education and Certification
Goldbelt Building
801 West 10th Street, Suite 200
Juneau 99801-1894, 907-465-2831
www.educ.state.ak.us/
    teachercertification

Arizona
Department of Education
Teacher Certification Unit
1535 West Jefferson
Phoenix 85007, 602-542-4367
www.ade.state.az.us/certification

Arkansas
Department of Education
Teacher Education and Licensure
#4 State Capitol Mall, Rooms
    106B/107B
Little Rock 72201, 501-682-4342
www.arkedu.state.ar.us/teacher.htm

California
Commission on Teacher
    Credentialing
1812 9th Street
Sacramento 95814-7000,
    916-445-0184
www.ctc.ca.gov or
    www.calteach.com

Colorado
Department of Education
Educator Licensing, Room 105
201 East Colfax Avenue
Denver 80203-1704, 303-866-6628
www.cde.state.co.us/
    index_license.htm

Connecticut
State Department of Education
Bureau of Certification and
    Professional Development
P.O. Box 2219
Hartford 06145, 860-566-5201
www.state.ct.us/sde/

Delaware
State Department of Education
Office of Certification
Townsend Building, P.O. Box 1402
Dover 19903-1402,
    302-739-4686
www.doe.state.de.us

District of Columbia
Teacher Education and Certification
   Branch
Logan Administration Building
215 G Street, N.E., Room 101A
Washington 20002, 202-442-5377
www.k12dc.us/dcps/home.html

Florida
Department of Education
Bureau of Teacher Certification
Florida Education Center
325 West Gaines Street, Room 203
Tallahassee 32399-0400,
   904-488-5724
www.firn.edu/doe/edcert/
   home0022.htm

Georgia
Professional Standards Commission
1454 Twin Towers East
Atlanta 30334, 404-657-9000
www.gapsc.com/
   TeacherCertification.asp

Hawaii
State Department of Education
Office of Personnel Services
P.O. Box 2360
Honolulu 96804, 800-305-5104
http://doe.k12.hi.us/teacher.htm

Idaho
Department of Education
Teacher Certification and
   Professional Standards
P.O. Box 83720
Boise 83720-0027, 208-332-6884
www.sde.state.id.us/certification

Illinois
State Teacher Certification Board
Division of Professional Preparation
100 North First Street
Springfield 62777-0001,
   217-782-2805
www.isbe.net/teachers.htm

Indiana
Professional Standards Board
251 East Ohio Street, Suite 201
Indianapolis 46204-2133,
   317-232-9010
www.state.in.us/psb/

Iowa
Board of Educational Examiners
Teacher Licensure
Grimes State Office Building
East 14th and Grand
Des Moines 50319-0146,
   515-281-3245
www.state.ia.us/educate/
   programs/boee/index.html

Kansas
State Department of Education
Certification and Teacher Education
120 South East 10th Avenue
Topeka 66612-1182,
   913-296-2288
www.ksbe.state.ks.us/cert/
   Welcome.html

Kentucky
Office of Teacher Education
   and Certification
1024 Capital Center Drive
Frankfort 40601, 502-573-4606
www.kde.state.ky.us/otec/cert/
   default.asp

Louisiana
State Department of Education
Bureau of Higher Education,
   Teacher Certification, and
   Continuing Education
626 North 4th Street
P.O. Box 94064
Baton Rouge 70804-9064,
   504-342-3490
www.louisianaschools.net

Maine
Department of Education
Certification Office
23 State House Station
Augusta 04333-0023,
   207-287-5944
www.usm.maine.edu/coe/
   etep/certify.htm

Maryland
State Department of Education
Division of Certification
   and Accreditation
200 West Baltimore Street
Baltimore 21201, 410-767-0412
www.msde.state.md.us/
   certification/testinfo.html

Massachusetts
Department of Education
Certification and Professional
  Development Coordination
350 Main Street
P.O. Box 9140
Malden 02148-5023, 781-388-3300
www.doe.mass.edu/cert/regs.html

Michigan
Department of Education
Office of Professional Preparation
  and Certification Services
608 West Allegan, 3rd Floor
Lansing 48933, 517-335-0406
www.state.mi.us/mde/off/ppc/
  miteach.htm

Minnesota
State Department of Children,
  Families, and Learning
Personnel Licensing
610 Capitol Square Building
550 Cedar Street
St. Paul 55101-2273, 612-296-2046
www.educ.state.mn.us/licen/

Mississippi
State Department of Education
Office of Educator Licensure
Central High School Building
359 North West Street
P.O. Box 771
Jackson 39205-0771, 601-359-3483
www.mde.k12ms.us/license

Missouri
Department of Elementary
  and Secondary Education
Teacher Certification Office
205 Jefferson Street
P.O. Box 480
Jefferson City 65102-0480,
  573-751-0051
www.services.dese.state.mo.us/
  divteachqual/teachcert

Montana
Office of Public Instruction
Teacher Education and Certification
1227 11th Avenue East, Room 210
Box 202501
Helena 59620-2501, 406-444-3150
www.opi.state.mt.us/Cert/
  Index.html

Nebraska
Department of Education
Teacher Education and Certification
301 Centennial Mall South,
  Box 94987
Lincoln 68509-4987, 402-471-0739
www.nde.state.ne.us/tcert/
  tcmain.html

Nevada
Department of Education
Licensure Division
700 East 5th Street
Carson City 89701, 702-687-9141
www.academploy.com/cert/
  certnv.htm

New Hampshire
State Department of Education
Bureau of Credentialing
101 Pleasant Street
Concord 03301-3860,
  603-271-2407
www.academploy.com/cert/
  certnh.htm

New Jersey
Department of Education
Office of Professional Development
  and Licensing
Riverview Executive Plaza,
  Building 100, Rte. 29
Trenton 08625-0500, 609-292-2045
www.state.nj.us/njded/educators/
  license/index.html

New Mexico
State Department of Education
Professional Licensure Unit
Education Building
Santa Fe 87501-2786,
  505-827-6587
www.sde.state.nm.us/div/ais/
  lic/index.html

New York
State Education Department
Office of Teaching
Cultural Education Center,
  Room 5A47
Nelson A. Rockefeller
  Empire State Plaza
Albany 12230, 518-474-3901
www.nysed.gov/tcert/
  homepage.htm

North Carolina
Department of Public Instruction
Licensure Section
301 North Wilmington Street
Raleigh 27601-2825, 919-733-4125
www.ncpublicschools.org/
employment.html

North Dakota
Department of Public Instruction
Educational Standards
and Practices Board
600 East Boulevard Avenue
Bismarck 58505-0540,
701-328-2264
www.state.nd.us/espb/

Ohio
Department of Education
Division of Professional
Development and Licensure
65 South Front Street, Room 412
Columbus 43215-4183,
614-466-3593
www.ode.state.oh.us/tp/ctp/

Oklahoma
State Department of Education
Professional Standards Section
Hodge Education Building
2500 North Lincoln Boulevard,
Room 212
Oklahoma City 73105-4599,
405-521-3337
www.octp.org/index.html

Oregon
Teacher Standards and Practices
Commission
Public Service Building, Suite 105
255 Capitol Street, N.E.
Salem 97310, 503-378-3586
www.ode.state.or.us/
supportservices/careers.htm

Pennsylvania
State Department of Education
Bureau of Teacher Preparation
and Certification
333 Market Street, 3rd Floor
Harrisburg 17126-0333,
717-787-3356
www.tcs.ed.state.pa.us

Puerto Rico
Department of Education
Certification Office
P.O. Box 190759
San Juan 00919-0759,
787-754-0060

Rhode Island
Department of Education
Office of Teacher Preparation,
Certification, and
Professional Development
Shepard Building
255 Westminster Street
Providence 02903, 401-222-2675
www.ridoe.net

South Carolina
State Department of Education
Office of Organizational
Development
Teacher Certification Section
Rutledge Building, Room 702
Columbia 29201, 803-734-8466
www.scteachers.org/cert/
index.cfm

South Dakota
Division of Education
and Cultural Affairs
Office of Policy and Accountability
Kneip Building,
700 Governors Drive
Pierre 57501-2291, 605-773-3553
www.state.sd.us/deca/OPA/
index.htm

Tennessee
State Department of Education
Teacher Licensing and Certification
Andrew Johnson Tower, 5th Floor
710 James Robertson Parkway
Nashville 37243-0375
615-532-4880
www.state.tn.us/education/
lic_home.htm

Texas
State Board of Educator Certification
1001 Trinity Street
Austin 78701-2603, 1-888-863-5880
www.sbec.state.tx.us

Utah
State Office of Education
Certification and
   Personnel Development
250 East 500 South
Salt Lake City 84111, 801-538-7741
www.usoe.k12.ut.us/

Vermont
State Department of Education
Licensing and Professional
   Standards
120 State Street
Montpelier 05620, 802-828-2445
www.state.vt.us/educ/
   license/index.htm

Virginia
Department of Education
James Monroe Building
P.O. Box 2120
Richmond 23218-2120,
   804-371-2522
www.pen.k12.va.us/VDOE/
   newvdoe/teached.html

Washington
Superintendent of Public Instruction
Professional Education
   and Certification Office
Old Capitol Building
600 South Washington Street
P.O. Box 47200
Olympia 98504-7200,
   360-753-6773
www.k12.wa.us/cert/

West Virginia
Department of Education
Office of Professional Preparation
1900 Kanawha Boulevard East
Building #6, Room B-252
Charleston 25305-0330,
   304-558-7010
http://wvde.state.wv.us/certification

Wisconsin
Department of Public Instruction
Teacher Education
   and Licensing Teams
125 South Webster Street,
   P.O. Box 7841
Madison 53707-7841,
   608-266-1879
www.dpi.state.wi.us/dpi/
   dlsis/tel/index.html

Wyoming
Professional Teaching
   Standards Board
Hathaway Building, 2nd Floor
2300 Capital Avenue
Cheyenne 82002, 307-777-6248
www.k12.wy.us/ptsb/

St. Croix District
Department of Education
Educational Personnel Services
2133 Hospital Street
St. Croix, Virgin Islands 00820,
   340-773-1095

St. Thomas/St. John District
Department of Education
Personnel Services
44–46 Kongens Gade
St. Thomas, Virgin Islands 00802,
   340-774-0100
www.usvi.org/education

**United States
Department of Defense
Dependent Schools**
Certification Unit
4040 N. Fairfax Drive
Arlington, Virginia 22203-1634
703-696-3081, ext. 133
www.odedodea.edu/pers/

Glossary

academic engaged time   The time a student spends on academically relevant activities or materials while experiencing a high rate of success.

academic freedom   The freedom of teachers to teach about an issue or to use a source in teaching without fear of penalty, reprisal, or harassment.

academy   A type of secondary school during the early national period that tried to combine the best of the Latin and English grammar schools. During the nineteenth century it took on a college preparation orientation.

acceleration   A method of teaching gifted and talented students in which they do the same work as other students, but at a faster pace.

acceptable use policy   A statement of rules governing student use of school computers, especially regarding access to the Internet.

active learning   Learning in which the student takes control of or is positively involved in the process of his or her education; strongly associated with constructivism.

aesthetics   A branch of philosophy that examines the perception of beauty and distinguishes beauty from that which is moral or useful.

alternative licensure   A procedure offered by many states to license teachers who have not graduated from a state-approved teacher education program.

American Federation of Teachers (AFT)   The nation's second largest teachers' association or union. Founded in 1916, it is affiliated with the AFL-CIO, the nation's largest union.

assimilation   The absorption of an individual or a group into the cultural tradition of a population or another group.

assistive technology   The array of devices and services that help people with disabilities to perform better in their daily lives. Such devices include motorized chairs, remote control units that turn appliances on and off, computers, and speech synthesizers.

at-risk students   *See* Students at risk.

authentic (performance) assessment   A recent trend in student evaluation that attempts to measure real student performance on significant tasks; the focus is on what we want the student to be able to do. Also called *performance assessment.*

axiology   The philosophical study of values, especially how they are formed ethically, aesthetically, and religiously.

behaviorism   A psychological theory asserting that all behavior is shaped by environmental events or conditions.

bilingual education   A variety of approaches to educating students who speak a primary language other than English.

block grants   Federal aid to education that comes with only minimal federal restrictions on how the funds should be spent; *compare* Categorical grants.

block scheduling   An approach to class scheduling in which students take fewer classes each school day but spend more time in each class.

breach of contract   A failure to fulfill the requirements of a legal agreement.

Brown v. *Board of Education of Topeka*   U.S. Supreme Court ruling in 1954 holding that segregated schools are inherently unequal.

Buckley amendment   The shorthand name for the Family Educational Rights and Privacy Act, which outlines who may and may not have access to a student's records.

call to excellence   An educational slogan pointing students to high standards.

career ladder   A series of steps in an occupation. Usually the higher steps ("rungs" on the ladder) bring new tasks, more responsibility, increased status, and enhanced rewards.

categorical grants   Federal aid to education that must be spent for purposes that are specified in the legislation and by the federal agency administering the funds.

CD-ROM   An acronym for Compact Disc–Read-Only Memory, a type of computer disk that stores several hundred megabytes of data and is currently used for many kinds of multimedia software.

certification   Recognition by a profession that one of its practitioners has met certain standards. Often used as a synonym for *licensure,* which is governmental approval to perform certain work, such as teaching.

character education   Efforts by the home, the school, the religious community, and the individual student to help the student know the good, love the good, and do the good and, in the process, to forge good qualities such as courage, respect, and responsibility.

charter schools   Public schools in which the educators, often joined by members of the local community, have made a special contract, or charter, with the chartering agency. Usually the charter allows the school a great deal of independence in its operation.

chief state school officer   The executive officer of a state's board of education who is usually responsible for the administration of that state's public education. This person is also the head of that state's department of education. Also called *superintendent of education, commissioner of education,* and *superintendent of public instruction.*

child-centered curriculum (society-centered curriculum)   A curriculum that tends to stress the needs and development of the individual student rather than the mastery of fixed subject matter; also called *society-centered curriculum.*

choice theory   A theory articulated by psychiatrist William Glasser holding that humans have fundamental needs such as survival, love, power, freedom, and fun, and that throughout our lives our actions are attempts to satisfy these needs.

civic learning (civic education)   A part of social studies that emphasizes preparing students to be good citizens by becoming aware of our common heritage and engaging issues related to character and values. Students learn to apply principles of democracy to everyday concerns they will face as citizens.

classroom management   The set of teacher behaviors that create and maintain conditions in the classroom permitting instruction to take place efficiently and effectively.

cognitive tools   Computer applications that are used to engage and enhance thinking.

common schools   Public elementary schools that are open to children of all classes. During the nineteenth century, the common school became the embodiment of universal education.

compensatory education   Educational support to provide a more equal opportunity for disadvantaged students through such activities as remedial instruction and early learning.

constructivism   A theory, based on research from cognitive psychology, that people learn by constructing their own knowledge through an active learning process rather than by simply absorbing knowledge directly from some other source.

content standards   Statements of the subject-specific knowledge and skills that schools are expected to teach and students are expected to learn.

continuing contract   An agreement between a school district and a teacher outlining the conditions and terms of work.

contract   A binding agreement between parties.

cooperative learning   An instructional approach in which students work together in groups to achieve learning goals. A variety of cooperative learning strategies exist.

core curriculum   A common course of study for all students, often called for by essentialist reforms in the 1980s.

core knowledge   *See* Cultural literacy.

credential file   A file established by college students—typically with the school's career planning and placement office—that contains materials important for securing a teaching job, for example, letters of recommendation, a transcript, and a résumé.

critical thinking   A general instructional approach intended to help students evaluate the worth of ideas, opinions, or evidence before making a decision or judgment.

cultural literacy   Being aware of the central ideas, stories, scientific knowledge, events, and personalities of a culture; also known as *core knowledge.*

culturally responsive teaching   A method of embracing students' cultural backgrounds by modifying classroom conditions or activities to include elements that relate to the students' culture.

cultural pluralism   An approach to diversity of individuals that calls for understanding and appreciating cultural differences.

culture shock   The feeling of disorientation experienced by individuals when initially immersed in a society with different values, customs, and mores.

curriculum   All the organized and intended experiences of the student for which the school accepts responsibility. *See also* Formal curriculum; Informal curriculum.

dame school   A school run by a housewife during early colonial days.

database   A software program that organizes and stores complex sets of information in the form of records that can be sorted according to different criteria.

deductive reasoning   A type of reasoning from the general to the particular; reasoning in which the conclusion follows from the premise stated.

***de facto* school segregation**   Segregation in the schools resulting primarily from residential patterns.

***de jure* school segregation**   Segregation in the schools that occurs by law.

democratic reconstructionists   Subscribers to an educational perspective that focuses on developing students who are prepared to make positive changes in a democracy.

differentiated instruction A variety of techniques used to adapt instruction to the individual ability levels and learning styles of each student in the classroom.

distance education The use of technology to link students and instructors who are separated in terms of location.

district school The type of school that succeeded the town school and moving school in New England. A township was divided into districts, each with its own school, its own schoolmaster, and funding from the town treasury.

drill-and-practice In educational technology, software programs that give students a series of tasks to reinforce a concept or to initially diagnose a student's level. These programs monitor progress, provide feedback, and present tasks accordingly.

due process The deliberative process that protects a person's constitutional right to receive fair and equal protection under the law.

economic reconstructionists Subscribers to an educational perspective or motivation that focuses on developing students who take a critical stance toward the dominant social and economic status quo.

education The process by which humans develop their minds, their skills, and their character. It is a lifelong process marked by continual development and change.

effective schools Schools that provide a significantly better education (usually measured by student test scores) for a much larger percentage of their students than do other schools serving similar student populations.

1890 institutions Colleges and universities created for African Americans as a result of the second Morrill Act passed by Congress in 1890.

Elementary and Secondary Education Act (ESEA) The federal government's single largest investment in elementary and secondary education, including Title I. Originally passed in 1965, Congress reauthorizes it periodically, most recently in 2001 as the "No Child Left Behind Act."

English grammar school A form of secondary education in the latter half of the colonial period that provided a practical alternative education for students who were not interested in college.

enrichment A method of teaching gifted and talented students in which they are allowed or assigned to do additional work to make regular class assignments more challenging or meaningful to them.

epistemology A branch of philosophy that examines the nature of knowledge, its origins, its foundations, its limits, and its validity.

equality of educational opportunity A concept that students from less advantageous backgrounds should have equal opportunities to experience success in school. Disagreement exists on whether this implies simply providing equal resources or ensuring equal success as more privileged students.

essentialism An educational philosophy that emphasizes a core body of knowledge and skills necessary for effective participation in society. Proponents believe that an educated person must have this core of knowledge and skills and that all children should be taught it.

ethics A branch of philosophy that examines the right and wrong of human conduct. The term can also refer to a particular moral code or system.

extrinsic rewards Rewards to an individual that are external to the activity itself, such as grades, gold stars, and prizes.

fair use A legal principle defining specific, limited ways in which copyrighted material can be used without permission from the author.

formal curriculum Those subjects that are taught in school and the instructional approaches used to transmit this knowledge; also known as *explicit curriculum.*

gifted and talented children Children who demonstrate or give evidence of potential for high achievement or performance in academic, creative, artistic, or leadership areas. The term *gifted* typically includes high intellectual ability; the term *talented* usually applies to creative or artistic abilities.

Goals 2000 *See* National Education Goals.

grievance A formal complaint about working conditions. Procedures for filing grievances are often part of teachers' employment contracts.

Head Start A federally funded compensatory education program, in existence since the mid-1960s, that provides additional educational services to young children suffering the effects of poverty.

hidden curriculum *See* Informal curriculum.

home schooling Parents teaching their children, rather than sending them to school. Home schooling is a growing trend in the United States.

inclusion The commitment to educate each child, to the maximum extent appropriate, in the regular school and classroom, rather than moving children with disabilities to separate classes or institutions.

individualized education program (IEP)
A management tool required for every student covered by the provisions of the Individuals with Disabilities Education Act. It must indicate a student's current level of performance, short- and long-term instructional objectives, services to be provided, and criteria and schedules for evaluation of progress.

individualized family services plan (IFSP)
Similar to an individualized education program for school-aged children, the IFSP specifies the services to be provided to developmentally delayed children from birth through age two. The IFSP is authorized by PL 99–457, the Education of the Handicapped Act Amendments.

inductive reasoning   A type of reasoning, from the particular to the general, in which one can make a general conclusion based on a number of facts.

informal curriculum (hidden curriculum)   The teaching and learning that occur in school but are not part of the formal, or explicit, curriculum; also called the *implicit* or *hidden curriculum.*

in loco parentis   The responsibility of the teacher to function "in the place of the parent" when a student is in school.

INTASC   The Interstae New Teachers Assessment and Support Consortium, an organization that has identified standards for beginning teachers.

integrated curriculum   *See* Interdisciplinary curriculum.

interdisciplinary curriculum   A curriculum that integrates the subject matter from two or more disciplines, such as English and history, often using themes such as inventions, discoveries, or health as overlays to the study of the different subjects. Also known as *integrated curriculum.*

intrinsic rewards   Rewards to an individual that come from within, such as personal satisfaction or happiness.

junior high school   A separate kind of school created typically for grades 7, 8, and 9. The first junior highs were founded in 1909–1910. In recent years, they have been gradually replaced by middle schools.

Kalamazoo case   The 1874 U.S. Supreme Court decision (*Stuart and Others v. School District No. 1 of the Village of Kalamazoo and Others*) that upheld the right of states to tax citizens to create public high schools.

kindergarten   A division of school for children below the first grade, usually for children between ages four and six; the concept, which means "garden of children" was imported into the United States from Germany during the nineteenth century.

Latin grammar school   First type of secondary school in the American colonies, whose main purpose was to prepare students for college.

law   The system of rules that governs the general conduct of a particular community's citizens.

learning communities   Organizations in which all members are engaged in continuous learning and improvement efforts.

learning style   Characteristic way a student learns, including such factors as the way an individual processes information, preference for competition or cooperation, and preferred environmental conditions such as lighting or noise level.

learning to learn   Acquiring a set of skills or competencies that enable one to learn more and to learn with greater efficiency.

least restrictive environment (LRE)   A requirement of the Education for All Handicapped Children Act that students with disabilities should participate in regular education programs to the greatest extent appropriate.

liability   A legal obligation.

licensure   The approval given to an individual by a governmental agency, usually the state, to perform a particular work, such as teaching.

limited English proficient (LEP)   Term for students whose native language is not English and who have difficulty understanding and using English.

local school board   The policymaking body of a school district, which represents the citizens of the district in setting up a school program, hiring school personnel, and generally determining local policy related to public education.

logic   A branch of philosophy that involves the study of reasoning or of sound argument. In a more specific sense, logic is the study of deductive inference.

looping   An educational practice of multiyear teaching in which the teacher follows students to the next grade level and stays with the group for several years.

magnet school   An alternative school that provides instruction in specified areas such as the fine arts, for specific groups such as the gifted and talented, or for using specific teaching styles such as open classrooms. In many cases, magnet schools are established as a method of promoting voluntary desegregation in schools.

mainstreaming   The practice of placing special education students in general education classes for at least part of the school day while also providing additional services, programs, or classes as needed.

McGuffey Readers A six-volume series of readers developed by William Holmes McGuffey that sold more than 100 million copies between 1836 and 1906. The readers served to create a common curriculum for many students.

mentor, mentoring A person who gives both personal and professional guidance to a novice.

metaphysics A branch of philosophy devoted to exploring the nature of existence or reality as a whole rather than to studying particular parts of reality as the natural sciences do. Metaphysicians try to answer questions about reality without referring to religion or revelation.

middle school A school that bridges the grades between elementary school and high school, usually grades 6–8. It differs from a junior high school in that it is specifically designed for young adolescents, with a strong emphasis on personal growth and development, rather than mimicking the high school's emphasis on academics and sports, as junior high schools often did.

Morrill Act Federal legislation passed in 1862 that granted each state federal land to establish colleges for the study of agriculture and mechanical arts. A second Morrill Act, passed in 1890, provided similar federal support to create "separate but equal" colleges for African Americans.

multicultural curriculum Several approaches to multicultural curriculum exist, but at its essence it promotes an understanding of and appreciation for cultural pluralism. It attempts to address issues of social injustice related to racism, sexism, and economic inequality by reducing prejudice and fostering tolerance through the formal curriculum.

multicultural education An approach to education that recognizes cultural diversity and fosters cultural enrichment of all children and youth.

multiple intelligences A theory of intelligence put forth by Howard Gardner that identifies at least eight dimensions of intellectual capacities that people use to approach problems and create products.

National Assement of Educational Progress (NAEP) A congressionally mandated survey of American students that is the primary source on educational achievement, and that has become known as "the nation's report card."

National Board for Professional Teaching Standards (NBPTS) A professional agency that is setting voluntary standards for what experienced teachers should know and be able to do in more than thirty different teaching areas.

national curricular standards Nationally dictated or recommended curriculum and levels of educational achievement.

National Education Association (NEA) The nation's largest teachers' association, founded in 1857 and having a membership of over 2.2 million educators.

National Education Goals (Goals 2000) Goals for U.S. education, established by the president and the fifty state governors and legislated by Congress, that were intended to be reached by the year 2000.

New Basics A label given to a proposed agenda of curricular reforms that hope to teach students how to *apply* knowledge.

New England Primer The basic text used in schools during the eighteenth century. It was an illustrated book composed of religious texts and other readings.

news group A worldwide electronic network of users who share a common interest and post messages to one another.

normal school A two- or four-year institution devoted entirely to preparing teachers that gained great popularity in the nineteenth century and faded out in the twentieth century.

Northwest Ordinances Passed by Congress in 1785 and 1787, these ordinances were concerned with the sale of public lands in the Northwest Territory (from present-day Ohio to Minnesota). Every township was divided into thirty-six sections, one of which was set aside for the maintenance of public schools. The 1787 ordinance reaffirmed that religion, morality, and knowledge were necessary to good government.

Old Deluder Satan Act A Massachusetts law passed in 1647 that strengthened an earlier law requiring parents to educate their children. It required every town of fifty or more families to pay a teacher to teach the children reading and writing so they could read the Bible and thwart Satan, who would assuredly try to keep people from understanding the scriptures.

parent-teacher organization (PTO) A local organization, usually centered around each school, that consists of both parents and teachers at that school. Its purpose is to serve as a communication mechanism between the school and the parents of the school's students.

participant observation In teacher education, the process of observing a class, recording one's observations, and comparing notes with other observers.

pedagogical content knowledge Teachers' knowledge that bridges content knowledge and pedagogy with an understanding of how particular topics can best be presented for instruction given the diverse interests and abilities of learners.

perennialism   A particular view of philosophy that sees human nature as constant, with few changes over time. Perennialism in education promotes the advancement of the intellect as the central purpose of schools. The educational process stresses academic rigor and discipline.

performance assessment   *See* Authentic (performance) assessment.

performance pay (pay-for-performance) A financial reward given to teachers, based on the special quality of their work.

personal practical knowlege   The set of understandings teachers have of the practical circumstances in which they work.

philosophy   The love or search for wisdom; the quest for basic principles to understand the meaning of life. Western philosophy traditionally contains five branches of philosophy: metaphysics, ethics, aesthetics, epistemology, and logic.

phonics   An approach to reading that teaches the reader to "decode" words by sounding out letters and combinations of letters.

Plessy* v. *Ferguson   A Supreme Court decision in 1896 that upheld the constitutionality of separate but equal accommodations for African Americans. The ruling was quickly applied to schools.

portfolio   A collection of a person's work. For students, portfolios are being used as a relatively new form of authentic assessment. They can contain a great range of work, from paper and pen work to sculpture.

private venture school   A type of school in the middle states during colonial times, licensed by the civil government but not protected or financed by it.

privatization   A movement to contract with private organizations, often for profit, to operate particular public schools whose students have been performing poorly on academic tests, or to provide specific educational services to public schools. The Edison Schools and Sylvan Learning Centers are examples of such providers.

problem solving   The process of either presenting students with a problem or helping them to identify a problem and then observing and helping them become aware of the conditions, procedures, or steps needed to solve the problem.

profession   An occupation or occupational group that fulfills certain criteria. Among other things, it must require training and knowledge, must perform a social service, must have a code of ethics, and must have a sense of autonomy and personal responsibility.

professional development   *See* Staff development.

progressivism   A form of educational philosophy that sees nature as ever changing. Because the world is always changing and new situations require new solutions to problems, learners must develop as problem solvers.

public comprehensive high school   The predominant form of secondary education in America in the twentieth century. It provides both preparation for college and a vocational education for students not going on to college.

real encounters   Face-to-face experiences that are powerful sources of learning.

reduction in force (RIF)   The elimination of teaching positions in a school system because of declining student population or funding.

reflection   Conscious and analytical thought by an individual about what he or she is doing and how the action impacts others.

reflective teaching   A teacher's habit of examining and evaluating his or her teaching on a regular basis.

reward dispensers   A function of teachers in classrooms in which they provide rewards for good work. Also a role of principals and other administrators in supervising teachers.

romanticism   A child-centered philosophy of education that condemns the influences of society and suggests a child's natural curiosity and the natural world should be used to teach, instead.

scaffolding   Providing assistance—some structure, clues, help with remembering certain steps or procedures, or encouragement to try—when a learner is on the verge of solving a problem but can't complete it independently.

school choice   Allowing parents to select alternative educational programs for their children, either within a given school or among different schools.

school culture   The prevailing mores, values, and rituals that permeate a school.

schooling   Formal instruction typically conducted in an institution, adhering to standardized practices.

schools-within-schools   In large schools, the establishment of "houses" of teachers and 100 to 400 students.

school vouchers   A type of educational choice plan that gives parents a receipt or written statement that they can exchange for the schooling they believe is most desirable for their child. The school, in turn, can cash in the received vouchers for the money to pay teachers and buy resources.

search engine   A large database that has searched and indexed millions of web pages and helps users navigate the World Wide Web and pinpoint the information they need.

self-fulfilling prophecy   Students' behavior that comes about as a result of teachers' expectations that the students will behave in a certain way. Teachers expect students to behave in a certain way; they communicate those expectations by both overt and subtle means; and students respond by behaving in the way expected.

sexual harassment   Unwelcome sexual attention.

simulation   A technique for learning or practicing skills that involves dealing with a realistic but artificial problem or situation. Typically, it provides an opportunity for safe practice with feedback on performance.

site-based decision making   A school reform effort to decentralize, allowing decisions to be made and budgets to be established at the school-building level, where most of the changes need to occur. Usually teachers become involved in the decision-making process. Also known as *site-based management, school-based management,* or *school-based decision making.*

social bet   The idea that the school curriculum represents a best guess or wager on what students will need to know to function in their society in the future.

social distance   The psychological relationships between individuals, ranging from the formal to the familiar.

socialization   The general process of social learning whereby children learn the many things they must know to become acceptable members of society.

social reconstructionists   Proponents of the theory of education that schools and teachers need to engage in the restructuring and reforming of society to eradicate its ills and shortcomings.

society-centered curriculum   *See* Child-centered curriculum.

socioeconomic status (SES)   A system for measuring the economic conditions of people using the family's occupational status, income, and educational attainment as measures of status.

special education   Educational programming provided by schools to meet the needs of students with disabilities.

spreadsheet   An interactive software program allowing users to perform multiple calculations and view more than one answer at a time.

staff development   The efforts by a school or school district to improve the professional skills and competencies of its professional staff. Also called "in-service" training in education.

standards   Exemplary performances that serve as benchmarks of what students or teachers are expected to know or be able to do.

state board of education   The state's primary education policymaking body for elementary and secondary education.

state department of education   The state bureaucracy, operating under the direction of the state board of education, whose responsibilities typically include administering and distributing state and federal funds, licensing teachers and other educational personnel, providing educational data and analyses, and approving college and university educational licensure programs.

students at risk   Students judged to be in serious jeopardy of not completing school or not succeeding in school.

subject-matter curriculum   A curriculum that focuses on bodies of content or subject matter, usually the traditional subject disciplines.

submersion model   A method of learning English in which students receive instruction in all-English-speaking classes.

superintendent of schools   Typically, a professional educator selected by the local school board to act as its executive officer and as the educational leader and chief administrator of the local school district.

teacher competency testing   Examinations given to teachers to assess their professional knowledge and skills.

teaching journal   A professional record of reflections, instructional ideas, and observations by a teacher or future teacher.

teaching portfolio   Collection of such items as research papers, pupil evaluations, teaching units, and videocassettes of lessons to reflect the quality of a teacher's teaching. Portfolios can be used to illustrate to employers the teacher's quality or to obtain national board certification.

teaching to the test   Instruction that is driven by the requirements or characteristics of a test, rather than the needs of students or the substance of a particular subject.

telecollaborate   To use telecommunications technology, such as the Internet, telephone, or television, to bring individuals from remote locations together to work on a project.

telecommunication   Communication through electronic transmission of messages, as by telephone, television, or computer network.

tenure   A legal right that confers permanent employment on teachers, protecting them from dismissal without adequate cause.

TIMSS   The Third International Mathematics and Science Study, the largest and most extensive international study of academic achievement in mathematics and science.

Title I   The section of the 1965 Elementary and Secondary Education Act that delivers federal funds to local school districts and schools for the education of students from low-income families and supplements the educational services provided to low-achieving students in those districts.

Title IX   A provision of the 1972 federal Education Amendment Act that prohibits discrimination on the basis of sex for any educational program or activity receiving federal financial assistance.

town school   A New England elementary school during the early colonial period, required in every town of fifty or more families.

tracking   The homogeneous grouping of students for learning tasks on the basis of some measure(s) of their abilities.

tutorials   A software application designed to provide initial instruction in a given topic, check for understanding throughout the process, and evaluate the learner's grasp of the topic once the program is completed.

universal education   Schooling for everyone.

vicarious experiences   Learnings gained not through direct experiences, but through observations or readings.

virtual fieldtrip   Computer software that simulates the experience of an actual fieldtrip with the use of digital images and multimedia tools.

wait-time   The time a teacher spends waiting for an answer after posing a question. Research indicates that good questioning practices involve giving students sufficient time to think about and respond to each question.

whole language approach   A teaching approach emphasizing the integration of language arts skills and knowledge across the curriculum. It stresses the provision of a literate environment and functional uses of language.

word processor   A software application that allows users to create, store, and edit text. These programs often come with additional writing aids such as on-screen dictionaries or spell checkers.

World Wide Web (WWW)   A collection of sites on the Internet that users can access using a graphical interface called a web browser. In addition to text, the sites often contain graphics, sound, video, or other multimedia applications, and many are connected to one another by hypertext links.

writing across the curriculum   An instructional approach using writing as a tool for learning in all subject areas.

zero-tolerance policies   School policies calling for automatic suspension or expulsion of students who bring forbidden items, such as drugs or weapons, to school.

zone of proximal development   A range of tasks that a person cannot yet do alone but can accomplish when assisted by a more skilled partner. This zone is the point at which instruction can succeed and real learning is possible.

Index

A comprehensive support package offers both print and media ancillaries for both instructors and students:

Houghton Mifflin Guide Series

This new series, edited by James M. Cooper, offers brief paperback guides that examine various topics in depth. There are currently five titles in the series with more to be announced. Any of these guides may be packaged with this text:

An Educator's Guide to Diversity in the Classroom
Carl A. Grant, University of Wisconsin, Madison

An Educator's Guide to Classroom Assessment
Terry TenBrink, Educational Consultant

An Educator's Guide to Inclusion
Kristen Sayeski, University of Virginia

An Educator's Guide to Technology Tools
Cheryl Mason Bolick, University of North Carolina at Chapel Hill

An Educator's Guide to School-based Interventions
James Garbarino and Ellen de Lara, Cornell University

Kaleidoscope: Readings in Education
Tenth Edition, ©2004 by Ryan/Cooper

This book of readings is a perfect companion to *Those Who Can, Teach.* Its comprehensive scope, effective pedagogy, and high-interest readings from a wide range of sources invite readers to participate in important discussions about education in a more informed way.

Instructors' Resource Manual with Test Bank

This manual provides complete instructional support. It includes a transition guide, sample syllabi, learning objectives, chapter overviews and outlines, supplementary lecture and discussion topics, class activities, student study guides, practice quizzes, selected references and media resources, school observation activities, and case studies with discussion questions. The test bank contains multiple-choice, short answer, and essay questions. The manual includes a cross-reference to *Kaleidoscope: Readings in Education,* **10/e,** the companion reader.